SENSUS SPIRITUALIS

Sensus Spiritualis

STUDIES IN MEDIEVAL SIGNIFICS AND THE PHILOLOGY OF CULTURE

FRIEDRICH OHLY

EDITED AND WITH AN EPILOGUE BY SAMUEL P. JAFFE

TRANSLATED BY KENNETH J. NORTHCOTT

The University of Chicago Press
Chicago and London

* *
*

FRIEDRICH OHLY was professor of Germanic philology at the University of Münster and the author of books and studies on literature both medieval and modern, Latin as well as German. His latest publications include *Ausgewählte und neue Schriften zur Literaturgeschichte* (1995), *Zur Signaturenlehre der Frühen Neuzeit* (1999), and *Die Perle des Wortes: Zur Geschichte eines Bildes für Dichtung.*

SAMUEL P. JAFFE is professor emeritus of Germanic studies and a member emeritus of the Committees on Medieval Studies and Interdisciplinary Studies in the Humanities at the University of Chicago.

KENNETH J. NORTHCOTT is professor emeritus of Germanic studies and of comparative studies in literature as well as a member emeritus of the Committee on Interdisciplinary Studies in the Humanities at the University of Chicago.

The University of Chicago Press, Chicago 60637
The University of Chicago Press, Ltd., London

Printed in the United States of America

14 13 12 11 10 09 08 07 06 05 1 2 3 4 5
ISBN: 0-226-62089-1 (cloth)

Published with the support of the Center for Interdisciplinary Studies in German Literature and Culture and the Department of Germanic Studies, the University of Chicago.

Library of Congress Cataloging-in-Publication Data
Ohly, Friedrich, 1914–
Sensus spiritualis : studies in medieval significs and the philology of culture / Friedrich Ohly ; edited and with an epilogue by Samuel P. Jaffe ; translated by Kenneth J. Northcott.
p. cm.
Includes bibliographical references.
ISBN 0-226-62089-1 (cloth : alk. paper)
1. Signs and symbols. 2. Philology. 3. Civilization, Medieval. I. Jaffe, Samuel P., 1934– II. Title.
P99.O37 2005
302.2'223—dc22

2003018993

♾ The paper used in this publication meets the minimum requirements of the American National Standard for Information Sciences—Permanence of Paper for Printed Library Materials, ANSI Z39.48-1992.

CONTENTS

ILLUSTRATIONS

FOREWORD

Friedrich Ohly was born on January 10, 1914, in Breidenbach (Hesse) in the vicinity of Gießen, the son of a Protestant minister. Ohly grew up in the vicinity of Gießen and in Frankfurt am Main; from 1932 to 1938 he studied Germanics, classical philology, and history at the Universities of Frankfurt am Main, Vienna, and Königsberg. In later years Ohly never spoke of his teachers with anything but the deepest respect and gratitude. It was surely Julius Schwietering, the eminent Germanist and medievalist in Frankfurt, who most decisively affected Ohly's life and work, but something of most, if not all, of his teachers remained with him; reminiscences of their life and work may be found in his own. In Königsberg Ohly studied with Hans Rothfels, the historian of German politics from Clausewitz and Bismarck to "the German opposition to Hitler." He was especially devoted to the literary historian Paul Hankamer, under whose guidance he intended to do his doctoral work until National Socialist authorities deprived Hankamer of his professorship in 1936—on account of the latter's refusal to entertain "any compromise and reconciliation with a system that went against his fundamental convictions" as a "committed . . . Catholic."

When the student intervened on behalf of his teacher, he had to face a trial, financial support was withdrawn, and he was obliged to leave Königsberg and return to Frankfurt. There Ohly was able to resume his studies. His teachers included among others the historian of Roman antiquity Matthias Gelzer, the classical philologist Karl Reinhardt, the literary historian, critic, and poet Max Kommerell, and, above all, the Germanistic medievalist Julius Schwietering, under whose supervision Ohly wrote his dissertation, "Sage und Legende in der *Kaiserchronik*" (1940).[1]

1. Ernst Friedrich Ohly, *Sage und Legende in der Kaiserchronik: Untersuchungen über Quellen und Aufbau der Dichtung*, Forschungen zur deutschen Sprache und Dichtung, no. 10 (1940; reprint, Darmstadt, 1968).

Ohly received his doctorate in 1938. Shortly after the publication of his dissertation in 1940 he was inducted into the army and suffered an eye injury in France; in 1941 Julius Schwietering brought Ohly to Berlin as an assistant. During the next three years Ohly prepared his *Habilitationsschrift,* a second, more substantial dissertation required to qualify for a university teaching post; it focused on medieval theology and exegesis, especially in commentaries on the Song of Songs. The fruits of this research were Ohly's studies of Song of Songs exegesis to 1200, his *Hohelied-Studien.* Although this work was finished and approved by 1944, it was not published until 1958.[2] Directly after the habilitation proceedings Ohly was recalled to active duty and sent to the eastern front. He was taken prisoner in Rumania and spent the next nine years, 1944 to 1953, in the "worst," "most dreaded" of Soviet labor camps, a length and form of internment directly proportionate to Ohly's resistance to a second attempt to exploit him—this time not as a passive bystander of Nazistic intimidation but rather as an active tool of Communist indoctrination.[3]

Upon Ohly's repatriation in 1953 he accepted a position as a lecturer at the University of Frankfurt; in 1954 he became an associate professor. In the autumn quarter of 1956 Ohly came to the University of Chicago as a visiting assistant professor in the Department of Germanic Languages and Literatures. In 1957 he accepted an appointment at the University of Mainz, and in the following year was called to a full professorship at the University of Kiel. It was there that he delivered, in July 1958, his epoch-making inaugural lecture, "On the Spiritual Sense of the Word in the Middle Ages."[4] In 1964 Ohly left Kiel to assume a professorship at the University of Münster, a position he held until his retirement in 1982, a retirement that marked the transition to yet another new beginning.

The esteem in which Professor Ohly was—and is—held by scholarly peers, colleagues, and students is extraordinary. It is documented in the po-

2. Friedrich Ohly, *Hohelied-Studien: Grundzüge einer Geschichte der Hoheliedauslegung des Abendlandes bis um 1200,* Schriften der wissenschaftlichen Gesellschaft an der Johann Wolfgang Goethe-Universität Frankfurt am Main, Geisteswissenschaftliche Reihe 1 (Wiesbaden, 1958; originally Habilitationsschrift, Universität Berlin 1944).

3. Cf. Ohly's bittersweet reminiscence of forced labor: Friedrich Ohly, "Glück eines Gefangenen mit Puschkin und mit Steinen," in "All das Lob, das du verdient: Eine deutsche Puschkin-Ehrung zur 150. Wiederkehr seines Todestages," *Zeitschrift für Kulturaustausch* 1 (1987): 87–92; reprinted in Ohly, *Ausgewählte und neue Schriften zur Literaturgeschichte und Bedeutungsforschung,* ed. Dietmar Peil and Uwe Ruberg (Stuttgart, 1995) (henceforth *AusgNSchr*), here pp. 931–937.

4. Cf. in this volume Friedrich Ohly, "On the Spiritual Sense of the Word in the Middle Ages" (with publication history).

sitions he occupied,[5] in the honors he received,[6] by his own scholarly achievements and, what Ohly would surely have prized most of all, by the achievements of generations of younger scholars inspired and instructed by his example: "In teaching prior to his retirement in 1982, in the research he did far beyond that point, he gave fruitful stimuli, as he did also through his editorships for the 'Schriften des Frühmittelalter-Instituts' and the 'Special Research Area 7 (Medieval Studies)' in Münster, through his role in initiating and presenting scholarly conferences and his membership in the Rhenish-Westfalian and the Austrian Academies of Sciences as well as in other scholarly institutions at home and abroad. His impetus as a researcher remained alive to his last days—despite painful suffering toward the end. He left behind a treasure chest of materials not yet prepared for publication, not yet unlocked by his words: an emblem of 'patience . . . for assembling evidence over a long period of years.'"[7] Many of the fruits of Ohly's research from his retirement in 1982 until his death in 1996 have been published, with selected earlier contributions, in the collection *Ausgewählte und neue Schriften zur Literaturgeschichte und Bedeutungsforschung,* the preface to which now follows, in grateful acceptance of Ohly's offer, as a "Preface" to the classic essays contained in the present volume.[8]

5. Cf. Ohly's editorship or coeditorship of: *Zeitschrift für deutsches Altertum und deutsche Literatur, Medium Aevum: Philologische Studien, Münstersche Mittelalter-Schriften, Frühmittelalterliche Studien,* and *Arbeiten zur Frühmittelalterforschung.* Cf. *AusgNSchr,* pp. 946–947 for additions to the preceding. For the most complete bibliographies of Ohly's work hitherto published cf. ibid., pp. 939–947, and the Web site bibliography accompanying the present volume.

6. Friedrich Ohly has been honored by no fewer than four Festschriften: (1a) Hans Fromm, Wolfgang Harms, and Uwe Ruberg, eds., *Verbum et Signum,* vol. 1, *Beiträge zur mediävistischen Bedeutungsforschung* (Munich, 1975); (1b) Hans Fromm, Wolfgang Harms, and Uwe Ruberg, eds., *Verbum et Signum,* vol. 2, *Beiträge zur mediävistischen Bedeutungsforschung: Studien zu Semantik und Sinntradition im Mittelalter* (Munich, 1975); (2) Christel Meier and Uwe Ruberg, eds., *Text und Bild: Aspekte des Zusammenwirkens zweier Künste in Mittelalter und früher Neuzeit* (Wiesbaden, 1980); (3) Klaus Grubmüller, Ruth Schmidt-Wiegand, and Klaus Speckenbach, eds., *Geistliche Denkformen in der Literatur des Mittelalters,* Münstersche Mittelalter-Schriften, no. 51 (Munich, 1984); and (4) Wolfgang Harms, Klaus Speckenbach, in Verbindung mit Herfried Vögel, eds., *Bildhafte Rede in Mittelalter und früher Neuzeit: Probleme ihrer Legitimation und ihrer Funktion* (Tübingen, 1992). See now a fifth homage: *AusgNSchr.*

7. Christel Meier, "*De thesauro suo nova et vetera:* Friedrich Ohly, 1914–1996," *Frühmittelalterliche Studien* 30 (1996): 419–424, here p. 420.

8. Cf. *AusgNSchr,* pp. vii–x. Ohly's original preface ("Geleitwort") was modified only slightly, by Ohly himself, to serve as "Preface" in the present volume. That Ohly proposed using essentially the same preface for two almost totally different collections bespeaks firm confidence in the consistency of his teaching and research—as a "philologist"—over a whole life of scholarship. In reading Ohly's "Preface" it is important, above all, to realize that there, as in many other

Before turning to that preface, however, one pleasant duty remains: to acknowledge those without whom this book would never have come to pass. Its seeds were sown with Ohly's visiting appointment in the Department of Germanic Languages and Literatures of the University of Chicago in 1956 and the bonds of "fond knowledge of one another" forged between University of Chicago scholars of American origin like Helena Gamer and George Metcalf, their German emigré colleagues, Hanns Stefan Schultz and Matthijs Jolles, and Friedrich Ohly. The bonds were further strengthened on the occasion of Ohly's return to the University of Chicago, where he received the honorary degree of doctor of humane letters on June 14, 1985. Our publication project grew out of the department's renewed contact with Ohly after the conferring of the honorary degree, for which the department recommended him, as it had recommended his teacher, Julius Schwietering, almost four decades earlier.

Heartfelt thanks and much gratitude are due to all who have contributed to this project. Without Kenneth Northcott's wonderful translation of a long and challenging text there would, of course, have been no book at all, and without the benevolent oversight, patience, and good counsel of Alan Thomas, editorial director at the University of Chicago Press, there would have been no publication. Many thanks are due to James Nitti, formerly director of computational services in the Humanities Division of the University of Chicago for his unflagging enthusiasm, skill, and inventiveness in pouring the fine wine of Ohly's scholarship into new bottles. A fresh wave of excitement has been brought to the project by his contribution: the prospect of addressing—via the World Wide Web—an intellectual curiosity and hunger for learning on the part of viewing and reading publics we would otherwise never have been able to reach. Here too, to refer to the words of Ohly's "Preface" yet once more before encountering them, and him, directly, there is "interest in what others are doing, the stimulating attention to voices that become more familiar, conversation at a distance, the fond knowledge of one another."

Samuel P. Jaffe

---

contexts, he identifies himself as a "philologist" and his calling as "philology," not in the sense of "the study of language history, as carried on by 'comparative philologists' since the late 18th century" (David Crystal, *A Dictionary of Linguistics and Phonetics* [Oxford, 1992], p. 257), but rather in an earlier sense that goes back to Greco-Roman antiquity: the interpretation and criticism of texts and other significative materials, with the aim of establishing the textual basis for a whole range of human activities that rely on signification, especially historical reconstruction. Cf. further the epilogue below, which uses Ohly's "Preface," as well as other self-reflective writings by Ohly, to help understand his sense of himself as a "philologist" and of his vocation as "philology."

PREFACE

I want in all sincerity to express a word of thanks at the very beginning of this book. It is spoken to my colleagues at the University of Chicago: Samuel Jaffe, for his manifold efforts in arranging for the publication of this volume, and Kenneth Northcott, who devoted himself to the translation. Both of them acted in that spirit of friendly and mutual knowledge that one scholar has of another and that informs and stimulates scholarship. I have written about this in the preface to my *Selected and New Writings on Literary History and Significs*.[1] I was able to use this preface as an essay in writing a sketch to characterize my life as a scholar; and I am grateful to have the welcome opportunity of also including it in this volume—designed as it is to serve the process of stimulating our knowledge of one another. What follows is a slightly modified text of my preface to the German volume.

I watched this book come into being with special interest. I was glad it happened. For did this not accord with my own ideas of bringing together what had been published in scattered places over the course of half a century to make one collective view that could lead to the emergence of an overarching unity in the multitude of topics that were dealt with? If I am now, at the editors' request, writing a preface, I shall use it as an opportunity to look back over long years of work that have brought me great joy, and of which not a few fruits are collected in this volume. I hope that the reader will make allowances for the personal distillate that has been precipitated from an octogenarian's view of what has been, and of the way in which it constantly inspired, moved, and propelled him into activity. What the author has done, what is most closely connected with the person who did it, reveals more than all those claims for the future for

1. [Significs is the study of meanings.—Ed.] Friedrich Ohly, *Ausgewählte und neue Schriften zur Literaturgeschichte und Bedeutungsforschung*, ed. Uwe Ruberg and Dietmar Peil (Stuttgart, 1995), vii–x. The self-portrait was preceded by one in *Geometria e Memoria* (Bologna, 1985), 21–32.

something—all too willingly put into programmatic form—that are not fulfilled in what is later produced. This book affords the reader the opportunity of meeting me as a self-possessed philologist who, in times of restless changes in the assumption of methodological and theoretical positions, always remained the same, and whose activity offered no clues for forecasting the professional climate. The serious reader understands, and will certainly not mistake the seeming peace of the tableau which I present for a still life.

The young man, like the old man, was always fascinated by the new, the unknown, places where the first furrows could be plowed in virgin territory. Medieval significs offered a scholarly field for research that could be cultivated according to plans that could with time grow broader. This could not be done single-handed. Cooperative work with a group of devoted younger colleagues, a group that grew more and more closely knit, managed to get us to the point where, today, the ground has in many sectors been cleared, and in some cases the cultivation may even be regarded as completed. Significs was not originally in my stars. When I took the opportunity of introducing it as the main field to be worked on by the "Middle Ages" special research area in Münster,[2] I regarded it as my duty to engage in serious research in this area. With its links to art history, the history of theology, and the sciences, and especially its involvement in the study of metaphor (in its function as a way of opening up the world through cognitive insights), it fascinated me as a field for interpreting the world. At the same time, I did not want to be labeled a "semiologist." My heart beat more strongly when I was involved with poetic art [*Dichtkunst*], which I see as a vessel that contains more secrets to help us understand what is human, in the fullness of all its developments throughout the course of history. What is common to the two fields is provided by the interest in the illumination of existence by means of those possibilities of the spoken word whose aim is meaning—something that is also a task of art. My project of considerably enlarging the scope of the significs of the early modern period by means of a lengthy article entitled "Observations on the Theory of Signatures"—I had been lecturing on this since 1987—had to give way to my putting the final touches on the completion of the edition of the St. Trudpert Song of Songs that was already in the process of being printed. Illness prevented me from completing the present volume, as I had intended, with the "Observations."[3]

2. "Sonderforschungsbereich 'Mittelalter,'" at the University of Münster.

3. But cf. now Friedrich Ohly, *Zur Signaturenlehre der Frühen Neuzeit. Bemerkungen zur mittelalterlichen Vorgeschichte und zur Eigenart einer epochalen Denkform in Wissenschaft, Literatur und Kunst*, ed. Uwe Ruberg and Dietmar Peil (Stuttgart, 1999), with "Vorwort der Herausgeber," vii–x.

The unchanging physiognomy of my scholarly character, with its eye whose guiding concern is curiosity, corresponds to the far-reaching unity of the subjects that arouse and hold my interest. I use my freedom of choice in these subjects as an opportunity to start—by the use of smaller forms of presentation—to work on things that are not then always subject to a complete and exhaustive treatment, for in this way I can assert the rights of certain areas and points of view to be considered in a scholarly way. And so, by avoiding the "magnum opus," I favored things that were smaller in scope; I preferred to cut a path into the distance, engage in the pursuit across open country and bring the more general into sight on the basis of the particular. It was only with the edition of the St. Trudpert Song of Songs, for which I also wrote a commentary, that I was able to combine many disparate elements and present the whole as a closed work. In this connection, I also devoted myself to the philologically informed editing of texts with an eye to helping criticism of form find its rightful place within the framework of medieval textual criticism.

In seminars and lectures, I gave free rein to my true inclination, which was to pursue the study of philology as an aesthetic science. My publications are, however, less concerned with the work as an art form. In a general phase of research into interpretation there was less need for that.

In Bible exegesis, as the mother of philology and the main area in which significs is applied, the problem that exists for classical and secular literature scarcely arose—in view of the immense abundance of written interpretations in commentaries and sermons—the problem, that is, of the history of interpretation as a key to intellectual history and the history of form, something that I pursued in my interpretation of the Song of Songs. This exercise in the history of the primarily, though not exclusively, theological interpretation of a poetic text over the span of a thousand years is like an inclination that I had already followed in my historical research into the history of the subject matter of the *Kaiserchronik,* where I pursued the history of the comprehension of narrative elements in order to understand the specifics of their position within the context of the work at a given point. The historical changes in the constants of a statement that has been handed down, in whatever form, can increase their yield in proportion to their transparency as a dictum for a period in which a new tradition and a new foundation are formed into one. My ultimate concern in this case was, in particular, with formulas of a varied explication of the world, in which a form, a sense, or a maxim is opened up. The dicta of which I am thinking offer solutions for universal contexts—in quite a different manner from the way in which Biblical precepts give directions for living life—in the form of thought images that can also be found as paintings. The conception of the world that is handed down from classical antiquity to Goethe, Homer's golden chain, presents the cosmic contexts to our view in such a way that both antiquity and Christianity can immediately make it their own. The pictorial concept of the constellations of salvation that started with Origen presents the totality of the history of salvation from the first day of Creation to the end of the world, as a cosmic course of events from "Let there be light!" to Christ's return as the sun that will be visible for all eternity. God's work of creation has been made visible in the idea of the *Deus geometria* that has existed from Plato till modern times under the aspect of ordered beauty. The book of nature as the metaphor for God's first revelation has, from the time of Augustine, had more effect than any of the thought images already mentioned and and is still valid today. The thought image of the inner-trinitarian conversations of the Trinity, one of the smaller, extrabiblical myths in which man allows God to think his thoughts, lasted from the twelfth century to the eighteenth. The doctrine of reverence for what is above us, beneath us, in us, and near us that endured from Augustine to Goethe belongs to those historically highly valued maxims—with which mankind has been charged—relative to a process of placing oneself into a referential position vis-à-vis the world in all the dimensions of an *ordo caritatis.*

I cannot propose a method of working on such problems that will always be valid. There comes a moment when the fascinating concept of a thought image appears to one at a given point in history; when we come across it again we are also conscious that it endures as part of tradition. Patience and more patience are necessary for assembling evidence over a long period of years. The only help in discovering it is reading—reading that covers large fields of history, which often yield an unexpected harvest. "I have the habit common to all those who cannot think: I can reflect only when I have a pen in my hand," says Italo Svevo. The philologist may cull blossoms in the manner of an anthologist, but they must not be combined philosophically, but rather in such a way that colors and forms fall into place as patterns of the historical process as it emerges from intellectual changes of climate that permit the determination of the time and place of a growth that has been discovered. The broken chain and the snapped string each show a particular sort, or phase, of the independent thought image of the golden chain or the harp; the unreadable page is an historical event in association with the eternal book of nature. Such thought images or imaged thoughts—metaphor is generally at the origin—are, as statements about human self-understanding, just as legitimate and necessary a theme of philology as a human science as are literary dealings with basic human givens in poetic art. I have tried to bring into view those things peculiar to human beings, such as guilt and atonement, love and betrayal, like the search for, or the ideal of, the holy as basic and motivational elements of poetic art. The philologist, as the guardian of *memoria,* would otherwise be guilty of dereliction of duty as one of the preservers of human culture. If he ignores this horizon of his commission—something that is well on the way to becoming more and more manifest in the growing denial of thematic areas of this sort—this denial signalizes an avoidance on the part of literary scholarship of the study of humanity as what has been, since antiquity, the most worthy subject of art after God. Grounded in reverence, my association has been with what has been entrusted to us, the subjects of linguistic tradition about mankind, its possibilities, and determinations that are given form in the arts and that are worthy of *memoria.* To a greater extent than usual, I have entered into my work, as a human being, mainly beneath the surface of what has been said. The scholar joins the reader over a tertium quid in the middle, across the subject whose choice may say something about the author. What aided and supported me in this was the thought that scarcely anyone else would do what I was doing. Everyone can accept the fact that the *ordo caritatis* determines the tone of my writing, everyone, that is, who counts learning among the goods that are placed in our hands and by which human existence schools itself. Under the sign of loss of reverence for the memorable wealth of history, the opportunity for scholarship to develop the inherent right of subjects to be interpreted by the method suited to them individually is dissipated. What constitutes the freshness of our method of working is the discovery and application of suitably different methods for individual cases. The space available for historical literary and linguistic observation to move in is as large as what history makes available to us, from the nuance in the particular, by way of the oeuvre, the author, his place and his time, right up to the phase of the history of form and style in which the cosmic feeling toward God and man in all its historical conditions finds its expression.

The conspectus of the philologist, working with thoughtfully eventful sobriety, combining imagination with meticulous precision, and concerned with what has been given form in the course of history, prepares a ground for righteousness. The enduring dialogue in history about what is enduringly human reveals to him in the arts possibilities of human existence, what has become reality in forms charged with meaning. In change he finds constants of the human condition that are never outlived—neither in good nor in evil. I carry on my craft without scruple—I hoped to do it right—it was supported by an unforced confidence. A weighty, trustful solace supported me in my choice of objects, of countenances in the image of the world and of human beings. The man without illusions needs them as a gift if he, like many of his spiritual forebears, is pursuing rays of humanity in the darkness of history.

It might appear, with my smaller works ordered in the way they are here, that they were written according to a deliberate plan. Not a bit of it; they are the fruits of a joy in this or that subject that flared up spontaneously over a long period, an imagined path into a new territory. The fact that a certain terrain offered points of view that held out the promise of the possibility of finding out further details is part of the magic of a progress through decades, whereby things that were imagined or suspected for good reason were kept in one's memory in the hope that they could one day be investigated. The scrupulousness that cost me much time in my attempt to achieve, at least, a representative completeness in my citations acted as a brake on my activities to the point where I was about to give up much that I had attempted. The fact that the ensemble of these writings—having followed the siren song of the time and finally emerged—reveals tacit interrelations, may accord with a unified intellectual need, extracting what is earnest from what is joyful, as the word "philologist" suggests. I never thought that I was alone; I felt myself to be a member of a pedagogical province into which everyone brings the art of his instrument, according to his ability and his skill at it, according to his knowledge and his conscience. If this comes about through mutual inclination, as in a chamber music ensemble, then that honorable and basic feeling of existence emerges that is given to us in *gaudere cum gaudentibus*. This is the reason for my interest in what others are doing, the stimulating attention to voices that become more familiar, conversation at a distance, the friendly knowledge of one another.

Friedrich Ohly

ONE

ON THE SPIRITUAL SENSE OF THE WORD IN THE MIDDLE AGES

When, in his lectures on aesthetics, Hegel described the art of sublimity, he determined its forms according to the different nature of the relationship of "substance, as meaning, to the phenomenal world" (p. 363).[1] Hegel distinguishes the "art form of sublimity, strictly so-called," which is determined by meaning and its clear understanding from pantheistic poetry, whose historical phenomena he sees as being linked by the experience of the "substantial existence of God in things" (p. 371), so that it recognizes only symbols of indistinct content. In the art of sublimity, the work of art is the "outpouring of the pure Being as the meaning of all things": the meaning of God which is here "present in the mundane, yet transcending everything mundane" makes the art of sublimity into a sacred art. Its content is the "relationship of God to the world created by him," since the creator who has no form can be represented artistically neither in what has presently been created nor by what is created. By being raised above the transitory man can encounter the sublimity of God, as in the "sacred verse" of the psalm (p. 373f.). In explaining the sublime on the basis of Hebrew monotheism, Hegel has brought us to the root of the sublimity of Christian art, which he now leaves out of consideration. The basis of the sacred art of sublimity is set not in antiquity—which Hegel also leaves out of consideration—but in the Bible as the revealed word of the relationship between God and man. The task which the revelation sets art and exegesis, that of making the word transparent as regards its signification, persists in the realm of Hegel's sublime. That is, if we

This essay is a somewhat extended version of Friedrich Ohly's inaugural lecture at the University of Kiel in 1958. Published as "Vom geistigen Sinn des Wortes im Mittelalter," in *Schriften zur mittelalterlichen Bedeutungsforschung*, by Friedrich Ohly (Darmstadt: Wissenschaftliche Buchgesellschaft, 1977), pp. 1–31.

1. The English edition that has been used is G. W. F. Hegel, *Aesthetics: Lectures on Fine Arts*, trans. T. M. Knox (Oxford, 1975).

are, in what follows, not to see what is "present in the mundane, yet transcending everything mundane" in the "pure existence" of "substance," the "absolute" of Hegelian philosophy, but are to understand it, in a Christian sense, as Christian, as the meaning of the created world revealed by God in the integument of the word.

The question of the spiritual sense of the word is not only common to Judaism, Christianity, and Islam as revealed religions but is also, in the Christian Middle Ages, which we are dealing with here, the common property not only of German but of all languages. The problem is a common hermeneutical one, which affects the universal church languages just as it does vernaculars and even the "languages" of art forms which are not tied to the word. Its development will show us the inner connection of all the learned disciplines—including the scientific ones—in the common service of the understanding of the world and its meaning as represented in the word, an understanding with which we are here and now concerned.

If we ask about the spiritual signification of the word, then we must start with the Bible, the understanding of which the Middle Ages struggled with in church service and instruction, in innumerable commentaries, and through all the arts, including poetry. The pressure to understand Holy Writ presented Christianity with the greatest task that had, up to that time, been attempted by mankind, not only in the narrower historical-philological sense, but also as an interpretative act pure and simple. And we philologists are as a rule not aware—as Dilthey was in his *Entstehung der Hermeneutik*—how much our art of interpretation owes to biblical exegesis both by the church fathers and during the Middle Ages.

The effort to reach an understanding of the word of revelation includes, within itself, a lofty task that goes further than any effort made in nonbiblical literature. There is, at the beginning of every Bible interpretation, from the time of the church fathers onward, the conviction that Holy Writ is unique, and different from all secular literature—from this point of view, all the literature of classical antiquity. The constantly reiterated principle is that while all profane literature includes only a historical or literal sense, the word of Holy Writ contains, side by side with the historical or literal sense, a spiritual one as well, a *sensus spiritualis*. Established in the New Testament, formulated in principle in Origen's "Peri Archon" and Augustine's "De Doctrina Christiana,"[2] sanctioned and validated by the exegetical

2. H. I. Marrou, *Saint Augustin et la fin de la culture antique* (Paris, 1938), with an addendum (Paris, 1949), esp. pp. 444–453, 478–494, 646–651.

tradition established by the church fathers—until Luther broke with the spiritual interpretation of the Bible and in so doing had to reject the tradition—the doctrine of the *sensus spiritualis* of the biblical word dominated the Middle Ages. It presented medieval philology—if we may include in this concept the efforts of theology vis-à-vis the written word—with two fundamentally different tasks. The one consisted of correctly comprehending the literal sense of the word which the Bible had in common with all profane literature, by means of textual criticism and the other methods of textual interpretation that were carried on in the trivium, which had been developed since Hellenistic times and handed down to the Middle Ages from classical antiquity. This is then the task which modern philology has taken over and which it continues to fulfill with its richly developed methods. Particular schools and periods of the Middle Ages made this task peculiarly their own, like the school of Antioch in the early Middle Ages and, in the twelfth century, certain representatives of the school of St.-Victor in Paris. Here we already meet with demands, now taken for granted by our own philology, for account to be taken of the context, place and time of provenance, genre, person and more intimate circumstances of the author—everything with the express aim of understanding the meaning which the author intended: "sententiam litteralem scripturae ab auctore principaliter intentam" [the literal sense of what is written, primarily intended by the author].[3] These things are something with which we have again become familiar, at least since the Dilthey school of interpretation, and will not occupy us any further. The second task, and the one which was more essential to the Christian philology of the Middle Ages, lay in the uncovering of the spiritual signification of the word that lay hidden in the letter—a meaning which was revealed, according to Bernard of Clairvaux, with the Crucifixion, for the Old Testament as well, when the "veil of the dead word was rent."[4]

3. An anonymous introduction to the *Allegoriae* of the pseudo-Hrabanus (12th c.), in *Spicilegium Solesmense,* ed. J. B. Pitra (Paris, 1855), 3:436–445, written at the latest in the fourteenth century, treats the hermeneutical principles of medieval exegesis clearly and extensively.

4. Bernard of Clairvaux, *Sermones in Cantica* 14, 4, in *Patrologia Latina* (hereafter *PL*), 183, 841 B. Peter of Poitiers also says in his *Allegoriae* (see below, nn. 9, 11) that on the day of the Passion the *velum* (veil) which up to that point had been spread throughout the world was rent: "revelata sunt fundamenta orbis terrarum" [unveiled are the foundations of the world]. Cf. in the *Distinctiones monasticae:* "Quod leo de Juda libri signacula solvit, Hoc est quod Christus, surgens a morte revolvit Velum scripturae: vero cessere figurae" [That the Lion of Juda opened the seals of the scroll, means that Christ, rising from death, rolled back the veil covering the scroll: then, in truth, the figures ceased to be] (III, 54).

The doctrine of the spiritual sense of the word is based on the principle of the difference in nature of the signification of the word in profane and sacred writing. I present it here, in a twelfth-century formulation, since what concerns me here, and in what follows, is not historical derivations, but a description of conditions, especially in the twelfth century, from which essential conclusions which lie outside the interests of theology may be drawn by medieval studies. The initiated will not fail to recognize where I owe a debt to the Anglicist H. H. Glunz, theologians like J. Daniélou, H. deLubac, M.-D. Chenu, and C. Spicq, and the historian Beryl Smalley—just to name a few.[5] Richard of St.-Victor formulated the principle, "Therein is the word of God far superior to worldly wisdom, so that not only the sounds of the word, but also things [sc. those meant by the word] are the vehicles of meaning": "non solum voces, sed et res significativae sunt" [not only words, but things too are significative].[6] The meaning of this sentence cannot be overestimated. Without it there is no spiritual sense of the word in the Middle Ages. It means that the profane word has only a surface, superficial meaning, or as Hugh of St.-Victor says, a meaning written on its forehead, the historical or literal meaning, that consists in the fact that the sound of the word (the *vox*) has a thing (*res*) as its content. Thus, the sound of the word "stone" is exhausted in its literal sense in the thing which we know from nature. It is the essence of Holy Writ which causes this thing only to have an actual meaning, after the literal sense is exhausted. Everything that is called into language by the sound of a

5. Earlier versions of this chapter refer here to a bibliographic essay, which has not been included.—Ed.

6. Richard of St.-Victor, *Excerptiones* II, 3, *De scripturae divinae triplici modo tractandi,* in *PL,* 177, 205 B; cf. *Speculum ecclesiae* (in the appendix to Hugh of St.-Victor), in *PL,* 177, 375 B: "In libris autem ethnicorum voces tantum mediantibus intellectibus res significant. In divina pagina non solum intellectus et res significant, sed ipsae res alias res significant. Unde claret scientiam artium ad cognitionem divinarum scriptuarum valde esse utilem" [In the books of the Gentiles, furthermore, words signify things only through the medium of intellectual cognition. In Sacred Scripture not only does cognition continue to signify things, but the things themselves now signify other things. Whence it is manifest that knowledge of the arts is especially useful for gaining knowledge of the Holy Scriptures]. Hugh of St.-Victor, *De scripturis et scriptoribus sacris,* cap. 3, in *PL,* 175, 12 A: "Habet enim sacrum eloquium proprietatem quemdam ab aliis scripturis differentem, quod in eo primum per verba quae recitantur de rebus quibusdam agitur, quae rursum res vice verborum ad significationem aliarum rerum proponuntur" [For sacred eloquence has a certain characteristic feature that differentiates it from all other writings, namely, that therein, first of all, particular things are presented by means of the words mentioned, things which, however, are in their turn propounded to function exactly like words in signifying other things].

word, every one of God's creatures that is named by a word, points to a further, higher sense, is the sign of something spiritual, has a *significatio,* a meaning. Thus, we differentiate a twofold meaning, once from the sound of the word to the thing, from the *vox* to the *res,* and a higher one, linked to the thing, which points from the thing to something higher. Whereas antiquity (both Jews and non-Jews) had been concerned only with the meanings of words, the Christian philology of the Middle Ages goes beyond that and is concerned with the "thing significations" of everything present in creation. "Every created being has a meaning" is Alanus ab Insulis's concise formulation;[7] or in the words of Hugh of St.-Victor,[8] "Omnis natura Deum loquitur. Omnis natura hominem docet. Omnis natura rationem parit, et nihil in universitate infecundum est" [All of nature speaks of God. All of nature teaches man. All of nature brings forth reason, and nothing in the universe is unfruitful]. The thing, however, does not have only *one* meaning, like the word—except in the cases of homonymity, where more than one meaning arises—but a diverse range of meanings. Every single thing meant by the word has itself a host of meanings, the number of which is identical with the sum of the properties of the thing. For this is the second principle, which again we shall not pursue historically: the thing has as many meanings as it has properties. Concisely formulated by Peter of Poitiers: "Quaelibet enim res, quot habet proprietates, tot habet linguas aliquid spirituale nobis et invisibile insinuantes, pro quarum diversitate et ipsius nominis acceptio variatur" [Indeed every created thing has as many meanings suggesting to us something spiritual and invisible as it has properties, in proportion to the diversity of which even acceptance of the name itself varies].[9] Those properties

7. *PL,* 210, 53 A. The words of St. Paul, "Invisibilia enim ipsius a creatura mundi per ea quae facta sunt intellecta conspiciuntur" [For since the creation of the world his invisible attributes are clearly seen . . . being understood through the things that were made] (Romans 1:20 Vulg.), are quoted by Petrus Cantor (II, 17) in the form "Invisibilia Dei a creatura mundi per ea quae facta sunt, visibilia conspiciuntur" [The invisible things of God are clearly seen from the creation of the world on through those that were made visible]. On this cf. Hugh of St.-Victor, *De arca Noe morali* II, 12, in *PL,* 176, 643 D. The Creation is the "opus Dei, quod numquam desinit esse, in quo opere visibili invisibilis sapientia creatoris visibiliter scripta est" [the work of God that never ceases to exist, in which visible work the invisible wisdom of the Creator has been visibly written] (cf. ibid., II, 16, col. 645).

8. *Eruditio didascalica* VI, 5, in *PL,* 176, 805 C.

9. Petri Pictaviensis, *Allegoriae super tabernaculum Moysi,* ed. Ph. S. Moore and J. A. Corbett (South Bend, Ind., 1938); cf. *Speculum ecclesiae,* in *PL,* 177, 375 D: "Res . . . tot figuras quot naturas et quot habent proprietates tot significationum habent diversitates" [Things . . . have as many [*tot*] figures as they have [*quot*] natures and as many [*tot*] diversities of signification as they

of the thing that contain meaning are given in the external form of its appearance (*visibilis forma*) and in its inner being (*invisibilis natura*).[10] Snow signifies something because of its form, inasmuch as it is white; because of its nature, inasmuch as it is cold. It has to be the fundamental concern of medieval philology to determine the essence of both the *voces* (words) and the *res* (things). Both take place in the framework of the seven liberal arts. The *voces* are treated in the trivium (grammar, rhetoric, dialectic), while on the other hand it is the task of the quadrivium to determine the thing according to its form and its nature, that is, according to its properties as a bearer of meaning. Thus, for example, mathematics treat the *forma exterior* (exterior form), physics the *interior natura* (interior nature) of things. Or, if we use the tripartite division—which was familiar to the Middle Ages since Origen—of logic, ethics, and theory: "logica de vocibus, ethica de moribus, theorica de rebus tractat. Item theorica subdividitur in mathematicam, physicam, theologiam" [logic treats of words, ethics of morality, theory of the nature of things. Likewise theory is subdivided into mathematics, physics, theology].[11]

---

have [*quot*] properties]. Richard of St.-Victor, *Excerptiones* II, 5, *De significatione vocum et rerum*, in *PL*, 177, 205 D: "Voces non plus quam duas aut tres habent significationes. Res autem tot possunt habere significationes, quot habent proprietates" [Words have no more than two or three significations. Things, however, can have as many significations as they have properties]; cf. Guibert de Nogent, in *PL*, 156, 29 B.

10. Richard of St.-Victor, *Excerptiones* II, 5, in *PL*, 177, 205 D: "Res duobus modis significat, natura et forma. Natura, ut nix, quia frigida est, exstinctionem designat libidinis. Forma, quia candida est, munditiam designat boni operis" [A thing signifies according to two modes, nature and form. According to nature inasmuch as snow, since it is cold, signifies the extinction of desire. According to form since it is white and signifies the purity of good works]. As an example from the *Distinctiones monasticae* (II, 482):

> Natura aquilae cognoscere non puto vile,
> Cuius naturas sacras reor esse figuras.
>
> [Knowing the eagle's nature I think not base,
> Whose natural traits I esteem as holy symbols.]

11. *Speculum ecclesiae*, in *PL*, 177, 375 D. It goes on to say (376 A): "Mathematica de visibilibus formis rerum visibilium agit, physica de invisibilibus naturis rerum visibilium, theologia de invisibilibus essentiis et earumdem naturis. Sic ergo per artes iuvamur in divina pagina, ubi vocum significationem attendimus propter litteralem sensum et rerum significationem consideramus, ut capiamus mysticum intellectum per formam visibilem, ubi iuvat mathematica, aut secundum naturam invisibilem, ubi physica et theologia serviunt" [Mathematics treats of the visible forms of visible things, physics of the invisible natures of visible things, theology of the invisible essences and natures of the same things. And so, therefore, we are sustained in Holy Scripture by the arts, when we attend to verbal signification for the sake of the literal sense and

Thus, it is not the philological disciplines in the narrow sense of the trivium, but rather mathematics and physics which are sisterly to theology. The trivium serves the science of the meaning of words, the quadrivium the science of the meaning of things that builds upon it. All the disciplines of medieval learning serve the disclosure of the spiritual sense of the word: "Omnes itaque artes subserviunt divinae sapientiae et inferior scientia recte ordinata ad superiorem conducit" [And so all the arts attend divine wisdom, and the lower science in its due order leads on to the higher].[12] Or "In hoc enim quod in divina pagina tam rerum quam vocum necessaria est significatio, artes ei subserviunt, dum trivium vocum, quadrivium phisicarum rerum administrat notitiam" [In this respect, to be sure, that in the sacred page the signification of things is as necessary as the signification of words, the arts render it their service, when the trivium tenders it the knowledge of words, the quadrivium a knowledge of things physical].[13] The specifically philological disciplines, which treat words, are the preliminary stages of the disciplines of the quadrivium, which treat things so as to clear the way to the spiritual sense of the word. Thus, the disciplines which treat the form and nature of things have no self-sufficient meaning as "pure" sciences but are the forerunners of the written meaning. The *Physiologus,* the bestiaries, the treatises on gems and plants, indeed the whole encyclopedic activity of the Middle Ages, starting with the massive work *De universo* by Hrabanus Maurus, who himself entitles it *De sermonum proprietate et mystica rerum significatione,* perform no

ponder the signification of things that we may grasp mystical understanding through the visible form, when mathematics comes to our aid, or according to invisible nature, when physics and theology serve us].

12. Richard of St.-Victor, *Excerptiones* II, 4, in *PL,* 177, 205 C: "quod scriptura mundana subserviat divinae" [that worldly scripture serves the divine]. It goes on to say: "Sub eo igitur sensu, qui inter voces et res versatur, continetur historia, et ei subserviunt tres scientiae, dialectica, rhetorica, grammatica. Et sub eo sensu, qui inter res et facta mystica versatur, continetur allegoria. Et sub illo, qui est inter res et facienda mystica, continetur tropologia. Et his duabus subserviunt arithmetica, musica, geometria et physica" [In that sense, therefore, which dwells between words and things, history is contained, and three sciences serve it, dialectics, rhetoric, grammar. And in that sense which dwells between things and mystical actualities allegory is contained. And within the one which lies between things and things-to-be-made-into-mystical-actualities is contained tropology. And it is these latter two [allegory and tropology] that are served by arithmetic, music, geometry, and physics].

13. *Speculum ecclesiae,* cap. 8, *De occultis scripturarum Veteris et Novi Testamenti,* in *PL,* 177, 375 C; cf. Hugh of St.-Victor, *De scripturis et scriptoribus sacris,* cap. 13, in *PL,* 175, 20 C: "Septem liberales artes huic scientiae subserviunt. Trivium ad significationem vocum, quadrivium ad rerum significationem respicit" [All seven liberal arts serve this form of knowledge. The trivium looks to the signification of words, the quadrivium to the signification of things].

other service.[14] The description of things is the intention of all knowledge directly concerned with what has been created so as to prepare the ground for the spiritual understanding of things by the determination of the properties of all creation. But it is not only the visible objects which belong to these *res primae res secundas significantes* (first things that signify second things), but also persons, numbers, places, times, and the facts of history as well.[15] Even those things which have taken place since the Creation are vehicles of meaning, something of far-reaching consequence for the typological thought of the Middle Ages.

"Those things which happened in truth are said to have prefigured the form of another sacrament."[16]

In what follows we shall not distinguish between a signification of events—on which the typological elements of medieval art are to a very large extent grounded—and the signification of words and things, which is fundamentally related to it. In this way we shall stay within the framework of a science of signification that could be represented lexicographically even by the Middle Ages.

Because the thing has as many meanings as it has properties, but because there are good and bad properties, the same thing can signify good things and bad things or, as the church fathers say, *in bonam partem* (in a good sense) as well as *in malam partem* (in an evil sense), or, as is often said, there are words that can be written in golden or in black ink. The same thing designated by

14. In the preface addressed to King Ludwig, in *PL*, 111, 9 B: "Nuper quoque quia vos, quando in praesentia vestra fui, compertum vos habere dixistis aliquod opusculum me noviter confecisse de sermonum proprietate et mystica rerum significatione . . . Sunt enim in eo plura exposita de rerum naturis et verborum proprietatibus nec non etiam de mystica rerum significatione" [Since you, also recently, when I was in your presence, said you had found out I had newly put together some small work on the peculiar nature of words and the mystical signification of things . . . [let me say that] within it many points concerning the nature of things and the peculiar qualities of words and, indeed, also concerning the mystical signification of things are expounded].

15. Richard of St.-Victor, *Excerptiones* II, 5, in *PL*, 177, 205 D: "Hae autem res primae res secundas significantes sex circumstantiis discretae considerantur, quae sunt hae: res, persona, numerus, locus, tempus, gestum" [These first things, however, that signify second things, are considered to be distinguished from one another according to the following six circumstances: thing, person, number, place, time, motion].

16. Hrabanus, in *PL*, 112, 331 A, on Galatians 4:24: "quae sunt per allegoriam dicta" [[those things] which are said by way of allegory]. Since this is the only instance of the use of *allegoria* in the Bible, the exegesis of Galatians 4:24 promises a wealth of information about the theological understanding of allegory.

one word can signify both God and the devil, just as, in its different significations, it can traverse the whole range of values which lies between them.[17] The lion can signify Christ, because according to its nature it sleeps with its eyes open: just as Christ as a human being died while God was still alive (III, 54), but, according to its nature, it can also signify the devil because of its bloodlust and because it goes about roaring and seeks whom it can devour (1 Peter 5:8; III, 54). It signifies the just man, who is confident as "a young lion" (Proverbs 28:1; III, 53) (figs. 1, 2, 3). It signifies the heretic because of the smell of its teeth, which issues from its mouth just as the word of blasphemy issues from the mouth of the heretic (III, 55), and so on. The signification of a thing at a given moment is determined by the property of thing which is brought into play, and the context in which the particular word appears. The signification of the word is exhausted with regard to the thing. The thing, on the other hand, has a universe of signification, which stretches from God to the devil and which is potentially present in everything which is designated by a word.[18] It realizes itself at a given moment only in a direction that is determined by the context and the property adduced to the thing. Thus, in the concrete textual case the lion cannot signify "God *or* the devil," but only one, but in another textual context it can signify the other. An interpretation of meaning from the context is also necessary in the case of the signification of things, so that we find the signification which is correct, in the given case, from among all the possible ones. It is the task of the Middle Ages to reveal, in the thing, all the possibilities of spiritual sense that it has been charged with since Creation, in order, by finding the right meanings, to use it in the concrete textual case. For this reason the Middle Ages created poetic catchphrases for individual things, which concisely catalogued the properties of a thing like, for example, the thing "sea" in the works of Anonymous of Clairvaux (II, 156):

17. "Dentes et tetris et aureis litteris scribuntur in hac pagina" [Teeth are written both in black and in golden letters on this page] (II, 212; cf. II, 251, 499, 504, etc.). Pseudo-Hrabanus, *Allegoriae*, in *PL*, 112, 850 B: "una eademque res non solum diversam, sed et adversam aliquando in scriptura sacra significationem habere potest" [at any time in Sacred Scripture one and the same thing can have not only a different but also an opposed meaning].

18. If F. Scheidweiler (*Zeitschrift für deutsches Altertum* 79, p. 264) noted that we find in the Middle Ages "in a way that is no longer acceptable to us the same words, with meanings that not only vary but also have completely different meanings, and this next to each other in the work of one and the same author," then this "iridescence of meaning" (265) corresponds to the nature of the poetic word (J. Schwietering, ibid., 265, n. 1) and to the resistances that are offered to a written language in the process of formation. May we not perhaps ask whether the polysemy of the word is not in the final instance also promoted by the spiritual sense?

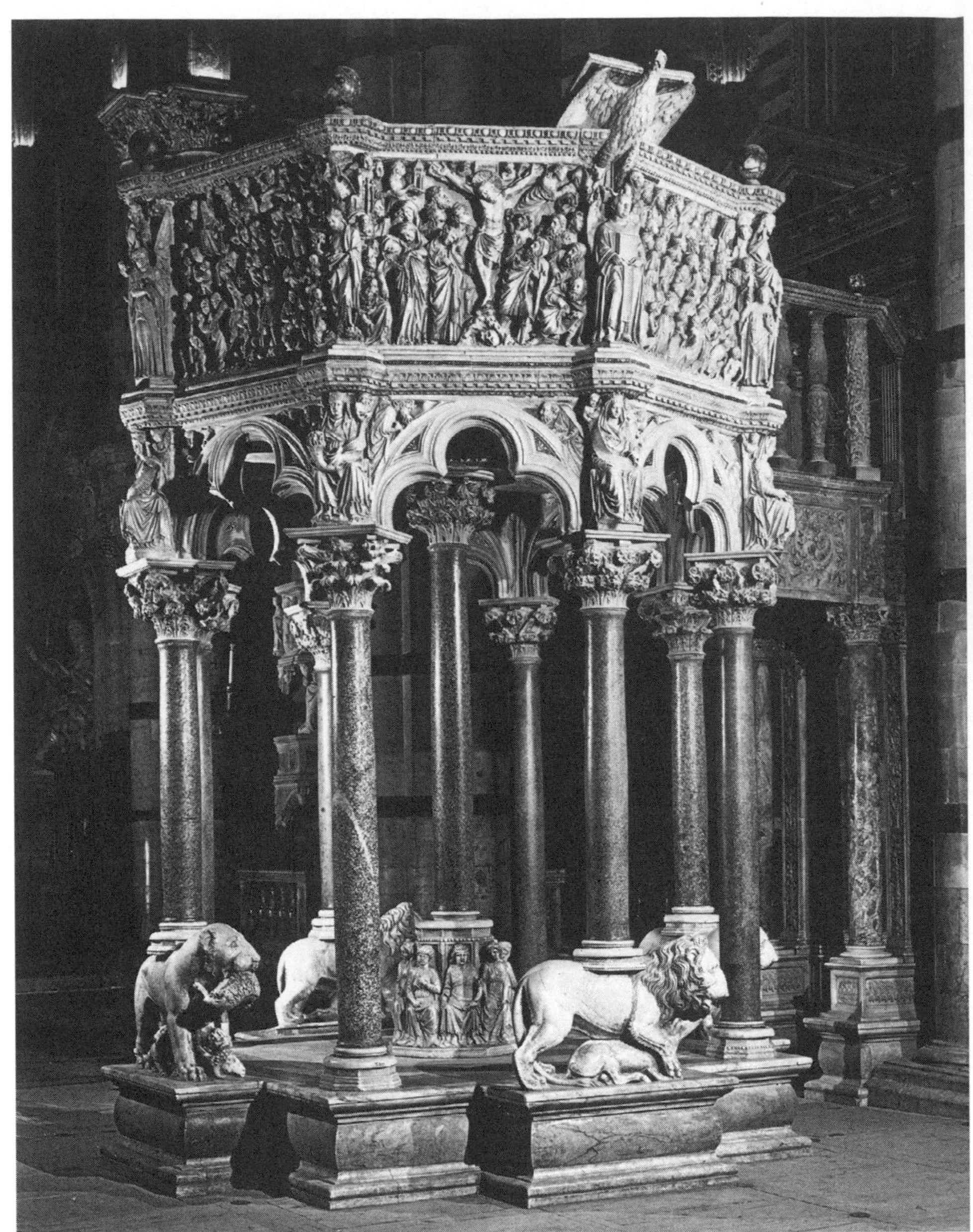

FIGURE 1

The lion can signify, these signified things/thing-signifiers, lions/lionesses, in their context on the edge of Nicola Pisano's pulpit, Siena Cathedral.

Est mare diffusum, fervens, salsum atque profundum,
Absorbens, fluidum, lucidum, foetens et amarum
Atque procellosum, rugit, gignitque periclum.

[The sea is spreading, seething, salty and deep,
Hungry, flowing, gleaming, stinking, and bitter
And stormy as well, it roars, and gives birth to peril.]

Or for the thing "oil" in the *Distinctiones monasticae* (II, 381):

Oleum multa significat in sacra scriptura, quia multae sunt eius proprietates, quae notantur his versibus:
Est oleum pingue, calidum, nitidumque, suave;
Mitigat et reficit, lucet, superenatat, ungit.

[Oil signifies many things in Sacred Scripture, since many are its properties, which are indicated in these verses:
Oil is fatty, warm and shiny, pleasant;
it soothes and refreshes, glitters, swims to the top and anoints.]

In an appendix these properties are interpreted in the same order.[19] If these are properties which can be used for interpretation, then also, to give

19. Thomas Cantipratanus, in *De naturis rerum* XVII, 3 and 7, seems to have written the verses *De proprietatibus lunae* (3) and *solis* (7) himself. In cap. 7 on the sun: "De eius proprietatibus septem versus sunt":

Fulgidus, effundit radios, fons ipse caloris;
Attrahit hic nubes, specimen vel forma caloris;
Illustrat lunam, noctemque diemque ministrat;
Fructus maturat; ac humida cuncta resiccat;
Intrat, si reseras; glacies et dura relidit;
Laetificat sanos oculos, lippos quoque claudit;
Occidit, et oritur; descendens, hinc quoque scandit.

In cap. 3 on den Mond: "Sunt ergo isti versus et lunae proprietates":

Humorum mater, solisque refrigerat aestum;
Eclipsim patitur, Phoebo faciente recessum;
Huic sol dat lumen; tenebras de nocte relidit;
Illustrat mundum, sol pristina quando revisit,
Inter planetas magis haec terris propiavit;
Crescit, decrescit, candet, tempus mediavit.

an example for this as well, in a catchphrase for the signification of things, in the *Distinctiones monasticae,* we have twelve different meanings of the thing "stone," which traverse its field of signification from the heights of Christ to the depths of the heathen (II, 330):

Christus, et angelica virtus, Christi quoque sponsa,
Iustus, iustitia, carnalis sensus, et usus
Pravus, peccatum grave, daemon, falsus hebraeus,
Verus gentilis dicitur esse lapis.

[Christ, and angelic virtue, Christ's bride as well,
The just man, justice, carnal sense, and depraved
Habit, grave sin, demon, false Jew,
True Gentile—each is said to be stone.]

The customary descriptions of things, which serve as the basis for the revelation of meaning in the Middle Ages, can display an elegance, characterized by a poetic devotion to the essence of things, precisely at that point where they remain prose. We may take as an example Anonymous of Clairvaux's particularly beautiful descriptions of dew: "Ros invisibiliter descendit,

---

[In cap. 7 on the sun: "On its properties there are seven verses":

Shining, it sheds its rays, itself the fount of warmth;
It draws to itself the clouds, a visible sign and form of warmth;
It makes bright the moon; and it ministers to night and day;
It ripens fruit; and humid garments it redries;
It enters, if you open; it beats back ice and hardness;
It gladdens healthy eyes, it also closes the watery;
It sets and it rises; descending, it also rises up again.

In cap. 3 on the moon: "These, then, are the verses and the properties of the moon":

Mother of humors she, and she cools the warmth of the sun;
She endures the eclipse, when Phoebus recedes;
To her the sun gives light; she beats back the dark of night;
She is the light of the world, when the sun revisits ancient origins,
Among the planets she has favored earthly lands;
She increases, decreases, shines, she stands in the midst of time.]

Each of the properties of the sun and the moon mentioned in these verses is used subsequently of the Virgin Mary (II, 63ff., 66ff.).

FIGURE 2
Lion tearing a horse to pieces (detail of fig. 1).

refrigerat, fecundat; clarus, suavis; modico calore siccatur; terram mollescit, semini placet; nocte fluit et silentio, minutatim ac sparsim" [Dew descends invisibly, cools, fructifies; clear, sweet; with moderate warmth it dries up; softens the earth, pleases the seed; flows at night and in silence, bit by bit and here and there] (II, 90). The temporal, as a creature of God's hand appointed for the purpose of praising him, is not extinguished by the process of spiritualization, but, on the contrary, is dedicated with the word of the creature which is enshrined in the thing and is, for this reason, described with pious devotion. It is the task of the Middle Ages to reveal the meaning of the essence of things comprehended in this manner. For—and herein lies the rationale for all this effort—the meaning of words is determined by man and serves man's expression of his will. The meaning of things, on the other hand, is determined by God. Man uses the word to speak to man; God uses things, and it is our business to understand the word of God in things: "Words signify by

FIGURE 3
Lioness tearing a lamb to pieces while giving suck (detail of fig. 1).

virtue of human institution, things by divine institution. For just as a human being makes its will known to another through words, so does God make His will known through the things He has created."[20]

Now what is the nature of the spiritual sense hidden within things—the *sensus mysticus* insofar as it is concealed—the *sensus spiritualis* insofar as it is revealed? At this point we can no longer avoid mentioning the word which we have up to this point omitted: we must now enquire about the nature of allegory. There is no concept, in the whole history of literature from antiquity to

20. *PL*, 177, 375 C; cf. Hugh of St.-Victor, *Eruditio didascalica* V, 3: "sed excellentior valde est rerum significatio quam vocum, quia hanc usus instituit, illam natura dictavit. Haec hominum vox est, illa vox Dei ad homines. Haec prolata perit, illa creata subsistit" [the signification of things is, after all, by far more excellent than the signification of words, since the latter was established by usage, the former dictated by nature. The latter is the word of men, the former the word of God to men. The latter, once brought forth, perishes, the former, creature of God's creation, persists].

Romanticism, and beyond, into modern scholarly terminology, that is more shifting and causes more misunderstandings than this. What literary history, particularly of the late Middle Ages, calls allegorical literature, like the *Roman de la rose* or the *minne* allegories, has nothing to do with what we understand by allegory here. Each excludes the other. In the one case we are dealing with allegories of personification:[21] the sense is the given, and the thing that serves to embody it is sought for, and found, by being set poetically.[22] Ever since C. S. Lewis wrote his *Allegory of Love*, literary history has been particularly devoted to this type of "allegorical" literature as well, and the danger of conceptual confusion which Lewis clearly avoids is obvious today. Personifying allegory is a literary technique which has been used since antiquity and is at home in poetics, where its name still lives on in the Middle Ages.[23] What the Middle Ages understands by allegory in the interpretation of Holy Writ is of quite a different sort and has quite different origins. If poetic allegorization is concerned with the arbitrary literary representation of a thing by personification or reification, it is quite the reverse in Christian word interpretation. Here we are dealing with the unveiling of the meaning of the language of God which was sealed into the creature at the Creation, with *revelatio*, with a *spiritualis notificatio* (spiritual knownmaking), as Hugh of St.-Victor calls it (*PL*, 175, 20 D), which hears the language of divine proclamation out of the mute universe of things.

In general, the Middle Ages distinguishes three stages of the spiritual sense of the word and, as a rule, calls the first stage allegory. What the Middle

21. We are dealing with that sort of Hegelian "conscious symbolism" (*Aesthetics*, p. 398ff.) "in which it is especially the domination of the abstract meaning over the external shape which appears" (p. 397).

22. The meaning of things here too—but not things designed at the Creation, but *ex humana institutione*, the concretization by literature of the abstract or the inner. It does not live by "nature" (*physis*) but by "convention" or "positing" (*thesis*).

23. On the history of allegory among the Greeks, Romans, and Hebrews and in Christianity to the time of Augustine, see J. C. Joosen and J. H. Waszink, "Allegorese," in *Reallexikon für Antike and Christentum* (Stuttgart, 1950), vol. 1, cols. 283–293 (with bibliography); K. Borinski, *Die Antike in Poetik und Kunsttheorie* (Leipzig, 1914), 1:21ff.; Leiva Petersen, *Zur Geschichte der Personifikation in griechischer Dichtung and bildender Kunst* (Würzburg, 1939); J. Bonsirven, *Exégèse rabbinique et exégèse Paulinienne* (Paris, 1939), pp. 207–251, 301–311; H.-I. Marrou, *Saint Augustin*, pp. 494–498; R. van Marle, *Iconographie de l'art profane au moyen-âge et à la renaissance*, vol. 2, *Allégories et symboles* (The Hague, 1932); R. Gruenther, in his review of H. Kreisselmeier, "Der Sturm der Minne auf die Burg" (*Euphorion*, vol. 51 [1957]), where he is concerned with the clarification of concepts, rightly calls the allegorical procedure in the medieval *minne* allegories "above all a literary technique to present inner action and emotional processes in the guise of concrete happenings."

Ages itself calls a superstructure of the three stages of spiritual written meaning—allegorical, tropological, and anagogical meanings—is built on the foundation of the historical or literal meaning of the word.[24] In accordance with the aspect under which the word is questioned, as to its meaning, it reveals itself to the exegete in the historical, the allegorical, the tropological, or the anagogical dimension of its meaning. If we ask the text questions about what has been, historically, it answers us with the historical literal sense. If we ask about the meaning of the text in terms of the doctrine of salvation, then it will answer on the level of allegorical meaning. Here allegory has the same meaning as the modern concept of typology, in other words, the relationship of meaning between prefiguration and fulfillment, as between the Old and the New Testaments. This form of thinking, anchored in the doctrine of salvation, left a strong mark upon the historical consciousness of the Middle Ages. Among other things, this was because it could be transferred to the idea of antiquity as prefiguration and Christianity as fulfillment, thus intensifying the exultation of the consciousness of living in a time that was so superior to antiquity that it was precisely to this consciousness that profound urges toward the artistic surmounting of antiquity were ascribed. This was something that Schwietering discovered and that Auerbach and Glunz developed and substantiated.[25] It is not from the aspect of the doctrine of salvation, but with respect to the life of the individual soul in the world that the word is revealed in the tropological or moral meaning that points out a way of leading one's life, by indicating to the soul the path to, and the destination of, its salvation. And, finally, if it is questioned as to its statement about the promises

24. Rupert of Deutz, in *PL*, 168, 839f.: "Non ignoro, quantum vel quale susceperim negotium, scilicet historiae sive rei gestae aliquod ponere fundamentum et super illud magnum, quod sub istis vocibus continetur, superaedificare mysterium. Tunc enim expositio mystica firmius stat neque fluitare permittitur, si super historiam certi temporis vel rei demonstrabilis rationabiliter superaedificata continetur" [I am not ignorant of how great or what sort of a task I have undertaken, namely to put in place some kind of foundation for history or, if you will, for the happenings that comprise it—and over the great basis which is contained in these words to build the superstructure of divine mystery. For then mystical explanation stands more firmly, nor is it permitted to idly flow hither and thither, when it is based upon the history of a certain time or is rationally built up upon the substructure of demonstrable preconditions].

25. J. Schwietering, "Typologisches im mittelalterlicher Dichtung," in *Festschrift für G. Ehrismann* (Berlin, 1925), *Deutsche Dichtung des Mittelalters* (Potsdam, n.d.), and *Anzeiger für deutsches Altertum* 70 (1957): pp. 2ff.; H. H. Glunz, *Die Literarästhetik des europäischen Mittelalters* (Bochum, 1937); E. Auerbach, "Figura," *Archivum Romanicum* 22 (1938): 436–489; *Typologische Motive in der mittelalterlichen Literatur* (Krefeld, 1953); F. Ohly, *Sage und Legende in der Kaiserchronik* (Münster, 1940).

which will be fulfilled in the afterlife, the anagogical meaning of the word is discovered, and that is meaning that leads us up to heaven. An example which is constantly given in the Middle Ages is the word Jerusalem: historically, it is a city on earth; allegorically, it is the church; tropologically, it is the soul of the believer; anagogically, it is God's heavenly city.

According to an image familiar to the Middle Ages, from the time of Jerome onward, the walls of allegory are built up on the foundation of the understanding of the letter (beyond which the Hebrews and the heathens were unable to go), arched over by the roof of anagogical understanding with its view of the afterlife, while it is the task of the colors of Moralitas to adorn the walls of the edifice of the understanding of the word, both inside and out. If it was previously our lot to introduce the concept of a *world* of meaning, we now see our lot as the new concept of a *space* filled with the meaning of the word, an edifice of spiritual meaning erected on the foundations of the historical sense. The stages and dimensions of medieval significs furnish the spiritual perspective of the world of what has been created, and this becomes language in the word. The Middle Ages, which is alleged not to have known perspective, has its own sort of perspective, one that is appropriate to it in the spiritual transparency of what exists. It arises in the upward vision and the visual penetration that detaches itself from the earthly to join the spiritual reality of the signification of the sign that is present in the creaturely. It is perspective in the truest sense of the word, in that it looks through the visible to the invisible, through the *significans* (signifier) to the *significatum* (signified). It leads from the foundations to the vault, from the earthly to the heavenly. Its essence is not foreshortening, but extension to the sublime. It does not relativize by means of a vanishing point on earth but orientates itself to the absolute, and makes what has been created transparent to the eternal. Its nature is not physiological-visual but theological-spiritual, and, as such, it determines the art of the sublime. Without a knowledge of the spiritual perspectives of the universe of signification and of the scope of signification, which take the measure of the relationships between man and God, we cannot expect to understand a literature which presupposes such a knowledge. Hugh of St.-Victor says that whoever lacks the right "manner" (*modus*) and "order of reading" (*ordo legendi*) is like someone who has lost his way in a dense forest and whose efforts are all in vain.[26]

German literature, just to take it as an example, was—apart from a few remnants of pagan literature—for centuries, from about 770 to 1150 almost

26. *Eruditio didascalica* V, 5, in *PL*, 176, 793 D.

exclusively, and even after that to a large extent, Bible literature. The modern secular science of word signification is limited, when it comes to the interpretation of this literature, because it is restricted to the literal sense of the word. Modern lexicography, which asks only what the literal meaning of the word is, is not in a position to reveal the spiritual meaning of the word. In the same way, most modern etymology would lead us astray, if we were to use its methods to approach the medieval word with a view to determining its spiritual meaning. The Middle Ages practice a form of etymology that is speculative, belongs to theology, and serves the illumination of the meaning of the word that is concealed within it. Even where it is historical, speculative knowledge is projected into the historical, and its chief task lies in that interpretation of meaning, by means of etymology, that flourished far into the Middle Ages, from the time of Isidor of Seville onward. Its interest is only apparently developmental, that is, only insofar as it serves the science of signification. If the word *mors* (death) is derived in the Middle Ages from *amarus* (bitter) or from Mars, the god of war, this was an interpretation of meaning that was possible for pagans as well, but the third etymology of the word is conditioned by Christianity, when the word is derived from the bite of the apple at the Fall of Man: "a morsu primi hominis qui vetitae arboris pomum mordens mortem incurrit" [from the bite of the first man, who, biting the apple of the forbidden tree, incurs death] (*PL*, 177, 134 C). It would be foolish to deride such an etymology as unscientific if it helped the people of its time to arrive at a deeper signification of the meaning of the word, since it was precisely the task of etymology at that time to illuminate the spiritual meaning of the word.[27] Our modern etymology would have appeared questionable to the Middle Ages, because it is bogged down in the literal meaning of the word and does not give any explanation of the meaning of the world or of life. The spiritual meaning of the word with its universe of signification, and its scope of signification, contains an interpretation of meaning that derives from the Christian spirit and is thus a guide to life, as the often quoted catchphrase that concisely formulates the four stages of the written meaning tells us:

Littera gesta docet, quod credas allegoria,
Moralis quid agas, quo tendat anagogia

27. Anonymous of Clairvaux (12th c.) remarks of his alphabetical dictionary: "In hoc libello continentur etymologiae nominum, rerum proprietates, et earumdem distinctiones scripturarum testimoniis confirmatae" [In this little book are contained the etymologies of names, the properties of things, and their distinctions confirmed by the witness of the Scriptures] (III, 488).

[The letter teaches what's been done, allegory what's to believe,
Morality what to do, whither thy course is bent—anagogy]

The writing of a history of Christian etymology in the Middle Ages has yet to be undertaken. The etymological substantiation of the signification of words, is—if I see it aright—reduced in the Middle Ages to the extent that the vernaculars gain in importance, because the etymological grounding of words, as our example of *mors* shows, cannot be transferred from Latin to the vernacular languages, or at least can be transferred only in exceptional cases, as in the *Wiener Genesis* (603f.) where we read: "maget sol sie haben namen, want si fone manne ist genomen" [she shall be called a maiden because she is taken from man].[28] If, then, medieval etymology contains itself within the framework of one language, it is on the other hand the nature of the signification of *things* that the spiritual meaning of the word is the same in all languages, since it does not proceed from the sound of the individual languages, but from the language of things, which is the same for the whole of mankind in God's creation, as Alanus ab Insulis tells us in a verse about the rose (*PL*, 210, 579 A):

Omnis mundi creatura
Quasi liber et pictura
Nobis est et speculum;
Nostrae vitae, nostrae mortis,
Nostri status, nostrae sortis
Fidele signaculum.
Nostrum statum pingit rosa,
Nostri status decens glosa,
Nostrae vitae lectio—

[The whole world of things created is,
As if it were a book and picture,
For us a mirror too;
Of our life, of our death,
Of our status, of our fate

28. Behind which already stands a biblical etymology: "haec vocabitur virago, quoniam de viro sumpta est" [she will be called woman because she is taken out of man] (Genesis 2:23). In Luther's translation: "man wird sie Männin heißen, darum daß sie vom Manne genommen ist" [They will call her woman because she was taken from man].

The faithful sign.
Our fate is painted by a rose,
On our state a fitting gloss,
It is the lesson of our lives—]

Looked at theologically, it turns out that the Babylonian confusion of languages continues only in the literal meaning of languages, while it is resolved by the spiritual meaning of the word—which is to be elicited from things—which is common to all languages. All languages participate in the Pentecostal secret by virtue of the spiritual meaning of the word, and by it historical ages—just like languages—are also resolved in eternal truth, which is announced by the whole of history.[29]

It is essential that all branches of scholarship devoted to the Middle Ages—from philology through the study of art and history to the natural sciences—not leave questions of the spiritual meaning of the world of creation, which becomes word through the medium of language, to theology alone, but make it their own concern and fructify it in the way that art history has pioneered, and historians (P. E. Schramm) have shown us with their research into symbols.

The Middle Ages did not create only a Christian etymology; they also created a Christian grammar, which—as Smaragdus expresses it in a commentary on Donatus, which Charlemagne commanded him to write—was to surpass what was shadowily prefigured in antiquity with the fulfillment of the spirit of truth, to change the *paganorum ritus* (rite of the pagans),

29. On the subject of the suspension of time: Gregory, *Moralia* XX, 1, in *PL*, 76, 135 C: Scriptura . . . scientias tamen omnes atque doctrinas ipso etiam locutionis suae more transcendit, quia, uno eodemque sermone dum narrat textum, prodit mysterium; et sic scit praeterita dicere, ut eo ipso noverit futura praedicare; et non immutato dicendi ordine, eisdem ipsis sermonibus novit et ante acta describere et agenda nuntiare [Scripture . . . nevertheless transcends all sciences and doctrines through the manner of its own locution since, in one and the same discourse in which it narrates a text, it also presents a mystery; and thus it knows how to tell of things past in such a way that through that very narration it will at the same time have found a way to foretell the future; and without having changed around the order of its discourse, it is capable of both describing the past and predicting things to be done in the future in the very same utterances]. Hugh of St.-Victor, *De scripturis et scriptoribus sacris,* cap. 3 (*PL*, 175, 12 A): "Est autem allegoria, cum per id, quod ex littera significatum proponitur, aliud aliquid sive in praeterito, sive in praesenti sive in futuro factum significatur" [It is, moreover, allegory when through that which is set forth as signified by the letter another thing is signified as done, in the past, or in the present, or in the future].

in this area as well, into a *sacrificium domini* (sacrifice of the Lord).[30] But it is not my intention here to pave the way for a critical judgment—appropriate to its time (not one which grew out of the developmental thinking of the nineteenth century)—of the Christian etymology and grammar of the Middle Ages, which could also serve the purposes of the science of signification,[31] but to point to another area of concern which is, in my view, more important.

It could quite easily become part of the daily devotions of anyone who was accustomed to ask about spiritual sense to allegorize the things of the world which met his gaze, as we are told that Gregory of Nazianz did.[32] And

30. Quoted by J. Marillon, *Vetera analecta* (Paris, 1676), 2:420f. On the aims of this commentary cf. also the introductory poem (*MG Poetae latinae,* ed. E. Duemmler [1881]), pp. 607ff.:

Dulcia depromit, promittit et aurea regna,
 Lactea cum solido, pocula pane dabit.
Muneribus sacris plenus est iste libellus,
 Scripturam retinet, grammatica redolet.
Nunc scriptura docet domini perquirere regnum,
 Linquere terrena, scandere regna poli.
Promittit cunctis coelestia dona beatis.
 Vivere com domino semper et esse suo.
Grandia retribuit caro seduloque legenti
 Praemia grammatica ars miserante Deo.

[It promises sweet things, golden spheres as well,
 Will offer milky goblets along with solid bread.
Brimming with sacred gifts this little book,
 Filled with Scripture, redolent of grammar.
Now Scripture teaches us to search the kingdom of the Master,
 To leave behind terrestrial parts, to scale the heavenly realms.
It promises to all the blessed heavenly gifts,
 To live with the Master forever and to be forever his.
So richly the art of grammar requites the dear, diligent reader, God taking pity.]
(vv. 33–42)

31. J. Leclercq, "Smaragde et la grammaire chrétienne," *Revue du moyen âge latin* 4 (1948): 15–22.

32. Guibert de Nogent, *Quo ordine sermo fieri debeat,* in *PL,* 156, 29 D: "Gregorius Nazianzenus, vir mirabiliter eruditus, in quodam suo libro testatur se id habuisse consuetudinis, ut quidquid videret ad instructionem animi allegorizare studeret. Quod acumine rationis si facere assuescat aliquis, non modo in voluminibus divinis, sed etiam pene in his omnibus quae subiacent oculis, comparationes satis idoneas in exemplum et significantias utiles illarum quas ex usu assiduo nihili pendimus rerum uberrime invenit, quae tanto utilius cogitantur, quo benevolentia

when Bernard of Clairvaux sets the sermons of the trees or the stones above the sermons of books, we have to look at this in the same light.[33] The book of creation must be read and its letters interpreted by meditating upon them. Here, too, the saying holds good: "Principium ergo doctrinae est in lectione, consummatio in meditatione" (The origin of doctrine lies, thus, in reading, its consummation in meditating).[34] The essence of pious edification lies in the elevation of the scope of signification to the realm of devotion.[35] Exegesis and sermon educate not only the spiritually educated, but everyone who is affected by this preaching, in the methods of the discovery of the spiritual meaning that is hidden in things. The achievement of the centuries, from St. Paul to the church fathers, in raising the universe of the created world—to the extent that it appeared in the vocabulary of the Bible—up to the light of its spiritual meaning was the enormous product of

---

illis ampliore dicuntur, tantoque sunt gratiosiora quanto minus auditoribus usitata" [Gregory of Nazianz, a man of marvelous erudition, declares in a certain one of his books that he had the habit of striving to make an allegory of whatever he saw for the instruction of his spirit. This is something which if anyone becomes habituated to doing with all the sharpness of one's reason, not only within the canon of divine books but also with regard to almost everything that comes before one's eyes, then one finds in abundance comparisons fitting enough to serve as examples and advantageous meanings of those things which, because they are invoked so assiduously, we regard as of little or no value; these are considered all the more helpful insofar as they are described with greater good will and all the more pleasing insofar as they are less well known to their audience].

33. *Epistola* 106, 2, to Henricus Murdach, in *PL*, 182, 242 B: "Experto crede: aliquid amplius invenies in silvis quam in libris. Ligna et lapides docebunt te, quod a magistris audire non possis. An non putas posse te sugere mel de petra oleumque de saxo durissimo? An non montes stillant dulcedinem et colles fluunt lac et mel et valles abundant frumento?" [Believe one who has experienced it: you will find anything represented more amply in the forests than in the books. Trees and stones will teach you what you cannot hear from the mouths of the masters. Or do you not think yourself capable of sucking honey from a stone and oil from the hardest rock? Do not mountains drip sweetness and hills flow milk and honey and valleys abound in wheat?].

34. Hugh of St.-Victor, *Eruditio didascalica* III, 11, in *PL*, 176, 772 C.

35. Pseudo-Hrabanus (12th c.), *Allegoriae*, in *PL*, 112, 849f., talks in detail about this *spirituale aedificium* (spiritual edifice). The passage begins: "In nostrae ergo animae domo historia fundamentum ponit, allegoria parietes erigit, anagogia tectum supponit, tropologia vero tam interius per affectum quam exterius per effectum boni operis variis ornatibus depingit" [In the house of our spirit, therefore, history lays the foundation, allegory erects the walls, anagogy props up the roof, tropology, then, employing various adornments, paints the interior with the affect as well as the exterior with the effect belonging to good works] (849 C). This dictionary asks about the signification of the words *Ad nostram aedificationem* (To our edification) (851 A); cf. *moralis aedificatio* (moral edification) in the works of Richard of St.-Victor, *Sermones centum* 69, in *PL*, 177, 1114C.

a meditation that dwelt upon the essence, and the ways, of salvation. In a tension between tradition and freedom that spanned a millennium—sometimes latent, sometimes in evidence—which includes in itself the intellectually profound problem of the change in signification of the spiritual meaning of the word—as it reveals itself at the crux of the change from Romanesque to Gothic with the dehistorification and the mystical internalization of religion[36]—the continuity of interpretation which owes much to tradition is so great that it could end up as the lexicographical codification of the spiritual meaning of words, and the history of this lexicography is no less alive than that of medieval exegesis.[37] The Middle Ages in both the monastic and the scholastic areas produced many dozens of allegorical dictionaries which point to the spiritual meaning of biblical vocabulary—naturally almost exclusively of nouns, names, and numbers—by systematically establishing the space and by measuring the universe of signification and making that universe transparent to the spiritual force underlying it. They begin in the fifth century with *Formulae spiritualis intelligentiae* (Formulas of spiritual understanding),[38] are significantly expanded after 820 in the *Clavis* of the pseudo-Melito,[39] become more frequent after the middle of the twelfth century, and are maintained in an unbroken chain as an aid to sermons and exegesis until the eighteenth century. As far as the Middle Ages are concerned, they are for the most part unedited (very little is to be found in Migne). Up till now they have been referred to almost exclusively by theologians, and we would have known little of them were it not that the stupen-

36. The question, which is related to this change in signification, of the abandonment of a paratactic style that aimed, while having only loose connections in a horizontal context, at a higher goal, by means of word, thing, and event signification, may at least be hinted at here.

37. F. Ohly, *Hohelied-Studien: Grundzüge einer Geschichte der Hoheliedauslegung des Abendlandes bis um 1200* (Wiesbaden, 1958).

38. Ed. C. Wotke (Vienna, 1894), vol. 31 of *Corpus scriptorum ecclesiasticorum latinorum.*

39. In Pitra, *Spicilegium Solesmense,* vols. 2, 3. The allegorical dictionaries are not as old as it might have seemed, when Cardinal Pitra discovered the lost κλεῖς (key) of Bishop Melito of Sardes in the Latin glossary *Caput domini* and thought, in this way, to have shown the existence of a Bible dictionary as early as the second century. Pitra, who is still the best scholar on questions of this sort, unearthed a host of valuable materials but in his pardonable joy at his discoveries allowed himself to be misled in their historical evaluation. Criticism has regarded the alleged *Clavis* of Melito as a Bible dictionary that was compiled from the works of Augustine, Gregory the Great, and other Latin church fathers (O. Rottmanner, *Theologische Quartalschrift* 78 [1896]: 614–629; E. Amman, *Dictionnaire de théologie catholique* X, 546). The *terminus ante quem* is the year 821, as this work is placed before Theodulf of Orleans's (d. 821) Bible. Tradition, editions, bibliography of *Clavis* in F. Stegmüller, ed., *Repertorium biblicum,* nos. 5574–5578: on the Theodulf Bible, ibid., no. 8005f.

dous scholarship of Cardinal Pitra in the last century, on the occasion of his editon of the *Clavis* (Key), made a breach in our lack of knowledge of the materials, then on its own and with few successors to this day. Besides the *Artes praedicandi* and the hints for reading the Bible from Hrabanus Maurus's *De institutione clericorum* (based on Augustine's *Doctrina christiana*) and Hugh of St.-Victor's *Eruditio didascalica* (*PL*, 176, 739–838) up to the appearance of Flaccus Illyrius's *Clavis*[40] in the sixteenth century, what has been said above about the spiritual sense of Scripture is largely drawn from the prefaces to these works.[41]

We distinguish three main sorts of lexicographical interpretation of the spiritual sense of the word according to their literary form. These dictionaries follow the order in which the word appears in a particular text, particularly the Psalter, as is the case in the collections of *distinctiones,* which have been known since early scholasticism and which are very like the continuous exegesis of the biblical commentaries. Then, in the twelfth century—for example, in the works of Alanus ab Insulis, Petrus Cantor, or the pseudo-Hrabanus—a new form is developed which treats the vocabulary alphabetically, thus serving the needs of the preacher, and it is this method that later predominates. The third form of allegorical dictionary, which orders the vocabulary according to groups of things rather like a summa, is older and is structured more ideologically than practically. These summae are older than, and different in form from, the summae of early and later scholasticism and are, on the contrary, closer to the attempts at an ordered comprehension and interpretation of the world like Hrabanus's *De universo* and closer in time to the *Clavis.* The twelve books of the *Clavis* in order treat the vocabulary ac-

40. G. Moldaenke, *Schriftverständnis und Schriftdeutung im Zeitalter der Reformation,* pt. 1, *Matthias Flaccus Illyrius* (Stuttgart, 1936).

41. See, e.g., the *praefatio* to Hrabanus's *De universo,* in *PL,* 111, 9ff.; the prologue *Quisquis ad sacrae scripturae notitiam desiderat pervenire* (Whoever desires to arrive at a knowledge of Sacred Scripture) to the *Allegoriae* by the pseudo-Hrabanus (thought to be Adam Scotus or Garnerius of Rochefort), in *PL,* 112, 849ff.; Guibert de Nogent, *Quo ordine sermo fieri debeat,* in *PL,* 156, 21–32; the prologue of the *Allegoriae* of Peter of Poitiers, 1ff.; the prologue of Hugh of St.-Victor's *De sacramentis,* in *PL,* 176, 183ff.; Alanus ab Insulis, prologue to the *Distinctiones dictionum theologicalium,* in *PL,* 210, 687f.; Sicardus of Cremona, *Mitrale* I, 13, in *PL,* 213, 47f. We do not need to consider here the line that leads from Aristotle via Boethius to Abelard's dialectic, as this is concerned only with the *voces.* On this, see M. Grabmann, "Aristotle in the Twelfth Century," *Medieval Studies* 12 (1950): 123–162, "Die geschichtliche Entwicklung der mittelalterlichen Sprachphilosophie und Sprachlogik: Ein Überblick," *Mélanges J. de Ghellinek II* (Gembloux, 1951), pp. 421–433; H. Roos, *Die modi significandi des Martinus de Dacia: Forschungen zur Geschichte der Sprachlogik im Mittelalter* (Münster, 1952).

cording to object groups—first the words for God, then those for the son. After this come the things that are between heaven and earth—from the angels to the dew—then the earth with all that concerns it, and then man with the parts of his body and his activities. The next books, which treat metals and the tools made from them, flora, birds, and fauna, give us to understand that the *Physiologus,* the medieval herbals, bird books, and lapidaries are to be taken, according to the idea incorporated in them, as specialized allegorical dictionaries, which tend either to become parts of such universal dictionaries or to split off from them. The next book deals with man as a social being in the family and the church, the next is entitled "De civitate," in which the city is understood as an architectural and social structure—important for art history because of its architectural allegoreses. The twelfth book treats—like the numerous special treatises *de significatione numerorum*—number symbolism. The thirteenth book, which is an appendix, finally treats historical and geographical names according to the example of St. Jerome.

There is also a mixed form among the alphabetically arranged dictionaries, where the vocabulary is ordered under the different letters of the alphabet, again as a sort of summa, that is, first the words beginning with *A* which are most closely connected with God, then descending, through the cosmos of things beginning with the letter *A,* to those words which designate the devil, as in Peter of Capua's *Rosa alphabetica* (ca. 1200), in which, for example, the words with the initial *I* begin with *iustitia* and end with *infernus.* The idea of the summa is incorporated again in the arrangement of the individual articles in the dictionary, in that, after the description of the thing—which can of itself be not only beautiful but also of interest for cultural history[42]—we traverse the world of signification of individual things, again from God down to the devil—something that we saw *in nuce* in the catch verse about the signification of *lapis.*

I have to restrict myself here to the hints contained in such tables of contents and to a general indication of the significance of such allegorical dictionaries for all the disciplines of medieval studies. The spiritual magnificence and the astonishing compactness of the science of Christian significs, together with the etymologies that are adduced in the dictionaries and the Christian grammar that belongs to them, are an impressive historical testimony to a science that penetrated the world with the spirit. It will not deflect the modern linguist from the path that is prescribed for him by historical conditions, but they may make an impression on him and cause him to pause

42. E.g., the article on *scutum* (II, 300), or on the bishop's crook (*baculus;* II, 387).

and think, for example, about the limits of the validity of the application of the modern word field theory of meaning to the Middle Ages, if he compares the medieval principles of the ordering of vocabulary in the summa with modern principles, for example, in the lexicographical scheme of Hallig and von Wartburg.[43] Research tasks in medieval scholarship which we see lying ahead of us are (1) a catalogued stocktaking of allegorical dictionaries, (2) the editing of at least the most important of them, and (3) their utilization by all disciplines for their own particular areas of interest.[44] Medieval theologians, like Thomas Aquinas,[45] held fast to the principle that the spiritual sense of the word distinguished the Bible from all secular literature and was not applicable to the latter. But, in practice, this principle could not be defended, as the allegorical method of textual interpretation in the Middle Ages—and this is true of antiquity as well—was applied to nonbiblical texts like Homer, Virgil, and Ovid, as well as to vernacular texts like the *Ovide moralisé.* The allegoresis of the *minne* grotto in Gottfried von Strassburg's *Tristan* is the first application *expressis verbis,* in German, of the methodology of the spiritual interpretation of a text applied by a poet to his own work. Dante described the same method in the *Convivio* and described it in his dedicatory epistle to Cangrande as applicable to the *Divine Comedy* and gave examples for the *Par-*

43. R. Hallig and W. von Wartburg, *Begriffssystem als Grundlage für die Lexicographie: Versuch eines Ordnungsschemas: Abhandlungen der deutschen Akademie der Wissenschaften zu Berlin,* 1952/54 (Berlin, 1952). For example, "Glaube" and "Religion" appear at the end of section 4, "L'organisation sociale" (pp. 79ff.). As examples of medieval research on synonyms the discussions of words for chambers within the church in Sicardus of Cremona, *Mitrale* I, 5, in *PL,* 213, 26f. and in Belethus's *Rationale,* in *PL,* 202, 15 D, 108 D, can be mentioned. The synonyms permit the same object to appear under different aspects.

44. Pitra already established the aim (2.ii) of making a "Biblioteca nova veterum de re symbolica scriptorum."

45. Prima pars, qu. 1, art. 9: "Cum in omnibus scientiis voces significent, hoc habet proprium ista scientia (theologica) quod ipsae res significatae per voces etiam significent aliquid. Illa ergo prima significatio, qua voces significant res, pertinet ad primum sensum, qui est sensus litteralis. Illa vero significatio qua res significatae per voces iterum alias res significant, dicitur sensus spiritualis; qui super litteralem fundatur et eum supponit" [Although in all branches of knowledge it is words that signify, this particular branch (theology) is distinguished from the rest in that the things therein signified by words also signify something. Therefore that first signification, by virtue of which words signify things, pertains to the first sense, which is the literal sense. But that signification by which things signified through words in turn signify other things is called the spiritual sense; which is based upon the literal sense and subordinates it]. According to M. D. Chenu, "Histoire et allégorie au douzième siècle," *Glaube und Geschichte (Festgabe J. Lortz),* vol. 2 (Baden-Baden 1958), pp. 59–71, the citation here is on p. 71.

adiso. If the distinction between material and signification holds good for Chrétien de Troyes's Arthurian romances, then we are entitled to consider whether he did not see—more consciously than we have yet done—beyond the distinction of material and idea that was appropriate to his work to a possible signification of the meaning of individual motifs in his materials.[46] For example, it was the allegorical dictionaries that first made it clear to me that the lion that defeats the dragon and goes around with Iwein after being defended by him signifies the right in the name of which Iwein emerges triumphant from his chivalric adventure.[47] Gottfried von Strassburg in his encomium on Hartmann von Aue gives voice to such a sentiment (4621ff.):

Hartman der Ouwaere
Ahi, wie der diu maere
beid ûzen unde innen
mit worten und mit sinnen
durchverwet und durchzieret!
Wie er mit rede figieret
der aventiure meine.

[Hartmann von Aue. Oh, how he colors and decorates his story both inside and outside with both words and sense! How well his words hit the target of the story's meaning.]

If the knowledge of the method of the spiritual illumination of the word is indispensable for the biblical literature of the Middle Ages, such knowledge can also bear fruit—with the proper care and the necessary sense for the poetic—for secular literature. We would have to set against a Bible literature which is consciously adhering to historical sense, and the literature of leg-

46. J. Schwietering mentioned the possibility "that secular literature could also be interpreted in the spiritual, symbolic sense" with reference to marriage poems and the Arthurian romance: "Crestien makes an express distinction between *matiere* and *san*—material and idea—and the poet's audience was so educated in the spiritually symbolic comprehension of a work that it would ask questions of the text—in the realm of secular narrative as well—as to its exemplary signification." In *Die deutsche Dichtung des Mittelalters,* 2d ed. (Darmstadt, 1957), p. 149.

47. Compare, for example, the interpretation of the lion as the *viri iusti securitas* (freedom from care of the just man) in the work of Gregory the Great, after Proverbs 28:1: "iustus autem quasi leo confidens absque terrore erit" [the just man, moreover, like the lion, will be confident, without fear] (III, 52). On the lion as the symbol of justice, A. Erler, *Das Straßburger Münster im Rechtsleben des Mittelalters* (Frankfurt am Main, 1954).

ends, which is coordinate with this and ignorant of allegoresis,[48] an allegorizing biblical literature which is something of a higher order.[49] When a literature goes over from pure narrative to allegoresis, like the *Wiener Genesis* in the biblical, and *Tristan* in the secular realm, we have to raise questions as to poetic function and aesthetic value. The fact that medieval poets—without fearing for their reputations as poets—could take over alien materials so that by further interpretation they could illuminate their inner sense, as, among many other examples, German poets did with the French romances, has to be seen in the context of the fact that the Middle Ages were less concerned with the invention of new material than with the interpretation of what existed—an essential difference from what is expected of a poet in modern times. Just as theology worked indefatigably to try to interpret the same texts creatively, so literature also did the same thing with the really few imaginative plots which it had at its disposal. The illumination of the sense of the given materials, even if it is, as in theology, brought about by the, here, poetic execution of its historical change in signification, is of hardly less poetic value to the Middle Ages than the inventiveness of the few really great poets like Chrétien, whose tale was given a final creative interpretation by Cervantes when he showed in the sadness of the lonely man, who had grown isolated in his enthusiasm, that time had run out in a world that could see in the knight nothing more than a lovable fool.

Since the Hebrews and the pagans stuck to the letter,[50] whereas, after

48. In principle what holds good for legends is what the exegetes call *historia.* E.g.,. pseudo-Hrabanus (12th c.), in *PL,* 112, 849 B: "Historia namque per perfectorum exempla quae narrat legentem ad imitationem sanctitatis excitat" [History, for example, through examples of the perfected which it narrates, excites the reader to imitate their sanctity].

49. Hervaeus of Bourg Dieu (d. 1150) remarks on the Book of Tobias, in F. Stegmüller, *Repertorium biblicum medii aevi* (Madrid 1951) vol. 3, no. 3256: "Liber Tobiae in superficie litterae est salubris. Maxime enim vitae moralis et exemplis abundat et monitis. Sed quantum poma foliis, tantum allegoria historiis praecellit" [The Book of Tobias is already salutary on its literal surface. For it abounds to the greatest extent in examples of, and admonitions to, a moral life. But as much as apples are better than leaves, by just that much does allegory excel histories]. The same passage appears in Hugh of St.-Victor, *Allegoriae in Vetus Testamentum* IX, 2 (*De mysteriis quae continentur in libro Tobiae*), and there follows: "Maxime enim ecclesiae sacramenta continet. Ipse enim Tobias populum Israel significat, qui caeteris idolatriae deditis fide recta et operibus Deo serviebat" [Indeed, it contains the greatest sacraments of the church. For Tobias himself signifies the people Israel which, when others were given over to idolatry, served God in upright faith and with their works] (*PL,* 175, 737 D).

50. An example from the *Distinctiones monasticae* may serve as one among many: "Plato, licet esset acutissimus, verba Moysis, quae potuit legere, non potuit multis in locis intelligere, quia caruit gratia adiutrice" [Plato, although he possessed the keenest intellect, was not capable, in

Augustine, spiritual understanding assures the believer of salvation,[51] a new Christian aesthetics in the Middle Ages looked beyond antiquity—with the help of allegory—and saw that a new beauty had entered the world. Otfrid von Weißenburg, the first poet of the *sensus spiritualis* in the German language, spoke of this in his interpretation of the Marriage at Cana. He interprets the changing of water into wine as the transition from the literal sense to the knowledge of the spiritual sense. The refreshing spring water of the word changes itself into magnificent wine, when the salvation which is contained within it is revealed. It was in such a clarification of and subsequent change in the word that Otfrid saw his poetic vocation. It is in the awakening of the letter to the spirit, the revelation of the hidden, the removal of the shadow in the light of knowledge, the changing of the water into wine, that Otfrid sees a new beauty given to us through Christ:

Deta er iz sconara al so zam, joh ziarara ouh so filu fram
(wir goum es nemen wollen), so win ist widar brunnen.

[He did it wonderfully as befit it, and beautifully too
To such high measure (we wish to mark it well),
As wine compared to water.]

(II, 10, 11f.)

In accordance with the demands of his teacher, Hrabanus Maurus, "in verbis verum amare, non verba" [in words to love what is true, not the words themselves], the beauty of the word is revealed in Otfrid not so much in its sound as in its spiritual sense. But the sound may not be unworthy of the spiritual sense. The modestly cultivated, formal beauty of his work is apparent to us only if we also understand the deeper meaning of form in Otfrid's work, which is revealed by the allegoresis of the terminology of the poetics of antiquity. Through Otfrid we know that what we call allegorical literature is what realizes a new beauty in a form that embraces meaning through the awakening of the letter to the spirit.

Luther said of himself that the time when he was a monk was the time when he allegorized everything. After that it was his concern "tradere scrip-

---

many passages, of understanding the words of Moses which he was able to read, since he lacked grace and her help] (II, 225).

51. This is how the anonymous author of the *Morales* still presents the task: "uti salubriter creaturis" [to make use of the things God created, to the end of salvation] (II, xxix).

turam simplici sensu" [to transmit the plain sense of Scripture].[52] This may well appear to be the end of the Middle Ages. Yet when the emblem books of the Renaissance—which in a single leap sprang over the Middle Ages and returned to antiquity—appeared side by side with the allegorical dictionaries and appeared to set aside their Christian allegorizing, the baroque period penetrated the emblems, which endured until the time of Winckelmann, with the medieval spirit of allegory, as in Filippo Piccinelli's *Mundus symbolicus* in the seventeenth century.[53] But Leibniz can already say: "Toute la nature est pleine de miracles, mais de miracles de raison" [The whole of nature is full of miracles, but of miracles of reason].[54]

It was only when an autonomous, natural observation of the biblical image of the world and a historicism which had been secularized put the history of salvation into question, found a revelation in discoveries, and left meaning to the senses and when the religious *experientia Dei* in the world was displaced by experiment to the point of the *experimentum suae medietatis*[55] that both the seven liberal arts and their sense of opening up the world to a creative interpretation, born of the spirit of mankind, disappeared. The liberal arts became an exact science. The disturbance of new knowledge—no longer of eternal but of historical verities—shook the sacred earnestness inherent in the artistic game of recreating the six days labor of creation by illuminating its sense in the process of meditation and shook, at the same time, the luminous edifice of the spirituality of things. Wherever the communality of peoples in the Pentecostal language of allegory was broken up, that was where the death knell of the Middle Ages was sounded.

52. H. Corbin, "L'intériorisation du sens en herméneutique soufi iranienne," *Eranosjahrbuch* 26 (Zürich, 1958): 57–187, here p. 63; P. Meinhold, *Luthers Sprachphilosophie* (Berlin, 1958).

53. Bibliography of emblems by H. Rosenfeld, in *Reallexikon der deutschen Literaturgeschichte* I², ed. W. Kohlschmidt and W. Mohr (Berlin, 1956), pp. 334ff.; H. Tintelnot, *Reallexikon der deutschen Kunstgeschichte* (1954), 3:1187; W. A. P. Smit, "The Emblematic Aspect of Vondel's Tragedies as the Key to Their Interpretation," *Modern Language Review* 52 (1957): 554–562.

54. Quoted by E. Cassirer, *Philosophie der symbolischen Formen* (Berlin, 1925), 2:318.

55. W. Rehm, *Experimentum medietatis* (Munich, 1947).

TWO

TYPOLOGY AS A FORM OF HISTORICAL THOUGHT

I have been invited as a philologist to talk at a meeting of a discipline that borders on my own: one that—in contrast to theology, art history, and the history of European and American literatures—has paid surprisingly little attention to the typological form of historical thought. I have at my disposal only the space of time allotted to the presentation of a paper in which to introduce you to this form of thought, perhaps to make its significance plausible to the historian and to suggest, if only in outline, some perspectives for possible research. Without giving a report on the state of scholarship in this area,[1] by resorting to much that is already known, and basing much of what

The lecture—this is an extended version of it—was given in section 7 of the Münstersche Sonderforschungsbereich "Mittelalterforschung" orientated toward "Mittelalterforschung im Verbund" (Interdisciplinary medieval studies). Other speakers were Karl Hauck on "Die historische Erforschung mündlicher Überlieferung mit Bildzeugnissen" (Historical research into oral transmission with pictorial examples), Ruth Schmidt-Wiegand on "Sprache und Geschichte im Spiegel historischer Bezeichnungen" (Language and history in the mirror of historical designations), and Joachim Wollasch on "Sterben und Tod in mittelalterlichen Vorstellungen" (Medieval representations of death and dying). Published as "Typologie als Denkform der Geschichtsbetrachtung: Vortrag gehalten auf den 34. Deutschen Historikertag in Münster am 7. Oktober 1982," in *Natur—Religion—Sprache—Universität: Universitätsforträge 1982/1983*, Schriftenreihe der Westfälischen Wilhelms-Universität Münster, Heft 7 (Münster, Westfalen: Aschendorffsche Verlagsbuchhandlung, 1983), pp. 68–102.

1. Let me point out one or two bibliographical aids: Sacvan Bercovitch, ed., *Typology and Early American Literature* (University of Massachusetts Press, 1972), pp. 245–337 ("Annotated Bibliography"—a treasure trove for sources as well); seventy-six titles of works, from the years 1954–72, on typology in different genres of English literature up to the fifteenth century can be found in Hugh T. Keenan, "A Check-List on Typology and English Medieval Literature through 1972," *Studies in the Literary Imagination* 8 (1975): 159–166; Joseph A. Galdon, S.J., *Typology and Seventeenth Century Literature* (The Hague, 1975), pp. 159–166 ("Bibliography"). Walter Haug, ed., *Formen und Funktionen der Allegorie*, proceedings of a symposium held at Wolfenbüttel,

I have to say on what I have myself published,[2] my task is to promote and awaken an understanding for a form of looking at history that has been effective from the time of the church fathers until quite late in the modern period. The typology of which I am going to talk has nothing in common with its homonym, in the sense that the latter denotes theories of types that serve the function of ordering knowledge in all the humanistic and social sciences, especially psychology, and thus in the historical disciplines as well.[3] The heightening of what has been experienced to the status of type, and the metamorphosis of the type, in Dilthey's morphological mode of historical thought, bear no relation to the theological typology which is our concern here.[4] Our typology is, first and foremost, a method of Bible exegesis. It consists in looking simultaneously at two happenings, institutions, persons, or things of which, in every case, one is taken from the Old, and one from the New Testament. The two are then linked as a pair of happenings in such a way as—by coordinating the two into a mutual illumination in which they mirror one another—to bring to light a relationship of meaning between them. The sacrifice of Isaac by Abraham in the Old Testament presages the Crucifixion of Jesus by God the Father in the New,[5] the passage of the Red Sea in the Old

1978 (Stuttgart, 1979), pp. 739–775 (bibliography); Paul J. Corshin, *Typologies in England 1650–1820* (Princeton, N.J., 1982), pp. 396–408 ("Typology: A Bibliographical Essay").

2. F. Ohly, *Sage und Legende in der Kaiserchronik: Untersuchungen über Quellen und Aufbau der Dichtung* (Münster, 1940; 2d ed., Darmstadt, 1968); F. Ohly, *Schriften zur mittelalterlichen Bedeutungsforschung* (Darmstadt, 1977), contains the essays "Synagoge und Ecclesia: Typologisches in mittelalterlicher Dichtung" (1966), pp. 312–337, "Außerbiblisch Typologisches zwischen Cicero, Ambrosius und Aelred von Rievaulx" (1976), pp. 338–360, and "Halbbiblische und außerbiblische Typologie" (1976), pp. 361–400; cf. the index of typology, pp. 420f. F. Ohly, "Skizzen zur Typologie im späteren Mittelalter," in *Medium Aevum: Deutsche Beiträge zur deutschen Literature des hohen und späten Mittelalters: Festschrift Kurt Ruh zum 65. Geburtstag* (Tübingen, 1979), pp. 251–310; F. Ohly, "Typologische Figuren aus Natur und Mythus," in Haug, *Formen und Funktionen der Allegorie*, pp. 126–166.

3. Wolfgang Ruttkowski, *Typologien und Schichtenlehren: Bibliographie des internationalen Schrifttums bis 1970*, Beschreibende Bibliographien no. 5 (Amsterdam, 1974). Among historians, the one I would mention is Theodor Schieder, "Der Typus in der Geschichtswissenschaft," *Studium Generale* 5 (1952): 228–234; and the chapter "Vergleich, Analogie, Typus" in Reinhard Wittram, *Das Interesse an der Geschichte: Zwölf Vorlesungen über Fragen des zeitgenössischen Geschichtverständnisses* (Göttingen, 1958), pp. 54–58.

4. On the concept "typos" in this connection, Rudolf W. Meyer, "Gestalt und Geschichte," in *Typologia Litterarum: Festschrift für Max Wehrli* (Zürich, 1969), pp. 11–28.

5. David Lerch, *Isaaks Opferung christlich gedeutet* (Tübingen, 1950), pp. 156–202. Hans-Jürgen Geischer, "Das Problem der Typologie in der ältesten christlichen Kunst: Isaak-Opfer und Jonas-Wunder" (theological diss., Heidelberg University, 1964). Finally, Ute Schwab, "Zum Verständnis des Isaak Opfers in literarischer und bildlicher Darstellung des Mittelalters," *Früh-*

Testament presages Jesus' baptism in the New,[6] the Passover sacrifice in the Old Testament presages the Last Supper of the New Testament. The Queen of Sheba's visit to Solomon in the Old Testament prefigures the journey of the Magi to the infant Jesus in the New.[7] It is to such relationships of meaning between happenings in the periods before and after the birth of Christ that we refer when we speak of typology.

The concept of typology, dating from the eighteenth century, is based on the biblical words *typos* and *antitypos* in the sense of prefiguration and affirmation. The type is also more frequently called *figura* or *forma;* we speak of prefigurations. Other metaphors for the relationship between the old and the new are, for example, the succession of shadow and form, childhood and adulthood, sketch and painting: in every case they mean the intensified fulfillment, as of a hint, by its interpretation at a later stage in the history of salvation. Typological thinking has its roots in the belief in the unity of God's revelation, which binds the Old and New Testaments together; the difference in time between the two is eliminated by the unity of their both being directed toward Christ. Early Christian synoptic power distinguishes what associates from what differentiates in such a way as to reveal—in the process of the revelation of God's temporal and universal will to salvation—a unity which embraces the ages: the product of a powerful fantasy directed toward an order that makes sense of history—something that is related to comparable concepts in the philosophy of history, to which we shall later make reference.

The theological exegete of the Bible relies on belief in the divine inspiration of its word and on the plan for the history of salvation that is contained in God's providence. This plan assigns everything that happens in the Bible to its immutable place and also to a meaning that is secretly ascribed to it and which points beyond it. The Old Testament's far-reaching silence on the subject of the idea of providential salvation, by which God invested biblical *happenings* with an actual prophetic quality that pointed to a fulfillment in Christ, was broken by the New Testament—apart from a few general statements—only in a limited number of examples that indicate a new direction. St. Paul and the Letter to the Hebrews indicate that the typological interpre-

---

mittelalterliche Studien 15 (1981): 435–494, with seven plates. Cf. fig. 21 from the Vienna *biblia pauperum* (ca. 1330) in F. Ohly, *Schriften.*

6. Jean Daniélou, *Sacramentum futuri: Études sur les origines de la typologie biblique* (Paris, 1950).

7. Cf. figs. 24 and 25 from the Klosterneuburg altar by Nicholas of Verdun (ca. 1180) in F. Ohly, *Schriften.* Cf. ibid., "Halbbiblische und außerbiblische Typologie," p. 365.

tation of history, something that Jesus practiced only with caution, is a theological task. As they considered the divine thought that had previously been sketched out, they aroused the theological desire to make revelations for their own time and for the whole future, beyond what was said in the Bible, in the sense of a growing number of examples that were yet to be discovered. Not only the early history of theological typology at the time of the church fathers, but also its history in the following epochs—right down to our own day—exerts a powerful attraction on the historian, just as all movements do that do not petrify into a systematic intellectual search. Corresponding to the *Work on Myth* (Hans Blumenberg) that has to be done by every age, something analogous takes place within the more limited space available for movements of thought permitted by the revelatory claims of the Bible—which was always good for surprises precisely in the most fertile epochs of Christian culture. It was not humanism or the Reformation, but it was very definitely the Enlightenment and the change to historicism that distanced us from every form of allegorizing interpretation of the world, to such an extent that there was a danger of drawing conclusions about the lively beginnings of such an interpretation from its faded late forms. It is the current interest in the metaphor—for the historian I need only mention the works of Demandt and Schlobach[8]—that leads us, by the shortest path, back to the insight that typological applications, as a sort of allegoresis directed at history, are, like every form of allegorization, the product of a combination of a bold and ingenious imagination that interprets the world. There is something artificial about every initial discovery of a typological connection, and it should not come as a surprise that it is precisely European literature (from about 800 to 1800 and beyond) and fine arts that adopted the typological form of thought as a possible form of synoptic organization. Unlike the rest of poetic allegorization, it was also protected from degeneration into a form of clever, intellectual game. Almost all the arts in the Middle Ages, from illumination, the art of the goldsmith, sculpture, and architecture to stained glass—and some even right down to the nineteenth century—reckon typological material among their subjects and developed some forms by which to represent it. Art history has not yet gone beyond iconographic study to make a systematic study of the possibilities of the language of forms by which typological con-

8. Alexander Demandt, *Metaphern für Geschichte: Sprachbilder und Gleichnisse im historisch-politischen Denken* (Munich, 1978). Jochen Schlobach, *Zyklentheorie und Epochenmetaphorik: Studien zur bildlichen Sprache der Geschichtsreflexion in Frankreich von der Renaissance zur Frühaufklärung* (Munich, 1980). Heinz Meyer, "Überlegungen zu Herders Metaphern für Geschichte," *Archiv für Begriffsgeschichte* 25 (1982): 88–114.

nections are made visual. There is still a need for elementary assistance to simplify a mutual recognition of what has already been achieved in fields of scholarship which are widely separated from each other. Theology, art history, and literary history and the various epochs into which all three are divided, branches of study directed at different creeds and continents, still know too little of each other's efforts vis-à-vis the same object for it to have been possible to gain, from a synoptic view, a complete picture of the history and effects of typological thought. After art history alone—from 1860 till about 1920—had cultivated the field of typological studies, the lead was taken, in the years from 1935 to 1965, by biblical and theological patristics, while the literary historical study of typology, which had at the same time got under way in Germany, had once more come to a halt and had to wait fifteen years to receive lively stimuli at the hands of American (and English) scholars of their own literatures. Lacunae in fields which had hitherto remained unstudied could certainly be found on every hand, and this is certainly true of the historians as well, who have been well aware of the problem since Herbert Grundmann's studies on Joachim di Fiore. As far as German historians are concerned, I shall mention only the name of Erich Meuthen.[9]

Older historiographical works, up to the time of historicism, are the result of a productive power of imagination, which endows what has happened with a spiritual form of which it itself probably hardly dreamed. It is part of the fascination of older historiography that it offers us *views* of history, specifically directed, and open-ended illuminations of what *has* been, from the impulses of an interest that is at once spiritually sympathetic and searching for a meaning. This is probably true of no age more than the Christian era, based as it is on biblical antiquity and indigenous antiquity. No epoch was as rich in highly varied genres of historical tradition and historiography, in literary forms whose generic aims in each case already contained precursors of a kind of contemplation of what had been and also the direction which the

9. Erich Meuthen, "Der Geschichtssymbolismus Gerhohs von Reichersberg (1959)," in *Geschichtsdenken und Geschichtsbild im Mittelalter,* ed. W. Lammers, Wege der Forschung, no. 21 (Darmstadt, 1965), pp. 200–246, esp. 234ff.; also Peter Classen, *Gerhoch von Reichersberg: Eine Biographie* (Wiesbaden, 1960), see *Typologie* in the index. Wilhelm Kölmel, "Typik und Atypik: Zum Geschichtsbild der kirchen-politischen Publizistik (11.–14. Jahrhundert)," in *Speculum Historiale: Geschichte im Spiegel von Geschichtsschreibung und Geschichtsdeutung: Festschrift für Johannes Spörl,* ed. Clemens Bauer, Laetitia Böhm, and Max Müller (Munich, 1965), pp. 277–302. Elisabeth Dahlhaus-Berg, *Nova antiquitas et antiqua novitas: Typologische Exegese und isidorianisches Geschichtsbild bei Theodulf von Orleans,* Kölner historische Abhandlungen, no. 23 (Cologne, 1975). Otherwise it seems as though our historians have only touched on typology point by point and occasionally.

sense of that contemplation was to take. These were different in popular histories from what they were in world chronicles, in the lives of rulers from legends, in annals from necrologies. Languages as well as literary genres have their own specific possibilities of a picture of history. The French *chansons de geste*, the heroic poetry of the Germani, and the Slavonic *byliny* have no counterparts in Latin, and various Latin genres had for a long time no analogue in the vernaculars. Each genre has it own view of the world, its own ideas of God and man, a specific view of history, and it is the same with languages, and certainly also with oral and written literatures, as it is with genres. There is a broad range of noninterchangeably developed forms of historical contemplation, and it is only the intellectual ordering of the whole field that makes it possible to survey the wealth of possibilities by which the past can be brought into a relationship by the way it is represented. Forms of thought determined by a philosophy of history can make their contribution to the intellectual ordering in the structure of this range of forms, since only certain genres open up the possibility of their use. The mental picture that comes to us from antiquity and is taken over by Christianity, thanks to its exegesis of the Book of Daniel, of a series of world empires of which the last, and present, one, the Roman, can be secured in its continued existence by the reworking of old materials provided the medieval present with an exultation of life in the fourth, Roman, Christian, and final world empire which was to endure until the coming of the Antichrist. The Augustinian doctrine of the six ages of the world—begun, it is true, earlier—the first five of which led from Creation to the birth of Christ, who introduced the sixth and final, Christian age, mediated the same consciousness of the present.[10] To live in the last and most perfect age was, at the same time, to live in the final and highest world empire. The old idea of the history of salvation that saw its ordering in a sequence of stages in the periods of salvation—*ante legem, sub lege,* and *sub gratia*—could only serve to emphasize this. The same is true of the ascription of ages to the persons of the Trinity, or to the seven gifts of the Holy Ghost after the twelfth century. The so-called Middle Ages, then, stood from every point of view on the final summit, looked back to what was lower, and saw before them nothing higher than the seventh age of being, with God, after the end of the world. Thinking in terms of world empires, ages of the world, and periods of salvation, the Old Testament and antiquity were seen as the pre-

10. Karl-Heinz Schwarte, *Die Vorgeschichte der augustinischen Weltalterlehre,* Antiquitas, ser. 1, no. 12, (Bonn, 1966); on typology, pp. 4–8.

history of a Christian history, in which all former ages are fulfilled. If historical research is sufficiently aware of world empires and the ages of the world, this holds good, if my point of view is the right one, less for the related and finally much more significant form of thinking about historical contemplation, which occupies us here under the name of typology.

The Bible places a beginning and an end on history, the Creation and the Last Judgment. Only God exists before and after this history, with Christ as cocreator and judge. Typological thought is Christocentric; the historically incarnate Christ is the center of the ages. The age stretching from Creation to the Last Judgment has, as history, two sides, the one before Christ and the other after. The Christian era corresponds to the latter. The age before Christ is the age of types, the age of Christ and the age after Christ are the ages of antitypes. The type is what is old, in the age before Christ, and the antitype what is new in the age after Christ. This crucial statement is intended, from the outset, to emphasize that, together with the doctrine of world empires and the doctrine of the ages of the world, typological thought simply excludes a concept "Middle Ages," for they lie in the center of the new age, in the final world empire, in the last *aetas mundi,* and look forward only to the last things, the eschatology. C. A. Patrides compares this Christian view of history with Jacob's Ladder.[11] The final rung leads to the gate of the heavenly city. For almost thirteen centuries, the genre of the world chronicle, richly represented in over a hundred works from Orosius (A.D. 417) to the end of the seventeenth century, usually started with the Creation and then proceeded to follow the progress of the six ages of the world. From the time of Bede, who was stimulated by Augustine, to Hartmann Schedel (A.D. 1493) and down to the seventeenth century, it was customary to close the chronicle with the end of history in the eschatology to which Otto von Freising, Joachim di Fiore, and Vincent de Beauvais—to name just three of the more well-known figures among many others in both the East and the West—had paid especial attention. Up to the eighteenth century, the genre of the world chronicle, which I

11. C. A. Patrides, *The Phoenix and the Ladder: The Rise and Decline of the Christian View of History* (Berkeley, 1964), p. 9. The dying and newly arising phoenix stand in Patrides's work for the Greek and Roman cyclical concept of history, Jacob's Ladder for the linear and upward-leading Christian idea of the history of salvation. Gert Melville, "Zur geschichtstheoretischen Begründung eines fehlenden Niedergangsbewußtseins im Mittelalter," in *Niedergang: Studien zu einem geschichtlichen Thema,* ed. Reinhart Koselleck and Paul Widmer, Sprache und Geschichte, no. 2 (Stuttgart, 1980), pp. 103–136, refers to typology (pp. 122ff.) but otherwise argues along other lines.

mention as an example, excludes the idea of a Middle Ages.[12] The genealogical trees of the periods of the history of salvation, painted by Joachim di Fiore in his *Liber figurarum* (*Book of Figures*)—with their series of generations and their synchronistic assignments of biblical and extrabiblical, of ecclesiastical and extraecclesiastical events—acquire a typological structure, when Joachim represents the concordance between the old and the new ages in such a way that the time from Christ to the universal peace after his coming again, at the Last Judgment, is an antitypical reflection of the age from Adam to Jesus, so that the whole of church history corresponds to the history of the chosen people in the Old Testament. His picture of the age is called—like other typological synopses—*Concordia veteris testamenti et novi* (*Concord of the Old Testament and the New*), where the New lasts until the end of the world.[13]

12. C. A. Patrides, *The Phoenix and the Ladder,* pp. 16–48, gives an overview of the world chronicle as well. But see also Anna-Dorothee von den Brincken, *Studien zur lateinischen Weltchronik bis in das Zeitalter Ottos von Freising* (Düsseldorf, 1957); and Karl Heinrich Krüger, *Die Universalchroniken* (Turnhout, 1976), with bibliography, pp. 10–12, and the synoptic tables A–D. Von den Brincken, pp. 37–45, inter alia, on the division into ages and empires of the world; on typology, pp. 28–30. Paolo Brezzi, "Cronache universali e storia della salvezza," in *Fontio medioevali e problematica storiografica: Atti del congresso internazionale tenuto in occasione del 90° anniversario della fondazione del Istituto Storico Italiano, Roma 22–27 ottobre 1973: I Relazioni* (Rome, 1976), pp. 317–336, with bibliography, pp. 335f. On the crossing of antiquity and the Old Testament in the world chronicles, see F. Ohly, "Typologische Figuren aus Natur und Mythus," p. 141 and n. 90. Beryl Smalley, *Historians in the Middle Ages* (London, 1974), pp. 95–105, "Universal History."

13. F. Ohly, *Schriften,* p. 372. On the subject of the Christian theology of history, I would point to the bibliographies of G. Thils, "La théologie de l'histoire: Note bibliographique," *Ephemerides Theologicae Lovanienses* 26 (1950): 87–95. Charles P. Loughran, "Theology and History: A Bibliography," *Thought* 29 (1954): 101–115. The article "Geschichtsphilosophie," by Alois Keil–Henri Irénée Marrou, in *Reallexikon für Antike und Christentum* (1978), 10:703–799, still takes no cognizance of typology. I add a few titles to the extremely rich bibliography there, also for the Middle Ages: Ernst Benz, *Ecclesia Spiritualis: Kirchenidee und Geschichtstheologie der franziskanischen Reformation* (Stuttgart, 1934). On relationships between typology and ideas about time see Robert C. Dentan, ed., *The Idea of History in the Ancient Near East* (New Haven, Conn., 1955), esp. Erich Dinkler, "Earliest Christianity" (pp. 169–214); and Ronald H. Bainton, "Patristic Christianity" (pp. 215–236). H. Butterfield, *Christianity and History* (New York, 1950). The acts of the colloquium "La théologie de l'histoire" in Rome, January 5–11, 1971, appeared in two volumes edited by Enrico Castelli (Paris, 1971): vol. 1, *Herméneutique et Eschatologie;* and vol. 2, *Révélation et histoire.* Yves M.-J. Congar, "Le sens de l'économie salutaire dans la *Théologie* de St. Thomas d'Aquin," in *Festgabe Joseph Lortz,* vol. 2, *Glaube und Geschichte* (Baden-Baden, 1958), pp. 73–122. Amos Funkenstein, *Heilsplan und natürliche Entwicklung in Formen der Gegenwartsbestimmung im Geschichtsdenken des hohen Mittelalters* (Munich, 1965). In Galdon, the chapter

With what has been said let us outline a horizon that will be broad enough to embrace what has yet to be said, but which limits its area sufficiently, within the field of possibilities of historical contemplation, for us to remain conscious of the fact that typology is one form of thought among others, and not simply a key to what is historical. A few thetically brief determinations will quickly suffice to sketch its characteristics without the necessity for presenting further justifications and evidence.[14] Typology sees history as the history of salvation, which proceeds according to God's plan for the salvation of man. For the Christian world, its home is in the Bible, where Jesus and Paul use it and bear witness to it. According to John 3:14–15, Jesus says, "And as Moses lifted up the serpent in the wilderness, even so must the Son of Man be lifted up: That whosoever believeth in him should not perish, but have everlasting life." The basic condition of all typology is the force of intensification. In the same process of lifting up, God the Father corresponds, in the intensification, to Moses, Christ corresponds to the brazen serpent, and, in the process of the salvation of those who believe in what has been uplifted, eternal life corresponds to health. According to the language of Paul, the lifting up of the serpent on the pole is the type, and the raising of Christ on the cross is the antitype. The biblical texts do not name the pole and the cross. The pictorial arts have added them, so as make clear to the eye what is

"Typology and History," pp. 54–69. Hans Werner Goetz, *Die Geschichtstheologie des Orosius* (Darmstadt, 1980). Frank Powell Haggard, "An Interpretation of Thomas Aquinas as a Biblical Theologian with Special Reference to His Systematizing of the Economy of Salvation" (Ph.D. diss., Drew University, 1972). Martin Henschel, "Figuraldeutung und Geschichtlichkeit," *Kerygma und Dogma* 5 (1959): 306–317. Wilhelm Kamlah, *Die mittelalterliche Auslegung der Apokalypse von Joachin von Fiore,* Historische Studien, no. 185 (Berlin, 1935). Ulrich Kühn, *Via Caritatis: Theologie des Gesetzes bei Thomas von Aquin* (Halle an der Saale, 1963). Walter von Loewenich, *Augustin und das christliche Geschichtsdenken* (Munich, 1947). Roger Mehl, "Philosophy of History or Theology of History," *Cross Currents* 3 (1953): 161–182. Robert L. Millburn, *Early Christian Interpretations of History* (New York, 1954). C. A. Patrides, *The Grand Design of God: The Literary Form of the Christian View of History* (London, 1972), with a wealth of literature, p. 10. Theo Preiss, "The Christian Philosophy of History: The Vision of History in the New Testament," *Journal of Religion* 30 (1950): 157–170. Joseph Ratzinger, *Die Geschichtstheologie des heiligen Bonaventura* (Munich, 1959). G. Scholtz, *Geschichte* II, "Der Geschichtsbegriff der Bibel, der Patristik und des lateinischen Mittelalters," *Historisches Wörterbuch der Philosophie* III (1974), pp. 345–352. John M. Steadman, *Nature into Myth: Medieval and Renaissance Moral Symbols* (Pittsburgh, 1979), pp. 185–212. Gert Wendelborn, *Gott und Geschichte: Joachim von Fiore und die Hoffnung der Christenheit* (Vienna, 1974).

14. See n. 2 and other Münster works on typology, which are indicated, on a continuing basis, in the reports of the actvities of the special research group Mittelalter, in its yearbook *Frühmittelalterliche Studien.*

common in the distinctions between the two cases of lifting onto wood. Type and antitype need a similarity in which what is common and what is different are both represented. The history of typological representation by the arts—which extends from the early Middle Ages to the nineteenth century—and a systematic investigation of the artistic means used to produce this representation have yet to be written. Typological thought underwent its great development in biblical exegesis, which—from the third to the eighteenth century and even beyond—interpreted the Scriptures typologically in all confessions. Typology puts the Old and New Testaments into a state of tension, in which the Old Testament is raised into the New by its fulfillment in the words of the Sermon on the Mount, "non veni solvere sed adimplere" [I have not come to release but to fulfill]: the fulfillment of a type in an antitype must be clearly distinguished from the fulfillment of the verbal prophecies of the Old Testament in the New Testament. The types themselves are a sort of prediction of what is to come, but *in factis* (in deeds) and not *in dictis* (in words). The type and the antitype are historical; typology is the interpretation of the historical and is, thus, a subject for the historian as well. Types are events, like the crossing of the Red Sea, or the raising up of the brazen serpent; they are persons like Moses or David, actions like the building of the Ark or the Temple of Solomon, which find their antitype in the church, and like institutions, for example, the temple cult, which is reflected antitypically in the church's liturgy, or the Jewish monarchy, to which the Christian monarchy placed itself in a typological relationship. A thousand Bible commentaries and a thousand sermons have practiced this form of thought for ages; they have drilled people in it and popularized it, so that it can be found in literature up to the end of the seventeenth century. The great typological pictorial cycles of the twelfth and thirteenth centuries placed more than a thousand types in a referential relationship with hundreds of antitypes. Art history can still point to such things in the nineteenth century.

The specific thing about typology lies in its synoptic view of what is divided in time, in the juxtaposition of two linked scenes out of the succession of time, in the rendering visible of a simultaneity of what is not simultaneous, in such a way that the old points to the new as a sort of intensification, always across the barrier of time and the historical appearance of Christ, as the center of the ages and as the turning point in the history of salvation. The Christian demonstration of the fulfillments of an Old Testament prophecy of facts by means of superfacts which took place in analogies on the other side of the great leap in time—if I may be allowed to emphasize the intensification of the type in the antitype in this manner—leads to a mutual illumination of the ages that links the two indissolubly together, for the new era would not be what it is without the old, and the old era finds its total meaning only in the new. Typological observation lifts the veil of the old era and lets the light of the new era fall on it. Freeing itself from the old era, the new era is at the same time linked to it anew. An appropriation and a takeover of what has been, by a self-reflection as a means of self-penetration, has never recurred so easily in history nor with such tremendous intensity. Contemplation of the old era and the new has long been preconditioned by talk of the Old and New Testaments and the old law and the new.[15]

Augustine already juxtaposes *vetustas* (the old era) and *novitas* (the new era) in this manner. He remarks of the Temple of Solomon, "Ibi enim diruebatur uetustas, ut nouitas aedificaretur" [for there the old was destroyed so that the new might be built].[16] The epoch, which had no idea that it might once be called the Middle Ages, lived in the orientation of the past to what was new in its own day, as a surmounting completion of what had been handed down to it. In Alcuin's new Athens, the seven gifts of the Holy Ghost were to set the crown on the seven liberal arts.[17] Biblical exegesis, as a form of thought, had a charisma that ranged far into the old and the new eras. As far

15. Giovanni Helewa, "La 'Legge vecchia' e la 'Legge nova' secondo S. Tommaso d'Aquino," *Ephemerides Carmeliticae* 25 (1974): 28–139, esp. pp. 125–128, on typological juxtapositions like the "lex nova dicitur lex veritatis, lex autem vetus umbrae et figurae" [the new law is called the law of truth, but the old one the law of shadow and figure] (p. 126).

16. *Enarrationes in psalmos* 95.1; *Corpus Christianorum, Series Latina* (*CCL*), 39, 1343. On Psalm 95:1, "Cantate domino canticum novum" [Sing unto the Lord a new song], under the heading "destruatur vetustas, novitas surgat" [let the old be destroyed, let the new arise], Augustine indefatigably extols the leap from the old era to the new as the step from the *vetus homo* to the *novus homo*, from the Old to the New Testament, from the old to the new song, from sin to grace. Henri Rondet, "La thème du Cantique Nouveau chez Saint Augustin," in *L'homme devant Dieu: Mélanges Henri de Lubac* (Paris, 1963), 1:341–354. The attribute *vetus* for the type and *novus* for the antitype is common in the early period right down to the seventeenth century and could be cited hundreds and hundreds of times. On the terminology (with bibliography), Rudolf Suntrup, "Zur sprachlichen Form der Typologie," in *Geistliche Denkformen in der Literatur des Mittelalters*, proceedings of a symposium held at Münster, 1982, ed. Klaus Grubmüller, Ruth Schmidt-Wiegand, and Klaus Speckenbach (Munich, 1983).

17. Étienne Gilson, "Le moyen âge comme 'saeculum modernum,'" in *Concetto, storia, miti e immagini del medio evo*, ed. Vittore Branca (Florence, 1973), pp. 1–10, here p. 3. In Gilson's essay, he presents the rise of dialectic, speculative grammar, the new logic, the arts (with Gothic as the first architectural style to be invented since the Greeks), the scholastic method, using the *quaestio*, as "the most original [and] the newest product of the thirteenth and fourteenth centuries—one that has no known predecessors and has never been continued" [l'oeuvre la plus originale, la plus neuve des XIIIe et XIVe siècles, celle à laquelle on ne connaît pas de prédécesseurs et qui n'a jamais été continuée] (p. 7); on the *quaestio*, cf. F. Ohly, "Die Suche in Dichtungen des

as the *corpus Christi mysticum* (the mystical body of Christ) was concerned, it was theologically unobjectionable to allow the age of the antitypical fulfillments beyond Christ and the New Testament to live on in the church, whose liturgy and sacraments, whose institutions and history, pretended to find things from the old era intensified in the new. Honorius Augustodunensis, Joachim di Fiore and, in part, Gerhoh von Reichersberg held up a typological mirror to the history of the Old Testament and the church. On the side of the new era, the Life of the Virgin and the legends of the saints were included in the system of typological concordances. Political history, which is closely enough connected with the history of the church, can also be included. I might mention Constantine as the new Moses, Charlemagne as the new David.[18]

It was more difficult to discover and to give a theological legitimation to types from the old era other than those which appeared in the Bible. The first divine revelation from Adam to Moses given to man only in the book of nature, as *lex naturae,* had not been replaced by the written law and the prophets, but had been expanded to the double testimony of God in the *liber naturae* and the *liber scripturae.* The principle that the two books of God, his work and his word, have to explain each other reciprocally supports the introduction of nature into the world of revelations before Christ: it is from among these that the types which point, forward in time, toward him can be taken. The inclusion of types from natural history—already present in patristics—increased considerably from the twelfth century onward. In the great typological cycle, *Concordantia caritatis* (*Concordance of Love*) dating from the fourteenth century, there are, in every case, two types from the Old Testament and two types from natural history which correspond to the 238

Mittelalters," *Zeitschrift für deutsches Altertum* 94 (1965): 171–184. Gilson sees an increasing distancing from Latin antiquity and quotes the *ars poetica* of Matthieu de Vendôme with its "vetera cessavere novis supervenientibus" [the ancients were stilled, when the new came upon the scene]. Gilson sees humanism as a countermovement to the old against the "modernity" of the Middle Ages (p. 8f.; "Dans le cas du moyen âge," sa modernité devait être dénoncée par les humanistes comme celle d'une décadence, mais pour ceux qui l'ont vécue, spécialement du XIIIe au XIVe siècles, elle fut sentie comme une ère d'innovation dans tous les ordres, une modernité de progrès" [In the case of the Middle Ages, its modernity was later denounced by the humanists as that of a decadence, but those who experienced it, especially from the thirteenth to the fourteenth century, felt the era to be one of innovation in all the orders of society, a modernity of progress], p. 10.

18. Literature on David as the type of Charlemagne in Michael Borgolte, "Papst Leo III, Karl der Große und der Filioque-Streit von Jerusalem," in *Byzantina* (Salonika, 1980), 10:401–427, here n. 1.

antitypes from the Bible and the legends (that is, 476 types in this field alone).[19] In the Mariological typological cycle by the Dominican Franz von Retz, done in the year 1420, five typical scenes derive from the Old Testament, twenty-one scenes from fable, myth, history, and legend, as well as thirty-four scenes from natural history. The mention of mythical scenes leads us to the problem of the inclusion of pagan antiquity, as well, in the store of types from the old era. A theological legitimation by the *logos spermatikos* made it easier to derive church doctrine from Jews and pagans, and from a preinspiration in antiquity. Thus, it came about that, after cautious beginnings in patristics from the twelfth century on, there was a strengthening of the movement toward introducing types from antiquity as well, though less from classical history than from mythology. The *Speculum humanae salvationis* (*Mirror of Human Salvation*) (1324) which is handed down in hundreds of manuscripts and translated into a number of languages, also included types from the secular history of antiquity. We find there, among others, the dream of Astyages, King Codrus of Athens, Antipater, and Caesar Augustus with the Tiburtine sibyl. The annunciation of the birth of King Cyrus to his daughter, which came to Astyages in his dream, is the type of the annunciation to Joachim that his daughter Mary would bear Christ. The supreme sacrifice by the legendary Greek king Codrus for the lifting of the siege of Athens is iconographically compared to its antitype in Christ's death. In the long view, the acceptance of antique mythology into the spiritual system of the typological concordance of old and new has greater significance. It was the High Middle Ages that first helped earlier beginnings in this field to achieve a complete breakthrough. The effects of this breakthrough were an essential factor in conditioning the Christian interpretation of antique myths up to the eighteenth century. The antique text on which typological interpretation was primarily carried out was Ovid's *Metamorphoses*, the Old French version of which, the *Ovide moralisé*, written after 1300, shows, in its more than seventy thousand lines, that the typological interpretation of the *Metamorphoses* had flourished widely (fig. 4). I have tried to represent the history of the introduction and the carrying out of this typological interpretation—and also of its continued influence into the seventeenth century, for example, in Calderon's Corpus Christi play—in two essays written in 1979, using the myths of Orpheus and Hercules as examples of prefigurations of Christ.[20] This sort of prefiguration facilitated a triangular typology where, for example, antique

19. F. Ohly, *Schriften*, fig. 22.
20. See n. 2.

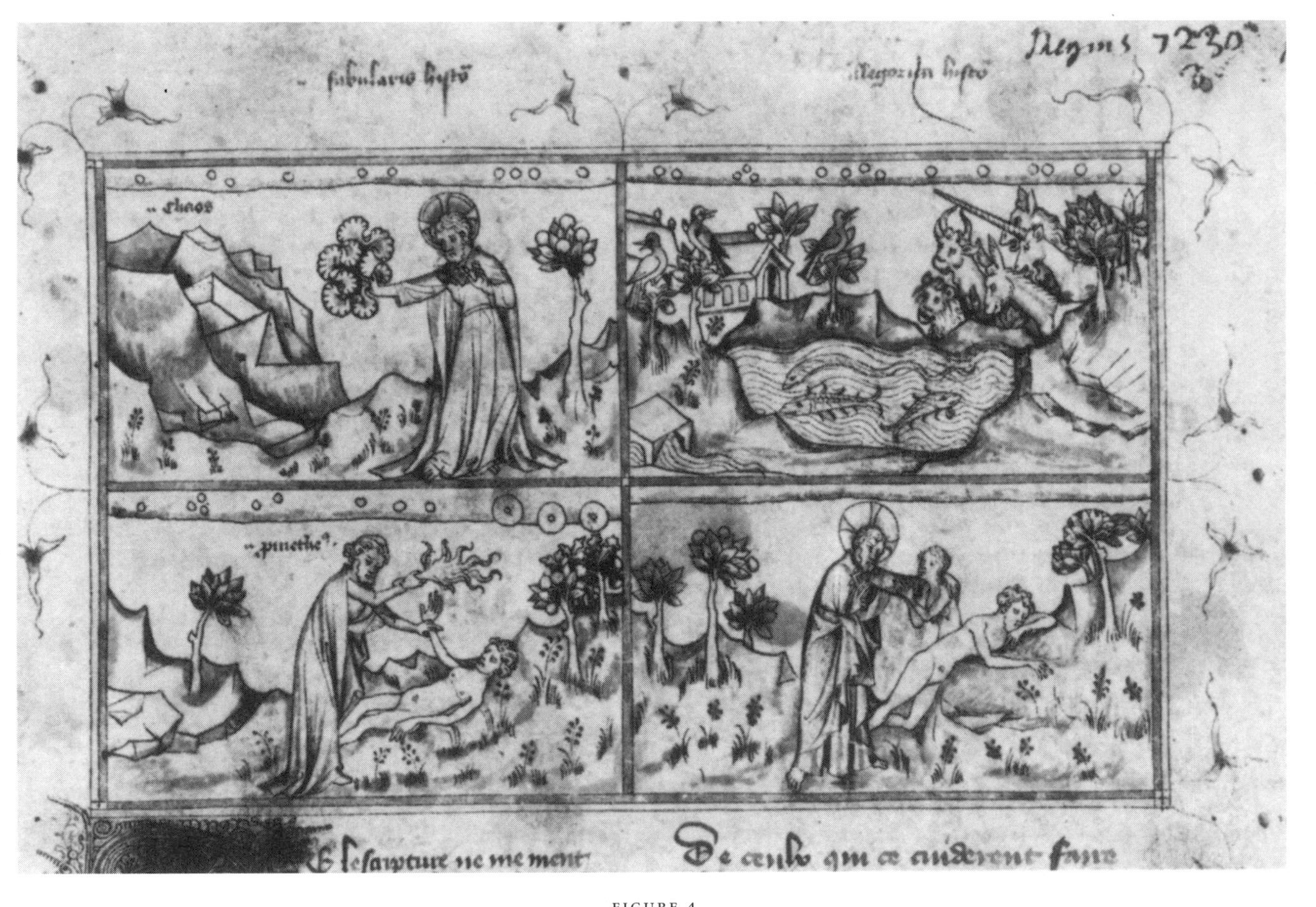

FIGURE 4

Anonymous, Prometheus (*fabularis*) and the biblical God the Creator (*allegoria historica*) in a Paris manuscript of the *Ovide moralisé* (fifteenth century).

pagan and Old Testament types, like the harpists Orpheus and David, are so approximated that both of them can point forward to Christ as the antitype. The juxtaposition of Orpheus and David, as types for Christ, paved the way for the monolithic Orpheus-Christ typology. The juxtaposition of Moses' brazen serpent on the standard, and of Aesculapius as a snake on his rod, promoted the Aesculapius-Christ typology. One picture (fig. 4) must suffice as an example for the whole field: the Paris manuscript, from the fifteenth century, of the *Ovid moralisé* (BN 871, fol. 1) shows, on two pictorial strips relating to the Creation on the left-hand side, the *fabularis* (fabulous story) and on the right the *allegorica historia* (allegorical history). The creator with a cruciform halo turns to a rocky chaos in the upper left corner, while next to it, on the right, there is a landscape filled with a river and a lake with fish, plants and trees, birds and animals, and a house. The strip below this one shows, on the left, in a scene which contains flowers and trees, Prometheus in the process of giving man fire. Man lies on his back in front of Prometheus, while flames emanate from Prometheus's right hand as he grasps the man's right arm with his left hand. On the picture on the right next to this, which exactly corresponds to it, Adam lies on the ground at the side while the Creator, with his cruciform halo, takes Eve from Adam's loins. The pictures on the left-hand side are explained by the inscription *chaos* and *prometheus*, while those on the right-hand side are self-evident for those familiar with the account of the Creation.[21] The juxtaposition of Prometheus and Christ the Creator (with the cross in his halo) suggests a step on the way toward reducing the typological distance between antique and Old Testament myth—something that Tertullian is familiar with in the case of Prometheus.

Finally, we have to consider the fact that from the time of Ambrose there

21. The typological interpretation of myths in painting is still virtually totally neglected by scholars: cf. F. Ohly, "Typologische Figuren aus Natur und Mythus," p. 143 and nn. 105f. On our picture of the Creation, Jürgen W. Einhorn, *Spiritalis unicornis: Das Einhorn als Bedeutungsträger in Literatur und Kunst des Mittelalters,* Münstersche Mittelalter-Schriften, no. 13 (Munich, 1976), pp. 135, 390 (no. 465A), fig. 135. Johannes Zahlten, *Creatio mundi: Darstellung der sechs Schöpfungstage und naturwissenschaftliches Weltbild im Mittelalter,* Stuttgarter Beiträge zur Geschichte und Politik, no. 13 (Stuttgart, 1979), p. 66, fig. 106: "In the scene of the creation of Adam, the Creator is replaced by the mythical figure of Prometheus"; p. 145: "A wild rocky formation, designated as chaos, is replaced in the second picture by a cultivated and inhabited landscape"; p. 198: "Two fourteenth-century French manuscripts of the *Ovide moralisé* in London (Cat. 222) and Paris (fig. 106) show, as something special—within a Creation cycle—the scene of the creation of man by Prometheus, who, according to legend, created men out of clay." Catalog number 222 calls the London manuscript "BM Add.10324 fol. 1 with a series of scenes from Ovid's *Metamorphoses,* French 14th cent."

is a third step in typology which takes its place beside the usual dual correspondence. Ambrose supplements *umbra* (shadow) and *imago* (image) with *veritas* (truth) as the highest stage of intensification, which is found only in the afterlife. In the second book of his ecclesiological work, *De domo Dei* (*On the House of God*) (ca. 1150), the monk Boto of Prüfening treats the phenomena of the House of God in the history of salvation. What was shadowy in the Old Testament (*umbra*), what became an image (*imago*) in the New, was completed in the future, in truth (*veritas*) in heaven.[22] The typological division of the history of salvation into the old era and the new era was thus given a universal completion by the provision of a final era. A half-biblical typology was added to the great core stock of biblical typology, in that, on the one hand, antique pagan types and, on the other, postbiblical antitypes extended the world that was involved, both that of the old and the new eras, into the era which was actually known. As an example, I would mention Moses and St. Benedict, the founder of the monastic order. The typological relationship between Moses, the old, and Peter, the new, lawmaker[23] was extended into the history of the church, when St. Benedict became the antitype of Moses, for antitypes of Old Testament types also came into the framework of church history out of monastic history. St. Benedict, the originator of the rule of his order, was frequently juxtaposed with Moses, the bringer of the old law. The sermon that Abbot Odo of Cluny gave at the grave of St. Benedict in Fleury, which seeks to rank Benedict above the saints, compares them both as lawgivers, the one for the Israelites, the other for the monks.[24] Hildegard of Bingen, in a vision, hears the voice of God the Father relating, typologically, the *primus Moses* (first Moses) with Benedict as the *alter Moses* (second Moses). Here, then, the voice of God gives authority to half-biblical typology: "Benedict, who lived in a cave and who in his love for life chastised his body with great severity and disciplined it, is at the same time a second Moses. I commissioned the first Moses to write a rough and harsh law on tablets and he gave it to the Jews. But when my son impregnated the law with the sweet-

22. Franz Josef Worstbrock, "Boto von Prüfening," in *Die deutsche Literature des Mittelalters: Verfasserlexikon*, 2d ed. (Berlin, 1978), vol. 1, cols. 971–976.

23. C. A. Kneller, "Moses und Petrus," *Stimmen aus Maria Laach* 60 (1901): 237–257. On the typology of Moses, see also Charles Pietri, "Roma Christiana," in *Recherches sur l'Église de Rome, son organisation, son idéologie de Miltiade a Sixte III (A.D. 311–440)* (Rome, 1976), pp. 317–320 and passim.

24. Joachim Wollasch, "Bemerkungen zur Goldenen Altartafel von Basel," in *Text und Bild: Aspekte des Zusammenwirkens zweier Künste im Mittelalter und früher Neuzeit*, ed. Christel Meier and Uwe Ruberg (Wiesbaden, 1980), pp. 383–407, here p. 399.

ness of the Gospel, then my servant Benedict—moved by the gentle inspiration of the Holy Spirit—made the beginnings of this vocation, which before him had been a most harsh way of living, into a smooth and easily passable path."[25] If the typological comparison between Moses, the saint of the old era, and Benedict, the saint of the new era, had not been a familiar one, Abbot Aelred of Riveaulx would not have been able to devote a whole ceremonial sermon on the founder of the order to a juxtaposition of *sanctus moyses* (holy Moses) and the *divus Benedictus* (godly Benedict), which was permeated with different typological characteristics.[26] Such selective references also stimulated a cyclical coming together. We have the original *Acta beati Benedicti in veteri lege figurata et per doctores novi legis luculenter approbata,*

25. Hildegard von Bingen, *Scivias,* vision 2, 5.20; *CCL cont. med.,* 43 (1978), 193, pp. 732–741; according to the translation *Wisse die Wege: Scivias . . . ,* trans. and adapted by Maria Böckeler (Salzburg, 1963), p. 189. It is certainly Hildegard von Bingen to whom God is talking in this vision. Even if persons of the rank of Odo of Cluny, in the tenth, and Hildegard of Bingen, in the twelfth, as well as John of Stablo, in the fifteenth century, represent this half-biblical typology for centuries, and with devotion, it should probably give those German scholars pause who, to this day, like to regard such half-biblical typology as impermissible; cf. F. Ohly, *Schriften,* p. 360 n. 1, and "Typologische Figuren aus Natur und Mythus" (see n. 2), p. 144.

26. Aelred von Riveaulx, *Sermo* 5: *In natali sancti Benedicti,* in *Patrologia Latina* (*PL*), 185, 238–245. For example: "Illos per ministerium Moysi eduxit Dominus de Aegypto: nos per ministerium S. Benedicti eduxit de saeculo. Illi erant sub Pharaone regi pessimo; nos sub diabolo. Illi servitute Aegyptiorum; nos in domino vitiorum" [The Lord led them out of Egypt by the ministry of Moses; he led us out of time by the ministry of St. Benedict. They were subject to Pharaoh, a very bad king; we are subject to the devil. They were enslaved to the Egyptians, we to the lord of vice] (239 C). "Moyses constituit illis legem" [Moses constituted the law for them] (with the promise of the Promised Land) (240 B); "beatus Benedictus constituit nobis legem" [The blessed Benedict constituted the law for us] (with the promise of eternity in Heaven) (240 B). "S. Moysis docuit filios Israel illas tres dietas . . . vos autem B. Pater Benedictus istas tres dietas spirituales docet" [S. Moses taught the children of Israel three regimens . . . you, however, the blessed father Benedict taught three spiritual regimens] (242 C)—"Merito ait sanctus Moyses . . . hoc docet beatus pater noster Benedictus" [Rightly says the sainted Moses . . . this teaches the blessed father, our Benedict] (244 B–D). Already in his *Dialogi,* Gregory the Great compared situations from the life of Benedict with ones from the lives of Moses, David, Elijah, and Peter, to show that Benedict was their peer. A rhymed office of the twelfth century on the feast of St. Benedict (March 21) mentions this in the second antiphon:

Huic iubilate, quo pater iste
par fit, Eliae, par quoque Moysi,
dum lapis illi flumina fundit
corvus obaudit.

[Rejoice in the one to whom this father
Is made equal, Elijah, equal to Moses as well,

in latino, gallico et teutonico et pictura . . . scripta et depicta (*Acts of the Blessed Benedict Prefigured in the Old Law and Clearly Approved by Doctors of the New Law, in Latin, Gallic, and Germanic Texts and Pictures . . . Written and Depicted*) by John of Stablo from the St. Lawrence monastery in Liège written in 1432. Thirty-five figures and events, mainly from the historical books of the Old Testament (*figurae*), are ranged in order with seventy similar events from monastic life and the life of St. Benedict, all drawn by the author's own hand, and each drawing is furnished with a Latin, French, or Dutch quatrain. (Liège's position on the linguistic boundary was, presumably, the reason for these polyglot texts, and later on this multilingualism also served, in the subscriptions in emblem books, to ensure their wider distribution.)[27] As an example from this cycle, I show the ascension of the Prophet Elijah as the prefiguration of the assumption of St. Benedict by angels on the heavenly ladder, which is decked out with torches (figs. 5, 6).[28]

I can make only marginal reference here to extrabiblical typology. It occurs when exemplary matter from antiquity is compared with analogous matter from the world of Christianity as something that is more significant in spirit and achievement. Perhaps originating as a rhetorical syncresis in comparing the lesser with the greater, it was the task of the presentation of such intensifications to demonstrate the theological change into a new quality, so that the old form was filled with a new meaning. When Ambrose in

---

When the stone pours forth its waters,
The raven obeys.]

Benedict is here like Moses, because he caused water to come forth from a rock (Peter Stotz, *Sonderformen der sapphischen Dichtung des lateinischen Mittelalters,* Medium Aevum, Philologische Studien, no. 37 [Munich, 1982], pp. 434–438). The comparison with Moses ("par quoque Moysi") is weaker than the typological juxtaposition. Apparently following the example of Benedict, people later pointed to St. Francis as the "new Moses," who precedes his people "walking with dry feet through the sea" into the Promised Land (Dietz-Rüdiger Moser, *Verkündigung durch Volksgesang: Studien zur Liedpropaganda und -katechese der Gegenreformation* [Berlin, 1981], p. 383, n. 179).

27. Albert Henry, "Une oeuvre trilingue de Jean de Stavelot," *Latomus* 1 (1937): 187–210.

28. The illustration is taken from the collected work edited by Dom P. Batselier, O.S.B., *Benedictus: Eine Kulturgeschichte des Abendlandes* (Geneva, 1980), p. 80, figs. 50 and 51; cf. also figs. 3, 6, 52, and 53 in the same work. In figure 49, Benedict is a new Jesse, with the root of the genealogical tree of the great Benedictine saints growing from his breast (cf. fig. 102). Other saints, too, were a new Moses. The sermon by Herbert of Bosham on the martyrdom of Thomas à Becket calls the saint an intensified Moses: "alterum se nobis Moysen exhibens nisi quia plus quam Moyses hic" [showing himself to us a second Moses unless it was the case that this one was more than Moses] (*PL,* 190, 1410 A).

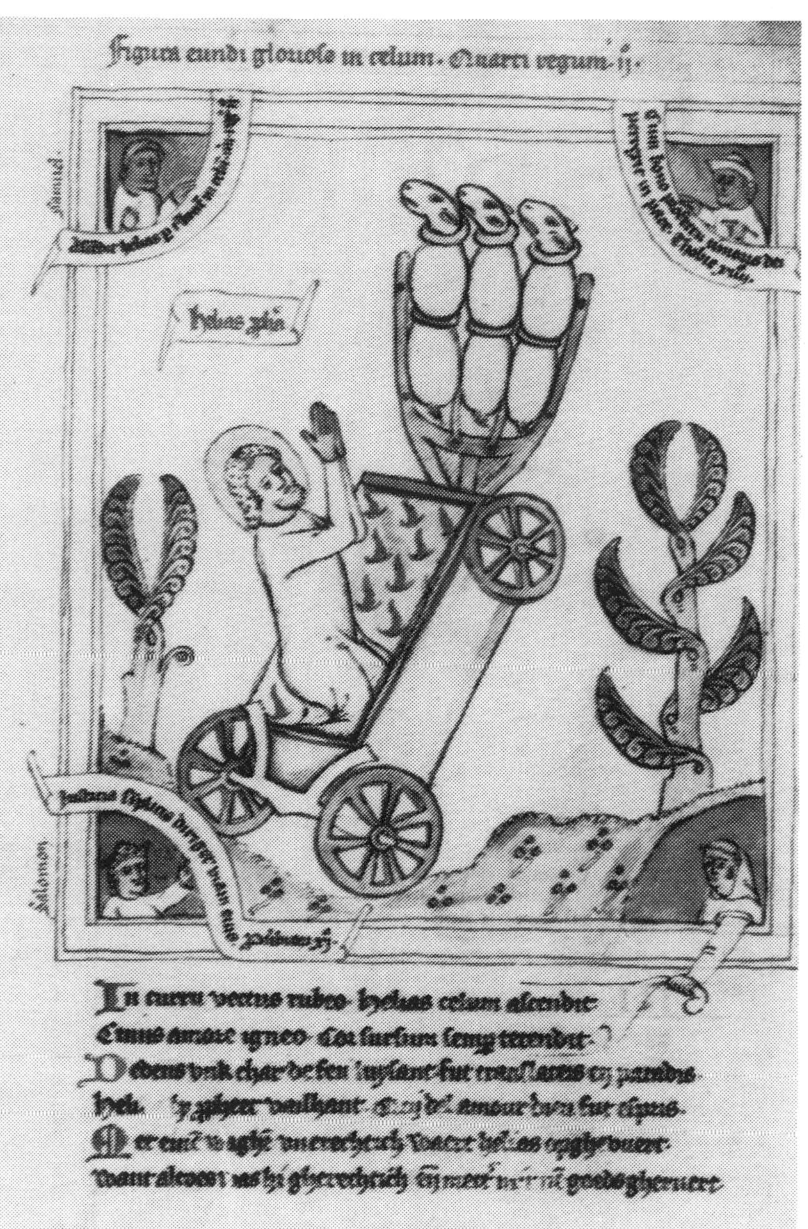

FIGURE 5

Johann von Stabio, The *figura* of the translation of the prophet Elijah in a chariot of fire (from *Acta beati Benedicti* [1432]).

FIGURE 6

Johann von Stabio, The *veritas* of St. Benedict's ascension into heaven upon a ladder of virtues lit by torches (from *Acta beati Benedicti* [1432]).

"De officiis ministrorum" ("On the Duties of the Clergy")—an extrabiblical antitype of Cicero's "De officiis" ("On Duties")—juxtaposes the Pythagorean virgin and St. Agnes, and Orestes and Pylades and SS. Sixtus and Lawrence, the typological meaning is clear. According to Tertullian, ancient and modern heroism are as different in value as glass and pearl. Extrabiblical typologization of this sort was practiced until the beginning of the eighteenth century. Side by side with the usual typology, with its intensification *in bonam partem* (in a favorable manner), there is, after all, a typological intensification *in malam partem* (in an unfavorable manner) as well—as in the case of the prefigurations (for example, Pharaoh, Goliath, Alexander, Antioch) which are fulfilled in the Antichrist.

If we take an overview of what we have sketchily described here, we see that the history of salvation—from Creation to the Day of Judgment—its progress through the old era and the new era, with a perspective on the final era, became in its totality, through typology, the object of a single, orderly interpretation as well as an assessment that accorded to each era what belonged to it, but put—as a major task—on the new era the burden of fulfilling what belonged to it. The genre of the world chronicle, as the form of a total view of history from Creation to the final era, served as a framework for such a view. Like almost no other theologian of his time, Rupert of Deutz (d. 1130), viewing the unity of the church from the Creation, through its middle period in Christ, to the end of the world, allotted a key role to typology in his Christocentric theology of the history of salvation as a means of illuminating conceptions of the unity of history.[29] This was also to be seen later—represented pictorially—in the work of Joachim di Fiore.

The field of typological interpretation of political happenings, which is an obvious one for the historian, should not continue much longer to be a no-man's-land between history and literary history. The latter has not always operated with great success in this field wherever, in the last three decades, it has tried to represent a ruler, antitypically, as an *Imitatio Christi*—whether it was Charlemagne or Charles I of England in the seventeenth century—as though it were thinkable that there could be a typological intensification of Christ. The misleading concept of postfiguration—which, in the meanwhile, is also haunting America—should finally be laid to rest, for it is something invented by philologists, as a legendary or historical successor to Christ, that implies an intensification of Christ. Of necessity refusing to ascribe the character of an antitype to each and every successor to Christ, we must lend all the

29. Mariano Magrassi, *Theologia e Storia nel Pensiero di Ruperto di Deutz* (Rome, 1959).

more weight to Christian historical superelevations of what is in the Old Testament or in antiquity—superelevations which were understood, or were later interpreted, as being truly antitypical fulfillments of pre-Christian prefigurations. Just as the group Synagoga and Ecclesia represents the understanding of the church as the antitype of the old-type synagogue, something already understood in the pre-Christian era, only the church in the form of a cathedral can fully be made out to be an antitypical intensification of its prefigurations in the Ark, the Tabernacle, and the Temple of Solomon. Types are also fulfilled in the church's sacrament and liturgy. The fact that Charlemagne, as the new David, antitypically exceeded the old king, was given expression, at his canonization in 1165, by the fact that St. David had to give up December 29 as the day of his liturgical veneration in favor of Charlemagne. The archbishop of Trier and teacher at the court school in Aix-la-Chapelle, Amalarius of Metz, closes the foreword to his *Liber officialis*, which is directed to Louis the Pious, with wishes that the emperor may be blessed, wishes that commend him, as the glory of the church and the keeper of the faith, to Christ and wish him salvation as the "new"—that is, now Christian—David and Solomon: "Divo Hludovico vita" [Life to the Blessed Louis]. "Novo David perennitas" [Perpetuity to the New David]. "Da principi, Domine, vitam [Give to the ruler, Lord, life]. Ipso novo Salomoni felicitas. Pax mundi vos estis" [Blessedness for the New Salomon himself. You are both the peace of the world] (reference to the title "Salomo pacificus").[30] In the same work, Amalarius gives a second example of typological reference between the Old Testament and the present, when, following Bede and emphasizing the essential difference, he derives the liturgy of the hours from a practice in the Book of Esdras. With the counterpoint of "them" and "us," and "formerly" and "today," which marks typological thought, he points out that it was once the walls of the city of Jerusalem that were to be built; today it is the walls of the church.[31] Amalarius elucidates what is specific about Christian

30. *Amalarii episcopi opera liturgica*, tomus 2, *Liber officialis*, ed. Johann Michael Hanssens, Studi e testi, no. 139 (Vatican City, 1948), p. 21, praef. 7.

31. *Liber officialis* 4.3.4 (p. 415): "Ex inspiratione qua inspiratus est dominus Beda, novimus cursum diei sive noctis habere exordium a libro Esdrae. Si enim iuxta eorum morem convenimus ad rogandum Deum, oportet nos scire quod habeamus opera murorum aedificandorum ecclesiae nostrae, sicut illi habuerunt Hierusalem, er in circuitu inimicos, sicut illi habuerunt. Murus nostrae ecclesiae habet in fundamento Christum, super quod fundamentum stabiliti sunt apostoli et qui per eos crediderunt, sive credunt, seu credent. Nos sumus hodierna die in structura huius muri, qui semper aedificabitur usque ad finem mundi" [From the inspiration

wall building in his interpretation. According to his interpretation, the elders, while teaching, support the younger brethren on Christ, the foundation of the wall, and on the apostles who are the socle, in the same way that the stones of a wall lie on the foundation. They cut them into ashlar and clad the wall so that the weaker brethren are protected, like uncut stones, in the inner part of the wall, while the lime of love, the water of the Holy Spirit, and the sand of earthly activity form the mortar that binds the wall for an entry into the Heavenly Jerusalem and as protection against the devils which attack it.[32]

No history has yet been written of the way in which persons, institutions,[33] and motivations to action conceive of themselves politically in Christian history, up to at least the seventeenth century, at least not in the sense of a stimulating comparison of themselves with the Old Testament, so as to surpass it in a new spirit. At the outset of the work, it would be necessary to distinguish as clearly as possible whether those who were active in this way consciously saw themselves in such a role, or whether it was only contemporary and later interpretations of their story by theology, historiography, and literature that set them in a typological light. In this case the historian and the literary historian would have to join forces. It was not until the Middle Ages that Peter and Paul were recognized as the founders of a new Rome who surpass the founder types, Romulus and Remus; it was only the Middle Ages that recognized in Benedict, the founder of the Benedictine rule, the church's new

with which Bede the master was inspired we know that the liturgical course of the day and night takes its origin from the Book of Esdras. For if it is according to their custom that we convene to supplicate God, it befits us to know that ours are also the tasks of raising the walls of our church, just as those [predecessors of ours] had [the tasks of raising the walls] of the city of Jerusalem, and of performing them encircled by enemies, just as those predecessors were. The wall of our church has Christ as its foundation, upon which foundation the Apostles are stabilized, as are whoever through them have come to have faith, or do have faith, or will have faith. We ourselves are held today within the structure of this wall, which will continue to be built higher and higher, until the end of world.]

32. *Liber officialis* IV, 3, 4–8 (pp. 415–417). On the vocabulary of typological reference, Rudolf Suntrup, *Die Bedeutung der liturgischen Gebärden und Bewegungen in lateinischen und deutschen Auslegungen des 9. bis 15. Jahrhunderts,* Münstersche Mittelalter Schriften, no. 37 (Munich, 1978), pp. 89–121, esp. p. 120; see Rudolf Suntrup, "Zur sprachlichen Form" (n. 16). Later interpretations of the wall, presumably inspired by Amalarius, in Joseph Sauer, *Symbolik des Kirchengebäudes und seiner Ausstattung in der Auffassung des Mittelalters* (2d enlarged ed., 1924; reprint, Münster, 1964), pp. 112–114. "Lapis qui portat portatur" [The stone that bears is itself borne] is the motto of wall building as early as Gregory the Great in his temple exegesis of the prophet Ezechiel (*Homilia in Ezechielem* 2.1.5., in *PL,* 76, 938f.). This was obviously in Amalarius's mind.

33. Johan Chydenius, *Medieval Institutions and the Old Testament* (Helsinki, 1965).

Moses and lawgiver. We have to distinguish such a subsequent typological mythologization of history—whose beginnings are already to be found in the New Testament—from a typological pragmatism of historical action that is certainly harder to comprehend. There is no question but that the typological myth of the theologians, the historiographers, and the poets is able once again to achieve its own historical efficacy. Luther, as the new Moses, is a different person from the monk of Wittenberg. When the Puritans made their exodus across the sea to New England, they were guided by the memory of the exodus from Egypt and the belief in the God-given foundation of a Christian New World. To what extent they acted in a conscious typological manner and oriented themselves in the belief that they were, on the new continent, acting as the Israelites had done in founding the new Jerusalem, and many other new-old places, does not seem nearly as certain to me as it does to American scholars, who are easily inclined to interpret such orientations of Puritan piety toward the Old Testament as being typological.

In what follows, I want to say a word about the continued existence of typology even in the modern era.[34] (To take this matter up as a medievalist also means looking at the question of how far the Middle Ages actually extend.) But before we start to give a brief sketch of the objective questions, we should give a short survey of research into this matter, so as to explain why England and the New World are more strongly represented. While German literary historians, after the earliest beginnings, made about fifty years ago, by the Germanist Julius Schwietering, the Anglist Hans H. Glunz, and the Romanist Erich Auerbach—whose status as an emigrant strengthened the well-deserved effect of his work because it came from America—showed only a measured interest in typology in literary history, the lead in the study of typology, from the late Middle Ages to the present, is, at the moment, held quite decidedly by American Anglists. Landmarks in recent research were the volume *Typology and Early American Literature* (1972) edited by Sacvan Bercovitch with a hundred-page bibliography, and then a colloquium which was held at Princeton in 1974, the results of which were published in Earl Miner's anthology *Literary Uses of Typology from the Late Middle Ages to the Present* (1977). After Americanists had proved the significance of typology for English and American literature in the sixteenth to eighteenth centuries, it was—again in America—George P. Landow's meritorious contribution in

34. My essay "Skizzen zur Typologie im späteren Mittelalter" pursues lines right up to the eighteenth century.

the seventies that showed the same to be completely true of Victorian England.[35] We can of course complain that the American impetus toward making new discoveries has resulted in considerable blurring of the clear definition of the boundaries between typology and other sorts of allegory, or of other, apparently related, sorts of historical imitation of Old Testament happenings. Yet today we can still affirm that, after the great achievements of theologians like Jean Daniélou and Henri de Lubac, who brought typology, as a form of thought in the understanding of the history of salvation, back into theological consciousness, it is not theology or art history—which in the hands of Émile Mâle was once in the forefront—but literary history which takes precedence over other disciplines in this field. Literary historians are today well on the way to studying typological thinking in all the centuries of the modern era, both in Protestant theology, which has yet to produce a reasonably thorough study of Luther's obvious typology, and in certain directions in art, but first and foremost in the whole history of modern literature. Meanwhile theology and art history have hardly been involved at all in research into typology in this area for the past three decades—that is since the

35. I will select just a few examples from the numerous Anglo-American works on the subject. For a more general background without a special interest in typology, Don Cameron Allen, *Mysteriously Meant: The Rediscovery of Pagan Symbolism and Allegorical Interpretation in the Renaissance* (Baltimore, 1970), with bibliography on pp. 312–338. In addition, Joseph A. Galdon, *Typology and Seventeenth Century Literature,* with bibliography on pp. 149–160; Paul J. Korshin, *Typologies in England 1650–1820* (Princeton, N.J., 1982), pp. 105–123. George P. Landow, *Victorian Types, Victorian Shadows: Biblical Typology in Victorian Literature, Art and Thought* (Boston, 1980). Ira Clark, *Christ Revealed: The History of the Neotypological Lyric in the English Renaissance,* University of Florida Humanities Monograph no. 51 (Gainesville, Fla., 1981).

English-speaking scholars who have worked on typology have to accept the reproach that their work suffers from an increasing obfuscation—even to the point of confusing the concepts—because of its increasing diffusion. This is possibly conditioned, in part, by the blurred use of traditional terms in modern sources; it has, nevertheless, assumed a proportion that leaves little possibility of new restraint, for in important publications almost no notice is taken of non-English-language research. Warnings by David S. Berkeley in "Some Misapprehensions of Christian Typology in Recent Literary Scholarship," *Studies in English Literature* 18 (1978): 3–12, had no effect upon Korshin's work, useful as it assuredly is, where evidence of Imitatio ("postfigurations," "christomimetic characterization," and the like) are simply mixed in with what is exemplary, or with other matter suited to the doctrines of types. Korshin's bibliographic synopsis, "Typology and the Visual Arts," p. 404, takes no notice of the art historical literature on this subject which has appeared on the Continent since the middle of the nineteenth century.

Everything that George P. Landow claims as political typology from the literature of the Victorian era, in his chapter entitled "Political Types," must be denied this quality.

work of Erwin Panofsky and since the publication of Joseph Coppens's historically broadly based, but largely uninfluential, work *Les Harmonies des deux Testaments* (1949). I am not in a position to say whether historians of the modern age have shown an equally energetic philological concern. Karlfried Gründer's important work on Hamann's typologizing history of philosophy was the work of a philosopher.[36]

The truism—taken over from theology by other disciplines of the humanities—that the Reformation put an end to allegorical and typological Bible exegesis is, in its lack of differentiation, simply untenable, both as far as the reformers themselves are concerned and for the whole period from the sixteenth through the eighteenth century. In the work of the reformer William Tyndale in England and, even more markedly, in the works of Martin Luther in Germany and John Calvin in Switzerland, typological thinking, together with its recognition in theory, is used in their own exegetical practice, so that a door was held open from the outset not only for a continuation, but also for a later burgeoning, of typology in Lutheran, Calvinist, Puritan, and, finally, Pietistic Protestantism. The end of the Middle Ages did not mark the end of typology and, by comparison, there is as yet nothing final to be said about the strength of its continued existence in the Catholic and Protestant churches, especially as, at any one time, the focal points do not coincide in time or place, as for example in Spain and New England, even if it does seem as though the seventeenth century was everywhere a renewed heyday of typological thought in both confessions. The state of research is so unevenly developed in different sectors that generally acceptable statements cannot, for the moment, be made.[37] The Protestant replacement of traditional exege-

36. On Hamann as the most significant representative of typological thinking in the eighteenth century—besides Bengel and others—Karlfried Gründer, *Figur und Geschichte: Johann Georg Hamanns "Biblische Betrachtungen" als Ansatz einer Geschichtsphilosophie*, Symposion, no. 1 (Freiburg, 1958). Urs Strässle, *Geschichte, geschichtliches Verstehen und Geschichtsschreibung im Verständnis Johann Georg Hamanns: Eine entwicklungsgeschichtliche Untersuchung der Werke zwischen 1756 und 1772* (Berne, 1970). Reiner Wild, *"Metacriticus bonae spei": Johann Georg Hamanns "Fliegender Brief": Einführung, Text und Kommentar*, Regensburger Beiträge zur deutschen Sprach- und Literaturwissenschaft, no. 6 (Berne, 1975), pp. 147–188. Völker Hoffmann, *Hamanns Philologie zwischen enzyklopädischer Mikrologie und Hermeneutik*, Studien zur Poetik und Geschichte der Literatur, no. 24 (Stuttgart, 1972), pp. 188ff.

37. On allegory and typology in sixteenth-to-eighteenth-century Protestantism, cf. Victor Harris, "Allegory to Analogy in the Interpretation of Scriptures," *Philological Quarterly* 45 (1966): 1–23, here pp. 5–17 (sixteenth and seventeenth centuries), pp. 17ff. (eighteenth century). On the period of the Reformation, James Samuel Preus, *From Shadow to Promise: Old Testament Interpretation from Augustine to the Young Luther* (Cambridge, Mass., 1969). In Bercovitch's an-

sis, according to the multiple senses of the Scriptures, by a "historical" interpretation of the Scriptures is, even well into the eighteenth century, an illusory process, at least inasmuch as the concept—propagated at this time—of the use, application, or accommodation of the single historical meaning of the Scriptures to the life of the faithful kept firmly alive the tropological and anagogical dimensions of the rules of existence from the understanding of the Scriptures while, on the other hand, the postulate that the firm foundation of the spiritual meanings of the Scriptures is found in the soil of the *sensus historicus* from the church fathers to the Middle Ages was never abandoned. In the Wittenberg history of the Reformation, typology achieved significance in one cardinal point. The fact that Luther developed his theology of justification by faith alone on the basis of the brazen serpent (especially between 1526 and 1528) and elucidated his conception of the value of figures on this basis ("for fulfillment of the figures must not be seen but believed") is what lies behind the wealth of figural representations of the brazen serpent. This is true of crucifixion typology in Wittenberg, as well as of the title pages of Luther's writings; it is found on the Saxon memorial plague *thaler* of 1528 and in the painting of Lucas Cranach as the theme of his *Law and Grace* (1529), the Prague version of which has the inscription "Figur unserer Rechtfertigung" [The figure of our justification], and on his son's altar paintings in the town churches of Wittenberg (1547) and Weimar (1555), both of which include Luther as a participatory figure in the paintings, where the reformer is standing side by side with John the Baptist.[38] Just as, in the Middle Ages, Joachim di Fiore had extended the typological concordance of the old and new ages, in ecclesiastical and imperial history, into his own days, or Gerhoh von Reichersberg, arguing typologically, had tried to set in motion the happenings of the time, so in the middle of the seventeenth century, English ecclesiastical parties using, on occasion, typological arguments fought

---

thology: Thomas M. Davis, "The Tradition of Puritan Typology" (pp. 11–45), and (on the medieval prehistory) Stephen Manning, "Scriptural Exegesis and the Literary Critic" (pp. 47–66). In E. Miner's anthology: Karlfried Froehlich, "Always to Keep the Literal Sense in Holy Scripture means to Kill One's Soul: The State of Biblical Hermeneutics at the Beginning of the Fifteenth Century" (pp. 20–48). On the philological side we should mention Steven N. Zwicker, *Dryden's Political Poetry: The Typology of King and Nation* (Providence, R.I., 1972). Richard Reinitz, "Symbolism and Freedom: The Use of Biblical Typology as an Argument for Religious Toleration in Seventeenth Century England and America" (Ph.D. diss., University of Rochester, 1967).

38. Donald L. Ehresman, "The Brazen Serpent, a Reformation Motif in the Works of Lucas Cranach the Elder and His Workshop," *Marsyas: Studies in the History of Art* 13 (1966/67): 32–47. Werner Busch, "Lucas von Leydens 'Große Hagar' und die augustinische Typologieauffassung der Vorreformation," *Zeitschrift für Kunstgeschichte* 45 (1982): 97–129.

the battle for religious tolerance, freedom of conscience, and freedom of the church that arose out of the separation of the Puritans from the state. At the same time they interpreted facts from the Old Testament for their own purposes—according to an already accepted goal—in the areas of state and faith, in order, as they thought, to legitimate their demands. If typological thinking put to use for political purposes could prove manipulable, this is something it has in common with the history of the realization of ideas in the secular world. In the ecclesiastical struggles, which, in New England, had far-reaching consequences, the question was whether Old Testament conditions could serve as examples or whether, from the Christian typological view, they were to be superseded, thus making room for innovations, something that, above all, Roger Williams tried to achieve in the middle of the seventeenth century for a New England which was, as the new Jerusalem, to surpass the old one.[39] Different determinations of the extent of the discontinuity in the typological continuity of old and new had far-reaching historical effects.

39. On Roger Williams, Reinitz, pp. 176–284. Insufficiently familiar with the doctrine of the four meanings of the Scriptures, Reinitz is surprised that Williams can illogically be indebted to the Old and the New Testament for both typological and tropological gleanings (pp. 228–237). Joseph Rosenmeyer's dissertation, "The Image of Christ: The Typology of John Cotton" (Ph.D. diss., Harvard University, 1966), has not been printed. Samuel Mather wrote a systematics of typology in *The Figures or Types of the Old Testament* (London, 1673; newly published by Mason I. Lowance, Jr., New York, 1967). On the revival of typology in Puritan New England in the seventeenth century, see Ursula Brumm, *Die religiöse Typologie im amerikanischen Denken* (Leyden, 1963). Helga Spevack-Husmann, *The Mighty Pan: Miltons mythologische Vergleiche* (Münster, 1963). Ursula Brumm, *Puritanismus und Literatur in Amerika* (Darmstadt, 1973), index. On Edward Johnson, Sacvan Bercovitch, "The Historiography of Johnson's 'Wonder-Working Providence,'" *Essex Institute Historical Collections* 104 (1968): 138–161. The special spring 1970 number of *Early American Literature*, the "Special Typology Issue," contains works on Roger Williams, Edward Taylor, Jonathan Edwards, and the exegetical tradition of typology. They appeared in a slightly expanded form in the anthology, edited by Sacvan Bercovitch, *Typology and Early American Literature* (see n. 1). A bibliography—not restricted to the Puritans—"Selective Check-List on Typology"—appeared in supplements to *Early American Literature*, vols. 5 (1970) and 6 (1971). On the controversy between Roger Williams and John Cotton on tolerance: Sacvan Bercovitch, "Typology in Puritan New England: The Williamsburg Cotton Controversy," *American Quarterly* 19 (1967): 166–191. Samuel Sewall wrote a typological interpretation of the Revelation, *Phaenomena quaedam Apocalyptica . . . or some few Lines toward a Description of the New Heaven* (Boston, 1697). On Cotton Mather: Brumm, *Die religiöse Typologie*, pp. 33–48; and Mason I. Lowance, Jr., "Typology and the New England Way: Cotton Mather and the Exegesis of Biblical Types," *Early American Literature* 4 (1969/70): 15–37. There is a rich treatment of typology in the works of Edward Taylor: Brumm, *Die religiöse Typologie*, pp. 49–72. Ursula Brumm, "Der Baum des Lebens in den Meditationen Edward Taylors," *Jahrbuch für Amerikastudien* 12 (1967): 109–123; a contrary view in Cecilia L. Halbert, "Tree of Life Imagery in the Poetry of Edward Tay-

In the art history of England, artists of the Pre-Raphaelite school not only show traces of an aftereffect, but clear evidence of a theoretically applied typology in their iconography. The combination of the historical guarantee of types and antitypes on the one hand, and of the historical context of the liberated ability of the factual, in typological thinking, to be used symbolically on the other, could not but afford a welcome counterpart to the Pre-Raphaelite efforts to create a combination of realism and symbolism, sensuality and mysticism, materialism and spirituality (fig. 7). In an epoch when the comfort—especially of faith—was increasingly diminished, a painter like William Holman Hunt—by his pictorial realization of the metaphor of the type as the shadow of truth, which none but the world first sees (*The Shadow of Death,* 1869–73) marks a restorative recourse to the Middle Ages, in whose "videmus nunc per speculum et in aenigmate" [now we see through a mirror and in an enigma] we cannot fail to see a feature of symbolistic modernity, so that George P. Landow could talk of the painter's typological symbolism as anachronistic modernism (fig. 6).[40] John Ruskin's 1846 interpretation of Joseph in Tintoretto's *Annunciation,* as the architect of the church on the ruins of the synagogue, stimulated Hunt's demand that art should "mirror the unknown spiritual truth," as poets do in metaphors.[41] The survival of typology in the Victorian church service in hymn and sermon, its treatment in Thomas Hartwell Horne's introduction to Bible studies, a definitive text for English universities, or its great presentation in Patrick Fairbairn's two-volume *Typology of Scripture,* a work which was constantly reprinted between 1852 and 1976, guaranteed typological thinking a widespread understanding—in spite of all its ineffectiveness—even in the contemplation of history, at least till the end of the century.[42] This Victorian art form is distinguished

lor," *American Literature* 38 (1966): 23–34. Thomas Werge, "The Tree of Life in Edward Taylor's Poetry: The Sources of a Puritan Imagery," in *Early American Literature* 4 (1969–70), pp. 27–47. Robert Reiter, "Poetry and Typology: Edward Taylor's Preparatory Meditations, Second Series, Numbers 1–30," *Early American Literature* 5 (1970): pp. 111–123. Karl Keller, "The World Slickt Up in Types: Edward Taylor as a Version of Emerson," ibid., pp. 124–140. On Jonathan Edwards, see Ohly, "Skizzen zur Typologie im späteren Mittelalter" (see n. 2), pp. 302–310.

40. George P. Landow, *William Holman Hunt and Typological Symbolism* (London, 1979); on the *Shadow of Death,* pp. 2ff., 65, 102, 111, 114, 116–125; George P. Landow with Ruth M. Landow, "William Holman Hunt's 'The Shadow of Death,'" *Bulletin of the John Rylands University Library of Manchester* 55 (1973): 197–239. The English bishop Joseph Hall had compared the type to a rough draft of a sketch, and the antitype to a picture completed in colors by a painter; Reinitz, "Symbolism and Freedom," pp. 46f.

41. Landow, pp. 4ff., 61, 165.

42. Landow, pp. 8ff. Emphasizing the orthodox nature of typological Bible interpretation,

FIGURE 7
Holman Hunt, *The Shadow of Death* (1869–73).

from that of the German Nazarenes by the types and artistic means of their introduction into Hunt's painting *The Finding of the Saviour in the Temple* (1854–62),[43] his stained-glass window depicting Melchizedek done in 1865,[44] or his *Triumph of the Innocents* (1883–84)[45] could be cited as examples of a particularly English—and, in their use of artistic means, not uninspired—typological unification of two worlds in pictorial simultaneity: the Nazarenes do not have this typological memory. We have also taken into consideration the fact that the typological pictorial thought of Pre-Raphaelites like Hunt or John Ruskin,[46] and also the work of an agnostic like Dante Gabriel Rossetti, who explained his watercolor *Passover in the Holy Family* with a sonnet beginning, "Here meet together the prefiguring day / And day prefigured . . ." correspond, with a symbolism which is integrated into reality, to the poetry of the day.[47] From this, we see that English nineteenth-century thought bears the not inconsiderable stamp of an old tradition, for which George P. Landow's book on biblical typology in art and literature that appeared in 1980 provides an overall view.[48] The *Annunciation,* by Edward Burne-Jones, shows stimuli from fifteenth-century painting (figs. 8, 9). The time when Anglo-Saxon research overlooked Continental, and German and French research overlooked the intensive English and American research in this field should now be past, and so should the unconnected coexistence of literary and art history, on the one hand, and history, on the other, where the European tra-

---

Landow also stresses the fact that it was universally known. "During the reign of Victoria any person who could read, whether or not a believer, was likely to recognize allusions to typological interpretations of scripture, and, in fact, the major Victorian poets had frequent recourse to them. Ignorant of typology, we misread many Victorian works—including those of Ruskin and Tennyson, Browning and Hopkins—and the danger is that the greater the work, the more our ignorance will distort and reduce it" (pp. 11f.).

43. Analysis in Landow, pp. 75–103. "Hunt has employed glosses, symbols on the frame, texts within the picture itself, the symbolic potential of Pre-Raphaelite composition, and a complex series of typological images and actions to create a painting that is 'truly replete with meaning'" (p. 103).

44. Landow, pp. 113–116.

45. Landow, pp. 125–138.

46. George P. Landow, *The Aesthetic and Critical Theories of John Ruskin* (Princeton, N.J., 1971), chap. 5, "Ruskin and Allegory" (pp. 319–457). Herbert L. Sussman, *Fact into Figure: Typology in Carlyle, Ruskin, and the Pre-Raphaelite Brotherhood* (Columbus, Ohio, 1979). Linda Haenlein Peterson, "Biblical Typology and the Poetry of Robert Browning" (Ph.D. diss., Brown University, 1978).

47. Landow, pp. 141–161; on Rossetti's typological artistic creations and his picture-poem sonnets to his own and others' work, see pp. 148–161.

48. See above, n. 35.

FIGURE 8

Studio of Fra Angelico, The *typus* of the angel with a flaming sword driving man and woman out of paradise (*background, above left*) and the *antitypus*, the angel of annunciation in an "Annunciation" (ca. 1435). (Photograph: Museo del Prado, Madrid. Copyright Scala/Art Resource, New York.)

FIGURE 9

Edward Burne-Jones, *The Annunciation* (1879), with the *typus* of the exile from paradise (*above right, in relief*). The model for Mary was Julia Jackson Stephen, the mother of Virginia Woolf and Vanessa Bell.

dition of typology, as a way of contemplating history, continues to be given up as a common object by all the arts and humanistic disciplines.

As a historical phenomenon that survived for two millennia, typology was also affected by the fact that everything historical changes in the course of time. The inclusion of nature and antiquity in the old era, and of ecclesiastical and secular history in the new, bears witness to this, just as, later on, secularized applications in nineteenth-century English literature do.[49] Even applications to natural historical processes may surprise us. Among nineteenth-century theologians there was no lack of adaptations of this form of thought to objects outside the history of salvation—within the framework of scientific thought—when they saw in man the antitype of a God-given, typical vertebrate history.[50]

The talk of an extended secularized, satiric, or parodistic typology in nineteenth-century politicizing authors, where even a formal structure is no longer to be found, should not, by creating the impression that it is a question of epigonal degeneration, obscure the fact that there is a falling-off in typology as there is in everything historical. Victorian biblical knowledge, even of the unbelievers, like that of Marx, does not legitimate, for example, Swinburne's blasphemous exploitation of the Bible for the propagation of national social gospels of freedom and of England's role as savior, by classifying the slogan "God is dead"[51] as "ironical" typology.[52] The pallor of Victorian typology in our eyes, accustomed as they are to the power which it enjoyed

49. Landow, *Victorian Types* (see n. 35), pp. 89ff., 95–118.

50. Landow, *Victorian Types*, p. 10ff.; F. Ohly, *Typologische Figuren* (see n. 2), p. 145 (n. 12).

51. Swinburne's poem "Before a Crucifix" (1871) reproaches Christ: "The nineteenth wave of the ages rolls / Now deathward since thy death and birth" (Landow, *Victorian Types*, p. 157).

52. Landow, *Victorian Types*, pp. 159f. Landow's chapter "Political Types" (pp. 143–176) even admits some dubious matter. "What is new, however, is that this Victorian political poet who often makes effective use of typology does not believe in Christianity. Nonetheless, he can use types because he reinterprets his major terms and makes, for example, England, Italy and Garibaldi, or the people take the place of Christ" (p. 154). "Resurrection becomes equivalent to the Risorgimento" (p. 155). "Like Swinburne writing two decades later, Carlyle masterfully uses typological images to attack the religion on which they are based" (p. 167). Where Landow espies typology, it is usually no more than biblical allusions and quotations for political ends. He admits that God is left out completely in the "Exodus" movements of the time (p. 168), emphasizes "the crucial fact, that there is no Christ at the center of his typology" (p. 176). In the polemics against the erection of a monument to the railroad king, Hudson, Carlyle made reference, in an article, to the brazen serpent. Landow evaluates this: "His pamphlet, which both warns the public about the consequences of false worship and instructs them in true belief, exists as the antitype, the true fulfillment of the original brazen serpent" (p. 175). Argumentation of this sort discredits the whole thing and leads it *ad absurdum*.

from the Middle Ages until the eighteenth century, points to the late nature of the revival of a form of thought that was largely outmoded in the age of historicism, and the loss of which took with it the possibility of there being a productive, synoptic view of the ages that could stimulate the present. The loss, too, of a humanistic source of power from what is always exemplary and which is, otherwise, used for the realization of what is classic and outside time, seems today to be the consequence, and it is widespread. And so we find ourselves more and more dependent upon self-regard and on a notion, to which the renunciation of a productive historical memory—which would be more than an always dubious "learning from history"—might lead us.

Typology as a hermeneutic principle for understanding the past and the present—with the unified synoptic view that points to both of them—makes a great claim upon the new era by demanding that it not only keep pace with the whole of the old era, including antiquity, as it does in renaissances, but that it change it, by intensification into a new era, and also raise it, at the height of a return, in such a way as to make the old era remain unforgotten even in the moment that it is being surpassed. The heightened return, after the gap in time between the old era and the new has been bridged, is not to be understood either as being cyclical or as being a spiral—thanks to the unsurpassable finality of the antitype for the whole of history, up to its final change into the new eternity. Unsurpassability, it is true, does not mean a state of being finished and released from tasks and possibilities, but is, rather, the supposition that there is the framework of a demand of the highest order: a framework created by the state of being called to and of being placed into the new era from the point of view of the typological contemplation of history. In spite of Christian history's constancy of aim, typology does not see permanent progress as a linear progression, but as leaps and bounds into a new period of salvation—effected by divine acts of revelation—limited in each case as from nature in Adam, to the Law in Moses, and to grace in the son of God. It is the same with the empires and ages of the world, to the extent that the change into the antitypical final age and empire will not extinguish the typical stages of time but will lift, enrich, and extend them. Typology would mark an end and not a beginning if the unsurpassable finality of the incarnate antitype were permitted to paralyze history. The new era, on this side of the appearance of Christ, remains a demand that is always unfulfilled—a stimulus to change what is historically present in its mission into possibilities of surpassing it. There is competition between the antitypical and the typical, so as to leave behind the marks which have been left by the old. The old era retains its exemplarity as a spur to its being surpassed by a new spirit, something that Augustine and later writers demonstrated in the heroism of the old heroes and the new saints. Discontinuity in continuity emerges from the accumulation of dimensions of value, which try to push the possible to the brink of the impossible, so as to gain for the new era, as a heyday, a perfection that is worthy of it, in theology and the church, in literature and all the arts, in the many forms of a new configuration of the world that would be uncontrollable without the spurs to creative imagination which are set in motion by typology (or which at best would be controllable only in a different historical manner).

Historical portrayals of typological Bible exegesis in commentary, liturgy, and sermon, in Latin, Greek, and vernacular literature, as well as in all the fine arts, have not been written by theologians, philologists, or art historians either for the Middle Ages or for the modern era, which has hardly begun. The problems of semibiblical and extrabiblical typology have, it is true, been adumbrated, but they are far from being treated in depth and are still a task which has to be performed. Where the subject goes beyond biblical or patristic theology, whole periods and sources simply lack the documentation, the formal analysis, the description of changes conditioned by the history of piety, and the evidence of their effect on the conception of history held by theologians, historians, and literary and art historians. What we have been able to provide here is an attempt to sketch out an area which has for the most part still to be developed.

Up till now, medieval studies have lacked a clear sense of the fact that notions of history of this sort—that represented the present as the true summit of the ages according to the divine plan—not only had to give wing to an age that expresses so elevated an emotion in many different arts, but was also flatly opposed to a consciousness of a renaissance which is felt at the time. Common concepts of medieval studies, like those of the *renovatio* of antiquity and the renaissances which follow, a "Carolingian," or an "Ottonian," "the twelfth-century renaissance," and then the early fixing of the date of the beginning of the Italian renaissance, needed to be investigated as to the true facts of the relationship to antiquity suggested by these concepts, especially in a heyday of typological thinking like the twelfth century. Typology and renaissance are opposing concepts; they are mutually exclusive. A present which sees itself as insufficient seeks, by introducing and reviving a past that is recognized as greater, to refresh and renew itself by means of a renaissance. A typological view of history exists in the elevated sense of the knowledge that everything that happened in the pre-Christian era lives to see its fulfillment in a present that takes it over and surpasses it, by transporting it—by means of an increasing number of metamorphoses—to its final possibilities, possibilities that have long since been determined. A typological view of history and the classical concept of a renaissance exclude each other because they are irreconcilable.[53] It is true that epochs do not exist on spiritual roots alone. Typological and renaissance thinking could just as easily enter into a relationship of multifarious tension, since both have stood—from late antiquity up to the period of historicism—as fundamental givens, and even rival possibilities, of the historical consciousness. The more recent history of typology has been investigated far less than the idea of renaissance. The future will have to take a comparative look at the historical power of both of them.

53. Renovation and renaissance are more than what is usually understood by them, if antiquity is to be surpassed at the same time. Gerd Tellenbach urges a sober judgment of *renovatio* even though he closes with the words "Thus, it is less turning back and restoration of the past that speaks out of the constant desire for *renovatio* than, in spite of all illusions, the will to a new formation" ("Kaiser, Rom und Renovatio: Ein Beitrag zu einem großen Thema," in *Tradition als historische Kraft: Interdisziplinäre Forschungen zur Geschichte des frühen Mittelalters: Festschrift für Karl Hauck,* ed. Norbert Kamp and Joachim Wollasch [Berlin, 1982], pp. 231–253, here p. 248). Willy Hirdt notices in the Renaissance, even where no pronounced typology is in play, a fundamental tendency: "Imitation which is intent upon surpassing what it imitates is the élan vitale of the Renaissance" (*Gian Giorgio Trissinos Porträt der Isabella d'Este: Ein Beitrag zur Lukian-Rezeption in Italien,*" Studien zur Fortwirkung der Antike, vol. 12 [Heidelberg, 1981], p. 55, in the section "Nachahmung und Überbietung"). Reinhart Staats, *Theologie der Reichskrone: Ottonische "renovatio imperii" im Spiegel einer Insignie,* Monographien zur Geschichte des Mittelalters, no. 13 (Stuttgart, 1976), pp. 36–43, presents numerous examples of the designation of the ruler as the "new David" or the "new Solomon" (when discussing the David and Solomon plates in the imperial crown) without, as a theologian, taking a typological explanation into account, because he is thinking along the lines of *imitatio/renovatio.*

THREE

PROBLEMS OF MEDIEVAL SIGNIFICS AND HUGH OF FOLIETO'S "DOVE MINIATURE"

I

One of the reasons why medieval art is so fascinating is that it abounds in mystery. Its meaning is seldom obvious. What it offers to the eye and to the other senses has the charm of both seductive promise and hermetic denial. The beautiful foreground not only signifies itself but is at once opaque and transparent with respect to a background, and it is only through this—as its true ground—that the foreground is substantiated. What is visible to the senses is a sign for something invisible that expresses itself mutely in what is visible. What is created as the "trace of God" (*vestigium Dei*) entices us to take part in a "search" (*investigatio*) for what is hidden within it. As a sign, it gives hints of the directions in which we must move in order to find the meaning. The sign is the hint of a goal of understanding that keeps itself hidden, because signs are still mute. To hear and understand the language of these mute signs is the goal of medieval involvement with what is created, both God's creation itself and an art that is inspired by the spirit of God. What is created has—as a *signum* (sign)—a *significatio,* or, as it is called in Middle High German, a *bezeichenunge* (signification). Recognition and understanding, as the creative replication of the act of creation, lie in the discovery of the semantic relationship between the *significans* and the *significatum,* which we call the "signifier" and the "signified." The doctrine of the *significatio* of signs—what is meant here by significs—is founded upon those medieval sciences that describe the world as nature and history: it is the doc-

Part 1 of this article was in the form of a lecture in the Münster Early Medieval Colloquium on April 28–30, 1966. Part 2 is written in the hope that what was only indicated on that occasion can be made convincing by the use of this example. Published as "Probleme der mittelalterlichen Bedeutungsforschung und das Taubenbild des Hugo de Folieto," in *Schriften zur mittelalterlichen Bedeutungsforschung,* by Friedrich Ohly (Darmstadt: Wissenschaftliche Buchgesellschaft, 1977), pp. 32–92.

trine of the spiritual superstructure of this indispensable foundation—to employ a much-used medieval image. In our search for the essence of historical periods we allow ourselves to be guided by the language of those periods. The Middle Ages talk of the "world of the spirit," the *mundus spiritualis*, that seeks to be revealed—as a *sacramentum* (sacrament)—out of the mute text of creation. This revelation takes place through a wealth of metaphors for the relationship between the spiritual meaning and the creaturely essence of things that the senses encounter as intimation and sign, hint and tip, and these insist on the recognition of their meaning as a means of release from their mute language. This "metaphorics" is a key to the representation of the tasks of significs as the discipline concerned with the spiritual exegesis of the created world. The superstructure of spiritual sense has to be erected on the foundation of the letter and of history. The walls of understanding must—in accordance with the history of salvation—be built upon the foundation of things: they support the roof of eschatological knowledge and are painted over with depictions of the moral dimensions of spiritual truth. The basic metaphor of "revelation" (*revelatio*) knows many varieties of figurative concretization; the seals of the scroll must be broken in order to unroll the written text which is inside it; the veils or coverings of the letter must be raised so as to find the new within the old. The veil of the temple must be rent; shadow must give way to light in order to depict change from age to age, from the age of law to the age of grace, from *littera* (letter) to *spiritus* (spirit). The sweetness of the spiritual sense must be extracted from the wax of the honeycomb. The rind must be peeled off to find the pulp within; the shell must be cracked to get at the kernel of the nut. The metaphors of wheat and chaff, of breaking the crust of the loaf to find the crumb, of grinding the letter between the millstones of the Old and New Testaments so that the preacher can prepare the bread of understanding from the meal, are on the borderline between a metaphorics of revelation and a metaphorics of nourishment. The metaphors of turning water into wine, of the transformation of milk into solid food, of the table with its four legs, that correspond to the multiple senses of the Scriptures and the bread of knowledge which they bear, are all metaphors of nourishment. The botanical metaphor of root and fruit, the landscape metaphors of forest and open field, of cloud and sky, metaphors of the quest—especially those of hunting for spiritual meaning by pursuing its traces—the whole wealth of this metaphorical language directs our thoughts to an abundance of aspects of the quest for traces of spiritual truth.[1] The quest

1. Since this was written there has appeared H. J. Spitz, *Die Metaphorik des geistigen Schrift-*

for the meaning of all things in the created world, and for the meaning of all the words used to name them, was a spiritual stimulus that kept a great age creative as it followed the path of the discovery of God and the meaning of life. There is an intellectual intensity at work here of search and discovery, finding and edifying, passing through surfaces into what is hidden, through foregrounds into backgrounds, a creative disclosure of the world which never flags because the dimensions of what is perceptible are infinitely rich. The metaphorics used in extracting the *sensus spiritualis* (spiritual sense) from the historical letter of the written text and from the things in a world created by God or by art discloses that what we are seeking is concealed within what is visible, as the spirit is within the body, as what is concealed and must be revealed, as the goal of the quest that motivates the age. Metaphorical language indicates the spiritual nature of the occurrence that it signifies, and this does not take linguistic shape in any other way. We discover the nature of sin from the metaphors for sin, the nature of love from the metaphors for love, and we discover the change in meaning, and the breadth of meaning, of these abstractions from the historical change in, and the richness of, the metaphorics. We recognize the complex nature of the problem of spiritual sense from the wealth of its metaphorics, the abundance of which (and we have mentioned only a few of the metaphors) indicates all the possible aspects of the problem. The selection and number of metaphors for a single phenomenon is by no means arbitrary. Their number and the kinds of metaphor used correspond to the sorts of essential features that are expressed by the metaphors in question. A single metaphor can signify something that the most diverse phenomena enjoy in common, while one and the same phenomenon can be signified by the most diverse metaphors, depending upon how rich its essential features are. Fire can stand for love, hatred, ambition, and much more. Love can be signified not only by fire but also by metaphors of captivity, service, and many others. A metaphor attaches itself to many aspects of signification, and a complex phenomenon can be signified by the many metaphors which are bound up in it. The reason we have brought up this question of metaphor is so that we can understand the nature of spiritual signification and its discovery from a metaphorics appropriate to that nature. At the same time, it

sinns: Ein Beitrag zur allegorischen Bibelauslegung des ersten christlichen Jahrtausends, Münstersche Mittelalter-Schriften, no. 12 (Munich, 1972). See also K. Lange, "Geistliche Speise: Untersuchungen zur Metaphorik der Bibelhermeneutik," *Zeitschrift für deutsches Altertum* 95 (1966): 81–122.

was our intention to suggest that the metaphorics itself constitutes an object of semiological investigation.

The metaphorics of the theory of signification (unveiling, metamorphosis, heightening, and other basic metaphors) only characterizes tasks and trends; it does not provide a systematic method for discovering a signification. I attempted to give a picture of this medieval method in my inaugural lecture at the University of Kiel, "On the Spiritual Meaning of the Word in the Middle Ages."[2] The characteristics of the thing are what bear its signification, and the number of possible meanings of a thing is fixed by the number of its properties. The description of a thing serves the perception of its properties from which the meanings can be derived. It emerges—from the large number of different characteristics of a thing—that the thing has its own world of signification, while the *word* for the thing always means only the one thing. God's eternal word within things opens up into the different dimensions of its signification, the allegorical—as to the history of salvation—the tropological and moral, and the anagogical and eschatological dimension of its spiritual meaning. "The stages and dimensions of medieval significs furnish the spiritual perspective of the world of what has been created, and this becomes language in the word."[3] The Middle Ages, which are alleged to have no sense of perspective, have, in the spiritual transcendence of what exists, their own perspective that is suited to themselves. It emerges in the glance and the view that penetrates to the spiritual reality of the signification of the sign that is present in everything creatural: a view that frees itself from everything earthly. It is perspective in the truest sense, since it looks through the visible to the invisible, through the signifier to the signified. It leads from the foundations of the sense structure to its vault, from the earthly to the heavenly. Its essence is not foreshortening, but extension to the sublime. It does not relativize by means of an earthly view but is directed to the absolute and makes what has been created transparent vis-à-vis the eternal. It is not physiological-visual in form, but theological-spiritual and determines, as such, the art of sublimity.[4] The patristic and medieval interpretation of the Scriptures, in thousands of commentaries, serves to open up this perspective. The exegete and the preacher are aided by allegorical dictionaries. "Modern lexicography, which asks only what the literal meaning of the word is, is not in a position

2. See chap. 1 of this volume.

3. See p. 17 for a more detailed treatment of this perspective.

4. See above, p. 1.

to reveal the spiritual meaning of the word."[5] We are faced with the task of presenting—by the use of exemplary monuments—the possibilities of a dictionary that would also be charged with portraying all those dimensions of the spiritual meaning of a word that go beyond the fundamentals of philological lexicography in the more narrow sense. For every naming word we would have to go beyond its philological-historical meaning and include its allegorical, tropological, and anagogical dimensions of signification, if we do not wish to relinquish the possibility of also embracing the spiritual perspective of the vocabulary—something that dozens of medieval allegorical dictionaries did. A dictionary of this sort for *Otfrid's Gospel Harmony* would be a pioneering philological achievement. Just as modern secular meaning theory, which takes no account of the spiritual perspective, opens the article on a word with its etymology, so a dictionary that is directed at medieval meanings, which can be acquired or supported just as easily by etymological discussion, could do the same thing. When, on a former occasion, I used the example of the etymology of the Latin word *mors* (death) which is derived in the Middle Ages from the bite into the apple ("a morsu primi hominis, qui vetitae arborem pomum mordens mortem incurrit" [from the bite of the first man, who biting the apple from the forbidden tree met death]), I will now give an example that shows that this is not unknown in the vernaculars. The apple tree in the Song of Songs 2:3 is interpreted, in the St. Trudpert Song of Songs, by considering five of its properties: its leaves, its shade, its blossom and fruit, and its trunk. When it said of the leaves "daz loup bezeichenet die ze der geloube komen sint" [its leaves signify those who have come to the faith] (25, 26f.), there is obviously an etymological relationship between leaves (*loup*) and faith (ge*loub*e), which could not correspond to anything in Latin (*folium—fides*). The green color of the leaves could also be mute support for this etymologizing interpretation, for the chief signification of green in the framework of color meanings is "faith."[6]

I am not here going to treat either the allegorical dictionaries of the Middle Ages—which cry out for definitive editions—or related works like the *Physiologus* and other bestiaries, the treatises on gems or plants, indeed the whole encyclopedic activity of the Middle Ages that begins with the massive work *De universo* by Hrabanus Maurus—who gives it the title *De*

5. See above, pp. 23ff.

6. Roswitha Klinck, *Die lateinische Etymologie des Mittelalters,* Medium Aevum, Philologische Studien, no. 17 (Munich, 1970); and W. Sanders, "Grundzüge und Wandlungen der Etymologie," *Wirkendes Wort* 17 (1967): 361–384, both appeared after the original article was published.

sermonum proprietate et mystica rerum significatione (*On the Nature of Languages and the Mystic Signification of Objects*)—and finds its crowning achievement in the colossal "Speculum Maius" ("Greater Mirror") by Vincent of Beauvais, all of which serve as keys to unlock the spiritual meaning of earthly objects.

The interpretation of the jewels of the Heavenly Jerusalem in the commentaries on the Apocalypse and the interpretation of the precious stones on Aaron's breastplate in the exegesis of Exodus 28:17ff. served as stimuli for the interpretation of precious stones in the Middle Ages, even in treatises on gems. As is the case in all interpretations of things, so, too, in the case of precious stones, the spiritual perspective was arrived at by making the connection with natural properties. The interpretation of stones in scriptural exegesis and in treatises on gems is a main source for our understanding of the significance of colors in the Middle Ages (the word "symbolism" is alien to the Middle Ages and awakens inappropriate associations). The signification of plants, animals, or stones is revealed by the medieval bestiaries and treatises on stones and plants, or by the corresponding parts of allegorical dictionaries, insofar as these are ordered by subject group. For an obvious reason, there are no similar shortcuts for the study of the theory of color. All the medieval collections, ordered either alphabetically or by subject group, serve to interpret things. Color is not a thing, but a property the interpretation of which has to be sought in the allegoresis of colored objects like precious stones, flowers, or animals. It is sad but true that art history possesses no adequate account of medieval color signification.[7] The compilation of a dictionary of medieval color signification would not be too onerous a task, and it would be an invaluable gift, not only for the art historian. We can cite dozens of instances for green as a characteristic of jasper and, as such, as the color of faith. There are colored pictures from the Middle Ages which we can understand only when we know this. The Virgin of the Annunciation, or the evangelists offering themselves to inspiration, those who are listening to the

7. The important work by H. Roosen-Runge, *Farbgebung und Technik frühmittelalterlicher Buchmalerei*, 2 vols. (Munich, 1967), p. 16 (and n. 19) remarks on the lack of knowledge of medieval color signification from the point of view of art history: "The medieval symbolic value of color that we sense on all sides in miniatures without, up to the moment, having been able to grasp it with sufficient certainty could not be examined in this work from the point of view of the iconography of color. A discussion of these questions would be of the greatest significance for a further understanding of medieval book illumination, but it lies outside our present purposes. Even though we are conscious of this, the present investigation can be only a first step on the road to a comprehensive theory of color in early medieval book illumination."

voice of God in the faith, are represented in book illumination in a great field of green as in the faith with which they are listening to God. The Annunciation in a Cologne sacramentary (Bibliothèque Nationale lat. 817, fol. 12r) (fig. 10) represents Mary and the angel in a concrete scene of bold architecture in front of a cloudlike abstract green that stands in space like a miracle, and the angel tidings brighten it, from the left, with the sapphire color of the sky. This astonishing color structure signifies the acceptance of the Annunciation in the faith.[8] Knowledge of medieval color signification would throw a new light on our understanding of a great many things. In no matter what field of significs, important support is always given when the Middle Ages breaks the silence with which creative artists are at work. There are texts in which painters of the twelfth century substantiate their use of colors with the most desirable precision while they are explaining the colors' spiritual sense. The Cologne Annunciation makes us aware of an important problem for medieval significs, for it deals in both theory and practice with the meaning of things on the basis of their properties. Furthermore, there is the phenomenon that properties, like colors, no longer visibly linked to a thing, seem to have a meaning of their own. Thus, at the time of the Annunciation, in a scene filled with objects, buildings, towers, cupolas, and Mary's throne, in the presence of a sort of numinous miracle in a deobjectifed green—one indeed that prevails vis-à-vis everything in the scene—color has acquired a life of its own that is only itself, in order, as such, to signify something. The task of painting faith ("Ecce ancilla Domini, fiat mihi secundum verbum tuum" [Behold the handmaid of the Lord, be it unto me according to thy word]) called for green and also the gesture of the receptive hands in the green of faith. The adjective

8. H. Schrade, *Vor- und frühromanische Malerei* (Cologne, 1958), pp. 225f. (with fig. 83), weighs the question of whether the "completely atectonic" ground, which is like malachite, could be a cave but decides, however, to assume that it is a "color phantasmagoria" of a painter who thinks that he can create forms "with color alone." If the upper margin of the structure were formed "according to white, pink, and brown bands with a golden outline," then he would recognize the band as a painterly motif also in *The Descent of the Holy Spirit* by the same artist. The pictures in the sacramentary are described and reproduced in P. Bloch and H. Schnitzler, *Die ottonische Kölner Malerschule,* vol. 1 (catalog and plates) (Düsseldorf, 1967), pp. 37–44, color plates VII and VIII, figs. 87–111, 500. Here we read (38) of the picture of the Annunciation: "In the background, a green hill on violet ground, above it the buildings of Nazareth in purple, violet, blue, and olive-green tones." In the related Annunciation in the Hitda-evangeliary from Meschede (ca. 1000–1020); cf. Bloch and Schnitzler, *Die ottonische Kölner Malerschule,* p. 47, plate 125. I can see Mary as standing not "in front of a pale blue mountain scene," but in front of a curtain, which Gabriel's *revelatio* is opening.

FIGURE 10
Anonymous, The Annunciation in Cologne (ca. 1000).

that designates the "proprietates rerum" [properties of things], out of which it is possible to develop the thing's world of meaning can, thanks to the tradition of interpretation, detach itself from the thing. Since every spiritual sense depends upon a property of the thing at a given time, a property can carry its own meaning, as in the case of stained glass, where colored panes can have meaning simply as color and do not have to be part of an objective pictorial body. What is true of color in pictures is also true for a whole list of adjectives in literature. We can demonstrate from the Latin *dulcis* (sweet) and the German *süeze* (sweet) how increasingly rarely the word is used as an adjective to describe a thing in religious literature—and not only there. By an intensification and heightening of its sensual meaning into the dimensions of the *sensus spiritualis*—and this is not to be confused with metaphorical or abstract usage—*dulcis* arrives at, among other meanings, its predominant meaning of "gracious, beneficial." The "sweet nails" that pierce Christ on the cross are, like Longinus's *süeze sper,* that is, "sweet spear" (Mechthild von Magdeburg), not an oxymoron, but nails in the service of redemption. I hope soon to complete a study, based on examples, of the use of *süeze* and *dulcis* from the ninth to the thirteenth centuries, with the aim of starting a dialogue on the problem of the *sensus spiritualis* of adjectives.

The case of numbers is similar to that of colors and other properties of things. As mathematical quantities, they live a life of their own, but in the Bible and in medieval texts they are usually encountered as the quantitative determination of objects, and their spiritual sense is predominantly codetermined by things that have the characteristic of certain numbers. Seven, as the number of the Holy Spirit, is supported by the seven gifts of the Holy Spirit, to which other groups of seven attach themselves, like the petitions in the Lord's Prayer, the Beatitudes, the days of Creation, the arms of the menorah, the pillars of wisdom, and many others. However, numbers acquire their own meanings, like things with properties, and in the process their mathematical qualities serve to display their meanings. The operations that can be carried out with them, as their properties, condition the fact that numbers, like objects, can have a world of meaning of their own. The literature on the meaning of numbers in literature, which has proliferated wildly in the past decades, suffers from the fact that its potentialities and its laws are not sufficiently observed and, as a result, what is serious is also misunderstood as mere game playing. Certainty that the procedure is the correct one can be assured only in the few cases where medieval authors themselves explain—by pointing out the meaning—the significance of their works on the numerical basis of their composition. A study of psalm commentaries of the twelfth century[9] was able to show how exegetes recognized that the form of the text of the psalm that is to be interpreted is based on numbers and then knew how to interpret the form that they recognized. Medieval analysis of form itself is able to open up a sure path to the interpretation of medieval texts when their form is based on the signification of numbers. In Honorius and Gerhoh's process of perceiving and interpreting the numerical structure immanent in the Psalter it transpires that the number of words, sentences, and larger textual units were understood as signs of something higher and can be interpreted from different points of view, in the process of which they can also be understood as parts of revelation by the psalm text that is structured in this manner. In addition, there is the totally new observation as to how the exegetes go about presenting the appearance of the structure, determined by numbers and observed in the biblical text, in the form of their own interpretation. The spiritual function of the meaning of the beautiful in the form of their language is determined, even in their syntax, by numbers. When speaking of God, the language is ordered in triads, of the Holy Spirit in heptads, of mortal things in tetrads, and of the Passion in pentads. Parts of the German St. Trudpert Song of Songs are formed according to a numerical pattern, and this is also true of its style and syntax; they form an artistically complete structure of a kind unknown to me in any Latin text of this sort.[10] The purity of a form that is based on numbers can even be used as a text critical argument. Forms based on the meaning of numbers in liturgy, music, and architecture are already under consideration by scholars. The allegorical dictionaries of the Middle Ages generally contain words for objects, but the "Clavis" of the pseudo-Melito of Sardis—ordered according to groups of objects—devotes a whole book to the meaning of numbers, and, similarly, there are numerous special tracts "De significatione numerorum" [On the signification of numbers] that treat the question and so show us the way in which numbers were regarded as things. Other parts of speech, like adjectives and verbs, were, as far as I can see, included, to any significant extent, only in baroque allegorical dictionaries like the *Silva Allegoriarum* by Hieronymus Lauretus,[11] which was in print from 1575 until the eighteenth

9. W. Köster, "Die Zahlensymbolik im St. Trudperter Hohelied und theologischen Denkmälern der Zeit" (dissertation, University of Kiel, 1963).

10. This is true not only of the prologue: cf. F. Ohly, "Der Prolog des St. Trudperter Hohenliedes," *Zeitschrift für deutsches Altertum* 84 (1952/53): 198–232.

11. Cf. in the meantime Hieronymus Lauretus, *Silva Allegoriarum totius Sacrae Scripturae* (Barcelona, 1570), a photomechanical reprint of the 10th edition (Cologne, 1681), with an introduction by F. Ohly (Munich, 1971).

century. The inclusion of verbs also suggested itself insofar as—side by side with the meanings of objects and their properties—from the beginnings of Christian allegoresis, significs had an object that had to remain outside lexicography, namely, the meaning of historical facts. The science of the meaning of happenings that we call, by the modern term, typology was now added to the study of the meaning of things—the doctrine of the relationship of meaning, in the sense of prefiguration and fulfillment,[12] between events separated from one another in time. I shall not here treat the subject of typology, the doctrine of the meaning of events, because I have recently dealt with it elsewhere.[13] But let this serve as the occasion for looking at a broader field of significs. What links type and antitype can rest in something significant that is common to both of them: the wood of the tree of paradise is conquered by the wood of the cross; the waters of the Red Sea prefigure the water of baptism. Type and antitype are also frequently linked by a common gesture: Isaac carries the wood to the place of sacrifice in the same form and with the same bearing that Christ carries the cross. Type and antitype in this case are linked by gesture and thing; in other cases the link is only in the gesture. The Annunciation of the Virgin Mary is the antitype to the temptation to the Fall in paradise.[14] Just as Satan, the fallen angel, approaches Eve and tempts her to eat of the apple, so the angel of the Annunciation approaches Mary with the lily. The gesture of temptation with all its consequences is offset, in the history of salvation, by the gesture of annunciation to Mary with all of its consequences. If research in legal and liturgical sciences has devoted itself, for its own purposes, to gestures, art and literary history have neglected, to a deplorable degree, studies that would permit us to hear the language of gesture in the arts as we should like to understand it. There are, without doubt, constants of meaning in the language of gesture that last for centuries, just as there are in the meaning of things and events. Research into the art and literary history of gestures in such a clear and manageable scene as the Annunciation of the Virgin alone would provide a rich source of information. Whether Mary answers the angel with a gesture of belief, fear, humility, obedience, modesty, or joyful thanks can be read quite wonderfully from the gestures of the hands. Restriction and freedom in the treatment of

12. For more on this, see pp. 16–17 above.

13. "Synagoga und Ecclesia: Typologisches in mittelalterlicher Dichtung," *Miscellanea Mediaevalia: Veröffentlichungen des Thomas Instituts der Universität Köln* 4 (1966): 350–369.

14. Maria Elisabeth Gössmann, *Die Verkündigung an Maria im dogmatischen Verständnis des Mittelalters* (Munich, 1957), pp. 22f., 79, 108, 125f., 139, 148f., 157, 163f., 176, 212f., 245; and now, especially, E. Guldan, *Eva und Maria: Eine Antithese als Bildmotiv* (Graz, 1966).

the language of gesture are presumably represented differently in the fine arts from the way they are in literature, even if it is true of both that the measure of freedom that exists between gesture and meaning could be greater than in the other, more strictly codified areas of significs. In art history, as in the history of literature, the language of gesture is most visibly subject to change of style. A history of gesture would furnish us with a history of style of convincing clarity precisely because, by it, we could pursue the relationship between obligation and freedom throughout the centuries, in the same motifs, like annunciation, inspiration, or others. The Middle Ages is an epoch of the expressive, forthcoming, and meaningful gesture whose language we have to learn. The whole of creation becomes gesture through the character of its signs. The verb *innuere* (to give a nod to) is one of the most frequent synonyms for *significare*. Under the word *nutus* (nod) in the *Silva Allegoriarum*, Lauretus says, "Creatures can be labeled both as nods and as traces of God."

Scholars have still almost entirely neglected the stylistic history of those works which go a thousand times further than patristics, mysticism, or scholasticism and are devoted to the interpretation of the Scripture and the created world. Bible commentaries and sermons, treatises on animals, stones, and plants or similar books, allegorical lexica, figure poems or meditations on things, and all the other genres that are devoted to a spiritual elucidation of a hidden revelation are not formal constants but are part of the life of the history of piety and theology. The style of perception and description, the interpretation of things, and their transmission in works is realized within the open bounds of the tradition and freedom in which historical life has its place. Romanesque and Gothic, scholasticism or mysticism, monastic and clerical piety create their own forms of interpretation of what *is* on the basis of God's idea of creation and salvation, the understanding of which is the task of significs: for the forms make it possible to track down the living meaning of the search for the meaning of the word and of the thing which it denotes.

Between the heyday of the church fathers and the creative freshness of the twelfth century—and especially after Bede—exegesis had become more rigid. The damp soil started to crack; the exegetes grew short of breath, proceeding from word to word and from thing to thing so as to see them in isolation, only to go on and look at the next one. This all changed in the twelfth century, when exegesis which proceeded from one word to the next was felt to be a mere syllabification (*syllabicare*) that did not go far enough. Rupert of Deutz succeeded magnificently in doing this beneath the great arches of his conceptions of the history of salvation. Stirred by emotion, the twelfth century follows Bernard de Clairvaux along the paths of his spiritualizing psychagogy through the world of the word. Another possibility, that of transforming the loose parataxis of an older observance into a cohesively smooth sequence in which every member is part of an immutably ordered spiritual whole, may be hinted at by Adam Scotus's commentary on the Tabernacle, written about 1180. He and John of Kelso, who commissioned the work, were concerned with the exegetical reconstruction of the Tabernacle as a whole—something that would surpass Bede's exegesis of the Tabernacle, which was no longer felt to be adequate. What they were out to avoid was allowing the text to disintegrate into its constituent letters, which would make the commentary into a loose conglomeration of words and word meanings, in order to combine an articulated set of building materials into a higher unity. The type of scriptural exegesis that builds up to a larger whole was, apparently, first tested on biblical edifices like Noah's Ark, the Tabernacle, the temple in Jerusalem, and the Heavenly Jerusalem. Adam Scotus's efforts to overcome the exegetical staccato of word-by-word explication and to offer a holistic as well as a spiritual view of the Tabernacle brought him to the consideration of a unique idea. As a painter on parchment, he created—after he had described its genesis in precise language—a great picture of the Tabernacle so that, besides the historical Tabernacle, the spiritual meanings of all its structural elements were represented by painterly means in such a way as to represent, pictorially, the salvational and tropological dimensions of meaning of all its parts and their properties. Even though the painting is lost to us, we can still reconstruct it with precision and can interpret the meaning of every brush stroke, because Adam's great commentary on the Tabernacle assumed the literary form of a comprehensive interpretation of every piece of his massive painting. We do not have time here to let the author himself explain his extraordinary work, nor to hear from Adam's own mouth what would integrate all that has been said into a marvelous unity and eliminate the loose parataxis from our comments. The metaphorics of his language, the artistic mastery of the problem of spiritual perspective, the purely descriptive representation of things in the first part of the work, the painterly application of the allegorical dimension in the second, and the addition of the tropological dimension in the third part of his "Tripartitum tabernaculum una cum pictura" [The tripartite tabernacle together with a picture] (*Patrologia Latina* [*PL*], 198, cols. 609–796) make the application of all that we have discussed appear to us as a true *theoria* of reflective contemplation. We see him drawing lines and explaining the significance of their extent and numerical values, we hear him accounting for the meaning of every one of the colors that he has chosen—Bede speaks of the "sacramentum coloris" [sacrament of color]

(*PL*, 921, 426 B)—he gives us an explanation of typological relationships, the four points of the compass, the etymology of this word or name, the significance of woods and metals, of curtains, coverings, and hides, and—with astonished admiration—we experience, before our very eyes, the transformation of the Tabernacle and its surroundings into a picture of the world, its mystical history, and the history of its salvation. Adam's Tabernacle, as a picture of the world whose pictorial space embraces a space of time extending over millennia, is a spiritual cosmos that we can now no longer pace out in our thoughts. His "Tripartitum tabernaculum" is the greatest interpretation of a medieval work of art by its own creator that I know of, and it is invaluable to us, because he employs every conceivable possibility of spiritual interpretation.

A reconstruction and an all-embracing analysis of Adam's lost picture (a project upon which we are engaged in Münster) is made simpler not only by his text and an older tradition of pictures of the Tabernacle, but also by works from the twelfth century that are closely related in character and which confirm, as Adam's spiritual neighbors, the new Gothic-holistic principle of exegesis using a picture and its interpretation. In their case, the interpretative texts are preserved in the manuscripts, in part with pictures, whether of a bird like the dove that is interpreted with respect to all of its properties that appear in the picture, or one or another edifice from the Bible which, like the Tabernacle, reveals itself as the pictorial and temporal space of a cosmic mappemonde from the Creation to the End of the World—a pictorial and temporal representation which the Middle Ages also deployed architecturally. From other sources, too, there is a rich, but still untapped, documentation of the semiological importance of medieval architecture.[15] Nature and its spiritual

15. I presented a preliminary analysis of the most important of the methodologically similar models for Adam's "Tripartitum Tabernaculum," Hugh of St.-Victor's *Arca Noe mystica*, in a lecture entitled "Stilwandel in der Exegese des 12. Jahrhunderts" at the conference of the Constance study group for medieval history, which took place on October 10–14, 1966, on the island of Reichenau. After this, there appeared J. Ehlers, "Arca significat ecclesiam: Ein theologisches Weltmodell aus der ersten Hälfte des 12. Jahrhunderts," *Frühmittelalterliche Studien* 6 (1972): 171–187.

Theodulf of Orléans (d. 821) already begins to interpret, as part of a poem, pictures of the seven arts (*Carmina* IV, 2, in *PL*, 105, 333ff.; *Monumenta Germaniae Historica, Poetae* I, 544ff.) and the earth (IV, 3) according to their poetic description, to reveal what the artist's *docta manus* (learned hand) intended by the gestures, attributes, and composition, "for the nourishment of the spirit that is observing the picture of the earth" (336 D):

Totius orbis adest breviter depicta figura:
Rem magnam in parvo corpore nosse dabit.

meaning constitute the whole of an existence that is filled with significance. The Middle Ages worked tirelessly at surveying that infinite plenitude of meaning—hidden at the Creation as the trace of God in nature—in the knowledge that grace does not cancel nature out but complements it. What is valid for the West is, incidentally, also valid to a large degree for medieval piety and poetry in the Orient. The interpretation of the trace of God is, both in the East and in the West, not a science but a hermeneutic path to salvation in accordance with the will of God, who—in the words of a Persian mystic—"devised door and lock and also invented the key."[16]

II

The reconstruction and systematic analysis of the Tabernacle picture cannot be anticipated here. However, I cannot resist the temptation, at once attractive yet necessarily linked to a hermetic disappointment, of presenting here another example of a little picture interpreted by the artist himself that is encompassable—namely, that of a dove. It is the introductory picture to a treatise on birds from the twelfth century, in which—as was the case with Adam—picture and text belong together, and the picture which accompanies the text is to hand. The painter and explicator is Hugh of Fouilloy (Hugo de Folieto—d. after 1172), not far from Corbie; Hugh was, as a canon regular, prior of St. Laurent, near Amiens (fig. 11).[17] His spiritual oeuvre, which exists in a hundred manuscripts of the twelfth and thirteenth century, is widely

---

[Here is a figure, briefly depicted, of the whole world:
It will offer a way to know a great thing in a small body.]

16. Annemarie Schimmel, *Die Bildersprache Dschelâladdîn Rûmîs* (Walldorf, 1949), p. 54; the mystic writes (8):

He who loves God's creation, is highly honored,
An unbeliever is he who honors the creatures.

The thought returned in the work of his contemporary, the poet Saadi:

Who does not see today
Thy traces in creation,
For him is it certain that tomorrow
He will not see thy countenance.

A. Schimmel, ed., *Orientalische Dichtung in der Übersetzung Friedrich Rückerts* (Bremen, 1963), p. 137.

17. On his identity, biography, and works see H. Peltier, "Hugues de Fouilloy: Chanoine régulier, prieur de Saint-Laurent-au-bois," *Révue du moyen-âge latin* 2 (1946): 25–44.

FIGURE 11

Hugh of Folieto, Dove (twelfth century).

distributed especially in the convents and chapters of northern and eastern France,[18] was generally, and for a long time, ascribed to Hugh of St.-Victor (and as good as assimilated into his work), and it is only today that we can survey a separate oeuvre.[19] Like the treatise on birds, Hugh also wrote another work, *De rota verae religionis* (*Concerning the Wheel of True Religion*), as an interpretation of two pictures of a wheel which stand at the beginning of the two parts of his work. One of them is interpreted in "bonam partem" [in a favorable manner] as to the virtues, the other in "malam partem" [in an unfavorable manner] as to the vices: "axle, hub, spokes, rim, creaking, and lubrication, everything is the object of allegoresis"; in these wheel pictures "the virtue—or the vice—which a particular part symbolizes is written on every such part of the wheel."[20]

Hugh states, in the prologue to his work,[21] that it is written for one Rayner, who as a knight (*miles*) became a convert, just as Hugh himself did, when he moved from the secular clergy (*de clero*) to the monastic life (*vita regularis*). Both now sit upon the perch of a life bound by the rule, the falcon and the dove, the plain man and the man of letters, the nobleman and the man of God who is called to introduce the man of the world to the secrets of life on the perch. Hugh paints them next to each other in the prologue that is addressed to Rayner: "E c c e , in eadem pertica sedent accipiter et columba. Ego enim de clero tu de militia ad conversionem venimus, ut in regulari vita quasi in pertica sedeamus" [Behold the falcon and the dove both sit on the same perch. For I came from the clergy, you from the military, to be converted, so that we may sit in the monastic life as if we were on the perch] (figs. 12, 13, 14). He writes on the ground, "This is the perch of the regulated life," and above the two birds he writes *clericus* and *miles.* The wall next to the knight is that of good works (*activa vita*), the cleric's wall is that of pious thoughts (*contemplativa vita*).[22] What the one perceives with his spiritual eye, by his sense of hearing, the other takes in with his actual eye by seeing.

18. On the dissemination of the manuscripts, see ibid., p. 34 n. 34. Peltier indicates numerous manuscripts and their present location that are in the possession of Benedictines, Cistercians, and Premonstratensians, of which more than thirty-five are now in Paris alone; cf. below, pp. 129–135.

19. The works are listed and characterized by Peltier, ibid., pp. 41–44.

20. Ibid., p. 43; Peltier (n. 54) indicates that the pictures of the wheel are in Paris, B.N. lat. 17468: on Hugh's *De rota* see below, n. 26 and pp. 126–128.

21. The text which is printed in *PL*, 177, 13–20, is based on the old edition of Hugh of St.-Victor (Rouen, 1648) and could be emended. I quote these emendations tacitly where they are confirmed in the manuscript without intending to make a "critical" decision.

22. Cf. 22 C: "Pertica accipitris designat nobis rectitudinem vitae regularis quae a terra longe

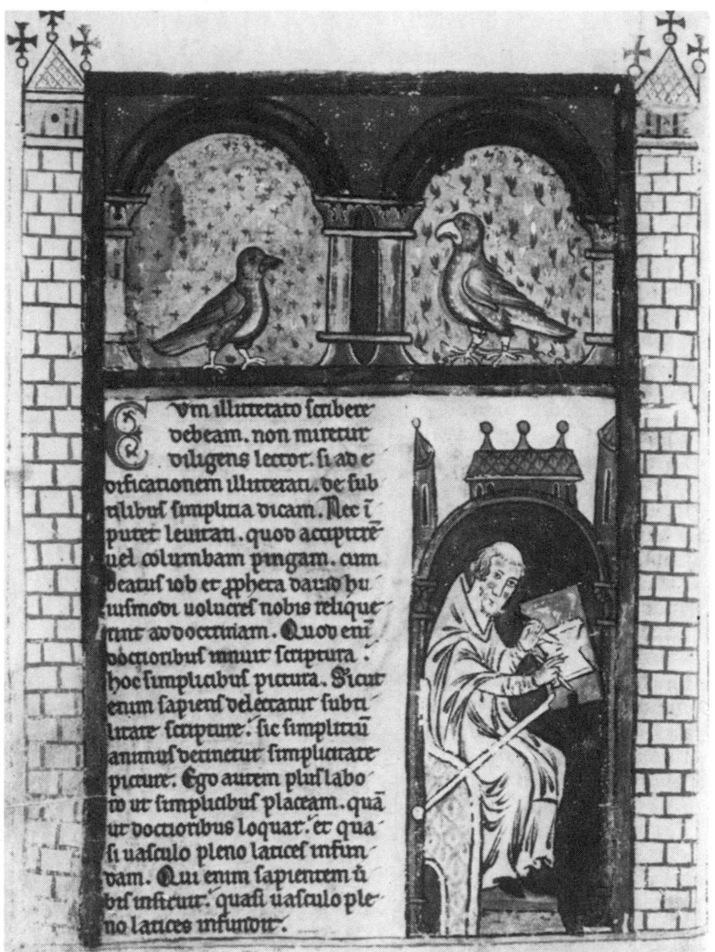

FIGURE 12

Hugh of Folieto, The dove and falcon on the pole of life lived according to a rule (from the prologue to a twelfth-century Paris manuscript).

---

suspenditur, quia a terrenis desideriis huismodi vita separatur. In hac pertica ligatus sedet, quia regularis vitae statuta firmiter tenet. Duobus parietibus inhaerere dicitur, a quibus ex utraque parte sustentatur. Duo parietes, qui perticam sustenant, sunt activa et contemplativa vitae, quae pie viventium rectitudinem portant" [The falcon's perch, which is suspended far from the ground, designates for us the righteousness of the monastic life because a life of this kind is separated from earthly desires. He who sits fixed on this perch holds firmly to the statutes of the monastic life. It is said to adhere to two walls by which it is held up on each side. The two walls which support the perch are the active and the contemplative life that sustain the righteousness of those who live piously].

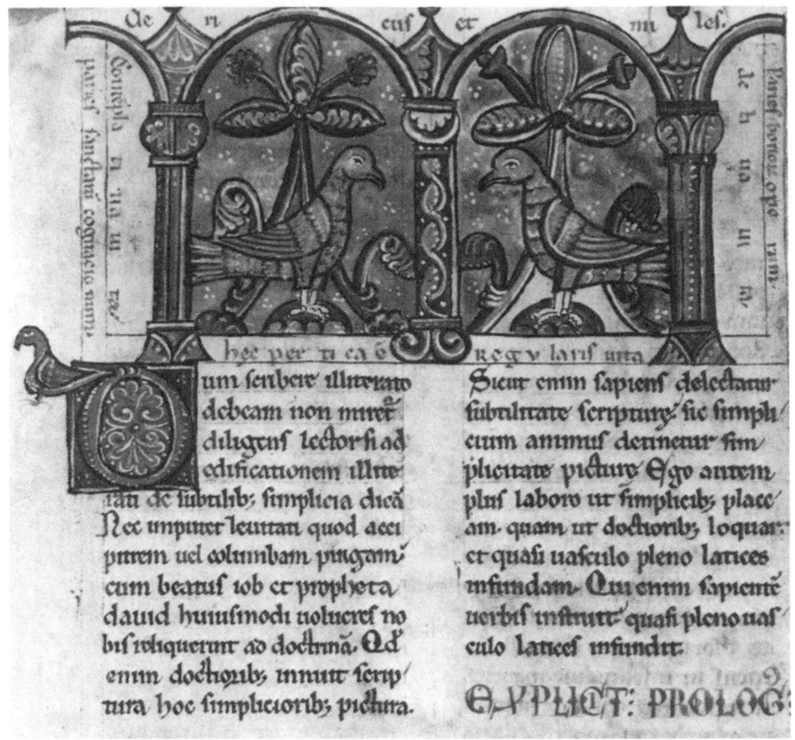

FIGURE 13

Hugh of Folieto, The dove and falcon on the pole of life lived according to a rule (from the prologue to a twelfth-century Paris manuscript).

Hugh therefore wants to serve Rayner with a picture, to paint the dove from Psalm 67 (68): 14, so as to edify the heart of the simple man with this picture. "But I did not just want to paint the dove to create a likeness, but also to describe it in words, to explain the picture with the text, so that even if someone did not like the simple picture, he could enjoy the interpretation of the text." "Thus, I placed at the head of this work the dove through which the grace of the Holy Spirit is always at hand for the penitent, and grace alone leads to forgiveness."[23] The picture stands at the beginning of the work; the

23. The Paris B.N. manuscript lat. 2495 does not read like *PL* and lat. 2495 B, but has *qua* instead of *quia* in the sentence: "In principio huius operis iccicrco columbam preposui, qua sancti spiritus gratia semper preparatur cuilibet penitenti—" [For that reason, I have placed the dove at the beginning of this work, by which the grace of the Holy Spirit is always ready for anyone who repents—].

FIGURE 14
Hugh of Folieto, The dove and falcon as priest and knight (twelfth century), *vita comtemplativa* and *vita activa.*

text is its interpretation. Hugh mediates grace for Rayner through the picture of the dove. Paris manuscript 2495 B clarifies the office of the painter and the interpreter, in that in the prologue it has a painting of the pelican that feeds its young with the blood of its breast (fig. 15). But we should not make the mistake of misunderstanding the picture as a vehicle for teaching laymen (like the later *biblia pauperum*) or as a sermon for the illiterate—any more than the *Physiologus* should be regarded in this light, even if the prologue does make this out to be the case. Hugh says that he is writing at the request of the

FIGURE 15
Hugh of Folieto, The author gives his heart's blood like a pelican (in a twelfth-century Paris manuscript).

knight Rayner "illiterato . . . ad aedificationem illiterati" [for an illiterate . . . for the edification of an illiterate] who has need of the picture in order to understand: "What writing gives to the understanding of the educated, pictures give to the illiterate. As, indeed, the wise man finds pleasure in the written word, so the heart of the simple man is captivated by the picture."[24] Older and contemporary picture-text works of the twelfth century whose texts interpret pictures—well-known ones like the *Hortus deliciarum* (*The Garden of Delights*) by Herrad von Landsberg, the works of Hildegard of Bingen, and the *Liber figurarum* (*The Book of Figures*) of Joachim of Fiore, as well as others that have yet to be discovered by scholars, in their way equally magnificent works (see above, pp. 79ff.)—leave us in no doubt that they are monastic in origin and intention.[25] Hugh's treatise on birds, which begins with the dove

24. 15/16: "Quod enim doctioribus innuit scriptura, hoc simplicibus pictura. Sicut enim sapiens delectatur subtilitate scripturae, sic simplicium animus detinetur simplicitate picturae" [For as the written word is to the learned, so the picture is to simple men. For just as the wise man is delighted by the subtlety of what is written, so the mind of the simple is engaged by the simplicity of the picture].

25. When Richart de Fornival, a doctor and a canon, wrote, in the first half of the thirteenth century, his *Bestiaire d'Amours* for a learned woman (from whom he was willing to accept a work in return)—it was a contrafacture of a bestiary with overtones of the spirituality of courtly love—he also emphasized in his prologue that text and picture belong together in his work. C. Segre, ed., *Li bestiaires d'Amours di Maistre Richart di Fornival e li Response du Bestiaire* (Milan, 1957), pp. 3ff. The German translation is by Gudrun Eichholz:

> And for this reason God, who loves man so much that he wants to take care of him to the extent that he needs it, has given man a special sort of strength of soul that is called memory. This memory has two doors—seeing and hearing—and a path, by which we can reach them, leads to each of these doors—namely, picture and word. Pictures serve the eyes, and words serve the ears. And it is apparent that we can reach the house of memory both by pictures and words, because the memory that stands guard over the treasures that the human mind acquires through the quality of its intellect recalls what is past. And it is precisely by means of pictures and words that we arrive at this result. For when we see a story pictured—the story of Troy or some other—then we see the heroic deeds that once took place, as though they were taking place in the present.
>
> And it is the same with the word. For when we hear a story read, we hear the adventures as if they were taking place before our eyes. And since we actualize by these two means—word and picture—what has gone before, it is evident that we can arrive at memory by both word and picture.
>
> And I, my lovely and lovable friend, whose memory you cannot quit without the trace of the love that I bore you immediately deteriorating, so that I could not be cured of it, without at least the scar of the wound's being visible, no matter how well I were to behave, I would be worthy of remaining for ever in your memory if that were possible. For this reason I send you these two things in one. For in this work I send you both picture and word,

and the falcon, is intended for the falcon that is already bound to its monastic perch and already looks like the dove in the picture in Paris manuscript 2495 (different from B.N. 2495 B). The treatise is handed down only in Latin in manuscripts that in part are theological and in part, like the *Physiologus*, present allegorized natural science (fig. 13).[26]

---

so that if I should not be present, this work, by means of its picture and its words, will make it seem as though I am present in your memory.

And I will show you how this work contains both picture and word. For it is certainly clear that it contains words because every piece of writing is done to show the word and to have it read: and when we read it, it becomes words again according to its nature. And the fact that, on the other hand, the picture is contained in it becomes clear from the fact that there is only one letter if it is painted.

And in the same way this piece of writing makes a statement that calls for a painting. For it is in the nature of birds and beasts that they are better recognized when they are painted than when they are described. (Color facsimile from a manuscript of 1277 in Segre, *Li bestiaires d'Amours*, before the title page)

26. The first short analysis of the dove portion of Hugh's book was presented by C. de Clercq in the *Gutenberg-Jahrbuch* (1962), pp. 23–26, on the Oxford (Bodleian, Lyell, 71) and St. Omer (94) pictures of the dove. The essential parts of what he has to say are as follows: The meaning that Hugh ascribes to the picture in the prologue emphasizes the fact that, at that time, author and illustrator were seldom the same person and stresses the significance of the picture as an essential part of the work (23; cf. 30). The rich inscriptions on Hugh's pictures of the wheel in the *De rota verae religionis* (C. de Clercq published six of them, here 28f.; *Archivum latinitatis medii aevi* 29 (1959): 222f.; *Revue du Nord* 45 (1963): 31–42, figs. 2 and 3; there is a seventh in F. Unterkircher, *La miniature autrichienne* (Milan, 1954), plate, 35; a better example in A. Katzenellenbogen, *Allegories of the Virtues and Vices in Medieval Art* (London, 1939), figs. 70, 71, discussed on pp. 70f. The picture of the dove proves to de Clercq "qu'ils n'étaient pas destinés à des religieux 'tellement simples que cela,' cependant ils résument et facilitent la compréhension du texte" [that they were not destined for clerics "as simple as that"; nevertheless, they sum up and facilitate the comprehension of the text] (p. 30). The picture in the prologue of the Oxford manuscript shows a knight and a cleric underneath the perch with the dove and the falcon "en dessous de l'épervier un guerrier à cheval tenant un glaive, au dessous de la colombe un clerc debout tenant un livre" [beneath the falcon a knight on horseback holding a sword and beneath the dove a cleric standing holding a book].) [According to this, the picture would be closer to a crusader and its turrets suggest a connection with Paris 2495 B. The picture of the author beneath the falcon (fig. 12) may have introduced only the knight, which completes the pair as an afterthought.] C. de Clercq writes of the dove pictures in the Oxford manuscript: "Elle reproduit dans un cadre rectangulaire, où se lit le verset 14 du psaume 67, une grande roue et un petit médaillon dans chaque coin. La grande roue est composée de plusieurs cercles concentriques, reliés par des bandes verticales qui pourraient signifier les rais de la roue. Au milieu du plus petit cercle figure une colombe. Les rais et les espaces entre les divers cercles sont couverts d'inscriptions empruntées aux chapitres 2 à 4 du traité. Tandis que celles des quatres médaillons et les deux textes intermédiaires rappellent les six symboles des couleurs, que nous avons évoqués. Ainsi cette miniature

In his introduction to *De tribus columbis,* Hugh takes as his starting point the three biblical doves, the careful observation of which can lead simple hearts to perfection: the doves of Noah, David, and Christ, which bring mercy, forgiveness, and grace. The etymology of the names of Noah, David, and Christ, the biblical story of the doves of the Ark, the verse of David's psalm (67:14) and the dove at Jesus' baptism, together with their properties, permit him to know three things that have been communicated: from Noah's dove, peace from sin and the return to the peace of the heart and the attainment of mercy; from David's, the promise of forgiveness after being steadfast in God's

facilite l'intelligence des dix premiers chapitres de l'ouvrage. L'alternance des inscriptions entre les rais semble suggérer la différence des circonstances, selon que tourne la roue de la vie" [It reproduces within a rectangular framework where Psalm 67:14, can be read, a large wheel with a small medallion in each corner. The large wheel is composed of several concentric circles, joined by vertical bands which could be seen as the spokes of the wheel. In the middle of the smallest circle is the dove. The spokes and the spaces between the various circles are covered with inscriptions borrowed from chapters 2 to 4 of the treatise, while those of the four medallions and of the two intermediate texts recall the six symbols of the colors which we have evoked. Thus, this picture facilitates the understanding of the first ten chapters of the work. The alternation of the inscription between the spokes seems to suggest the difference in the circumstances according to which the wheel of life turns]. The fact that the dove picture is also a picture of the wheel of life is assumed—though he gives no grounds for the assumption—by C. de Clercq as an analogy to Hugh's wheel pictures in *De rota verae religionis,* which he treats in the same essay (pp. 27–30). While there is no doubt that the iconographic tradition of the wheel of fortune is in the background of these pictures, the association should certainly be kept at a distance (see below, pp. 126–128): "Au fol. 4v de notre manuscrit commence le texte du corps de l'ouvrage. Le chapitre 1 parle des trois colombes mentionnées par l'Écriture: celle de Noé, qu'il décrit comme de couleur noire; celle de David, c'est-à-dire celle du psaume 67 et qui est donc de multiples couleurs; celle qui survola le Christ au moment de son baptême, qu'il indique de couleur blanche. Ces trois colombes sont répresentées au fol 5.r" ["The body of the work begins on fol. 4v of our manuscript. Chapter 1 talks of the three doves mentioned in Scripture: that of Noah, which he describes as being black in color, that of David—in Psalm 67—which is parti-colored, and the one that flew over Christ at the moment of his baptism, which he indicates as being white in color. These three doves are represented on fol. 5r] (p. 26). The rest of this passage is concerned with the remaining text of the treatise on birds, which I am not going into here, interesting as the relationship between picture and text is in that part of the work.

C. de Clercq treats Hugh's treatise on birds somewhat more extensively in his article "Hugues de Fouilloy, imagier de ses propres oeuvres?" *Revue du Nord* 45 (1963): 31–42, here pp. 31–36, discussing tradition (pp. 31f.) and the dove picture (pp. 33f.); the rest is concerned with sources, *Physiologus,* Gregory of Tours, Isidor of Seville, Bede, and Hrabanus Maurus (pp. 35f.). His readings of the inscriptions of the dove pictures can be improved here and there. Here, too, he calls the central part "la grande roue" [the big wheel]. Also on *De rota* (pp. 36–40) and *De pastoribus et ovibus* [On shepherds and sheep] (pp. 40ff., fig. 4) he asks whether, and in what form, the author may have drawn the bird, wheel, and shepherd pictures in the original.

cause; from the dove at Jesus' baptism, the receipt of grace after the search for peace and the expectation of salvation: "Poenitenti igitur fit misericordia, operanti promittitur venia, diligenti datur gratia" [for the penitent, therefore, compassion is found, the one who strives is promised remission, the one who loves is given grace] (15 C). Without referring later on to Noah's dove and Christ's dove and without giving a reason for this omission, Hugh gives a broad interpretation only of David's dove because its many colors ("columba varia; columba amicta varietatibus" [the multicolored dove; the dove cloaked in many colors]; see n. 26) corresponded to what he wanted to do with the picture. The illustrated manuscripts[27] have three differently colored pictures of the three doves in medallions placed one above the other, in part with inscriptions which act as frames,[28] but without any interpretation of their colors (fig. 16). In the manuscripts, the medallion pictures then follow, as opposed to the order of the text which begins with "De tribus columbis" [On the three doves], in which they appear only in the first chapter, that is, after the main picture, to which they are definitely subordinated. It is this picture only that will be the object of our closer attention[29] (Hugh's dove picture, original size 14 × 21 cm. according to Paris, B.N. lat. 2495, fol. 2r, on colored plate 2).

27. E.g., Paris B.N. lat. 14429; B.N. 2495, fol. 7r; B.N. lat 2495, fol. 3r; Cambridge, Sidney Sussex College, ms. 100, fol. 2r.

28. According to the catalog of Sidney Sussex College library, 118, they read in the Cambridge picture: "f.2*b*. Three medallions, each containing a dove facing *R*. The uppermost is red on blue ground, the second white on red, the third, grey and pink on blue. Round the first is, *Columba unica est spiritus sancti gratia* ('the singular dove is the grace of the Holy Spirit'): round the second, *Columba uaria est sancta ecclesia* ('the variegated dove is the Holy Church'): round the third: *Columba est a ma nigra sed formosa* ('the dove is black but beautiful'). On the frame is *Columba Christi data gratis non pro meritis: Columba noe formosa opere nigra tribulatione* ('the dove of Christ is given freely, not for the sake of merits; the dove of Noah, is beautiful through completion of its work, black with distress at having to do it'). For *columba unica* in Paris 2495, I read *columba rubea,* which corresponds to *columba varia,* the multi-colored dove." There are no inscriptions in Paris 14429, 2495 B; in 2495 the inscriptions for the last two medallions are missing.

29. Let me point out from the beginning some of the rich material on the allegoresis of the dove, which in general I shall not adduce for commentary: H. Messelken, "Die Signifikanz von Rabe und Taube in der mittelalterlichen deutschen Literatur: Ein stoffgeschichtlicher Beitrag zum Verwesungscharakter der altdeutschen Dichtung" (Ph.D. diss., University of Cologne, 1965): in this work see the dove at the time of the Flood, p. 241 (index); on the dove in Psalm 67:14, pp. 59, 108, 125, 143; on the dove at Jesus' baptism, p. 237 (index). Unfortunately, Messelken, in spite of the fact that he refers to Hugh's work in other places, totally neglected his interpretation of the dove. On the dove, see (apart from the literature in Messelken's bibliography) V.-H. Debidour, *Le bestiaire sculpté du moyen âge en France* (Paris, 1961), pp. 344f., 389 (index); G. Penco,

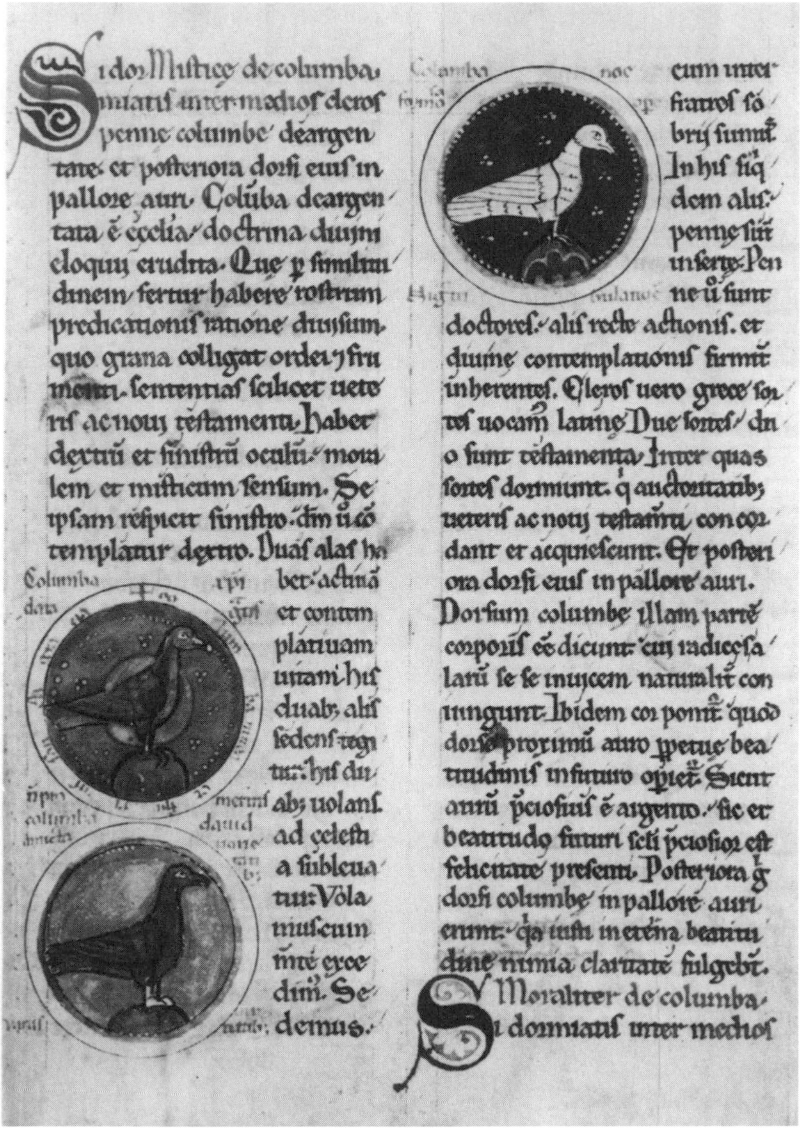

FIGURE 16

Hugh of Folieto, The doves of Noah, David, and Christ bring mercy, forgiveness, and grace (in a twelfth-century Paris manuscript).

The person looking at the painted dove is surprised that its nature is barely portrayed by the picture. It merely typifies and does not emphasize its properties in the way that we might expect in a text that is to serve as a stimulus to interpretation. The natural picture of the dove is the center of a spiritual view of being and determination of location in an order which is determined by circles and squares, the circular movement of which within the framework determines the picture. Whether it leads from the framework to the center, or from inside to outside, or is merely resting after coming to a conclusion is not immediately obvious. The natural picture rests in the spiritual one that manifests itself above what is organic in the preponderance of lines and writing. The picture presents itself to the viewer as a task that requires the viewer to read the solution to the problem from out of it. It is unthinkable that a lay brother like Rayner could do this, if writing were still a closed book to him. The picture's microcosm can be unlocked only by the key of totally absorbed contemplation, by the pursuit, in the picture, of all the lines of thought that are fulfilled in writing. If it were really intended for laymen, they would have needed the experienced hands of an initiate to guide them if they were to unlock its meaning. It is not more simple, but more demanding than the *Physiologus* tradition, so that we have to take into account the fact that Hugh, in the prologue, has entreated the knight, Rayner, now a lay brother, to give legitimation, on this occasion, to the unusual and demanding form of the interpretation of picture and text.[30] The fact that the tradition of treatises on birds generally dispenses with pictures[31] is an indication that the intention, which may once have been entertained, of presenting the work to laymen was never carried out.[32]

"Il simbolismo animalesimo nella letteratura monastica," *Studia Monastica* 6 (1964): 7–38, here 24–28.

Abundant older references in F. Sühling, *Die Taube als religiöses Symbol im christlichen Altertum* (Freiburg, 1930); on the interpretation of the dove, new material in D. Schmidtke, "Geistliche Tierinterpretation in der deutschsprachigen Literatur des Mittelalters (1100–1500)" (Ph.D. diss. Freie Universität, Berlin, 1968), pp. 417–426.

30. I intend to treat other larger examples from the twelfth century elsewhere. Precursors are Hrabanus Maurus's figure poem *De laudibus sanctae crucis,* and Hincmar's *Ferculum Salomonis;* see F. Ohly, *Hohelied-Studien: Grundzüge einer Geschichte der Hoheliedauslegung des Abendlandes bis um 1200* (Wiesbaden, 1958), pp. 89–91; J. Rathofer, *Der Heliand: Theologischer Sinn als tektonische Form* (Cologne, 1962), pp. 290–295.

31. Peltier, "Hugues de Fouilloy," p. 43 n. 54: "En fait, dans la plupart des Mss du Volucraire, les miniatures et dessins annoncés n'ont pas été exécutés" [In fact, in most of the treatises on birds, the miniatures and drawings that are announced have not been executed].

32. Even Hugh's most ambitious work, *De claustro animae* (*PL,* 176, 1017–1182), was not di-

Even today, the picture on its own is still mute, as far as the layman is concerned, if it is not interpreted for him on the basis of the Latin explanation. We shall attempt to look at the picture and interpret it from the text. Within a decorative molding, the words of Psalm 67:14 form a square framework, beginning at the top left and running clockwise, and they can be read inside this framework: "Si dormiatis inter medios cleros, penne columbe deargentate, et posteriora dorsi eius in pallore auri" [When you rest easy in the midst of your sheepfolds, [yours are] wings of the dove covered with silver, and pinions of its tail shimmering pale yellow with gold]. The picture's function is to interpret the writing that forms the framework. Everything within the framework that lies on the surface of the parchment, like a spiritual latticework directing the eye to its center, serves the understanding of the biblical dove, with its silver feathers and golden tail, and not a dove that has been observed from nature. Hugh lets the verse stand on its own but may also have in mind the ones that precede it: God sends the rain of grace to his "heritage" [*hereditas*] (67:10). "Animalia tua habitant in ea; parasti in dulcedine tua pauperi, Deus" [Your animals live therein; in your sweetness you have made them ready for your poor man, O God] (67:11). The picture is divided into upper, middle, and lower and right and left parts. There is a central, vertical, axis that extends, uniquely and oddly, above and below the framework and the ornamental molding out to spigot-like appendages which could, if they were unambiguous, modify the formal pictorial character in favor of what appears to be an object or implement. As a wheel or a mirror, for example, the picture would gain additional meaning as a thing. Both, common as titles of books, would teach their own lesson. There is, however, no suggestion in the text of such an interpretation.

The picture relates the upper and lower central bar to the eyes and the feet of the dove. From the bottom up (reading from the right) we read "rubor pedum cruor martyrum" [the red of the feet the blood of the martyrs],

---

rected at laymen but at religious brothers, whom he regards equally as "simplices" [artless] and whom he wishes to delight with the "simplicitate eloquentiae" [artlessness of eloquence], that is, by renouncing Greek and other equally difficult expressions "quae turbant simplices" [which disturb the artless] (1131 AB). He excuses the length of his work: "quando aliquis simplicibus loquitur, oportet ut eis diffusius et verbis planioribus loquatur. Ideo tractatum longius extendi, quoniam simplicioribus fratribus intendebam loqui" [when one addresses the artless, it is fitting that one speaks to them in a rather diffuse manner and using rather simple language. Therefore I have extended what I had to say at some length, since my intention was to address the more artless brothers] (1181 B). Thus, Hugh is not thinking of laymen, but of those who know Latin, even if they are not theologically advanced.

and above, "oculus croceus maturitas sensus" [the saffron-colored eye the ripeness of perception]. The eyes and the feet emphasize the top and the bottom of the picture of the dove, which *is* also a dove. We will consider the bottom and then the top. The text says of the dove's red feet (18 AB): "This dove is the church, which had feet with which it traversed the whole world. The feet are the martyrs, who traverse the earth with as many steps as examples of good works that they show to them who follow them. They touch the earth when they chide earthly acts and wishes with due scolding. But their feet are wounded when they tread the earth because it is rough with the cruelty of earthliness, and in the same way the feet of the church became red because the martyrs had shed their blood in the name of Christ. *Rubor igitur pedum est cruor martyrum.*"[33] The text gives the explanation of the inscription in the picture, which emerges in the form of a result (*igitur*). The lower edge of the picture, with the red feet, is thus the earthly world from which the inner motion of the picture emanates—leading first of all to the center—when we read what is written on it: "fugiens mundum mansi in solitudine." These words from Psalm 54:8 lead from the world into solitude, from restlessness to repose, from the edge to the middle.

The eyes above are over the feet at the bottom: "oculus croceus maturitas sensus" [the saffron eye is the maturity of perception]. The text also points these toward the church, taking its cue from the eyes of the watchful dove looking over the waters in the Song of Songs (5:12).[34] Just as the dove escapes from the falcon by looking at its shadow in the waters, so the church escapes the snares of the devil by arming itself with the Scriptures. "This dove has saffron-colored eyes,"[35] because the church in ripe consideration looks attentively ahead to what is to happen in the future. The saffron color of the eyes signifies the discernment that comes from mature consideration (*discretionem maturae considerationis*). When someone regards his deeds or his thoughts maturely, he adorns his spiritual eyes with the color of saffron, for

33. Debidour, *Le bestiaire sculpté*, p. 344: "Dans les sculptures polychromées, en Bretagne notamment, on ne manque guère à lui donner les pattes et le bec rouges—allusion au sang versé par les martyrs soutenus par l'Esprit (et l'on sait que la couleur de la Pentecôte est le rouge)" [In the polychrome sculptures, especially in Brittany, there is scarcely one where the bird is not given red feet and a red beak—an allusion to the blood shed by the martyrs, sustained by the Spirit (and we know that the color of Pentecost is red)].

34. On the dove in the Song of Solomon cf. Messelken, *Die Signifikanz von Rabe und Taube*, p. 237 (index).

35. Messelken knows of no statement about the color of the dove's eyes or feet.

saffron has the color of ripe fruit. "Croceus igitur oculus est maturitatis sensus" [the saffron-colored eye is, therefore, maturity of perception] (19 B). The conclusion of the explanation is again the inscription. Like the red of the feet, the saffron color of the eyes is not observed from the nature of the dove; it is also not taken from the Bible, but placed there by Hugh, so that it can signify: *cruor martyrum* and *matura consideratio.* Endowing the traditional, or observed, nature of the dove with properties freely taken either from the Bible or the imagination allows the interpreter to extend their world of meaning for his own purposes. The sense of the whole precedes the organic unity; what is natural is expanded into a cosmos of sense (for example, the dove receives six wings; see below, pp. 114–116). The medieval mode of observing nature—with its reciprocal view of thesis and physis—that enlarges what it has seen for reasons of sense and, contrary to appearances, preserves the traditional, has a poetic and spiritual attraction wherever its function fits in with something higher.

To the left and right of the upper central bar—bearing the inscription "oculus croceus maturitatis sensus"—there are two golden dots surrounded by a dark color (possibly a silver solution: the upper circles talk of gold and silver). These dots, separated abstractly from the organic whole, are apparently the eyes of the dove. Recognized as such, they observe *matura consideratione* the observer who can scarcely escape their effect. They lend an intensity to the picture that seems masklike and magically invigorating to us, but this is probably unintentional: a purely isolated property of the dove which in a spiritual way is not magic but speaks more *in* the picture than *out* of it and also demands *maturam considerationem* from the viewer. These eyes are golden instruction and yet, though they are completely isolated, still contrive to give life to the spiritual picture.

In the upper and lower bands of the picture, in the corners of the framework, there are rings that surround a circular space with two concentric circles. At the top they are in contact with the sides of the framework and with the outermost circle of the center; at the bottom, because they are larger, they impinge upon the framework, something that—together with other departures from symmetry—enlivens the picture and lends more weight to the bottom part than the top, so that it appears to be standing rather than lying. The rings and the circular surfaces that they enclose have writing on them. Just as in the framework and in the large rings in the center, so in the four corner rings, too, the beginnings of the inscription, each reading clockwise, are marked with a cross. Just as the inscription in the framework is a closed text, so the four corner rings contain a unified psalm text which can be read from left to right, first at the top and then at the bottom (54:7f.): "Quis dabit michi pennas sicut columbe? Et uolabo et requiescam. Ecce elongaui fugiens et mansi in solitudine" [Who will give me wings like a dove? And I will fly and I will rest. Behold I am wandering far off and I have remained in solitude]. The upper rings speak of wings and flight into peace; the lower ones of flight and refuge in solitude. The heavy movement (of the dove's feet) at the bottom seems to correspond to the lighter flight (of the dove's wings) at the top. Trusting in help from persecution, David is speaking in the psalm as one filled with desire for deliverance. The "pennis uirtutum uolabo desiderio" [on the wings of virtue will I fly with desire] beneath the upper edge of the picture corresponds to the alliteration—which changes the text of the psalm—on the bottom edge of the picture: "fugiens mundum mansi in solitudine" [fleeing the world I remained in solitude]. The personal first person form used by the psalmist in the corner rings corresponds to the impersonal third person form in the framework. The viewer adopts the first person form and repeats to himself: "On the wings of virtue will I fly, full of desire! On my flight from the world I would stay in solitude!" Hugh's text gives no explanation of the text (54:7f.) in the picture. The dedication to Rayner does, however, make a reference to it when Hugh writes: "Tibi igitur, cui datae sunt pennae columbae, qui elongasti fugiens, ut in solitudine maneres et requiesceres, . . . , tibi inquam, non tantum ad praesens columbam, sed et acippitrem pingam" [For you, therefore, to whom are given the wings of a dove, who withdrew taking flight, that you might remain in solitude and rest yourself, . . . for you, I say, I will paint at present not only a dove but also a falcon] (13, 14). The recipient of the picture has already run, fled, and found peace in the convent. The falcon already flew "with the wings of the dove." The work is addressed, beyond him, to those who ought to follow him. Just as the dove speaks first of all, from the outer edges, of the desire to leave the world, it speaks afterward, from the inner edge of the center, of the goal of the fulfillment of its desire in solitude. Corresponding to the medieval (and again modern) possibility of the pictorial simultaneity of what takes place at different times, the dove speaks from the framework and from the middle, in the process of which the space between the edge and the center also indicates a space of time: the dove speaks *first* from the edge (from the world), and *then* from the center (from solitude). Between the corner rings and the outer central ring, and conforming to this, we now find written below, "elongaui mente, perseueraui in contemplacione" [I withdrew mentally, persevered contemplatively], and above, *simplicita(te)* [in simplicity].[36] In pictorial space as space of time (we shall only hint at it in this small picture: the twelfth century knew the *mappa mundi* as a picture of the history of the world's salvation), the space from the edge to the center is also the path of internalization that leads to duration and rest in contemplation and peace. The "requiescam in pace" [I shall rest in peace] imparts an anagogical dimension to the upper part of the picture: above the center it makes visible eternal repose, behind the repose of the convent. The movement is from below to above, from time through mystic duration to eternity.

The inscriptions on the corner medallions interpret the four colors of the dove. Just as the red of the feet was interpreted between the lower medallions, and the saffron color of the eyes between the upper ones, so, too, the colors of air and water are added below, and those of gold and silver above. These are all properties of the dove—the color of the tail (gold), of the feathers (silver), of the wings (air), and of the rest of the body (sea). All are interpreted *in extenso* in the text. We begin at the bottom right: "Color maris in reliquo corpore[37] tribulationem designat in carnali mente" [The color of the sea in the rest of the body signifies tribulation in the carnal mind]. The breast of the dove is "the color of the sea when it is churned up." The text explains this (19 BC):

Color reliqui corporis imitatur colorem turbati maris.

Mare motu fluctuum saeviens ebullit.
Caro motu sensuum ebulliens saevit.
Mare perturbationibus suis arenas movet et sublevat.
Caro delectationibus suis animi levitatem pulsat.

Mare terminos suos egrediens aquis dulcibus occurrit.
Caro lasciviens lacrymarum dulces rivulos obtundit.
Mare diversis procellarum turbinibus navigantium cursus impedit.
Caro procellosa recte viventium mores in profundum mergit.

Dum tantis mare tempestatibus agitatur,
undarum collisione terra fluctibus immiscetur,
et sic ex collisione maris et terrae colorem mistum recipit mare.

36. Ms. *simplicitas;* also in the Cambridge ms. On the dove's *simplicitas* see Messelken, *Die Signifikanz von Rabe und Taube,* p. 241 (index).

37. The Cambridge ms. has *tempore.*

Similiter dum caro suggerit et animus non consentit,
quasi ex nigro et niveo quidam in corpore color efficitur,
qui ex diversis factus color medius appellatur.

Marinus igitur color in pectore columbae tribulationem designat in humana mente.

[The color of the rest of the body imitates the color of the sea when it is churned up.

The sea boils up, raging with the agitation of the waves.
The flesh rages, boiling up with the agitation of the senses.
The sea through its disturbances moves and tosses the sands.
The flesh through its pleasure excites the inconstancy of the spirit.

The sea when it goes beyond its bounds passes into sweet waters.
The wanton flesh dulls the sweet rivulets of tears.
The sea stays sailors' voyages by its manifold and tempestuous whirlwinds.
The tempestuous flesh drowns in its depths the ways of those who live righteously.

When the sea is agitated by such great tempests,
The earth is merged into the billows by the clash of the waves,
And thus out of the clash of sea and earth the sea assumes its mixed color.

Similarly when the flesh proposes and the spirit does not consent,
A certain color is produced in the body, made as it were from black and white,
Which—having been composed of different constituents—is called the middle color.

Therefore the color of the sea on the breast of the dove signifies tribulation in the human soul.]

The color of the churned-up sea on the breast of the dove signifies the bewilderment of the heart. "Dove grey" was unknown to the Middle Ages, which always called the dove simply "white."[38] Hugh's dove—as the bearer of color significations—is parti-colored (*amicta varietatibus*—"clothed in diversity" cf. n. 28 above); it is red and yellow, gold and silver, and the color of

38. While the etymology of the words for *dove* in many languages suggests a dark color, in all the citations used by Messelken, *Die Signifikanz von Rabe und Taube*, pp. 63ff., it is white—often "snow white."

sea and sky. The diversity and the number of properties determine the extent of its world of signification. The conception of the interpretation of "dove grey" by etiological-metaphorical interpretation has something about it of the structure of a baroque sonnet[39] that begins with an antithetical juxtaposition, proceeds to an explicit statement of comparisons, and finally culminates in a *pointe.* The suggestively organized parallels of sea and flesh meet in the final comparison of the endangered shore of the moral world with that of a heart in disorder. A poetic intelligence combines tradition and its own contribution within an original way of expressing the *conditio humana,* in a world always exposed to attack, without any further tropological instruction.

In the medallion at the lower left is written: "color aerius in alis est amor divine contemplacionis" [the air-color in the wings is the love of divine contemplation]. Just as the sea grey of the breast is oriented downward, so the sky blue of the wings is oriented upward—the one toward the world, the other toward God. The text, remarking on the sapphire color of the wings, says (18 D): "I found nothing written about the color of the wings;[40] but from a comparison with a natural dove you can be assured that when you look at the painted dove you, too, will agree that it is the same color as the natural dove. In particular, the surface of the wings is covered with the color of sapphire because the spirit of the contemplator resembles the appearance of the heavens. The sapphire color is, however, hatched with lines of white so that the color of snow is mixed with the sapphire. For the color of snow that is mixed with sapphire signifies purity of the flesh and love of contemplation." Only where the Bible is silent is nature consulted to supplement the Scriptures, but only out of concern for spiritual rather than organic coherence. The color of sapphire, which is always interpreted elsewhere as the color of the (cloudless) sky, is the color of contemplation in other places, too. The hatching-in of white lines on the sapphire color—in our picture it also serves to suggest plumage—points to a form of painting that is also practiced elsewhere for the purpose of signification; these are the only reasons we can think of for the introduction, in twelfth-century book illumination, of cirrus or snowflake white in sapphire-colored backgrounds to portrayals of the Virgin Mary, the angel of the Annunciation, or the Crucifixion. The white in the sapphire blue of the dove's wings as the *munditia carnis* (the purity of the flesh) shows that

39. I have taken the liberty of printing the poetry in this way to reveal its artistic form.

40. The same is true of the silver of the *pennae* (pinions, wings) and the gold of the *posteriora dorsi* (rear back) in Psalm 67:14; there is no other mention of the color of the dove in the Bible.

the sea-gray *tribulatio carnis* (the tribulation of the flesh) has been overcome. It is in this that the superiority of the wings over the breast lies. Independent of their color, the two wings signify the *vita activa* and the *vita contemplativa* in the church. They cover the dove on its perch and lift it up in its flight to the heavens. "We fly when we are outside ourselves: we sit when we are soberly among our brethren" (16 A, after 2 Corinthians 5:13). For the soul, the wings are the love of one's neighbor and the love of God: "The one is spread out in compassion to one's neighbor, the other is raised in contemplation to God" (17 A). The left side of the body is for one's neighbor, the right for God.[41] Contrary to everything in nature, we find, in the Middle Ages, angels and birds depicted as having one wing pendent and one raised; the pendent wing is turned toward man and the raised one toward God. The dove of the *hortus deliciarum* has one dorsal wing folded and the other raised. The doves of the Paris, Cambridge, Oxford, and St. Omer pictures have both wings folded. The same dove in the picture in the Paris manuscript B.N. lat. 2495 B, folio 6r, which is without inscription, has, however, one wing raised at an acute angle.[42]

Written on the medallion at the upper left are the words "color argenteus in pennis est in linguis docentium sermo sancte exhortacionis" [the silver color of the wings is a discourse of holy exhortation on the tongues of those who teach]. Three of the four inscriptions in the upper-left-hand part of the picture are about wing feathers. The interpretation of their silver color, like that of the gold of the tail, is more detailed than that of the sea grey and the sky blue of the breast and the wings. The point of departure is the phrase "pennae columbae deargentatae" of Psalm 67:14 [the wings of a dove covered in silver]. Corresponding to the modern proverb "Speech is silver; silence is golden," which has its roots in the medieval signification of things (silver signifies speech; gold signifies silence), silver is interpreted as meaning the speech of Christ, the church, the preacher, and the individual soul. The silver dove is the church, instructed in the knowledge of God's word (*ecclesia doctrina divini eloquii erudita*), whose "preacher's beak" gathers up corns of

41. Ohly, *Hohelied-Studien*, pp. 211, 221f. After I had written this, an article by Ursula Deitmaring appeared, "Die Bedeutung von Rechts und Links in theologischen und literarischen Texten bis um 1200," *Zeitschrift für deutsches Altertum* 98 (1969): 265–292.

42. The doves in the tympanum of Estagel (1125–50) in the Louvre have one wing pointing to heaven and one to earth; see Debidour, *Le bestiaire sculpté*, figs. 30, 32f., 54, 56, 65, 68; W. Hansmann, *Kunstwanderungen in Westfalen* (Stuttgart, 1966), p. 268, fig. 19; doves with one wing up and one down are to be seen as early as the Gregory-David diptych in the sixth century: Frauke Steenbosk, *Der kirchliche Prachteinband im frühen Mittelalter* (Berlin, 1965), pp. 72f. and fig. 9.

barley and wheat—the words of the Old and New Testaments. Seated on the wings of the active and the contemplative life are the silvered feathers, the teachers of the church (16 AB). Taken tropologically, they refer to the good repute—based on virtue—of the believer, who consumes, as nourishment for his own good works, the corns of the example offered by the righteous. "These feathers shine with the luster of silver when—according to the nature of silver—they sound sweetly for the listener in the speech that belongs to good repute" (17 A). Just as the picture of the king that is stamped on the silver coin is intended as an example, so also "the coin of the word of God teaches the imitation of the life of Christ" (18 A). The silver feathers are also preachers: "God's word is silver, the sound of silver the sweetness of his word, its warmth a shining luster." The luster of the preacher's utterance lies in his own words' purity, in the active love of his teaching. The word of God is pure silver refined in the fire. "Thus, the bright luster of silver on the feathers is the soft charm of speech in the mouth of the teacher" (18 C).

In a shift from the thing "feather" to the property "silver-colored" that, because of its frequency, might almost be called characteristic of the interpretation of things, the interpretation then finds its way to the thing "silver," which is well suited to the spiritual and pictorial conception under discussion. The possibility of being able to move easily from a thing, by way of its property, to a related thing associated with this property established a multifaceted elasticity, an apparently arbitrary variability of the interpretation of things that is, nonetheless, the result of regulated trains of thought and multiplies the number of significations which can be developed out of it. Interpretation is even more loosely bound to the thing, if it has even further ramifications and adduces as proof things from related biblical passages, thus raising the multiplicity to an even higher power. This is the case, for example, in the artistry of Thomas Cisterciensis's analytical studies of meaning, whose almost rankly spreading associations run the risk of pulverizing all coherence of meaning—despite the discipline exercised on the author by early scholasticism.[43] Hugh's procedure, whereby he chooses among all possible meanings by judiciously considering their medial sense, not only contributes to the lucid structuring of his picture, but is also conditioned by the very nature of color signification. Since a color is not a thing per se that possesses any property other than itself, it assumes a significance only by means of some other thing that has the color—as one of it properties—and determines the direction of the color's signification on a given occasion: the red of the feet by way

43. Cf. Ohly, *Hohelied-Studien*, pp. 188–197.

of blood, the saffron color of the eyes by way of the color of ripe fruit, the sapphire color by way of the color of the sky, the grey of the breast by way of the color of the sea. This mental step suggests itself even more readily in the case of the colors of metals, which are used by an idealizing metaphorics only to stand for similar colors ("golden hair"), but which otherwise refer to the true color of the metal of the same name. The interpretation of the colors silver or gold can follow no other path than that of silver or gold or things made of such metals, like—in our case—a crown or a coin, where plumage and tail are not thought of as "silvery" or "golden," but as "covered with silver" and "[covered] with gold": "in pennis igitur argentum, quia in linguis eloquium; in posterioribus vero aurum, id est post labores præmium" [the reason why there is silver on the wings is because there is speech on tongues; in the tail, though, there truly is gold, that is, rewards after labors] (17 C). The significations of colors emerge by way of things that have color as a property; the significations of colors that are specific to a particular thing, by way of the things they specifically belong to. If a thing's world of signification develops from the aggregate of its properties, that of the property "color" develops from the aggregate of things to which it may refer.[44]

The medallion in the upper-right-hand corner interprets the gold color on the tail: "color aureus in posterioribus est in futuro eterne retributionis munus" [the golden color on the tail is the gift of eternal reward in the future]. Thus, in the fourth medallion, disorder, instruction, and contemplation are joined by promise. The gold (in the framework; Psalm 67:14, "posteriora dorsi eius in pallore auri" [the pinions of his rear back with the pale gleam of gold]) excels all other colors and opens up the anagogical dimension of the picture. Silver is the here and now; gold is the future. The heart of the dove beneath its back, where the wings commence, will be covered with the gold of eternal bliss after the silver of present happiness: on the left the transient present, on the right the eternal future. "The just man will shine with luminous clarity in eternal bliss" (16 B). Since the back bears burdens of sorrow, its end is the expectation of future reward for God's saints, "post labores præmium" (17 C). "You will have gold on the pinions of your tail, when the coming glory of the divine majesty shall appear." Gold, the metal from which kingly crowns are made, will be given as a reward, as a

44. I have to thank Christel Meier for her suggestions. After this was written her works on the theory of color appeared: "Die Bedeutung der Farben im Werk Hildegards von Bingen," *Frühmittelalterliche Studien* 6 (1972): pp. 245–355; *Gemma Spiritualis: Methoden und Gebrauch der Edelsteinallegorese vom frühen Christentum bis ins 18. Jahrhunderts*, pt. 1, Münstersche Mittelalterschriften, no. 34 (Munich, 1976).

crown of victory when it no longer has need of the silver of speech, when the dove lives eternally in the purity of perfection" (18 A). The gold of the pure heart has the pallor of the suffering of the mortification of the flesh even unto death. The gold of the back upon which the sapphire-colored wings of contemplation are folded allows eternal glory to follow that contemplation. "Color igitur aureus in posterioribus designat aeternae retributionis munus" [Thus the color of gold on the tail denotes the gift of eternal reward] (19 A). The silver on the left and the gold on the right are separated in the same way that this world and the next are separated, and so are the wings and the tail. The limbs are not joined organically but only spiritually. The picture of a natural dove is divided into a structure of spiritual figures and coordinations. Feet, eyes, breast and wings, feathers and tail pinions, signs uncannily heightened in color proclaim meanings, teach, make demands for themselves alone and in concert. The "spiritual bonding" sets the stasis of the picture into a motion of such strength that it goes along with life as it is being lived. The creature interpreted in word and picture becomes a binding rule for the viewer. Struck by the spiritual look—whose train of thought turns the language of nature into writing—mute revelation can now be seen, and it becomes speech. A sovereign, interpretative contemplation of nature turns it into a picture, the birth of whose meaning is aided by the word. Nature gives an answer to the questions which are put to it—as it does in all ages.

Does the picture allow us to determine, of its own accord, whether left and right in the picture are to be seen as from the picture or from the point of view of the viewer? (This question, which is important for the determination of the signification of left and right in medieval pictures, is often hard to answer.) Even if the central composition of the picture does not permit the two halves of the picture—which are separated by the central axis—to control the whole, they are not filled in capriciously. Leaving the central medallion and the framework out of consideration, the vocabulary of the inscriptions divides into the left and right halves of the picture in the following manner (numbers indicate the number of occurrences):

Left	Right
mundus	*solitudo* 2
fugere 2	*manere* 3
elongare 2	*perseverare*
mens	*contemplatio*
simplicitas	*pax*

Left	Right
virtus	*volare 2*
pennae 3	
columba 2	
argentum	*aurum*
lingua	
sermo	
docentes	
sancta exhortatio	*retributio*
quis dabit mihi	*munus*
	futurus
	aeternus
	posterioria
	desiderium
amor	tribulatio
alae	reliquum
corpus	
divinus	carnalis
aer	mare
contemplatio	mens

The words in italics allow us to recognize—as corresponding to one another on the right and the left—present and future, time and eternity, *vita activa* and *vita contemplativa,* our neighbor and God, unrest and rest, value and what is more valuable, desire and fulfillment—while the words printed in Roman characters reverse the relationship. The vocabulary is taken from the inscription in the lower medallions. Although the pictures in Cambridge, Oxford, and St. Omer place them in the same spot, I am convinced that the reversal of left and right in the manuscripts is intentional, especially as all the pictures contain other textual errors in the inscriptions, and we do not possess the original picture. Anyone who thinks that placement on the left or the right is a daring argument to use in textual criticism should consider that the double *mansi* "mansi in solitudine" in the right-hand corner medallion, and in the framework adjacent to it, does not fit in, in any way, with the "tribulatio" inscription on the framework above, and by changing them we harmonize the two texts on either side, and should also consider that even today it is still easy for the historian to allocate a speech to the "left" or "right" side of a Parliament, or even to identify a "left" insertion into a "right" speech. The signification of left and right in the art, theology, and literature of the Middle Ages, for which there is endless material, still awaits thorough research (this is also true of the points of the compass).[45] But it is easy for the person well read in the Middle Ages to distinguish between what belongs on the right and what belongs on the left. We have but to reverse the columns printed in roman letters to reach a clear verdict that left and right are determined in the picture from the point of view of the viewer. It is only with the text that interprets the picture of the dove that we are in a position to complete our knowledge of the significance of right and left, and this can easily be developed from pairs like parts of the body, here in the wings (see above, pp. 101–103) and the eyes. Hugh distinguishes the left eye from the right as "moralem et mysticum sensum" [the moral and mystic sense]: the left "*respicit*" [looks around]; the right "contemplatur" [contemplates];[46] the left eye looks at itself; the right at God (16 A). The left eye, "memoria," weeps for the past; the right eye, "intellectus" [perception], foretells the future. Of the two eyes in the upper part of the picture, the left eye is directed to "sermo sanctae exhortationis" [the discourse of divine exhortation] of the present and of man; the right eye to "requiescam" [I shall rest] and "in futuro aeternae retributionis munus" [the gift of eternal recompense in the future], a future with God. The eyes in the picture are in mute repose, and speak only through their place in the whole.[47] The direction of the dove in the center of the picture, looking toward the right, is simply irreversible, because it alone is fully significant. The

45. The article by Ursula Deitmaring that deals with this subject appeared subsequently (see n. 41); Barbara Maurmann, *Die Himmelsrichtungen im Weltbild des Mittelalters: Hildegard von Bingen, Honorius Augustodunensis und andere Autoren,* Münstersche Mittelalter-Schriften, no. 33 (Munich, 1976).

46. The Middle High German words that correspond are *besehen* and *warten;* Ohly, on the St. Trudpert Song of Songs, 3,1ff. op. cit., p. 211:

de winstere ouge consilium besach den nâhesten.
de zeswehe ouge intellectus besach sich selben.
de houbet sapientia wartet allezane hin ze gote.

[The left eye, counsel, looked at its neighbor.
The right eye, intellect, looked at itself.
The head, wisdom, looks at God all the time.]

47. We will leave to the art historian the daring question whether a "squinting" position of the eyes in book illumination (for example, of affliction) could be explained by the fact that one eye is directed to God and the other to man.

Hugh reflects on the falcon that sits on the perch with the dove and wonders why the hunting falcon is carried on the left hand and transferred to the right when he makes his kill: "Laeva

fact that the placement of the feet in our picture shows it, additionally, as moving toward the right corresponds to the words of fugitive desire ("Who will give me wings?") on the left-hand side, and to those of reposeful fulfillment on the right, while its static position in the pictures of Cambridge, St. Omer, and Oxford does not satisfy us, whereas the other Paris picture shows the dove with one wing raised up steeply and moving to the right.

The parts of the picture on the left and the right, above and below, were devoted to the properties of the dove, the colors, and their motion from left to right, from below to above, from outside to inside.[48] The other parts of the picture relate to the circular central part—which is not only optically central but can also be regarded as the heart of the picture—as paths to the picture's intention. The words of Psalm 67:14 stand on the top of the framework as a sort of title to the picture: "si dormiatis inter medios cleros" ("when you rest easy in the midst of your sheepfolds"). Hugh helps us to this literal understanding; Greek κλῆρος is Latin *sors* (share), and this is why a heritage that has been bequeathed in a will is called *cleronomia.* For example, among the sons of Israel, the sons of Levi did not possess "sortem [a share], id est haereditatis partem" and therefore lived from tithes (17 D, 16 B). In replacing *cleros* with *sors,* Hugh is probably thinking back to Psalm 67:9f.: "Pluviam voluntariam segregabis, Deus, haereditatis tuae: et infirmata est; tu vero perfecisti eam. Animalia tua habitant in ea" [Thou, O, God, didst send a plentiful rain, whereby thou didst confirm thy inheritance, when it was weary. Thy congre-

---

sunt bona temporalia, dextera vero sunt aeterna. In laeva igitur sedet qui bonis temporalibus praesidet. In dexteram vero volat qui toto mentis affectu aeterna desiderat. Ibi capit accipiter columbam, id est quilibet mutatus in melius sancti Spiritus gratiam recipit" [Things on the left hand are temporal good things, those on the right are truly eternal. On the left is seated whoever deals with temporal good things. The one who flies to the right desires, with his whole mind, things eternal. There the falcon seizes the dove; that is to say, whoever is changed for the better receives the grace of the Holy Spirit] (22 C).

48. On the interpretation of birds see the wealth of material in the section "De avibus" in the pseudo-Melito in the work of J. B. Pitra, *Spicelegium Solesmense* (Paris, 1855; reprint, Graz, 1963), 2:470–520: on the dove, pp. 484–487, with a catalog of the dove's properties (see below, pp. 111f.) from the *Distinctiones Monasticae* and Anonymous of Clarevallensis, who also cites "pedes rubeos habet; osculis instat; gemellos pullos nutrit" [it has red feet, seeks kisses, and nourishes twin offspring]. In Pitra see also "alae" [wings], 2:475ff.; on "argentum," 2:283ff., 3:401, 420; on "aurum," 2:275–278, 3:420; on "dormire," 2:19f.; on "dorsum," 2:235f.; on "oculus," 2:lxxiv; on "pennae," 2:475ff., 3:480; on "rota" (see below, pp. 126–128ff.), 2:174ff. These references avoid my having to give individual references to the traditional nature of Hugh's interpretation, which could easily be produced from psalm exegesis. I do not intend to write a commentary that simply consists of piling up parallels—something that could easily be done.

gation hath dwelt therein]. Now it is not a question of properties, but of the particular point of location determined by *inter* as "in the middle of"; not the "how," but the "where" of the dove. By a playful reinterpretation of "haereditas, quae defertur ex testamento" [disposition of heritage] (17 D) into the biblical Testament, the first determination of place emerges: inheritances are the Testaments, and between the two Testaments sleep those "who stand and rest in harmony with the statements of the Old and the New Testament" (16 B). The word *concordare* for this harmony with the two Testaments has a typological overtone: *concordantiae* of the Old and the New Testaments are the names for typological cycles which flourish in the twelfth century. We read in the outermost circle from right to left at the bottom: "in medio sorcium ueteris et noui testamenti dormit, qui eorum auctoritatibus adquiescit" [in the midst of shares in the Old and of the New Testament he sleeps who assents to their twofold authority]. And further, up above, reading to the right: "Inter expectacionem celestium et contemptum terrenorum dormit, qui inter hec duo moriens vitam finit" [Between expectation of heavenly and contempt for earthly things he sleeps who amid these two, dying, finishes his life]. Resting, sleeping, and dying between the earthliness of the Old Testament and the eternal heritage of the New Testament, between the expectation of heaven and the rejection of the world, means "not to seek tempestuously for what is in the present, but to wait patiently for what is to come" (17 D). There are *duo sortes* opposite one another in each of the fields between the outer and the inner ring, arranged in the form of a cross: "expectacio [celestium]"[49] (above) and "contemptus terrenorum" (below) and also "novum testamentum" (left) and "uetus testamentum" (right). New on the left and old on the right is a surprise. The position in the Paris, Cambridge, and Oxford pictures has reversed that of St. Omer: the Old Testament on the left and the New Testament on the right. It would be appealing to give this reading preference because of the signification of left and right. Then the dove is looking at the New Testament. (Of course it would also be possible to make the point that the golden "posteriora dorsi" [pinions of the back] were also turned toward it in a meaningful way. But what we have seen in the upper left and right corner medallions would argue against this). The way the St. Omer picture reads means that, on the cross, we have heaven above and earth beneath, on the left the mortal and on the right the eternal heritage. The shares of the inheritance lie in the middle fields like plots of land, just as twelfth-century pictures of the Tabernacle show the tribes of Israel encamped around the center in similar

49. Completed on the basis of the pictures in Cambridge, St. Omer, and Oxford.

fields.[50] "Sortes sunt, quia paternae haereditatis locum distribuunt" [They are shares, since they allot the area belonging to the paternal legacy] (17 A). In addition to four in the shape of a cross, there are four corresponding middle fields in the shape of an X. The fields which lie thus—/—are called *extreme* (extreme, outermost); those which lie thus—\—*medie sortes* (medial, innermost shares). The ones in the cross, which are more determined by the history of salvation, are augmented in the diagonal and correspond to plots that are determined more by the history of the soul. The "extreme" ones are called in the picture "timor pene" [fear of punishment][51] (top right) and "desiderium gloriae" [the desire for glory] (bottom left). The text explains: "Fear confuses the spirit, desire torments the heart, so that if nothing intervenes, the spirit gives up its repose." The *medie sortes* have to intervene between fear and desire, in the picture, "amor gracie" [love of grace] and "spes venie" [hope of reward] (bottom right). The text comments: "hope refreshes fear; love moderates desire. Thus, he who is awake and out of his senses between the extreme portions—fear and desire—sleeps peacefully between hope and love. If you are a dove, or a dove's feather, you stay awake between the outermost plots if you are fearful and desirous; you sleep peacefully between the middle ones if you hope and love (17 B). "For this reason, the inscription on the innermost circle of the picture, on the right, runs: "Inter medias sortes dormit, qui sperat et diligit" [Between innermost shares sleeps he who hopes and loves]; and on the left: "Inter extremas [*sortes*][52] uigilat, qui timet et desiderat" [Between outermost [shares] keeps watch he who fears and desires]. The dove watches and sleeps, because it hopes and fears, desires, and loves. It could say "ego dormio et cor meum uigilat" [I sleep and my heart keeps watch] (Song of Songs 5:2). The dove's waking sleep is the state of being held between God and the world, expectation and patience, contemplation and activity. This is not a well-balanced balance: halted movement, stationary walking is in the picture. What is below and above, left and right, the edge, the middle, do not stand in the same place: a yearning goes to the right, to what is above, to what is within; that is where it rests in wakeful sleep. The apparently static system of the picture's structure lives as a spiritual vision that is ordering a world. It designs a life while giving it meaning. The chosen

50. P. Bloch, *Nachwirkungen des Alten Bundes in der christlichen Kultur: Monumenta Judaica: 2000 Jahre Geschichte und Kultur der Juden am Rhein,* handbook for an exhibition in the Cologne Municipal Museum, October 2, 1963–February 2, 1964 (Cologne, 1963), pp. 753–781, here, pp. 755ff., figs. 75ff.

51. Ms. *penne* emended according to Cambridge and St. Omer.

52. Completed from St. Omer.

confinement of the monastic life—its "lots" surround it like walls—opens up that life by making a promise. The "mansi in solitudine" [I remained in solitude] is not abandonment, lonely as the dove may seem to be in its encirclement. It lives for the falcon which is next to it on the perch. The picture is a mirror for the brethren, a growing crystal.

The dove's properties—their location in space—are part of the picture: how does the dove live? The dove's idiosyncratic ways of life could hardly be represented in the picture. We have already heard: "it walks on the rough earth, looks with a mature eye, flees and flies, fears and hopes, demands and loves, is awake and sleeps." The text twice touches upon its nourishment: its beak is in the service of the church's preaching as it gathers up grains of wheat and barley, words of the Old and the New Testament (16 A). For its food, the dove gathers as many grains of seed as it gathers examples of just men who do good (16 C). The picture places the corns which are the dove's food in the radii that join the outer and the inner rings in between the lots. The words "Grana frumenti et ordei sunt sentencie ueteris et noui testamenti" [the grains of corn and barley are the sentences of the Old and New Testament] stand in the upper radii and run from the top toward the right. The dove lives on the word of the Scriptures, just as the falcon is to live on the text of the psalm that the picture is interpreting for it. The words "grains of wheat;" frame the expectation of heaven; "barley" stands between fear and the Old Testament; "old" stands between desire and disdain; "New Testament" frames the New Testament. This relationship between radii and lots might furnish a possible explanation of the new situated on the left (see above, p. 109). Where the order of ideas and the order of the picture compete, there may be shifts as the one starts to determine the other. Some occasional mild asymmetry in the picture, and in the train of thought, serves to enliven the whole.

In connection with his explanation of the picture, Hugh gives us a further list of ten properties (*proprietates*) of the dove that he has found "in different places" and which he lists and explains for the brother (19 D):

Property	Interpretation
1. pro cantu gemitum profert [instead of a song, she brings forth a sigh]	quod libens fecit, plangendo gemit [what she did gladly, mournfully she bemoans]
2. felle caret [she lacks gall]	id est irascibilitatis amaritudine [that is, the bitterness of wrath]
3. osculis instat [she insists upon kisses]	delectatur in multitudine pacis [she delights in peace manifold and on all sides]

Property	Interpretation
4. gregatim volat [she flies in flocks]	coventus amat [she loves gatherings]
5. ex raptu non vivit [she lives not from ravage]	non detrahit proximo [she does not detract from her neighbor]
6. grana meliora colligit [she gathers grains of better sort]	meliora dicta [things better said] (see above, pp. 102–103, 111)
7. non vescitur cadavere [she feeds not on the dead]	desideriis carnalibus [carnal desires]
8. nidificat in petrae foraminibus [she builds her nest in crevices of stone]	spem ponit in Christi passione [she puts her hope and trust in the Passion of Christ]
9. super fluenta aquarum residet, ut visa accipitris umbra, venientem citius devitet [she takes her rest over flowing waters, so that, the shadow of the closing hawk once seen, she quickly avoids the oncoming threat]	in scripturis studet, ut supervenientis diaboli fraudem declinet [she studies the Holy Scriptures so that she may shun the treachery of the devil, should he attempt to fall upon her unawares]
10. geminos nutrit pullos [she nourishes her twin chicks]	amorem Dei et amorem proximi [the love of God and the love of one's neighbor]

Catalogs of the dove's properties that signify virtues—analogous to the seven gifts of the Holy Spirit that also appear with the dove—are common in Latin and, later, German sermons from the eleventh century onward.[53] At the end of his Whitsuntide sermon, Hildebert of LeMans interprets "septem virtutes in columba" [seven virtues in the dove],[54] and they also form the theme of a sermon on the Purification of the Virgin Mary[55] that introduces the subject in this manner: "These two birds [*turtur* and *columba*], dear brethren, are an example to us. Those of you who cannot read books, can read in them what you should do. God's creatures serve you not only as food, but also as precept. The heavenly teacher gives you daily to understand this through his creatures. In these birds the just man finds the object of his imitation; these birds teach the sinner what he is to do. The dove that instructs us *spiritualiter* gives us an

53. Messelken, *Die Signifikanz von Rabe und Taube,* pp. 89–95.

54. *PL,* 171, 592 AB.

55. *PL,* 171, 611–615.

example of the seven virtues" (612 B). They are the subject of the sermon. Hugh has expanded the usual series of seven to a group of ten, the members of which are more or less frequently documented.[56]

It was difficult to introduce certain properties of the dove into Hugh's picture: properties which could not be expressed by adjectives, like words for color, active ways of life and behavior ("it flies in flocks"), or characteristics that could not be described with one word ("it lacks acrimony" [*felle*]); the introduction of such properties could be accomplished only with one of Hugh's "choice grains" [*ausgelesene Körner*] that appear in the picture (and there only in the inscription). For this we should require a picture of the scene rather than the object—this was already represented quite simply in Hugh's picture

56. In Messelken, *Die Signifikanz von Rabe und Taube,* we find the following evidence of 1: pp. 77–81, 242; to 2: 66–69, 242; to 3: 89; to 4: 84f.; to 5: –; to 6: 73ff., 242; to 7: 74; to 8: 86–89, 243; to 9: 81ff., 242; to 10: 77. Some properties seem to have been found in contrast to similar ones in the raven. On the raven as the eater of carrion, see Messelken, pp. 31–35, and Hugh himself in the treatise on birds (31 C), where he assumes that the raven at the time of the Flood preyed upon floating carcasses like the sinner, "qui carnalibus desideriis pascitur" [who feeds on carnal desires] (cf. 41 D), while the dove flew back to the Ark. The raven is regarded as a thief (cf. Messelken, pp. 47–49). Messelken (p. 89) cites only one place for the *osculis instat*—from Cyprian ("oris osculo concordiam pacis agnoscere" [to acknowledge the concord of peace by a kiss of the mouth]) and from the richest catalog of the dove's properties in the fourth book of *De bestiis et aliis rebus,* an anonymous and alphabetically ordered encyclopedia: "Columba simplex est, osculis instat, felle caret, pedes rubros habet, visum prae ceteris avibus, habet acutum, nullum ore vel unguibus laedit, pauper est, pullos rostro pascit his quibus pasta est, morticinio non vescitur, puro grano vescitur, alienos pullos ut suos fovet, super fluenta residet, ut accipitrem videat venientem, in petris nidificat, alis se defendit, gregatim volat, fecunda es, gemitum pro cantù dat, geminos pullos nutrit" [The dove is artless [or innocent], it desires kisses, it lacks bitterness, it has red feet, it has an acute vision beyond other birds, it hurts no one with its beak or its claws, it is poor, it feeds its young from its beak with the things which it has eaten, it does not feed upon the dead, it eats pure grain, it succors the young of others as though they were its own, it lives over rivers so that it can see the bird of prey when it is hunting, it makes its nest in rocks, it defends itself with its wings, it flies in flocks, it is fertile, it makes a sigh for its song, it feeds twin offspring] (142 B).

The Genesis illustration shows Noah's dove and the raven sitting on the carcasses in the same picture; we find the same thing in Simon of Tournai's psalm commentary in the Morgan ms. 338, where a pictorial cycle of Genesis is distributed among the psalm texts (F. Deuchler, *Der Ingeborgpsalter* [Berlin, 1967], plate 45, fig. 132); also the picture of the Flood in the Jena manuscript of Otto of Freising's *Weltchronik,* in Edith Rothe, *Buchmalerei aus zwölf Jahrhunderten* (Berlin, 1966), plate 23.

Only three of these eighteen properties seem to have been known in the twelfth century from Hugh's treatise on birds ("osculis instat" [it desires kisses]; "pedes rubros habet" [it has red feet]; "geminos pullos nutrit" [it feeds twin offspring]), which would suggest that Hugh's work was used for the fourth book of *De bestiis et aliis rebus.* This is also suggested by the falcon article.

of the pelican—something that develops extensively in the emblem books of the high baroque.[57] In early emblems, and in their prototypical forms, it is often left to the motto attached to the picture of the object to express what is happening as to the way an object lives; in late emblems it is possible to do this by means of a scene filled with people or objects that calls for a poetic or other sort of commentary—this is not the case with Hugh's dove. Again, the preacher welcomes the properties of a thing that are to be found in its way of life, for they can be used to illustrate didactic points, to the disadvantage of the attributive properties that the painter prefers. This is one point where the treatises on animals are superior to the herbiary or the lapidary,[58] whose more silent life pulses even more silently into the arts. In Hugh's work, the "ten properties of the dove" have to stand outside the picture in an appendix, the last sentence of which closes the work on the dove: "Anyone who has these properties, let him put on the wings of contemplation and fly with them to heaven."

Hugh of Folieto's method of interpreting the dove, and other birds, with the help of a picture is used only a little later by Herrad of Landsberg in the *Hortus deliciarum.* Herrad's picture of the dove, with the same psalm text, also shows the bird as silver in the front and golden at the back, but distinguishes it from nature by giving it three pairs of wings—on the head, the back, and the feet—in order to fulfill the ecclesiastical interpretation.[59] Herrad took the explanatory text to the picture (fig. 17) from *Ex sermone cuiusdam doctoris.*[60] In

57. Examples of high quality are to be found, among other places, in the work of Jacob Cats, *Alle de Wercken* (Amsterdam, 1712); and Johannes David, *Veridicus Christianus* (Antwerp, 1606). I hope to treat medieval precursors of the emblem elsewhere.

58. The possibilities and limits of illustrations in a lapidary are shown by the invaluable *Lapidario del rey D. Alfonso X,* facsimile edition (Madrid, 1883), and the widespread lack of stones in emblematics.

59. The picture on folio 240v of the codex that was burned in Strassburg in 1870 is preserved in sketches which were made earlier in the nineteenth century. Our reproduction is to be found in Herrad de Landsberg, *Hortus deliciarum* (a selection), ed. J. Walter (Strassburg, 1952), p. 97. It is taken here from A. Straub and G. Keller, *Herrade de Landsberg* (Strassburg, 1879–99), plate 60 (see p. 47) and is also in the excerpts which were made from the manuscript by A. de Bastard d'Estang between 1830 and 1848. The manuscript material of de Bastard which refers to the dove is in Paris, B.N., N.A.F. 6044, 6045, where Gudrun Eichholz kindly consulted it on my behalf. As Herrad's interpretation of the dove has, up till now, been known only from a short extract (Straub, p. 47; Walter, p. 98), I am printing it here according to the extract from de Bastard.

60. The excerpt from de Bastard from fol. 240v reads as follows:

> De columba aurea cuius dorsi posteriora in pallore auri per quam significatur ecclesia. Columba aurea et argentata de qua legitur in psalmo est sancta ecclesia que habet sex

precipuas pennas sive alas. Duas pedestres, duas laterales, duas capitales. Pedestres ale sive penne due sunt cordis contricio et oris confessio. . . . . laterales ale sunt timor et spes . . . . capitales ale que sunt humilitas et caritas . . . . Columba ista ut prediximus est sancta ecclesia. de qua in canticis canticorum dicitur. Una est amica mea. una est columba mea. Notandum est duas ecclesie partes. Una est que adhuc militat in terris. alter jam triumphat in celis. que sine macula est et ruga. Columba ista deargentata dicitur. et non plena argentea. Argentum est es (i.metallum) sonorum. per quod significatur eloquentia. Sed quia eloquentia sine sapientia multum nocet. sapientia etiam sine eloquentia parvum prodest. juncta vero eloquentie multum prodest. . dicitur ecclesia deargentata id est divis eloquentiis erudita et sapientia exornata . . . . . . Hec columba non tantum deargentata dicitue. verum etiam aurea. id est caritate splendida. Est enim aurum ceteris metallis carius. quod significat caritatem ceteris virtutibus preciosiorem. Notandum est. quod cum propheta deberet dixisse. erunt nobis penne columbe deargentate, et auree. in commendationem caritatis ultimi temporis circumloquendo dixit. et posteriora dorsi eius in pallore vel in rubore auri. videlicet fidelium qui era[=u]nt tempore antiXρῑ id est dorsum posterioris temporis vel posteriorum hominum. caritas videlicet fidelium qui erunt tempore antiXρῑ. erit in pallore vel in rubore auri. id est comparabitur auro rubro vel auro obrizo. id est auro preciosissimo. Per dorsum enim caritas designatur. qe (?) sicut in dorso onera portamus. sic per caritatem gravis toleramus.

Hec columba significat ecclesiam que per divinam eloquentiam quasi argentum est sonora. et erudita. et sapientia exornata ut alios erudiat. Hec etiam columba est aurea. id est caritate splendida. et posteriora dorsi eius sunt in pallore vel rubore auri. id est caritas fidelium qui erunt in posteriori tempore antiXρῑ. comparabitur auro rubro vel auro obrizo. id est auro preciosissimo.

[Concerning the golden dove the rearmost parts of whose back are pale gold which signifies the church.

The golden and silver dove of which we read in the psalm is the holy church, which has six special wings (*pennae*) or wings (*alae*). Two on the feet, two on the side, two on the head. The wings on the feet are the contrition of the heart and the confession of the mouth. . . . . the side wings are fear and hope . . . . the wings on the head are humility and love . . . . This dove, as we have already said, is the holy church of which it is said in the Song of Songs. One is my friend. One is a dove. We must note the two parts of the church. One is the one who reigns up to this time on earth, the other already triumphs in heaven, and this is without spot or wrinkle. The first dove is called silver plated and is not completely silver. Silver is the sonorous ore (that is, metal) by which eloquence is signified. But because eloquence without wisdom does great harm. wisdom on the other hand without eloquence does little good. But joined to eloquence it does indeed do lot of good. It is called the silvered-plated church, that is, skilled in divine eloquence and adorned with wisdom . . . . . . This dove is not merely called silver plated but truly golden. That is, shining with love. For gold is more precious than other metals. Which signifies that love is more precious than other virtues. We must note. what should have been said with the prophet. You will have silver-plated wings of a dove. And golden ones. to commend love he spoke, in circumlocution, of the last days. and the rearmost things of its back in the pallor or redness of

Hugh's treatise on birds, pictures and interpretations ("non tantum scribam, sed et pingam" [I shall not merely write but also draw] [23 B]) of a further twenty-six birds follow the dove and the falcon. This teaching about life on the basis of birds[61] really merits an edition containing the colored pictures that are essential to the work, at least of the first four (dove, falcon, turtledove, and sparrow), the pictures of which are especially remarkable (figs. 18, 19). The critical evaluation of the tradition of the pictorial part of the work that can go from parchment to another more freely than the text can, and through different hands, promises to have a charm all of its own. Where does the picture lose its "spigots" and its "eyes"; who turned the "wheel" so that two radii lie on the central axis; who made the picture square; who changed and exchanged inscriptions; where were inscriptions lost; who moved them into the framework and the medallions (fig. 20)? The history of the tradition of the picture seems to be one of a loss of meaning and of attempts to win it

---

gold. that is, of the faithful who will be in the days of the Antichrist. That is, the rear of the last days or of the last men. that is, the love of the faithful who will be in the days of the Antichrist will be in the pallor or redness of gold. that is, it will be compared to red gold or refined gold, that is, the most precious gold. For love is signified by the back. which ("suggests that"?) just as (*sicut* = "just as") we carry burdens on our backs, so also by love do we bear onerous things.

This dove signifies the church that resounds with divine eloquence as though it were silver. and it is skilled. and decorated with wisdom so that it may teach others. For this dove is golden. that is, shining with love. and the rearmost parts of its back are in the pallor or redness of gold. that is, the love of the faithful who in the last days of the Antichrist will be compared with red gold or refined gold. that is, with the most precious gold.]

Herrad of Landsberg's source may have made use of an interpretation of the six-winged seraphim. In the appendix to the printed *Miscellanea* of Hugh of St.-Victor there is written about their six wings "Seraphin, sex alae uni sunt: duae pedales, pudor de praeteritis et metus de futuris; laterales duae quibus volat, timor deprimens et spes sustollens; capitaneae duae, humilitas provehens at charitas perficiens" [Seraphim each have six wings: two at the feet are fear of things past and hope for things future; two at the side, with which it flies, fear that casts down and hope that sustains; two at the head humility that carries us forward and love that perfects].

61. At the end of a chapter, Hugh often emphasizes the relationship of his bird texts to his readers and listeners, for example, in the case of the swallow: "Ecce qualiter simplex avis nos instruit, quos ab initio divina providentia discretos facit" [Behold how a simple bird instructs us, whom divine providence made different from the beginning] (43 B); on the goose: "Divina autem providentia naturas volucrum nobis, ut opinor, non proponeret, nisi eas in aliquo nobis prodesse vellet" [However divine providence would not, as I see it, set before us the natures of birds, unless it might wish them to be of some use to us] (47 B); on the phoenix: "Ecce volucrum natura simplicibus resurrectionis argumentum praestat et, quod Scriptura praedicat, opus naturae confirmat" [Behold the nature of birds is presented to the simple as an argument for the resurrection and, what the Scriptures state, the work of nature confirms] (49 A).

FIGURE 17
Herrad von Landsberg, Six-winged dove (from *Horus deliciarum* [1167–95]).

back with "improvements" that only make things worse. But, above all, how was it possible to retain the original colors of the picture when copies were made?

The colors were jeopardized because Hugh does not name them in the text and so does not fix them as other interpreters of their own pictures did in the twelfth century. Their texts describe exactly where and how each color is used and why it is so used. Hugh names only the colors of the dove: red and

FIGURE 18

Hugh of Folieto, The sparrows that nest in the branches of the cedar (in a twelfth-century Paris manuscript).

FIGURE 19

Hugh of Folieto, The sparrows that nest in the branches of the cedar (in a twelfth-century Paris manuscript).

saffron, gold and silver, sea and snow color, sapphire. The feet in the picture are not painted red, as the text and inscriptions say they are, perhaps because they are on a red field. The grey of the breast is only a little darker than the sapphire blue of the wings with their white lines. The silver of the feathers at the ends of the wings seems to have been darkened by decomposition, while the gold at the end of the tail has remained intact. Gold and saffron colors do not seem to be differentiated, as the "eyes" in the upper field are the same color, perhaps because a color was missing.[62] The text describing the picture of the dove makes no mention of the red in the center. The text describing the other birds makes only a few mentions of color;[63] it expatiates only on the goose and the peacock, where perception joins forces with tradition: "Wild

62. In "Quellengeschichtliche Untersuchungen zur *Schedula diversarum artium des Theophilus,*" *Münchener Jahrbuch der bildenden Kunst* 3/4 (1952–53): 145–171, St. Waetzold presented a "Systematic List of the Names of Colors" (pp. 150–158). Here p. 152, *croceum:* "Saffron is used in imitation of gold leaf."

63. *Color phoenicus* (48 C); *saphirinus* on the breast of the peacock (*coeleste desiderium,* 53 A); *aurum* (*sapientia,* 52 A); *argentum* (*eloquentia,* 52 A; *doctores,* 52 B), *argenteus* (*verba lucis nitore patentes,* 34 C); *nigredo* of the raven (*humilitas,* 31 C; *peccatorum fuligo* 33 A), of the old crane (*dolor,* 40 D, 41 C), of the blackbird (*peccatum,* 44 A), of the swan's flesh (*peccatum carnis,* 51 AB); *albus, niveus, candidus* of the swan (*simulatio,* 51 B), of the domestic goose (47 A), of the heron (*munditia,* 47 D), of the *caladrius* (*ab omni peccato immunis,* 48 A), of the blackbird (*purus,* 44 D); *cinericius* of the wild goose (*poenitentia* 47 A), of the heron (*poenitentia,* 47 D); *viriditas* (*aeterna,* 35 C); *viridis* on the tail of the peacock (53 B); *ruffus subrubens* on the peacock (*amor contemplationis,* 53 B); *varius* of the domestic goose (47 A), of the peacock (53 B).

Hugh drops a pretty glimpse of convent life as he describes the jackdaw fluttering about chattering, with a warning not to admit painters, doctors, and minstrels to the community without checking them out first. They will not be tied down; accustomed as they are to wandering, they are scarely capable of *stabilitas* (46 A–D). "The painter's art is extremely pleasant. That is to say, when the painter has finished painting a church, a chapter house, a refectory, or a workshop, he goes, if someone asks him and he is given permission, to paint in another convent. He paints the works of Christ on the wall—would that he would also keep them in his heart in the same way that he knows how to paint them with colors, that is, by behaving in an exemplary fashion!" Doctors are needed everywhere, they also have to bring a whole apothecary's shop with them (with *aromata*!). If the abbot refuses to allow him to practice in the neighborhood, the abbot incurs the doctor's anger and the anger of those who are sick. If he lets him practice, the convent doctor gets to see and touch more than he should. Medical practice forces the man who should speak the truth to lie. He promises his church his fee, but keeps silent about the "scandalum et animae suae damnum" [scandal and damage to his soul].—Minstrels are mostly backsliders, because those who are accustomed to the world and to traveling soon find that the convent is a burden.

At the beginning of *De claustro animae* (I, 1, in *PL,* 176, 1019 D), Hugh pillories the houses of the bishops, large as churches, the rooms painted: "They clothe the pictures there with valuable colored clothes, while the poor man comes with nothing on his back and cries at the door with his stomach empty. O wonderful, fundamentally perverse luxury! The painted wall shows the

geese are all ash colored; I have not seen any that are speckled or snow colored. In the case of domestic geese they are not only ash colored, but are also speckled and white. In the case of wild geese there is ash color, that is, the simple robe of repentance for those who are outside the world. Those, however, who live in villages or towns wear clothes of a more beautiful color" (47 A). "The peacock has a hideous voice, a simple gait, a snake's head, a sapphire-colored breast; it also has reddish feathers on its wings [*aliquantulum ruffas*] and a long tail which is, so to speak, filled with eyes" (53 A). Everything is interpreted—"Varietas igitur colorum designat diversitatem virtutum" [The variety of colors designates the diversity of virtues] (53 B)—the red color in the wings as well; "color ruffus subrubens in pennis amorem significat contemplationis" [the color red blushing on the wings signifies the love of contemplation] (53 B). It seems to be the red of the field of the dove, for which "the love of contemplation" would be the suitable color. (Whether the three-point pattern has more than ornamental significance, like the white drawing in the wings, remains an open question but is scarcely to be assumed.) The considerations which follow are necessarily hypothetical, as they try to make sense of what is in the realms of possibility. They are based upon experience with other twelfth-century texts that interpret pictures and do not claim to be complete evidence. Around the red field of the dove, there is a golden ring within a green one. The outer rings in the corner fields are green; the inner ones golden. Perhaps the green of earthliness lies around the gold of summons or promise in the four fields, whose number—like the four elements—points to earthliness. Are the elements also perhaps present in the picture? At the bottom there would be *aer* (air) and *mare* (sea), at the top gold (fire?) and silver (earth?).[64] Bede interprets the golden rings on the Tabernacle: "the *cir-*

Trojans clad in purple and gold, while the Christian is denied even some old rags. The Greek army is given weapons, Hector a gleaming golden shield, but the poor beggar at the gate is not given even a crust; indeed, to tell the truth, the poor are often plundered, so that stones and wood can be clothed."

The convent, too, should not be painted: "Genesis should be read in a book not on the walls." Painting may be allowed in the towns and villages for the body of the people, "ut simplicitas eorum teneatur delectatione picturae, qui non delectantur subtilitate scripturae" [That those who cannot delight in the subtlety of the Scriptures may be held fast in their simplicity by the enjoyment of a picture]. "But for us who delight in solitude, horse and ox are more useful on the fields than on the wall" (1053 BC).

64. It is true that I do not know of the application of gold and silver for fire and earth; the "aurum ignitum probatum" [gold tried in the fire] would be a connection. Psalm 11:7 could have paved the way for this connection between silver and earth: "Eloquia Domini eloquia casta; argentum igne examinatum, probatum terrae, pergatum septuplum" [The words of the Lord are

culi aurei signify the bliss of heavenly life that is justifiably compared to gold because of the glory of its brilliance."[65] The golden rings within the green ones may signify a summons to and a promise for man. The sapphire blue ring around the innermost ring of writing, whose color radiates in the radii (sapphire next to blue) out to the next gold ring that is contained within a green one, diffuses the color of heaven from within into the portions of the dove's inheritance. The ring that circumscribes the radii on the outside is gold within green. The relationship of gold and green seems to intensify as it moves from the outside to the inside: in the corners the golden ring is circumscribed by a larger green one: the green (outside) and gold (inside) form a unified double ring. The relationship of what is of this earth and of what is promised to man is gradually brought into harmony, by a series of approaches, until it reaches a resting point in the center, where we "do not strive impetuously for the present and await the future with patience" (17 D).[66]

---

pure words: as silver tried in a furnace of earth, purified seven times]; cf. Hrabanus Maurus, *De universo* XVII, 13 (*PL*, 111, 476 B); "argentum terrae igne examinatum" [the silver of earth tried in the fire].

65. *PL*, 91, 443 D.

66. Hugh speaks of green in *De claustro* IV, 23, when he refers to the jasper of the wall of the Heavenly Jerusalem, which signifies for him "perseverantia in proposito" [perseverance in purpose]. The green of the painter and the dyer, however, pales and disappears like that of the tree. Only the "color creatus" [the created color] endures in the jewel that is not harmed by time and circumstances (*PL*, 176, 1162 B–D, 1163 C). Green is the area of law, in the middle of the heavenly cloister, because green heals the eye. It refreshes the eyes of the citizens of heaven and constantly strengthens them by its freshness, because there—away from time—it represents the "identitas aeternitatis" [the identity of eternity]. It does not need rain, but the dew of the contemplation of God (IV, 34; 1172 Dff.).

There are few colors in *De claustro*. Upon the pearls of heaven's gates shines a lustrous white (chastity unbesmirched, IV, 24). The cloister of heaven has four rows of columns in four colors—saffron, rose, snow white, and sky blue—for the four orders of the chosen—the fathers, the martyrs, the confessors, and the virgins. The fathers who are entering heaven become like living stones there ("Saffron columns") ("Habet enim crocus similitudinem maturi fructus" [for the crocus has a similarity to a ripe fruit]). The rose color is the blood of the martyrs. The angels admire the "rubrum colorem Stephani" [the red color of Stephen] and the "flammeum colorem Laurentii" [the flame color of Laurence]. The snow color signifies the "munditia confessionis" [the purity of confession] of the confessors. The color of the clear sky, which is like the violet, stands for the "integritas virginum" [the integrity of virgins] (IV, 30).

The connection between green and gold is established in the Temple of Solomon (according to 2 Par. 3:5f.), where the gold-covered tablets stand on marble. Hugh and the Scriptures say nothing about the color of the marble, but we can gather from his interpretation that he imagines the floor of the temple as being made of green marble, for he interprets the marble as the "fortitudo fidei" and "propositi firmitas" [the strength of faith and the firmness of purpose].

Within the framework of the inner world, it is only the outermost ring of the central part that is *only* gold. Its gold continues, in a strange way (like the sapphire of the radii), up and down into the central axis and into the "spigots." I do not know how to explain this. Does the picture—above and below—have an opening into the life hereafter, through which passes the gold that surrounds the middle?[67] The window on the right-hand side of the wall of the northern transept of Strassburg Cathedral, a series of medallions treating the judgment of Solomon, shows pictures (dating from between 1190 and 1200)—also furnished with spigots—has a yellow (pearl) margin that runs round the circle, and it too enters and exits (fig. 20).[68] The great central pane of the picture extends on all four sides beyond an almost square, blue-colored rectangle that is placed beneath it: the color is darker than the sapphire color and can be regarded as hyacinth blue. The frequently developed

---

However, these are common significations of green. Gottfried von Strassburg, who is quite reliable in these things, says therefore of the floor of the "Love grotto" in *Tristan:* "der marmelîne esterich der ist der stæte gelîch an der grüene und an der veste; diu meine ist ime diu beste von varwe und von slehte" [The marble floor is like constancy in its greenness and its firmness; this is its best meaning both as to color and as to its evenness] (*Tristan,* 16969ff.). From the interpretation of "marble"—which can be of many different colors—we can deduce the color in which it is thought of even where there is no actual color adjective (III, 23: "de pavimento templi" [concerning the pavement of the temple]. Where Hugh imagines marble to be white, as it is on the walls of the temple ("de marmore Pario" [concerning Parian marble]), we necessarily have in mind the other meaning of marble—"munditia in mente" [purity of thought] (III, 20: "de parietibus templi" [concerning the walls of the temple]). The gold on the green floor is interpreted by Hugh as "pretium caritatis" [the reward of love] and "intentionis puritas" [purity of intent]. "Whoever strives to enter into heaven has to walk on this" (1125 B). The conjunction of green and gold in the dove picture is explained perhaps by the combination of gold and green marble in the Temple of Solomon.

67. The golden ring could also mean something like the prayer of the anonymous English Cistercian who prefaces his *Distinctiones Monasticae* with these lines that refer to Revelation 1:13 (Pitra, *Spicelegium Solesmense,* 3:453):

Sint mihi cuncta bona quae circuit aurea zona,
Quae pectus cingit, quae cor cum corpore stringit,
Ut sit clausa malis dilectio spiritualis.

[May I have all goods that are surrounded by a golden girdle
That encircles the breast, that binds the heart to the body,
So that my spiritual delight may be closed to evil things.]

68. According to P. Ahnne and V. Beyer, *Die Glasmalereien des Straßburger Münsters* (Strassburg, 1960); L. Grodecki, *Mémorial du voyage en Rhenanie de la Société des Antiquaires de France (1953)*, pp. 241–248, sees in this the influence of the Meuse area and of the Rhenish area around Master Gerlach.

FIGURE 20
Medallion from the Solomon window, Strassburg Cathedral (1190–1200).

signification of this color—it is the color of one of the precious stones of the Heavenly Jerusalem—as the color of the sky, or of the air, indicates (in a number of different variations) what comes from heaven or leads to it, and is thus close to the gold and sapphire of the center of the picture. The poem—probably composed in 1071 for the dedication of the church on Monte Cassino—on the Heavenly Jerusalem, "Cives caelestis patriae (Citizens of the Heavenly Land) by Amatus of Montecassino,[69] devotes a strophe to each of the precious stones and says of the sapphire and the hyacinth:

3
Saphirus habet speciem
caelesti throno similem
designat cor simplicium
spe certa praestolantium;
quorum vita et moribus
delectatur altissimus.

12
Iacinthus est caeruleus
virtute medioximus;
cuius decora facies
mutatur ut temperies;
vitam signat angelicam
discretione praeditam.

[The sapphire's appearance
Is like the heavenly throne:
It represents the heart of the simple
Waiting in certain hope;
By whose life and behavior
The most high is pleased.

The hyacinth is dark blue,
Of moderate strength,
Whose decorous form
Changes like moderation
It signifies the angelic life
Endowed with discernment.]

The framework of the picture, filled with the inscription and a decorative margin of an acanthus leaf pattern[70] in sapphire on blue, is limited both

69. A. Lentini, "Il ritmo 'Cives caelestis patriae' e il 'de duodecim lapidibus' di Amato," *Benedictina* 12 (1958): 15–26.

70. Lucia N. Valentine, *Ornament in Medieval Manuscripts* (London, 1965), p. 35.

internally and externally by graduated red margins. In the face of the multiplicity of red colors and significations it is hard to say what their meaning is. It could be a color of suffering because of the external world in the sense of "Quis dabit mihi pennas sicut columbae?" But there is nothing to exclude the possibility that it could be interpreted as being the same as the identical color of contemplation that is in the center. The psalm text of the framework and the inscription of the circle that extends into it is surrounded by a stripe of the most delicate gold: wisdom. Our consideration of colors, however uncertain as it may be in the interpretation of individual cases (even though each one of them could be supported by parallels), does allow us to recognize this much for certain: they are used according to an intellectual plan that reinforces or completes the statements the picture is making. It is not easy to understand their language so long as we still lack a lexicon of medieval color significations. If we had Hugh's original picture, we could probably be more certain. We may also expect number signification to come into play in the picture. The eight cruciform signs in the rings of the picture—four in the corners and four in the center—not only mark the beginnings of the inscriptions, as an aid to reading them, but are probably also signs of benediction: the number eight that also appears in the radii in the center promises eternal blessedness.

The sequence of picture and explanation is also the form of Hugh's *De rota verae religionis.* The wheel pictures are placed at the beginnings of the two parts that constitute the explanation of the pictures. The parts of the wheel, like axle, hub, spoke, rim, and their creaking and lubrication, determine the division of the text, which also broadly interprets the turning and running of the wheel. We must not impose the wheel idea on the dove picture—and see in the dove picture the great wheel of life going round and round—without subjecting it to a close examination.[71] The wheel vocabulary that dominates the wheel picture and the wheel treatise is totally lacking in the dove picture and the dove text. There is nothing to suggest the idea of turning: the ordering of the left- and right-hand sides is opposed to such an idea. The not entirely peaceful quietude is far from the restlessness of a wheel of life with its vicissitudes, the "up and down" in *De rota.* It is a pulling and a being pulled in the direction of an expectation that stems from a promise. If we assume that the picture has the character of a thing and if, as result of the formal relationship of its center to that of the center of the *rota,* we wish to

71. See also C. de Clercq, n. 26 above.

determine that it is a wheel—it is a makeshift: the text makes no statement about it and I cannot interpret the spigots in the picture (they are not the end of an axle, and the wheel pictures show nothing of this sort)—the idea of the turning wheel of the *rota* must be left on one side, and we are left with, at the best, the possibility of a stationary, halted wheel. The "rota in medio rotae" [wheel within a wheel] (two concentric wheels, according to Ezekiel 1:15ff.) that has been depicted since the twelfth century is a favorite image of the concordance of the Old and New Testaments[72] (cf. in our text "Inter quas sortes dormiunt qui auctoritatibus veteris et novi testamenti concordant et acquiescant" [among which shares do they sleep who are in accordance with, and assent to, the authorities of the Old and of the New Testament] [16 B]). Their eight (or sixteen noncoincident) spokes—Hugh's has twelve—would be closer to our picture. "Cumque adspicerem animalia, apparuit rota una super terram iuxta animalia habens quattuor facies" [Whenever I looked at the animals, one wheel appeared next to the animals having four faces] (Ezekiel 1:15). If the magnificent vision of the summoning of the prophet Ezekiel were to be behind our picture, it would be there silently yet scarcely simply as a formal pattern. We would be facing a mystical reinterpretation of a picture that has, up to now, been interpreted from the point of view of the history of salvation as the effect of the word upon the four parts of the world (or of the fourfold sense of language), just as we often find the history of salvation in the twelfth century reinterpreted as the history of the soul, as the private quest for salvation instead of by means of the public way into the church.[73] Just as Hugh tacitly assumes a knowledge of the verses that precede Psalm 67:14 for the understanding of his picture, he could also have enriched the picture by awakening the memory of Ezekiel's wheel—without putting it into words—for those cognoscenti who would not confuse the summoning of the dove with the summoning of the prophet, but who might perhaps see a trace of the latter falling upon the former.[74] Bearing in mind that Hugh was

72. The typological cycle *Pictor in carmine* (The painter in the poem) that comes from England at the end of the twelfth century was transformed, a century later, in Austria into a *Rota in medio rotae:* on the subject of this title, see F. Röhrig, "Rota in medio rotae: Ein typologischer Zyklus aus Österreich," *Jahrbuch des Stiftes Klosterneuburg* 14=NF 5 (1965): 7–113, here pp. 34–39.

73. Ohly, *Hohelied-Studien*, pp. 154ff.

74. If the picture were lost, we could not reconstruct Hugh's explanation of its form. Others who have interpreted their own pictures that are now lost to us are fortunately more precise in their descriptions. But we have to take into account the fact that the text does not deal with every aspect of the picture.

drawing a picture of himself as well as the dove—a self-portrait of a highly idiosyncratic and most impressive sort that was possible only in his time[75]—we should be listening, in this connection, to that wordless medieval language that speaks only to the initiated, and then often as a last word without "language" (even in literature). Its understanding comes from the practice of contemplative immersion in the spiritual vision of the time.[76]

Omnis mundi creatura
Quasi liber et pictura
Nobis est et speculum—

[Every creature in the world
Just like a book and a picture
Is for us a mirror—]

Situated as it is on the threshold of the Romanesque and the Gothic, there is a very restrained mysticism alive in the picture, whose patient desire for God tries not to shorten the path trodden on earth, but to turn it inward. Without an affective or speculative approach to God—achieved by intensifications of language or an upsweep of thoughts—Hugh treads the soberly ennobling path of interpreting creation as the trace of God in order to pursue it. The form of seeing or of thinking about creatures, *matura consideratio,* reads the book of nature as strengthening the Scriptures: "quod scriptura praedicat, opus naturae confirmat" [What the Scriptures proclaim, the work of nature confirms] (49 A). The spirit's insight into the letter does not extinguish it; it awakens in it unthought-of life, which rises out of it without looking away from it. Hugh looks beyond the heart of things to God. This wakefully immersed contemplation does not skim over anything in a mystical, immediate way, but has need of the creature as it searches for its transparence. This mediate path to God leads from the world into its center, where God is closer but has not yet been reached. The centripetal motion of the picture determines its position as a central composition. Previously, Romanesque central composition proved to be "a form that is transparent as to spiritual sense,

75. "See, the dove and the falcon are sitting on the same perch. Namely, me from the clergy, you from the service of the world, we were both converted so that now we sit, according to the rule, on this perch" (13/14). While not forgetting the typical nature of the "I" and the pedagogical nature of turning to the brother, we certainly cannot entirely exclude the personal element.

76. W. von den Steinen (*Symbolon* 4 [1964]: 22) speaks, when talking of the signification of animals, of "thoughts that are seen or spiritual contemplation."

that is based on a typological meaning of history perceived from a creative point of view; the form of central composition with the system of symmetrically intensified mirroring as a consequence of typological thinking."[77] Here we are now becoming aware of an early Gothic possibility of reinterpreting the basic form that is preserved and turning it into a mystical central composition, where the Gothic path to the "final summit" presents itself as the way to the center that points further to a new stylistic future.

The Pictorial Tradition of Hugh's Bird Book

Without having systematically investigated the manuscript tradition of Hugh's bird book, I will list the *illustrated* manuscripts of Hugh's *Aviarum* that I know of—not according to the history of their tradition but according to their research history. In this particular case, where the author has drawn the pictures himself, the pictorial tradition has a text critical significance of its own—beside the manuscript tradition—that has its own editorial attraction. As I do not intend to make an editon, I restricted myself to looking at the dove picture in the manuscript Paris 2495, which seems to be very close to the original in age and quality. The following list of manuscripts, grouped according to the people who discovered them, is offered only with the intention of putting what had previously been communicated in scattered sources (and consequently largely hidden from the most recent scholarship) at the disposal of an editor as an indication of the extent of the tradition and as a means of presenting the idea that a systematic search could promise success.

Manuscripts where catalogs give no information about the miniatures are ignored here; other manuscripts that, on the basis of other information, seem to include miniatures whose catalogs I have not seen are in parentheses.

I. L. Thorndike, *A History of Magic and Experimental Science during the First Thirteen Centuries of Our Era* (New York, 1923), 2:16f. pointed out

1. Cambridge, Sidney Sussex College, ms. 100, thirteenth century, fols. 1–26. The pictures are described by M. R. James, *A Descriptive Catalogue of the Manuscripts in the Library of Sidney Sussex College* (Cambridge, 1895), pp. 117ff.
2. Vitry-le-François, 23, thirteenth century, fols. 1–23v, "De tribus

77. F. Ohly, "Die Suche in Dichtungen des Mittelalters," *Zeitschrift für deutsches Altertum* 94 (1965): 171–184, here p. 182.

columbis," in *Catalogue général des manuscrits des bibliothèques publiques de France, Départements* (hereafter *CGMDép*), vol. 13 (Paris, 1891), pp. 20f.: "Le traité *de tribus columbis* est orné de vingt-neuf figures d'oiseaux peintes aux fol. 1–22" [The treatise *De tribus columbis* is decorated with twenty-nine paintings of birds, on folios 1–22].

In addition to the manuscripts cited by Thorndike, Vendôme,156; Dijon, ancien fonds 225; Vitry-le-François, 63; Paris, B.N. 12 231; Bourges, 121; Munich, 15 407 and 18 368, the catalogs do not list any other miniatures. I could not see the catalog for Cambridge, University Library, 1574, 1823, 2040. Thorndike says of Cambridge University Library 1823, *Liber bestiarum:* "The numerous figures of animals in outline 'are remarkable for their finish and vigor'") (bird pictures also?).

II. Manuscripts of our bird book are probably listed in M. R. James, *The Bestiary,* edited for the Roxburghe Club, publication no. 100 (Oxford, 1928). The work, which lists about forty English bestiary manuscripts, was not available to me.

III. A. Katzenellenbogen, *Allegories of the Virtues and Vices in Medieval Art,* Studies of the Warburg Institute, no. 10 (London, 1939), p. 62, cites the following:

3. Frankfurt, Stadtbibliothek, ms. Batt. 167, second half of twelfth century, East French, fol. 66r. The dove picture in this manuscript is reproduced in Katzenellenbogen, plate XXXVII, fig. 62.
4. Stift Heiligenkreuz im Wiener Wald, ms. 18 (226), thirteenth century, fols. 129–145r. On this: *Die Handschriftenverzeichnisse der Zisterzienerstifte* (*Xenia Bernardina*), pt. 2, vol.1 (Vienna, 1891), p. 178: "with many illustrations"; mentioned by C. de Clercq in *Gutenberg-Jahrbuch* (1962), p. 62, and in *Revue du nord* 45 (1963): 31: "The complete series of miniatures." The pen drawing of the dove and the falcon on the perch (fol. 129r) is reproduced in F. Unterkircher, *La miniature autrichienne* (Milan, 1954), plate 34; W. von den Steinen, "Altchristlich-mittelalterliche Tiersymbolik," *Symbolon* 4 (1964): 218–243, here p. 229, with 11 illustrations; W. von den Steinen, *Homo caelestis: Das Wort der Kunst im Mittelalter,* vol. 1, *Textband* (Berne, 1965), pp. 199, 292f., with plate p. 281 (in vol. 2, *Bildband*). The manuscript also contains *de rota:*

an illustration of the wheel picture on fol. 146r in Unterkircher, *La miniature autrichienne,* plate 35.

5. St.-Omer, Bibliothèque publique, ms. 94, thirteenth century: see *CMGDép* (Paris, 1861), 3:55f.: "No.2, *De columba argentata* or *De avibus* includes all the pictures of birds noted in the text, painted on a colored background with an inscription around each painting (4 to 5 centimeters.)" The well-preserved dove picture in this manuscript, colored only in the midfield with the dove and in the frame, is reproduced in monochrome in C. de Clercq, "Le rôle de l'image dans un manuscrit médiéval," Bodleian, Lyell, 71 (*Gutenberg-Jahrbuch* [1962]), pp. 23–30, here p. 25; H. Peltier (see n. 17), pp. 42f.; C. de Clercq, in *Revue du nord* 45 (1963): 31: "The complete series of miniatures."
6. Brussels, Bibliothèque Royale, 1491, beginning of thirteenth century, "De significatione avium," in *Catalogue des manuscrits de la bibliothèque royale de Belgique,* by J. van den Gheyn, vol. 2 (Brussels, 1902), p. 387: "Some strange miniatures drawn by pen represent the subject of Hugh de Folieto's treatise . . . fols. 124, 124r, 1265, 127v, 129, 129v, 131, 132v." C. Gaspar and F. Lyna, *Les principaux manuscrits à peintures de la Bibliothèque Royale de Belgique,* vol. 1 (Paris, 1937), p. 129: "fol. 124, 124v, 125 doves on perches in wheels and circles . . . There is nothing remarkable about this illustration; these are pen drawings, that use, very prudently, only black, green, gold, and silver. It is provincial art of a style that is still totally Romanesque." C. de Clercq, in *Archivum latinitatis medii aevi* 29 (1959): 219 n. 2.
7. Cambrai, 259, thirteenth century, fol. 192, "De quarumdam avium significatione mystica et morali." A. Molinier, *Cambrai* in *CGMDép,* vol. 17 (Paris, 1891), p. 92: "Pretty little paintings, depicting the mystical dove and different animals." C. de Clercq, in *Revue du nord* 45 (1963): 32.
8. Douai, 370, twelfth century, fols. 102–108: "De tribus columbis et de avibus," *CGMDép,* vol. 6 (Paris, 1878) p. 201: "miniatures depicting birds." C. de Clercq, in *Revue du nord* 45 (1963): 31: "with one or other miniature, among them, dove, falcon and turtledove" (p. 42).
9. Paris, B.N. ms. 2495, twelfth century, fols. 1–30; Ph. Lauer, *Bibliothèque Nationale, Catalogue général des manuscrits latins,* vol. 2 (Paris, 1940), p. 489: "Numerous miniatures in frames and two paintings (2 and 10v)." Katzenellenbogen differs from Lauer in placing our dove picture in the mid-thirteenth century.

10. [London, British Museum, Royal ms. 10. A. vii, fol. 150v, late thirteenth century.]
11. Bordeaux, 995, thirteenth/fourteenth century, fols. 62–79, "De natura avium." C. Couderc, Bordeaux *CGMDép*, vol. 23 (Paris, 1894), p. 545: "This part is decorated with numerous pictures of birds. We would draw attention in particular to that on folio 62v, which is surrounded by numerous inscriptions and so occupies the whole page." Katzenellenbogen places this dove picture in the late thirteenth century.

IV. S. Ives and H. Lehmann-Haupt, *An English Thirteenth Century Bestiary* (New York, 1942) have an extensive treatment of:

12. A thirteenth-century manuscript now in the possession of P. Hofer (Cambridge, Mass.) but at that time in the hands of H. P. Kraus (New York). This contains, on fols. 3–16 preceding the text, a closed series of seventy-five miniatures, of which forty are published in the appendix (the first birds are the sparrow and the turtledove, which should be preceded by the dove and the falcon); fols. 17–58: text of Hugh of Folieto, *De bestiis,* bk. 1; fols. 58–60: *Tractatus Hugonis prioris de diversis coloribus ac naturis columbarum;* fols. 60–89: *Dicta Chrysostomi.* Cf. F. McCulloch (see no. VI), p. 31 n. 33.

V. A. Wilmart, *Codices Reginenses Latini,* vol. 2 (Rome, 1945), 111, pointed out

13. Troyes, 177, twelfth century: "De tribus columbis et aliis multis avibus (cum imaginibus avium)." *CGMDép* vol. 2, no. 1 (Paris, 1855), p. 87. C. de Clercq, in *Revue du nord* 45 (1963): 31: "The complete series of miniatures."

VI. Florence McCulloch, *Medieval Latin and French Bestiaries,* University of North Carolina Studies in Romance Languages and Literatures, no. 33 (Chapel Hill, N.C., 1962), pp. 29f., points to illustrated bird book manuscripts from the Isidor of Seville extended *Physiologus* tradition B:

14. [Oxford Bodleian, p. 602, fols. 1–36, late twelfth century with bird book, fols. 36–65.]
15. [London Sion College L $^{40.2}/_{L\,28}$, fols. 73–116, thirteenth century; bird book, fols. 1–54.]

16. [(Dyson) Perrins, p. 26, fols. 67–120v, thirteenth century, bird book, fols. 1–45 (sold in 1958 to H. P. Kraus, New York).]

F. McCulloch, pp. 30ff. and 211, refers to illustrated bird book manuscripts that are handed down together with the anonymous (printed under the name Hugh of St.-Victor in *PL*, 177, cols. 55–84) second book of *De bestiis et aliis rebus.*

17. Paris, B.N. lat. 2495 A. According to P. Lauer, *Bibliothèque Nationale, Catalogue des manuscrits latins,* vol. 2 (Paris, 1940), p. 489, this manuscript from the twelfth/thirteenth century has only the text of *PL*,177, cols. 26–56 and 67–82 (with gaps), and a few defective miniatures. C. de Clercq, in *Revue du nord* 45 (1963): 32: "The miniatures have been removed."
18. Paris, B.N. lat. 2495 B, thirteenth century, fols. 1–29. Lauer, *Bibliothèque Nationale,* p. 490: "Two paintings, one of which has a portrait 5^v and 6"; "numerous miniatures in frames." C. de Clercq, in *Revue du nord* 45 (1963): 32: "complete series of miniatures."
19. Valenciennes 101, thirteenth century, fols. 171–189. *CGMDép,* vol. 25 (Paris, 1894), p. 231: "For each chapter a small figure representing the animal that is described." C. de Clercq, in *Revue du nord* 45 (1963): 32: "complete series of miniatures."
20. Paris, B.N. lat. 14429, thirteenth century, fols. 96–109. All that it says about the dove picture is something about marginal miniatures that are rather larger than the size of an initial in the framed squares.
21. Chalons-sur-Saône, 14, twelfth/thirteenth century, *CGMDép.* vol. 6 (Paris, 1887), p. 365: "Bestiary with miniatures." Incomplete at beginning and end.

VII. C. de Clercq has published

22. Oxford Bodleian, Lyell, 71, ca. 1300. The dove picture on fol. 4r is completely colored; reproduced without colors in *Gutenberg-Jahrbuch* (1962), p. 24. C. de Clercq, in *Revue du nord* 45 (1963): 31: "contains only some of the miniatures."
23. Namur, cod. 48, dated 1424, fols. 87r–111v, "De significationibus avium," has pictures in the prologue and the dove section; cf. C. de Clercq, in *Archivum latinitatis medii aevi* 29 (1959): 228; P. Faider et al. *Catalogue*

des manuscrits conservés à Namur, vol. 1 (Gembloux, 1934), p. 116, after C. de Clercq, in *Revue du nord* 45 (1963): 32; a copy of Brussels, Bibliothèque Royale, II, 1076.

24. Brussels, Bibliothèque Royale, 3241, twelfth and thirteenth centuries, fols. 43–4711v (= *PL,* 177, cols. 13–23); fols. 48–71v (= *PL,* 177, cols 23ff.). J. van den Gheyn, *Catalogue des manuscrits de la bibliothèque royale de Belgique,* vol. 5 (Brussels, 1905), p. 248: "fols. 48–71^v^, pictures of animals."; cf. C. de Clercq, in *Archivum latinitatis medii aevi* 29 (1959): 219 n. 2.
25. London, British Museum, Sloane, 278; *Catalogus librorum manuscriptorum bibliothecae Sloanianae* (n.d., n.p.): "sec. XIV.; nitide exaratus et picturis plurimis adornatus ('brightly written and decorated with several pictures')." De avibus et bestiis. C. de Clercq, in *Revue du nord* 45 (1963): 31: "complete series of miniatures." Ives and Lehmann-Haupt, *An English Thirteenth Century Bestiary,* p. 18.
26. Charleville, 166 B. thirteenth century, *CDMDép,* vol. 5, no. 2 (Paris, 1879), says nothing about pictures. C. de Clercq, in *Revue du nord* 45 (1963): 32: twelfth century, "with one or two miniatures."
27. Brussels, Bibliothèque Royale 8536–43, thirteenth century, fols. 73–98, "De naturis avium." J. van den Gheyn, *Catalogue des manuscrits,* vol. 3 (Brussels, 1903), pp. 385f.; C. de Clercq, in *Revue du nord* 45 (1963): 32: "Has only a most unusual ornamental letter at the beginning. It depicts a dove and a sparrow hawk; beneath the dove there is a monk in a grey-blue habit; beneath the sparrow hawk another monk in a white habit with a brown cape."
28. Brussels, Bibliothèque Royale II, 1076. C. de Clercq, in *Revue du nord* 45 (1963): 31: thirteenth century; "contains only some of the miniatures." C. de Clercq reproduces this manuscript's dove picture in fig. 1, preceding p. 31.
29. Brussels, Bibliothèque Royale 18421–29. C. de Clercq, in *Revue du nord* 45 (1963): 32: thirteenth century, "complete series of miniatures."

VIII. Further:

30. Oxford Bodleian, 3522 (32), thirteenth century, Dutch (?). *A Summary Catalogue of Western Manuscripts in the Bodleian Library at Oxford,* vol. 2, no. 2 (Oxford, 1937), pp. 669f.; "A compendium of Hugo de Folieto's 'De bestiis'"; "with many slightly coloured drawings of men and ani-

mals"; "There are numerous illustrations slightly coloured in green, red, brown etc., some with pricked outlines, one full page."

On the transmission of Hugo de Folieto's works, see further *Histoire littéraire de France,* vol. 13 (1869), pp. 492–507; M. Manitius, *Geschichte der lateinischen Literatur des Mittelalters,* vol. 3 (Munich, 1931), pp. 227f.; L. Thorndike, *A History of Magic and Experimental Science,* vol. 2 (New York, 1923), pp. 17f.; H. Peltier, "Hugues de Fouilloy"; F. McCulloch, *Medieval Latin and French Bestiaries,* n. 33, remarks, "A study of the various manuscripts of the *Aviarium* has been undertaken in Paris by M. Yves Lefèvre." C. de Clercq, "Le 'liber de rota verae religionis,'" *Archivum latinitatis medii aevi* 29 (1959): 219–228, here 219f., 228; *Archivum latinitatis medii aevi* 30 (1960): 15–37; C. de Clercq, "Le 'liber de pastoribus et ovibus' d'Hugues de Fouilloi," *Archivum latinitatis medii aevi* 31 (1961): 77–107, here p. 77; R. Grégoire, "Le 'de claustro' animae' est-il clunisien?" *Studia monastica* 4 (1962): 193–195; M. de Marco, "Per la Storia della tradizione di Ugo di Fouilloi 'De claustro animae,'" *Aevum* 36 (1962): 172–174; C. de Clercq, "Hugues de Fouilloi, imagier de ses propres oeuvres?" *Revue du nord* 45 (1963): 31–42; M. de Marco, "Codici Vaticani del 'De claustro animae' di Ugo di Fouilloi," *Sacris Erudiri* 15 (1964): 220–248; R. Baron, "Note sur 'de claustro,'" *Sacris Erudiri* 15 (1964): 249–255; J. Gorky, *Hugonis de Folieto "De claustro animae"* (edition and translation), 2 vols. (Paris, 1965), pp. 235 and 142 (typewritten complementary thesis not seen.)

I had at my disposal colored photographs of the manuscripts listed above under 1, 9, and 18. The dove picture in 18 is hurried and rough and painted without inscription. The dove pictures published by C. de Clercq from mss. nos. 5 and 22, as well as the one from ms. 18, have in common the fact that they have no spigots on the upper and lower edge of the picture; this is in contrast to no. 18. Only no. 9 has preserved the "eyes" of the dove. "Eyes" and "spigots" are a *lectio difficilior* that relegates the pictures without these criteria to a second class.

H. Silvestre, in his review of the book by Florence McCulloch (*Revue d'histoire ecclésiastique* 58 [1963]: 720ff.), gives a great deal of further information about the *Physiologus* tradition.

FOUR

THE CATHEDRAL AS TEMPORAL SPACE: ON THE DUOMO OF SIENA

1. The Twelfth Century: Seeing the Whole

The Signification of Spatial Dimensions

The twelfth century, during which the foundation stone of the cathedral in Siena was laid, had an unequaled creative vigor. Its impetus gives it an epochal significance, as a turning point, within the Middle Ages, which are too readily regarded as a global unity. Its significance can be compared with the Renaissance. It is the cradle of Gothic, the mother of mysticism and the foundation stone of scholasticism. The vernacular literatures owe to it novel possibilities, of creative interpretation of the world, in previously unknown genres, with effects that are felt for more than five hundred years. The works of Ariosto and Tasso still echo the *chanson de geste,* which begins in grandiose fashion with the *Chanson de Roland.* The Arthurian romance, given to the world by Chrétien de Troyes, dies a noble death in Cervantes's *Don Quixote.* The Minnesang discovered possibilities of love that had been alien to antiquity and popular culture but that set an indelible stamp on the feelings and behavior of the whole Western world. The Christian hero, because of his readiness to sacrifice himself for the faith, the Arthurian knight as the incarnation of a humanity which was striving to please God *and* the world, and the man devoting himself—and the woman—to a boldly drawn image of the lady and living according to its awakening demands, represent the possibilities for an ennobled human existence that were the vision of the poets of this

I was able to write this article in the German Art Historical Institute in Florence and in the Zentralinstitut für Kunstgeschichte in Munich. I offer my hearty thanks to the directors of both institutes, Herr Herbert Keutner (Florence) and Herr Willibald Sauerländer (Munich). Published as "Die Kathedrale als Zeitenraum: Zum Dom von Siena," in *Schriften zur mittelalterlichen Bedeutungsforschung,* by Friedrich Ohly (Darmstadt: Wissenschaftliche Buchgesellschaft, 1977), pp. 171–273.

century. They live by drawing a bow at the target of a love-inspired search that is aimed at preserving the faith, at finding the right way to be a man, and at perseverance in the face of ideal images of the woman, so as to set a dynamically tense example for mankind's potential to realize a daring dream by such an effort. The motif of quest in literature, of the quaestio in scholasticism, and the urge to unification in mysticism reveal one of the fundamental movements of the piety of the age, a piety that is directed toward the meaning of the world, truth, and God and that suffuses all the movements of its spirit. This movement, which brings about a stylistic change in the twelfth century, disturbs what has been a statically peaceful world, ordered around spiritual and formal centers, because it is seen as being predominantly historical and typological. This world now changes as it moves from Romanesque to Gothic and with the rise of mysticism and scholasticism—in the sense of the history of form as the expression of the history of the experience of the image of God and of man. Change in style, as the manifestation of the change from piety, can be explained in this way. The study of these spiritual bases teaches us how to understand a stylistic epoch on the basis of its entire origin. Closer to this than the mostly later examples in art are the most immediate stirrings of human piety toward God in the inner movements of theology too, especially in the way that they treat the word of God. The genres of exegesis that are devoted to the spiritual illumination of God's hidden revelation are not formal constants, but are part of the change in the life of the history of piety and theology that realizes itself, like art, in that borderland between history and tradition where the life of history has space to draw breath. The forms of exegesis which are marked—always in transitions—by mysticism or scholasticism, Romanesque or Gothic, monasticism or clericalism, which reveal God's notion of creation or salvation, show the changing sense of the search for the meaning of revelation in Scripture and creation. This can be seen in the history of the interpretations of the Song of Songs.[1]

In different ways, for example, in the forms of the sermon cycle, of the dramatic self-interpretation of the word, or of the drama of universal salvation—with great dramatic panache (in the works of Honorius Augustodensis) and elsewhere—the first half of the twelfth century succeeded in trans-

1. Friedrich Ohly, *Hohelied-Studien: Grundzüge einer Geschichte der Hoheliedauslegung des Abendlandes bis um 1200* (Wiesbaden, 1958), "Die Suche in Dichtungen des Mittelalters," *Zeitschrift für deutsches Altertum* 94 (1965): 171–184, "Synagoge und Ecclesia: Typologisches in mittelalterlicher Dichtung," in *Schriften zur mittelalterlichen Bedeutungsforschung* (Darmstadt, 1977), pp. 312–337, and, on what follows, "Problems of Medieval Significs and Hugh of Folieto's Dove Miniature" (see chap. 3 of this volume).

lating the loose parataxis of an older traditional observance into a binding uninterrupted succession, where every member participates in a noninterchangeable, ordered spiritual whole. The effort to overcome the earlier exegetical staccato of word-by-word explication, and the accomplishment of a total spiritual view in the interpretation of a text, was realized uniquely in the interpretation of biblical structures like Noah's Ark, the Tabernacle, the temple in Jerusalem, or the Heavenly Jerusalem. This happened as exegetes like Hugh of St.-Victor, Adam Scotus, and others began to represent the structure to be interpreted, together with the dimensions of its signification, by painting it on parchment, so that the verbal interpretation served as a commentary on the picture of the structure that was attached to it.[2] Here exegesis took the form of a spiritual architecture that sees the world, through theological and architectural eyes, as a unified continuum of meaning and interprets the dimensions of its signification in every direction.

The view of the whole that could be made visible in book painting,[3] in the rod of Jesse, in the systematizing trees of vices and virtues, in every conceivable sort of formation of cycles in cathedral art, and in much else will also be only briefly considered here with a few remarks about German literature. This literature shows a stylistic change in which loosely aggregating forms, consisting more or less of blocks, were replaced by forms that aimed at a continuous unity. In sentence structure, hypotactic ligatures replace paratactic series. Strophic structures give place to continuous narrative verse. A stylistic continuum was promoted just as much by the interlacing of syntactical units in rhymed couplets, so as to form an enjambment, as it was by superseding a style, derived from individual lines, by strophes made up of long lines that aspire to totality in both content and in form. Episodic series give way to continuous contexts in the development of plot, with sequences of facts, ideas, and lives. Conceptions of gradation and intensification represent a threshold in the history of style between the aggregation of episodes and of series that proceed toward something higher. The gradualism of the twelfth century is dominated by the idea of ascent or of movement toward the interior, which, as it strives toward the summit or the center, combines the succession of steps into a whole. The story of the poetic hero is no longer fulfilled in *one* critical phase of his life, but strives toward biographical sequentiality and completeness. The transition from lay to epic, the extension of the early

2. See the essay on Hugh of Folieto, above, pp. 79ff.

3. See the essay on Hugh of Folieto, above, pp. 82–135.

Arthurian romance into the life of the knight, the legend form of the *conversio* or the *passio,* the *visio,* the *miracula,* and *translatio* all seek the unifying context of the meaning of the vita. The legend, the romance, and heroic verse show how the poet strives to pilot his plot not just through one life, but through a whole series of generations. The genealogical introduction and the continuation of the plot into the story of the children, even the grandchildren, can serve different poetic purposes, but they always establish a context and a continuity. The poetic concept of the cycle (in the grouping of legends, and in the Minnesang) provides one possibility of large-scale poetic forms whose seeds are to be found in the twelfth century and which comes into full bloom in the next. The treatment of space and time manifests a striving to get away from the possibilities of a parataxis—that is constantly jumping from one time or place to another—and to achieve a consistent continuum of time and space. This has been achieved, in large-scale poetic forms, by about 1230, where—for example, in the prose *Lancelot*—the writer, for the first time, creates an all-round unity of scene, in the decisive context of place and time, even in the atmosphere of the time of day, and of the term of an individual life or of the stage that it has reached, on into the psychological mood. It is less easy to explain the deeper causes of the stylistic changes in the altered image of man and God than it is to portray the formal elements mentioned above, and we shall not concern ourselves with them here. Tendencies toward the construction of systems in early scholasticism and, above all, the mysticism of the twelfth century—which seeks the way and goal of unity—would have to be considered here.

Let us return to buildings; the vision of entireties apparently made it necessary for theologians of the twelfth century, who were endowed with an artistic sense, not just to put into words what they had apprehended in their spirit but to show it "una cum pictura" [as one with a picture]—as Adam Scotus puts it—with an accompanying picture that represents the relation of the whole as a universe. We know Hugh of St.-Victor's and Adam Scotus's view of the world from their own descriptions, and Hildegard of Bingen's and Joachim of Fiore's views have been preserved in both word and picture. At the end of *De arca Noe morali,* Hugh of St.-Victor introduces us to *De arca Noe mystica,* the work that is appended to it, which describes and interprets his picture of the Ark in such a way as to lead us, with impressive words, to the Ark as a cosmos:[4]

4. *PL,* 176, 679 D–680 D.

What, then, is this Ark of which people talk so much and in which so many paths of knowledge are contained? Should we believe that it is a labyrinth? It is not a labyrinth, not a place which causes us troubles; it is a place of rest (*nec labor intus, sed requies intus* [and within there is no labor, but rather there is rest within]). How do I know this? Does not he who says "Come unto me all ye that are weary and heavy laden and I will refresh you. You shall find rest for your souls" (Matthew 11:28ff.) live in it? But if the place where he is, is a seat of troubles, how shall they who come to him find rest? Now however, "His place is prepared in peace and his dwelling in Sion. There breaks he the arrows of the bow, the shield, the sword, the battle" (Psalms 75:3f.). All noise and confusion are remote from that place; there joy, peace, and tranquillity persist. What then is this Ark, would you like to know? Keep still so that I may tell you a little of much. This Ark is like a richly endowed treasure-house of all the joys. You cannot seek anything in it which you will not also find. In it are contained, in all their fullness and complete in number, the works of our salvation from the beginning of the world until its end; it represents the status of the universal church (*status universalis ecclesiae figuratur* [the condition of the universal church is presented figurally]). The history of happenings is there linked one to the other; there you will find the secrets of the sacraments; in it are ordered the stages of the movements of the soul and thoughts, observations, and sights of good works, virtues, and their reward. What we are to believe, what we are to do, what we are to hope for, is shown us there.[5] The example of human life and the peak of perfection

5. What follows calls to mind the usual discourse regarding the functions of multiplicity in scriptural meaning:

> Littera gesta docet, quid credas allegoria,
> Moralis quid agas, quo tendas anagogia
>
> [The letter teaches what happened, allegory what you should believe, the moral sense what you should do, the anagogical whither you are on the way.]

The formula for this thought has become second nature to us in the course of the centuries. As late as 1780, G. Chr. Lichtenberg says in his *Gedankenbücher,* ed. Franz H. Mautner (Heidelberg, 1967), p. 149, "What am I? What shall I do; what can I believe and hope? All philosophy is reduced to this." In a somewhat earlier passage, Hugh of St.-Victor found that the threefold meaning of the Scriptures was contained in the spatial dimensions of the Ark (678 D): "In his tribus dimensionibus omnis divina scriptura continetur. Historia enim longitudinem arcae metitur, quia in serie rerum gestarum ordo temporis invenitur. Allegoria latitudinem arcae metitur, quia in participatione sacramentarum constat collectio populorum fidelium. Tropologia altitudinem arcae metitur, quia in profectu virtutum crescit dignitas meritorum" [In these three dimensions all of divine Scripture is contained. For history measures the length of the Ark, in that the temporal order is found in a series of things that have happened. Allegory measures the width of the Ark, in that the assembly of peoples of faith consists in their participation in the sacraments. Tropolis contained there. That which is hidden becomes radiantly visible there, what is heavy seems light, and what seemed less clear when looked at reveals itself, in its order, as meaningful. The whole represents itself as a body, and the harmony of the individual becomes clear within it (*Ibi quoddam universitatis corpus effingitur, et concordia singulorum explicatur* [There a certain body is fashioned representing the whole, and the concord of its individual features is explicated]). There we find a second world contrasted with this transitory and fleeting one, because whatever is transitory in the ages of this world exists simultaneously in that world, as if in the

---

ogy measures the height of the Ark, in that the worthiness of their merits grows with the progress of their virtues].

Deriving a manifold doctrine from the same truth ("doctrina multiplex fiat manente eadem veritate" [let a manifold doctrine be made on the basis of the same enduring truth]), Hugh recognizes even in the dimension of height alone three steps. For the three stories of the Ark designate the sequence, *figura, res,* and *veritas,* or shadow, body, and spirit (679 A–C): "In primo ordine quasi in prima mansione est umbra. In secundo ordine quasi in secunda mansione est corpus. In tertio ordine quasi in tertio mansione est spiritus, vel, si mavis hoc modo dicere, figura, res, veritas, ut idem intelligas esse umbram et figuram, idem corpus et rem, idem spiritum et veritatem" [At the first level, as it were, in the first suite of rooms, dwells the shadow. At the second level, as it were, in the second suite of rooms, dwells the body. At the third level, as it were, in the third suite of rooms, dwells the spirit, if you prefer [for all three] the following mode of speech: figure, thing, truth, so that you understand that shadow and figure are the same, that body and thing are the same, that spirit and truth are the same]. The shadow is what has happened before Christ and is the corporeal prefiguration—under the laws of creation ("lex naturalis" [law of nature]) and of the tablets. "Corpus vocantur ipsa nostra sacramenta, quae nunc in ista ecclesia visibiliter geruntur. Spiritus autem est id quod gratia Dei sub visibilibus sacramentis invisibiliter operatur" [These sacraments of ours, which are now being performed in this church for all to see, are called body. Spirit, however, is that which by the grace of God under the visible sacraments invisibly works its effects]. The shadow of the Red Sea prefigures the body of the sacrament of baptism, whose spirit abrogates sin. Hugh distinguishes three further stages of the height: The works of salvation occur down below among men, above among the angels, in the heights as the works of God. Looked at morally, the order is faith, hope, and charity; looked at anagogically, the order is "cogitatio recta" [right thinking], "meditatio provida" [circumspect meditation], and "contemplatio clara" [clear-sighted contemplation]; looked at ethically, it is "scientia" [intellectual knowledge], "disciplina" [instruction], and "bonitas" [goodness]. As for the positions in time with respect to grace—nature, law, and grace itself—nature is at the bottom, law above it, and grace on top. What with respect to height presents itself as an ordering of values that ascend by steps can also present itself with respect to length as a sequence of times: "Haec enim tria si secundum tempus considerantur, longitudinem arcae metiuntur, si secundum dignitatem discernuntur, altitudinem arcae distinguunt, quia sicut tempore se subsequuntur, ita dignitate se praecedunt" [For if these three are considered according to time, they measure the length of the Ark; if they are demarcated according to their worthiness, they characterize the height of the Ark, for just as they follow one another in time, so also do they take precedence over one another in worthiness].

condition of eternity. There the present does not follow the past, what is to come does not dissolve the present, but whatever is always there is ever present. Thus, they (presumably, the people gathered together for eternity) also remain there and will live forever and rejoice forever, without suffering pain for the past, or fear for the future, having what they love, seeing what they desire, and it is perhaps in this sense that the apostle said: "The essence of this world fades away"[6] (*Praeterit figura huius mundi;* 1 Corinthians 7:31), the appearance of this world, the manifestation of this world, the beauty of this world, because there is a second world whose form is endless, whose appearance is not transitory, whose manifestation does not wither, whose beauty is without end. That world is in this world and this world is smaller than that world, because that world embraces one whom this world is not in a position to embrace. The eyes of the flesh see this world; the eyes of the heart see that world in its innermost being. Men have their satisfactions in this world; the joys of that world are ineffable. In this world men run and applaud the spectacles of vanity; in that world they are practiced by eternal (inner?)[7] silence and have, in the purity of their hearts, joy in the contemplation of truth.

In the structure of the Ark, the succession of time is transformed into simultaneity and the transitory is changed into the permanent. Its universal cosmos represents the categories of time, space, and value in terms of length, breadth, and height: "Igitur ordo dignitatis ad altitudinem arcae pertinet, ordo temporis ad longitudinem arcae, ordo loci ad latitudinem[8] simul et longitudinem" [Therefore, the order of worthiness refers to the height of the Ark, the order of time to the length of the Ark, the order of place to the breadth and at the same time to the length].[9] The structure—because it assembles times into simultaneity—affords us the opportunity to survey infinity as though with the eye of God, something impossible for the natural eye. Thus, it also collects infinite spaces into one space and the world of values into the order of precedence of height. Just as God, who—as the one who embraces the whole world—has no exterior around him[10] ("incircumscrip-

6. Thus Luther; Hugh's concepts *figura, forma, species,* and *pulchritudo,* which I render as "form," "appearance," "manifestation," and "beauty," could be explained on the basis of Hugh's aesthetics in book 7 of the *Eruditio didascalica* (*PL,* 176, 811–838).

7. Paris ms. Maz. 729 (twelfth century) fol. 201r reads instead of "aeternum" (*PL,* and Merton College ms.) "internum silentium."

8. *PL* has *altitudinem.*

9. *De arca Noe morali* IV, 9, in *PL,* 176, 678 C.

10. Barbara Bronder, "Das Bild der Schöpfung und der Neuschöpfung der Welt als *orbis quadratus,*" *Frühmittelalterliche Studien* 6 (1972): 188–210, p. 193.

tus omnia in se continet" [uncircumscribed he contains all things within himself]),[11] and holds the whole world in his hands, so man—who also achieves the unbelievable in representing the one who embraces the world, seen from the point of view of the nonexistent exterior of God—can, in the microcosm of the building, survey the universal cosmos of time, space, and values. He needs, for this purpose, the *oculus cordis* (eye of the heart) that sees supernaturally and is able to recognize, in this world, the world that already appears in our own as the totality of space, time, and values—thanks to a spiritual creative power that is peculiar to him and that forms his thought. In the preface to Hugh of St.-Victor's didactic dialogue between a master and a pupil, *De vanitate mundi,* he develops the doctrine of the natural and the spiritual eye (*oculus carnis* [eye of the flesh] and *oculus cordis*):

"You have within you another eye that is far superior to this one in clarity, that perceives the past, the present, and the future simultaneously, that pours out the light of its viewing and its gift of sight over everything, penetrates the hidden, pursues what is elusive, and does not need an external light in order to be able to see, but perceives by virtue of its own light."[12] The master assigns a point of view to the eye of the heart that is expressly outside, and above, the world and that permits it to survey the whole:

"Go then, as to a watchtower of the spirit, and direct its vision to the Ark of this world, which is to be seen on all sides, so that the whole world lies before the onlooker, and from there I will show you the whole [*universa*], that you either previously did not see or recognize or, if you did see it, you considered it inappropriate. . . . For the eyes of mortal beings are cast down and they care not for the course of worlds, but fixated upon the most trifling bits of things, they pay slight attention to what is happening in the universe as a whole" (cf. excursus 1, pp. 228f.).[13]

11. Amalarius of Metz, *Liber officialis* IV, 3, 18,in *Amalarii episcopi opera liturgica omnia,* ed. Johannes Michael Hanssens, Studi e Testi (Rome, Vatican City, 1948–50), pp. 138–140, here volume 2, p. 418, on the *Lektio* as hymnic praise of God: "Ibi maiestatem Domini invenimus, quomodo incircumscriptus omnia in se contineat" [There we come upon the majesty of God, in the way he contains—uncircumscribed—all things within himself].

12. Hugh of St.-Victor, *De vanitate mundi,* in *PL,* 176, 704 B: "Habes alium oculum intus multo clariorem isto, qui praeterita, praesentia et futura simul respicit, qui suae visionis lumen et aciem per cuncta diffundit, qui occulta penetrat, subtilia investigat, luce aliena ad videndum non indigens, sed sua ac propria luce prospiciens."

13. *PL,* 176, 704 B, "Constitue igitur te quasi in quadam mentis specula et eius aciem in arcam huius mundi circumquaque lustrandum dirige, ut totus contemplanti coram positus sit mundus, et inde tibi universa demonstrabo, quae prius vel non visa ignorasti, vel visa non quomodo oportuit considerasti." Cf. 711 C: "Sunt enim oculi mortalium depressi, et cursum uni-

The ingathering of past and future into a whole that is visible to our eyes turns the flow of history into a permanent possession by the process of recollection. The history of the world becomes a picture of the world—"contemplanda rerum universitas" [a universe of things to be contemplated][14]—just as water forms itself into a ball, dew becomes a pearl, humidity changes into a jewel. What is mutable acquires form and permanence in an artistic spirit. In the picture of the world, the fullness of ages, spaces, and values has become a cosmos that one eye surveys. The moment of creative vision that—with God and the world—contains eternity achieves permanent form in the work of art, and, in the work of art, the picture of the visible world also achieves permanence.

The fact that the powerful pictures of Hugh of St.-Victor and Adam Scotus have, nevertheless, not been preserved can probably be explained by the fragility of the large, unwieldy parchment formats, for the authors themselves presumably wanted their pictures to be permanent. The smaller pages and formats of Hildegard of Bingen and Joachim of Fiore survived. A picture of the world would have more hope of permanence if it were realized not on parchment but on stone. We hope to show that the Middle Ages also built, as architecture, the pictorial and temporal space of the cosmic *mappa mundi*—from Creation to the end of the world—that it first saw in the Ark.

But, as preparation, we have something further to consider. The Middle Ages were able to survey, as a formal unit in more than one picture, the course of the history of salvation in its individual steps, measured according to the ages and epochs of salvation. The portrayals of the cosmos of the history of salvation, as in Hildegard von Bingen's wheel of the eternal ages with God—"who embraces the whole creation and history of salvation from before the act of creation to after the Last Judgment, including all the time in be-

versorum non respiciunt, atque in exiguis rerum particulis defixi quid agatur in toto non attendunt."

14. Hugh of St.-Victor, *De vanitate mundi*; *PL*, 176, 704 C; Hugh calls the Ark a *mappa mundi* in *De arca Noe mystica* 14, in *PL*, 176, 700 C: "In hoc spatio mappa mundi depingitur ita, ut caput arcae ad orientem convertatur et finis eius occidentem contingat, ut mirabili dispositione ab eodem principio" (Migne; *principe* and Paris ms. B.N. 14506, fol. 28r; *principio* in other manuscripts, e.g., Paris Maz. fol. 7r) "decurrat situs locorum cum ordine temporum et idem sit finis mundi qui est finis saeculi" [In this space a map of the world is painted in colors in such a way that the head of the Ark is turned toward the east and its tail touches upon the west, so that through a wondrous disposition worked by one and the same principle . . . the geographical position coincides with the temporal order and the boundary of the [Western] world is the same as the boundary of the [pagan] age].

tween"[15]—are not painted metaphors or personifications of time. Pictures conceived in a bold spirit represent to the eye, as a finite form, what is, in the human conception, the infinity of time from the Creation to the Last Judgment—the point at which time relapses into eternity: God holds the cosmos of space and time in his hands.[16] Or, revelation makes it possible for man, who is legitimized by the vision inspired by God, to see—as though from a vantage point outside God and the cosmos—the way in which God holds the cosmos of time and space in his hands. Hildegard in her own way, though—if we think of related efforts in the work of Hugh of St.-Victor, Adam Scotus, and Joachim of Fiore in the twelfth century—her way is not an isolated one, has shown us the cosmos of eternity and time in a vision of the wheel of eternity and the ages. She pictorializes this in the *Liber divinorum operum* in the form of a series of colors of the history of salvation which, through the medium of art, she makes into a viewable whole.[17] The representation—in the miniatures inspired by Hildegard which accompany her works—of the process of the history of salvation, as it has been guided by God through the ages and states of grace (creation, law, and grace), by tracts, zones, sectors or series of colors, by figures, things—above all, human forms—but in animals as well, represents a maximum of almost crystalline condensation in the process of making the spiritual visible. There is here such a high degree of abbreviation of the world—this is not abstract, for it always signifies its meaning—that the picture needs explanation in words, and this is true of Hugh of St.-Victor, Adam Scotus, and Joachim of Fiore. The "universal formulas" (Karl Hauck) of medieval art[18] that embrace, time, space, and eternity often require an interpretative context if their visible secrets are to be revealed completely. The miniature is basically to be read in the context of the codex.

We still lack the study of the spiritual signification of spatial dimensions—length, breadth, and height—in the Middle Ages, which would be desirable for our understanding of medieval architecture. Yet, as far as I can see, it is probably almost without exception true that, from the time of the Fathers to the High Middle Ages, the spatial dimension of length would be

15. Christel Meier, "Die Bedeutung der Farben im Werk Hildegards von Bingen," *Frühmittelalterlichen Studien* 6 (1972): 14.

16. Bronder (see n. 10), figs. 34–39.

17. On the "colors of the history of salvation" in the works of Hildegard, Hugh, Adam, and Joachim, which were discovered here for the history of art, cf. Meier, pp. 320–355.

18. The *orbis quadratus* (squared world) that Barbara Bronder treats is also one.

interpreted as length of time, both in architecture and in the allegoresis of the cross, which develops the interpretation of dimension particularly richly. In this connection, it makes no difference whether we choose the tropological aspect—the fundamental signification is then *longanimitas perseverans* (persevering forbearance) or *perdurans* (enduring)—or whether we bring the allegorical aspect into play, where spatial length represents the course of the history of salvation. We can illuminate this last by a few examples.

Just as Hugh of St.-Victor recognizes that the course of the history of salvation from the Creation to the end of the world is established in the length of Noah's Ark, he also sees the upright of the cross as extending from the beginning (alpha) to the end (omega). The Middle Ages often saw the plan of a church—like the Ark or the cross—as a depiction of the body of God, for example, in the works of Rupert of Deutz and Adam Scotus. According to Hugh of St.-Victor, the body of God from the head to the feet signifies the time from before the beginning of the world to a future time after its end;[19] Hildegard von Bingen, too, sees the whole temporal extent of the history of salvation in the human body stretched out from head to feet.[20] Wherever the form of the church was interpreted anthropomorphically,[21] the suggestion was to see it as space-time. Rupert of Deutz sees the *status temporis* (constitution of time) from Adam to Noah in the outer portico of Solomon's palace and temple complex, the area containing the judge's throne, the time from Noah to Abra-

19. Bronder, p. 191 n. 13.

20. Meier, p. 328f. The early Middle High German Song of Songs (ed. Hermann Menhardt [Halle, 1934], 77:23–86:32), ca. 1160, interprets the length of the body of the *sponsus* from the hair to the feet and the length of time to the Last Judgment as divided up according to the seven gifts of the Holy Ghost:

Head and hair	Trinity	wisdom
Eyes	Mary	intellect
Cheeks	Apostles	counsel
Mouth	Martyrs	bravery
Hands	Church fathers	knowledge
Torso	Present church	piety
Legs and feet	Time left till the Antichrist and the Last Judgment	fear

In the works of Hildegard, the strip of girdle which hangs down from the breast to the feet signifies the time "ab exordio mundi . . . usque ad finem saeculorum" [from the beginning of the world . . . up to the end of the ages]. The jewels and colors of the girdle represent the epochs of the history of salvation; *Scivias* III, 9, in *PL*, 197, 688 D–689 A.

21. Then the head of Christ lay in the holy of holies of the Tabernacle or the Temple of Solomon, that is to say, in the choir of the church, so that the passage of time differing from that in the cathedral—which is oriented to the east rather than the west—goes from east to west.

ham in the inner portico, and the period of time from Abraham to Christ in the temple itself.[22] The house that Solomon built for the Queen of Sheba was to make room for the church of the heathens.[23] Rupert reads the divine qualities of Christ in the dimensions of the Temple of Solomon—"et templum illud manufactum templum corporis Dominici significat" [and the temple that was built signifies the temple of the body of the Lord][24]—the height being the majesty, the breadth charity, and the length the "antiquitas. . . . quae per longitudinem . . . intelligitur" [antiquity . . . which is understood through length].[25]

We may mention Sicardus of Cremona's (ca. 1155–1215) work on the liturgy of the church *Mitrale seu de officiis ecclesiasticis* as being representative of a whole number of similar statements about the tropological and anagogical interpretation of dimensions—in this case of the church as a building. The chapter on the allegorical signification of the parts of the church building says: "Longitudo eius langanimitas est quae patienter adversa tolerat, donec ad patriam perveniat; latitudo charitas est quae dilatato sinu mentis amicos in Deo et inimicos diligit propter Deum; altitudo spes est retributionis futurae, quae prospera et adversa contemnit, donec videat bona Domini in terra viventium" [The length is his longanimity, which patiently bears adversity, until it reaches the homeland; the breadth is the charity which—in the expanded bosom of the soul—loves both our friends in God and for the sake of God our enemies too; the height is hope for a future retribution which disdains prosperity as well as adversity, until it sees the good things of God in the land of the living]. In this explanation there is a tacit inclusion of the frequent interpretation of the dimensions as the theological virtues, faith, hope, and charity,[26] just as length is interpreted as perseverance on the long journey to the eternal resting place. We may adduce a few more examples here; just as the wanderings of the Israelites through the desert lead into the promised land, so, in Siena, is the goal reached along the floor of the cathedral right up to the space in front of the altar. The choice of the theme of the wanderings

22. 1 Kings 6, in *PL*, 1157 D–1159 C, cf., on *domus Salomonis*, 1165 A–1157 C.

23. *PL*, 167, 1159 C–1161 A.

24. *PL*, 167, 1156 B; the interpretation of the temple as the body of Christ in extenso in cap. III, 6 (1147 C–1148 A).

25. *PL*, 167, 1153 B.

26. For example, in the early Middle High German poem on the "Heavenly Jerusalem" (vv. 434–443) the length, breadth, and height of the celestial city are interpreted as faith, charity, and hope; Friedrich Maurer, ed. *Die religiösen Dichtungen des 11. und 12. Jahrhunderts*, vol. 2 (Tübingen, 1965), p. 152.

in the desert[27] could also have been inspired by the interpretation of length as "perseverance to the very end in the time of wandering." It makes no difference whether the length of structures like Noah's Ark, the Tabernacle, and Solomon's temple, or of things such as the cross, the Ark of the Covenant, and the table of the Tabernacle, are interpreted as prefigurations of the church, since the understanding of the dimension as such, independent of what it represents, is as good as definite. In a Christianity that views the world and the soul historically, "length" as a spatial metaphor for time predominates in the interpretation of the spatial dimension—length—at every level of spiritual interpretation throughout the Middle Ages.

A sermon of Ivo of Chartres (d. 1116) views the length of the upright of the cross, tropologically, as the "longa et perseverans laborum et persecutionum sustinentia, quam patienter ferre debet ad patriam suspirans nostra peregrinatio" [long and relentless burden of travail and persecutions, which our pilgrimage ought, patiently sighing, to bear to the heavenly homeland].[28] A sermon of Bede's sees the length of the Ark as the period of the wanderings: "quidquid in hac peregrinatione (length) pro Deo geritur, totum hoc in illa mansione patriae perennis (height) . . . sustollitur, in sola dilectionis amplitudine (breadth) perficitur" [whatever during this pilgrimage [length] is borne for the sake of God, all these things, . . . are removed in that habitation of the eternal homeland [height], are perfected in the unadulterated amplitude [breadth] of love alone].[29] And Hrabanus Maurus, adopting Bede's words, says of the length of the Temple of Solomon: "longitudo domus longanimitatem designat ecclesiae, qua in exilio peregrinationis hujus patienter adversa quaque tolerat, donec ad patriam, quam exspectat, perveniat" [it is the length of a house that signifies the longanimity of the church by virtue of which it patiently bears all the adversities enountered in this wandering exile, until it finally arrives in the homeland, the long awaited].[30] Hugh of Folieto took this up in the twelfth century.[31] As early as Gregory the Great's interpretation of Ezekiel's description of the temple, length signifies the long patience exerted in the expectation of the heart burning with the desire for heaven:

27. See below, pp. 178f., 207f., 226.

28. *PL*, 162, 565 B; also under the name of Augustine: *PL*, 39, 2202 A, and *PL*, 40, 1193 A.

29. *PL*, 94, 438 D.

30. *PL*, 111, 398 A, after Bede, in *PL*, 91, 749 A.

31. *De claustro animae* III, 12, in *PL*, 176, 1118 C, on the Temple of Solomon: "longitudo domus est longanimitas boni operis in exsilio huius *peregrinationis*. . . . Sic fit ut moraliter sis in bona operatione longus . . . ita scilicet ut perseverentia duret usque ad ultimum vitae finem" [The length of the house is the longanimity of striving for the good during this wandering exile. . . .

"[Longitudo] longanimitatem exhibet ad exspectandum Deum et patienter portat moras longitudinis. . . . Potest etiam ipsa longitudo longanimitatem patientiae, quae exhibetur proximo, designare" [[Length] represents longanimity to the end of waiting for God and patiently bears the delays of long duration. . . . Length is also itself capable of signifying the longanimity of patience which is shown to one's fellow man].[32] Hrabanus Maurus sees a divine quality in the idea of length as forbearance: "habet longitudinem, quia ad vitae patriam nos longanimiter tolerando perducit" [[God] has length, since He guides us to the heavenly fatherland of life, longanimously tolerant].[33] Maximus of Turin understands the length of the upright of the cross, which the later interpretation of the cruciform church sees as being contained in the nave and the side aisles, as the "perseverandi longanimitas" [longanimity of persevering] in Christ's hanging on the cross, according to Matthew 24:13: "qui perseveraverit usque in finem, hic salvus erit" [whoever perseveres to the end, he shall be saved].[34] The Ark, viewed anagogically, was already seen by Gregory of Elvira (before 360/62) as the *figura crucis,* and for the dimensions he inferred that "quo mysterio et longitudo vitae credentibus datur et latitudo terrae novae tribuitur et altitudo caelestis regni praeparatur" [through this mystery both length of life is given to believers, breadth of the newfound earth is bestowed upon them, and heights of the celestial kingdom are made ready for them].[35] The length of the upright of the cross as length of time is elucidated by Augustine in his commentary on St. John's Gospel: "et significat perseverentiam in longitudine temporis usque ad finem" [and it signifies perseverance in the length of time all the way to the end].[36] And Alcuin and Haimo of Auxerre both adopted the wording of this formula.[37]

Thus, it comes about that one is morally active for the good in the long run . . . so, namely, that perseverance on behalf of the good endures to the very end of life] (cf. 1119 A); for bibliography for *De claustro animae,* see above, pp. 120ff., 135.

32. *PL,* 76, 963 B.

33. *PL,* 112, 423 A.

34. *PL,* 38, 904 D (under the name of Augustine).

35. Gregory of Elvira, *Arca Noe,* ed. André Wilmart, *Révue bénédictine* 26 (1909): 1–12, p. 10, lines 192ff.

36. Corpus christianorum, series latina 36, 657, 10.

37. Alcuin, in *PL,* 100, 983 C; Haimo, in *PL,* 118, 440 C. The Gospel promise in Matthew 24:13, "qui persevaverit usque in finem, hic salvus erit" [whoever perseveres to the end, he shall be saved], was doubtless the background of the usual interpretation of length as *perseverantia.* I am including a number of other examples of the interpretation of length in this sense: Hrabanus Maurus, in *PL,* 122, 424 D; "longitudo itaque perseverentiam boni operis significat" [and so length signifies the perseverance of good works]. Augustine, in *PL,* 34, 64: (Christ) "persever-

The signification of the three spatial dimensions as time, space, and value speaks loud and clear in the works of Hugh of St.-Victor, where he relates them to the dimensions of the spiritual sense of the Bible: "In his tribus dimensionibus omnis divina scriptura continetur. Historia enim longitudinem arcae metitur, quia in serie rerum gestarum ordo temporis invenitur. Allegoria latitudinem arcae metitur, quia in participatione sacramentorum constat collectio populorum fidelium. Tropologia altitudinem arcae metitur, quia in profectu virtutum crescit dignitas meritorum" [In these three dimensions all of divine Scripture is contained. For history measures the length of the Ark, inasmuch as in a series of deeds the *temporal order* is disclosed. Allegory measures the breadth of the Ark, inasmuch as through participating in the sacraments the *assembly of peoples* of faith is constituted. Tropology measures the altitude of the Ark, inasmuch as with the increase of the virtues the dignity attached to their merits grows].[38]

---

anter inhaerere" [to cleave to with perseverance]. Thiofried of Echternach, in *PL*, 157, 338 C: "perseverantia usque in finem" [perseverance to the end]. Rupert of Deutz, in *PL*, 169, 787 B, and *PL*, 170, 159 D: "perseverantia." Bede, in *PL*, 91, 407, on the table of the tabernacle: "perseverantia nobis coeptae religionis" [perseverance in [our] religious undertakings]. Hugh of St.-Victor, in *PL*, 176, 634 D: "perseverare usque in finem." Honorius Augustodunensis, in *PL*, 192, 193 A, on hanging on the cross: "ipsa statio perseverentiam significat" [the station itself suggests endurance]. Hildebert von Lavardin, in *PL*, 171, 685 C: "perseverantia bonorum operum." Somewhat less frequently than *perseverantia* we find that length stands for *longanimitas* or *patientia.* Augustine, *Epistolae* 140, 25; Corpus scriptorum ecclesiasticorum latinorum 44/3, 208, on the cross: "Nunc longanimitate adversa tolerat et in eo quod veraciter tenuit perseverat—et haec longitudo est" [Now with longanimity it endures adversities and in that which it truly has accepted it perseveres—and this ["it"] is length]; cf. pp. 175f. On standing on the cross: "ibi enim quodam modo statur, id est persistitur et perseveratur, quod longanimitati tribuitur" [there is, indeed, in a certain way a question of standing, that is, of something being persisted in and persevered in, and of this "standing" being assigned to longanimity]. Bede, in *PL*, 91, 401 C on the length of the Ark of the Covenant: "longanimam Domini ac Redemptoris nostri patientiam, qua inter homines conversatus est, insinuat [longitudo]" [[length] implies the longanimous patience of our Lord and Redeemer, with which he conversed among human beings]. Bede, in *PL*, 91, 88 A, on the length of the Ark: "patientia, qua fortiter adversa tolerantur" [patience, through which adversities are bravely endured]. Bede, in *PL*, 91, 793 A: "patientia longanimitatis" [the patience of longanimity]. Bede, in *PL*, 91, 401 D: "humanae tarditas fragilitatis" [the sluggishness of human fragility]. Eugippius, in *PL*, 62, 892 C: "longanimiter . . . molestiae tolerentur" [longanimously . . . vexations are tolerated]. The word used least often is *perdurare* (to hold out). In the works of Bede, the length of the Ark refers to the cross beneath which the church "invicta et stabilis inter adversa perdurat" [invincible and enduring holds out among adversities] (*PL*, 91, 88 B). Bede, in *PL*, 92, 616 A, on the cross: "In longitudine . . . persistere, hoc est longanimiter permunere" [In length . . . to persist, this is what it means to abide longanimously].

38. *PL*, 176, 678 D. Hugh seems to be thinking of a circular temple as time-space in his inter-

There are only a few instances where length goes beyond temporality and signifies eternity; these are in Bernard of Clairvaux,[39] Gerloh von Reichersberg, and Hildegard von Bingen.[40]

In the world of dimensions, love, as one of the theological virtues, has for centuries encompassed only the dimension of width as the *amplitudo chari-*

---

pretation of Isaiah 6:1: "vidi Dominum sedentem supra solium excelsum et elevatum, et ea, quae sub ipso erant, replebant templum" [I saw the Lord sitting upon a throne, raised up and elevated on high, and those things that were under him, were filling the temple] (*PL*, 176, 623 BC); "Templum in hoc loco intelligi potest circuitus temporum et ambitus saeculorum. Tempora namque dum cursu suo in seipsa redeunt, quasi quemdam templi ambitum gyrando circumscribunt. Quid ergo dicit: Ea, quae sub ipso erant, replebant templum, sic intelligendum est, quod omnia saeculorum tempora plena sunt operibus Dei, et omnis generatio narrat mirabilia eius" [The temple in this passage can be understood as the cycle of times and the orbit of the ages; the times, namely, insofar as they return to themselves in due course, as they complete their passage around the circumference of the temple. What he goes on to say, therefore—"those things that were under him, were filling the temple"—is to be understood thus: that all the times of all the ages are filled with the works of the Lord, and every generation tells of his wonders] (*PL*, 176, 623 BC). The same thing is found in Alanus, *De sex alis Cherubim*, in *PL*, 210, 269 D; cf. Bertha Widmer, *Heilsordnung und Zeitgeschehen in der Mystik Hildegards von Bingen*, Basler Beiträge zur Geisteswissenschaft, no. 52 (Basel, 1955), pp. 106, 122f.

Hugh's interpretation of the circular church as a temporal circle contradicts the usual interpretation of the circular church which was prevalent in the Middle Ages from the time of Honorius, when it was viewed as a spatial terrestial globe, as in the works of Sicardus 1.4, in *PL*, 213, 19 D: "quae fiunt in modum circuli, ecclesiam dilatam per circulum orbis significant, unde in fines orbis terrae verba eorum" (Psalm 18:5), "vel quod de circulo orbis perveniamus ad circulum coronae aeternitatis" [things that are made in the fashion of a circle signify the church spread abroad throughout the circular globe, whence "to the ends of the globe of the world their words" . . . or that from the circle of this world we will arrive at the circle of the crown of eternity]; further examples in Joseph Sauer, *Symbolik des Kirchengebäudes und seiner Ausstattung in der Auffassung des Mittelalters*, 2d ed. (Freiburg, 1924; reprint, Münster, 1964), p. 110.

39. *Epistolae* 18.3, in *PL*, 182, 121, on Ephesians 3:18: "longitudo . . . hoc est aeternitas" [length . . . this is eternity]; cf. Gerhoh von Reichersberg, in *PL*, 194, 963 C, on God: "cujus latitudo charitas, longitudo aeternitas" [whose width is charity, length eternity]; on the dimensions of love, John of Ford (d. 1214), *Super extremam partem Cantici canticorum sermones, CXX*, edited by Edmundus Mikkers and Hilarius Costello, Corpus christianorum, series latina, continuatio medievalis 17/18 (Turnhout, 1970), sermo 26, pp. 112–161; 82, pp. 80–103. On the dimension of love, Friedrich Ohly, "Gottes Ehrfurchten—ein ordo caritatis," *Euphorion* 55 (1961): 113–145, 405–448 (see also n. 135), pp. 121, 145.

40. *PL*, 197, 1045 B, on Ephesians 3:18: "Per longitudinem istam divina essentia, quae sine fine et initio est, intelligitur; quoniam ipsa ab opere suo, quod initium habet, in nulla ascensione ullius scientiae comprehendi potest" [What is understood by this length is the divine essence, which is without end and without beginning; since it [the divine essence] cannot be understood from his work, which does have a beginning, neither can it be comprehended within the progression of any branch of knowledge]. Width is God's *potestas* (power), height his *claritas* (clar-

tatis. It is not until the twelfth century—in an echo of Augustine—that the world as a whole becomes a space of love whose extents are love alone. They are visible on the cross as the length and breadth, the height and depth of love, by means of which "love also has length, breadth, and height in us."[41] What appears on the cross is "the length of love which must endure to the end."[42]

The interpretation, in the High Middle Ages, of the length and breadth of the church as worldly time and space and its height as the world of the saints does not surprise us at all. It is set out in the church fathers in the interpretation of a biblical structure that has always been seen as the prefiguration of the church. The *forma, figura,* or *imago ecclesiae* was repeatedly seen in Noah's Ark, from the time of Tertullian and Origen,[43] and Origen paved the way for the understanding of its dimensions, breadth, length, and height as time and place and everlasting holiness, something that later writers were able to consolidate into a firm tradition. Augustine recognizes the Ark as *orbis terrarum,* its length as time stretching out from the beginning of the world ("sicut sex aetatibus omne hujus saeculi tempus extenditur"), its height as the gathering of those who have departed this life for union with Christ.[44] Isidor of Seville and Hrabanus Maurus took over Augustine's actual words in interpreting the length of the Ark as the six ages of the world: Christ's teachings were not confined to one single age; they were proclaimed in five ages by the prophets and disseminated in the sixth by the gospels.[45] Later Bruno of Segni

---

ity). The three dimensions fight in unison against the *abyssus aquilonis.* Gerhoh on Psalm 144:2, in *PL,* 194, 963 C: "Cujus [God's] latitudo charitas, longitudo aeternitas, altitudo vel sublimitas potentia insuperbilis, profundum sapientia inscrutabilis" [Whose [God's] breadth is charity, length is eternity, height or sublimity is insuperable power, depth is unfathomable wisdom].

41. Petrus Lombardus, in *PL,* 192, 194 B.

42. *PL,* 192, 194 B; with reference to the words of our Lord, John 13:1, "cum dilixisset suos, usque in finem dilexit," Bernard of Clairvaux talks of the soul's extension of itself so that it can grasp length, breadth, height, and depth (after Ephesians 3:18), and he goes on, "these four dimensions of God can be embraced by our two arms, namely, true love and true fear [*vero scilicet amore at vero timore*]; of fear, height and depth, that is, power and wisdom; of love [*amor*] breadth and length, that is, love [*caritas*] and truth"; *Sermones de diversis,* no. 117, in *PL,* 183, 741f.

43. Hartmut Boblitz, "Die Allegorese der Arche Noahs in der frühen Bibelauslegung," *Frühmittelalterliche Studien* 6 (1972): 159–170, pp. 163ff.; "Arca figura ecclesiae."

44. *Contra Faustum* 12.14, in Corpus scriptorum ecclesiasticorum latinorum 25/1, 344. Hartmut Boblitz, pp. 167ff., on the Ark as "structura ecclesiae."

45. Isidor, *In Genesin* 7.5, in *PL,* 83, 230 AB, 232 B. The building of the Ark in the sixth age corresponds to the building of the Ark in the sixth century of Noah's life; Hrabanus Maurus, *In Genesin* 6, in *PL,* 107, 515 D. The breadth signifies here, as so often, the "amplitudo caritatis" [breadth of love] after the opening up of the heart to love by Pentecost (515 D). The sixty-ell length of the Temple of Solomon is interpreted in one of Bede's sermons as the perfection of God's six-day

(canon in Siena until 1079, d. 1123) again renewed the thought: "Trecentorum vero cubitorum est longitudo arcae, quia a principio primae aetatis usque ad ultimae aetatis finem Ecclesiae extenditur longitudo. . . . Tanta est igitur Ecclesiae longitudo, quanta est hujus vitae dimensio" [The length of the Ark is three hundred cubits, since the length of the church is extended from the beginning of the first age until the end of the last age. . . . The length of the church is thus as great as the extent of this life, "the length of life on earth"]. The significations of the length and breadth of the church, for which the foundations are laid in the Ark, are derived from the signification of the numbers contained in God's statements about the dimensions of the Ark (300 × 50 × 30 ells): "Haec sunt enim maximae et principales causae, quibus Ecclesiae longitudo et latitudo crescit at dilatatur" (These are indeed the greatest and principal causes, through which the length and the breadth of the church extend and expand). The length of three hundred ells provides fifty ells for each age, so that the breadth of the church—fifty—corresponds exactly to the length of an age ("ut unicuique aetati aequalis inveniatur"). Thus, the length of each of the six ages of the world fills out the breadth of the entire world: "Tanta enim est Ecclesiae latitudo, quantum est spatium mundi" [The breadth of the church is indeed as great as the space occupied by the world].[46] A few years after the death of Bruno of Segni, Hugh of St.-Victor in *De arca*

---

work of creation: "et sex sunt huius saeculi aetates, in quibus sancta ecclesia pro aeterna requie piis actibus instat" [and six are the ages of this milennium, in which the Holy church earnestly demands pious deeds for the sake of eternal restfulness] (*PL*, 94, 437 C).

46. Bruno of Segni, *In Genesin* 8, in *PL*, 164, 178 D–179 C. In the allegoresis of the cross, too, the upright has repeatedly been understood as time, and the crosspiece as space. There is a wealth of citations on the interpretation of the dimensions of the cross in Hartmut Freytag, "Kommentar zur frühmittelhochdeutschen *Summa Theologia*," *Medium Aevum* 19 (1970): 104f. and 110–115.

The idea that the church stands in all parts of the earth, and for all time, and that it covers all the parts of the world beyond the Roman Empire, already leads Augustine to the idea of the "orbis terrarum aedificatus" [the orb of the world as a building]. The flexibility of such transitions in the idea makes palpable, for example, an interpretation of Psalm 92:1, 5; "Domum tuam decet sanctificatio, Domine. Domum tuam, totam domum tuam: non hic, aut hic, aut ibi, sed domum tuam totam per totum orbem terrarum. Quare per totum orbem terrarum? Quia correxit orbem terrae qui non commovebitur. Domus Domini fortis erit; per totum orbem terrarum erit: multi cadent, sed domus illa stat; multi turbabuntur, sed domus illa non movebitur. Domum tuam decet sanctificatio, Domine. Numquid parvo tempore? Absit. In longitudine dierum" [Sanctification befits your house, Lord. Your house, your whole house: not here, nor here, nor there, but your whole house throughout the whole orb of the world. Why throughout the whole orb of the world? Because the one who conferred order upon it is the one who will not be moved. The house of the Lord will be strong; throughout the whole orb of the world it will be [strong]: many fall,

Noe mystica developed, in the greatest detail and in truly magnificent fashion, the idea of the Ark-church as a representation of the time and space of the world.[47] From Origen to Augustine to the High Middle Ages the Ark, a *figura ecclesiae,* was known to be interpreted as a building that embraced the time, and often the space, of the world in its length and breadth,[48] so that we should not be surprised if the church as a building showed traces of a representation of this thought, especially as the history of the interpretation of the Tabernacle and the Temple of Solomon—certainly more important prefigurations of the church than the Ark—could obviously lend strong support to the amount of evidence, which could easily be multiplied.

What historiography, as a literary *mappa mundi,* a history of the world in the chronicle genre, offered as reading material, artistic spirits of the twelfth century like Hugh, Hildegard, Adam, and Joachim presented visually in representations where word and picture could not be interchanged. It would be surprising if architecture—after word and picture had already mastered the prefigurations of the church as pictures of the world—were to remain unaffected by these visible worlds of thought, and were not to have participated—using its own means—in developing them in the succeeding century. Here we have to take into account nothing more than that certain time lag that emerges in the series *word-picture-building,* where we find differing degrees of resistance offered by the materials used to form an intellectual movement that creates a unified style when the conception is turned into communicated reality. The preservation of the idea on parchment needs the materials of writing. Even the communication of the *mappa mundi,* which has become a subject for meditation, occurs—if the colors and parchment surface have been made ready—with a certain ease as the production of the image of an idea that has already been created. The realization of the spiritual conception of a cathedral whose pillars go as deep into the earth as they rise high into the air,[49] calls for immense resources, the participation of

but that house stands; many are thrown into confusion, but that house will not be moved. Sanctification befits your house, Lord. For just a little while? Perish the thought. Rather, for the length of days] (*PL,* 37, 1189); commentary in Dominique Sanchis, "Le symbolisme communautaire du temple chez St. Augustin," *Revue d'ascétique et de mystique* 37 (1961): 3–30, 137–147 (the section "Domus Dei per omnem orbem terrarum").

47. Joachim Ehlers, "Arca significat ecclesiam: Ein theologisches Weltbild aus der ersten Hälfte des 12. Jahrhunderts," *Frühmittelhochdeutsche Studien* 6 (1972): 171–187.

48. Further evidence in Hugh of St.-Victor's *De vanitate mundi;* see below, pp. 210ff.

49. In the case of Cologne Cathedral it is possible to descend into the depths and see the abysses into which the bases of the pillars, underground towers of endless masses of stone, are sunk.

all the arts, a will to participate in a creatively changing intercourse with the most unyielding materials, extending over many human lifetimes, and the active patience of generations.

II. The Cathedral of Siena as Temporal Space

The leap in time that occurred when the Son of God was born represents the midpoint of the history of salvation, the point where antiquity changes into modernity. The church, as a building, stands on our side of the center of the story of salvation that appears in Christ and takes a point of view of historical consciousness, from which antiquity has already disappeared. From this vantage point, the Christian present and the promised future can—thanks to the new revelation—all be surveyed in a unified spiritual perception. This view of the whole time that lies between the origin in the Creation and the end in the Day of Judgment, with its center in Christ, acquired its total form in the Middle Ages in different arts and can also be seen, in the architecture of the period, as space of time. The creative conception of revealing to the eye, in the space of a building, the whole of the history of salvation was realized in different ways by different artistic means.

When an image of the Heavenly Jerusalem can be seen in parts of a cathedral, one aspect of many different possibilities of the depiction of the history of salvation as temporal space of time has been touched upon. Its splendor consists in the linguistic muteness of its artistic means, whose peculiar language is to be understood if seeing eyes are not to be blind. If we are permitted to see into different structural parts of a cathedral and recognize the Heavenly Jerusalem, the possibility that other prefigurations of the church may be recognized in other significant parts of the cathedral is not ruled out. By participating in the Heavenly Jerusalem, the cathedral stands for the eschatological and anagogical dimension of the history of salvation as a promise of a future in heaven. At the same time, we recognize that other spiritual dimensions of the time have been incorporated in the church as representational models, the exemplary character of which does not lie in an architectonic anticipation of the future, but lies more in a sense of projecting the past into the present. Even prefigurations of the church from the Old Testament entered the present as the enhanced architectural fulfillment of objective prophecies of the Old Testament. If the cathedral signifies, in a few of its characteristics, the Heavenly Jerusalem, it can, in other characteristics, always using an accentuation that signalizes their presence, imitate the Ark, the Tabernacle, the temple seen by Ezekiel in a vision, or the Temple of Solomon. The way to recognize this fully will be prepared only when more account than has been the case up to the present is taken by art history of the Christian exegesis of the buildings erected, according to God's will and his plan, in the Old Testament. There are dozens of patristic and medieval commentaries on the Old Testament descriptions of the Ark, the Tabernacle, Ezekiel's temple vision, and the Temple of Solomon, which the world of Christian faith has so read into the buildings of the Old Testament that the sum of the old and the new, of Jewish buildings or architectural visions and their Christian interpretation, results in a third, higher, factor which one would like to call the cathedral. If we disregard the New Jerusalem of the Apocalypse, which is not thought of as an earthly place of worship, the New Testament has produced no model for the form of the cathedral. If it could be shown that, like the Heavenly Jerusalem, the Tabernacle in the desert, and the Temple of Jerusalem, had also entered the cathedral in essentials which were currently obvious, we could see, in its architectonic form, a picture of the history of salvation of the Old and New Testament and the anagogical promise of what is to come. The architectonic space of the church, as a given, would offer the hermeneutic evidence of its interpretation of space as time, which would incorporate within itself the origin of the church in the Old Testament, its present in Christ, in the middle, and its future in the promised New Jerusalem, as a total, unified form. The church building would be a tangibly architectonic body—with limbs of different substance according to their origin in the history of salvation—which would offer points of departure for its interpretation in all the dimensions of a spiritual significance. As a space of time, combining within itself the Ark, the Tabernacle, the temple, the church, and the Heavenly Jerusalem, it would be an eloquent architectonic image of the history of salvation simply through its distinctive forms, which would follow in biblical steps, just as elsewhere, the Chronicles—in literature—and the painted picture of the world are an eloquent architectonic history of this secular world.[50] In principle, the forms that derive from different periods of

50. This is not to say that the points of departure for a spiritual transparency of the church building would have to lie separately in the architectonic space, according to the allegorical and anagogical dimensions of signification, as, for example, architectural metaphorics could suggest for the fourfold meaning of the written word, according to which the foundations would designate the historical, the walls the allegorical, the roof the anagogical, and the wall paintings the tropological dimensions of designation. Such a division of the periods of the history of salvation into the temporal space of the cathedral may suggest itself and even derive from itself, insofar as the place of the specifically Christian present of the church is not at any point in the building so pregnantly condensed as it is at the altar, which is the liturgical and sacramental centerpoint of

the history of salvation can prevail to such an extent that new forms are established in which the sum of the periods becomes the fulness of time. If we are able—by means of our understanding of its form through the history of salvation—to recognize a temporal space in the church building in which all periods of time and grace in the history of salvation unite in one order of meaning, so that the law also finds an architectonic solution in grace, then the cathedral is to be understood as being built as a temporal space in which the ages unite to form an image of the whole period of world history, which centers on Christ and lies between the Creation and the end of the world. The language of forms which points to this contains—as a mute language—something arcane, which does not reveal itself to us and remains, therefore, hard to comprehend.

We could try to show that the temporal status of the history of salvation under the law which lasted from Moses to Christ is incorporated in the cathedral by trying to show essential elements of the Tabernacle that was built by Moses according to God's plans and directions. But let us defer that, and let us pursue a methodologically different, and simpler, way of achieving it that is more certainly suited to proving convincingly that a cathedral is built as a temporal space. The pictorial representation of historical happenings speaks more clearly of the progression of time than does architectural form that does not interpret itself. An overall cyclical program of the pictorial appointments of a cathedral can, by using means other than mere forms, do much more to make evident the vision of that age of the world that is actualized in the building than the possibility that we have already taken into consideration of rediscovering Old Testament forms and architectural ideas can. In this case that means ones commanded by or revealed by God in the Christian church. A cathedral's pictorial program that creates a space devoted to the periods of the history of salvation can be seen here in the Cathedral of Siena in Tuscany, a powerful building of imposing size which towers above the city and casts its brilliance far and wide. If we bear in mind that medieval exegesis of the Temple of Solomon relied not only on the Old Testament but also on the description of the temple in Josephus's *Jewish War,* we may recall, as we look at the Cathedral of Siena from the distance, Josephus's words about the distant prospect of the Temple of Solomon: "Truly it looked like a snow-covered mountaintop to the stranger approaching Jerusalem, for where it had not

---

the church. On the building metaphor for the dimensions of the *sensus spiritualis,* Hans-Jörg Spitz, *Die Metaphorik des geistigen Schriftsinns: Ein Beitrag zur allegorischen Auslegung des ersten christlichen Jahrhunderts,* Münstersche Mittelalterschriften, no. 12 (Munich, 1972), pp. 205–218.

been gilded it was dazzlingly white."[51] In Siena—as opposed to the almost completely gilded facade of the cathedral in Orvieto, which was modeled on the Temple of Solomon—only the three tympana of the facade were gilded.

The Cathedral at Siena is dedicated to the Virgin Mary. The plastic pictorial program of the cathedral's facade (fig. 21) acts as the multivoice prophecy of the Virgin: "The facade of the cathedral at Siena is the first in Italy to have every part of it filled by sculpture and, at the same time, to elevate architectural sculpture to the position of one of the most important elements of architectonic creation."[52] The lowest zone shows animals: horse and ox, griffin and lion. The first story is for the prophets of Mary, from Jewry and classical antiquity. The main facade has the plastic figures of David and

51. Flavius Josephus, *De bello Judaico,* ed. Otto Michel and Otto Bauernfeind, vol. II/1 (Darmstadt, 1963), p. 141 (bk. V, 223). On the subject of the snow-white marble from which the temple was constructed and its origin in the Cyclades cf. Bede's interpretation of the Templum Salomonis where he refers extensively to the Old Testament and to Josephus (*PL,* 91, 746 D–746 A). He relies on Josephus's *Jewish Antiquities* (VIII, 3, 2): "Up to the height of the ceiling, the structure was built of white marble, to a height of sixty ells, a length of sixty ells, and a width of twenty ells"; *Des Flavius Jospehus Jüdische Altertümer,* trans. Heinrich Clementz, vol. 1 (Halle, 1899), p. 478. Archaeologists say that the temple was built of indigenous limestone mainly from the so-called Quarry of Solomon. The "meleki" [royal] limestone that is found there, "so called 'because of its sheen and its versatility,' is a grainy white marble that was frequently used later (in Mamre) for capitals, pillars and bases." "Perhaps the stones needed for the construction of the temple and for the other buildings of the citadel were quarried in the great quarries near the Damascus Gate in the old city. That is where the *meleki* limestone is found"; Th. A. Busink, *Der Tempel von Jerusalem von Salomo bis Herodes: Eine archäologisch-historische Studie unter Berücksichtigung des westsemitischen Tempelbaus,* vol. 1, *Der Tempel Salomos* (Leyden, 1970), pp. 219ff.

52. Harald Keller, "Die Bauplastik des Sieneser Doms: Studien zu Giovani Pisano und seiner künstlerischen Nachfolge," *Kunstgeschichtliches Jahrbuch der Bibliotheca Hertziana* 1 (1937): 138–220, p. 148; in addition, Ulrich Middeldorf, *Art Bulletin* 20 (1938): 327ff. Also on the facade, Ludwig Justi, "Giovanni Pisano" (1903), in *Im Dienste der Kunst* (Breslau, 1936): 37–65, pp. 44–52; W. R. Valentiner, "Observations on Sienese and Pisan Trecento Sculpture," *Art Bulletin* 9 (1926): 177–220, pp. 177f.; Renate Rieger, "Siene und Ruvo: Ein Beitrag zur Baugeschichte der beiden Dome," in *Festschrift für Anselm Weissenhofer* (Vienna, 1954), pp. 97–111, pp. 99–102; Wolfgang Braunfels, *Mittelalterliche Stadtbaukunst in der Toskana* (Berlin, 1953), pp. 167ff. (the meaning of the church facade), 155ff. (the cathedral and city palace in Siena), pp. 230ff. (Giovanni Pisano); John Pope-Hennessy, "New Works by Giovanni Pisano I," *Burlington Magazine* 105 (1963): 529–533: the bust of the Prophet Haggai on the cathedral facade; Anna Rosa Garzelli, "Problemi di scultura gotica senese," *Critica d'arte* 13 (1966), fasc. 78, pp. 17–26; fasc. 79, pp. 17–28; 14 (1967), fasc. 89, pp. 22–37; 15 (1968), fasc. 94, pp. 55–65. "Scultura del trecento a Siena e fuori Siena"; on Pisano's sibyl on the facade, Angelina Rossi, "Le Sibille nelle arti figurative italiane, *L'Arte* 18 (1915): 209–221, 272–285, 427–458, pp. 273ff.; Michael Ayrton, *Giovanni Pisano, Sculptor* (Frankfurt am Main, 1970), pp. 103ff.; Max Seidel, "Die Rankensäulen der Sieneser Domfassade," *Jahrbuch der Berliner Museen* 11 (1969): 81–160.

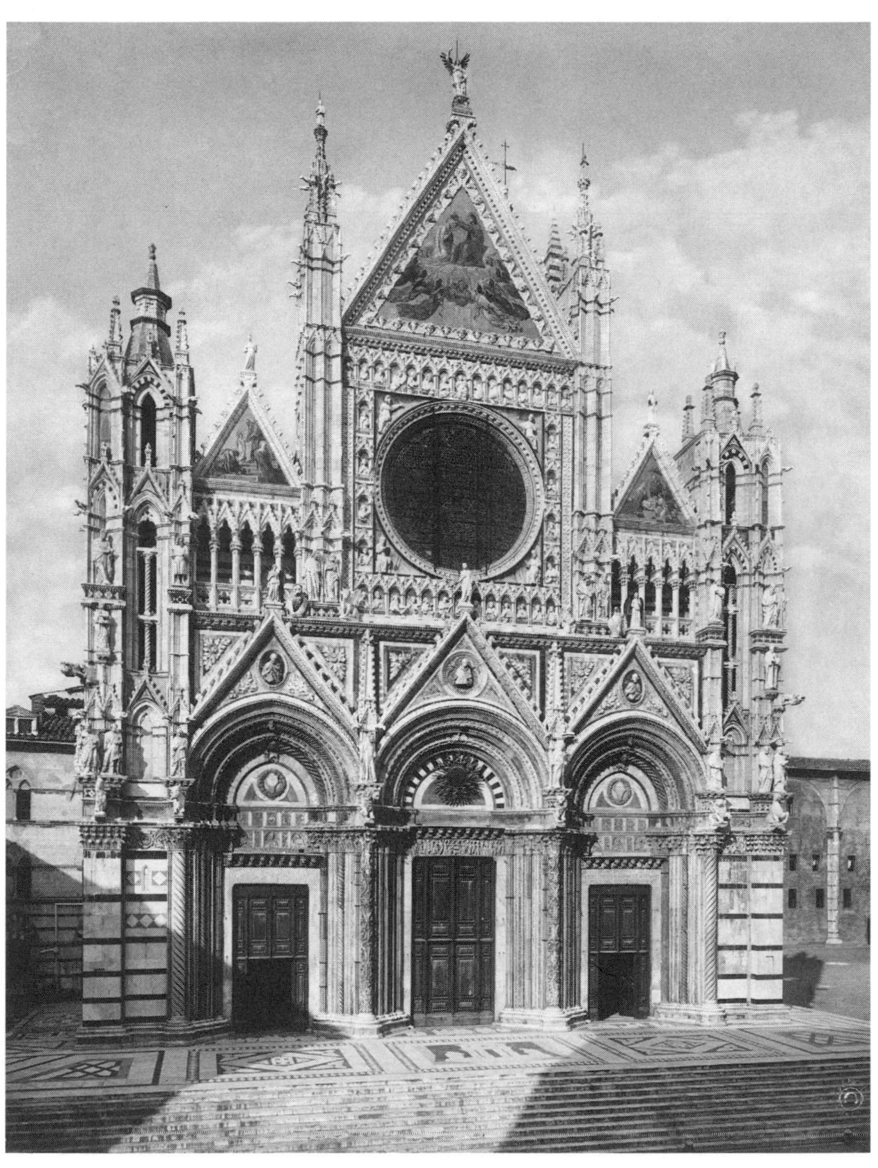

FIGURE 21
Facade of Siena Cathedral. (Photograph: Exterior. Duomo, Siena, Italy. Copyright Alinari/Art Resource, New York.)

Solomon in the center: Daniel and a sibyl are on David's right, with Plato on the outside; Moses and Joshua are on Solomon's left, with Habakkuk on the outside. Haggai, Isaiah, and Balaam are on the north side behind Plato, and, on the south, Simeon, Mary (Moses's sister), and Aristotle are next to Habakkuk. The images of the animals on the bottom, with the prophets and sibyls above them, represent the prehistory of the proclamation of the Virgin by the dumb animals and the mouths of the prophets and philosophers from the Jewish and pagan world. The mariological prophecies of the Old Testament are familiar to Christianity. The scrolls in the hands of Balaam, the sibyl, Plato, and Aristotle, which contain the text of their prophecy, make clear—just as they do in the hands of all the other figures—that they had proclaimed Mary in advance and owe their place on the facade of the Cathedral of the Virgin to this fact.[53] Thirty-five busts of Mary's genealogical ancestors, encircling the great rose window, stand on the upper story of the facade. The plastic pictorial program is completed in the middle above the rose window by the figure of Mary, holding the Christ child in her arms, standing between two apostles who are turned toward her. The design of the facade is by Giovanni Pisano, who was responsible for its erection from the year 1287 onward, but who did not survive to see its completion. It was never finished as he intended it should be. Not until after his death (ca. 1320) were the evangelists, some apostles, and the four patron saints of Siena added. If we disregard St. Michael, the protector of the church, on the highest triangular gable above the rose window,[54] the program draws our attention to Mary and those who are standing nearest to her. The lintel above the main portal shows reliefs with scenes from Mary's youth. However, what was done later, in the

53. The text of Aristotle's scroll is "Indefexa datura Dei nativitatis non habens principium et exitum verum potentissimum substantialis verbi" [Unwearied bearer of the nativity of God, having no beginning nor end but rather more puissant than any other of the substance of the word]; of Plato's, "Ex matre puella immaculatissime virginis debes ad . . . dei solum fecit" [Of a maiden mother, a most immaculate virgin, thou shalt be . . . the sole [son] of God he made]; of Balaam's, "Orietur stella ex Jacob" [A star will arise out of Jacob] (Numbers 24:17); and of the sibyl's, "Et vocabitur Deus et homo" [And he will be called God and man]. Keller, p. 157, was unable to find the sources of the nonbiblical texts and could not completely resolve them.

54. On St. Michael on the west fronts of the church, see Jürgen Fischer, *Oriens-Occidens-Europa: Begriff und Gedanke 'Europa' in der späten Antike und im frühen Mittelalter,* Veröffentlichungen des Instituts für Europäische Geschichte, Mainz, no. 15 (Wiesbaden, 1957), pp. 67ff.: "Michael is protection against the Occident in the western towers. But the Occident is not only that western area of demons; it is ruin pure and simple; it is the *populus infidelium* in every form; it is unbelief and heathenism," p. 70.

fourteenth century, could fit in with Pisano's conception.[55] From bottom to top there is an ascent from the prophetic annunciation by dumb creatures, Jewry, and classical antiquity, through the generations of Mary's ancestors, to the Mother of God as the termination of these periods. The facade, as the outside of the church, leads up to its beginning in the birth of Christ from Mary. It traverses the prophetic prehistory of the church, among the Jews and the pagans, as the external space in front of its outer door. This space belongs to it and is drawn into it in what is anything but a purely decorative facade. It is the elevated anteroom of pre-Christian times, which the upward-directed eye of the observer traverses before he enters the realm of the Christian age.

The vertical, as a dimension of the succession of ages, is known to us from the typological cycle, insofar as this cycle lets the old support the new. The horizontal, as a dimension of extended time, is less frequent in art history.[56] In his interpretation of the relationship of Noah's Ark to the church,

55. Keller, p. 157: "The Sienese facade keeps strictly to themes of the High Middle Ages. The whole of creation that has foretold the coming of the Mother of God is gathered here—no matter whether human being or animal, Jew or heathen. In the impost zone, there are six representations of four different animals that symbolize individual characteristics of Christ. The prophets from God's chosen people and the heathens, who have spoken of the birth of God's mother, then follow in the first story. They are joined in the upper zone by the apostles, their sons, who have gathered, from all parts of the world, to be round them on their deathbeds. They are finally joined by the patron saints of Siena."

56. Werner Hager says of church building in Italy in the sixteenth century: "And since the axis (= the long axis of the nave and the side aisles) contains a hiatus, space is addressed in its relationship to time" (*Religion in Geschichte und Gegenwart,* 3d ed., vol. 3 [Tübingen, 1959], col. 1374).

Gunther Bandmann, "Früh- und hochmittelalterliche Altaranordnung als Darstellung," in *Das erste Jahrtausend: Kultur und Kunst im werdenden Abendland an Rhein und Ruhr,* vol. 1, ed. Viktor H. Elbern (Düsseldorf, 1962), pp. 371–411, explains, "the multiplication of altars in the medieval church, as (being) a result of older commemorative, allegorical, and representative intentions" (p. 380). He points to the fact that in Centula, the cruciform altars that are erected at all four points of the compass also represent a temporal succession of events, when an altar of the Nativity is set up in the west, an altar of the Passion in the center, an altar of the Resurrection in the north, and an altar of the Ascension in the south (p. 377); on p. 380, he talks of "commemorative stations in the life of Christ"; cf. p. 377 n. 37: "Unfortunately, to the best of my knowledge, there is no research that considers the question of whether the stations which are established in the church edifice were also present in the prayers of the canonical hours." The edifices, which were often cruciform in shape and united "in one ecclesiastical family were formed into a unit by the so-called stational divine service" (p. 383f.). Bandmann also sees an architectural representation of time in the ordering of important altars on the central axis from west to east. For example, from John the Baptist across the lay altar, in the center, to the main altar, in the east, and the apsidal picture with its suggestions of the parousia, if this is so, then the main stations, both

Hugh of St.-Victor represented the length of the church—which is prefigured by the Ark—theologically as the historical dimension of salvation, and pictorially as a clear succession of historical ages (cf. above, pp. 140–142). Thus, it is not surprising that we can read the same thing into the cathedral space. The most magnificent example is offered by the pavement of the cathedral in Siena. It starts in the forecourt under the facade. And, as we walk through the portal, the mighty expanse of parti-colored marble pavement stretches out before us like a brilliant sea flowing into the great space. After its completion in the sixteenth century, Vasari praised it as the most beautiful, greatest, and most magnificent pavement that had ever been created (figs. 22, 23, 24).[57]

The cathedral is faced from pavement to vault with marble both inside and out (figs. 21–28; see also figs. 1–3). The covering of the cathedral with marble, which gives it an incomparably different appearance from the cathedrals of France, is not characteristically Italian and is justified only in those areas where there is ample marble available. The reason for the treatment is theological, because it is based on the Bible and on the imagistic character of the space within the church. The Heavenly Jerusalem knows nothing of marble, but the Temple of Solomon does. David leaves his son gold and silver, brass and iron, wood and stones of all sorts, precious stones in all colors "et marmor Parium abundantissime" [and Parian marble in the greatest abundance] for the building of the temple (1 Chronicles 29:2). It is an old tradition of the church that this marble served Solomon for the walls of the temple. The Bible says of Huram, the architect of the temple, that he knew how to use marble as well as other materials (2 Chronicles 2:14). But the Old Testament says of the pavement of the temple in Jerusalem: "stravit quoque pavimentum templi pretiossimo marmore decore multo" [but the pavement of the temple he covered most decoratively with the most precious marble] (1 Chronicles 3:6). We see and set foot upon this marble pavement—which introduces the old era into the church—when we cross the threshold of the cathedral in Siena. Made of the most precious marble, it forms the gigantic area *decore multo* as a great work of art.[58] It consists of inlay work of marble,

---

of the life of Christ (baptism, crucifixion, resurrection, parousia) and of the life of the Christian (baptism in the west, burial at the high altar, purgatory, and second coming of Christ and resurrection) were represented.

57. In the vita of Domenico Beccafumi (1486–1551) he evaluates his contribution to the pavement of the cathedral in Siena as "al più bello ed al più grande e magnifico pavimento che mai fusse stato fatto"; Giorgio Vasari, *Le vite dei più eccellenti pittori, scultori ed architettori*, vol. 5 (Florence, 1880), p. 646.

58. Honorius says of the church floor in a consecration sermon (using as his text Song of

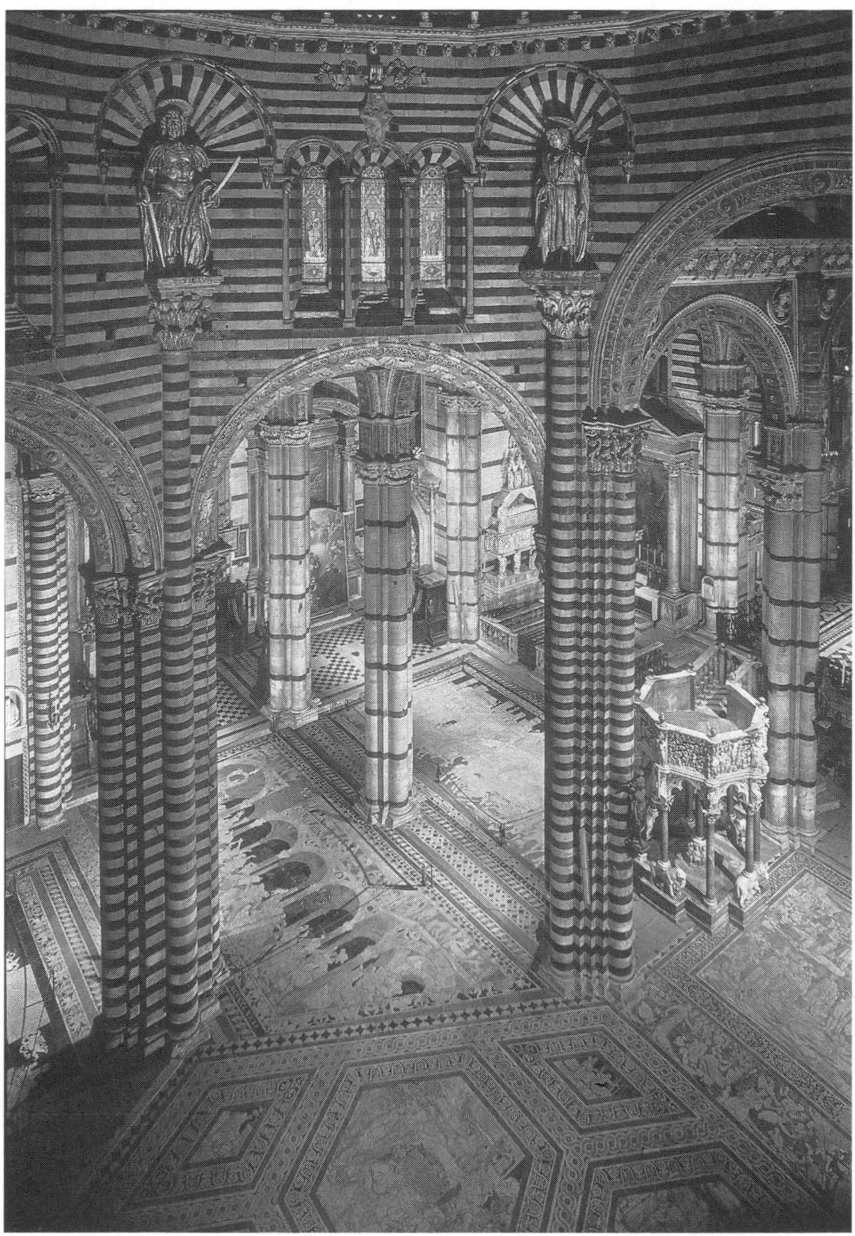

FIGURE 22

View from the dome space into the north transept, Siena Cathedral. (Photograph: Interior view. Duomo, Siena, Italy. Copyright Scala/Art Resource, New York.)

or of marble treated with various colors, and is a work upon which forty, mostly named, artists—only four or five of them are not known to us by name—worked for two centuries (1369–1562). What it achieves is more than an artistic dividing up of the surface that clarifies the architectural rhythm of the building and seeks beauty in itself—in the way in which a former pavement also did—namely, now a grand pictorial program (fig. 23) has been realized.[59] The most recent monograph on the medieval decorated

Songs 3:9f.): "media caritate constravit" [the midst he covered with charity]: *PL,* 172, 1100 D, "Media id est pavimenta, crustis marmorum aut tapetibus vel palliis erant strata, in quibus cuncta quae ad caritatem pertinent, mira sunt pictura atque textura variata. Per quae reliqua plebs accipitur, cui legem et prophetas in duobus praeceptis caritatis implere praecipitur" [The midst, that is, the pavement, was overlaid with pieces of marble or tapestry or coverlets, in which all things that pertain to love are wondrously impressive as pictures as well as through their varied textures. In this way the remaining populace is received into the fold, being instructed to fulfill the law and prophets in the form of the two precepts of love [God and one's neighbor]].

59. With reference to the floor, Alfonso Landi's "Descrizione del Pavimento del Duomo di Siena," from the seventeenth century, is printed in Guglielmo della Valle, *Lettere Senesi,* vol. 3 (Rome, 1786), pp. 124–157: Johann Dominicus Fiorillo, *Kleine Schriften artistischen Inhalts,* vol. 2 (Göttingen, 1806), pp. 198–241, writes, "Über die Kunst, verschiedene Steine und Cameen nachzuahmen, den Marmor zu färben und ihn zur Mahlerey anzuwenden; verbunden mit einer Beschreibung des Fußbodens im Dom von Siena" (pp. 218ff.). With reference to the marble technique of the Sienese floor, pp. 223ff. This description is according to Landi in della Valle. Historical material in Gaetano Milanesi, *Documenti per la storia dell'arte Senese,* 3 vols. (Siena, 1870) (not available to me); H. J. Wagner, "Das Dompaviment von Siena und seine Meister" (diss., Göttingen, 1898) (only a partial printing of pt. 5 [on Domenico di Bartolo Ghezzi] was available to me); Robert Henry Hobart Cust, *The Pavement Masters of Siena (1369–1562)* (London, 1901) (the most important publication); Alfredo Melani, "Pavimenti artistici d'Italia," *Emporium* 23 (1906): 428–447, pp. 443–446; G. Marangoni, "Il più bel pavimento del mondo," in *La Cultura Moderna* (1925), pp. 508–517; Giovanni Cecchini, *Il Pavimento della Cattedrale di Siena* (Siena, n.d. [ca. 1930])—good illustrations—likewise, anonymous, *The Pavement of Siena Cathedral: Wonder of the World* (Milan, 1968) (a well-illustrated guide).

The pavement is sometimes treated in works on the cathedral as a whole; thus, the great monograph by V. Lusini, *Il duomo di Siena,* 2 vols. (Siena, 1911, 1939); and further, in the well-illustrated pamphlets by Enzo Carli, *Il duomo di Siena,* in the series I Tresori (Florence, 1966); Silla Zamboni, *Siena/duomo,* in the series Tresori d'arte cristiana, fasc. 55 (Bologna, 1967); not available to me: Zita Pepi, *Il duomo di Siena* (Siena, 1964), pp. 17, 192 figs.

The literature about the pavement has as good as ignored the concept of temporal space which will be developed in what follows. In its succession of point-by-point pictorial observations it has not succeeded in taking an overall view of the formative idea behind the whole; rather, it has allowed itself to be guided largely by the idea of the tour around the cathedral—which dismembers the relationships—or else it has been concerned with the more than forty named artists who participated in the undertaking, thus placing the historical point of view before the iconographic. Points of view of chronology, of the quality of the work, of the achievement of the individual artist—even in monographs on such important participants as Becca-

FIGURE 23

Pictorial program of the pavement, Siena Cathedral. (Photograph: Giovanni Paciarelli [19th CE]. Design of the Pavement of the Duomo in Siena. Museo dell'Opera Metropolitana, Siena, Italy. Copyright Scala/ Art Resource, New York.)

pavement—it disregards Siena[60]—enables us to understand for the first time what it meant to break away from the tradition of the precious ornamental pavement as it is found in Monte Cassino, in San Marco in Venice, in Rome, and in many other churches, in order to execute a new pictorial program. The fact that Hiltrud Kier takes into account the pavement in Roman antiquity but does not recall the marble pavement of the Temple of Solomon in the Bible, as a prefiguration of the church, is symptomatic and disquieting.

The pictorial program begins under the facade in a forecourt in front of the portals. In front of the central portal, the picture in the marble shows a temple, turning toward which, on the left, is the Pharisee and, on the right, the publican at prayer (Luke 18:10): "Duo homines ascenderunt in templum ut orarent: unus pharisaeus et alter publicanus" [Two men went up into the temple to pray; the one a Pharisee and the other a publican]. As tax collectors for the Romans, the Jewish publicans are, as a rule, generally considered to be heathens. Even the Jewish tax collector Matthew speaks of tax collectors and heathens in the same breath: "but if he neglect to hear the church, let him be unto thee as a publican and a heathen" (Matthew 18:17). Thus, we interpret those who are praying in front of the temple as Jews and heathens. The next picture, on the left of the Pharisee, shows a vessel in a mandorla with the inscription "mel" [honey]; on the right-hand side, next to the publican, an analogous vessel bears the inscription "fel" [gall].[61] Gall and honey appar-

---

fumi—have not, in the past seventy years, shown the least awareness of the spiritual relationships of the pictorial program. The only indication given in Cust's 1901 volume on the artists involved in the pavement (p. 4), of an inner connection within the whole has never been taken up anywhere else: "Although the order in which the stories meet our eyes does not in the least agree with the chronology of their execution, a sense of fitness in position seems to run through them even from the great West door itself." According to Cust, the path leads from Hermes Trismegistus and the sibyls, via half-pagan symbolic pictures and through the history of Jewish heroes and prophets, to the high altar as the scene of the sacrifice of Christ. "But this suggestion must not be pressed too far, because . . . many variations for which at first sight the reason is not very obvious have from time to time crept in. For general purposes, however, the student of the floor may fairly start with some such complete conception." Cust himself did not revert to the idea in the remainder of his work.

60. Hiltrud Kier, *Der mittelalterliche Schmuckfußboden unter besonderer Berücksichtigung des Rheinlandes*, Die Kunstdenkmäler des Rheinlandes, Beiheft 14 (Düsseldorf, 1970).

61. We hear this in the seventeenth century. Landi, p. 157. Bernardus Lamy portrays the Pharisee and the publican at the entrance to the temple in Jerusalem in *De tabernaculo foederis, de sancta civitate Jerusalem et de templo eius*, 7 vols. (Paris, 1720), plates after p. 817; see also 815E, 816 A, according to which the publican, as a heathen, was not permitted to cross the threshold of the temple: there is a discussion of the gestures of the Jew and of the heathen at the entrance to the temple.

ently stand for Jews and heathens.[62] On the extreme left, beyond the Pharisee and the "mel," there was, in the marble, a picture of a sacrifice, but this has been lost; a kneeling figure raises its hands to the altar where a ram was being sacrificed in the fire. Since the seventeenth century this has been interpreted as Abel's sacrifice.[63] Even then there was no corresponding picture on the extreme right, on the heathen's side, which could have helped us interpret the sacrifice taking place on the left-hand side.[64] On the left- and right-hand sides the forecourt is bounded by the pillars of the facade with the she-wolf—the heraldic animal of Siena—nursing the two children. Like the facade, the forecourt is also the site of the prehistory of Christianity, the Jews and heathens, of biblical history and Roman antiquity. It is only between the lintels of the portal that the pavement shows scenes of the ordination of a deacon, a priest, and a bishop and so becomes the threshold of the transition from the temple of the Jews and the heathens into the space of the church.

When we cross this threshold, we are faced with fifteen massive marble statues, five on the pavement of the nave up to the transept and five in each of the side aisles (figs. 23 and 24). They show the whole pavement of the nave to be the historical and, at the same time, temporal space of heathen history—excepting the Jews—functioning as a prophecy of the church. We may assume that Giovanni Pisano's great concept of building the facade as the temporal space of the prophetic prehistory of the Jews and the heathens, up to the time of the birth of the Virgin Mary, may have given rise to the creative idea of realizing an analogous program on the pavement. This conception must have exercised such a powerful fascination that it gave birth to the plan of removing the old, geometrically patterned marble pavement of the cathedral, which had been in place for more than a century, and of replacing it with the present one, with its pictorial program of temporal space. The fact that this idea held sway, over the course of two centuries, until it was fully realized

62. As this is no longer understood, a modern restoration changed the word *fel* to *lac,* so that it could be read as "milk and honey."

63. Landi (see n. 58), p. 157; Cust (see n. 58), p. 16; Cecchini (see n. 58), p. 5.

64. The Tabernacle and the Temple of Solomon have in their anteroom next to the sacrificial altar (Exodus 171.ff. and Exodus 29:1ff., with reference to the sacrifice at the consecration of a priest; 2 Chronicles 4:1) a basin for the purification of the priests (Exodus 30:17ff.: "labrum aeneum" [basin of Aeneas]); (Chronicles 4:22ff.: "mare fusile" [molten sea]). In the Temple of Solomon, this basin stands "on the right-hand side" and "toward the south" (2 Chronicles 4:10). Thus, it is easy to assume that the sacrificial altar, like the basin (which is missing on the right-hand side), was taken from these Old Testament prefigurations of the church as Jewry (sacrificial altar) and heathendom (basin, an allusion to fulfillment in baptism). Thus, they simultaneously prepared the scenes that are on the floor between the doorposts of the portal.

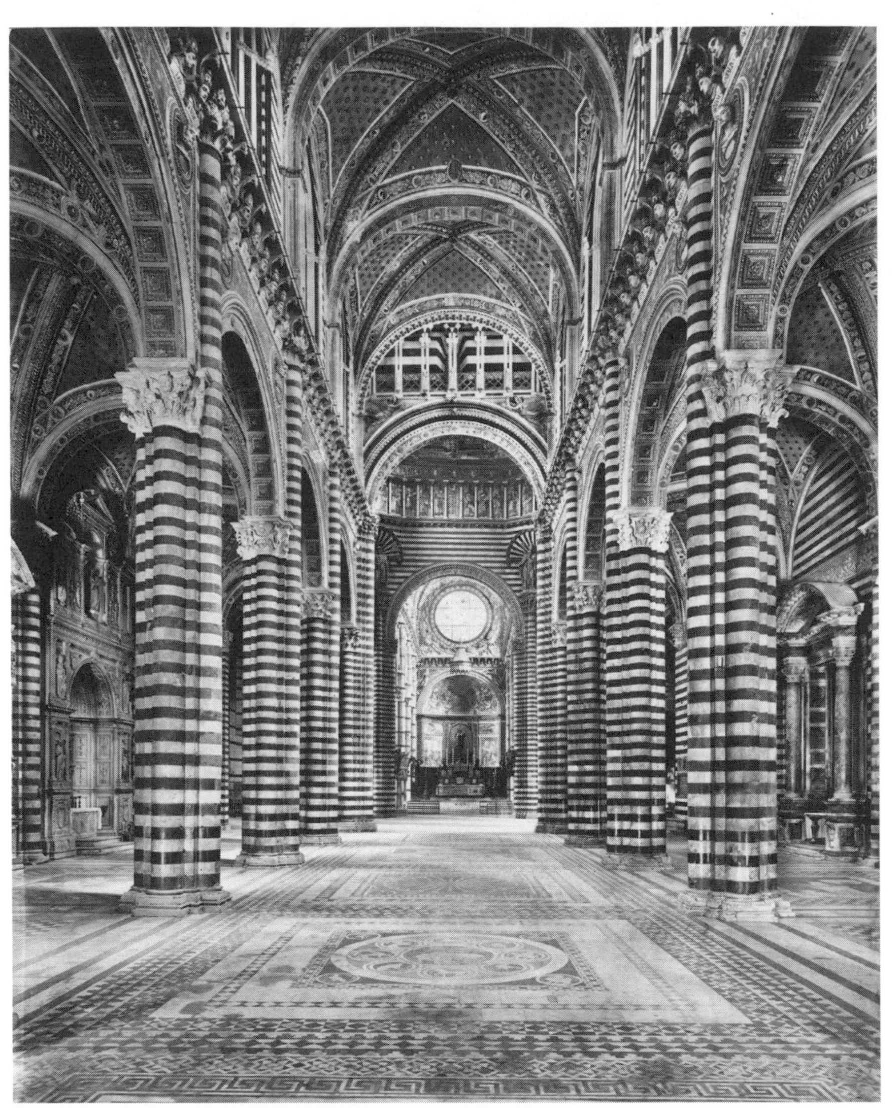

FIGURE 24
Interior view of Siena Cathedral, toward apse. (Photograph: Duomo, Siena, Italy. Copyright Alinari/Art Resource, New York.)

is testimony to the far-reaching idea behind it. I will give a description of the complete thing and leave the question of the stages of development unanswered.

When we enter through the middle portal we are confronted by the massive first statue, the most recent in the nave, from the year 1488, on which the subscription reads: "Hermes Mercurius Trismegistus Contemporaneus Moyse." We are standing at a place far more than a thousand years before Christ. The sphinxes under the scroll in his left hand and the words "Receive the Scriptures and the laws of Egypt" in the open book that he holds in his right hand and that he is handing to two figures—probably seekers after knowledge from the East and the West—prove that Moses' contemporary, Hermes Trismegistus, is an Egyptian.[65] The *translatio sapientiae* from the hand of the old Egyptian, as its origin, to the other peoples at the time that Moses received the law from God's hand shows, on the threshold of this church pavement, the beginnings of worldly wisdom.[66] The text of Hermes Trismegistus's scroll begins with the words "God, the creator of all things. . . ." and thus places us at the very beginning of the whole of world history. The legendary Hermes Trismegistus, who is given a rank equal to the Egyptian god

65. The two persons receiving the book of Hermes have been interpreted in a number of different ways. Cust, p. 22, sees two men, perhaps "the learned men of East and West"; Cecchini, p. 5, accepted this. In the seventeenth century, Landi, p. 140, saw a woman in the rear half-covered figure. He regarded both figures as representatives of heathendom, which had received the knowledge and law of God but once and only in the words of this book.

66. The translation here attempts to make sense out of a nonsensical misprint in both the first (1977) and second (1983) printings of the original German text of Ohly's *Schriften zur mittelalterlichen Bedeutungsforschung.* The correct text is as printed in the very first publication of "Siena" in *Frühmittelalterliche Studien* 6 (1972): 116 n. 62: "Acta 7, 22 *Et eruditus est Moyses omni sapientia Aegyptiorum.* Zur translatio der Schrift und des Wissens aus Ägypten an die Griechen und weiter an die Römer Franz Josef Worstbrock, Translatio artium. Über die Herkunft und Entwicklung einer kulturhistorischen Idee (*Archiv für Kulturgeschichte* 47, 1965, S. 1–22) bes. S. 6 und 13ff.: 'Im Quadrivium läßt man, nach griechischer und patristischer Überlieferung, überwiegend Ägypten bzw. den Orient den Griechen vorangehen' (mit Belegen aus Josephus, Augustin, Cassiodor, Isidor, Hugo von St. Viktor und Otto von Freising)." In English: "Acts 7:22: 'Et eruditus est Moyses omni sapientia Aegyptiorum' [And Moses was erudite in all the wisdom of the Egyptians]. On the transfer of the script and the knowledge from Egypt to the Greeks and then on to the Romans cf. Franz Josef Worstbrock, 'Translatio artium: Über die Herkunft und Entwicklung einer kulturhistorischen Idee,' *Archiv für Kulturgeschichte* 47 (1965): 1–22, esp. pp. 6 and 13ff.: 'In the quadrivium especially Egypt, or, as the case may be, the East in general, is given—according to Greek and patristic tradition—precedence over the Greeks themselves (this on the basis of citations from Josephus, Augustine, Cassiodorus, Isidor, Hugh of St.-Victor, and Otto von Freising).'"—Trans.

of wisdom, is deemed to be the author of Poemander's hermetic treatise *Shepherd of mankind* (second to third century A.D.), from whose visionary cosmogony the words of the scroll are taken:[67] "God the creator of all things created at his side a visible God and made him into the first and the only. He was well pleased with him and loved him greatly, as his own son, who is called the word of God."[68]

In the side aisles, the pictures of the ten sibyls are, like the Egyptian, also given scrolls, the texts of which point prophetically to Christ. But let us first proceed along the nave. The next statue, dating from a century earlier, in 1373, takes us into the time and space of Rome. It depicts the she-wolf suckling Ascius and Senius, the sons of Remus, the symbol of Siena, which is supposed to have been founded by them. Twelve other animals, symbols of the cities that are allied to Siena, encircle the she-wolf. The third, coeval statue (1373) in the nave, like the former one, shows that the cathedral is situated upon Roman ground: it is a wheel with twenty-five pillared spokes with the imperial eagle in the center, just as Rome is the center of the world. The fourth picture is a work of Pintoricchio from the year 1504:[69] Fortuna has driven the seekers after wisdom onto the rockbound island, to the high seat of wisdom, which gives virtue its reward:

Huc properate viri, salebrosum scandite montem,
Pulchra laboris erunt premia palma quies.

[Men, hasten hither, climb the rugged mount,
Beautiful will be the rewards of your labor, the palm of victory, rest.]

Seated on a throne under this scroll, wisdom gives a palm to Socrates and a book to the philosopher Crates. After Egypt and Rome, for which there are

67. Cust, p. 22.

68. Erik Iversen, *The Myth of Egypt and Its Hieroglyphs in European Tradition* (Copenhagen, 1960), p. 60: "According to Ficino, Hermes Trismegistus was a sage of the Egyptians, a contemporary, or maybe even a predecessor, of Moses. He had attained a knowledge of things surpassing even that which was revealed to the Hebrew prophets, and comparable only to that of the Evangelists. Pythagoras had become acquainted with his teachings in Egypt, and through his transmission they had been transmitted to Plato who was a student of Egyptian wisdom himself, and had eventually based his own philosophy on the doctrines of Hermes."

69. Enzo Carli, *Il Pintoricchio* (Milan, 1960), p. 68: the best color reproduction of the picture is to be found in front of the title page; Evelyn M. Phillips, *Pintoricchio* (London, 1901), pp. 110f.; Pietro Rossi, *Il Pintoricchio a Siena* (Siena, 1902); Michèe Beaulieu, "Un bas-relief allégorique de la seconde moitié du XVIe siècle," *La revue des arts* 5 (1955): 121–123.

symbols of dominion, we enter the space of the Greeks as the land of wisdom. Pintoricchio's rockbound island with Fortuna balanced on the rolling sphere of fortune on its shores leads us to the last and oldest picture in the nave (1372): the well-known medieval Wheel of Fortune, which is surrounded, in the corners of the picture, by the Greek and Roman poets and philosophers Aristotle and Euripides, Seneca and Epictetus. Their four half-figures hold, in their hands, scrolls with quotations from their works that comment critically upon the belief in the fatal qualities of the Wheel of Fortune—its medieval motto is "Regnabo, regno, regnavi, sum sine regno" [I shall reign, I reign, I have reigned, I am without a reign].[70] Aristotle's quotation (upper right) is "Fortuna prospera petulantes magis facit. (Aristotle, *Politics,* book 7)" [Fortune's favor leads only to presumption]; Euripides' (bottom right), "Tibi dixi o fili ut fortunam laboribus indages. Eurip. *Elek.*" [I have told you my son that you should study fortune with great care]; Seneca's (top left), "Magna servitus est magna fortuna. Sene. *De consol. lib VN*" [Great good fortune is great servitude]; and Epictetus's (top left), "Non fortunae muneribus sed animi bonis gloriandum. Epict. *Enchyr.* cap. lxvi." [You may not boast of the gifts of fortune, but of the goods of the spirit].[71]

70. *Carmina Burana,* ed. Alfons Hilka and Otto Schumann, vol. 1 (Heidelberg, 1930), p. 37 (no. 18[a]), with a miniature of Fortune on the title page.

71. The quotations from the poets and philosophers of antiquity come from the following writings (I am indebted to Christel Meier for this information):- Aristotle, *Politics* 1334a 26ff.: "war compels men to be just and temperate, whereas the enjoyment of good fortune and the leisure which comes with peace tend to make them insolent." The text is not in Euripides *Electra,* but in Euripides fragment 233; *Tragicorum Graecorum Fragmenta,* rec. Augustus Nauck, supplementum . . . adjectit, Bruno Snell (Hildesheim, 1964), p. 430. Seneca, *Ad Polybium de consolatione* VI, 4: "Multa tibi non licent, quae humillimis et in angulo iacentibus licent: magna servitus est magna fortuna." Cf. IX, 5: "Mihi crede, is beatior est cui fortuna supervacua est quam is cui parata est. Omnia ista bona quae nos speciosa, sed fallaci voluptate delectant, pecunia, dignitas, potentia aliaque complura ad quae generis humani caeca cupiditas obstupescit, cum labore possidentur, cum invidia conspiciuntur, eos denique ipsos quos exornant et premunt; plus minantur quam prosunt; lubrica et incerta sunt, numquam bene tenentur" [Many things are not allowed to you, which are allowed to the lowest and those lying in the worst straits: great good fortune is great wretched servitude. . . . Believe me, that man is happier to whom good fortune is superfluous, happier than the man to whom she is always ready to lend her assistance. All those good things which delight us with a splendiferous but fallacious pleasure, such as money, high standing, influence, and several other things in the face of which the blind cupidity of the human species is struck senseless, are possessed only with hard labor, are beheld only with envy, and in the end only suffocate those whom they adorn; they are more threatening than advantageous; slippery and elusive as they are, they are never safely retained]. The quotation attributed to Epictetus is not to be found in this form in his works.

Julius von Schlosser, *Quellenbuch zur Kunstgeschichte des abendländischen Mittelalters* (Vi-

FIGURE 25
Pact between Elijah and Ahab, pavement, Siena Cathedral. In Ahab's presence, Elijah points in the direction of the main altar at the sacrificial steers. (Photograph: Domenico Beccafumi [1486–1551]. Duomo, Siena, Italy. Copyright Scala/Art Resource, New York.)

The pavement of the nave traverses the temporal space of pagan antiquity in Egypt, Rome, and Greece. It is dominated by the idea of law and wisdom, of power, virtue, and fate conquered by wisdom. Pintoricchio's picture of the wise men who have been taken by Fortune to the rockbound island in the midst of a storm in the course of which the mast of their ship has been broken, and who, turning their backs on their Fortuna, follow the path of the search for wisdom, is like an interpretation of the picture of the Wheel of Fortune, drawn a century and a half earlier, on which the words of poets and philosophers teach us how to conquer fate. The nave depicts an antiquity that implies more than itself.

enna, 1896), pp. 331ff., quoted by Hartman Schedel, *Sprüche des Aristoteles, Sokrates, Seneca, Plato und Hieronymus,* which also comments similarly upon the *Regnabo, regno, regnavi, sum sine regno* of the Wheel of Fortune.

The fact that the pavement of the nave and the side aisles—like the facade—represents the temporal space of the prehistory of Christianity and, in fact, up to the crossing point only of pagan antiquity is confirmed by the pictorial program of the side aisles with the pictures (all from the year 1482–83) of five sibyls who, like the wise men of Egypt, Rome, and Greece, are all given scrolls. As we enter through the right-hand portal, we reach, one after the other, the Delphic, Cimmerian, Cumaean, Erythrean, and the Persian, and in the left side aisle, the Libyan, Hellespontine, Phrygian, Samian, and Tiburtine sibyls.[72] The scrolls of all the sybils contain prophecies about Christ.[73] The sibyls stand for different lands and places in Greece and Italy, the Aegean and Asia Minor, Africa and Persia, and also for different epochs of pre-Christian history which are linked in predictions about the Son of God. I shall mention just one as an example: the Hellespontine sibyl from Troas in the period of Cyrus: "Sibylla Hellespontica in agro Trojano nata, quam scribit Heraclides Cyri tempore fuisse" [the Hellespontine sibyl, born in Trojan territory, whom Heraclides records as having existed in the time of Cyrus] (fig. 26). Her prophecy speaks of the offering of gall and vinegar and the rending of the veil of the temple: "In cibum fel, in sitim acetum dederunt. Hanc inhospitalitatis monstrabunt mensam. Templi vero scindetur velum, et medio die nox erit tenebrosa tribus horis" [For food gall, for thirst they gave [him] vinegar. They will reveal this table of inhospitality. Truly, the temple curtain will be torn, and at midday the night will be as dark as at the third hour]. This Sibylline prophecy comes from Psalm 68:22f.: "Et dederunt in escam meam

72. On the subject of these pictures of the sybils, see Cust, pp. 31–53; literature on the sibyls in Keller, p. 158 n. 84.

Angelina Rossi treats the sybils of the pavement, pp. 437–440. Her treatment permits us to see them in a medieval relationship. As early as the *Dies irae* hymn of Thomas of Celano (d. 1253), we find the sibyls placed side by side with the prophets: "Dies irae, dies illa, Solvet saeclum in favilla. Teste David cum Sibyl" [Day of wrath, that day, Will dissolve the world to a glowing ash, David bears witness together with the Sibyl]. Giovanni Pisano's sibyl on the cathedral facade (ca. 1290) carries the banderole "Et vocabitur deus et homo" [And he will be called god and man]. Rossi (p. 275 and n. 3), referring to the sibyl's standing there with Aristotle, as the prophet of Christ, points to the work of Thomas Aquinas, who, in the *Summa Theologiae* and in his maxims, mentions the sibyl—and "several pagans who were visited with a revelation of Christ"—as a prophet of Christ. One manuscript mentions the sibyl together with Thucydides, Sophocles, Aristotle, and Plato. Even Honorius Augustodunensis places the pagans among the prophets of Christ in his work on the liturgy written in 1125, *Gemma animae* III, 1:172, 642 D: "per legem, prophetas, psalmos et gentilium libros Christi adventus praeconabatur" [by the law, the prophets, the psalms and the books of the Gentiles the advent of Christ was heralded].

73. Cust has the texts.

IN CIBVM FEL. INSITIM ACE
TVM DEDERVNT. HANC
IN HOSPITALITATIS MOSTR
ABVNT MENSAM; TEMPLI
VERO SCINDETVR VELVM
ET MEDIO DIE NOX ERIT
TENEBROSA TRIBVS HORIS
SIBYLLA HELLESPONTICA INA
GRO TROIANO NATA QVĀ SCRIBIT
HERACLIDES CYRI TĒPORE FVISSE

FIGURE 26

Anonymous, The Hellespontine sibyl. (Photograph: Italian School, marble inlay on the floor of the Siena Cathedral. Duomo, Siena, Italy. Copyright Alinari/Art Resource, New York.)

fel et in siti meo potaverunt me aceto. Fiat mensa eorum coram ipsis in laqueum et in retributiones et in scandalum" [They gave me also gall for to eat; and in my thirst they gave me vinegar to drink. May their own table be a snare before them and a punishment and a stumbling block]. Beneath the scroll, a dog and a lion join paws. They have been interpreted as wolf and lion, the animals of Florence and Siena, which had become allies at that time.[74] However, the theory that a political alliance is being celebrated beneath this scroll is refuted by the biblical references which contain aspects of the Passion, to which the rending of the veil of the temple also belongs. The Roman soldiers offer Christ wine with gall on Golgotha (Matthew 27:34), but it is a Jew who offers the sponge filled with vinegar (Matthew 27:48). The heathens and the Jews are allied at the Passion: as dog and lion they join paws. The dog is a very common symbol for the heathens, the "catulus leonis Juda" [Judah the whelp of a lion] is biblical (Genesis 49:9). The picture in the forecourt also joins the Pharisee and the publican.[75]

The marble pictorial cycle in the nave shows the pavement as the temporal space of pagan antiquity on whose foundation the cathedral stands in a very real sense. Whether the sparse evidence about the early history of the city of Siena permits us to assume an Etruscan, Gallic, or Roman origin must remain moot, since medieval Siena believed in its Roman origin and cultivated this belief. The symbol of Rome—the she-wolf nursing the founders of the city—became the symbol of Siena. As such it was incorporated in the pavement of the cathedral on the basis of a legend according to which the two sons of Remus, Ascius and Senius, who were persecuted by Romulus made their sacrifices to Diana and Apollo on the site of what was later to become Siena. According to the legend, Senius was riding a white horse and Ascius a black one, or else white smoke rose from the altar of Diana and black from the altar of Apollo. Thus, black and white became the heraldic colors of Siena. If the etiological legend of the city founders played a part in determining the choice of black and white marble in the cathedral at Siena, then Roman elements of the legend are at work, in the background behind the biblical, Hebrew-Solomonic ones, in the marble cladding of the cathedral. The combination of green and white in the marble cladding of the cathedral at Flo-

74. Ibid., p. 50; Cecchini, p. 6: "simbolo della pace allora vigente fra Firenze e Siena" [symbol of the peace then in force between Florence and Siena].

75. This relationship between word and picture has a counterpart in the Phrygian sibyl. The text on the tablet, a prophecy of the Resurrection and the Last Judgment, is illustrated by a group of people rising from the depths beneath the tablet, from *The Pavement of Siena Cathedral* (cf. n. 58), fig. 13.

rence shows that other combinations of color are possible. In Siena the cathedral has white and dark green on the outside, but, inside, it has the Sienese black and white. As far as the Sienese were concerned, the cathedral stood on Roman ground. The pavement of its nave and side aisles represents and is, at the same time, in a very concrete sense the pagan-classical foundation of the building. For the benefit of strangers, the guide to the cathedral museum—which is located in the basement beneath the choir—knocks on a wall there and alleges that this is a Roman temple of Minerva.[76] In the pictorial idea of the pavement of the nave and side aisles, the foundation of the church is the whole world of pagan antiquity, upon which—just like the cathedral—the whole Christian church rests, at least to the extent that this antiquity foretold the coming of Christ. There is scarcely another place where antiquity has been incorporated, architectonically, into the church in a more magnificent, more lively manner, though also, it is true, with more reflective power. Antiquity is part of its foundation and its soil, even in the forecourt and on its facade.

When you have traversed the nave and the side aisles as far as the crossing, your feet have covered more than a thousand years, from Moses to Seneca, from Egypt to Roman Siena, from the Cuman sibyl, whom Aeneas visited, to the Tiburtine sibyl, whom Augustus went to see. When we reach this last sibyl, who stands below Augustus and prophesies, "Christ will be born in Bethlehem . . . ," we are standing at the left-hand front end of the nave and of the pagan prehistory of the church, which begins, as a church, with Christ, who was born in the reign of Augustus.

Between the nave and the altar the whole space—the crossing, with the transept and almost the whole choir—is taken up with pictures from Old Testament history. Pagans and Jews, who stand next to each other at the same height as they do on the facade and the forecourt, follow one another on the pavement. The nave belongs to the pagans of antiquity, the transept and the

76. Titus Burckhardt, *Siena: Stadt der Jungfrau* (Olten, 1961), p. 10: "According to its site, the city is of Etruscan, but perhaps also, as John of Salisbury maintains, of Gallic origin. In any case, it existed in Roman times and regarded itself throughout the Middle Ages as Roman. It is supposed that a temple, dedicated to Minerva, stood on the hill above the sunken center of the city—where the cathedral now stands—which would give a doubly true sense to the designation of Siena as 'vetus civitas Veneris' [the old city of Venus], since Minerva was the virgin goddess of wisdom." On the medieval traditions of the Roman origin of Siena, see Nicolai Rubinstein, "Political Ideas in Sienese Art: The Frescoes by Ambrogio Lorenzetti and Taddio di Bartolo in the Palazzo Pubblico," *Journal of the Warburg and Courtauld Institutes* 21 (1958): 179–207, pp. 200–204.

choir to the Old Testament Jews, who stand nearer the Christian mysteries of the chancel. The system of bays in the nave had suggested an arrangement of the pictures in groups of five in each aisle. This arrangement was so closely dictated by the architectonic arrangement that we would not question the significance of the number five for these cycles if it were not for the fact that, as we step from the temporal space of the nave into the Jewish period, we notice that this is linked to a sevenfold arrangement of the pictorial cycles. The transition is obvious in the artistic manner in which a cycle of seven hexagonal pictures is incorporated into the hexagon which is formed on the pavement by the pillars supporting the dome. This cycle is completed by six rhomboid pictures in the corners of the hexagon (fig. 22f.). This cycle (1519–24)—based on designs by Domenico Beccafumi, who worked on the pavement from 1517 to 1546, and was the most important of the artists engaged on it at the time—is devoted to the prophet Elijah and his struggle with King Ahab.[77] Beccafumi was responsible for the middle picture of the group of seven and the three hexagons which extend in front of it toward the altar, as well as for the two rhombuses which lie in front of them.[78] Beccafumi's four hexagonal pictures treat the miraculous fight between Elijah and Ahab's

77. On Beccafumi's work on the pavement in Siena: Hans von Trotta, "Das Leben und die Werke des Sieneser Malers Domenico Beccafumi, known as Mecarino" (diss., Berlin, 1913), pp. 20–24, 29, 35f., 41ff.; Jacob Judey, "Domenico Beccafumi" (diss., Freiburg, 1932), pp. 87–100; Maria Gibellino-Krascheninnicova, *Il Beccafumi* (Florence, 1933), pp. 96–100, figs. 34 (the sacrifice of Elijah), 35 (Moses striking water from the rock), 36 (Abraham sacrificing Isaac), 44 (Moses on Mount Sinai—outline), 45f. (worship of the golden calf—outline); Anna Maria Francini Ciaranfi, *Domenico Beccafumi* (Florence, 1966), p. 39, figs. 70–74 (outline drawings for the pavement pictures in front of the high altar); Donato Sanminiatelli, *Domenico Beccafumi* (Milan, 1967), pp. 16f., 21f., 38, 40, 86f. (the Elijah cycle), 92f., 105 (Moses on Mount Sinai), 144, 146, 150, 154, 156, 159, 161, 167f., fig. 18 (Ahab's sacrifice), fig. 18a (Elijah's sacrifice), fig. 18c (compact between Elijah and Ahab), figs. 32 and 32a–d (Moses strikes water from the rock together with outline drawings), figs. 48 and 48a–n (Moses on Mount Sinai and relevant scenes, together with drafts), fig. 69 (biblical figures, prophets, and sibyls; underneath, the wanderings of the people of Israel), fig. 76 (sacrifice of Isaac, and beneath it the wanderings of the people of Israel).

78. The remainder of the hexagon under the dome was occupied, until 1522, by the high altar and was therefore not used by Beccafumi. The plan to place the high altar in its present position, in the choir, was already in hand at the beginning of the century, so that Beccafumi was already able to execute his cycle in the direction of the apse, in the same way that earlier artists had treated the pavement behind the altar. The three remaining hexagonal and the four rhomboid pictures beneath the dome were not executed until the nineteenth century. Sanminiatelli, p. 195; on the text of the scrolls on Beccafumi's Elijah pictures, p. 196. Originally the parable of the mote in the eye was linked to the rear of the Wheel of Fortune in the hexagon (this was already done by 1375); on the left of this was the parable of the blind leading the blind and, on the right, a man

priests of Baal from 1 Kings 16:16–40. The middle picture, under the lantern of the dome (fig. 25), shows the compact that Elijah made with Ahab, that each should lay a sacrificed bullock on the wood and call upon God for fire (1 Kings 18:16–25). In front of this, and toward the left, Ahab's sacrifice to God remains unheeded (18:26ff.), in the middle in front, God grants Elijah's prayer and sacrifice (18:38f.), and toward the right the unsuccessful priests of Baal are murdered. Elijah's gesture, in the middle of the picture indicating the high altar, points, in the picture, to the site of the sacrifice that—in the main picture of the Elijah cycle which is in front of it—shows God heeding the prayer and sacrifice of the prophet while the prophets of Baal are being murdered.[79]

The altar sacrifice introduces a theme that is foreign to the "pagan" nave, and this is repeated in the direction of the high altar; we shall now pursue it. A Moses cycle, again by Beccafumi, follows the Elijah cycle between the dome and the choir. A strip painting between the two eastern pillars that support the dome shows Moses, in the center, during the wanderings of the people of Israel in the wilderness, striking water from the rock (Exodus 17:1–7). This painting together with the six scenes around Moses on the massive picture which is behind it forms a sevenfold cycle consisting of three pictures of Moses, one above the other, and two accompanying pictures on each side.[80] Three scenes of Moses at the rock form the central axis: in the upper one he is receiving the tablets of the law on Mount Sinai (Exodus 24:12f.), below that he is breaking the tablet at the foot of the mountain (Exodus 32:29f.), and beneath that one he is striking water from the rock. In the upper-left-hand corner, the Israelites are awaiting his return from the rock (Exodus 24:12f.), beneath that, the golden calf is being melted down, on the right, next to this, Moses' anger has been vented on the makers of the calf, and above it they are being slain by the children of Levi (Exodus 32:26–29). (The large picture has to be read counterclockwise). The sevenfold Moses cycle underneath the first

---

giving alms to a woman holding a child in her arms (1433). The pictorial ideas behind these remains (now in part in the museum) are treated on p. 179 n. 81. These pictures, which were replaced in the nineteenth century by a completion of Beccafumi's Elijah cycle, are reproduced by Cecchini, fig. 24.

79. Beccafumi's two rhomboid pictures in front of the hexagonal pictures belong to the Elijah cycle. They show Elijah ordering Obadiah to bring Ahab to him (1 Kings 18:7–15) and Obadiah bringing Ahab before Elijah (1 Kings 18:16–19).

80. In order to recognize the cycle as an entity we have to place fig. 31 in Sanminiatelli—who treats the pictures separately—under fig. 48.

step up to the choir shows the godless sacrifice of the stiff-necked people on their journey through the wilderness, where they had already encountered a prefiguration of the altar sacrament when Moses struck water from the rock. Moses' receipt of the law from the hand of God is of a higher order than the receipt—from the hands of Hermes Trismegistus—of the laws of Egypt by the sages of antiquity at the threshold of the cathedral.[81]

Moses and Elijah are followed, in the central axis, by David, in a cycle dating from the year 1423: David is sitting on a throne, in the middle of a circle with his zither in his hand, surrounded by four musicians. In the left-hand rhombus David is depicted with his sling; in the right-hand one, Goliath is seen falling down: there are seven figures in all. The picture of the royal psalmist prefigures the liturgical music of the church. The David cycle is framed on the left by Joshua and on the right by Moses, the two who led the Israelites out of the wilderness into the promised land. When we reach the picture of David we are standing in front of the three steps to the choir which contains the high altar. The middle of the space between the "pagan" nave and the steps to the chancel is filled by the prophet Elijah, the lawgiver Moses, and King David. It seems that with David, the battle of the leader with God's people is brought to a peaceful concluson.

The "Jewish" space in the side aisles is filled mainly by battles from Israelite history: on the right, at the level of David, Samson's victory over the Philistines, on the left, Joshua's victory over the Amorites; on the left-hand side at the level of Moses, Judith is seen cutting off the head of Holofernes and the Battle of Bethulia is taking place; on the right lies the picture of King Sigismund (which the Sienese placed next to the Old Testament wars of liberation on the occasion of Sigismund's visit to Siena in 1431, because they may have hoped for the king's aid in their war against Florence).[82] We find, on the same level as the Elijah cycle under the dome on the left-hand side, the massacre of the Innocents, and on the right, Jethro's victory over the Ammonites; beneath

81. The scene in the upper-left-hand corner of the Moses cycle—which is easily overlooked—where a blind man is moving toward a fall (Sanminiatelli, fig. 48a), could help to interpret the old pictures, from the fourteenth century, of the blind between the Wheel of Fortune and the Elijah cycle (now in the cathedral museum) as pictures of the blindness of the people of God, who follow false gods and therefore suffer death.

82. On the particular occasion see, Lusini, 2:25f.; on the picture of the emperor Sigismund, a work of Domenico Bartolo Ghezzi (ca. 1400–pre-1446), Wagner, pp. 9–14; James H. Beck, "The historical 'Taccola' and Emperor Sigismund in Siena," *Art Bulletin* 50 (1968) 309–318, pp. 314f. on King Sigismund's stay in Siena, pp. 316f. on his picture on the pavement.

these are two pictures which do not belong in the Old Testament framework: a cycle of the seven ages of man, which is probably there not simply because of the proximity of the other sevenfold cycles (see below, p. 217). Then, because of an extension of the space, we find on the right the four theological virtues, faith, hope, charity, and religion which also do not fit in with the program. They date only from the eighteenth century, which was unaware of the mistake it was making.

Between the nave and the chancel, seven pictures of battles are set into the pavement. It is unlikely that the recurrence of the number seven in the Elijah and Moses pictures, the seven figures in the David cycle, and the seven battle pictures from the history of the Israelites is coincidental, the more so since the chancel offers two more sibyl cycles, so that, in the biblical part of the pavement, there are seven groups of seven that are clearly demarcated from the groups of five in the nonbiblical nave. We may see—in the mute language of forms—the number five of the senses in the "antique" nave, and the number seven of the Holy Spirit in the "Old Testament" space.

Behind the David cycle, three steps lead up to the main choir, which functions as the chancel. The pillars that support the final bay link this to the nave, and, on the sides, there is a strip painting with the people of Israel wandering in the wilderness. Beccafumi takes up this motif from the Moses cycle again at the altar, at which point Israel has reached the promised goal after wandering through the historical space of the history of God's people.[83] The person who walks over the pavement, representing the space of time, also reaches his final goal when he is in front of the altar. The surface in front of the altar is taken up with the sacrifice of Isaac, as the most noble prefiguration of the sacrifice of the Son of God. There are seven pictures corresponding to one another and forming a framework to the right and left of the sacrifice of Isaac and the altar. They are

7. Tobias with his son and the archangel Gabriel
6. A sibyl
5. Adam kneeling
4. A prophet gazing up to heaven

7. Elisha raising the son of the Shunammite
6. A prophet seated with an open book
5. Eve kneeling
4. A sibyl resting her right hand on an open book

83. Vasari saw in these three strip paintings a sacrificial procession. Faluschi's explanation of them, cautiously expressed in 1784, as the migration into the promised land has become the accepted one. Cf. Sanminiatelli, p. 205.

3. A seated sibyl reading a book	3. A seated sibyl reading a book
2. The sacrifice of Abel	2. The sacrifice of Melchizedek
1. A seated woman with a child	1. A seated woman with a child[84]

The Old Testament space contains the scenes of the sacrifices of Abel, Melchizedek, Abraham, the Israelites in front of the Golden Calf, the Prophet Elijah, King Ahab, and the daughter of Jephtha (Judges 11:34–40; small, in the upper-left-hand corner of the Jephtha picture). The seven scenes of good and evil sacrifices thread their way through various cycles of seven.[85] On the outside, to the left and right of the altar, there are squares containing medallions with the figures of the four cardinal virtues, Fortitudo, Justitita, Prudentia, and Temperantia, and these are completed by a Misericordia behind the altar. Behind the altar, a fifth specifically Christian virtue—mercy—is added to the four of the Greek-Stoic and Old Testament (Wisdom 8:7) traditions, which Ambrosius first called the cardinal virtues. The number five dominates in the nave; the number seven in the Old Testament space. In the choir surrounding the altar, where prophets and sibyls now stand side by side, where all ages, Jews and pagans, the sacrificers and the moralists are united in Christianity, the cycle of five embraces the two cycles of seven at the sides of the altar, so that what was formerly separated in space is here united. The numbers speak of the progress of the history of salvation.

Christ and Mary, the Mother of God, to whom this cathedral is consecrated, are not present in the pictorial program of the pavement. There is one place where we might have expected to see them represented pictorially. The Albunian (Tiburtine) sibyl prophesies, "Christ will be born in Bethlehem. He will be proclaimed in Nazareth when Taurus, the peaceful, the founder of peace, is in the ascendancy. Happy the breasts of the mother that suckle him." But it is the pictures of Herod and the massacre of the Innocents that are immediately next to this picture. The birth of Christ remains outside. The choir, too, shows only Old Testament prefigurations of the church's altar sacrifice. From the facade to the apse, the pavement of the cathedral in Siena signifies only the old era. If we walk from the portal to the altar, we traverse more than a thousand years, walking over the paganism of Egypt, Rome, and Greece,

84. According to Sanminiatelli, pp. 204f., the explanation of the pictures is not entirely certain.

85. On cycles of seven in the Middle Ages, see Hugh of St.-Victor's writing on "de quinque septenis" (175, 405–414); Friedrich Ohly, "Der Prolog des St. Trudperter Hohenliedes," *Zeitschrift für deutsches Altertum* 84 (1953): 198–232; Barbara Tillmanns, "Die sieben Gaben des Heiligen Geistes in der deutschen Literatur" (diss., Kiel University, 1963).

over the Jewry of the Old Testament right up to the typological fulfillment of what was prophesied in its history. The pavement, as temporal space, stands both for historical times and geographical spaces. It is covered by the Egypt of Hermes Trismegistus and of Moses, the Roman Empire with Seneca and Siena, the Greek empire with its poets and philosophers, the Jewish empire of the Old Testament, and the sites of the ten sibyls from Africa to Persia, Troas to Naples. Whoever walks across the pavement walks over the temporal space of the known historical and spatial world of antiquity. "He who does not know how to take account of three thousand years, let him remain in the dark, inexperienced; he can live from day to day."

The pavement up to the threshold of the altar is the open book of the prehistory of Christ, which, by virtue of its prophetic character among pagans and Jews, is the foundation of the church and the soil on which it is built. This book asks to be read for its content, like a *chronica mundi* of the first five ages of man. From the portal to the altar, almost all the pictures—even in the sixteenth century—have a banderole let into the marble, without which the prophecy of the pavement would be almost mute. Pictures and words form a unit. A purely formal look at this work of art would lead past it into a vacuum. The fact that artists from several centuries clung to the use of banderoles could have its own significance. Up to the sacrifice of Isaac in front of the altar, the floor is the era of the law (*sub lege*). At the portal, Hermes Trismegistus hands over the *litteras et leges* of Egypt. On Mount Sinai, Moses receives the tablets of the law. *Litterae et leges,* letter and law, belong together. The pavement, as the base of the law, is the also the base of the letter, of the deadening letter, above which the church, even as a building, must rise into the space of its life-giving spirit. The era of the law and of the letter, present in the banderoles, is also not to be read literally; it belongs to the church as a spiritual member that supports it, not simply as a pavement, but as the base of the church itself. It is as though it is raised up, above and beyond itself, into the church, and thus, its pictorial text is to be read and understood transparently in the superliteral, spiritual sense. As verbal prophecies, its texts *cry out* for the space to raise itself above the flat surface of the law and into the new dimension of its fulfillment through grace, as the specifically Christian dimension of the church. With the transition from the "pagan" nave to the "Hebrew" chancel, the verbal prophecies of Hermes and the sibyls are replaced by prophecies from Old Testament Hebrew history in the form of typological actions. Elijah, Moses, David, and Abraham are active, not speaking prophets, whose deeds—battles, miracles, and the service of God in sacrifice—could prefigure the life of the church (cf. figs. 25 and 26). Beyond their literal sense, the pictures of sacrifices, at least those leading toward the altar, also have a typological dimension of meaning that is lacking in the pictures in the nave. The fundamental possibility of also understanding happenings in antiquity as types of Christian antitypes—the history of which has yet to be written—is not made use of here. It would perforce have blurred the distinction between antiquity and the Old Testament, which is what is being sought after in this space. As a prefiguration of what is Christian, the Old Testament is indispensable in its place in the temporal space of this cathedral. We can scarcely go wrong if we observe that, in the Middle Ages, prophecy by action enjoyed a more far-reaching significance than verbal prophecy. This impression is forced upon us by the arts, because it is easier to give shape to a happening than to mere words. But theology, too, would do well to note that, as far as the Middle Ages are concerned, typological thought played a more important role than prophetic thought in theology. Its intellectual attraction was also more productive. In Siena, the transition from pagan verbal prophecy to Hebrew action prophecy marks a stage in the history of salvation that, by virtue of the spiritual significance of its being present in space, is demonstrated by its closer proximity to the altar.[86]

This stage is not made apparent by any difference in level; there is a flat marble surface from the forecourt to the end of the Moses cycle. It is only after the Moses cycle, one bay before the choir, that the level of the floor—for this one single bay—is raised by one step. What is there in the meaning of this surface that calls for it to be raised above that of Moses? The verbal prophecy of the "pagan" nave and side aisles is monological and solitary. The sibyls stand alone without partners; their prophecy reverberates in empty time. In the space filled by antiquity, there is not a single scene in which people converse. Mute gestures of offering link the few figural groups. The sentences of the poets and philosophers of antiquity are individual voices that are linked by the framework of the piece and not by anything scenic. The Old Testament space is filled with scenes of groups as they are linked by combat, fate, division into parties, conversation, and the common service of God or of idols (cf. figs. 25 and 26). The language of weapons, actions, or words reverberates within this space. The space of the pagans is silent; the space of the Hebrews

86. On particular forms of "placement in the building" as a key to the signification of architectural parts, see Günter Bandmann, *Mittelalterliche Architektur als Bedeutungsträger* (Berlin, 1951), pp. 39f.

is filled with language. This is followed by the space filled with music, raised up by the step. David, the royal singer, is valued by the church as the singer of psalms, the founder or orderer of a cult filled with music. The picture on the pavement shows him—and this corresponds to an old tradition in book painting—as a king sitting on his throne, holding a zither, and surrounded by four players with an organ, tambourine, lute, and viol. David's right hand is pointing to a book with musical notation. (Perhaps the musicologists can read this and interpret it?).[87] The step raises the space allotted to David and Solomon, the kings and builders of the temple. Solomon is placed on the same level—on the extreme left above Moses—as the space of the temple, above that of the Tabernacle, in the furnishing of which there are no musical instruments. The picture of David in the pavement has the following circumscription: "Decantabat populus Israel alleluja et universa multitudo Jacob canebat legitime et David cum cantoribus citharam percutiebat. In domo domini laudes Deo canebat alleluja alleluja" [The people of Israel were chanting alleluia, alleluia, and the whole congregation of Jacob was singing in the prescribed manner, and David with his singers was striking the lyre. In the house of the Lord, he was singing praises to God, alleluia, alleluia].[88] When Saul was struck down by the evil spirit, "David tollebat citharam et percutiebat manu sua" [David took up his lyre and struck it with his hand] (1 Samuel 16:23). David organized the service of song in the tabernacle for the period when Solomon was building the temple (1 Chronicles 6:31). He arranged the "psaltae canentes Domino in organis, quae fecerat ad canendum" [singers singing to the Lord on instruments that I made for singing] (1 Chronicles 23:5). He created the service of the sons of Asaph, Heman and Jeduthun, "qui prophetarent in citharis et psalteriis et cymbalis secundum numerum suum dedicato sibi officio servientes" [who should prophesy with harps, with psalteries, and with cymbals according to their number serving in their appointed office] (1 Chronicles 25:1). The background to the pavement picture in Siena is apparently the report of the altar sacrifice of King Hezekiah, according to David's direction, "coram rege et

87. On the pictorial tradition of David with the players, see Hugo Steger, *Philologia musica: Sprachzeichen, Bild und Sache im literarisch-musikalischen Leben des Mittelalters: Lire, Harfe, Rotte und Fidel*, Münstersche Mittelalter-Schriften, no. 2 (Munich, 1971), figs. 3–9.

88. The remainder of the circumscription places the date of the picture as 1424, when the cathedral architect was Bartholomaeus Cecchi: "Hoc opus factum fuit spectabilis militis domini Bartholomei Joannis Cecci operarii anni mille CCCCXXIII" [This work was completed by the worthy soldier of the Lord, Bartolomeus Joannis Cecci, architect, in the year 1424].

universa multitudine" [in the presence of the king and the whole congregation] (2 Chronicles 29:23):[89] "Constituit quoque levitas in *domo Domini* cum cymbalis et psalteriis et citharis secundum dispositionem David *regis*[90] et Gad videntis et Nathan prophetae; siquidem Domini praeceptum fuit per manum prophetarumn eius. *Steteruntque levitae tenentes organa David et sacerdotes tubas.* Et iussit Ezechias ut offerrent holocausta super altare; cumque offerrentur holocausta, coeperunt *laudes canere Domino* et clangere tubis atque in diversis organis, quae *David rex Israel* praeparaverat, concrepare. Omni autem turba adorante, cantores et ii qui tenebant tubas erant in officio suo, donec compleretur holocaustum" [And he set the Levites in the house of the Lord with cymbals, with psalteries, and with harps, according to the commandment of David, and of Gad the king's seer, and Nathan the prophet, for so was the commandment of the Lord by his prophets. And the Levites stood with the instruments of David, and the priests with the trumpets. And Hezekiah commanded that the burnt offering be made upon the altar. And when the burnt offering began, the song of the Lord began also with the trumpeters, and with the instruments ordained by David, king of Israel. And all the congregation worshipped, and the singers sang, and the trumpeters sounded: and all this was continued until the burnt offering was finished.] (2 Chronicles 29:25; cf. 8, 14).

The biblical origin of the picture teaches us to understand David's music as being the praise of God during the sacrifice on the altar. The step raises the picture of David, as the locus of liturgical music, into the space devoted to the altar sacrifice, without raising it to the actual height of the altar. Three further steps lead up to the choir behind David and his liturgical musicians; thus, the choir is four steps higher than the nave. The site of the Christian altar sacrifice is higher than the slightly raised site of the musical offering of praise in the temple at Jerusalem.

We are amazed to notice that two centuries took part in the realization of a great idea that was not expressed in Siena except by the language of art. Perhaps the association of cathedral masons—we know the names of the master masons for centuries after 1226—was the custodian of an idea in whose service dozens of artists, of name and rank, worked—sometimes for decades—as though it were their own creative idea (more on this on pp. 204ff.). Their own creative contributions were certainly not insignifi-

89. The emphasized words are reminiscent of the circumscription on the picture of David.

90. The title of the pavement picture is *David rex.*

cant. The high demands of the task must have worked as an inspiration. The facade that was conceived by Giovanni Pisano as the temporal space of the prophetic prehistory of the church may have been the inspiration for the realization of a similar pictorial program on the pavement, when the first pictures in marble were laid fifty years after Pisano's death.

The grandiose nature of the pavement in Siena—a combination of intellectual clarity and historical spontaneity and artistic perfection—makes an even deeper impression if we compare it with the duller character of the pictorial cycle of an older Italian cathedral pavement. In the years 1163–66, a good two centuries before the beginning of the pictorial pavement in Siena, the archbishop of Otranto had already laid a mosaic pavement that filled the whole floor of that city's cathedral with a pictorial cycle.[91] The pavement in Otranto has one thing in common with Siena: here, too, the enormous pictorial program does not contain a single picture from the New Testament or the Christian church. The subjects fall into the following categories: first of all, natural ones in the nave and the side aisles: animals and monsters, trees and plants, a bestiary, the animal signs of the zodiac. The tree that traverses the whole of the central nave, from its roots at the portal to its top at the beginning of the choir—trees also fill the side aisles—awakens, in the century in which the rod of Jesse is extended, a conception of time, and yet only here and there can we see a historical succession in the pictorial series. The scenes represented belong to antiquity and the Old Testament: Alexander the Great's attempt to fly through the heavens, the equally daring construction of the Tower of Babel, Adam and Eve, Cain and Abel, the story of Noah and his salvation in the Ark as a prefiguration of the church, in the space behind the altar the stories of Jonah and Samson, a dragon, Apuleius's ass, and other animals. It is only the picture of King Arthur before the gates of paradise—where a panther is jumping up at him—that leads us out of the world of nature, of antiquity, and the Old Testament. Apparently it is the similarity in the nature of the two that makes this connection—Arthur as an intensified Alexander—for there is nothing to identify him as a Christian. Lying, then, on the pavement of the nave and the side aisles, we see "the tree of world history regarded as nature and fate. . . . It is the world of the descent of the second Adam. His work does not belong on the pavement. The fate of mankind, which is unfolded in the tree, is entwined, in all its characteristics, with life

91. Grazio Gianfreda, *Il mosaico pavimentale della basilica cattedrale do Otranto,* 3d ed. (Otranto, 1970); Wolfram von den Steinen, *Homo caelestis: Das Wort der Kunst im Mittelalter,* vol. 1, *Text* (Berne, 1965), pp. 204ff.; vol. 2, *Bildband* (illustrations), table 298/III.

on earth and with the course of the stars: every characteristic of the animals reflects, most meaningfully, the fate of mankind. They are beasts when man goes to his ruin because of his vain desires; they are pious before Noah's Ark; in the Zodiac, they serve as signs for the divinely determined course of nature."[92] The aisle on the right-hand side is filled with a tree full of monsters: it bears Atlas on its tip, and Ephialtes and Antæus, as well as Samuel, Nimrod, and the Gigantes. In the branches of the tree, in the left-hand aisle, we see, on one side, hell with animals, Satan, the Erinyes, Charon, Cerberus, and examples of sinners and, on the other, paradise with a stag and, above it, Abraham, Isaac, and Jacob.[93]

The space that represents the old era in the pavement of Siena makes sense only when we see it as the basis of the space allotted to the church that is constructed above it and that spans—as an undivided entity—the history of salvation, which is divided up on the pavement. The new era has its space above, between the pavement and the cupola. Gregory the Great says of the Temple of Ezekiel: "Intellecta ergo lex, quae in latitudine jacuit, in altitudinem surrexit" [Hence the law is understood that lay horizontally, and rose vertically].[94] Nicolas Pisano's pulpit (1265–68) is a hundred years older than the oldest pavement pictures (figs. 1, 28), and it, too, is a representation of a temporal space.[95] The octagonal pulpit is supported by one central pillar and eight others, one at each corner. The base of the pulpit is formed by the bases of the pillars; at four of the corners there are two nursing lionesses and two lions tearing a horse to pieces; beneath the central pillar we find the seven liberal arts and philosophy. The base of the pulpit also stands for the creatural world and the world of antiquity. Giovanni Pisano was still a young man

92. Von den Steinen, p. 206. Melani, p. 438, wrote: "al primo vederlo sembra una grande bizarria, con animali, figure, alberi, un cumulo di cose; e tosto lo sguardo si fermi paziente, scorge l'albero della vita ritto su due elefanti a'qauli si avvincevano esseri di tutte le razze."

93. As we consider the trees on the pavement that represents the old world, may we be permitted to recall that Augustine, on several occasions, calls the world of pagan belief, filled with idols and demons, a forest that covers the world, against which the church has to be deployed by using the wild wood of the forest as building material for the church? Citations in Dominique Sanchis, *Le symbolisme communautaire du temple chez saint Augustin,* pp. 143ff.

94. *PL,* 76, 179 A.

95. On the pulpit, see G. H. and E. R. Crichton, *Nicola Pisano and the Revival of Sculpture in Italy* (Cambridge, 1938), pp. 68–85; Giusta-Nicco Fasola, *Nicola Pisano* (Rome, 1941), pp. 113–138; Cesare Gnudi, *Nicola, Arnolfo, Lapo* (Florence, 1948), p. 140 (index); Martin Weinberger, "Nicola Pisano," in *Encyclopedia of World Art,* vol. 10 (1965), cols. 641–647; Max Seidel, *Die Sieneser Domkanzel des Nicola Pisano* (Milan, 1971), p. 7, calls the Pisanos' pulpits "great systems of instruction."

when his father brought him to work on this pulpit, and, presumably, he developed ideas for the cathedral facade from it that, in their turn, could further affect the program of the pavement. Thus, we can look upon Nicola Pisano's cathedral pulpit as the creative idea that was the source of the entire Sienese pictorial program. Above the capitals of the pulpit's pillars, in a higher order and supported by the cardinal virtues, the theological virtues, prophets, and a sibyl, the body of the pulpit represents the period of the history of salvation in the church, from the birth of Christ to the Day of Judgment. The reliefs on the octagon show the life of Christ up to the Passion, the evangelists, and church fathers, with the Day of Judgment at the end. Today, the pulpit stands on the cathedral pavement to the left of the Moses cycle, on a diagonal toward the right-hand corner, behind Herod's massacre of the Innocents, on the site of the birth of Christ, which is the beginning of the history of salvation. It is conceivable that the pictures of Herod on the pavement were placed here, between the last sibyl in the nave and the pulpit, with an eye to the latter, whose relief depicting the massacre of the Innocents looks down at the picture of the massacre on the pavement. It is true that the pulpit was moved here only in the sixteenth century—prior to this it had been on the right of the central nave under the cupola.[96] Pisano's pulpit shows how the cathedral in Siena distinguishes, by different heights, between the old and the new world, the creatural and antique below, the prophetic above, and the Christian at the very top.[97] Even before the completion of the marble pavement in the chancel, Beccafumi had, between 1535 and 1544, painted frescoes in the apse: on top, Christ ascending between angels, and underneath, the Virgin Mary among the Twelve Apostles.[98] The theme of angels and apostles that testifies to the idea of height encompassed the whole area. The eight central pillars between the cupola and the apse bear—at exactly the "Christian" height of the pulpit

96. On the various positions of the pulpit, Max Seidel, "Die Verkündigungsgruppe der Sieneser Domkanzel," *Münchener Jahrbuch der bildenden Kunst*, vol. 21, pp. 19–72, pp. 56f.

97. On the transition from the Old to the New Testament in the vertical planes of the cathedral, see P. de la Ruffière du Prey, "Solomonic Symbolism in Borromini's Church of S. Ivo alla Sapienza," *Zeitschrift für Kunstgeschichte* 31 (1968): 216–232, p. 227: "Thus, the interior of S. Ivo might be compared to the mystical mill in which the grain of the Old Testament (as represented by Solomonic references in the lower part of the church) is transformed by Christ (whose cross appears in the vault) into the flour of the New Testament." "In its motion upwards, the church of S. Ivo represents the progression from the wisdom of the Old Testament to the dissemination of the New Testament through the Dove of Pentecost, the Apostles, and Petrus's successor, Pope Alexander VII" (p. 228).

98. The frescoes, which are only partially preserved, have been described with great precision by Vasari: see Sanminiatelli, pp. 114f. (figs. 65f.) and the colored plates after p. 160.

rail—the eight bronze candelabra angels (fig. 28), one and a half meters in height, that date from the last years of Beccafumi's life (1548–51).[99] The effect of hovering that these convey lends a light and delicate height to the space. Four older candelabra angels, on the high altar, bring the number of angels to twelve, the same number as the apostles on the fresco in the apse.

The remaining pillars in the nave and side aisles carried twelve marble statues of the apostles. In accord with the allegorical meaning of *columna* (apostle), the medieval church saw the apostles as standing in the pillars that support the church. When people no longer had faith in the mute language of the pillars, it was given voice in a number of different cathedrals—from the thirteenth century onward—by adding statues of the apostles to the pillars.[100] Twelve apostles who were sculpted by Giuseppe Mazzuoli at the end of the seventeenth century stood on the pillars until 1870 (today they are in London). These baroque apostles had displaced the Gothic marble apostles that were, perhaps, by Giovanni Pisano and his school from the pillars onto the southern roofs of the nave and the side aisles, where today only copies of them are to be seen: the originals are in a museum in the cathedral crypt. A plan, already in existence in 1505, to replace them with twelve bronze statues in the nave, so that the whole space would have been surrounded by twelve

99. Ibid., p. 122, figs. 79 and 79a, b.

100. Bandmann, p. 37: "The relationship of the forms to these predetermined, or underlying, meanings changes as they try—increasingly in the High and late Middle Ages—to make the hints that are, at first, only associatively effective become more and more visually apparent." Hans Jantzen, *Kunst der Gotik* (Hamburg, 1957), pp. 153f.: "The fact that the *columnae* mentioned by Suger in the choir of St. Denis contain an inherent symbolism, and that it lives on, seems to derive from the fact that, in the course of the thirteenth century, what was signified still appeared in physical form. The classic cathedrals, it is true, still have no monumental sculpture in the interior (except for the decoration of the rood screen); however, in the Ste.-Chapelle in Paris (1245–48) the figures of the apostles, turned inwards, appear, for the first time, on pillars. At the beginning of the fourteenth century, in the choir of Cologne Cathedral, we can see pillars, with the figures of the Twelve Apostles that, because of the growing orders of magnitude of Gothic architecture, can now hardly be interpreted anthropomorphically but that still correspond to the spiritually perceived context that Suger suggests in his description of the choir of St. Denis."

In the Freiburg Minster, Christ and thirteen apostles, partially characterized by their attributes, stand on pillars dating from 1300–1310; Ernst Adam, *Das Freiburger Münster* (Stuttgart, 1968), p. 74. In the Church of the Virgin in Trier, the pictures of the apostles were painted on the twelve central pillars in the center of the building.

The example of the apostle pillars makes it emphatically clear—since dozens of examples of the signification of *columna* as "apostle" are to be found in the exegetical literature of medieval architecture—how much we still feel the lack of a dictionary of the spiritual significations of architectural members. It would not be difficult to compile such a dictionary.

angels and twelve apostles, all in bronze, was never realized. The number twelve in the space above is a sum of the sevens and fives of the pavement. Just as, on the floor of the chancel, the cycles of five and seven merge, so, too, the pillars in the choirs show seven light and, above them, five darker, more modestly accentuated, tambours (figs. 27, 28). In this way, the white marble apostles led right up to the space under the cupola, and the angels of the candelabras, in bronze, went as far as the apse, in the same way that the holy of holies of the Tabernacle could be regarded as the space of the angels.[101] The space above belongs to the angels, the apostles, and other saints, who have gathered under the cupola. The four patron saints of the city of Siena (Ansanus, Savinus, Crescentius, Victorius) and SS. Catherine and Bernardine, who lived in Siena (figs. 22, 27), stand in a circle, monumental and gilded, at the nichelike corners of the hexagon above the capitals of the pillars supporting the cupola. These statues date from the year 1490.[102] Twelve further figures of saints in stained glass stand between them, at the same height, in three small window niches (fig. 22). A cycle of forty-two painted—though the effect is one of sculpture—Old Testament patriarchs and prophets, dating from 1482 (fig. 27) and standing between forty-two delicate pillars, runs above these eighteen saints underneath the ceiling of the cupola.[103] This cycle, the highest of all the pictorial cycles in the cathedral, which was painted while the pictures of the sibyls were being inlaid into the marble of the pavement, seems, with its patriarchs and prophets, to contradict the fundamental observation of this present study. Apparently, we have here an isolated illogicality that runs counter to the basic idea that the old era is represented in the pavement and the new era in the superstructure. The patriarchs and prophets in the cupola cycle all have haloes, but these are absent from the pictures on the pavement. The haloes incorporate them into the *communis sanctorum* of the church, which even today—when the medieval worship of Old Testament saints is still only partially preserved—still invokes these saints from

101. Enzo Carli, "Le statue degli apostoli per il duomo di Siena," *Antichità viva* 7, no. 6 (1968): 3–20, with a bibliography of older literature.

The commentary on the Tabernacle by Peter of Poitiers (d. 1205) interprets the sky-blue curtain between the shrine and the holy of holies in the Tabernacle as the entrance to the paradisal part of the church, "because the church is partly on earth, and partly triumphant in heaven. . . . The curtain is hung up in front of the four pillars, that is, before the angelic spirits who nurture the four cardinal virtues that we attempt to follow with all our might"; Philip S. Moore and James A. Corbett, *Petri Pictaviensis Allegoriae super tabernaculum Moysi* (Notre Dame, Ind., 1938), p. 122.

102. Lusini, 2:141ff.

103. Ibid., 2:142f.

FIGURE 27
View through the cupola space into the choir, Siena Cathedral.

FIGURE 28
Pulpit of Nicola Pisano, Siena Cathedral.

the old era in the litany for All Saints' Day. The patriarchs and prophets of the cupola cycle are saints of the church and have a right to their place on high.[104] Beneath the cupola, just as in the chancel, the saints of the old era are linked to those of the new era. Above them, there is a narrow strip of forty putti, representing the world of the angels, of whom six once again hover under the lantern. The cupola, built in 1264, was painted at the end of the fifteenth century when the rest of the vault was painted sky blue, and it was divided into a hundred sky-blue fields with a hundred golden stars as the perfect space of eternity that arches over the old and the new eras. The five coffers of the Pantheon vault that taper into rings (just as in Siena) were originally decorated with stars.[105] The niches in the Pantheon that hold the statues of the gods and surround the coffer vault apparently inspired the cycles of patriarchs and prophets that are painted in the same position in Siena. In the spatial context of the church, the saints and angels in the cupola baptize the classical form—which was consciously created as such by Renaissance decoration—into the Christian heaven. Like the Temple of Solomon, the Pantheon is also present in the cathedral. The acceptance of the cupola of the Pantheon into the cathe-

104. Henri-Irénée Marrou, "Les saints de l'ancien testament au martyrologe romain," in *Mémoire J. Chaine* (Lyon, 1950), pp. 281–290; Jean de Menasce, "Notes sur la dévotion liturgique aux saints de l'ancien testament," *Bulletin catholique de la question d'Israel* (1929), no. 27: 1–11; no. 29: 11–15. D. B. Botte, "Le culte des saints de l'ancien testament dans l'église ancienne," *Cahiers Sioniens* 4 (1950): 38–47; M. Simon, "Les saints d'Israel dans la dévotion de l'église ancienne," *Revue d'histoire et de philosophie religieuse* 34 (1954): 98–127. On the cult of David, Robert Folz, *Études sur le culte liturgique de Charlemagne dans les églises de l'empire* (Strassburg, 1951). Chrétien de Troyes speaks of St. Abraham (*Graal* 2966) and St. David (*Graal* 4234); cf. Paul Imbs in *Les romans du Graal dans la littérature des XIIe et XIIIe siècles* (Paris, 1956), p. 36; on the worship of the Old Testament saints, Raymond Kottje, *Studien zum Einfluss des Alten Testaments auf Recht und Liturgie des frühen Mittelalters (6–8. Jahrhundert),* Bonner Historische Forschungen, no. 23 (Bonn, 1964), pp. 19–28.

The cycle of pictures of standing prophets, as the uppermost row of pictures in St. Peter's, corresponds to the highest pictorial cycle of patriarchs and prophets in the cathedral at Siena; J. Garber, *Wirkungen der frühchristlichen Gemäldezyklen der alten Peters- und Paulsbasiliken in Rom* (Berlin, 1918), p. 24; "erant in summitate ad planum fenestrae prophetae stantes" [there were prophets standing at the highest place, on the level of the window], so that both the Pantheon and St. Peter's are linked here. On the relationship between the Pantheon and St. Peter's in Goethe's work, see Friedrich Ohly, "Römisches und Biblisches in Goethes *Märchen,*" *Zeitschrift für deutsches Altertum und deutsche Literatur* 91 (1961): 147–166.

105. M. Zeph, "Der Mensch in der Höhle und das Pantheon," *Gymnasium* 65 (1958): 355–382, p. 373: "there is still an echo, in the Renaissance, in the ceiling vaults, decorated as the firmament, in Agostino Chigi's Villa Farnesina at the point where, spatially too, antiquity and the Renaissance once again come most closely into contact" (taken from Arnold von Salis, *Antike und Renaissance* [Erlenbach, 1947], pp. 190–207).

dral in Siena also had a liturgical significance, for if the central space of the Sienese cupola was conceived, from the outset, as a shrine to Mary, it had a lofty predecessor in the Pantheon, which was rededicated as the Church of S. Maria Rotonda.[106] The area covered by the cupola has a certain life of its own from the pavement up to the lantern. Its floor shows the cycle of seven in its most pure form. The cycle of Old Testament saints numbers six times seven patriarchs and prophets. The program of the pillar statues, before and after it, leaves the space of the cupola untouched. The transition from the saints to the angels in the vertical lines of the cupola corresponds to the horizontal leap of the apostles, in the nave, to the angels of the candelabra beyond the crossing. The progression from the saints (apostles) and the angels, in the pillar and cupola programs, shows the unified space as having been graduated

106. Antje Middeldorf-Kosegarten, "Zur Bedeutung der Sieneser Domkuppel," *Münchener Jahrbuch der bildenden Kunst* 21 (1970): 73–98, esp. pp. 84ff: "Whether the architect of the Sienese cathedral actually intended to make a reference, with his cupola, to the church of S. Maria Rotonda, that is, the Pantheon, is of course undemonstrable since, as we have said, no information has been handed down on the subject. But such a view is not to be dismissed out of hand" (p. 84). Scepticism of this sort where the appearance is convincing, and where only an authenticating piece of paper is lacking, weakens the trust in one's own vision and robs the eye of the intellect of its most beautiful power. The assumption, by the writer, that the cupola was inspired "by small pieces of architecture from the field of liturgical fixtures," like the tabernacle or the baldachin (pp. 86ff.), can, in view of the monumentality of the cupola, scarcely be regarded as convincing.

On the new respect for the Pantheon—which was also godfather to Bramante's Santa Maria della Grazie (1492–97)—that has existed since Petrarch (who believed it to be the oldest church of the Virgin to be preserved from destruction), see Tilman Buddenseig, "Criticism and Praise of the Pantheon in the Middle Ages and the Renaissance," in *Classical Influences on European Culture A.D. 500–1500*, ed. R. R. Bolgar (Cambridge, 1971), pp. 259–267.

With regard to the cathedral as the Church of the Virgin, we have to bear in mind that before work was started on the new pavement, and on the new ornamental sculptural cycles, its pictorial decoration was strongly influenced by panel painting. In the middle of the fourteenth century it contained four major works of Sienese painting: under the cupola on the high altar, Duccio's great *Maestà* (1311), which was followed, on the altars of the chapels, by Simone Martini's *Annunciation* and, in 1342, by Pietro Lorenzetti's *The Birth of Mary*, and by the *Purification of the Virgin* by his brother Ambrosio Lorenzetti. Ever since these valuable monuments to the Marian cult were removed to the cathedral museum and to the Uffizzi, much of the visual character of the cathedral as a church of the Virgin has been lost. After the great panel paintings were removed from the high altar, Mary dominated the inner space only from the huge round windows above the apse and on the facade. On the pictures of Mary, see H. W. van Os, *Marias Demut und Verherrlichung in der sienesischen Malerei 1300–1450* (The Hague, 1969), pp. 3ff. (the altar pictures in Siena Cathedral), 37ff. (Simone Martini's *Annunciation*). I am grateful to Frau Dr. Middeldorf-Kosegarten for this reference.

vertically as well as horizontally. There are, however, two other sculptural cycles running round the building from the portal to the apse that are a completely ungraduated, and paratactically similar, unit that shows us the whole era of the church on earth. As a rectangle that fills the whole space from the wall of the portal to the rear wall of the choir and encircles the whole church, they are the highest cycles outside the area of the cupola, and that they skip.

Under the bright clerestory, at the height of the main cornice, there is a cycle of 172 terra-cotta busts of the popes (figs. 24, 27) from Peter to Lucius III (1181–1185), representing within the cathedral the unbroken progression of church history, from Christ to the year 1185. After two centuries, the main cornice, dating from the thirteenth century,[107] and going back to Nicola Pisano—the architect who may also have been engaged in the design of the cupola—acquired, with the addition of this cycle of busts, a significant and

107. Wolfgang Krönig, "Toskana und Apulien: Beiträge zum Problemkreis der Herkunft des Nicola Pisano," *Zeitschrift für Kunstgeschichte* 16 (1953): 101–144, emphasizes the fact that the creative novelty of the form of the basilica, with its corbeling, is a specifically Italian art form, and, in Siena Cathedral, he sees a cardinal point of its history; he is also inclined to accord to the person of Nicola Pisano a key position in the development of Italian corbeling. "Ultimately the later addition of the plastic series of portraits—in the form of the busts of the popes—in the quattrocento gave a further peculiar pictorial interpretation to the corbeled cornice, which is architecturally so significant" (pp. 104f.). Krönig (pp. 120f., 129) would like to derive corbeling from antiquity. The double-storied central nave, accentuated by the horizontal corbeling that he ascribes to all Italian basilical church spaces containing corbeling (pp. 103, 127), may perhaps be related to the two stories of the Temple of Solomon. Antje Middeldorf-Kosegarten also considers the possibility that Nicola Pisano may have been the builder of the cupola of Siena Cathedral—he was also well known as an architect (pp. 89f.). Giusta Nicco Fasola, in his "Induzioni su Nicola Pisano architetto," *L'Arte* 41 (1938): 315–343, pp. 331ff., thinks that Nicola Pisano was involved as an architect, not only with the capitals of the columns that came out of his school, but also with the pioneering cornice in the nave and the design of the cupola. Renate Rieger also sees "the possibility that Nicola played a decisive part in determining the form of the cornice" (p. 103). We also have to take into consideration the change in the original spatial effect that was not effected until the nave was raised in 1396: "Because of the raising of the nave in the second phase, the corbeling, both in Siena and Ruvo, was raised into a position half the height of the nave. This use of the corbeling, which is common to Siena and Ruvo, as opposed to other Italian buildings, suggests that they belong together" (p. 108). Rieger believes "that both go back to a common prototype. We can, with some certainty, assume that Siena was dependent on the architecture of Poitiers." Rieger thinks that Siena was dependent on French architecture, especially that of Poitiers, in the facade as well, so that the part played by Giovanni Pisano was restricted to the sculptural program, "but, at the same time, because of the rich plastic decoration of the facades in Poitiers, we would have to ask ourselves whether stimuli from Poitou were not also to be held responsible for the decoration of the facade in Siena."

emphatic interpretation of the importance attached to these horizontals. The popes look down upon the church, from the bright upper area, as though they helped support it. Starting with the bust of Christ, in the middle of the apse, and the bust of Peter on its left, the long series of likenesses of the popes encircles the huge space and ends in the apse with the final bust, Lucius III, next to Christ. The diverse quality of the busts in this cycle, which dates from the end of the fifteenth century, has certainly not earned it any great esteem; on the contrary, people have tended to turn up their noses at it.[108] However, the judgment cannot be only an aesthetic one—from whom could one expect 172 busts of high quality? It also does not fulfill a decorative function, for analagous main cornices of other churches, like the cathedral in Florence, manage to achieve the same effect of spatial division without busts. The idea of placing the popes in the niches between the corbels of the molding, where they are in poor light, was done not with any thought of ornamentation but, apparently, with the idea of representing an era. The busts show the temporal space and the continuity of the church, as it is represented, from Christ onward, by the popes. Encircling the church, and returning to Christ, the series is, ideally, endless, even if it does not go beyond Lucius III. The number 172—the number of popes to be seen here—is idealized. One hundred is the number of perfection, seventy-two the number of the peoples of the earth.[109] The number can lay claim to a certain universality. It cannot be a coincidence that the pillars of the nave have, as a rule, seventy-two black and white stripes between base and capital, and the same number of stripes, in white and green, are also to be found on the campanile between its "base" and "capital," that is, in the six fenestrated stories of the spire.[110] In contrast to the nave

108. Lusini, 2:147f., regards the addition of the main corbeling, as a gallery, around the church as an "unfortunate" burden and an interruption of the verticality of the nave, which the idea (*sfogo ornamentale*) of adding the busts of the popes beneath it only made worse. With few exceptions, he regards the busts, which were colored between the years 1499 and 1505, as mass-produced wares. The fact that the controversial bust of Pope Joan was removed in the year 1600 (pp. 148ff.) is mentioned today only as a curiosity. According to Lusini (2:148), the cycle of the popes was to have ended with Lucius III at the wall of the portal. I am guided by the evidence of my own eyes and by Aldo Lusini and Sandro Chierichetti, *Siena: Guida artistica illustrata*, 5th ed. (Siena, n.d.), p. 69, according to which the cycle ends in the apse on the right of Christ.

109. We may perhaps consider whether the fact that the end of the series is Lucius III may bear some relationship to the date when the cathedral was started—something which has been obscure up till now. The initial dedication of the unfinished building, in 1215, for the purpose of holding divine services, could suggest a beginning in the 1180s.

110. The number of stripes on the campanile is not derived simply from 6×12; the individual stories from bottom to top have 10, 12, 12, 12, 14, and 12 (= 72) stripes.

and the area of the cupola the stripes on the pillars start beyond the crossing. It is here that the space grows brighter, because the pillars and walls are predominantly white. In the area of the cycles of seven on the pavement, the pillars have seven tambours between their base and their capital; every tambour is set off by black stripes (figs. 22, 27).[111] The exterior wall of the cathedral, with its marble cladding, also participates in this transition to groups of seven stripes (fig. 24).

At the time when the cycle of the 172 busts of the popes was added in Siena, mosaic cycles of half-length portraits of the popes in medallions were to be seen, at a corresponding height above the arcades, in the Roman Churches of S. Paolo fuori le mura and the old St. Peter's. Siena thus took its place as a successor to the most venerable churches of Rome,[112] something no other place had dared to do. But literary tradition must also be taken into account. In the worldview of the *Arca Noe mystica,* written by Hugh of St.-Victor, the half-length portraits of the twelve sons of Jacob were painted with their names beneath them, "quasi quidam senatus Dei civitatis" [as though it were a sort of senate of the state of God],[113] and opposite them, painted in similar fashion, were the portraits of the Twelve Apostles. However, the series of names of all the popes from Clement to Honorius II—that is, all the popes up to the date when the work was composed (prior to 1130)—was joined to Peter. "And the rest of the space, to the end of the Ark, will admit those who come after us until the end of the world."[114] The series of names of popes on the Christian length of the Ark stands for the era of the church from Peter until its end. Half a century later, Adam Scotus (ca. 1180), in his view of the world of the Tabernacle, encircled the inner world of the church—which is distinguished from the world of the laity that surrounds it on the outside—by enclosing the whole rectangular Tabernacle in a rectangle, in which there are pictures of all the popes from Clement to Alexander II (i.e., up to 1180, the date of the composition of the work). This is done in such a manner that the picture of the last pope completes the circuit by ending up next to the picture of Peter. Adam's description and explanation of his pictorial cycle of popes reads like a description and explanation of the Sienese cycle:

111. Krönig, pp. 102 and 104, regards this only as a "simplification of the black and white stripes of the pillars" on the east side of the cupola.

112. See below, p. 202 and n. 121.

113. *PL,* 176, 686 D.

114. *PL,* 176, 687 D.

Post haec omnia ad orientem supra patriarcham Jerosolymitanum pono nomen et imaginem Petri apostoli. . . . Post Petrum vero intra quamdam quadraturam, quae per circuitum usque ad eamdem Petri imaginem undique porrigitur, aliorum apostolicorum virorum, qui suae post eum sedis apostolicae in Ecclesia Romana fuere successores, ponuntur icones, easdem tenenetes in manibus claves; ita ut singulorum nomina singulis iconibus subtus ponantur, hoc modo: Petrus, Linus, Cletus, Clemens [what follows is a catalogue of Papal names up to Alexander III]. Hos viros apostolicos una cum Petro, cujus et locum tenent et officium exercent, idcirco in tam sublimi loco posuimus, quia ipsi sunt sanctae universalis Ecclesiae capita et praelati omnium praelatorum ejus. . . . Quos ideo in pictura nostra super omnes Ecclesiae personas in eminentibus et summis locis, in quibusdam excelsis thronis et subliminibus consistoriis posuimus, quia eis vice beati Petri apostolorum principis praesidentibus omnis ordo ecclesiasticus obtempererare debt; qui soli singulari praerogativa praecelsae dignitatis claves habent ligandi et solvendi omnia super terram. [After all these things, [turning to] indications of the ascent on high of the patriarch of Jerusalem, I set the name and the image of the apostle Peter. . . . And indeed, after Peter within a certain rectangular figure which, closing the circle, makes contact in every respect with that same image, icons of other apostolic men are set up, post-Petrian men, who after Peter were successors to his apostolic seat in the Church of Rome, holding those selfsame icons in their hands as keys to the kingdom; this in such a way that the names of the individuals are placed beneath the individual icons, in this fashion: Peter, Linus, Cletus, Clement [what follows is a catalogue of papal names up to Alexander III]. These apostolic men, together with Peter, whose position they occupy and whose offices they exercise, we have put in so sublime a place since they are the heads of the holy universal church and the prelates of all its prelates . . . men whom we have placed, therefore, in our picture above all persons of the church in eminent and even in the highest positions, on their exalted thrones and in sublime cohorts, inasmuch as every ecclesiastical order ought to obey them as presiding in place of the blessed Peter; they alone, who with their singular prerogative of august dignity, have in their possession the key of binding and loosing all things upon this earth.][115]

Adam drew the popes on the parchment as half-length figures, so that he could give them the keys of office. Even if we are reluctant to derive the Sienese cycle of popes from Adam Scotus's Tabernacle commentary, written three hundred years earlier, it is nonetheless true that the pictorial cycle of all

115. Adamus Scotus, *De tripartito tabernaculo una cum pictura,* pars 2, cap. 106, in *PL,* 198, 710 B–711 B.

the popes contained in a rectangle surrounding the whole church is—apart from Siena—known to us only from Adam's worldview of the Tabernacle.

A cycle of emperors just below the cycle of popes serves the same function. This also dates from the fifteenth century: there are thirty-six bas-relief busts of Christian emperors in medallions (figs. 24, 27). There are two busts over each arcade in the nave between the molding and the pillar, and they traverse the nave on both sides from the portal to the apse, without—like the popes—also impinging upon the short sides of the cathedral. These busts, of which scholarship—giving up trying to solve a puzzle—notes that they are the Roman emperors from Constantine to Theodosius,[116] could have a significance analogous to the busts of the popes immediately above them, namely, that of representing the world and the temporal space of the Christian empire within the cathedral. We cannot here take up the question of the spiritual relationship of the cycle of emperors to the royal galleries, or to the other cycles of rulers in the stained glass windows and on the exterior of the cathedral. But we can refer, once again, to Adam Scotus's view of the world and the temporal cosmos of the Tabernacle. On the concentrically rectangular world of the Tabernacle, with its five areas, we found—after the holy of holies, the shrine, and the atrium—the fourth area, next to the outside, to be that of the clergy surrounded by the cycle of popes from Peter to the time of the composition of the work (ca. 1180). Corresponding to the festoon, in the fourth area, of 156 popes, the next area, the fifth, the world of the laity, is framed by the pictures of kings and emperors that protect the Tabernacle on all sides against an empty world which is no longer shaped by it. Each of them is, like Constantine—the first of the series of Christian rulers—painted with the insignia of his office:

Sic clericis circa tabernaculum ordinatis laicos fideles circa idem tabernaculum, foris tamen a clericis, dispono; quia nimirum laici fideles, licet in ipso tabernaculo sanctae Ecclesiae officium spirituale sicut clerici non habent, ad eam tamen per fidem et bona opera pertinent. Primum itaque antiqui temporis laicos videlicet per tribus circa praedictum tabernaculum et intra quamdam magnam quadraturam, quam modo facio, per quatuor ejus partes cum nominibus et iconibus suis pono. [Just as the clerics were arranged around the Tabernacle, so too do I arrange the faithful lay people around the same Tabernacle, nonetheless, however, beyond the ranks of the clerics, since without doubt the faithful laity, although within the Tabernacle itself of the Holy church it does not have the same spiritual office as do

116. Lusini, 2:150; Lusini and Chierichetti, *Siena*, p. 72.

the clerics, nonetheless still relates to it ["the Tabernacle itself of the Holy church"] through faith and good works. And so first of all I post the lay people of ancient times, namely, by tribe around the aforesaid Tabernacle and within that particular great rectangular figure, which I just now make, according to its four parts with their names and icons.][117]

After having settled the way groups and families of pious laymen of the old era are to be distributed in the Tabernacle to all points of the compass, and after adding pictures of good works from the compassion of the New Testament, Adam proceeds with his description of the cycle of emperors:

Post haec ad orientem imperatorem Romanum, diadema in capite aureum, et in una manu evaginatum gladium, in altera vero sceptrum habentem aureum, armillam nihilominus in dextera brachio auream, et ipsum imperatorem purpura vestitum depingo: quia sicut Dominus papa caput est clericorum ita imperator caput est laicorum. . . . Haec autem imago, quae hoc in loco visibiliter depicta est, magnum et illustrem innuit imperatorem Constantinum. . . . Post hunc, de quo loquimur, Constantinum intra quamdam quadraturam, quae per circuitum usque ad eumdem Constantinum porrigitur, aliorum imperatorum ponuntur icones eisdem insignibus decoratae: ita ut singulorum nomina singulis iconibus subscribantur. [After these indications of the ascent of the Roman emperor, the diadem on a head of gold, in one hand an unsheathed sword and in the other, to be sure, a scepter made of gold, a golden ring on the finger, and nothing less than a gold bracelet on the right forearm, I also paint the emperor himself clothed in purple: since just as the Holy Father is the head of the priesthood, so is the emperor head of the lay people. . . . Moreover, this image, which is visibly depicted in this place, suggests the great and illustrious emperor Constantine. . . . After the latter, of whom we speak, Constantine within a certain rectangle, coming full cycle, extends himself to reach that very same Constantine, icons of the remaining emperors and decorated with the same insignia are laid down, so that the names of individual emperors are inscribed under their individual icons.][118]

The fifty-nine pictures of Roman emperors up to Frederick I are followed by pictures of thirty-six Frankish, nineteen English, and six Scottish kings, all with their names, and all with their insignia of office individually

117. Pars 2, cap. 13, section 108, in *PL*, 198, 712 BC.

118. Pars 2, cap. 8, section 110f., in *PL*, 198, 713 BC, 714 B.

interpreted.[119] Adam placed the kings of England and Scotland—as the kings of his homelands—in the Tabernacle after the emperors and the Frankish kings but left it to his imitators to place the kings of their homeland after the Frankish kings, just as long as the cycle of emperors was undisturbed.[120] In this work, which depicts the ideal and magnificent plan for the pictorial pro-

119. Pars 2, cap. 13, section 122, in *PL*, 198, 724 D. The symbols of the rulers are introduced again with the comment "Haec enim sunt quaedam dignitatis ornamenta regibus concessa, quibus et excellentia ordinis eorum ostenditur et sacramentum mysterii figuratur; non solum quippe visibilem exterius intuentibus repraesentant decorem, sed et spiritualem in se latentem continent significationem, quia singula nimirum ista insignia spiritualia, quae in sanctitate debent exercere conversationis innuunt ornamenta" [For these are certain ornaments of status to which kings are entitled, by which both the excellence of their order is shown and the sacrament of mystery is figurally represented; indeed, not only do they represent visible beauty to those looking on from the outside, but they also contain a spiritual signification hidden within them, since doubtless individual specimens among these spiritual insignia, which ought to exercise an effect within the sanctity of our social intercourse, seem to signal an ornamental effect]. Then follows the interpretation of the insignia (725 A–C).

120. Pars 2, cap. 13, section 120, in *PL*, 198, 723 C–724 A: "Hoc autem sciant inspectores picturae hujus, quod sicut nos pro eo quod in terra Anglorum et in regno Scotorum sumus, Anglorum in ea et Scotorum posuimus reges, ita quoque possunt ipsi, si forte aliam secundum formam istius facere voluerint, etiam Christianissimos in ea regionum suarum reges post Francorum reges ponere: hoc quidem duntaxat diligenter observato, ut magna illa quadratura, quae ab una parte imaginis Constantini Magni usque ad aliam ejus porrigitur, Christianorum regum iconibus impleatur, singulis iconibus singulorum regum nominibus subter (Migne supra) inscriptis" [Those who have examined this picture also know this, that just as we have included the kings of the Angles and the Scots for the reason that we ourselves are in the land of the Angles and the Scots, so also they too, if they perhaps wished to follow the form of this document further, could add to it, after the Frankish kings, the most Christian kings of their regions: given that, at least as far applies, that that great rectangle which is extended from one part of the image of Constantine the Great to the other is filled with the icons of Christian kings, each and every icon being inscribed below (Migne supra) with the name of the corresponding king]. As in the case of the series of popes, he intends to leave room for a series of additional pictures without names, so that the successors of those who are ruling at the moment can be entered into the series. "Et idcirco quod superius de iconibus et nominibus quatuor horum apostolicorum diximus, hoc per omnia et in isto loco de imperatoribus teneatur, ut ab una videlicet parte Constantini usque ad aliam ejus partem per circuitum nominibus suppositis sine aliquo spatio interposito imperatorum et regum ponantur icones; sed illis iconibus quae post eos, qui nunc regnant, ponuntur, nomina non subscribantur. Igitur horum principum nomina, imperatorum videlicet Romanorum et regum Francorum, Anglorum quoque et Scotorum cum singulorum iconibus supra depictis, in hac quadratura undique per circuitum porrecta scribimus hoc modo" [And therefore what we said before concerning the icons and the names of the four apostolic peoples, this holds for all and here in particular for the emperors, so that clearly one can proceed from one attribute of Constantine to the other by way of a cyclical movement, the names

gram of the Tabernacle-church, Adam saw the world of the church as being contained in two superimposed cycles of popes and rulers that encircled it on the outside, running from the east back to the east. The question of how far the program of the figures of rulers in the Gothic cathedral corresponds to the spiritual vision that Adam committed to parchment—at least as the beginnings of an ideal and typical realization—cannot be addressed here. This is particularly true since Adam's total view is by no means unique in the twelfth century, and the ways in which architecture and theology had a common part to play in an overarching spirit of the time often—and this too is fortunate—elude any attempt to prove dependence. Nevertheless, it is important to recollect that the cathedral in Siena realizes, with great precision, the cycle of popes that Adam describes, and that it also has beneath it—that is, spiritually, around it on the outside—a cycle of emperors that begins with Constantine and still awaits closer examination by scholars.[121] This form of architectural decoration, with cycles of portraits in medallions, has a venerable prototype in the painted medallions of the popes in the Roman basilicas of St. Paul and the old St. Peter's, as well as in the mosaic cycles in Ravenna.[122]

---

having been added, and this without any intervening space filled with the icons of emperors and kings; but to those icons which are placed after those who now reign, names are not added. Therefore the names of these leaders, emperors, namely Roman emperors and Frankish kings, also Angles and Scots, with the individual icons of each above depicted, we write in this rectangle everywhere extended cyclically in the fashion described]. This is followed by the catalog of all the names of the rulers that are to be entered.

The cycles—each consisting of twelve angels, with kings next to them and, on the outside, prophets—arranged concentrically around the Mother of Christ in the innermost part of the great rose window in Chartres can be compared with Adam's concentric pictorial cycles.

121. Lusini, 2:150: "I pennacchi delle sottosanti arcate . . . ricevettero l'ornamento di una nicchia circolare ben lavorata di stucco con entro un busto degl'imperatori romani da Constantino a Teodosio; queste teste ebber colore da Jacomo Pacchiarotti e da Antonio di Giovanni." There is no more to be learned about the cycle of emperors from this two-volume work on the cathedral at Siena. The busts of the popes and the emperors have also been completely ignored in the literature on the architectural sculpture of the cathedral that has appeared in the past few decades (in the works of E. Carli, P. Bacci, H. Keller, M. Seidel, and Antje Middeldorf-Kosegarten).

122. The old St. Paul's and St. Peter's basilicas in Rome have cycles of pictures of the popes in a position which corresponds to that of the cathedral in Siena. The basilica of St. Peter had the busts of the popes painted in medallions on the walls of the nave beneath the cycles of pictures from the Old and New Testaments: "Infra has historias spatiis distinctis in rotis picti erant summi pontifices a pectore sursum, nudatis capitibus cum orbiculari diademate et ipsorum nominibus" [Beneath these historical sketches in spaces demarcated by wheels the supreme pontiffs were depicted from the breast up, heads otherwise bared adorned by an orbicular diadem and their names] is the way they are described by Grimaldi in the reign of Pope Paul V (1605–21);

Garber, *Wirkungen der frühchristlichen Gemäldezyklen,* p. 23 and diagrams III, IV. The cycles of pictures in S. Paolo fuori la mura correspond, in order and theme, to those of St. Peter (pp. 52f. and diagrams I, II). The cycles of pictures of the popes stand (like the cycles of popes and emperors in Siena) in two rows one above the other, the lower one on the tympana and the upper one, twice as closely set, on the lower edge of the pictures on the wall of the nave (p. 20). Pictorial programs of other churches which are derived from St. Paul's and St. Peter's have cycles of panoramas of the apostles, abbots, or saints in corresponding positions (pp. 29, 33f., 36, 40, 48). The Sienese medallions of the cycle of emperors (which is in the same place as the lower series of the cycle of popes in St. Paul's and St. Peter's) apparently correspond to nothing in churches and may have their origin in antiquity. According to Garber (p. 21), the division of pictures on the walls of St. Paul's and St. Peter's has an analogue in antiquity in the so-called Esquiline basilica, which, instead of popes, had "round medallions with the heads of the emperors." In Siena, the busts of the popes had to be placed close together as, in contrast to Rome, two rows were not available for them, and the number of popes had, in the meantime, considerably increased. The combination of a row of popes and a row of emperors (instead of the two rows of popes as in Rome) in the cathedral at Siena confirms the tendency there to combine antique and Christian traditions. (A section of Garber's diagram I shows the etching of the drawing for the relief on p. 242.)

The early Christian cycles of portrait medallions are amply represented in Ravenna in S. Apollinare Nuovo, in the same position as in Siena; Friedrich Wilhelm Deichmann, *Frühchristliche Bauten und Mosaiken in Ravenna* (Baden-Baden, 1958), fig. 98f.; cf. the mosaic medallions of the saints and the apostles in the episcopal chapel, plates 219–223, 226–245, and the medallions in S. Vitale, plates 297, 301, 311, 334–339. The mosaic medallions above the entrance to the chapel of S. Zeno in S. Prassede in Rome date from the ninth century: Walter Oakshott, *The Mosaics of Rome from the Third to the Fourteenth Century* (London, 1967), plate 125; further, Rubinstein, p. 192. S. Apollinare in Classe in Ravenna has a much more recent painted cycle of half-length portraits in medallions over the arcades of the nave; André Chastel, *Die Kunst Italiens* (Darmstadt, 1961), figs. 42, 44. We now have outstanding copies in the work of Leonard von Matt, *Ravenna,* with text by Giuseppe Bovini (Cologne, 1971), figs. 32, 33 (S. Apollinare Nuovo), fig. 75 (San Vitale), figs. 99–101 (S. Apollinare in Classe).

Portrait medallions are often inserted, as groups, series, or frameworks, into the bindings of books—especially Byzantine ones. On the subject of medallion heads and busts in stained glass (the rose windows of the south transept in Strassburg Cathedral, ca. 1230) and in the Shrine of the Magi in Cologne, see Rüdiger Becksmann, "Das Jesse-Fenster aus dem spätromanischen Chor des Freiburger Münsters," *Zeitschrift des deutschen Vereins für Kunstwissenschaft* 32 (1969): 8–48, figs. 26, 28f. Carved wooden busts in medallions, dating from the early sixteenth century, are to be found on the wall of Magdalen College, Oxford; Royal Commission on Historical Monuments in England, *An Inventory of the Historical Monuments in the City of Oxford* (1939; reprint, 1951), pp. 73f., plate 127.

The rib vaults and the arches of the bays in the lower church of S. Francesco in Assisi are completely covered with painted cycles of portraits in medallions, squares, hexagons, and other frameworks, as are, in part, the arches and vaults of Sta. Croce in Florence. Similar extremely frequent series of portraits—to which we cannot here make reference—on the main lines of a building that serve the ends of architectural organization would be worthy of separate research on their doubtless more than ornamental meaning.

The bust in a medallion that is more or less a sort of relief is, however, also known in architecturally sculptured exterior cycles of the Italian Renaissance,[123] so that here in Siena old and new are also linked together (cf. excursus 2, pp. 229ff., on the Palazzo Pubblico in Siena).

We may, by presenting a few reflections, try to counter to some extent the reservation that may arise here—at the end of our detailed observations—as to whether it is credible that a spiritual conception could have been maintained and creatively sustained from the time of Giovanni Pisano (ca. 1290) to Beccafumi in approximately 1550. This is not an attempt to circumvent such a reservation or, as I fear, to sustain the hope that it will satisfy critical skeptics who would like to see the most concrete possible documentary proof for a program that is fixed and handed down on the spot: It is one of the charms of the Cathedral of Siena that, from the very beginning, there was no complete and binding pictorial program that was realized strictly and logically in the sense that, over the centuries, a building that was determined by a plan and elevation was finally completed according to that plan. People were, for example, flexible enough to place King Sigismund on the pave-

123. When the cycles of popes and emperors were added to the nave in Siena, the church of Sta. Maria della Grazie in Milan (built by Bramante 1494–97) also received a cycle of relief busts in medallions that surrounded all the exterior walls of the church at a corresponding height—something which has never been the object of scholarly research, perhaps because it is not known whether it is actually the work of Bramante; illustrations in Costantino Baroni, *Bramante* (Bergamo, 1944), p. 30 and plates 62–65; Otto H. Förster, *Bramante* (Vienna, 1956), pp. 112ff. and plate 44; Arnaldo Bruschi, *Bramante architetto* (Bari, 1969), pp. 194–207, esp. 206f. and fig. 139; André Chastel, *Die Ausbildung der großen Kunstzentren in der Zeit von 1460–1500* (Munich, 1965), p. 89; the illustration of a section in Chastel, *Die Kunst Italiens,* vol. 2, fig. 300, shows the busts of saints in profile in the medallions. At the end of the fifteenth century, a cycle of terra-cotta relief busts in medallions was added to the Cortile of the Palazzo Stanga in Cremona in exactly the same place; André Chastel, *Die Ausdrucksformen der Künste in der Zeit von 1460 bis 1500* (Munich, 1966), p. 33 and fig. 145. The medallion busts in the Church of L'Incoronata in Lodi (begun in 1488) take the same form, and are in the same place, as those in Siena; Staale Sinding-Larsen, "Some Functional and Iconographical Aspects of the Centralized Church in the Italian Renaissance," in *Acta ad archaeologiam et artium historiam pertinentia,* ed. Hans Peter L'Orange and Hjalmar Torp (Rome, 1965), 2:203–252, p. 246 (bibliography), plate VI, *a, b.*

In Siena itself it is possible that the *Maestà* of Simone Martini, in the Sala de Mappamondo of the Palazzo Pubblico, with the twenty medallions of Christ with patriarchs, prophets, evangelists, and church fathers that frame the whole picture, could have been a formal inspiration; on the *Maestà,* Irene Hueck, "Frühe Arbeiten des Simone Martini," *Münchener Jahrbuch der bildenden Kunst* 19 (1968): 29–60. The fresco depicting the crucifixion of Beato Angelico in the chapter house of S. Marco in Florence is framed, in hexagonal spaces on the arch, by half-length portraits of eleven patriarchs and prophets holding scrolls and by seventeen saints in medallions on the lower edge of the picture.

ment among the pictures of the Old Testament. What is really astonishing is that different creative impulses, separated by long periods of time, had, each in its own way and at its own time, their effect as a single spatial concept, so that the different initiatives brought into harmony, in the sense of a spiritual whole, what were—apart from the pavement—largely independent cycles that were realized over the short term. It is precisely this which suggests that we should view the Sienese phenomenon—which is not as unique as it may at first sight appear—within a universal context, so long as the eye has not yet been awakened to such a view. This is surely a better basis for believing in this visible and incontrovertible condition that we would prefer not to ascribe to coincidentally similar moods over a period of centuries, or to the discovery, in Sienese or Tuscan archives, of some document that substantiates the existence of a program—as though the eye were to be trusted less than a piece of paper. The art of the Middle Ages that trusts the mute language of form for the making of its spiritual claim is otherwise very discreet and does not lack spiritual bases, even if it is not holding them in its hand in a written volume.

In the cathedral at Siena, the world as space and time, with the eternal cosmos in the vault, became a unified artistic form; a view of the world became a building. The Middle Ages see creation in the hand of the creator, see the spiritual represented in the object, see the universal in what they survey and see totality in the microcosm. They see being in what is being. Hugh of St.-Victor had a sublime vision of a *mappa mundi* as the picture of the world in the structural form of Noah's Ark. Surrounded by the circles of the earth, the ages, and eternity, Hugh's picture of the Ark shows the Ark as *mappa mundi* in such a manner "that the beginning of the Ark points to the east, its end touches the west, and, according to a wonderful plan that stems from the same beginning, the order of the rooms coincides with the order of the ages, so that the end of the world in space is also the end of the world in time."[124] In

124. *De arca Noe mystica*, in *PL*, 176, 700 C: "Hoc modo arca perfecta, circumducitur et circulus oblongus, qui ad singula cornua eam contingat, et spatium, quod circumferentia ejus includit, est orbis terrae. In hoc spatio mappa mundi depingitur ita, ut caput arcae ad orientem convertatur, et finis ejus occidentem contingat, ut mirabili dispositione ab eodem principio decurrat situs locorum cum ordine temporum et idem sit finis mundi, qui est finis saeculi. Conus autem ille circuli, qui in capite arcae prominet ad orientem, Paradisus est, quasi sinus Abrahae, ut postea apparebit majestate depicta. Conus alter, qui prominet ad occidentem, habet universalis resurrectionis judicium, in dextra electos, in sinistra reprobos" [In this fashion a perfect Ark, encircling itself, forms an oblong circle which is closed at the meeting point of single horns, and the space which its circumference includes is the world itself. In this space a global map is

front of the Ark, in the east, lies paradise, behind it, in the west, lies the Day of Judgment. The merging of the categories of time and space, in which the category of time is also the category of space, is not completely new in this view of the world. The map of the world is also the history of the world, in that the flow of world history, from the Creation to the Day of Judgment, is seen by the eye as simultaneity in the space that has now become a picture. Millennia have been compressed like crystals not, of course, in such a manner as to suggest a mystic coincidence of the ages. Time, that is, in the eyes of God, a single day from sunrise to sunset, retains the dimension of length. Hugh of St.-Victor says: "If, then, the Ark signifies the church, the result is that the length of the Ark represents the length of the church. But the length of the church is perceived in the duration of the ages, just as its breadth is perceived in the number of peoples. This, however, is known as the propagation of the church; if the number of believers is increased, many are gathered together in the faith. Its length, however, consists in the extension of the ages that stretches from the past through the present to the future. The time of its length, however, lasts from the beginning of the world until its end, because the holy church started at the beginning and will last until the end of the world" (685 B).

Hugh takes one decisive step for the future when he puts in concrete terms the universal significance of length and breadth for "time" and "space," interpreting the Ark into the details of history and into a geography ordered according to the quarters of the heavens. The old era extends from the bow of the Ark to the middle of the history of salvation—Christ is the central pillar[125]—and Hugh articulates this by cycles of names and pictures. The *linea carnalis generationis* between Adam and Christ is depicted by sixty-one names, painted on the longitudinal axis—from Seth to Joseph—and these are crossed, on the latitudinal axis, by twelve names and half-

painted so that the head of the Ark is turned toward the east in such a way that its tail makes contact with the west, so that through some marvellous disposition from that very same point of departure the locale of sites runs down in an ordered flow of temporal intervals and the end of the world is the same as the end of the age. The cone, moreover, of that circle, which, at the head of the Ark, stands out in the direction of the east, is paradise, as it were, the bosom of Abraham, as it will appear afterward in the colors of majesty. The other cone, which stands out in the direction of the west, holds judgment over universal resurrection, on the right over the elect, on the left over the damned].

125. On the tree metaphor and the stylistic history of the significance of the central pillar of the Ark in Hugh's *De arca Noe morali*, in *PL*, 176, 647–664, see Friedrich Ohly, "Cor amantis non angustum: Vom Wohnen im Herzen," in *Schriften* (see n. 1 above), p. 137.

length portraits.[126] Thus, 12 + 62 (= 74) names represent the old era, from Adam to Joseph.[127]

The half-length portraits of the Twelve Apostles correspond, in the new era, to the patriarchs, so that both groups surround Christ in the center like the twenty-four seniors of the Apocalypse (687 A). The new series of generations, born of the spirit, starts with Peter and runs through the names of all the popes up to Honorius II (1124–30), that is, up to the time when Hugh composed his work. In the old half of the Ark, Hugh sees five ages with a total of 3,950 years, while the sixth, Christian, age will end, after an uncertain length of time, with the death of worldly time.

The remaining, open, length of the Ark belongs to the remainder of the sixth age of the world, and Hugh goes on to say: "These ages—filled with affliction and misery—that were conquered by a fortunate death, have already been taken up by the seventh age of the eternal sabbath and are awaiting the eighth age, that of spiritual resurrection, in which they will reign with the king in eternity" (668 A).

Hugh of St.-Victor distinguishes three stages in the time span of salvation. The space between Adam and the patriarchs is the period of natural law (*tempus naturalis legis*); the space from the patriarchs to Christ is the period of written law (*tempus scriptae legis*); the space from Christ, as the central pillar, onward is the period of grace (*tempus gratiae*).[128] The specific dimension of space in Hugh's work is the breadth of the Ark, and here there is also the same threefold division, when the children of Israel are wandering, from

126. 686d: Hugh places "imagines . . . semiplenas a pectore sursum, quales nonnumquamm in tabulis solent figurari, quas Graeci frequentiori (*sic*) Iconas εἰκόνας vocant" [images . . . half-length or half-full from the breast on upward of the kind that are sometimes accustomed to be shaped for tablets or panels, and which the Greek quite often (*sic*) call icons εἰκόνας]." Ms. Paris Maz. 717, fol 2v[a], reads "quas greci frequentiori usu iconias vocant" [which the Greeks with a rather frequent turn of phrase call icons].

127. According to Hugh's commentary on Genesis, the seventy-two peoples and languages have seventy-two ancestors (in *PL*, 175, 48ff.). According to Arno Borst, *Der Turmbau von Babel: Geschichte der Meinungen über Ursprung und Vielfalt der Sprachen und Völker,* vol. 2, bk. 1 (Stuttgart, 1959), p. 652, Luke, in his Greek Gospel, counts seventy-six forebears of Jesus (including Adam), the Vulgate seventy-five, while Ireneus Lucas ascribes seventy-two forefathers to Jesus, without clearly equating the number of peoples and languages with the number of Christ's forebears. The number of forefathers in Matthew, according to Borst (see above), vol. 1 (Stuttgart, 1957), pp. 222, 230, is forty-two.

128. On the precise description of the interlocking of these three periods (668ff.) see Meier, pp. 320f.; Ehlers, pp. 179f.

Egypt, through the wilderness to the promised land. Hugh inscribes, in his picture, the forty-two stations of the migration from Egypt to the Jordan: "quadraginta duae mansiones usque ad ripam Jordanis, per quas populus Dei spiritaliter ab Aegypto naturalis legis per desertum scriptae legis tendit ad terram promissionis gratiae" [forty-two halting places until the shore of the Jordan, through which God's people strive, departing spiritually from Egypt, the land of natural law, through the desert of the written law toward the soil of the promise of grace] (699 D). In Joachim of Fiore's *Liber figurarum,* the world views of the history of salvation of all ages, with their cycles of forefathers, rulers, and popes—depicted there as treelike unities—are incorporated into the picture, with length as the dimension of time, and breadth the dimension of space.[129]

When we look back from the Ark to Siena, the cathedral is made clear to us. Egypt, the wilderness, and the wanderings into the promised land recur on the pavement. The number—forty-two—of patriarchs and prophets under the cupola, as the number of stations of the migration (and, according to Matthew, of the forefathers of Jesus) here shows that the goal of the wanderings has been reached up above under the cupola. The nave of "antiquity," of natural law from Egypt, is resolved, in the written law of Moses, in the "Hebrew" space. The way from nature, through law, to grace explains why, on the bottom of the facade and on the base of the pulpit, as well as at the beginning of the length of the cathedral, animal creation predominates.[130] If we ignore the symbols of the evangelists, or the ass on the flight into Egypt on the pulpit, the space given to grace is reserved for human beings, saints, and angels.

Breadth is also the dimension of the promulgation of the Gospel among the peoples of the world in Siena, too. In the side aisles, the sibyls stand for their homelands as far as the borders of the antique world. The seven pictures of the battles of the chosen people against their enemies or persecutors are

129. Leono Tondelli, ed., *Il libro delle figure dell'abbate Gioachino da Fiore,* 2d ed. (Turin, 1953); on the question of whether the work is by Joachim, see Wilhelm Totok, *Handbuch der Geschichte der Philosophie,* vol. 2, *Mittelalter und Frühzeit* (Frankfurt, 1970), p. 212 (bibliography of literature on the controversy).

130. Lions and horses on the pulpit; lions, horses, griffin, and ox on the facade; next to the sibyls and Hermes Trismegistus, dog and lion, snakes, sphinx and mythical beasts; in the "Roman" space, besides the imperial eagle and the she-wolf of Siena, unicorn, panther, lion, horse, goose, elephant, and heron (in the ring round Siena), as well as lion, goat, dragon, and a bird of prey in the corners, as insignia of dominion. The animals disappear in the second half of the nave. The Hebrew space of the law shows animals only in the context of warhorse, sacrificial animal, in decorative molding, or in nature, as a bird on the tree or a cow in the meadow.

found only on the sides in the Hebrew world. The spirit of Dantesque epic form hovers in the Cathedral of Siena, and before the secular vision of this spirit[131] lies the infinite—as the universe that can be traversed—and what is boundless in the work, like God's creation between the day of Creation and the Day of Judgment, appears as a cosmic individual. Dante introduces into his work the worlds of history, by using portraits of men, and—like God at the Day of Judgment—passes a verdict upon them by sending them to heaven, purgatory, or hell.[132]

Siena Cathedral shows, as do Hugh's Ark and Adam's Tabernacle, that if works of art are not ornaments but a means of ordering a spiritual world, their location in space cannot be altered. Their cosmos would become chaos if we were to think of taking them and placing them in a museum. The aesthetic perfection, even of the individual work that is complete in itself, would suffer if we were to wish to displace it in space. It would, for example, amount to an act of madness that would destroy the whole space if we were to imagine Hermes Trismegistus in the chancel, the angels supporting the candelabra in the nave, and the popes on the pavement. The spirituality of the space gives the location of objects—externally and internally, longitudinally or latitudinally, high or low, left or right, east or west—a view into the world that illuminates the significance of the space, and this gathers itself in the building into an arcane present. This spiritual view expands the visible quality—what Hans Jantzen has called the diaphanous structure of the cathedral[133]—by what is at first an invisible characteristic but one that can become visible by means of spiritual observation and that is analogous to the spiritual diaphanousness of space. What is lacking in diaphanous struc-

131. Jean Paul says of Herder's works that their "explanatory and epic style . . . as a philosophical epic brings in an unbiased manner—with the great hand of a god—to the secular eye that measures years only by centuries, all the ages, forms, peoples, and spirits, thus setting it on the broadest possible stage" in his praise of Herder at the end of *Vorschule der Ästhetik, Werke,* ed. Norbert Miller, vol. 5 (Munich, 1963), p. 452.

132. His claim makes him seem to be God: he also knows—and this is incredible—like God's command and threat, his grace and his promise, and, anticipating his judgment, the concrete individual consequences, in the life hereafter, for those who have lived on earth. On the other hand, everything remains in God's hands, first in the legend of Gregory the Great's achievement of the salvation of the heathen Trajan—there is still a painting of this, as a deed that characterizes Gregory, on Michael Pacher's church fathers' altar in the late fifteenth century—and second in Wolfram von Eschenbach's trust that God's power will, miraculously, extend to the salvation of the heathens.

133. Jantzen, *Kunst der Gotik,* pp. 71ff.

ture in the plan of Siena Cathedral—conceived as Romanesque and later modified by Gothic—as compared with French cathedrals is made up for by a spiritual diaphanousness of space that is presented to our eyes by the depiction of a world of signification. The illustration of the invisible, which is made visible in pictures, is probably a later form. Architectural self-interpretation by pictures and architectural sculpture, however, facilitates insights into other cathedrals that are elucidated by the spiritual transparency of space—even when this is not done explicitly by texts like those of the Abbot Suger of St. Denis or by artistic means as in Siena. It was for insights into the "iconology of architecture"[134] such as these—which were not predictable when the written text and art were both examined—that new ground had to broken here (see excursus 3, pp. 232ff.).

We have finished our interpretative consideration of Siena Cathedral. We do not know what thoughts and feelings spiritually educated men may have had, centuries ago, when they walked through the completed church. The Middle Ages knew the value of spirituality as an aesthetic quality. Hugh of St.-Victor testifies to an artistic taste of this sort half a century before work was begun on the building of this cathedral. Assuming the role of master in his *de vanitate mundi,* he takes a student by the hand to introduce him to the structure that is Noah's Ark, and in doing so he is undoubtedly thinking of the church. Toward the end of the second book, which is dedicated to the Ark, the master says:

> "But this alone is still left to us, that we enter this salubrious dwelling, insofar as we not only flee the evil that is outside it, but can also find, within it, those joys of the divine sweetness that God keeps hidden for those who love him. More precisely, this is the house of the Lord and the wine cellar into which the king leads his bride so as to set his love in order within it.[135] Once we have entered, we shall, with God's help, be able, easily and joyfully, to despise all the pleasures of the world and also be safe and sound without fear of what is inimical."[136]

134. This [*Ikonologie der Architektur*—Ed.] is the title of Günter Bandmann's fundamental treatise written in 1951, now in a special edition (Darmstadt, 1969). There is certainly a positive answer to the question which Bandmann asks on pp. 67ff.: "Can allegorical interpretation have formal consequences, whether this lies in making certain members more pronounced and emphatic or whether it lies in the development of the other thing that is adduced as a metaphor?"

135. On the tradition of the *ordo caritatis* from Augustine to Goethe, Friedrich Ohly, "Gottes Ehrfurchten—ein ordo caritatis," *Euphorion* 55 (1961): 113–145, 405–448.

136. *PL,* 176, 717 D.

After a long and vivid chapter about the idyllic and paradisiacal joys of a child's growing up in its father's house which, like the house of the Lord, is a rich and loving home,[137] we are brought back:

"Let us now enter and let the Lord be our guide and guide our feet in the way of his commandments. But when we have entered, I will precede you and guide you through everything, beginning with the facade of the house and on into the innermost part of the holy of holies: we will look at the length and breadth and height in all three stories, and, finally, we will climb up and not rest until we have reached the king's throne. We will traverse all the works of the history of our salvation, from the beginning until the end of the world, according to the passing of the ages, to the order in which things occur, and to human deeds.[138] And when we have looked at

137. *PL*, 176, 717 D–719 D.

138. In *Wilhelm Meisters Wanderjahre*, Goethe furnished the shrines in the middle of the province of pedagogy with cycles of pictures from antiquity and from the Old and New Testament in such a way that—analogous to Dante's pictorial cycle behind the gate of purgatory—the similarity of the signification of actions and occurrences that are objectively in harmony in the different epochs of history should be obvious to us. Wilhelm Meister is led through the cycles so that, after he has seen the series of pictures from the old era that harmonize with and elevate the history of the world (which here takes the place of the history of salvation) into the present, it can be said (*Goethes Werke*, ed. Erich Trunz, 14 vols. [Hamburg, 1948–60], 8:160): "Our friend, in a short walk through these halls, had now recalled the history of the world: there was something new to him with respect to this occurrence. Because of the arrangement of the pictures and the reflections of his companion, he had given voice to many a new insight. He was glad for Felix to appropriate to himself, for his whole life, by such a worthy and sensitive presentation, those great, significant, exemplary happenings as though they were real and as though they had been alive and at his side."

On the shrines of the pedagogical province and their pictorial cycles that resemble Dante's, see Friedrich Ohly, "Gottes Ehrfurchten," pp. 425–443; cf. the remark made by Elizabeth M. Wilkinson, that here the "pictures themselves symbolize the progress of time through the centuries" ("Faust in der Logosszene: Willkürlicher Übersetzer oder geschulter Exeget?" in *Dichtung, Sprache, Gesellschaft: Acts of the IV. International Congress of Germanists, 1970, in Princeton* [Frankfurt, 1971], pp. 115–124, here p. 124).

We cannot imagine what the epochal effect upon Goethe's historical thinking would have been if he had seen the related phenomenon in Siena Cathedral, which he did not visit on his Italian tour. On October 22, 1826, Goethe wrote to Wilhelm von Humboldt about his work on the Helena act in *Faust*, part 2: "From time to time, I have continued to work on it, but the play could not be completed except in the fullness of time, for then it will play all its three thousand years from the fall of Troy to the capture of Missolonghi [i.e., Byron's death]. This can also be regarded as a unit of time in a higher sense; the unity of place and action is, even in the usual sense, most carefully observed" (*Goethes Werke*, vol. 3 [Hamburg, 1957], p. 436). It would be attractive to compare the unity of time and place in the cathedral and in Goethe's drama with a view to the

everything which is within, I will open the window of the Ark from time to time, and, taking turns, we will, by looking at what is outside, renew our spiritual eyes in the waters of the flood. It will be especially pleasant to look down by turns—as though from a sort of watchtower—with our eyes turned inward, now upon the evil which we have left behind and now at the good that we have found and possess." The student: "We shall love this good more emphatically if we try, in turn, always to be aware of misery and danger and always to allow ourselves to be told of it." The master: "It is now your task, no matter what wonderful sights you may see, whether inside or out, to ask questions as you may desire and as it seems right to you; my task, however, will be to give answer to the extent that I am able."[139]

The sort of answers to be expected are shown by the words of the master about the dimensions of the Ark which come just before this:

"Because, however, God has again brought about the works of the history of salvation, some through man, others through the angels, and others again by his own hand, we shall climb, as we proceed from the works of man to the works of the angels, and again to the contemplation of the works of God, in the spiritual Ark as we do from the first to the second and to the third story, and, finally, we shall come to the highest point itself, in which the Ark culminates,[140] when we come to the perception of God through his works. The Ark, however, extends to a length of three hundred cubits because, as we have already said, the works of our history of salvation, from the beginning to the end of the world, extend through the periods of nature, law, and grace as through three separate hundreds. Its breadth is, however,

---

possibilities of representing this unity in different arts at different periods. Both of them represent a universe that spans a period of millennia from antiquity, through the Middle Ages, into their own present.

139. *PL*, 176, 719 D–720 B. The last sentence of the quotation reads as follows: "Tuum ergo erit ex omnibus, quae vel intrinsecus vel extrinsecus videris mirabilia, quantum volueris et dignum judicaveris interrogare, meum autem erit quantum voluero tuis interrogatoribus respondere" [It will be up to you to decide how much of all the wonders which you have seen either within or without you will have wanted and deemed worthy to question; it will be up to me to decide, however, how much I will have wanted to answer your questions]. The master's "quantum voluero" [how much I will have wanted] does not accord well with the general tone of the conversation, so that I am inclined to read "quantum potuero" [how much I will have been able]; hence my translation, "to the extent that I am able."

140. We find on the pyramid-shaped Ark the "cubitus supremus" [supreme cubit], "in quo arca consummatur" [in which the Ark culminates], the one topmost surface, one square cubit in area, on which Hugh painted the Lamb of God: *De arca Noe mystica*, cap. 1, in *PL*, 176, 681 A–C.

set at fifty cubits and its height at thirty, because the whole host of the faithful, for whose sake all this has taken place, is expressed by seven times seven, and Christ, as the head, is added to that. Also, the whole sum of the deeds that God did for mankind since its beginning is contained in the thirty books of Holy Writ."[141]

Unlike its predecessors—the Ark, the Tabernacle, and the Temple of Solomon—the church is oriented toward the east and not toward the west. For this reason, the relationships of directions in the cathedral, as opposed to the cardinal points of the Ark that Hugh of St.-Victor mentions, are reversed. Thus, the passage over the length of the Ark leads from the entrance in the east facade through to the facade in the west.

"I will lead you first to the front side of the house, that is, in front of the facade that lies toward the east, so that our entrance will be simultaneous with the beginning of the world, both in time and space . . . the front facade stands . . . toward the east, but the back came to stand in the west. The left-hand side looks toward the south and the right-hand toward the north, for divine providence has so ordered the progression of things that what happened at the beginning of the world happened in the east and finally all things descend, in due course, to the end of time in the west, that is, at the end of the world in space."[142]

141. *PL*, 176, 717 AB. In another place as well, Hugh points to the three-hundred-cubit length of the Ark in relation to the three periods of grace: "Longitudo trecentorum cubitorum tria tempora, quibus praesens saeculum decurrit, tempus scilicet ante legem, sub lege et sub gratia . . . designat" [The length of three hundred cubits signifies the three temporal dimensions in which the present age runs its course, namely, the times before the law, under the law, and under grace] (*PL*, 175, 641 D).

142. *De vanitate mundi* II, in *PL*, 176, 720 BC: "Introducam autem primum te in partem superiorem domus, hoc est in frontem, quae est ad orientem, ut ingressus noster simul fiat ab initio mundi at ab initio saeculi. Nam . . . superior frons orientem tangit, inferiorem autem usque ad occidentem pervenit. Latus vero sinistrum ad austrum et dextrum ad aquilonem respicit, quia divina providentia decursum rerum sic ordinavit, ut ea quae in principio saeculi facta sunt, in oriente quasi in principio mundi fierent, tandemque decurrentibus temporibus ad finem saeculi rerum summa ad occidentem descenderet, hoc est ad finem mundi" [Now I shall lead you first into the higher part of the house, this is into the forepart which faces toward the east, so that our entry is accomplished both from the beginning of the world and from the beginning of the age. For . . . the higher forepart touches the east; the lower, however, comes through to the west. The left side is borne to the south and the right looks to the north, since divine providence has ordered the course of things in such a way that those things that were created in the beginning of the secular age were made, as it were, at the creation of the world in the east, and then, times finally dwindling to the end of the secular age, the entirety of all things descended to the west, this is to say, to the end of the world].

The course of events leads, therefore, from paradise in the extreme east, across the empire of the Assyrians, to the Roman empire in the west.[143] Mutatis mutandis and, above all, assuming that the cardinal points in the cathedral are reversed, we can relive, in our passage over the pavement in Siena, what Hugh of St.-Victor says of the passage along the temporal length of Noah's Ark:

"When we start at the origin of all things and proceed along the length of the Ark, across the works of the history of salvation to the end and completion of all things, we find that a way has been made through the middle of the ages of the world so that, when we pass through, both sides are open, both to the north and to the south, that is, on the right-hand and on the left-hand sides, as though they were lying outside the Ark, in the Flood. Such a journey would, it is true, be of considerable extent, but it would not be tedious, because the persons walking through would find abundant pleasure in any number of things. And again: when we look out of the window, our eyes that look out from the high watchtower, and the most secure station, would see at our feet—from far and wide—the miraculous confluence and waves of the mutability of the world."[144]

III. Temporal Space and the Commemoration of the Ages in the Liturgy

The representation of the history of salvation, through the medium of the ecclesiastical building, in Siena Cathedral has a meaning that rests within it-

143. *PL*, 176, 720 C.

144. *PL*, 176, 720 CD: "Incipientibus ergo nobis ab origine rerum omnium et per opera restaurationis secundum longitudinem arcae decurrentibus ad finem et consummationem universorum, semita strata est per medium saeculi, ut transientibus a latere hinc inde pateant quaecumque sive ad aquilonem sive ad austrum, hoc est ad dextram et sinistram, quasi extra arcam in diluvio fiant. Spatiosa quidem, sed non fastidiosa erit ista deambulatio, ubi intrinsecus tantarum rerum varia oblectatio transeuntibus erit obvia, et rursum per fenestram prospicientibus foris tam mirabilis confusio et fluctuatio mutabilitatis mundanae oculis longe lateque de alta specula ac firmissima statione intuentibus erit subjecta" [For us, therefore, beginning from the origin of all things, and coursing by all the works of restauration along the entire length of the Ark to the end and consummation of whole worlds, for us, I say, a path has been laid down through the midst of the secular age, so that for us passersby, to each side, on this side and on that, everything lies open, be it to the north or the south, that is, to the right or to the left, as if outside the Ark all were again overwhelmed by the Flood. Lengthy indeed but not for the squeamish will be this trip, when the travelers within will be met by the varied delights of so many things on the outside and, on the other hand, those peering out of their windows will have as their objects such wondrous confusion and fluctuation of worldly mutability subjected far and wide to eyes gazing down from a high watchtower and the firmest of stations].

self. Eternity rests within the microcosm of the cathedral as though it were a single day. A further and—for the church as the place of divine service—specific dimension of the meaning of the history of God's action in the world, a history that can be paced out by the feet and calculated by the eyes, emerges when we recall that something analogous takes place in the liturgy that is heard every day. According to medieval liturgists, a passage through the ages of the world also takes place, in the course of a single day, in the liturgy as well, and it is this that fulfills the most noble destiny of ecclesiastical space. They repeatedly express the idea that the ages of history are passed through in the canonical hours. The hours are sung in the cathedral choir, and the liturgist Sicardus of Cremona (d. 1215) says of these in his *Mitrale seu de officiis ecclesiasticis,* toward the end of the book which is dedicated to the prayers of the canonical hours: "And, finally, we must not overlook the fact that many people say the following when speaking of the offices: the midnight office recalls the age from Adam to Noah, matins from Noah to Abraham, prime from Abraham to Moses, terce from Moses to David, sext from David to the coming of Christ, nones from the first to the second coming of Christ, when he will come to judge. Vespers they understand as the sabbath of the soul, on which they will rest from their labors; in compline that age of the great celebration to which the elect will come to receive the kingdom, when the joy of the saints will be completed, the struggle will cease, and eternal peace will come. In this age, the bridegroom will give the bride sleep and immutable rest."[145] As a microcosm of the ages, the day whose course is formed by the rhythm of the canonical hours recalls the macrocosm of the ages: "Quilibet enim dies repraesentat hujus saeculi tempus, quod per septem intervalla distinguitur" [Indeed, whoever represents this our worldly time as a single day will find it is distinguished by seven intervals].[146] Honorius Augustodunensis expressed it in this way a good half century earlier:

Matutina illud temporis nobis memorat,
    quo primi parentes Deum in paradiso laudabant.
Prima illud tempus indicat,
    quo Abel, Enoch et alii justi Deo laudes solvebant.

145. Sicardus of Cremona, *Mitrale de officiis ecclesiasticis* IV, 9, in *PL,* 213, 185 D.

146. Ibid., IV, 3, in *PL,* 213, 159 D. Matins represents and recalls the praise of our parents in paradise; prime, Abel; terce, Noah; sext, Abraham; none, the prophets; vespers, the apostles; compline, the just at the Day of Judgment.

Tertia illud tempus insinuat,
quo Noe et alii de arca egressi Deum benedicebant.
Sexta illud tempus denuntiat,
quo Abraham et alii patriarchae Deum glorificabant.
Nona illud tempus demonstrat,
quo prophetae sub lege Deum magnificabant.
Vespera illud tempus revocat,
quo apostoli et illorum sequaces Deo hymnizabant.
Completorium illud tempus monet,
quo in novissimo sub Antichristo justi Deo gratias referent.

[Matins reminds us of the time,
when our first parents praised God in their Paradise.
Prime denotes the time,
when Abel, Enoch and other just people paid God their praises.
Terce suggests that time,
when Noah and others, having emerged from the Ark, blessed God.
Sext announces that time,
when Abraham and other patriarchs glorified God.
None shows that time,
when the prophets magnified God under the law.
Vespers recalls that time,
when the apostles and their followers praised God in hymns.
Compline admonishes of that time,
when most contemporaneously the just will give thanks to God under the reign of the Antichrist.][147]

The hours of the day can be understood as the time span of the ages of the world and, at the same time, as the totality of the seven ages of man or of Christ's life, Passion, and salvation.[148]

147. *Gemma animae,* in *PL,* 172, 632 D–633 A.

148. *PL,* 213, 161 A–162 A. Rupert of Deutz, in his first work, *De divinis officiis* (1111), lays particular emphasis upon the commemorative representation of the stages of our salvation through Christ: *Liber de divinis officiis,* Corpus christianorum, continuatio medievalis, no. 7, ed. Hrabanus Haacke (Turnhout, 1967); here, for example, 1, pp. 1–15 on the canonical hours. Honorius Augustodunensis sees in the canonical hours, like the progress of the history of salvation and the ages of man, the *Christi mysteria* as the representation of the stations of his Passion and salvation from his being taken prisoner to the journey to Emmaus: *Gemma animae* II, pp. 55–57, in *PL,* 172, 633 D–634 B.

Dies etiam vitam uniuscujusque hominis representat, quae septem aetatibus variatur . . . (*Matutin* infantia, *Prim* pueretia, *Terz* adolescentia, *Sext* juventus, *Non* senectus, *Vesper* senium, *Komplet* finis vitae). . . . Ergo septies, id est semper: quia dum septies in die laudem Domino dicimus, totum saeculi tempus et totam vitam hominis ad Deum referendam notamus. [A day also represents the life of each and every human being which changes in the course of seven ages . . . (matin, infancy; prime, childhood; terce, adolescence; sext, youth; none, old age; vespers, senility; compline, the end of life). . . . Therefore, septies, that is, "always": since when seven times a day we sing praises to the Lord, we mark the whole time of the [existence of the] world as well as the whole life of man as things to be attributed to God.][149]

Here we come to grips with a meaningful reason for the introduction of the cycle of the seven ages of man into the pavement of Siena Cathedral. Even before Sicardus of Cremona, Johannes Beleth in *De ecclesiasticis officiis* (1160–64)[150] and, even a generation before him, Honorius Augustodunensis in the *Gemma animae* saw the seven ages of man as passing through the prayers of the canonical hours:

Ergo per Matutinam commemoramus infantiam,
in qua quasi de nocte ad diem orti sumus, dum de matribus in hunc mundum nati sumus.
Juste itaque in hac hora Deum laudamus, qua de nocte erroris ad lucem veritatis in baptismo nos renatos exsultamus.

On the question of the interpretation of the ages of man and the days of the week as epochs, millennia, and periods in history, see Bernhard Kötting, "Endzeitprognosen zwischen Lactantius und Augustinus," *Historisches Jahrbuch* 77 (1958): 125–139. Hippolytus interprets the length—five and a half cubits—of the Ark of the Covenant as the 5,500 years from Creation to the birth of Christ, after which the world will last for another five hundred years to the total length of world history, which is six thousand years (p. 128). On Kötting's evidence for the birth of Christ in the middle of the sixth millennium (pp. 128ff.) see, most recently, Ruth Schmidt-Wiegand, "Die Weltalter in Ezzos Gesang," *Zeiten und Formen in Sprache und Dichtung: Festschrift für F. Tschirsch* (Cologne, 1972), pp. 42–51.

149. *PL*, 213, 160 A.

150. *Summa de ecclesiasticis officiis*, cap. 28, in *PL*, 202, 39 CD. Every day, in the canonical hours, the individual traverses the seven ages of his life: matins, *infantia;* prime, *pueritia;* terce, *adolescentia;* sext, *iuventus;* none, *aetas virilis;* vespers, *senectus;* and compline, *aetas decrepita et finis humanae vitae.* They are equally designed for the praise of the Creator. In the three readings of the individual hours, too, Johann Beleth also sees the ages of man; 34 D: "Tres postremo lectiones tres connotant aetates, videlicet pueritiam, iuventutem et senectutem" [In the end three readings connote three ages, that is, childhood, youth, and old age].

Per Primam pueritiam recolimus,
qua aetate libros discere coepimus,
Merito ergo in hac hora laudes Deo solvimus, qua ejus servitio imbuti sumus.
Per Tertiam adolescentiam recolligimus,
qua ordine suscepimus.
Juste in hac hora Deum glorificamus, qua ejus ministris associati sumus.
Per Sextum juventutem innuimus,
qua ad diaconatus vel presbyteratus gradum promoti sumus.
Et in hac ergo hora non incongrue Deum benedicimus, qua duces et magistri populorum electi sumus.
Per Nonam senectutem notamus,
qua plerique ex clero ecclesiasticas dignitates quasi graviora pondera subimus.
Convenit itaque nos in hac hora Deum magnificare, qua nos voluit super plebem suam exaltare.
In Vespera decrepitam ducimus ad memoriam,
qua plurimi ex nobis ad melioris vitae conservationem in primis venimus, qui quasi tota die in foro otiosi stetimus (Matthew 20:3), dum tota vita in vanitate viximus.
In hac hora decet nos Deum laudibus extollere, qua nos dignatus est suis laudatoribus adjungere.
Per Completorium finem nostrae vitae retractamus,
quo per confessionem et poenitentiam salvari speramus

[Thus through matins we commemorate infancy,
In which we are risen, as it were, from night to day, when we are born from our mothers into this world.
And so justly do we praise God in this hour, in which we, reborn in baptism, leap from the night of error into the light of truth.
Through prime we recall childhood,
The age in which we began to read.
Rightly, therefore, will you repay God with your praises in this hour, in which we were instructed in his service.
Through terce we recollect adolescence,
In which we accepted our vocations.
Justly do we glorify God in this hour, in which we were accepted among his servants.
Through sext we recognize our youthful maturity,
In which we were advanced to the rank of deacon or presbyter.

And in this hour not improperly do we bless God, in which we were chosen to be leaders and teachers of peoples.
Through none we mark the maturity of age,
In which many of us from the clerisy undertake high eccelesiastical ranks as they were heavy burdens;
And so it befits us to magnify God in this hour, in which it has been his will to set us over his people.
In vespers we call to mind the infirmity
Through which many of us first come to be acquainted with a better life, we who, as it were, the whole day long had stood idle in the market place [Matthew 20:3], while we lived a whole life in vanity.
In this hour it befits us to extol God with our praises, the hour in which he has deemed us worthy of being among those who praise him.
Through compline we reconsider once again the end of our lives,
Hoping to be saved by confession and penitence.][151]

The three periods of grace, before the law, under the law, and under grace, were recognized in the sequence of the three nocturns by Honorius,[152] John Beleth,[153] and Sicardus.[154] As early as the ninth century, Amalarius of Metz had also written an extensive treatment of the representation of the history of

151. *Gemma animae* II, p. 54, in *PL*, 172, 633 B–D.

152. Honorius, *Sacramentarium*, cap. 47, in *PL*, 172, 771 C: "Nox pro ignorantia ponitur: ab Adam usque ad Christum quasi nox erat, quia lux scientiae deerat; quae nox dividitur in tria tempora, ante legem, sub lege, sub gratia; quae tempora per tres nocturnos significantur, qui in nocte cantantur" [Night is understood to stand for ignorance: from Adam to Christ it was as if there were nothing but night, since the light of knowledge was absent; this night is divided into three periods, before the law, under the law, under grace; these intervals are signified by three nocturns, which are chanted in the night]. Three psalms are sung in each nocturn, because the Trinity was prayed to by the patriarchs *ante legem*, was invoked by the prophets *sub lege*, and was preached to the world by the apostles *sub gratia*.

153. Johannes Beleth, cap. 22, in *PL*, 202, 33f.: "Illud quoque notandum est, quod in his trium nocturnarum officiis tria tempora representamus" [Also to be noted is the fact that in these rites of the three nocturns we symbolize three temporal periods]. The three ages, before the law, under the law, and under grace, each divide up into a further three ages: *ante legem*, the ages from Adam to Noah, from Noah to Abraham, from Abraham to Moses; *sub lege*, from Moses to David, from David to the Babylonian captivity, from the captivity to Christ; *sub gratia*, the age of the apostles and the preaching of the gospel, the age of attack and the heretics, the age of peace without heresies. The three times three psalms, readings, versicles, and responses of the three nocturns for feast days correspond to the three times three ages of the history of salvation.

154. Sicardus, *Mitrale* IV, 5, in *PL*, 213, 166 A: "Tempus ante nocturnum significat tempus

salvation in the night office: The night office of feast days goes through time from the beginning to the end of the world, on workdays, the office goes through the period of the wanderings in exile.[155] Six antiphons follow the psalms in the nocturn because God's protection covers the six ages of the world. Three readings and three responses follow, because the six ages of the world are contained in the three ages of the law, the letter, and grace. The five antiphons at matins on feast days depict the period of the church from the beginning of its steadfastness in the apostles up to the perfection of the elect, who will come at the end of the world. During the week, the periods of the history of Christian salvation are once again traversed.[156] Amalarius argues that the inclination to see the cosmos of the history of salvation in the

---

mortis ante legem, in quo silebant homines a laudibus Dei. Tempus nocturni significat tempus legis datae Moysi. Tempus laudis matutinae significat tempus gratiae, a resurrectione usque ad finem mundi, in quo tempore Deum laudare tenemur" [The time prior to the nocturn signifies the time of death before the law, in which human beings held back from the praises of the Lord. The time of the nocturn signifies the time of the law given to Moses. The time of the matutine praise signifies the time of grace, from the Resurrection to the end of the world, in which we are required to praise God]. Previously, Sicardus interpreted the three ages tropologically: *Mitrale* IV, 4, in *PL*, 162 B.

155. *Liber officialis* IV, 11, II, 454: "Ut enim dominica nox recolit cives Hierusalem ab initio mundi usque in finem, ita cotidianae noctes peregrinationem mortalium et abalienationem a patria inter inimicos degentem" [Just as the Lord's night commemorates afresh the citizens of Jerusalem from the beginning of the world to the end, so too do the weekly nights [commemorate] the wandering of mortals and, living among enemies, their lifelong alienation from the fatherland].

156. IV, 13 (see n. 11), II, 457: "Tertia feria illud tempus recolit, quando ab impiis imperatoribus persequebatur ecclesia. . . . Tempus illud praecipue fuit a prima persecutione Neronis ad tempus Diocliciani et Maximiani" [The third day of the week [Tuesday] recalls the time when the church was being persecuted by impious emperors. . . . Such a time was especially the interval from the first persecution of Nero to the time of Diocletian and Maximian]; IV, 14, II, 458: "Feria quarta tempus illud recolit, in quo sancta ecclesia exaltata est super inimicos suos" [The fourth day of the week [Wednesday] recalls the time in which the Holy church was exalted above its enemies]; IV, 15, II, 459: "Iste articulus sub una virga, id est sub uno regimine, suscipit populum Iudaicum et populum gentilem" [This moment under the rod, that is, under one government, begets the Jewish people and the Gentile people]; IV, 16, II, 459: "Sexta feria caelebratur in memoriam passionis salvatoris nostri . . . *In the period there appears the* victoria summi et solius triumphatoris illius [The sixth day of the week [Friday] is solemnized in memory of the passion of our savior. . . . On it appears the victory of the highest and sole victor]; IV, 17, II, 460: "Sabbatum recolit memoriam electorum Iudaeorum, qui erunt iuncti ecclesiae in fine mundi" [Sabbatum recalls the memory of the chosen Jews, who will be joined to the church at the end of the world]. In *De ordine antiphonarii,* cap. 1, Amalarius says of the reading of twelve psalms in the nocturns: "duodenarius numerus universitatem temporis et rerum continet in se" [The number twelve [of those psalms] contains within itself the universality of time and the things within it].

liturgy of feast days, and the cosmos of the history of the soul in the liturgy of workdays—in the former allegory, and in the latter tropology—derives from the fact that man is a microcosm: "Quoniam homo pars est mundi, apud Graecos appellatur microcosmos, id est minor mundus, et ideo non immerito statui temporum comparatur rota nativitatis humanae" [Since the human being is part of the world, among the Greeks it is called a microcosmos, that is, a little world, and, therefore, an orb of human birth, is not undeservedly compared to the status of temporal succession].[157] In the introduction to his work on divine service, Rupert of Deutz emphasizes, in general terms, that "Haec vero sacramenta celebrare et causas eorum non intelligere quasi lingua est et interpretationem nescire" [Truly, celebrating these sacraments and not understanding their causes, is as if all that is a language and not knowing its proper interpretation]. And a dozen years later, Honorius Augustodunensis says the same thing in the introduction to his work *De officiis ecclesiasticis,* entitled *Gemma animae,* but using a different metaphor: "qui enim non intelligit, quae agit, est ut caecus, qui nescit quo vadat; et ut Tantalus in mediis undis siti deperit" [indeed, whoever does not understand what he is doing is like a blind man who does not know whither he walks and, like Tantalus, in the midst of waves perishes for thirst].[158]

The question of how far the magnificent idea of representing the time of the history of the world in the events of the liturgy was involved in its development, or whether it became an additional effective force only in the course of its history, or whether it left its mark on it as the interpretation of an independently evolved phenomenon—the liturgy does not have this spiritual meaning written all over it as its idea of the Creation—may be easier to determine for the history of the liturgy, which has verbal texts at its disposal, than it is for analogous forms in the history of art. It is not out of the question that the body of Siena Cathedral—like that, no doubt, of many other churches—was erected, at first, without any thought for spiritualizing speculation and was interpreted only subsequently, when pictures were added. Ten thousand Bible commentaries treated the Bible in this way in the Middle Ages,[159] and the interpreters of the authors of antiquity and of Dante do the same. In the three books of his *Tripartitum tabernaculum una cum pictura,* Adam Scotus, the architectural interpreter, follows the historical Tabernacle,

157. *De ordine antiphonarii,* cap. 5, vol. 3, p. 26.

158. Rupert of Deutz, *De divinis officiis* 5, pp. 29f.; Honorius Augustodunensis, *Gemma animae,* in *PL,* 172, 543 A.

159. The evidence for this is adduced by Friedrich Stegmüller, *Repertorium biblicum medii aevi,* 7 vols. (Madrid, 1950–1980).

first with the allegorical and then with the tropological Tabernacle. In the case of a church, it is difficult to decide whether we are dealing with a building's freedom from, or simply inexplicitness of, interpretation, when there is no sign to correspond to its signification. What would we say of the cathedral facade in Siena, if Pisano had not interpreted it and it had remained raw and bare like that of San Lorenzo in Florence and many another church? Before the language of its marble integument was laid upon it, clearly suggesting, for the first time, the Temple of Solomon, was the facade, and with it the whole cathedral, then void of signification? Our discretionary judgment is restricted only by the extent of the critic's acquaintance with the theological tradition of the interpretation of architecture, and of the manner in which architecture interprets itself. We are still far from both of these.[160]

When we talk about circumstantial evidence of a subsequent process of interpretation in Siena, we are not faced with a decision on whether this clarifies something by awakening what was formerly mute and dormant, or whether new meaning is given to something that was already there. Either way, we would recognize that the cathedral had not previously been completed, for even what has come about historically is completed if, like the tower of the Strassburg Minster, the completion does indeed go beyond the idea of its inception. In Siena, perhaps as the result of the impulse that emanated from Pisano's facade, the century-old ornamental floor, whether without signification or with a hidden one, was replaced by the present pavement with its powerful exegetical statements. In Siena and only there busts of the popes were added to the corbels of the cornice, the medallions of the emperors were added to the arcades, the angels and apostles were added to the pillars, the cycles of saints were added to the space below the cupola, and the vaults received the paintings which opened up the heavens. The aesthetic and

160. The problem which is presented here is elucidated by Sinding-Larsen, "Some Functional and Iconographical Aspects," p. 241: "It has to be admitted that in both the architecture and the reproduction of buildings these symbolical implications are rarely conspicuous in the articulation of an individual building. After all, the same kind of building may generally serve as a tabernacle of the Holy Eucharist or as a *martyrium* on the site of St. Peter's crucifixion, or it may represent the Temple of Jerusalem or even the Temple of Diana at Ephesus. The buildings reappear in many contexts, between which there is no obvious common denominator as regards significance or function. The buildings alone do not normally provide a basis for the interpretation of their possible signification. When stripped of their images and decorative details these structures, both in architecture and art, may often be freely interchanged with each other, without affecting their appropriateness in the particular context. It is their images and decorative details and above all their context that would invest them with a definite significance."

spiritual heightening of the space forms a unit that is self-determinative and self-explorative.

We saw that Sicardus of Cremona is not the only figure of the twelfth century to allegorize the litany: a process that was begun with Amalarius of Metz (ca. 775–ca. 850) was carried on in the twelfth century by Rupert of Deutz, Johann Bethel, and Honorius Augustodunensis and expanded in the thirteenth century by Durandus, so that by the later Middle Ages it was quite common and was even treated in the vernaculars. The allegorizing liturgical scholars who linked the allegoresis of the church building, in part, with that of divine service were not outsiders or eccentrics, but leading churchmen and theologians. The allegoresis of biblical structures, like the Ark, the Tabernacle, and the temple, in which the church is prefigured, or in which it is fulfilled, as in the Heavenly Jerusalem, was pursued by important minds like Origen, Gregory the Great, Bede, Rupert of Deutz, Hugh of St.-Victor, Hugh of Folieto, Adam Scotus, and hundreds of other writers. As Christians they interpreted Genesis (with the Ark), Exodus (with the Tabernacle), the historical books (with the Temple of Solomon), the prophet Ezekiel (with the vision of the temple),[161] and the Apocalypse (with the Heavenly Jerusalem) in relation to the church.[162] We surely do not need to adduce proof that the intellectual world of an episcopal city like Siena, which was a rival to Florence and which counted within its walls—besides a cathedral—churches and

161. Gregory the Great's Ezekiel commentary, which gives an extensive interpretation of the vision of the temple, served in the thirteenth and fourteenth centuries as mealtime reading in the convent of St. Denis; in other words, it was not kept secret; Ph. Schmitz, "Les lectures de table à l'abbaye de saint-Denis vers la fin du moyen-âge," *Revue bénédictine* 42 (1930): 163–167.

162. The literature of architectural exegesis, which has its place, outside biblical exegesis, in the sermon delivered at the dedication of a church and also in the literature of the Middle Ages, as in the interpretation of the *Minne* grotto in Gottfried von Strassburg's *Tristan*, as well as in poems about the spiritual convent, or the castle of love, in a number of different literatures, lasts well into modern times. In George Herbert's *Temple* (1633) the stones and colors of the floor in the poem "The Church Floore" are interpreted as the virtues of patience and humility, trust and love:

But the sweet cement, which in one sure band
Ties the whole frame, is *Love*
and *Charitie* . . .
Blest be the *Architect,* whose art
Could build so strong in a weak heart.

The poem "The Church Window" sees the sermon of the windows as linked to the sermon of the priests:

convents, a university, and artists of the highest quality, would know those conceptions of temporal space and of the liturgical representation of historical periods, which had in any case been developed since the twelfth century. Stimuli from the upper Rhine and from Poitou that were incorporated into the cathedral, and that are architectonically visible, bear testimony to the breadth of its intellectual horizons.

The liturgy of the hours is an abbreviation of historical time, the ages of man, or the stations of the Passion of Christ. What is past, what is present,

---

Doctrine and life, colours and light, in one
When they combine and mingle, bring
A strong regard and awe: but speech alone
Doth vanish like a flaring thing,
And in the eare, not conscience, ring.

This idea is taken up by an anonymous poet in a longer poem, written in 1656, which defends the decoration in Christ Church Cathedral in Oxford. It says of the windows, for example,

Windows are Pulpits now; though unlearned, one
May read this Bible's new Edition . . .
The cloudy mysteries of the Gospel here
Transparent as the Christall do appear . . .
The Scriptures rayes contracted in a Glasse
Like Emblems do with greater vertue passe . . .
Both edifie: what is in letters there
Is writ in plainer Hieroglyphicks here.
Tis not a new religion we have chose;
Tis the same body but in better clothes . . .
A Christian's sight rests in Divinity,
Signes are but spectacles to help faiths eye . . .

Just as the window presents a world to our sight, so too the marble floor is more than mere ornament:

Thus as (in *Archimedes* sphear) you may
In a small glasse the universe survey . . .
But if the window cannot shew your face
Look under feet, the marble is your glasse,
Which too for more than Ornament is there;
The stones may learn your eyes to shed tear . . .

H. J. C. Grierson and G. Bullough, eds., *The Oxford Book of Seventeenth Century Verse* (Oxford, 1968), pp. 367f., 805–808. L. Gougaud collected evidence—from medieval theologians and liturgists from Gregory the Great to Villon—of the fact that the task of church decoration was mutely to serve the uneducated as *laicorum lectio et scriptura* in "Muta praedicatio," *Revue bénédictine* 42 (1930): 168–171. However, this topos, which lasted for more than a thousand years, did not, by any means, always hit the target of what was the main function of the pictures.

and what is promised to us are linked to a simultaneity that can be paced out and that makes the parts into members of a body. The spiritual edifice of the liturgical day is a compression of the ages. The divine service for the day, the week, or the church's year (here in the form of the *lectio continua* of the Bible) is the abbreviated progression—presented to our memory in a number of stations—of the periods of salvation from the Creation to the Day of Judgment. The liturgists of the Middle Ages, recognizing this, try, by means of cultic imitation, to collect the temporal sequence of the millennia, which is experienced as anything but endless, into a present which can be surveyed, just as the celebration of the mass replayed for us the life of Christ from his birth to Emmaus.[163]

The ruling commemorative understanding and celebration of the mass in the idea of the life and Passion of Christ was able to incorporate completely the memory of their prefigurations in the Old Testament, just as we are taught by Honorius Augustodunensis's *Gemma animae* (post 1125).[164] The seven offices of the mass also celebrate, in the seven stations of Christ's life (his being sent into the world, the beginning of the church, his preaching, the entrance into Jerusalem, Crucifixion, descent into hell, and Resurrection),[165] the anticipation of these happenings in the Old Testament, so that the Old and the New Testament are brought into harmony in the mass. The seven stations of the mass from the Old Testament are (1) Moses, the messenger of God in Egypt, collects and liberates his people and leads them to the promised land; (2) Mary, Moses' sister, sings to the liberated people, who answer her song; (3) Moses receives the tablets of the law on the mountain and explains them to his people; (4) God's people bring gifts for the building of the Tabernacle and the altar to Moses when he descends from the mountain; (5) Moses prays on the mountain with outstretched hands, while Jesus-Joshua defeats Amalek; (6) Moses blesses Israel before his death; he com-

163. On the allegorical explanation of the mass in the Middle Ages, from the time of Amalarius of Metz, see Josef Andreas Jungmann, *Missarum Sollemnia: Eine genetische Erklärung der römischen Messe* (Freiburg, 1952), 1:114–120, 143–156, here p. 154: "The basic theme of all allegoresis of the mass is the Passion, or rather, the life and Passion of Jesus, and this was something to which the Middle Ages—in spite of all vacillations—held fast." On the memory of the ages in the liturgy, see also Sarah Appleton Weber, *Theology and Poetry in the Middle English Lyric: A Study of Sacred History and Aesthetic Form* (Columbus, Ohio, 1969), pp. 7–25 ("Three Reformulations of Sacred History by the Liturgy of the Church").

164. On the dating, see Hermann Meinhardt, "Der Nachlaß des Honorius Augustodunensis," *Zeitschrift für deutsches Altertum* 89 (1958/59): 23–69, p. 68.

165. On the *septem officia* of the mass, Honorius, *Gemma animae* I, 3, 13, 19, 26, 44, 60, 61, in *PL*, 172, 543 B, 548 C, 550 C, 552 D, 557 B, 562 B, 562 D.

mands Jesus-Joshua to lead Israel into its homeland; (7) Jesus-Joshua has led the Israelites home and disposed of the new lands by lot.

Moses' sister on the facade and the great Moses cycle in front of the chancel in the Cathedral of Siena now appear in a new light. Honorius once more interprets the mass as the battle and victory over the Amalekites and Joshua's preparation of the way into the homeland and declares the office of bishop, down to its very last detail, to be the office of a spiritual emperor.[166] He also understands the battle between David and Goliath, which likewise appears on the cathedral pavement in Siena, as an anticipation of the celebration of the mass.[167] Honorius's interpretation of the mass as Moses' liberation of God's people from Egypt and their battle-torn repatriation into the promised land by Joshua, which is sustained by David when he defeats Goliath, gives rise to the question of whether the addition of these events on the pavement, between the cupola and the altar in Siena Cathedral, might have linked the idea of peregrination through the historical ages to a representation of the Old Testament prefiguration of the mass. Honorius introduces the historical time of the world into the mass just as he does into the canonical hours, insofar as he understands the six signs of the cross in the mass in this way: "Per sex ordines (sc. crucum) cuncta mundi tempora comprehendimus, quae per crucem Christo unita exprimimus" [Through the six orders (sc. of crosses) we comprehend all the temporal orders in the world, which we express as united to Christ through the cross].[168] The first three series of signs of the cross signify the ages *ante legem, sub lege,* and *sub gratia;* the fourth, the Passion; the fifth, the original church; the sixth, the church from the heathens. "Item per quinque ordines crucum quinque aetates mundi designantur, quae per crucem et Christi corpus salvantur" [Likewise through five orders of crosses five ages of the world are signified, which by the cross and the body of Christ are saved].[169]

Historiography, in the form of the world chronicle,[170] book illumination in the picture of the one who embraces the world and in the pictures of the

166. I, 72–77, in *PL,* 172, 566 C–568 A.

167. I, 79–81, in *PL,* 172, 568 A–569 D.

168. *PL,* 172, 559 A.

169. *PL,* 172, 560 B.

170. Walther Lammers recognizes, as the special feature of a chronicle like that of Otto of Freising, "the whole historical picture of the world, the subdivided universal concept and the rationale for the universal drama as a whole." Otto, Bishop of Freising, *Chronik, oder die Geschichte der zwei Staaten,* trans. Adolf Schmidt, ed. Walther Lammers (Darmstadt, 1960), XLI. "The

Ark and the Tabernacle as the *mappa mundi* and the cosmos of the ages, architecture in the cathedral, and word, melody, and gesture in the liturgy represent the universe as a surveyable form. The conception of the cathedral as temporal space has an analogy in the understanding of the liturgy as a memory of the ages. The space of the divine service and the divine service itself, in which its meaning is fulfilled, harmonize in the realization of the ages.

Human memory cannot achieve a simultaneity of the ages, even if its progress through time does take flight. It is dependent on movement through temporal space. Even the architectonic assemblage of the ages in the simultaneity of space cannot compress them into one point of memory. As a cathedral, too, time has its space, which the spirit perceives only through the eyes and not through the spirit. The microcosm of the ages still has to be perceived, *deambulando*, with the spirit and all the senses. It is only the eye of perception—as it recreates—that knows that everything is in its right place. We recall the words of Hugh of St.-Victor: "What is hidden becomes brilliantly visible there, what is difficult seems easy, and what, when looked at as itself, seemed less obvious proves, when seen in its right order, to be meaningful. *Ibi quoddam universitatis corpus effingitur, et concordia singulorum explicatur*" [There a certain body is fashioned representing the whole, and the concord of its individual features is explicated].[171] The prayer of the canonical hours does not preserve time, but articulates eternity, the ages of man, or the Passion of Christ—whose epoch is also spatially represented by the stations inside or outside the church—in the temporal space of the day, just as the lection of the twelve prophecies in the mass for Easter Saturday leads from Creation to the rebirth in baptism, and the *lectio divina* of the Bible, in the church's year, runs from Creation to the end of the world. The church—as the space of the liturgically represented celebration of the memory of the ages

---

world and mankind with all the scenes of their activity are seen in context. . . . Not only the survey of the world, as a unified, local scene, but also the whole knowledge of the beginning of history and the end of the ages belong to the universality of the historical picture . . . the closed uniqueness of the historical progress of the world . . . history is fundamentally the history of salvation. It is a temporal, surveyable, and by no means limitless process that is inserted between Creation and the law, between eternity and eternity. . . . If history is the history of salvation then the direction leads toward salvation. . . . This direction to the fulfillment of time is explained from the plan of divine, providential order" (XLIIf.). "Like fate, man, too, as an autonomous or heroic force, lacks a history that is designed by Providence. Man is, above all, a tool in the hands of God" (XLIV).

171. See above, p. 141.

in the service of the praise of God—takes part, as a building, in the representation of the ages. The cathedral as temporal space is the place of the liturgical memory of the ages.

Excursus 1 (see p. 143)

The bliss of Lynkus the Watchman ("Faust," part 2, act 5, "The Depths of the Night") is changed into horror when he sees Philemon and Baucis consumed by fire:

You blissful eyes
What you have ever seen,
Whatever it may have been,
It was so beautiful!
(Pause)
Not merely for my own delight
Have I been placed here,
What a cruel horror
Threatens me from the dark world!

The same reversal of a sight from bliss to horror is encountered by the pupil when he meets the master, who is also on watch, in Hugh's didactic conversation *De vanitate mundi:* "D[ocens]: Vides igitur mundum istum? I[nterrogans]: Video et bene. Numquam tam bene vidi, quia numquam tam bene diligenter consideravi. D: Quid ergo tibi videtur? Qualis est species ejus? I: Pulchra valde. Miror tale opus Dei" [T[eacher]: You see, therefore, this world? Q[uestioner]: I see it and see it well. I have never before seen so well, since never before have I reflected so well, so diligently. T: How, then, does it look to you? What kind of a world is it? Q: Very beautiful. I am full of wonder at this work of God] (705 A). The master directs him away from the view of the world, as the work of God, in order to allow the pupil to recognize the works of man in the world. He turns him in all directions and every time the result is "D: Quid tibi videtur, quale est hoc opus hominis? I: Vanitas est et vanitas vanitatum" [T: What does it look like to you, what kind of work is this work of man? Q: What it is, is vanity and vanity of vanities] (707 A; cf. 709 C, 712 A, 713 B).

In the second book of Hugh's work *De vanitate mundi,* he gives a third interpretation of the Ark, after the first and the second, *De arca Noe morali* and *De arca Noe mystica,* that is mainly concerned with the heart and so brings more strongly into play what is mystical in the more up-to-date sense of the word: the eyes of the spirit that see the visible as the path to the perception of the invisible recognize, in the rise of the Ark to the heights, the inner road to God in the heart (715 A–716 A).

It is not as if Hugh in *De vanitate mundi* were here retracting his earlier view of the Ark, as the world in the hands of God, in the sense of a disillusion, as was the case with Jean Paul when he added the shot tower of his satire to the biographical holy city of his novels.[172] His vision *Die Mondfinsternis* reveals what he thinks of as his shot towers.[173] A "shot tower filled with silent, black death" is here the "black genius" of the seduction of the eighteenth century that has been petrified by the "genius of religion: The infinite sends an evil genius to every century to tempt it." Jean Paul apparently gives voice to the most frightful temptations of his century in order to banish, to "petrify" them, by the act of saying to them, "'I want to protect you.' It was the genius of religion. The giant undulating serpent coagulated in front of him and, petrified, it stood on the earth and on the moon, a shot tower filled with silent black death." Jean Paul says of Herder in his speech in praise of Herder at the end of the *Vorschule der Ästhetik:* "How magnificently, unreconcilably he flew into a passion against . . . every scepter held in a claw; and how he conjured up the snakes of the day!"[174]

Hugh of St.-Victor contrasts the ordered cosmos of the world of the Ark—as a saving force—with the anticosmos of the Flood and its throng of ages, deeds, and *vanitates.* It is the one firm point in a sea of fluctuations. The mutability of the world can be seen from the window of its high watchtower. The firmly based spiritual universe floats on a sea of insubstantiality. The view from the window leads here—in contrast to panel painting, in the Renaissance and in the age of Romanticism—not into the beautiful world or the cosmos, but to the uncertainly flowing sea of evil. The Ark and the cathedral are crystals in an amorphous environment.

Excursus 2 (pp. 199–204)

In relation to the cycle of emperors in the cathedral, we should say a few words about the possible connections between the cycles in the cathedral and the city hall in Siena.

172. Jean Paul, *Werke,* ed. N. Miller, vol. 4 (Munich, 1962), p. 361.

173. Jean Paul, *Die Mondfinsternis,* in *Werke,* 4:38–42.

174. Jean Paul, *Vorschule der Ästhetik,* in *Werke,* vol. 5 (Munich, 1963), p. 453.

If the circular, revolving *Mappamondo,* of which mention has been made since 1344 but which was lost in the eighteenth century, was really a cosmographic representation of the inhabited earth and not, as is believed today, a representation of the world of the Sienese state, with Siena in the center of the surrounding lands, then it was—as a total representation of a universe—probably related formally to the universal conception found in the cathedral, but as a secular representation of a world conceived as being centered on Siena, it was a completely different object, for the center of the temporal space of the cathedral is the altar.[175] In the cathedral pavement there were at first only a few marble pictures—the five virtues in the chancel, the first of the seven hexagons under the cupola and the Wheel of Fortune in the nave, the wheel of the Roman empire and the picture of Siena with its allies. This was the case until, between 1408 and 1414, Taddeo di Bartolo created a cycle of frescoes in the narthex of the chapel in the city hall—the "anticappella," which should not be denied this name in scholarly literature—which linked the Christian era with antiquity. St. Christopher on the one narrow side corresponds to a medallion with the map of the city of Rome over the other entrance, Jupiter and Mars on this side, Apollo and Minerva on that, Aristotle on this side, and Caesar and Pompey on the other: Religio is above the picture of Rome. Fortitudo (with Judas Maccabeus underneath it) and Prudentia (with the Sienese saint, Ambrogio Sansedoni, beneath) are on one of the long sides, and opposite these are Justitia (with Cicero, Cato, Scipio Nasica beneath) and Magnanimitas (with Curius Dentatus, Furius Camillus, and Scipio Africanus underneath). In addition, sixteen heads of famous Romans serve as a frame for the four virtues.[176]

As both a humanistic and republican work, the wall cycle, consisting mainly of public-spirited Roman virtues, together with mainly Roman heroes, is different in character from the later prophetic sermon in the cathedral pavement. On the character of the Anticappella, [Rubinstein says:] "The Sienese citizen who, coming from the Sala de'Nove, entered the antechapel from the Sala di Mappamondo found himself in a hall commemorating republican heroes and pagan divinities, which formed a curious contrast to the adjoining chapel"[177] (p. 206). Rubinstein emphasizes the discrepancy when

175. On the *Mappamondo,* see Aldo Cairola and Enzo Carli, *Il palazzo pubblico di Siena* (Rome, 1963), p. 139.

176. On this cycle by Taddeo di Bartolo, see Rubinstein, pp. 189–207; good illustrations in Cairola and Carli, pp. 185f., plates XXXVII and XL, as well as illustrations 97–103.

177. Rubinstein, pp. 200–206.

he states that the picture of St. Christopher, which was painted six years before the rest, stands outside the cycle. "On the wall facing the entrance to the Sala di Mappamondo, the St. Christopher, painted six years earlier remains unconnected with the program of the new frescos" (p. 192). On the other hand, we must bear in mind that—apart from the great names of Greece and Rome—with the inclusion of Judas Maccabeus we have a hero of the Old Testament and, with Ambrogio Sansedoni, a saint from Siena. St. Christopher, as the holy giant in a heathen world, is also not ill placed next to the heroes of antiquity, particularly as the Christ child and the globe are opposite the picture of ancient Rome. The globe that the infant Jesus is balancing on the tip of his raised index finger could have been the inspiration for the medallion shape of the picture of Rome. What is worth noticing is St. Christopher's rod in the form of an oar, from whose shell-shaped blade three drops are falling.[178] Is there a special legend concerning this? The usual version—that the rod is planted and bears leaves—seems improbable if the rod is shaped like this.

The fact that the cycle in the antechapel unites antiquity, the Old Testament, and the Sienese saints, as well as St. Christopher, relates it to the program of the cathedral facade. What argues against the inclination, expressed by Rubinstein and Cairola and Carli, to separate the antechapel from the chapel proper and assign it a function as a corridor or vestibule between two council chambers is the fact that antiquity and the Old Testament do indeed belong in the anteroom of the church, and St. Christopher, too, often has his place there on the outside wall. This intermediate hallway has a meaningful connection with the chapel, from which it is separated only by a screen, in that it gives the effect of a single space, and should therefore continue to be called "anticapella," even if it does, at the same time, fulfill the function of joining the two main chambers in the city hall.

The title under the picture of Aristotle affords a nicely etymologizing and numerically significant reason for the use of the hexameter in the *senarum urbs:*[179]

Magnus Aristoteles ego sum, qui carmine s e n o ,
E s t e t e n i m n u m e r u s p e r f e c t u s , duxit ad actum
Quos virtus tibi signo viros, quibus atque superne
Res crevit romana potens, celosque subivit.

178. Cairola and Carli, fig. 103.
179. Rubinstein, p. 193 n. 93.

[I am the great Aristotle, who with a song o f s i x,
F o r i t i s i n d e e d a p e r f e c t n u m b e r, led to finding,
By a sign, men to be your men of virtue, for whom also upward
Grew the Roman cause and its power, and subjected itself to the heavens.]

Excursus 3 (p. 210)

Geza de Francovich, in *Il palatium di Teodorico a Ravenna e la cosidetta "architettura di potenza,"* pillories the "grave errors" of the so-called "method" of "interpreting architectonic forms" in the sense of an "iconology of architecture" and those who represent this method: Dvoràk, Dyggve, Krautheimer, Grabar, Kitschelt, Stangte, Sedlmayr, Weckwerth, Bandmann, Smith, Haute-coeur, and Lavin, as well as "many others."[180] His demand that the reading of the language of forms precede the question of signification, and that the two be allowed to interact, comes straight out of the Middle Ages and is one that should be heeded. "Significato e forme devono intimamente compenetrarsi, il significato dev'essere tratto della forme in un diretto ed immediato rapporto reciproco perché il risultato critico appaia persuasivo" (p. 67). The related, and thus indisputable, reproach against "the direction taken by scholarly research which has, in recent decades, become more and more popular" reads as follows: "Concetti prestabiliti e speculazioni incontrollabili si alleano allora nell'elaborare fragili construzioni critiche che poggiano su fondamenta d'argilla" (p. 67). It is unjust, if not iniquitous, for every error made by a legitimate and fruitful method to be charged with being symptomatic, and for every overexertion to be called an innate error. De Francovich is fighting a battle that has already been won, wherever the attempt is made to solve, with methodological care, the difficult problem of bringing into view what—on the basis of mere forms alone—is no longer perceptible by the modern eye, which is often blind to what is "spiritual" in the Middle Ages. Research into the sacred art of the Middle Ages which considers only spontaneously—that is, in the literal sense of form—colors, dimensions, and proportions, gestures, materials (jewels, ivory, metals, woods, and stones), and buildings and their members runs the danger of shutting the door on essential questions of meaning. Art history and the philology of the world of the spirit, whose inspirational breath penetrates the work of art and, metamor-

180. Geza de Francovich, *Il palatium di Teodorico a Ravenna e la cosidetta "architettura di potenza": Problemi d'interpretazione di raffigurazioni architettoniche nell'arte tardoantica e altomedievale* (Rome, 1970), pp. 67ff.

phosed, issues forth again as a productive part of the world of the spirit, can most readily discern where, and how far, the question of signification can legitimately be posed and can also concern itself with the answers to this question. The meeting of disciplines and their discourse does not have to be easy at the outset but can exert a stimulating force. Even de Francovich does not seem to exclude this possibility: "Art history as the history of forms and as intellectual history"—"sarebbe l'esigenza critica ideale ma, come tutti gli ideali, difficilimente realizzabile" (p. 69.).

Theodor Klauser, who called my attention to de Francovich in his *Kleine Abendländische Liturgiegeschichte,* calls for "a history of church structure as of the house that is created for the liturgy" and considers the efforts of the art historian to find, in the structure of the church, representation of biblical themes or of other ideas which are incorporated in the liturgy to be false: "In our opinion all of these theories are mistaken."[181] Certainly we should bear in mind his warning: "People read just as much into the completed churches as exegetes of the liturgy, like Amalarius, did into the interpretation of the actions of the divine service. Primary intention and secondary interpretation must therefore be kept scrupulously apart. Of course, it is conceivable that certain secondary interpretations of the church do enter completely into the consciousness of an age. But then they determine and modify the liturgical concepts of that age. The commission, however, that the congregation gives to the architect, is always the same: "Build us a church, to which we are used and which we understand!" (p. 141). Klauser's attempt to ascribe a formative monopoly to this main motif of the church building, by which, however, the "accessories," such as the portal, the pulpit, the choir stalls, the stained glass windows, the towers, and so on, are not affected and can thus be made available for "allegorical trains of thought" (p. 142), surely, for its part, strains the nuclear idea of the church in a manner that removes the complexity of the historical process from our view. The very history of the building of Siena Cathedral, which is so richly documented by written sources, from minutes of decisions taken, down to the very record of how each person voted, gives rise to doubts about purely liturgical motives like that of "turning the cathedral like a weather vane" (Wolfgang Braunfels) so that it lies on a north-south axis—a colossal plan which was pursued for decades and into which huge sums of money were poured.

181. Theodor Klauser, *Kleine abendländische Liturgiegeschichte* (Bonn, 1965), pp. 140–150 ("Liturgie und Gotteshaus"), p. 141.

FIVE

DEW AND PEARL: A LECTURE

"Now let fire descend!" This is the way Hölderlin's poem "Der Ister" ("The Hister") begins. An arc of a thousand years spans tradition between Hrabanus Maurus's Easter hymn "Veni creator spiritus" and Klopstock, Milton, and Hölderlin, the last poets to pray for inspiration from the Holy Ghost, when they write. "Consecrate it, O creator spirit!" cries Klopstock at the beginning of *Der Messias,* and he is referring to his poetic art. Hölderlin's "Now let fire descend!" refers simultaneously to poetry and to the sun. Today we no longer talk of inspiration. For three millennia, from Homer onward, poets prayed for a divine gift; now the appeal to the muses, the prayer to the Holy Spirit, the cult of enthusiasm are all silenced. The history of poetic inspiration and its effects, as the history of piety and style, has yet to be written. We are scarcely conscious of the reasons for, and the consequences of, the loss of inspiration, the sinister nature of its drying up, indeed, of its already having been forgotten. As a philologist, I try to approach the question of language by what it says about poetry.

Almost two thousand years ago, Pliny reported, in his *Natural History,* that a drop of dew falling, at a favorable moment, from heaven is picked up by the oyster swimming on the sea; the oyster opens itself up to receive it and takes it down to the seabed, where the dewdrop changes into a pearl. The belief that the pearl originates in a marriage of heaven and earth—Pliny already says that the pearl contains more of heaven than of earth—is continuously expressed and repeatedly celebrated in verse right down to the eighteenth century, and a list of witnesses containing a hundred names testifies to this.

The form of this lecture, which was given in London in 1972, is unchanged. The theme is treated in greater detail in the essay "Poetry as the Necessary Fruit of a Suffering" (chap. 6 of this volume). Published as "Tau und Perle: Ein Vortrag," in *Schriften zur mittelalterlichen Bedeutungsforschung,* by Friedrich Ohly (Darmstadt: Wissenschaftliche Buchgesellschaft, 1977), pp. 274–292.

The *Physiologus* broadcast it throughout the whole world from the second century onward. There is quite a theology of the pearl in the early church in the works of Clement of Alexandria and of Origen, and, most beautifully of all, in the work of Ephraim the Syrian. The natural myth, of the origin of the pearl in the heavens, serves over and over again for the verbal expression of mysteries such as the Immaculate Conception of the Virgin Mary, and the Annunciation of the Virgin, to name but two theological themes that maintained a lively connection with the myth of dew and pearl, especially in the seventeenth century. The same century also took up a myth that had previously been known only to the world of the Greeks, the myth of the genesis of the pearl from lightning, which united with water to form a pearl in the oyster. There were related myths in ancient India about the genesis of the pearl in the clouds, but Indian traditions of the origin of the pearl in the forehead of the elephant, or in the raindrop in the bamboo reed, were not taken over by the West. In the Middle Ages, the idea of the heavenly origin of the pearl is handed down, in the lapidaries and bestiaries, by Isidor and Hrabanus Maurus, in the great encyclopedias, and in many other places. Over a period lasting more than a thousand years, the travel descriptions written by visitors to the Orient who traveled to Persia, India, Ceylon, and China, from the ninth century until the time of Olearius and Chardin—they provided Goethe with his knowledge of the dew and the pearl—scarcely ever failed to give particulars of the pearl and its origin. From the later Middle Ages onward, Mariolatry served as an inspiration to art history for the pictorial representation of the myth of the dew and the pearl in connection with the Annunciation of the Virgin and the Immaculate Conception. Then, from the fifteenth to the nineteenth century, emblem books established their own tradition, in the shape of hundreds of pearl emblems. It transpires, in this connection, that emblems—which are thought to have originated in the sixteenth century—have a not inconsiderable prehistory in medieval manuscripts.

The Christian allegoresis of the nature myth, for which there are attestations from the time of Origen, lasted until the eighteenth century and maintained itself side by side with the strand of tradition in natural history that experienced a resurgence especially in the Renaissance. Islamic explanations of the pearl as coming from the tears of Adam and Eve over the death of Abel, or from angels' tears, made no impression on the Occident. I will mention only one theologically remarkable legend from Ethiopia, according to which Mary, as a white pearl, was already resting in Adam's right loin and was passed on from man to man, as generation succeeded generation, up to the time of Joachim, from whom the pearl came to reside in Anne's womb. The pearl that

God had laid in Adam's loin at the Creation here stands for the seldom attested—it recurs once in the works of Goethe, and is so called by him—idea of an inherited grace that was handed down from Adam to Mary.

Various traditions of dew and the pearl, rain and the pearl, and storm-tossed drops of the sea and the pearl probably enjoyed their most poetic and active life in that part of the medieval Orient that lies between the Red Sea and India and coexists in a puzzling state of osmosis with the intellectual movements of the West. Its highlights are to be found in the works of Persian poets. The poet Saadi's thirteenth-century parable about dew and the pearl reached Goethe in three different ways and simultaneously. This happened in the wake of the not insignificant history of the reception of oriental literature in the seventeenth and, above all, the eighteenth century, in which, besides Sir William Jones, Herder also played his part. Thus, we encounter it in Goethe's *West-östlicher Divan:*

From heaven, a drop fell fearfully into the wild ocean waves,
The waves pounded it cruelly
But God rewarded the humble courage of belief
And gave the droplet force and stamina.
A silent oyster enclosed it
And now, to its eternal praise and reward,
The pearl shines in our emperor's crown,
Looking lovely and shining gently.

The question then arises, out of the myths about the origin of the pearl, as to how far the speech and thought of poetry also uses knowledge drawn from science to illuminate the world or whether it rejects it. Baroque emblem books often state that they record images that are fashioned by tradition, even though these images are shown to be contrary to nature, because what is false, but traditional, may seem more sensible than what has been newly learned. The problem is an old one and is discussed around the year 1000, at the time of Notker, in the *Book of Jewels* by Al-Beruni, an Arab born in Persia, who taught Greek philosophy in India. He quotes over a hundred pearl metaphors from the literature of the preceding centuries, in order to test critically whether the poets' pearl metaphors accord with the true nature of the pearl. It needed an earthquake to loosen pearl oysters from the sea bed, yet the poets wrote—and Goethe still did so—that oysters with pearls were cast up on to the shore by the waves. Al-Beruni presents a model of the critical reciprocity by which literature illuminates nature, and vice versa, and, as criticism of metaphors, his work penetrates and cleanses both fields while aiming at a metaphorical reality that parallels nature. The question also achieved theological relevance, as in the seventeenth-century works of the Jesuit Théophile Raynaud. His dictionary of metaphors for the Virgin Mary examines the most diverse traditions of the origin of the pearl from the point of view of their applicability to Mariological interpretation. He is concerned with closing the gap that had opened up in history between the theological truth of dogma and the scientific truth of the metaphor through which it is expressed. He is so successful in bringing about an agreement between dogma and language that the metaphor hits upon theological and scientific truth simultaneously. The nature metaphor must be true to nature if it is to express the truth of belief. He distances himself from the early Christian explanation of the origin of the pearl, from the union of lightning and seawater in the oyster, with the observation that the church fathers often explained mysteries by using familiar, even though false, stories because they were suited to the understanding of the common people. Raynaud seeks to achieve the congruence between the truth of faith and the truth of nature that he was striving for by involving the most famous scientific minds of the sixteenth and seventeenth centuries and by rejecting the myths of the Middle Ages and antiquity. This Jesuit father is opposed to the church fathers and the whole Middle Ages, he is opposed to a belief in the origin of the pearl that lasted into the nineteenth century, and so he stands on the side of the scientists, who make no claim that the development of the pearl in the oyster is dependent upon outside influences, "in the same way that the Virgin Mary brought forth Jesus Christ, from her own substance, by excluding any influence of an externally created father." The antique etymology of the name of the pearl, *unio*—the oyster produces only one pearl—is scientifically refuted and replaced by a new explanation of the name *unio* based on the true genesis of the pearl. This now refers to the pearl's perfectly circular and spherical form, which is the product of a developmental process.

Théophile Raynaud tries to make close contact with the natural history of his time so as to break down contradictions between theology and science in theological imagery. He works at language's eternal task, the preservation of intellectual purity and freshness in the metaphor, by insisting on the truth of its objective origin and ensuring that what is signified by the metaphor benefits from these qualities. The inexpressibility of many scientific truths in our own day, at least in the language available to us up to the moment, is such a strong deterrent to the refreshment and enrichment of our stock of metaphors from newly discovered truths that we still cannot see what the effects of this will be. Just as in Raynaud's lexicon, we also become aware of something further in Marracci's baroque lexicon of Marian metaphors, which lists, from its sources, no fewer than seventy oyster, pearl, and lightning metaphors for Mary. The baroque dictionaries of Marian metaphors are the final, hybrid form of what was present in the litanies and in the related Marian poetry of the Middle Ages. They make clear that all the aspects of a human or divine phenomenon—like the totality of experiences such as love, sin, or death—can be grasped only in the sum of the names, attributes, and metaphors that characterize it. The hermeneutic principle of illuminating being by metaphors is the ontological reason for the litany-like, cataloging, religious form of verse. What is varied in its incomprehensibility can be expressed, approximately, within the whole spectrum of all the designations that can be taken out of, and used from, the book of being and that, in every case, find their mark in one of the qualities of the divine or human phenomenon, but that can only try to grasp the whole, in the sum, by means of language. The baroque summas of Marian metaphors—in which the pearl metaphors are also to be found—that point to the origin of the pearl form a mosaic filled with the numinous, with margins that are capable of infinite expansion. We can come closest to complete descriptions of a phenomenon like deity, or an experience like love, that evade unambiguous definition because of their inexhaustibility, by means of the sum of the metaphors used to express them. Theology has constantly produced such poetic or systematic summas as a necessary form. Those emblem books that, for example, contain emblems only for the heart, or for love, are to some extent related to this. It is quite astonishing that, as far as I can see, no philologist has ever tried to make a summa of all the metaphors for the origin of poetry. The mosaic of metaphors for poetry is extremely rich and changes from epoch to epoch, from the Orient to the West, from genre to genre, and is one thing in rhetoric and poetics where craft metaphors like text, structure, and the like hold sway, and something else when we are talking of the poetry of inspiration. One of a hundred metaphors for the birth of a poem is the image of the genesis of the pearl in the oyster out of the dew of heaven. It is suited to the nature of the thing that is intended by the metaphor only if the genesis of the poem is recognized as the effect of being conceived from above. This is not the place to investigate oriental metaphors, especially those found in medieval Persia, for the poem as a pearl. All I can do is take a look at the echo in Goethe's *West-östlicher Divan.* Like the poet Saadi in the thirteenth century, Goethe likened the poet's creative efforts to God's help in the conglobation of water into a pearl. The *West-östlicher Divan* also varies the idea outside the parable of the dew and the pearl that is adopted from Saadi. In the *Buch der Sprüche* (*The Book of Sayings*), Goethe writes:

The flood of passion, it rages in vain
Toward the unconquered, *terra firma*—
It casts up poetic pearls onto the shore
And that already profits life.

Passion assaults what is unconquered, what has been attacked in vain, the land where force is pent up. The dividing line between passion and the state of being unconquered is the locus of the creative leap into form. What has matured frees itself; the depths come to light; life casts poetic pearls on to the shore. "Powerful surprise" was what he wrote in the sonnets written in the year 1807; there we have "the flashing of the waves as they pound the rock, a new life." In the *Buch der Sänger,* the artist "plunges his hand into the Euphrates . . . if the pure hand of the poet scoops up water, the water will form itself into a ball." Poetic pearls, as things which profit life, are not an increase, but a salvation into a higher being. The pearls are thrown up in swelling abundance. Released from the hard shell of the oyster, they descend on the land with the waves. Who could fail to be reminded of the *Book of Suleika,* where the full bunches of twigs on the chestnut tree with their fruits "cased in shells, prickly and green," which, like pearls cradled in the flood, form themselves, when ripe, into spheres (the water has to form itself into a sphere) and are ready to fall to earth as poetic kernels.

They have long been hanging in their round
Silent, unknown to themselves,
A branch, that gently swings them,
Rocks them patiently.

But ripening ever from within,
The brown kernel swells.
How it desires to breathe the air
How gladly would it see the sun.

The shell bursts open and, joyfully,
The kernel is released.
In the same way my songs
Fall into your lap.

This poem was written three days after Goethe's second pearl strophe, which was a thanks for Suleika. The date supports our hypothesis that the pearls that were cast up, and the kernels that fall, are poetically related. The image of the sphere and the pearl are linked in the following song; both are a passion that has been cast up and metamorphosed.

If you, Suleika
Gladden me rapturously,
Throw me your passion
As though it were a ball,
I shall catch it
And throw it back to you
Myself dedicated to you:
That is a moment!
. . . .
Here now, in exchange,
Are the poetic pearls
That the powerful breakers of your passion
Cast up to me on to the barren strand of life.
Daintily picked up
With tiny fingers
Threaded with jewelled
Golden ornaments
Put them on your throat,
On your bosom!
Allah's raindrops
Ripened in the humble oyster.

Threaded and interspersed with gold on the throat and on the bosom, the breakers are stilled; the element becomes a jewel. The pearl alone is not enough; it must be threaded, and that means that it must be pierced and, with a gesture of renunciation, be cyclically tied on to a string. Adopting a Persian metaphor for a lyric cycle, Goethe lets the pearl bewail its loss of perfection before it is pierced, and the goldsmith answers:

You must forgive me:
For if I am not now cruel
How shall the string be threaded?

Once more we are in the *Book of Parables.* Its use in conjunction with Saadi's dew-and-pearl metaphor is not unexpected: it is prepared for in the *Book of Sayings* and in the *Book of Suleika.* The laconism of the parable is not cryptic; it relies on connoisseurs whose memory is filled with what has been reduced. Allusion to the theme stimulates a continuation of the thought, invites and does not exclude, seeks interpretation as it is being listened to.

In the *Book of Suleika,* which is written in the form of a dialogue, the poet speaks, in the parable called "Relief" ("Hochbild"), of his position at a distance from the beloved. The sun and the rainbow, Helios and Iris, are separated from one another for the whole of their lives because that is the fate of their natures. Helios cannot attain Iris, because her being takes on color only when it is irradiated from afar by the sun. Light, as the sun god, suffers the experience of natural law, which decrees that, bathed in the light of his rays, the moisture that reflects him shines forth in the rainbow only when the light is at a distance from it. It is this distance alone that makes room for the miracle of the metamorphosis in which drops, called tears, become pearls. If the light does not strike them, they remain "my heart's grey tears": sky and cloud, light and moisture have need of each other, so that, in the heartless inhumanity of the cosmos, the color of humanity may emerge, when light penetrates the gloom. The preservation of distance makes room for the miracles, effected at a distance, of a growing awakening to the possibility—released by a look and the response to it—that promises us a "relief" in our existence.

Now she feels deeply the powers of the look
And looks up fixedly;
The pearls seek their form:
For each one of them assumed his image.

And thus, wreathed in color and by a bow,
Her brightened face lights up,
He comes toward her,
But he—alas—does not reach her.

Goethe authenticates certain findings in his theory of color by the myth of Helios and Iris. The mythicization of the natural law changes it into a metaphor of human experience, but Goethe created the myth, so that natural law should not be an immediate metaphor for human experience. The poem takes a triple step toward metaphorical perception: from nature, by way of myth, to the individual, and another triple step when it speaks of the pearl: the rain falling from the cloud is mythicized into the weeping of the goddess, and the drops are her tears. Initially it is pearls—called tears—that kiss the rays of Helios: "And her tears fall more frequently: / He sends joy into her sorrow / And gives every pearl kiss upon kiss." Iris's tears, previously mentioned only metaphorically as pearls, now become real pearls, as eyes that look back to Helios, when they reflect his colors. The natural drop that falls from the clouds is, first of all, mythicized into a tear pearl and undergoes the miracle of metamorphosis at the moment when the god's kiss of light awakens it to its final destiny, that of mirroring the god in its colored reflection. This pearl is also something pure and of miraculous origin; it owes its purity to the fact that, here on earth, it receives light from above, but not beneath the atmosphere. Pearls that are born in the clouds and that, like these, never touch the earth are otherwise known only in ancient India, in traditions that Goethe can scarcely have known. His myth is quite personal and is formed here, in the image of Helios and Iris—the lover and the unattainable beloved—by a perception from his theory of color. The distance between the lovers is overcome in the pearl by the reciprocity of the gift of light that has been received. Goethe is here treading his own path, changing the perception of nature into language for what is human. He follows the path of a new myth and clings to the idea of the pearl's origin from on high. Herder created a similar myth, probably on the basis of a painting by Titian, when he metamorphosed into pearls the drops that fell back into the ocean from the hair of Anadyomene-Venus and were picked up by oysters. In the meantime, science had been pursuing its own course, and it will be represented here by two great names. Linnaeus took up the idea, known to late antiquity in the twelfth century—but then only to Byzantium—that an oyster that has been wounded by being pierced covers up its wound and heals it with a pearl. The king of Sweden—on Linnaeus's advice—ordered masses of pierced oysters to be sunk into the sea, in the hope of adding to the state treasury by the pearls that would be produced in this way. And, in the year 1711, a lecture by Réaumur in the Paris Academy helped get a theory of the formation of pearls from endogenous forces within the oyster accepted into scientific thought—this theory had been advanced since the time of the Renaissance. With the end of a two-millennia-long tradition that believed in the origin of the pearl in the heavens—even Pliny had averred that there was more of the sky than the sea in the pearl—traces of this new thought are not long in coming into poetry. With the end of the old belief, the world also lost its belief in poetic inspiration, insofar as, up to the time of Klopstock, it had been understood as divine inspiration. The pearl and the poem are, in the future, no longer a gift arising out of the union of heaven and earth, as they had been up to the time of Goethe's "Relief," but both are now merely the fruit of a suffering untouched by heaven. Shortly before the turn of the century, Jean Paul wrote in his *Palingenesien* a chapter with the title "Mens sana in corpore insano" ("A Healthy Mind in an Unhealthy Body") in which we read: "Genius and sickness are such foster-brothers that, in our days, men of talent are most frequently subjected to the most poisonous excrescences, simply because they imagine they can help their satirical acuity by their scorbutic acuity and can help their nervous spirits with nervous fevers: Linnaeus did the same to pearl oysters: he injected them with artificially fruitful illnesses, and the sicker they grow the more pearls they conglobate and deliver."

From now on, poets recognize their writing as a salutary mobilization of their inmost self, with the purpose of staving off and overcoming the suffering perpetrated by a wound that threatens their very life, just like the process that affects the oyster, which, in resisting the crisis it faces, forms a pearl. Jean Paul, who was perhaps the first to interpret the formation of the pearl in the oyster as the union of genius and sickness, also spoke, in his *Siebenkäsroman,* when meditating about his verse, of a humorous defense in circumstances "where one totally covers one's inner self with philosophy, like Diogenes' tub, as a protection against external wounds, or to use a more beautiful metaphor, one insulates, with the pearls of maxims, the mother-of-pearl of our verse, like the pearl oyster that insulates the holes which worms bore into its mother-of-pearl. In the meantime pearls are better than an undamaged mother-of-pearl—a thought that I should really inscribe in golden ink."

In this way Jean Paul was the first to express a poetic metaphor—without a mythic integument—that he had acquired from a new knowledge of nature, something not unique in the nineteenth century. In Ludwig Tieck's novel of the same name, Vittoria Accorombona transforms herself into a wretched oyster in the darkest depths of the sea. A monologue spoken by the oyster ends: "No one knows, no one understands my longing. Everything is alien to me; tight-lipped, I have to eat my heart out in the fear of the unknown—a sigh, lament, sorrow, or death-bringing jubilation bursts from the wretched object, and, like a silent tear, the sorrow sets itself firmly on the shining covering. The tender sickness grows silently, just as the longing increases. The harsh house is already too small for it. Then comes release by death. A skillful fisherman breaks the walls, takes the exquisite, invaluable pearl, and carries it to the king, in whose crown it shines from that moment on, as the most valuable of jewels—O poor Torquato Tasso!" Here for the first time, there is an acknowledgement of the parthogenesis of the arts, of their birth from their own suffering and their own love, both of which are aimed so powerfully at a distant, enhanced satisfaction of their desire for themselves that only a work that has seen the light of day in this way touches the ineffable and takes light from its light. There is here a miraculous inner cosmic genesis that has to be borne by man to the very portals of mortal sacrifice, that transforms the pain of the moment into a quieted permanence, that turns tears into pearls, suffering into light. A hundred and fifty years previously, Sigmund von Birken had composed a pearl song to the tune of "Wie schön leuchtet der Morgenstern" ("How brightly shines the morning star!") and let the heart respond to the gift of heaven in song: "You want in me to give birth to yourself." Such notes are no longer to be heard. In 1818, the young Grillparzer compares his poetic existence with the suffering of the oyster:

And, just as pearls that adorn beauty,
Those bright adornments of the watery kingdom,
Rejoice the finder not the giver,
The silent, joyless oyster,
For sickness alone and long torment
Take from the oyster the treasure so fervently sought,
And what gives you such delight with its rays,
Was begotten in mortal distress and torment.

Only a few years later, Annette von Droste-Hülshoff, in a poem called "Poesy," compared her art with a turquoise, an amethyst, and, again, a pearl. If they are damaged by contact with something unworthy of them, the turquoise, amethyst, and pearl are subjected, in their purity, to clouding. As for poesy, it

is also like the pearl, the tender pearl,
Dewy clear on the healthy man
But, on the sick man,
Sucking out what was in his most secret vein;
Did you never see its sheen?
Greenish like a moldering rag?
It remains a pearl for ever,
But one that was worn by a sick man.

The seal is set upon the demythification of the pearl as a metaphor for poetry by Heinrich Heine:

Pearls that are world-famous
Are nothing but the pale slime
Of a poor oyster
That lies sickly silly on the seabed.

The pearl is, for Heine, like a memory from afar, now worn out by passing through several hands, grown blunt with the loss of its origin from above, even if he does go on:

But the pearls in this casket
Are sprung from a beautiful
Human soul that is deeper,
Out-and-out deeper than the ocean.

For they are the tear-pearls of Yehuda ben Halevi
Who shed them for the fall
Of Jerusalem.

Pearl-tears that,
Linked by the golden threads of rhyme,
Come forth from poetry's golden smithy, as a song.

The Latin word for pearl, *margarita,* has served again and again as an inspiration to the poet to regard women called Margaret as related, by meaning, to the pearl. This happened to St. Margaret and, especially, Margaret of Navarre, around whom a whole wealth of pearl poetry entwined itself. The only poet to make a woman with the name Margaret into a symbol of inspiration, the inspiration that comes from the love of a woman, was a fourteenth-century Englishman. The first literary work of the English Middle Ages to be written in prose, "The Testament of Love," by Thomas Usk, refers to the pearl at a climax of the work. Usk wrote the work in prison, where he was being held by the duke of Gloucester before being executed in 1388, so that "The Testament of Love" could be compared with Boethius's *De consolatione philosophiae,* which was written while Boethius was imprisoned by Theodoric the Great. Years after Usk's death, the beginnings of the chapters of "The Testament of Love" were found to form an acrostic which read:

MARGARETE OF VIRTUE HAE MERCY ON THIN USK. Usk himself accentuates the significance of the passage that emphasizes Margaret—whom he has already introduced—when he explains the work's structure at the beginning of the third and last book. The work, he says, takes three steps, through three ages, and three books: the detour that leads to sin and hell; the return from this detour to the right path of the age of grace; and finally resurrection into eternal joy, splendor, and peace at the end of transience. The first book of "The Testament of Love" shows error, the second the return from error, the third the joy and bliss of perfection. The analogy to the three parts of Dante's *Divine Comedy*—the inferno, purgatory, and paradise—is obvious. We may consider further stimuli from Dante when Usk, at the beginning of the third book, places the emphasis on Margaret, who has already been introduced to us: Dante's Beatrice also becomes of significance in the work only when she is at the threshold of paradise.

Usk links the progression of his work to the Margaret-pearl—he often uses this double name—for a special reason. He takes his cue from the scientists, who tell us, among other things, that the best pearls emanate from the dew on the coast of England—thus throwing light upon Usk's fictional Margaret (objections that there is also a woman of flesh and blood in the background are unfounded). The tradition surrounding the medicinal effects of the pearl ascribe special powers to it, and Usk sees this as referring to three sorts of philosophy: philosophy of nature, of morality, and of knowledge. His third book constructs an ideal world equally concerned with body and soul, a world of philosophy and love and justice over whose poets and truth the inspiring light of the Margaret-pearl shines. In his work, it is the pearl that, by the power of the heart, unites heaven and earth, letter and spirit, woman and grace, human and divine love, and the pearllike perception of the work is represented in the final sentence "Charité is love and love is Charité."

The inspirational light of the Margaret-pearl can stand as a symbol that denotes special possibilities for the obvious but ineffable secret—something that is disfigured rather than explained by the concept of sublimation—of woman's love as the inspirational force behind man's work. The human sensorium of sense and spirit that makes art possible, and other works of an exceedingly complexly constituted spirit, is something unknown to which language does justice only by hinting at the image of inspiration or of influence. Language thinks of the conception of a miraculous effect that creates forms as coming from a heaven that is experienced as God, nature, or man, just as the dew of that same heaven is the origin of the pearl—the incarnation of an intensified form—made possible in the element of corporeal nature. The female name Margaret can stand for the inspirationally poetic effect of a love whose biographical nucleus of experience sends out roots that will bring forth a blossom in which soil and light are united. Inspired metamorphosis of experience demands secrecy. The biographical reason, together with its inmost self, can be brought to light only by a process of metamorphosis in language and other arts. The miracle of the metamorphosis in the oyster takes place on the dark seabed, where no sunlight can penetrate. There are keys to hand that it is forbidden to use. Goethe wrote such a one in *Wilhelm Meisters Wanderjahre.* Wolfram von Eschenbach opens up one motive for his writing when he considers the completion of his *Parzival* in the last sentence of the poem: "If this came about because of a woman, / Then she has to admit that I spoke sweet words." Wolfram offers a key to the imagination, which at the end of the poem, where poets thank the sources of their inspiration, locks up one secret of his work. The inspiration that derives from Beatrice, Diotima, and Sophia has to be perceived from the works of Dante, Hölderlin, and Novalis. They formed these women for the lasting purity of their being. Thomas Usk secretly immortalized Margaret-pearl, and Wolfram von Eschenbach "a woman" as inspirations for their works.

In the Christian explanation of nature that was conceived as early as the second and third centuries in the work of Origen and in the *Physiologus,* and that took the form of an allegoresis, what is a natural given is rendered comprehensible on the strength of the dimensions of interpretation that are discovered and revealed by intellectual movements that are as methodical as they are creative. The spiritual transparency of what *is* in nature reveals itself by means of an active observation that adds, to the foregrounded thing, perspectives on horizons of meaning—inherent in the thing itself—by revealing its background meaning. The imaginative insight into a spiritual world, within the natural world, makes the thing into a kernel of spheres of signification and gives to the macrocosmic dimension of a spiritual world its microcosm of nature by making it comprehensible. Spiritual observation penetrates what *is* to the very core of its meaning. Its discovery is, however, not a primal discovery and can be called original only to the extent that its meaning was thought into the thing in its creative origin in God, and that what is revealed in the word is made audible—by the one who already knows it—out of the mute language of nature. It is in the perception of the harmony of revelation through the word, and its spiritually revealing rediscovery in the book of nature, that the hidden language that needs to be interpreted is guaranteed to be God's. The theological reason for the fact that one and a half millennia clung to this spiritual form of the revelation of being lies in Christianity, which, from its early history, was accustomed to read and explain creation as another revelation—beside the Bible—that confirms what is in the Bible. Reading nature through the eyes of the Bible, the knowing search for, and rediscovery of, the same revelation in the Creation—as God's second language—joined the word and the world firmly together, when they might easily have fallen apart. It is also human to experience a spiritual joy in rediscovery, since it expands the world, from one point of view, in the sense of the view of the world that accompanies it. The character of an epoch is determined by the extent to which it rediscovers itself in everything that is inherent in it. A creative disruption of this unity, of its style, to which it is bound to cling, creates a crisis for itself. Goethe's poem "Wiederfinden" ("Rediscovery") speaks of the unearthly quality of the solitude, for both creator and creatures, after an act in which "the cosmos broke into realities with a show of force." As God, in creating himself, had the world torn from his breast, he and what was new were "Without longing, without sound."

Everything was mute, silent, deserted,
God was alone for the first time!
Then he created the dawn
Which took pity on his torment;
It developed for the desolate one
A resounding play of colors,
And now what had first disintegrated
Could love again.

The possibility of rediscovery is a condition of culture. If tradition and foundation do not interweave, creative change makes the world unrecognizable, to the point where rediscovery is prevented, and solitude forces its way in, unless there is a dawn to "take pity on the torment" and permit the reestablishment of trust in, and of, what was created and, at length and after a long time, a new rediscovery as well. The modern age, grown uncertain, has initially caused the mutual rediscovery of self by word and world, through the spiritualization of God's creation, to die out and has renounced it in the face of the pressures of knowledge.

"Lending a hand to the unknown" is what Paul Claudel—with a specifying imagination—calls the medieval form of jewel interpretation in his "Mysticism of Precious Stones," an essay that looks at precious stones in the Bible in the old way of Marbod of Rennes and Cornelius a Lapide—that is, in order to see what was communicated by them. The spiritual eye penetrates these stones and changes their nature into language. Like Philip of Thaon, the first person to write about the pearl in French, Claudel, in his essay, also places the pearl immediately after the precious stones. In this the last great hymn of praise to the pearl, written in 1938, the Middle Ages again breathe the air of a new world. More restrained than Jean Paul and others, Paul Claudel interprets the emergence of the pearl from the oyster, in the sense of modern knowledge, as the fruit of a wound, as the "symbol of that injury that the wish for perfection calls forth in us." Like no one else in our century, Paul Claudel let his spiritual and ruminative eyes rest on the pearl, which nature and history concentrate into the miracle of what the individual can achieve and of what he is capable of experiencing. We may quote a few of his sentences about the pearl, which only implicitly call to mind the idea of the work of art:

All the marvels that we have recorded up to now cannot dispense with human collaboration. The human hand has to be involved in order to perfect the secret desire of the stone. Fundamentally they are something that has been made. But the pearl, at the bottom of the sea, is born, quite alone, from living flesh: pure and round, it breaks away, immortal, from the ephemeral being that has given birth to it. It is the image of that wound that summons up in us the desire for perfection and that, slowly, ends up in this inestimable globule. Here it is in the innermost recesses of our substance, the pearl that is the metaphysical kernel withdrawn, at one and the same time, by the silence of any vocation within it from the menace of the interior seed and from external criticism, a condensation of worth . . . a solidification of conscience, the abstraction of all the colors to the point of light, an immaculate conception. The wounded and fertile soul possesses in the very heart of itself an apparatus that allows it to solidify time into eternity. . . . It is something kind, sweet, soothing, affectionate, I was going to say, human, it is a summons to our flesh, divine and incorruptible! It is less of eternity than of persistence, something that we owe to time that is disengaged from the passing of time. The humble mollusc is dead, but what it has made within itself, without seeing it, that unheard of being that it has given us, that continues to live.[1]

In the same year, 1938, the Little Monk in Bert Brecht's *Galileo* says the following: "Don't come to me with the beauty of phenomena that have been gilded by the ages! Do you know how the oyster *Margaretifera* produces its pearl? By wrapping up—at the risk of a mortal disease—an insupportable

1. Paul Claudel, "La Mystique des Pierres Précieuses," in *Oeuvres en Prose de Paul Claudel* (Paris, 1965), pp. 350–351, 352.

foreign body, for example, a grain of sand, into a ball of mucus. It almost dies in the process. To hell with the pearl, I prefer a healthy oyster. Virtues are not tied to misery, my friend. If your people were wealthy and happy they could develop the virtues of wealth and happiness. Now these virtues of the exhausted come from exhausted fields, and I reject them." It must have been about the same time that Robert Musil wrote in *The Man without Qualities:* "Writing is like the pearl, a sickness."

The origin of what is perfect, what is lasting, remains a secret. The pearl cannot intensify any art into something higher. The history of thoughts about the origin of the pearl, which has lasted for millennia and crossed whole continents—the myth of dew and pearl like the explanation of their origin from sickness demanded again and again the discovery of their transparency in relation to meaning. It—and history in general—stands for the individual's potentials, which, thanks to human constants, are never worn out—neither in good nor in bad, neither in light nor in darkness.

SIX

POETRY AS THE NECESSARY FRUIT OF A SUFFERING

Our theme, "poetry as the necessary fruit of a suffering," is not one that characterizes the premodern period. The rhetoric and poetics which were in effect from antiquity until the eighteenth century teach us that literature is something that can be made if we follow the rules of a craft, and even when the poets of antiquity pray for their consecration as poets or, in the Christian era, for inspiration from the spirit of God, they are buoyed up by a confident faith in their ability to achieve what is imposed on them from above and into whose service they enter when they begin to give paradigmatic validity to something objective that is sanctioned by tradition and by genre. There is a wonderfully alien note struck by the poet Konrad von Würzburg when in a literature that thrives in an ambience of social relevance, he distances himself from the song of the lark—whose world-embellishing song is receiving little attention at that late date—because it is heard too much and on all sides. Nonetheless, a master of the high art of poetry should not remain silent, even in a world of fools, but should think of the nightingale that sings in the wood even when no one is listening, so devoted to its song for its own sake that it is a matter of life and death, "daz si ze tode singet sich" [that she sings herself to death].

The sweet passion of the nightingale's self-consuming devotion to its song, for the sake of love, has never been better expressed, since Ovid, than by the Franciscan John Peckham (d. 1292). His nightingale poem on the song of the liturgical hours offers the soul the example of the nightingale that sings itself to death, since it sacrifices itself in song—from before daybreak until evening—throughout the canonical hours, just as the soul should exhaust itself during the canonical hours in singing of Christ from his birth to his burial. I shall quote only five of the eighty-seven strophes of the *Philomena* poem:[1]

De hac ave legitur,
quod, cum deprehendit
Mortem sibi proximam,
arborem ascendit
Summoque diluculo
sursum rostrum tendit
Diversisque cantibus
totam se impendit.

Cantilenis dulcibus
praevenit auroram,
Sed cum dies rutilat
circa primam horam,
Elevatur altius
vocem in sonoram,
In cantando nesciens
pausam sive moram.

Circa verum tertiam
quasi modum nescit,
Quia semper gaudium
cordis eius crescit,
Ferre guttur rumpitur,
sic vox invalescit,
Et quo cantat amplius,
Et plus inardescit

Et cum in meridie
sol est in fervore,
Tunc disrumpit viscera
nimio clamore,
O c i O c i clamitat
illo suo more

1. *Analecta hymnica,* vol. 50, pp. 602–610.

Sicque sensim deficit
cantus prae labore.

Sic quassatis organis
huius philomenae,
Rostro tantum palpitans
fit exsanguis paene,
Sed an nonam veniens
moritur iam plene,
Cum totius corporis
disrumpuntur venae.

[We read of this bird (the nightingale) that, when it discovers that it is close to death, it climbs into a tree at first light and gives itself completely over to a diversity of songs.

It anticipates the dawn with its sweet songs, but when the sky begins to redden around the time of the first hour, it lets its voice swell higher and knows neither rest from, nor end to, its singing.

About the third hour all moderation is forgotten, because its heart is for ever swelling with joy, its throat is close to bursting, as its voice gains strength, and the greater its song the more it bursts with fire.

When at midday, with the sun at its height, its entrails are ready to burst open with the great sound, "oci, oci," it cries, in its own way, as if in the face of such effort its song is gradually losing power.

So when this nightingale has battered the organs of its song, its beak, pulsating, grows almost bloodless, and when the ninth hour comes round, it dies completely, while the veins in its whole body burst.]

Here the nightingale stands for the mystical power of love in the Song of Songs, where, because its own ability is insufficient, it consumes itself in the fervor of the soul's desire for the divine bridegroom and seeks for itself the voice of the nightingale. A poetic subjectivity, with its eyes turned away from the world, proclaims itself in the image of the nightingale singing itself to death with its isolated sense that it has the gift of surpassing itself. It is a subjectivity that, with the arrival of the modern age, has manifested itself in the concept of the *furor poeticus,* the power of suffering engendered by inspiration and, finally, of the visionary melancholy of genius.

The metaphor of the nightingale for the poet, forgotten by the world, singing himself out of life in his poems, is what will point our feet to the path of our methodological process. It is the process by which we shall seek an answer—on the basis of the metaphors by which poets characterize their artistic vocation and their art—to the question of whether there is a specific literary quality—here, "a necessary fruit of suffering." This philological process, which has, up to the moment, been as good as totally neglected is based on the recognition, in the philosophy of language, of the fact that the actuality of human conditions, like life and death, guilt and grace, but also art, is scarcely touched upon, let alone exhausted by conceptual language. Thus, the metaphor, as an indispensable instrument of self-revelation, exercises a Socratic function in the discovery of truth, and the literary scholar has to respect this by making the ability of metaphors to exhaust perception into a hermeneutic principle of his literary historical process, thus uniting the studies of language and literature.

Taking one out of the extraordinary wealth of metaphors for the literary art, the pearl, we are immediately made aware of the fact that it can be used for many aspects of that art. This depends on whether we are considering its natural origin, or its collection—by a diver or by being collected on the beach—whether we are considering its extraction from the oyster, or its dissolving in vinegar, its unpierced purity, or its being pierced to be set in a strand, whether we are thinking of its function in the story of the cock and the pearl, or in the biblical saying about not casting pearls before swine, its use as a gift or as an earring, its place in the crown or the puddle, the breaking of a strand of pearls, or the counterfeiting of pearls, the medical use of the pearl, or its passage through the digestive organs of the dove.

The metaphor of the string of pearls for the composition and the stylistic forms of poetry—common from ancient times, in ancient China, among the Persians, the Arabs, and the Turks, and in Moorish-Hebrew Spain—took hold in the rest of Europe only from the eighteenth century onward. The metaphor was combined, in an astonishing way, with the metaphor of the nightingale, in a strophe the bold invention of which ignores everything from the earlier tradition and—in a terrifying image—exceeds the whole capacity of metaphorical meaning that had previously been attached to the string of pearls, in the idea of a stringing together of poets who sang themselves to death. "Inexpressible" was the title given by Annette von Droste-Hülshoff to a strophe that has in it a breath of the Orient but is not borrowed from it. One single word in the vocabulary of the ineffability of poetry that is never satisfied with itself, whose language is only one voice among all the arts that treat the incomprehensible—as though they could ever grasp its finality—the pearl can stand for one note in the constant insufficiency of singing oneself to death, an insufficiency which, nevertheless, suffices in the sacrifice.

Unaussprechlich
Die Nachtigall in den Kampf sich gab
Mit der Lerche, der schwebenden Stimme,
Daß ihre Reize besängen sie
Und all ihre süße Gebärde;
Doch die Nachtigallen reihten sich
Und die Lerchen, wie Perlenschnüre,
All lagen sie tot in Gras und Strauch,
Verhaucht im süßen Gesange.

["Inexpressible." The nightingale challenged the lark, the hovering voice, to celebrate their charms and all their sweet gestures in song, but the nightingales strung themselves together, and so did the larks, like strings of pearls; they all lay dead in the grass and the underbrush, having breathed their last in sweet song.]

Strings of pearls have never been spoken of more boldly than here, where the completions of the incomplete—this is what art is about—are strung together.

We shall confine our attention to one characteristic of the pearl, its origin from its creation, and again we have to realize that at the same time that the natural concepts of the pearl's origin were changing, so were the poetic interpretations connected with it also undergoing a historical change. Almost two thousand years ago Pliny, in his natural history, told us that a drop of dew, falling from the heavens at an auspicious moment, is picked up by a shellfish swimming on the sea; the shellfish opens up to receive the dewdrop and takes it to the seabed, where the dew is changed into a pearl. This little nature myth and the related derivation of the pearl from lightning, both of which express a belief in the origin of the pearl in a marriage between heaven and earth, and both of which were handed down hundreds of times right up to the time of Goethe, served, wherever the pearl was seen as a poem, as an authentication of its origin from a divine inspiration received by the poet on earth. A surprisingly parallel development in both literary history and natural history is documented by the fact that, in the eighteenth century, the rejection of the natural historical tradition—that there was more of heaven than of the sea in the pearl—was linked to the end of the belief that the poetic gift stemmed from divine inspiration. After the eighteenth century had established a natural historical explanation of the pearl, as a disease of the oyster, we find a corresponding conception of literature as the necessary fruit of a suffering, which we shall now pursue with the aid of the metaphor. "Does not the best begin with sickness everywhere?" is the question that Novalis asked himself.

The thought that the oyster that presents the world with a pearl produces something permanent out of something transitory lay in the nature of things, but it is one of those things that epochs do not express until the hour has arrived when they have some meaning. The formation of jewels takes place in chemical processes that change what is present in nature into other states. Arising from the processes of organic life as an animal product, the pearl has a "mother-of-pearl" with a limited life span. The pearl that is produced by the oyster is also not a child, with a life of its own, that can pass on what it has received by a process of generation. The oyster produces oysters but forms sterile pearls. If it dies on the seabed, its flesh rots, whereas the shell and the pearl that are made of the same material decay, like human bones, only over a long period of time. But the oyster is sacrificed for pearls that are fished for, it is torn from its seabed, cooked in the sun to make it open, and, while its flesh putrefies and starts to stink, it is robbed of the pearl, and what is left is thrown away as rubbish. Man shortens the oyster's natural transitoriness, so as to separate the lasting from the transitory. What originated in the ephemerality of a biological cul-de-sac, as the final perfection of form, recommended itself for adoption as the property of the civilized world, whose desire for art and jewelry in the worship of God and the ruler, and in the service of women, accorded it a supernatural permanence. It was found in the tombs of ancient Egypt. Such considerations were applied to literature only to the extent that the anonymity of art was the object of concern, not as in Horace's "Exegi monumentum aere perennius" [I finished a monument more lasting than bronze][2] and subsequently and, above all, in more recent centuries, which have renounced the medieval anonymity of important areas of art and literature and go on to seek the immortalization of the names of artists, and those who were intellectually important, in their own works, or if they themselves did not do this, it was the intention of their contemporaries to do so. It was possible to visualize in the pearl oyster the way in which an artist's creation could outlive its creator. In a review of *Des Knaben Wunderhorn,* Joseph Görres wrote, thinking of the poems of the anthology that had been assembled from works spanning many centuries, "When the oyster has produced

2. Horace, *Carmina* III, 30.

its pearl, the oyster itself may decay; its jewel remains, lying in the sheen of mother-of-pearl." The way he talks shows that Görres did not believe in the impersonal soul of the people, as the creator of what was collected in this anthology.

The short-livedness of the oyster and the durability of the pearl do not suggest a contradiction, but rather a meaning, as in the section of Paul Claudel's essay "The Mysticism of Precious Stones" entitled "The Pearl,"[3] where he recognizes a creatural accomplishment in the formation of the pearl that makes possible the change of what is at hand into something of a higher quality, so that, in the course of a wonderful enhancement, something immortal emerges from the ephemeral, and eternity emerges from time. Claudel varies the formulation of the thought. Natural jewels need man's cooperation.[4] "The human hand has to be involved in order to perfect the secret desire of the mineral. Fundamentally it is something that has been made. But the pearl, at the bottom of the sea, is born, quite alone, from living flesh: pure and round, it breaks away, immortal, from the ephemeral being that has given birth to it."[5] "The wounded and fertile soul possesses within its very heart an apparatus that allows it to solidify time into eternity." He speaks of the oyster's "conceiving permanence" and of "its persistence, something that we owe to time but that is disengaged from the passing of time. The humble mollusc is dead, but what it has made within itself without seeing it, that unheard-of being that it has given us, continues to live." There is both a poetic and a theological explanation in this essay, which is included among Claudel's essays on art. We did not need the final word on the black pearl—"It is like a voice that has fallen silent, but the sight is there that reveals the song. Speak, word! This pearl is like a completely rounded word in the night!"—to turn our thoughts to poetry. The oyster's power to change the ephemeral into permanence is not something that is necessarily normal, but is linked to a provocation to produce the extraordinary in the form of a sort of fructification by wounding. The pearl in the oyster stands for us and our artistic power, no matter of what sort, a crisis created in an alien setting which has to

3. Paul Claudel, "La Mystique des Pierres Précieuses," in *Oeuvres en Prose de Paul Claudel* (Paris, 1965), pp. 350ff.

4. This section is part of the essay "The Mystique of Jewels," which looks at jewels—in the way the Middle Ages did—for what is mediated by them, so as to transform their nature into language by means of the spiritual eye.

5. There is an ancient Indian saying: "What is beautiful by nature needs no adornment; it is not necessary to rub down a pearl on the grindstone." *Indische Sprüche: Sanskrit und Deutsch*, ed. Otto Böhtlingk (St. Petersburg, 1870–73), no. 7297.

be overcome by the inner creation of form. Only the "wounded and fertile soul" achieves the realization of its essence in the pearl. "It is the image of that wound that causes in us the wish for perfection and that, slowly, ends up as that inestimable globule." "Here it is in the innermost recesses of our substance, the pearl that is the metaphysical kernel . . . a condensation of worth . . . a solidification of consciousness, the abstraction of all colors to the point of light, an immaculate conception of permanence, possessing no other value than its beauty and the perfection which is inherent in it, a perfection that emerges from its simplicity, from its purity and its luster, as much as from the desire that it arouses." Like no one else in this century, Claudel let his thoughtful and intellectual gaze rest on the pearl, so as to concentrate nature and history into the miracle of what man experiences, and of what is possible, in the process of which his sentences on the pearl awaken, only obliquely, thoughts of the work of art. Claudel—by linking theology and knowledge of nature, the old and the new, transcendence and immanence, in a manner that renews tradition by accepting new ideas and not by critically seeking to renounce it—elevates once more, by the poetic spirituality of his views, what is medieval into the atmosphere of a new world.

The poet's oyster fate—to create a poetic pearl within himself—was, in earlier epochs, a grace which had befallen him, a sign of inspirational selection, a favor bestowed by nature, and the possibility that it would ever occur to anyone to think of an author's suffering simply did not exist. Inspired by heaven, literary works—like Christ, the pearl, in the Virgin's womb—came painlessly into the world. Poetic metaphors were completely untouched—until modern times—by the modern notion of literature as the result of a productive melancholy, or a pathologically frenzied enthusiasm.[6] The ability, peculiar to the Middle Ages, to enable the experience of sorrow to achieve and master artistic form in the lament—in the High Minnesang in the lament for parting, in the dirge, in the lament for the division of faith in the world, in the dramatic passions—accepted this as a cosmic given and made it possible for the poet, especially when he was trying to bring order to something that had become out of joint, not to lose his footing. The poet is understood in a very broad sense as a "master"—a fundamental concept of poetic theory. It is only

6. Hans-Jürgen Schings, *Melancholie und Aufklärung: Melancholiker und ihre Kritiker in Erfahrungsseelenkunde und Literatur des 18. Jahrhunderts* (Stuttgart, 1977); Ludwig Völker, *Muse Melancholie—Therapeutikum Poesie: Studien zum Melancholie-Problem in der deutschen Lyrik von Hölty bis Benn* (Munich, 1978).

when the pearl is seen as the fruit of an oyster's mortal sickness that the poet also, as someone whose existence is endangered by his artistic vocation, really enters the view of the age. In more recent years, Claudel, together with Brecht and Musil, is among the most recent witnesses of this understanding of the poet as it conforms to a new scientific concept. We will outline its history.[7]

The scene of an elephant dance, within the framework of a description of a great feast, is part of the extensive chapters on jewels in Daniel Caspar von Lohenstein's colossal historical novel *Arminius und Thusnelda* (1689). While the elephants, representing the four elements and the four points of the compass, are dancing, Juno, as air, and Vesta, as fire, seated on them, sing songs that function as lyrical inserts and compete as to the origin of the pearl. While Juno's song sings of the pearl's origin from the dew—

Thus it is true the daughters of the oyster
Are a brood of the air, and the children of the stars

—and Vesta's song argues for its origin in fire—

the pearl in oyster shells
Milk in breasts, love in body and soul
Yes, love itself is my purest flame

—India, seated on a white elephant, enters and sings a song with five strophes about the pearl which, surprisingly, makes reference, for the first time, to the pearl as a product of sickness, which, it is true, it immediately condemns as

Slander, that regards the pearl,
As the glands of sick snails.[8]

7. I shall leave out of consideration the less frequent citations for the idea—apparently less applicable to literature—that it is precisely in the saline, or bitter, sea that pearls are formed, as we are told in the verses of the sixteenth-century Persian poet Saib: "Everyone, who—like the sea—has experienced only bitter days, is on the outside full of amber, on the inside full of pearls." Joseph von Hammer, *Geschichte der schönen Redekünste* (Vienna, 1818), p. 394.

8. Daniel Caspar von Lohenstein, *Großmüthiger Feldherr Arminius* (1689), ed. Elida Maria Szarota (Berne, 1973), pt. 1, p. 1377. In its song of praise to Thusnelda, India also has to proclaim that the German pearl is the most beautiful of all: "Although Thusnelda's beauty gives way to purple, pearl, and star, her spirit's inmost part is a hundred times superior to the externals. For her virtue is her treasure, her body the grotto, the oyster her figure, and the pearl itself her soul."

A competition in song about the origin of the pearl was possible only after the theory of the origin of the pearl in the dew of heaven, a theory uncontested until then, was challenged in the sixteenth century and a number of fantastic theories had arisen about the endogenous origin of the pearl in the oyster, and had been current for a whole epoch, as rivals to the antique myth of the pearl's origin. Lohenstein, the first author to show some knowledge of the theories of the origin of the pearl as the fruit of a sick oyster, rejects it as slander. The theory was unable to establish itself until the eighteenth century. Linnaeus took up an idea—which had appeared in isolated instances in late antiquity and, in one instance, in twelfth-century Byzantium—that proposed that an oyster paralyzed by having been pierced placed a pearl on its wound in order to heal it. The king of Sweden on Linnaeus's advice ordered hundreds of pierced oysters to be sunk into the sea in the hope of improving the state's finances by producing pearls in this way. In the year 1711, Réaumur, in a lecture to the Paris Academy, helped gain acceptance in scientific thought for a theory that had been propounded since the Renaissance that held that the pearl was the product of endogenous forces in the oyster. With the collapse of a two-thousand-year-old tradition that held, with Pliny, that the pearl had more of heaven than of the sea in it, traces of this were soon to be found in literature. With the end of the old belief, the world also lost its belief in poetic inspiration, insofar as this was, up to the time of Klopstock, understood as divine inspiration. In the future the pearl and the poem would no longer be a gift emanating from the combination of heaven and earth, as they had been up to the time of Goethe's *Hochbild,* but would both now be nothing but the fruit of a sorrow untouched by heaven.[9]

Jean Paul, ever sensitive to scientific upheavals, was a pioneer in subscribing to the new understanding, which is not to say that apocryphal writing was totally excluded from his work—as witness a saying in *Jubelsenior* in the year 1797. One thought sweetens the tears of an old woman looking back on her life: "that was, that every happy child whom she had brought up, and every pain that she had borne, her patience had made into a virtue, just as the

9. Such a dictum should not shock anyone. History knows of no radical ascents and descents without wide areas of twilight that slowly rise and fall, and the period of dawn or Enlightenment regarded itself as being one of these. The individual never emerges from one, from his twilight, the most characteristic in history. Even index fossils dissolve only slowly, but eventually they do. Of course we still find later appeals to the muses, perhaps even a poetic prayer for inspiration. But how can we then explain, for example, the motto for Mann's *Dr. Faustus,* which is an appeal by Dante to the muses?

pearl oyster lends brilliance to the grain of sand that is thrown into it and creates a pearl out of it."[10]

When we consider the sickness caused by the grain of sand in the oyster we must take note of the fact that it did not fall into the oyster, but was "thrown" into it, for even if we think of a restless surge on the seabed we still think rather of something falling into the oyster, rather than of its being thrown into it. Jean Paul, however, clings to the grain of sand thrown into the oyster in other, later passages, although he does not account for it anywhere, apparently remembering an emblematic tradition according to which the crab throws stones into the shell of a waiting oyster in order to prevent it from closing its shell, thus leaving it defenseless and in the crab's power.[11] The "sharp red grain of sand that is thrown into the life" of the pearl oyster (in the *Vorschule der Ästhetik*) does not stand for natural wrongs, but signifies, fatefully and mortally, what it is that attacks the sensitive interior of life by entering from the outside. The crisis that has to be overcome is not endogenous, but an additional suffering that wounds. This must be borne in mind when the poet is the oyster that, quietly and patiently creating a pearl, exerts all its power just to stay alive.

At the end of *Jubelsenior* Jean Paul—in looking back at his work—remembers to break away from this carefully, and that also means breaking away from the people he created in his work and whom he led to their fate. Just as, in the sixteenth century, du Bartas at the end of his epic on God's week

10. *Werke,* vol. 4, ed. Norbert Miller (Munich, 1962), p. 521.

11. Arthur Henkel-Albrecht Schöne, *Emblemata: Handbuch zur Sinnbildkunst des XVI. und XVII. Jahrhunderts* (Stuttgart, 1967), cols. 725ff. As early as the ninth century there is a report by pseudo-Aristotle of the crab that outwits the oyster by forcing a stone into it, and this was taken over by the Arabic lithologist Ahmed Teifaschi. S. F. Ravius, *Specimen arabicum continens descriptionem et excerpta libri Achmedis Teifaschii de gemmis et lapidibus pretiosis* (Utrecht, 1748), pp. 47ff. It also has a place in emblematics. Under the lemma *ne claudar* it stands for people who are morally obstructed by the devil from opening themselves up to religion. The oyster which closes up in good time, when a crab is approaching with a stone, is to be found under the lemma *vitat fallacias* for her clever defense against heretics and serves as the title of philosophical writings. Under the lemma *claustro tuta suo* (safe in her cloister) she befits the cloistered seclusion of the virgin. The oyster that is open, awaiting the dew, becomes the prey of the crab, just as those who are open to worldly joys are sacrificed to the devil (*Rorem quaerendo*). The crab swallows the pearl in the oyster, just as the devil sows discord in the convent and attacks it: "Nec unio servat ab hoste" [Nor does unity save it from the enemy]. Johann Michel von den Ketten, *Apelles Symbolicus* (Amsterdam, 1699), pt. 1, p. 720, no. 75; p. 722, nos. 85, 86; pt. 2, p. 86, no. 171; p. 87, no. 182. A further six emblems with the crab-and-oyster motif are to be found in Phillipus Picinelli, *Mundus symbolicus,* vol. 1 (Cologne, 1694), bk. 6, chap. 13, nos. 48–51, 53f.

of creation once more regards his work as a painting of the world and finds it good, the poet, as painter, here also looks at his "tableau"—which seems to him complete—even if he feels that he ought to examine it once more to see whether perhaps, at the end, it still lacks one stroke of the brush: "As an artist, I disassociate myself from the family, as a human being, it is with the family that I truly refresh myself: for I am not going to leave Neulandpreis in under eight days, eight days that I shall use for trimming the heart, the ears, and the lips of this little work, and I shall add—where they are lacking—extravagances, the most necessary as extravasations and lardaceous cysts, or, in a more beautiful metaphor, I shall adorn it with sets of baroque pearls."[12] Moving unexpectedly from the metaphor of painting to the anthropomorphic one of the body and then returning to the painting metaphor, Jean Paul considers extensions to the body he has created that a doctor would diagnose as life threatening: extravagances (not digressions—*digressiones*), bloodlettings, fatty ulcers. It is not the only place where Jean Paul leads us from an ugly metaphor of illness with an "or, to use a more beautiful metaphor" to the pearl metaphor,[13] and, in fact, it is not so surprising, for Jean Paul also understands the pearl as a product of sickness, and he considers the pear-shaped, or otherwise unevenly bulging, baroque pearls as misshapen formations which deviate from classical form. The fact that the settings of baroque pearls are supposed to ornament the poetic body reminds us of the use of the poetic ornatus. But, never one to employ a chance word, Jean Paul prophetically suggests something else: he adds to the "end of the story" the "appendix of the appendix"—the *Jubelsenior* already bears the subtitle "Appendix" (after "Biographical Entertainments")—with the title "My Christmas Eve,"[14] and only after this does he place the word "end." He uses the metaphors of sickness to announce the unclassical excrescence (appendix) at the end of the work, on whose first page the author is wearing a "cap of freedom on his head." He does not fashion an aesthetic conscience out of his baroque pearl, especially as, like other appendices in Jean Paul's oeuvre, this one constitutes the high point of the work.

Surprisingly, in the *Vorschule der Ästhetik* (1804), Jean Paul lights on the pearl, when he is talking about Greek poetry and its peace and serenity, as a condition of its beauty that extends like a blue ether over its world and its age and gives us an inkling of the eternal. Jean Paul admits, but only in an image,

12. *Werke*, vol. 4, p. 540.

13. See above, pp. 260–261.

14. See n. 10.

that the Greeks had probably known of troubled movement arising from suffering, and of quest in striving, but had transformed them into serene repose in poetry, when he shows, in the pearl, what Greek poetry can and should bring forth. It banishes death and suffering by an apotheotic metamorphosis, so that divine blood issues from poetic wounds. "Poetry should be, as it was formerly known in Spain, the happy science and, like a death, create divinities and blessed ones. Ichor alone should flow from poetic wounds, and poetry, like the pearl oyster, must cover every sharp or rough grain of sand that is thrown into it with the material of pearls." Just as the pain of its wound provokes the oyster to muster up all its strength to surmount that pain in a beautiful manner, so the world of poetry must be "the best, in which every pain is resolved into a greater joy." The wound caused by the grain of sand that falls into the oyster does not cause death as a permanent dissonance, but awakens a more beautiful harmony. Art elevates suffering; "then we are like people on mountains around whom what falls below, in real life, as heavy drops, is merely drizzle up above. Therefore every poem is unpoetical, just as any musical piece that closes with dissonances is incorrect."[15]

In the *Kleine Nachschule* to the *Vorschule der Ästhetik,* Jean Paul is mockingly irritated by formal poetic games like the acrostic, the alphabetic acrostic, the nonuse of certain letters in a poem, and, above all, a process in the composition of novels in which the stories have to be invented around prescribed main or root words, in the way that Kotzebue composed the life of his father around twelve prescribed words. The process—not common in poetics—is explained and condemned on the basis of a number of metaphors. Every chapter in the novel is arranged around a main word, like the "historical thread" on a wooden spool of thread, so that a skein of the story is produced. Or "Romantics believed that they could produce miraculous arbitrary and omnipotent works if they proclaimed their work beforehand by means of a root word and then crept and ran around a few demarcated word-pillars like ivy." An arbitrariness that reveals itself in this way proceeds like masons, who "build away with arbitrarily scattered nouns that are presented to them, like rhyme words, as building blocks." The metaphor of the mason, the agricultural metaphor, and the spinning metaphor for writing are each adapted

15. *Vorschule der Ästhetik* IV, *Programm,* par. 19, in *Werke,* vol. 5, ed. Norbert Miller (Munich, 1963), p. 77. In a comic chapter about "poetesses" who have swum into their own province, Jean Paul mentions three ways in which it is possible for a man to look upon them as pearl oysters. One admirer values them as pearl oysters "with pearls or brilliant ideas"; another looks on them merely as something to swallow with his eyes and his lips; the third, the husband, simply as an oyster of another sex. In the "Jubilate-Lecture" in the *Vorschule der Ästhetik,* p. 437.

so specifically that, instead of illustrating the different processes of writing, they appear as though they could all be applied to a unique process that had not been previously described, either metaphorically or conceptually. The superscription to the paragraph "Romanen-Musaik" and the talk of the romantic "musaicist" complete the group of metaphors that are concerned with the new phenomenon, both satirically and as explication of the further one of the "mosaicist" who has to complete the whole thing by using words that are prescribed for the work. If the pearl metaphor were to be applicable in this context, it too would be in need of a modification that is not present in its history, so that it could represent the way in which what is not poetical can be made poetical: "at least the writers should not prophesy to us that such foreign bodies have, both like seed pearls—which are placed into an oyster so that they can be covered with real pearl material—and like dead animals in a beehive that have to be covered over with beeswax when there is a difficulty in getting them out—so that, I say, foreign root words that have created the stuff of the story just as that has created the words."[16] It is only the knowledge of an alleged procedure, that of changing false pearls into apparently real ones, that makes the pearl metaphor comprehensible here. For this reason, Jean Paul added a note of explanation when he first used it in his early satire, *Flüchtige Mutmaßungen über die menschlichen Tugenden.* The point at issue was: if the desire to imitate examples allows us to have dealings with the society with whose virtues we seek to be tinged, we are like "false pearls" "that are refined and overlaid by real oysters with a real pearl skin." In his allegedly scientific explanation of this metaphor, Jean Paul is following Pliny's erroneous view, which states that oysters climb out of the sea in the spring in order to be fructified by the dew. By appealing—as the first writer in a two-thousand-year-long tradition—to an anonymous source, he considers this natural process so manipulable that it is possible for a false pearl to be substituted for the dew and for it to be refined by the oyster. "It is well known that the Chinese placed false pearls, fashioned out of mother-of-pearl, into open oysters that creep up out of the sea in the spring. The following year they find the false pearls covered in a skin which the oysters have provided."[17] There is no other evidence for the idea that oysters come up on to the beach in the

16. Par. 2, "Romanen-Musaik," in *Werke,* 5:460. Cf. in the *Palingenesien,* in *Werke,* 4:809: "The moment the ideas that make honey in the beehive of our heads can no longer throw a foreign body like a dead mouse, etc., over the threshold of the hive, they at least cover it with wax, so that it won't stink."

17. *Sämtliche Werke,* pt. 2, vol. 1, ed. Norbert Miller and Wilhelm Schmidt-Biggemann (Munich, 1974), p. 844.

spring. The wish was probably father to the thought. Human cunning has been engaged in finding recipes for the counterfeiting of pearls from time immemorial and finally seizes upon the services of the supposedly natural ability of the oyster to refine the cuckoo's egg of the seed pearl—like the grain of sand thrown by the crab—and adorn it with the brilliance of the real pearl. Imitating the innocent crab with his cunning, the counterfeiters and those people undertaking the culture of pearls by means of boring a hole in the oyster—when it was once known that by causing harm to the oyster it was possible to squeeze beauty out of it—did not hesitate to try to profit by such practices. Even if such procedures existed only in literature—traditions of prescriptions for the counterfeiting and treatment of pearls have, whatever the motives might be, reluctantly avoided the fantastic—such fantasies betray secret directions taken by the effort.

While the old metaphor of the sugarcoated pill of useful truth[18] permits the poet, as physician, to communicate the healing kernel of his work, the metaphor of the pearl covered with the appearance of authenticity belongs to the field of deception that deceives and does not help: it promises what it does not produce, like the mendacious "pearls" of the common courtier. It is not part of poetics, but of literary criticism. Its verdict in the chapter about the composition of the Romantic novel destroys—with a host of metaphors—what has already been censured, even if Jean Paul does still switch to the poet as creator: "In truth, wherever the true poet turns he encounters only lumps of earth and ribs, but he breathes life into them, and Adams and Eves emerge from them, while the false poet turns what is alive back into clay and makes the rib into a skeleton."[19] There are genuine and false poets, just as there are genuine and false pearls. The process by which pearl growers provoke, by a cunning use of their art, natural processes of suffering, so as to profit from the mastery effected by the tortured creature, is also a false process. Such a model nourishes its masters.

Shortly before the turn of the century, Jean Paul writes, in his *Palingenesien,* a chapter with the title "Mens sana in corpore insano" ("A Healthy Mind in an Unhealthy Body"), whose reversal of the ancient maxim is aimed at the disproportionate development of the head of the later scholar, who thinks better than he acts, so that it is "precisely physical decrepitude that repays us with

18. Hubert Gersch, *Geheimpoetik: Die "Continuatio des abentheuerlichen Simplicii" interpretiert als Grimmelshausens verschlüsselter Kommentar zu seinem Roman,* Studien zur deutschen Literatur, no. 35 (Tübingen, 1973), pp. 67–74.

19. See n. 10, p. 461.

intentions for what it takes from us in actions. Genius and sickness are all the more closely related, like foster brothers, that, in our time, men of talent undertake the most poisonous excesses, simply because they think that they can reinforce their satirical sharpness with their scorbutic acumen and can, with their nervous fevers, come to the aid of their nervous spirits; it was in the same way that Linnaeus injected pearl oysters—who the sicker they are, the more pearls they conglobate and produce—with artificial and fructifying sicknesses."[20] As though there were a self-mutilation of the oyster, so here the self-imposed sickness is supposed to stimulate spiritual sensibility to an extraordinary growth in thought. A few sentences further on, in a closely related image, the need for protection on the part of a delicate nature that tries at the right moment to compose itself as a citizen of the world is contrasted with this affected poetic vulnerability: "Thus it was, on Easter morning, that I was well served by exuding from my soft snail shell a stony carapace and covering myself with it; I was absolutely certain that I did not want to be touched until my return and then all the harder."[21] We are dealing, in the oyster's exudation, with an intensified survival; in the snail's, with spiritual self-control.

Looked at as part of a text, Jean Paul's metaphors can appear so embedded in contexts that it seems as if they are presenting the decoding of an inner constellation. In the *Palingenesien,* Siebenkäs takes responsibility for an offence against Hermina: "Oh, I did not understand this martyr of the heart, but merely wounded her."[22] Hermina behaves poetically in her suffering. She anticipates an apology with her letter, a "spiritual patent of nobility," which anticipates rather than forgives. And the recipient, "Oh," I said in my enthusiasm toward me and my kind, "if we have wounded you defenseless souls, then we shall continue to tear at the wound until you wipe away the blood and the tears and ask us to forgive you for having shed them both." Hermina's letter relates the great dream that she had toward daybreak, in which her mother, descending from heaven, offers her the sparkling chalice: "Drink the chalice of suffering to the dregs; then the veil will fall. I love you forever, for love is eternal, like God." Jean Paul, the writer who uses revelation in dreams par excellence, does not offer us this dream unmediated, but after an observation that contains something like a "Poetics of Female Dreams" and that is supposed to legitimate, out of Hermina's character and out of female dreams

20. *Werke,* vol. 4, p. 765.
21. *Werke,* vol. 4, p. 766.
22. *Werke,* p. 798.

in general, the dream which appears as a "fiction" and present it to us as truth. On dreams: "In male dreams we find worlds in wild ferment, Milton's working chaos and the clash of spirits,[23] but up to the moment, in most female dreams, I have come across idealistic and gently ordered compositions, the pallidly collected wreaths of pearls from the shattered seabed of masculine dreams—poetic and religious idylls of life." The metaphor of the pearl gives woman the gift of opening up to idealism, at night, what is kept closed during the day, of finding patiently what is placed on the "shattered seabed of the man," of seeing it and changing it into something that has vital potential. As the martyr of his heart, woman is man's poet when in dreams she gives form—as the fruit of a passion—to what he cannot achieve. She assumes the function of the oyster, when she, "wounded" and "injured" to the point of suffering, permits what is actually given to man to achieve, to develop vicariously in herself, while at the same time giving the appearance of collecting only "the wreaths of pearls from the man's shattered seabed." While she is forming "gently ordered compositions," she completes the work of art that is the string of pearls. This is done in order to overcome a vital crisis in the poetic form of the dream as the foundation of the idyll. The metaphor of the pearl appears in Jean Paul's works only as talk of achieving the ideal.

Poetry is a pearl, wherever it effects a reconciliation with life's suffering. Already in *Hesperus,* Jean Paul uses the motto of forgiveness and reconciliation for the development of the pearl. Flaminius and Victor rediscover—with an unexpected inner compulsion—their friendship, which had been so brutally shaken that they had reached the point where they contemplated suicide, and they find themselves in each other's arms, moved to the depths of emotion, "Now we shall not leave one another again, now we shall stay like this for ever." It is at this moment that Jean Paul seals what has just happened with a saying that brings into play the oyster's wound when it is bored into: "Nothing moves man more than the sight of a reconciliation, our weaknesses are not bought too dearly by the hours of forgiveness, and the angel who never felt anger would have to envy man, who overcomes it. When you forgive, the person who wounds your heart is the sea worm that makes holes in the oyster shell, which in its turn closes those holes with *pearls.*"[24] There is a not unrelated passage in the Siebenkäs novel. Siebenkäs, who bears the scars

23. Jean Paul's note on this, p. 798: "How wildly must the clouds of the dreams of, e.g., Callot, Dante, Cromwell, Robespierre, etc., clash together."

24. *Hesperus,* 32 *Hundsposttag,* in *Werke,* vol. 1, ed. Norbert Miller (Munich, 1960), p. 1015.

of his "thousand domestic vexations," is shaken by scenes of misfortune, falls asleep—"depressed and wounded by the day"[25]—on the eve of the auction of the things that he holds dear, has to reconcile himself with his own existence and with the loss of his worldly honor and takes the innocently sovereign step of taking the place of the auctioneer when it comes to offering his own things for sale. Jean Paul narrates the self-surpassing boldness of his action after prefacing it with "a lot of philosophy" so as to prepare the reader for the unusual scene. It takes place with these aphoristic considerations: "Nothing makes it more humorous and more cold to class honor than when you have to exchange the honor of your class with that of a person or a value, and if you always have to protect your own heart against external wounds by the use of philosophy, like Diogenes' barrel, or if, to use a more beautiful metaphor, you are like the pearl oyster and have to exude the pearls of maxims to cover the holes that are bored into our mother-of-pearl.—Meanwhile pearls are better than an intact mother-of-pearl—a thought that I should write down in golden ink."[26] When it is not a question of a grain of sand's being thrown into the oyster, but of its being bored into by a sea worm—a person "who wounds your heart"—the exudation of the pearl to save the oyster from a mortal affliction is a stronger defensive move against something involving existence itself. It is humorous in the sense of a cosmic spirit deriding finality with a superior and patient gentleness; it is that laughter "in which there is still a pain and a stature."[27]

Dr Katzenbergers Badereise, written in 1809, also refers to the new knowledge of the suffering undergone by the oyster in producing the pearl, where two temperaments, one sentient in love—and thus suffering—and one executing the inner movements without feeling, as though following the rules of an exercise, are concisely compared. Niess, unruffled by experience, enjoys his heartfelt grief, while Theudobach suffers painfully because of his feelings. "He melts pleasurably into tears in an orderly manner and clicks his tongue like a merry fish. The feeling that, in the case of a mathematicizing Theudobach, is an oppressive pearl in the oyster is worn by him, on the outside, as an adornment."[28] The pain suffered by the one as a first experience—it would be nice to have this as a reference to the poet—slips through the

25. *Werke,* vol. 2, ed. Norbert Miller (Munich, 1959), p. 214.

26. Pp. 216f.

27. *Vorschule der Ästhetik* VII, par. 33, in *Werke,* vol. 5, p. 129.

28. *Dr Katzenbergers Badereise,* 36 *Summula,* in *Werke,* vol. 6, ed. Norbert Miller (Munich, 1963), pp. 231f.

other's hand, as a completed form, like jewelry. The rhyme of *drückend* (oppressive) and *schmückend* (decorative) seems to say something about the poem that has yet to be composed and the one that is already written. We live with pearls of value and appearance that have grown in others.

The poem ripens in secret, in banks of pearls, as the oyster colonies on the seabed are called. The rank assigned to an author is determined by his pearl banks, his treasury of ability, patience, and maturity. Dian's friendly glance recognized the great gifts—here not of a poetic nature—that had been bestowed upon the youth Albano, "when he approached him passionately and saw, with a few glances, the pearl banks and the fertile ground in the youth's deep but pure sea."[29] Scribblers who are not blessed with banks of pearls—or imaginative riches—feign a miserably shabby treasure. Jean Paul speaks of the new Romantic mysticism in terms of suspicions that—in remembering true mysticism, lived in the deed—place his maxim, "the mystical is the holy of holies of the Romantic," against a relativizing background. The mystical is suited to a time that has neither heart nor substance; "it allows mystical, nocturnal moths to fly instead of the twilight moths of Romanticism or, to put it in another way, it does not dive down to the Romantic pearl bank, but dives more happily into the mystical fog bank."[30] Pearl bank, twilight, and immersion stand for what is poetic in Romanticism, whose claim is not met by a mysticism characterized by fog bank, night, and surface movement. In a world lacking both heart and God, philosophical absolutism and mysticism do, it is true, devise "an abyss both upward and downward . . . into both of which we look, suspended," until, finally, only after being whirled round and round in the empty space that we have discovered, "we actually see nothingness." The pearl banks, in contrast to the fog banks, conceal poetic cosmic substance. In *Museum* (1814), Jean Paul polemicizes against Romantic novelists—poetic nonentities—who inflate their books with a loose and fuzzy sentence placed above the pages in large characters as though they were as full as those of Klopstock, Baader, or Kant. He recommends that "small pearl type veil the lack of their pearl bank. . . . Heavens, would not many writers finally be best printed in so infinitely small and compact a type that they would be as unreadable, typographically, as they are aesthetically?"[31]

The dedication preceding the fantastic story "Der Mond" ("The Moon") in the *Leben des Quintus Fixlein* places astronomy as the subject in women's

29. *Titan*, 24. *Zykel*, in *Werke*, 3:129.

30. *Vorschule der Ästhetik*, in *Werke*, 5:426.

31. Prologue to *Museum*, in *Sämtliche Werke*, pt. 2, vol. 2 (Munich, 1976), p. 881.

education that will inspire nobility above the study of French and the chivalric novel. If the astronomer and the poet, the measurer and the imaginer, both turn to heaven, their professions are complemented by the formation of a new view of the world: "The astronomer inventorizes and assesses heaven and comes up a few pounds short; the poet furnishes and enriches it; the former compiles the register of water meadows into which the latter guides his stream of pearls together with a few goldfish; the former lays down measuring cords; the latter places garlands around the moon and around the earth.[32] Pearl streams are oyster pearls, that is streams that lead to fishing for poetic treasure, for imaginative stories. Jean Paul uses the nature metaphor for his writing when, in his "Mond" story, he gives an example of the combination of science and literature. It is the story of a holy family—"There is a holiness, which arises only from, and is purified only by, suffering"; Rosamunde is "a bright pearl who is transfixed by pain," who climbs from earthly depths to the highest alp, in order to find there, where earth and cosmos look at one another, solace for her innermost desire by striving for the moon. The change of the astronomical perspective by looking from the moon, where the shining earth was now "poised in the blue sky like a thin, white cloud"[33] and where a solar eclipse and the earth's darkness appear differently, completes the change of poetic perspective, in whose imagination the sight of the earth from the moon, which has been gained through death, sees the earth quivering in the hour of darkness. The poet's introduction of the pearl streams into the astronomer's lunar water meadows fills the experience of cosmic nobility with a movement of inmost inspiration.

In the earlier nineteenth century, the knowledge of sickness as the origin of the pearl must have been so widespread that different authors each independently used the oyster as a metaphor for the poet and, after Jean Paul, who had to communicate the knowledge of the natural process only when he came to introduce the metaphor, could now reckon with an understanding of it; we see this in Grillparzer (1818), Grabbe (1827), Heine (after 1835), Rückert (1836), Tieck (1840), and Droste-Hülshoff (after 1841).

32. *Werke,* 4:51.

33. Socrates imagines the earth when seen from on high as "like those balls, which are made of twelve pieces of leather, variegated, a patchwork of colors." Plato, *Phaedo,* trans. R. S. Black (London, 1955), 110 B. The view of the earth from the heavenly bodies has been revived to a considerable degree by literature about celestial travel in recent centuries. See Michael E. Winter, *Compendium Utopiarum: Typologie und Bibliographie literarischer Utopien,* vol. 1, *Von der Antike bis zur deutschen Frühaufklärung* (Stuttgart, 1978), pp. 64ff.

If, in the work of Jean Paul, the development of the pearl had to overcome an external wound in the oyster, a belief in a parthogenesis of literature is professed soon after that, in its condition as an endogenous suffering. In the poem "Farewell to Gastein," written in 1818, the young Grillparzer compares the state of being a poet with three natural sufferings and torments. The tree struck by lightning is gloriously transfigured in the flames which fell it. The rainbow stands above the waterfall, since the cliffs which oppose it make it more beautiful even as they are wounding it: "And, all around, diamonds shake themselves loose." No intervention from above, or resistance from below, brings about the development of the pearl in the oyster:

And just as pearls that adorn beauty,
Those bright adornments of the watery kingdom,
Rejoice the finder not the giver,
The silent, joyless oyster,
For sickness alone and long torment
Take from the oyster the treasure so fervently sought,
And what gives you such delight with its rays
Was begotten in mortal distress and torment.

In this clearly constructed poem, the three strophes of comparison are framed by an introductory strophe and a final one: the latter collects the statements:

The poet thus, if borne on high by happiness,
Praised on all sides by the loud sound of applause,
Is the withered tree struck by lightning,
The poor oyster, the waterfall;
What you consider songs are laments
Spoken into a joyless cosmos
And flames, pearls, jewels that hover round you
Are parts of *his* life separated from him.[34]

The pearl strophe, as the center of the poem, strikes a new note and one that, from now on, can no longer be ignored, whereas the lightning and the

34. F. Grillparzer, *Sämtliche Werke,* vol. 1, ed. Peter Frank and Karl Förnbacher (Munich, 1960), pp. 97f.

waterfall conjure up classical possibilities of the experience of a poetic existence that is chosen by fate and exposed to view. The poor poet pays with his existence in sickly seclusion for the profit that others derive from his torments. The motif of literature as a lament for torment already lay embedded in the theme of the poet's suffering solitude and alienation that is struck in Goethe's *Tasso:*

> One thing only remains:
> Nature has given us the tear,
> The cry of pain, when, finally, man
> Can no longer bear it—and to me above all else—
> It left to me, in pain, both melody and speech,
> With which to lament the greatest abundance of my afflictions
> And if man grows silent in his torment,
> There is a god that gave me tongue to say what I endure.[35]

Goethe still leaves a breath of comfort hovering over this more-than-private fate of the poet—and this is different from earlier laments—if nature *does* lend support in extremis, and if "a god" bequeaths language capable of speaking without foundering. The remembrance of such a final resting place of poetry in some form of transcendence, however weakened, is extinguished when we think of the mussel and the pearl. The joy of even a metaphysical resonance is lost when the all itself becomes alien to us. Song has [for Goethe] an aura of resonance. Grillparzer's laments, however, are "spoken into a joyless cosmos" without the expectation of a resonance either in this place or beyond. The dark seabed is a space without joy, where light no longer penetrates, and there are no reflexes to bear witness to life. If the oyster and the pearl stand for the poet, they do so in a joyless cosmos without reflex or resonance.

The darkness around the oyster is not absolute, if it has knowledge of a world bathed in light and joins itself with longing to that unattainable world, as is the case in Tieck's thoughts on Tasso. Poetry in Tieck's most important novel, *Vittoria Accorombona* (1840), which is set in late-sixteenth-century Italy, is represented by the figure of Tasso, who is drawn into the action in such a way as to represent it as the story of a suffering, so that the "poor, diseased" Tasso, who is—thanks to his work—as ennobled as he is humiliated and insulted, stands there as the most pitiable object of a tragedy

35. Goethe, *Tasso,* act 5, scene 5, lines 3426ff.

imaginable. He emerges a broken man after he has completed his work.[36] "He is the incarnation of a ruined, beautiful, and noble human being."[37] Vittoria, who high-spiritedly surpasses the normal level of human enthusiasm, and who still cherishes—at the very moment of its collapse—the golden age of the free spirit of the early part of her century, meets Duke Bracciano; it is a meeting that changes her whole life. The duke follows the dictates of his guiding spirit and wins her noble heart. She has just finished talking to him and a cardinal of the church, once more grown inflexible, about the decline of her century, and the men—the cardinal apprehensive, the Duke elated—have just left her. "When everything was quiet and still, she opened the door to the garden and looked at the light of the declining moon that shone mysteriously through the trees. Then, in her melancholy mood, she sat down and wrote down a few more poems." Tieck writes the four poems in prose.[38] The first two, about the tear of the dew in the rose—"Die Träne des Elends" ("The Tear of Wretchedness")—and about the tear of pain in the oyster, are elegies on the age. The next two believe in personal survival, by the power of a love unto death that is greater than the "you—I and I—you." Vittoria's pearl poem uses poetic means to accentuate her life within the age in which she lives[39] and consists of two strophes in prose, in the first of which the oyster laments the fate of its unavoidable banishment into a strange world: "In the broad sea, on the dark seabed, the oyster moves. 'How lonely I am!' it laments, 'How can plants and animals wander on earth in the joyous light? What a deserted neighborhood is mine! Wherever I look and think, only cold, mute monsters. Misery and repulsion on the dark bed: up above, at the borders of light, the sad race of scaly animals are moving to and fro swimming. No one knows, no one recognizes my longing. Everything is strange to me; enclosed within myself, I must pine away in fear of unknown joy.'"

36. Ludwig Tieck, *Werke,* ed. Marianne Thalmann, vol. 4, *Romane* (Munich, 1966), pp. 539–814, here pp. 648ff.

37. P. 687; cf. pp. 598ff., 707, 758f.

38. The suggestion that Tieck is here offering a prose version of the canzones of Vittoria Accorombona or of Vittoria Colonna (see Marianne Thalmann, p. 848, on this passage) has nothing to recommend it. The content of the pearl song speaks just as much against the sixteenth century as do Tieck's words: "Many have asked why I reduced to prose the poems that I inserted. It was hard to find the right form for these poems; the closest would have been the canzone form, but this is not easy to handle. I also did not want to interrupt the smooth flow of presentation by using verse." Rudolf Köpke, *Ludwig Tieck: Erinnerungen aus dem Leben des Dichters nach dessen mündlichen und schriftlichen Mitteillungen,* pt. 2 (Leipzig, 1855; reprint, Darmstadt, 1970), p. 176.

39. Pp. 709, 713, 716, 736f., 758, 777, 788, 791, 797.

The world of fish, plants, and animals—a world of light that the oyster envies—is, in its lack of suffering, incapable of rising above its own nature. The oyster—with no sense of its gift of surpassing itself and entering into a new value—has the power to change a suffering unto death into a treasure that will survive. The second strophe talks of that: "There the most miserable of things breaks into a sigh, a lament, groans, and, like a silent tear, the pain, holding fast, sets itself onto the shining coating. The tender sickness goes on growing in silence, just as the longing increases. Already the adamantine housing is too small. Then it is resolved into death. A clever fisherman breaks the walls, it dies, he takes the precious, priceless pearl to the king, in whose crown it will henceforth shine, as the most valuable jewel—O poor Torquato Tasso!—and may I say, unhappy Vittoria?—or am I too vain?"[40]

At the moment of a work's parthenogenesis as the product of an endogenous sickness, the suffering caused by the alien nature of life explodes into a new quality as it dies, when the suffering on the dark seabed is transformed into gain and ascends to the light of the crown. Tasso's poetic existence, declining as he produces his work, stands for a modern picture of the poet, whose rank is determined by the measure of his ability to wrest his work from suffering. The lyricist Vittoria follows in his footsteps. She takes her fate in hand and writes verse, as her strophes, and among them the pearl song, fix and illuminate stages along the lofty path of what is possible in her life—a path that leads higher and higher as it encounters growing opposition—and they enable her to survive, even if the base facts of the century force her back down into the depths. Like Tasso in his prison, Vittoria and Bracciano die at the hands of murderers.

Just as the fable and the fairy tale have always let animals speak and feel like human beings, Tieck wrote a richer and more intense monologue for the oyster than any earlier poet. Knowing of another world and recognizing its fate as an exile, then bursting to the fullest possible extent—full of longing and to the point of "fatal rejoicing"—the bounds of what had been set in it, the oyster can more easily stand for a special form of literary composition than would appear to be the case if we look at its soulless nature. The spectrum of the pearl's qualities, gathered from no matter what branches of tradition—qualities that were suited to the fanlike metaphorical extension of

40. P. 704 (bk. 4, chap. 1). When Vittoria first meets Tasso, his poetic gift fails him, for he is happy, whereas it is pain that conditions poetry (p. 584). Vittoria says later: "We mortals lack an expression for the highest happiness; joy is the sibling of pain; there are a thousand feelings in us for unhappiness and suffering" (p. 775).

literary idiosyncrasies—is now correspondingly extended, when it is not the formal qualities of the work, but the self-confidence of the author that is under discussion. With the shift of interest from the work, as object, to the author, as subject, greater attention is paid to the psyche of the oyster. The oyster confesses its responsibility for the birth of the pearl from its own suffering and from its own love, both of which are powerfully directed toward something distant, a heightened fulfillment of its own desire, to such an extent that only a work that has been born in this manner can touch the unattainable and draw light from its light. It is here that the miracle of a genesis from within the earth takes place: it is a miracle carried out by man to the very point of mortal sacrifice and changes the pain of the moment into peaceful permanence, tears into pearls, suffering into light.

The sickness and death of the oyster, as the pearl grows on the seabed, would belong to what is luxuriously superfluous in nature—in whose earth, unknown both to nature and themselves, precious metals and jewels originate and rest eternally in a hiding place, in whose universe, as the heavenly bodies continue in their flight, a stupendous beauty of preordained motion takes place, in whose organic life an excess of more-than-necessary beauty is squandered, were it not for man, the "clever fisherman," who raises up what appears perfect to his human eye to become part of his cultural possessions. It is precisely what the poet creates in the lost solitude of "everything is alien to me"—even if he is thrown away like an opened oyster shell, or like Tasso into prison and others into oblivion—that needs an inkling of the product of its suffering, its tracking down, and its acceptance into the memory of what is worth remembering. The motif of the elevation of the word as a pearl—from the time of Ephraim the Syrian to late Romanticism—to its predetermined place in the king's crown also says something about the duty of history. It is the duty of history to place in the treasury of what is humanly possible the legacies of what has fallen to it over time—what has been received from heaven, and what has been suffered to perfection on earth—to keep them pure and make it possible for them to be seen.

Not long after Tieck's novel, in the winter of 1841/42, Annette von Droste-Hülshoff wrote the poem "Poesy,"[41] which compares art with a turquoise, an amethyst, and, finally, a pearl. Turquoise, amethyst, and pearl, as pure objects, are liable to grow dim if they are harmed by coming into contact with what is unworthy. Droste's strophes about the three jewels that re-

41. Annette von Droste-Hülshoff, *Sämtliche Werke,* ed. Günther Weydt and Einfried Woesler, vol. 1 (Munich, 1973), pp. 118f.

veal one light broken up into three colors pass over the genesis and the writer of a verse that is characterized by jewels and speak only of their acquaintance with the completed work as a vulnerable treasure. Following old traditions about the sensitivity with which jewels reveal harm or unworthiness in their vicinity, the strophes also show how these treasures react to what is inappropriate for them:

Poesy is like the turquoise
Whose pious eye grows dim
When the fumes of hidden sorrow
Approach its light . . .

And like the amethyst
Which lets its violet raiment
Pale into a base grey
In the traitor's hand. . . .

It is also like the pearl, the tender pearl,
Dewy clear on the healthy man
But, on the sick man,
Sucking out what was in his most secret vein;
Did you never see its sheen?
Greenish like a moldering rag?
It remains a pearl for ever,
But one that was worn by a sick man.

Here the pearl does not originate in sickness. The pearl, however it came to be, remains flawless when worn on a healthy body, but it is susceptible to the sickness hidden away inside a body that is wearing it. A popular belief in its feeling for even a deep-rooted sickness, which the pearl reveals by sucking it out, ascribes a sympathetic sickness to the pearl, which dims its pure brilliance into a greenish color. A similar sensitive vulnerability is a characteristic of literature that is harmed by every false association. Droste warns that it may be endangered if it is subject to a careless reception. It is precisely as a jewel that literature is not intangible. It is dependent upon an atmosphere that is suited to it, so that the eye of the turquoise does not grow dim. It has need of morality that makes even the amethyst pale to a dull grey if it comes into contact with disloyalty. "Serving false and base gods" (taken into service by them) makes the jewel into a nonprecious stone. It rejects the misuse of its service. Thanks to its sensorium for what is here scarcely a physical sickness, the pearl shows its wearer to be someone who is sick. The specific sensibility of poetic jewels to what endangers them signalizes symptoms of unsuitability in those who are around them. By virtue of literature's seismic feeling for the quality of the relationship that people have to it, it provides a diagnosis of its environment:

Poetry is like the drinking cup
Made of Venetian crystal;
Pour poison into it and, buzzing,
It will sing the melody of a swan song;
Then it will shatter into a thousand pieces,
And the poetry is gone.

What Grillparzer, Tieck, and Droste-Hülshoff said, with their fingers on the pulse of the age, the virtuoso Rückert wrote in the harmless elegance of an epigram:

The fact that the oyster bears the pearl makes it sick;
Praise heaven for the pain that ennobles you.

The formation of the pearl does not serve as a convalescence after a wound or an illness out of some impulse to live and recover: it makes the oyster sick, as though it were involved in the pangs of a pregnancy. Rückert sees, in the association of the marriage of heaven and earth, which has been, since the days of Pliny, inspired by the myth of the dew and the pearl, a burden that has been placed on the oyster, even if in "Jewel and Pearl" he has the oyster—"summoning up its forces to the point of sickness"—change the dew that it receives from heaven into a pearl. The old myth of dew and pearl could not be reconciled with the new one in which the oyster's suffering is the origin of the pearl. Even the alexandrine does not suffice to form a bridge here.[42]

42. The pleasant wisdom of Eugen Roth's verse bestiary in our own day—with the poet in the back of his mind—has the following pleasantly ironic rhymes about the suffering of mother-of-pearl:

There upon the banks of oysters sit
The mothers, giving little thought;
It is dead certain that they are only talking
About how painful and how large

Grabbe was the first, and apparently the only, one to transfer the metaphor explicitly from the individual suffering of the poet to the general suffering of a body politic like Prussia, whose years of external political suffering were a source of inner fructification for him. He projects the private into the historical in a letter to his friend Kettembeil on August 3, 1827: "self-criticism is also profitable. Prussia was victorious for seven years (1756–63) and suffered for seven years (1806–13). It gained more in the seven years of suffering than it did in the seven years of victories. Artists and heroes are like the pearl oyster; pearls come out of suffering."[43] Inspired by the motto of self-criticism and referring, on the other hand, to the suffering of Prussia under Napoleon, Grabbe's sketchy reflection links the endogenous suffering of the artist with the exogenous suffering of Prussia, without giving voice to the thought, lying close to the surface, that a period of political suffering could prove to be a cradle of art.

Heinrich Heine plays his part in distorting the doctrine—demonstrated by the pearl—that suffering forms understanding and makes it into the stigma of an age that suffers from the pearl. As far as Heine is concerned, E. T. A. Hoffmann and Novalis give documentary evidence of this in that their writing was "actually a form of sickness," a fever in the former, and a consumption in the latter. "But do we have a right to make such remarks, we who are blessed with all too much health? And certainly now when literature looks like one great infirmary? Or is literature perhaps a human sickness, just as the pearl is, in reality, only the stuff of sickness from which the poor oyster suffers?"[44] The pearl is not an achievement provoked by suffering, but suffering itself. Literature is not the product of a wonderful, vital exertion to master an injury; it is sickness itself, the "stuff of sickness" that causes, not conquers, suffering. Heine's deliberate misunderstanding of the natural process unintentionally turns Jean Paul's thought upside down: literature is a bacillus, not a healing power.

The pearls are in their worthy intestines
From which they suffer.—
But still they form, as noble souls,
Their inner suffering into jewels.

Eugen Roths Tierleben für jung und alt (Munich, 1973), p. 428.

43. *Grabbes Werke*, ed. Spiridon Wukudinowic, pt. 5 (Berlin, 1913), p. 294. I am grateful to Ludwig Völker for pointing this out to me. The "self-criticism," a short piece of copy (p. 292), is quite unscrupulous and of course suggests that the author is a genius.

44. *Die romantische Schule* (1835), ii, 4, in *Sämtliche Schriften*, vol. 3, ed. K. Pörnbacher (Munich, 1971), p. 441. I thank Ludwig Völker for kindly drawing my attention to this.

Looked at as a whole, the new assumption that the origin of the pearl was the oyster's sickness—something which modern science has again made outdated[45]—remained in effect only until the middle of the nineteenth century, just as scientific knowledge—apparently in other cases too—can be at first epoch-making and then be covered over again by traditions. Apparently, the last person in the nineteenth century to bear testimony to this is, again, Heinrich Heine, who, in one of the strophes of his *Romanzero* (1851), robs someone of the illusion that the pearl is of a higher origin:

Pearls that are world-famous
Are nothing but the pale slime
Of a poor oyster
That lies sickly silly on the seabed.

The next strophe contradicts the suggestion that Heine is thinking of his own grave illness, which fetters him to his Paris mattress-grave: in this strophe, instead of talking of the natural pearl, he refers to the poetic pearls of the Spanish Jew Yehuda Halevi (d. 1141) that are preserved in manuscript form in a casket.

But the pearls here in this casket
Are sprung from a beautiful
Human soul that is deeper,
Out-and-out deeper than the ocean.

The natural pearl and the poetic pearl do not correspond to one another on the same level. The former outdoes the latter through intensification. In the one there is the poor animal, in the other the beautiful soul, there the seabed, here the fountain's source—"deeper, far, far deeper than the ocean"—not a sickness, but sorrow and lamentation, a suffering from history from whose sorrows the poem bursts forth as "a tear-pearl."

Almost sixty years pass, after this reference in Heine, before we again come across the metaphor of the poetic pearl as the fruit of sorrow, though it may be that my choice of readings led me to this. Then, quite unexpectedly, I encountered a classical love sonnet written in 1909 by Georg Heym, each of whose two strophes chooses as its medium of expression two traditions, an old one and new one, about the suffering of the oyster. Ever since antiquity,

45. See n. 52.

tradition has repeatedly related that when a pearl diver touches the oyster on the seabed carelessly, its open shell closes so rapidly and forcefully that the fisher's finger is bitten off. What is represented in tradition as a natural defensive reaction on the part of the oyster and, up to this time, as far as I can see, had not been used as a poetic image, Heym interprets as the gesture of suffering by the frightened heart, which cringes at the pain of an unexpected touch:

The oyster closes its open silver shells,
When children try cruelly to destroy them:
The tender flesh turns back upon itself
The animal cringes back deep within itself in the face of the torment.

I feel how my heart, wounded once more
By your hand, would close itself off from the world.
Into its chambers must flow the blood
That was scarcely purged by bitter untruth.

The neat form of comparison between the first strophe and the second is repeated in the two final ones about the metamorphosis of suffering into the pearl of the poem:

But just as the oysters who having suffered injury,
Form in their wombs the liquor that's been lost,
The brilliance of the pearl is wrested from suffering,

So this song grew from a bitter hour,
This song was created from a tear,
And I forgot the wound that scarce had been received.[46]

Why does this poem stand out so strangely among the examples that have existed since Jean Paul? The simple rhymed sonnet form—which makes it seem as though nothing has happened—makes us conscious of the fact

46. Georg Heym, *Dichtungen und Schriften,* ed. Karl Ludwig Schneider, vol. 1 (Munich, 1960), pp. 670ff.; I am grateful to Ludwig Völker for this suggestion. Gottfried Been talks of a resistance, against which the spirit has to test, overhaul, and renew itself, as "a deep wound, which should heal and intensify him." Gottfried Been, *Briefe,* ed. Harald Steinhagen and Jürgen Schröder, vol. 1, *Briefe an F. W. Oelze, 1932–1945* (Wiesbaden, 1977), p. 81.

that, apart from Grillparzer's stanzas in 1818, all other expressions on this theme were unrhymed: prose, a prose poem by Tieck, and unrhymed strophes in lyrics by Heine and Droste-Hülshoff, as though the divine inspiration of rhyme, too, had been lost along with new knowledge about the pearl. In the love sonnet, the theme is a private one, tied to a moment. All the other voices speak more generally and more seasonably of a *suprapersonal* confusion of art. This is true even when, in the decade after 1930, three major writers, Brecht, Claudel, and Musil—each in his own way—returned to the metaphor once more. We have already talked about Claudel.[47]

The idea occurs in Robert Musil's novel *The Man without Qualities* on the occasion of an unexpected conversation. In the streets, an agitated mob, anxious to cause an uproar, is marching to a demonstration against parallel action. The artistic device of looking out through the closed windows of the *palais* down onto the excited demonstration reveals what is going on, through the eyes of the uncannily disorienting psychology of such a mass action—seen in this way as a film behind the glass that deadens all sound—to be a comedy, since mouths, gaping open at directorially correct crucial moments, can be seen, but not a word of whatever they were shouting can be heard. The perspective does not change with the point of view, as Ulrich, who first looks out with Graf Leinsdorf from his *palais,* then looks out of the window in Diotima's house with Arnheim.

> . . . and so the two men fell silent after their words of greeting and finally went together to the window, where they looked in silence at the excitement beneath them.
>
> After a while, Arnheim said, "I can't understand you; isn't it a thousand times more important to be involved in life than to write?!"
>
> "But I don't write," rejoined Ulrich shortly.
>
> "Well, you're right not to!"—Arnheim suited the answer to himself—"Writing is like the pearl, a form of sickness." "Look!": He pointed with two of his carefully manicured fingers to the street, a movement that, in spite of its speed, had a little of the papal blessing about it. "The people are coming singly and in packs, and from time to time someone's mouth is torn open from within and he shouts! On another occasion the man would write; you're right!"
>
> "But you yourself are a famous writer?!"
>
> "Oh, that doesn't mean anything!"—But after this answer, which graciously left everything open, Arnheim turned to Ulrich.[48]

47. See above pp. 257ff.

48. Robert Musil, *Der Mann ohne Eigenschaften,* ed. Adolf Frisé (Hamburg, 1952), p. 649.

This is the beginning of the chapter entitled "The Talk." Carried on against the background of the demonstration, it includes Arnheim's—the magnate's—invitation to the man without qualities to join him in his business enterprises, before closing again with the question about writing.[49] Arnheim's idea about a piece of writing by Ulrich signifies—like the invitation he extends to him—that he is to participate in the age and have power in it, to tempt him to be Schiller's nonpareil. *Schreiben* (writing) rhymes in a strange way with *Schreien* (shout): ". . . and shouts. On another occasion the man would write." Arnheim carries on his enterprises and writes as well. His gesture at the window is involuntarily, at least in part, "blessing."[50] In the ambiguous conversation at the window the sentence that Arnheim applies to Ulrich, "Writing is like the pearl, a sickness," functions as a piece of self-knowledge by recognizing the fact that Ulrich does not write. Does the sickness of writing lie in the act of devoting oneself to the day?[51] Why then "like the pearl"? This hardly refers—as it did in the early nineteenth century—to the poet's enduring the exudation of the pearl. "But you, yourself, are a famous writer?!" Does Arnheim wear the sickness of writing like jewelry? "Oh, that doesn't mean anything!"

In 1938, Bertolt Brecht, in his *Life of Galileo,* chooses the genesis of the pearl, as an example, in a new context of argumentation uniting aesthetics and politics. The struggle of the church against the establishment of the truth about the cosmic system that has been revealed by Galileo's discoveries is also a part of the defense of the social system—in which the church holds the world captive—which, like the geocentric system, is also outmoded. In his conversation with the "little monk," the child of peasants who have been oppressed from time immemorial, who nevertheless sees a certain order in its passing, Galileo remonstrates against the glorification and embellishment of the deplorable social state of affairs, in which the wrong picture of the world is reflected, when he extorts from the person who is suffering from its op-

49. Pp. 660f.: "Do you write? No, I asked that already. But why don't you write? You're right. In the future the poet and the philosopher will make their entry across the running board of journalism! Has it not yet occurred to you that our journalists grow better and better, and our poets worse and worse. There's no question but that it's a regular development: there is something underway, and I have not the least doubt what it is: the age of great individualities is coming to an end!"

50. P. 643: Ulrich at Graf Leinsdorf's window: "he even believes from time to time that among the 'Heils' directed to Germany he has heard 'long live Arnheim!' but he was not entirely sure of himself, because the thick window glass made the sounds indistinct."

51. To journalism that is replacing poetry? See above, n. 49.

pression the virtue of tormenting himself to death. "Don't come to me with the beauty of phenomena which have been gilded by the ages! Do you know how the oyster *Margaritifera* produces its pearl? By encasing—at the risk of a mortal disease—an incompatible foreign body, for example, a grain of sand, into a ball of mucus. It almost dies in the process. To hell with the pearl; I prefer a healthy oyster. Virtues are not tied to misery, my friend. If your people were wealthy and happy they could develop the virtues of wealth and happiness. Now these virtues of exhausted people stem from exhausted fields, and I reject them. Good Lord! My new water pumps can perform more miracles in the fields than all your superhuman twaddle" (scene 8).

How far a key sentence, "Virtues are not tied to misery," that unhinges—by means of a Christian ethos of suffering, because it is based upon it—outmoded forms of government can also call into question the poetic aesthetics of suffering founded in the pearl metaphor is still a matter of doubt. The sociocritical negation of "the beauty of phenomena that have been gilded by age" may be directed toward art, but then it encounters the flat postulate of well-being, based on a social system free from suffering, as the fertile soil of poetic virtue, in other words, quality.

Brecht allows Galileo to anticipate, prophetically, the eighteenth-century state of knowledge about the genesis of the pearl. He might well believe, after the pearl—since the time of Jean Paul—had stood for the genesis of poetry from sickness, that he was having him speak on the present-day level of knowledge, since Galileo's physics are not outmoded. But Brecht surely scarcely dreamed that a mere four decades after his *Galileo* was written, a biochemist would feel himself critically amused at the dramatist's theory of the genesis of the pearl because present-day knowledge of biomineralization had rendered it out of date.[52] Once again the time seems to

52. Brecht's allegedly scientific foundation for his description of the pathological formation of pearls is again pilloried as mistaken by a present-day student of biomineralization. Heinrich Erben, "Von Zähnen, Perlen und Gallensteinen: Organismus produziert Minerale und Kristalle," *Deutsche Forschungsgemeinschaft: Mitteilungen* 4 (1978): 6ff., quotes the passage from *Galileo* and adds, ". . . Bertolt Brecht has his poor Galileo say. He would, however, scarcely have used biological facts so thoughtlessly as his careless author: The oyster *Margaritifera* is actually not an oyster at all, its real name is *Pinctada;* it does not use a ball of mucus to produce a pearl, but a sac of epithelial cells, and there can certainly be no question of danger to life! In the face of such a mass of products of the imagination, we are probably forced, involuntarily, to think of a second quotation which—piquantly enough—comes from the same work: "no more mercy for those who have not done their research and yet still speak!" Here, at least, God knows we would agree." I know mother-of-pearl only once as poetry. Ernst Jünger says in a note entitled "Books and Readers": "A Thousand and One Nights: the model of what is at once collective and anony-

have come when the sciences reject—as a romantic idea—what was once a revolutionary explanation of the genesis of the pearl that poets, moving with their times, had made into their own and into a symbol of their self-understanding. They demand a sober reorientation to the new natural truth. Whether we can also expect a metamorphosis of the pearl metaphor, at the moment when the history of styles should harmonize with intellectual and social history, and with the history of natural knowledge—and the closely related question about this is still moot—in the wake of the breaks in the history of style in this century, will probably depend upon whether the new knowledge of the biomineralization of the pearl is suited to act as a symbol for the diagnosis of our time.

---

mous authorship. The work could have been invented by a demon—built overnight like one of the castles in the air. You could also think of the mother-of-pearl in an oyster shell—of a cerebral trace, which hardened and iridized" (*Parerga zu "Annäherungen": Gesammelte Werke,* vol. 11 [Stuttgart, 1978], p. 439).

SEVEN

A PHILOLOGIST'S REMARKS ON *MEMORIA*

The need for love and friendship is so deeply imbedded in man that he perishes without them. Yet as long as his trust in his memory sustains him when he is among strangers, he can survive even long periods of separation in distant places without fearing that he will lose that love and friendship. Man's primal fear of being forgotten is not something that is confined to childhood, and whether or not he is endowed with a primal trust that he will be preserved in the memory of others—thus balancing out the fear—can be decisive as to whether the individual is happy or unhappy. The words "forget me not," whether they arise out of trust or out of the seeds of anxiety, constitute one of the most moving of pleas and are, unconsciously rather than consciously, a silent stimulus to many of those impulses in our lives that are directed toward other human beings. This is also true of a part of that desire, peculiar to man, to leave behind him something lasting to serve as a reminder of him: creations of his hands and spirit, buildings and books, works of art. The readiness of many medieval artists, in certain literary genres and many other areas of art, to give their works to the world without naming themselves and to conceal their authorship for all time, serves to document—particularly with regard to their rejection of memory—a self-sacrificing humility that goes far beyond a craft ethos. Today, as in earlier times, such self-sacrifice is practiced only by people like the builders of cathedrals and bridges, space shuttles and dams, and many other similar things, who, laboring under a great weight of responsibility for the success of their projects, soberly create

This article develops and supplements some observations by a philologist on the theme of the Münster colloquium "*Memoria:* The Historical Value of the Testimony of Liturgical Memory in the Middle Ages," which opened in Münster on May 28, 1980. What is presented here, in a loose form, by a German scholar is part of the dialogue between disciplines. Inspired by historians, it addresses itself no less to philologists. As it is here expanded it was my farewell lecture on the occasion of my retirement on February 10, 1982. A few sentences originated there.

major technical works. Not even a snippet of the most trivial verse preserves its anonymity. Both the sciences and the arts would suffer unthinkable consequences were a cosmic dictator inhumanly to decide that all their works were to remain anonymous. Would not the dialogue in art or science, which is carried on as a dispute and which is validated by the names of the disputants, perish if man's desire to participate in it with his own voice and to set his own mark upon the dialogue of his time were stifled? There would be no prospect of any great gain in excluding the by no means indecent effort to introduce the very best that is associated with the name—something that may outlast the person in the individual memory—by separating the search for truth from the person of the individual who is seeking to make discoveries in art and science. Would the sciences be furthered if purely objective arguments, unaffected by the imponderables of their protagonists, had to vie with each other? European intellectual history argues that it would not. True, it is aware of great works of art from earlier times that are anonymous, but it knows as good as nothing of any significant philosophy not tied to a named philosopher, and, by analogy, the same is true for theology and other sciences. It is the works that have engraved the names of their creators on the memory of history. The aspiration to survive in memory, by leaving behind a successor, is a property of humankind and must be recognized as a fact of human existence.

Religions and culture are tied to memory in the human world, and lively relationships between human beings do not come about in any other way. Human beings outlive their bodies as long as there are people alive who remember them. They promote this memory by the works that they leave behind. No memory, no history. The stream of time would flow on like Lethe. Memory changes happening into history, gives form to what is fluid. History as what is passed on (*memoriae traditum*) apparently arises out of a fundamental human desire to narrate what has been, and this creates a soil for culture. Memory forms our past by making an unconscious selection from what is worth preserving, but it also forms our future, insofar as what may be experienced is determined by the memory of what has already been.[1] The com-

1. William Stern, *Allgemeine Psychologie auf personalistischer Grundlage* (The Hague, 1950), p. 253: "Memory is the relative nature of experience in the past." The individual does not remember an experience passively and indifferently. His memory already has a spiritual force (*energeia*) according to Plotinus, 4.6.1f. (Willy Theiler, "Erinnerung," in *Reallexikon für Antike und Christentum,* vol. 6 [Stuttgart, 1966], cols. 43–54, here col. 50). Günter Kunert in his foreword to *Der andere Planet: Ansichten von Amerika* (Munich, 1975) explains it: "Memory and writing are identical. In principle. And what would this consist of, if not in the questionable process of se-

munity lives from its memory, in religion as well as in culture, and when this is lost the community dissolves. A community of action still develops its future projections on the basis of the memory of its historical experience. As a common memory, language establishes the community of those to whom it reveals the world. It is exciting to see that—however metaphorically—the sciences cannot comprehend a history of organic life without taking over the most arcane speech acts and the most secret products of memory.[2]

Man's desire to submit what he has caused to happen, and what has happened to him, to the judgment of tradition and thus establish his memory raises him, as does language as a fact of human existence, above other living creatures, who are concerned, it is true, with their descendants, but not with an afterlife. Animals can be unconcerned about passing on their experience in particular cases, since their instinct guides them more surely than it does a human being, who is less protected and is forced to rely on the transmission of experience and knowledge.[3] Man's education is also an introduction into

---

lection, repression, evaluation, judgment that colors and changes its objects—often to the point where they are unrecognizable? No matter how great the effort, it is not in our power to be objective. . . . It is only in writing that the patchwork of reality is joined together, as a perfection, and given significance (corresponding to the general human need for causality), whereby over the course of quite long periods the impression tends to arise that reality contains the same mechanism that appears in literature" (p. 7). "Only the moment, but that moment memorialized, preserved, stilled—and distilled—in the poem, remains." Murray Krieger, *The Play and Place of Criticism* (Baltimore, 1967), p. 121.

2. They consider memory a property of every living thing to such an extent that biophysical chemistry, in its dependence upon the metaphors of a language in use between molecules participating in biogenetic processes, ascribes to them a memory as a condition of the continuation of their existence. Manfred Eigen's statement "Without memory . . . there would be neither evolution of living beings nor of ideas" links natural and spiritual existence to the possibility—common to both—of language and memory as the condition of their history. Manfred Eigen and Ruth Winkler, *Das Spiel: Naturgesetze steuern den Zufall* (Munich, 1975), pp. 317–322, "Gedächtnis und komplexe Wirklichkeit." On "language" in genetics, pp. 291–316, "Vom Symbol zur Sprache"; Manfred Eigen, "Zeugen der Genesis: Versuch einer Rekonstruktion der Urformen des Lebens aus ihren in den Biomolekülen hinterlassenen Spuren," in *Max Planck Gesellschaft Jahrbuch* (Göttingen, 1979), pp. 17–54. Hans Blumenenberg, *Die Lesbarkeit der Welt* (Frankfurt, 1981), pp. 372–409, "Der genetische Code und seine Leser." F. E. Weinert, "Mnemismus," in *Historisches Wörterbuch der Philosophie*, vol. 5 (Basle, 1980), col. 1444. As the psychology of memory draws closer to biology, it speaks of engrams, coding, and decoding. On the scientific psychology of memory, see Weinert, "Gedächtnis," in *Historisches Wörterbuch der Philosophie*, vol. 3 (Basel, 1974), cols. 35–43.

3. In the first sentence of his second Unseasonable Observation "On the Advantage and Disadvantage of History for Life," Nietzsche says of the difference between animals and human beings: "Look at the herd, which is grazing its way past you: it does not know what yesterday is,

the store of experiences of his species, a store that has been handed down to him and that he has accepted so as to be able, in his turn, to pass it on. The Decalogue, the Beatitudes, the poetic legacies of doctrine, of didactic literature, the formality of mnemonic verse, gnomic literature, and exemplars are all designed to impress things upon the memory, and the rejection of rote learning is by no means the acme of pedagogy. Even education or culture are probably acquired less in the limited space of experience within our actual lives than in our association with the treasures of the possibility—which has achieved permanent form in the arts, been seen by thinkers in its design, and been raised into light by religion—of ensuring a developing anthropogenesis. We would not learn what it is to be a knight, a hero, a saint, even what gods or God are from the experience of our own petty existence without what has been handed down to us in words, in writing, in works of art, without the witnesses and the evidence that, as the soil of history, nourish the memory of our species. Community constitutes, to a large extent, the common memory of an experience that unites us. Our cultural memory, first oral, later written and, finally, documented in libraries and art collections, forms the basis not only of our humanities faculties but of all our doings. All genres of historiog-

---

what today is, it leaps about, eats, rests, digests, jumps around again, and it does this from morning till night, from day to day, bound, in its pleasure and its aversion tightly, to the peg of the moment, and for this reason it is neither melancholy nor disgusted with life. It is hard for men to see this, because they boast of their humanity in front of the animals, but yet look jealously at the animals' happiness. . . . Yet they are also astonished at themselves for not being able to learn to forget and for always having to cling to the past: no matter how fast and how far they run, the chain runs with them. It is a miracle: the moment is here and gone in a flash, nothing before and nothing after, yet it comes back as a ghost and disturbs the peace of a later moment. A leaf from the book of time is constantly being loosened, flutters away, and suddenly flutters back into man's lap. The human being says, "I remember" and envies the animal, which immediately forgets and sees death at every moment, a sinking back into the mists of the night and an eternal extinction. This is the way the animal lives unhistorically." Friedrich Nietzsche, *Sämtliche Werke, Kritische Studienausgabe,* ed. Giorgio Colli and Mazzino Montinari, 15 vols., vol. 1 (Berlin, 1980), pp. 248f. There are other groans about the great burden of history to be heard in the nineteenth century. Goethe says, in his *Maxims and Reflections:* "The spirit that is receptive to poetic and artistic creations feels—with regard to antiquity—that it has been placed in the most pleasing and ideal situation as far as nature is concerned, and even today Homer's songs still have the power to free us for a few moments from the terrible burden that several thousands of years of tradition have laid upon us." *Goethes Werke,* ed. Erich Trunz, vol. 12 (Hamburg, 1981), p. 483, no. 838. Günter Hess, "Memoriae Thesaurus, Predigttradition, ikonographischer Kanon und historische Realität beim Leichenbegängnis Kaiser Karls VII (Munich, 1745)," *Daphnis* 10 (1981): 3–46, points out a change in the function of *memoria* in a phase of historicization around the year 1750.

raphy serve the memory of periods, of a recollection that can change what has been into a living possession that characterizes the present. A historical thinker in the age of humanism says: "Historia rerum memoriam conservat" [History preserves the memory of things] and is scarcely ready to call someone a human being who does not develop the power of his memory.[4] Memory is peculiar to human beings and is also a necessity for them. History as the remembered past also includes an expectation of the future.[5] Just as loss of memory robs a person, as a sick man, of the comprehensive view of his own life and that of his fellow beings, of a life that was to be led as a whole, as feeling, experience, and duty, so our spiritual culture, which has sprung from indefatigable commemorative work in cloister and church, school and university, but probably most energetically in the arts, is deeply wounded by a loss, for example, simply of our memory of the Bible and antiquity in their

4. Francesco Patrizi, *Della historia diece dialoghi* (Venice, 1560) fols. 18f., discusses in detail the *memoria* character of history. The plastic, engraved, and written monuments (*memorie*) produce, "che le historie non sien altro ueramente che memorie . . . che la historia è memoria della cose humane" (fol. 18rv). The dialogue is inclined to view the *memoria* of a private man as *historia* (fol. 19r). Eckhard Kessler, *Theoretiker humanistischer Geschichts schreibung: Nachdruck exemplarischer Texte aus dem 16. Jahrhundert,* Humanistische Bibliothek, ser. 2, texts 4 (Munich, 1971), p. 94. Cf. Francesco Robortello, *De historica facultate disputatio* (Florence, 1548), p. 13: "History preserves the memory of things," p. 14: "the person who does not develop his *vis reminiscendi* [power of memory] is scarcely to be called a human being" (Kessler, p. 84). Dionigi Atanagi, *Ragionamento della istoria* (Venice, 1559), p. 75, states that memory as the most "worthy part of our mind" [la memoria digniss. parte dell'anima nostra] is what qualifies us for history (*istoria*), since it "conserves remembrance of past things" [conserva la memoria delle cose passiage] (Kessler, p. 88). Giovanni Antonio Viperan, *De scribenda historia liber* (Antwerp, 1569), p. 23, believes in the narrative transmission of what has happened even before the invention of writing, "lest the memory of things be extinguished" (Kessler, p. 109). Gerd Tellenbach, *Aus erinnerter Zeitgeschichte* (Freiburg, 1981) begins: "From time immemorial, historiographers have justified their work as intending to snatch the happenings of their time from oblivion and give them to posterity. These sketches . . . turn more against forgetfulness and lack of understanding of one's fellow men—things that continually make me uneasy."

5. Jacob Burckhardt speaks of the significance of the *transfigured picture of memory* in Restoration or Renaissance endeavors, like, for example, Epaminondas's efforts on behalf of Messenia, Cyrus's and Darius's efforts on behalf of Jewry, and the Sassanids' on behalf of ancient Persia: "their character: always ideal in the sense that it is not the actual past but the transfigured picture of the memory of that past that is to be restored; strong optical deception. Its justification lies in the effort that is made, by force, to desire something that is longed for, that is ideal: in fact it is likely that something quite different from what was there earlier will eventuate, because things have changed so much in the meantime." Jacob Burckhardt, "*Über das Studium der Geschichte": Der Text der "Weltgeschichtlichen Betrachtungen" auf Grund der Vorarbeitungen von Ernst Ziegler nach den Handschriften,* ed. Peter Ganz (Munich, 1982), p. 130.

substance—a loss of the memory, which is grown within us, of feeling for, experience of, and even duty toward the possibilities of the realization of humanity that appear to us in biblical and classical history.[6] Christianity is not the first religion in which the motive force of man's life has been the fear that God could forget him and the hope that God would remember him. The trust that God will remember him or the concern for God's *memoria* are a spur to prayer. The concern with questions about the mutual forgetfulness and remembrance of God and man, which stretches from the Old Testament to Dostoyevsky and Brecht, circles around a cardinal point of the relationship between God and man,[7] since just as God's devotion of his memory to man

6. Perhaps I may be allowed to refer to an earlier thought that I had on this subject: "Memory makes us humble and hopeful, is a condition of culture, of insight into what will survive change, of the possibility of recalling what has been that lives on to set its stamp on life. Its demands are not easy. Rilke saw the torso of Apollo: 'You must change your life.' Times which remember are creative; times which forget fall into excess" (Ohly, *The Damned and The Elect,* trans. Linda Archibald [Cambridge University Press, 1992], p. 139).

7. Christel Meier, "Vergessen, Erinnern, Gedächtnis im Gott-Mensch-Bezug: Zu einem Grenzbereich der Allegorese bei Hildegard von Bingen und anderen Autoren des Mittelalters," in *Verbum et Signum,* ed. Hans Fromm, Wolfgang Harms, and Uwe Ruberg, vol. 1, *Beiträge zur mediävistischen Bedeutungsforschung* (Munich, 1975), pp. 143–194 (with a rich bibliography).

The final part (pp. 187–194) offers a survey of fields of research on memory—beyond the actual investigation of forgetting and remembering in the God-man relationship—that is the richest one available as far as the different aspects treated are concerned and has the best bibliography. I shall not repeat what is said there, in great detail, on the metaphors of memory (n. 202f.), on Augustine (pp. 188f.), on the myth of forgetting and remembering (pp. 190f.), on forgetting, remembering, and memory in the liturgy, on theological meditation and religious literature (pp. 191f.), on memory in prayer (p. 192 and n. 224: "A separate treatise on remembering in prayer and commemorative prayer would probably be worthwhile"), on the *memoria Christi* (pp. 192f.), on rhetorical mnemotechnics (n. 231: "A special question, in which antique tradition and Christianity are linked in the Middle Ages and after, is the theme 'Poetry as Remembrance,' which I shall pursue").

Augustine begins the thirteenth book of his *Confessions* with the prayer "Invoco te, 'deus meus, misericordia mea,' qui fecisti me et oblitum tui non oblitus es" [I call upon you, O my God, my compassionate one, you who made me and whom forgetful of you have not forgotten]. Theodoric has lost his whole retinue, and says in the *Nibelungenlied* (strophe 2319), "And if all my men are dead, / then God has forgotten me—the miserable Theodoric that I am." Otto Gerhard Oexle, "Die Armut und Armenfürsorge um 1200: Ein Beitrag zum Verständnis der freiwilligen Armut bei Elisabeth von Thüringen," in *Sankt Elisabeth, Fürstin, Dienerin, Heilige: Aufsätze, Dokumentation,* catalog for an exhibition to celebrate the 750th anniversary of the death of St. Elizabeth, Marburg, ducal castle and the Church of St. Elizabeth, November 19, 1981–January 6, 1982 (Sigmaringen, 1981), pp. 78–100, p. 83. On the poverty of the godless (as *arme sêlen* or the like), Friedrich Ohly, *Sage und Legende in der Kaiserchronik,* Forschungen zur deutschen Sprache und Dichtung no. 10 (Darmstadt, 1968), p. 24. On "poor Judas," Ohly, *The Damned and the Elect,*

or his turning the grace of his memory away from him so too man's forgetting or remembering God decides whether he shall be damned or saved. The Bible and, after it, the church have both developed a rich theology of *oblivio* and of *memoria* in the relationship of God and man,[8] and liturgical memory in prayer, in the monastic intercession for the living and the dead, wishes to be embedded within its framework.[9]

---

pp. 71ff. (with bibliography). Walther Lipphardt, "*Laus tibi Christe—Ach du armer Judas*": Untersuchungen zum ältesten deutschen Passionslied," *Jahrbuch für Liturgik und Hymnologie* 6 (1961): 71–100.

8. Meier, pp. 146ff., on the Bible; pp. 149–156, 187–194, on Augustine and his successors; pp. 156–187, on Hildegard of Bingen.

The prohibition on eating the fruit of the tree in paradise—with which primal human guilt was explained—by the deafening of the memory to the commandment which had been given is opposed to the notion that a memoryless track leading back into a time in which there are no ages could be part of the paradisal life of the first human beings, just as it is of other living creatures, and that it was only the expulsion of Adam and Eve from paradise that imparted to them the memory of what they had lost and of their own suffering; at the same time it was in this way that they also received hope, which is also a part of memory. The theologoumenon of forgetting, memory, and remembering in the relationship between God and man says: If men live contrary to their memory, then the abyss is not far away. Memory, as a gift, should be able to function as a protection for the individual in small things as well as in large, when he makes memory into his conscience.

9. Out of the wealth of literature that has appeared most recently in the circle around Karl Schmid and Joachim Wollasch, I shall here mention only Otto Gerhard Oexle, "Memoria und Memorialüberlieferung im früheren Mittelalter," *Frühmittelalterliche Studien* 10 (1976): 70–95. Standing as it does in the closest proximity to my own work, the article mentions a wealth of literature that I shall augment only here and there.

On the positions of philosophers of history from Dilthey to Gadamer and Habermas, with a chapter on memory in psychoanalysis, Alice Kohli-Kunz, *Erinnern und Vergessen: Das Gegenwärtigsein des Vergangenen als Grundproblem historischer Wissenschaft*, Erfahrung und Denken, no. 40 (Berlin, 1973). Freud's discovery of the significance of forgetting is here introduced into the understanding of history: see the review of this work by Robert Anchor in *History and Theory: Studies in the Philosophy of History* 14 (1975): 326–335.

As a philosophizing challenger of the jurisdiction of philosophy, Odo Marquardt denies philosophy's jurisdictional monopoly in the area of worldly wisdom all the more rigorously because the old poets and, after them, the disciplines of the humanities, as the custodians of memory, cast doubt upon it in this field. "To be the experience of life for those who, as yet, have none, to be the wisdom of old age for those who are not yet old, that is, in the last analysis, possible not only as a partial definition of philosophy, but also as a partial definition of the humanities, at the point at which their task is to remember and precisely for that reason—and this is to their honor—that they are now under attack. For wherever reform is carried out that involves risk, we are plausibly interested in reducing that risk in the control of success by forbidding remembrance. Does philosophy have a better memory than the humanities? Scarcely: and thus it has a competitor

The interpretation of the liturgy of the mass as a celebration of the memory not only of Christ's life and Passion but also of the history of salvation, by recollecting its representation in religion—in the twelfth century, for example, according to the *Gemma animae* of Honorius Augustodunensis[10]—and the further development of the magnificent notion of recollecting the ages of the world in the liturgical happenings of the canonical hours created the theological conditions for the conception of the cathedral as temporal space, the architectonic universe of an assembled recollection of the epochs of world history which also serves as the site of the liturgical memory of those epochs.[11]

The Christian promise of eternal life, especially for someone who is not concerned whether his earthly name outlives him or not, made it possible for an individual's fellow Christians, on earth, and the saints, in the presence of God, to intercede for his eternal salvation. The liturgical intercession for the living and the dead is intended to transmit eternal life to those who are brothers in prayer. The significance of the entry of a name into monastic commemorative books that recommend the individual to the grace of God results

---

that has developed in those disciplines that remember, disciplines upon which philosophy—because of its loss of jurisdiction in other areas—has been building since the last century: a competitor that probably jeopardizes its last jurisdiction: the jurisdiction of remembering." Odo Marquardt, "Über Kompetenz und Inkompetenz der Philosophie" (1973), in *Abschied vom Prinzipiellen: Philosophische Studien* (Stuttgart, 1981), p. 26f.

10. Friedrich Ohly, *Schriften zur mittelalterlichen Bedeutungsforschung* (Darmstadt, 1977), pp. 368–372, 375–377.

11. See F. Ohly, "The Cathedral as Temporal Space," chap. 4 in this volume.

The *Rede vom Glauben,* written by Der arme Hartmann in the middle of the twelfth century, underlines the value of the Lord's Supper as memory on the basis of the command contained in his opening words ("da sult ir min mite gedenken / daz sult ir tun gewisse / in min gehugnisse" [There you should think of me as well / That you must certainly do / In memory of me] (1019ff.). "Christ ne hat unsir nit nevergezze" [Christ certainly did not forget us] at the Last Supper (928) that we celebrate in the Mass "daz man nit nevergezze" [that we should certainly not forget] (1045) what he suffered for the daily renewal of Christians till the end of the world. The liturgical gestures remind us individually of the happenings of the Passion. The chalice signifies Christ's burial: "alliz daz di prister da tut / iz ist gewisse / ein gehucnisse, / ein war urchunde / der gotis marterunge" [Everything the priest does there / Is certainly a reminder, a true witness / Of God's martyrdom] (1081ff.). The priest "gedenket" [remembers] the living and the dead (corresponding to Christ's plea on the cross), because the devil "uns vil gerne senket" [gladly sinks us] (1098f.). Friedrich Maurer, ed., *Die religiösen Dichtungen des 11. und 12. Jahrhunderts,* vol. 2 (Tübingen, 1965), pp. 588ff. On the interpretation of the mass as a function of memory in general, Rudolf Suntrup, *Die Bedeutung der liturgischen Gebärden und Bewegungen in lateinischen und deutschen Auslegungen des 9. bis 13. Jahrhunderts,* Münstersche Mittelalter-Schriften, no. 37 (Munich, 1978); on the symbolism of the burial in the *Elevatio,* pp. 390ff.

in the recording of the name of the person who is to be entered, stripped of its earthly qualities and bare as though clothed in the dignity of a dead person, just as we may imagine it being called out before God's judgment seat. In the lists of those to be remembered in Weißenburg the name *Otfridus* stands plain and unadorned, and without the attribute "poet," just as if, a thousand years later, in endless lists of names, we were to come across Johann Sebastian or Johann Wolfgang, without the names Bach or Goethe. The name is a challenge to God's memory to complete the person from his own knowledge. What makes the decoding of a person from his mere name so difficult for the historian has a reason, in the convent lists, in the fact of being dead in the world's eyes, for the sake of God, while bearing a monastic name. As it frequently does, on other occasions, a historical discipline reads its sources against the grain of what was originally intended, here to bring to light, for the purpose of research into the lives of individuals, what was deliberately hidden—because what was hidden was open to God.

Research into the function of commemoration in liturgical prayer, from the sources of monastic *memoria,* knows that persons not belonging to the convent could request that they be included in the intercession. "Donors and benefactors of spiritual and monastic communities expressly requested not only the entry of their names into *Libri vitae* and diptychs, but also the mention of their names in divine service."[12] Yet there has been no collective study of the evidence for individuals' seeking inclusion in the conventual lists of those whose salvation was being promoted by intercession. Let me give a few references here. When Otto the Great, in 936, confirmed the foundation of the convent in Quedlinburg—"so that the praise of almighty God and his elect could be carried on for all time" "et nostri nostrorumque omnium memoria perpetretur" [and our memory and the memory of all of ours might be recalled][13]—he apparently has in mind the commemoration, in prayer, of himself and of all his house.

12. Oexle (see n. 9 above), p. 78, cf. also p. 88 (with bibliography).

13. According to *Monumenta Germaniae Historica* (hereafter *MGH*), *DD* i. pp. 89f.; according to Achatz Freiherr von Müller, *Gloria Bona Fama Bonorum: Studien zur sittlichen Bedeutung des Ruhmes in der frühchristlichen und mittelalterlichen Welt,* Historische Studien, no. 428 (Husum, 1977), p. 111. Under the heading "Prayer as Gift," Oexle ("Memoria und Memorialüberlieferung") also treats the social function of giving, receiving, and reciprocation with reference to prayer and gift. Here, too, he remarks "that the request for prayer and the granting of benefactions on the part of the king are linked and that the benefactions of the king and the prayer of the clergy and monks correspond to one another as gift and reciprocal gift" (p. 91). Oexle traced the important roots of commemorative tradition in the diptych memento and

There is evidence for the requests of medieval poets and authors to be remembered in monastic prayers as early as the ninth century in German, in Otfrid of Weißenburg's final chapter in his Gospel harmony. This chapter is directed to his fellow monks Hartmut and Werinbert, is most artfully distinguished by an acrostic and a telestich, "Otfridus Uuizanburgensis monachus Hartmuate et Uerinberto sancti Galli monachis" [Otfrid of Weißenburg, monk, to Hartmut and Werinbert, monks of St. Gall], and is introduced by the poet's final prayer. In the telestich at the end of the chapter he beseeches the MONACHIS (monks), to give him love and brotherhood as company on his journey to heaven, and a climax is reached in the plea to be remembered in the brothers' prayers before St. Gall, with his own promise to remember them in his intercessory prayers before St. Peter, in the poet's own monastery, as a mutual escort to the glory of heaven.[14] Otfrid's name is not found only in the

---

diptych prayers for the living and the dead in the liturgy of the mass (pp. 71–76). The *memento Domine* (Remember me, O Lord!) for the living and also for the bringers of gifts may have promoted such an expectation on the part of donors.

14. *Otfrids Evangelienbuch*, ed. Oskar Erdmann, 3d ed., ed. Ludwig Wolff, Altdeutsche Textbibliothek, no. 49 (Tübingen, 1957), p. 270:

Mit karitate ih fergon—(so bruederscaf ist giwon,
  thi unsih scono, so gizam.—fon selben satanase na   M):
Ôfono thio guati—joh duat mir thaz gimuati
  in gibete thrato—iues selbes dat   O:
Ni lazet ni ir gihugget—joh mir ginada thigget
  mit minnon filu follen,—zi selben Sancti Galle   N!
Afur thara widiri—thiu mines selbes nidiri
  duat iu gihugi in wara—thaz ir bimidet zal   A.
Ci selben Sancti Petre,—ther so giang in then se,
  thaz er si uns ginathic,—thoh ih ni si es wirthi   C;
Hohi er uns thes himiles—(joh muazen frewen unsih thes!)
  insperre thara gileite mih—joh thar gefrewe ouh iui   H;
In himilisgo sconi,—thaz wir thaz seltsani
  scowon thar in wari—joh thio ewinigun ziar   I.
Simbolon in ewon—thes sint thie sine thar giwon:
  wir muazin frewen unsih thes—iamer sines thanke   S!
Krist halte Hartmuatan—joh Werinbrahtan guatan,
  mit in si ouh mir gimeini—thiu ewiniga heili;
Joh allen io zi gamane—themo heilegen gisamane,
  thie dages joh nahtes thuru not—thar sancte Gallen thionont!

[I ask you with love (as is the custom with brotherliness), which rescued us from the clutches of Satan for our salvation and in the right manner. May he show his goodness and you show me your love emphatically in the prayers that you yourselves offer. Never cease to remember or cease to seek grace for me. Pray to St. Gall with all love. But in return my humble person will remember you in truth so that you shall avoid all danger. For this I shall pray to St. Peter, who walked on the water, that he be gracious to us, though I am not worthy. May he open to us the heights of heaven (indeed we must rejoice in that!), lead me thither and also rejoice you thither. Into the glory of heaven that we may in truth see the wonders there and also eternal beauty, always in eternity, is what his chosen ones are accustomed to there. We may rejoice in this evermore through his memory. May Christ preserve Hartmut and Werinbert the good and with them may I also be included in eternal salvation and to the joy of all of those in the holy community who serve St. Gall with zeal by day and by night.]

On final prayers in Old High German, Friedrich Ohly, "Zum Dichtungsschluss *Tu autem domine miserere nobis* [Thou, O Lord, have mercy upon us]," *Deutsche Vierteljahrschrift für Literaturwissenschaft und Geistesgeschichte* 47 (1973): 26–68, pp. 28f. *Gihuggen,* "remember," and *githenken,* "remember," are already to be found as verbs of commemoration in prayers in the Old High German period. Julius Schwietering, "Die Demutsformel mittelhochdeutscher Dichter" (1921), quoted from *Philologische Schriften,* ed. Friedrich Ohly and Max Wehrli (Munich, 1969), pp. 140–215, here p. 141, "regards the brotherhood of monks of Weißenburg and St. Gall as extended to all listeners and readers."

Wolfgang Haubrichs has, most recently, applied the prosopographical method in the service of a literary history of "texts in the literary communication of people bonded in associations," using Otfrid as an example: Wolfgang Haubrichs, "Nekrologische Notizen zu Otfrid von Weißenburg: Prosopographische Studien zum sozialen Umfeld und zur Rezeption des Evangelienbuchs," in *Adelsherrschaft und Literatur,* ed. Horst Wenzel, Beiträge zur Älteren Deutschen Literaturgeschichte, no. 6 (Bern, 1980), pp. 7–113. The reference to Otfrid in the necrologies of St.-Denis, of St.-Germain des Prés, and of the cathedral chapter of Auxerre, apart from the intellectual connections between them, makes it almost certain that Otfrid visited West Franconia. Haubrichs explains Otfrid's request for *memoria* at the close of the Gospel harmony by the fact of its being embedded in a web of commemoration that linked monasteries and involved both a monastic and a lay upper class: "The fraternitas of the monks realizes an elite community, in which the evangelical command to love your neighbor was completely valid" (pp. 51–55).

In the poems by an Otfridus presbyter (*MG, Poetae* II, 407f.), which are ascribed to Otfrid von Weißenburg by Haubrichs in "Nekrologische Notizen" (pp. 33ff.), this Otfrid, as the scribe of a codex that includes the Epistles and the Gospel reading for St.-Denis, asks for St. Dionysius's intercession with God:

Presbiter ista tuo, Dionisi, Otfridus honori 1
  Optulit ex voto munera, sancte pater . . .
Horum, sancte, memor votum exhibet, auxiliator. 41
  Pro facto grates, munera seque vovens.
Hunc apud altithronum precibus meritisque iuvato.
  Ut compos voti fiat ubique boni.

[The priest Otfried offered these gifts in your honor, O Dionysius, Holy Father, as a vow . . .
Of these mindful, Holy One, He, the Helper, will honor the vow. In exchange for the
  deed—grace, and—Himself, vowing gifts.

lists of the monks of Weißenburg.[15] His name is also to be found in the fraternal books of the monasteries of Reichenau and St. Gall on Lake Constance, and thus we know that he was also remembered as a member of the community of love of the fraternitas in the monastic intercession in St. Gallen.[16] Often linked to the confession of their own sinfulness, the plea for intercession by listeners and readers is for many poets, and other medieval authors, one of the main motives for naming themselves in the expectation that their name will be presented in an intercession before God.[17] They emerge from anonymity in the hope that the reader or listener will pronounce their name in an intercession for eternal salvation and so recall them in the grace of God. Of course, only in a situation where the work is being recited in front of a group of listeners could this be a communal prayer for commemoration. When the work is read privately the author could hope only for individual intercessions. If the plea is made within the framework of a monastic brotherhood of prayer, it can go so far as to be a plea for the insertion of the author's name into the lists of the dead of that monastery—as is the case with the

---

Close to this high-throning one there is help with prayers and meritorious deeds, so that everywhere the master of the vow is also made master of the good.]

He repeats the same thing as the writer of a Bible:

Hanc seriem divinorum summamque librorum 1
Otfridus summi scripsit amore dei.
Sancte tua fultus, Dionisi, pace patrisque
Hiltwini et domini dulcis iussa sequens.
Illi, Christe, tuae praesta mercedis honorem.
Post mundana metat dona perenne bonum

[This series and summa of divine books Otfried wrote out of love of the highest God.
He, sustained by your peace, Holy Dionysius, by the peace of our father, Hiltwin, and following the sweet commands of the master.
To him [Otfried] give, O Christ, the honor of your reward, that after worldly gifts he may reap the eternal good.]

15. Wolfgang Haubrichs, "Die Weißenburger Mönchslisten der Karolingerzeit," *Zeitschrift für die Geschichte des Oberrheins* 118 (1970): 1–42, p. 30 and n. 95.

16. On the lists of St. Gallen, see Haubrichs, pp. 3–9; on the Reichenau lists, pp. 9ff. On fraternal relations with St. Gallen, Oskar Erdmann, *Otfrids Evangelienbuch*, Germanistische Handbibliothek, no. 5 (Halle, 1882), pp. 317ff. On the monks of St. Gall, Hartmut and Werinbert, Wolfgang Haubrichs, "Otfrids St. Galler 'Studienfreunde,'" *Amsterdamer Beiträge zur Älteren Germanistik* 4 (1973): 49–112, and "Ein prosopographische Skizze zu Otfrid von Weißenburg," in *Otfrid von Weißenburg*, ed. Wolfgang Kleiber, Wege der Forschung, no. 419 (Darmstadt, 1978), pp. 397–413, pp. 409–411.

17. Schwietering ("Demutsformel," pp. 141–150) writes about this whole complex.

Venerable Bede.[18] The same thing also happened half a millennium later. Just as at the end, Heinrich von Kleist dedicated a fragment of his *Penthesilea* to Goethe "on the knees of my heart,"[19] Adam Scotus, at the close of the twelfth

18. Schwietering, p. 145: "To what extent, when this plea to listeners and reader was made, there was a vision of a freer form of confraternity that was linked to the naming and entry into the *liber vitae,* cannot be determined in each individual case. Bede asks for a true confraternity of prayer—to which Otfrid also appeals—and as a reward for his literary achievement, in his prose life of St. Cuthbert, which was directed at the bishop and the monks of Lindisfarne (in *Patrologia Latina* [*PL*], 94, col. 734): 'also for my humble self remember to pray for divine mercy—but when I am dead pray and say masses for the redemption of my soul as though I were one of your own, and deign to write my name among your own.'"

19. Klaus Düwel, "Das Bild von den 'Knieen des Herzens' bei Heinrich von Kleist: Zur Geschichte der Herzmetaphorik," *Euphorion* 68 (1974): 185–197, 6 plates. The knees of the heart are at first to be bent to God; citations in Heinz Piesik, "Bildersprache der Apostolischen Väter," (diss. Bonn, 1961), pp. 30, 155.

The work of an author who is writing between Isidor and the ninth century, "Exhortatio poenitendi" ("Exhortation to Repent") admonishes the sinner:

> Dic "peccavi nimium," "parce miserere!" proclama.
> Curva cordis genua prostratus corpore terrae.
> Obsecrans assidue profusis lacrimis ora—

> [Say, "I have sinned grievously," Cry, "spare me, have mercy!" Bend the knees of your heart prostrate upon the ground, Pray beseeching continuously, with profuse tears—]

Karl Strecker, ed. *MGH, Poetae aevi carolini* IV/2 (Berlin, 1896; reprint, 1964), p. 765. The dedicatory gestures of the dedicator conclude a fourteenth-century Benedictine oration, "Coronula beatae Mariae virginis": "Eya ergo regina celi, reginarum imperatrix, exiguum munus quod dat tibi pauper amicus, accipito placide. Te enim cum hoc munuscululo, te cum hoc oposculo salutationum et benedictionum laudo et glorifico, genibusque cordis et corporis flexis capiti tuo nobilissimo hanc coronulam laudis supplex impone. Utinam tue sit acceptabilis maiestati." [O queen of heaven, empress of queens, gently accept what your poor friend gives to you. . . . For with this small present, with this small work of salutation and benediction, I praise and glorify you, and with the knees of my heart and my body bent, I, a supplicant, place upon your most noble head this little crown of praise. May it be acceptable to your majesty]. Gilles Gérard Meersseman, *Der Hymnos Akathistos im Abendland,* vol. 2, *Gruß-Psalter, Gruß-Orationen, Gaude-Andachten und Litaneien,* Spicilegium Friburgense, no. 3 (Freiburg, Switzerland, 1960), p. 187. I will add the following later citations: Ernst Ludwig Rathke, *Akridotheologie oder historische und theologische Betrachtungen über die Heuschrecken,* 2 pts. (Hanover, 1748, 1750), pt. 1, p. 139: "Sollen wir nicht die Knie unseres Herzens und unseres Leibes für solchen herrlichen Got beugen?" [Should we not bend the knees of our hearts and our body before such a splendid God?]. Goethe's letter to Herder of May 12, 1775: "Deine Art zu fegen—und nicht etwa aus dem Kehrigt Gold zu sieben, sondern den Kehrigt zur lebenden Pflanze umzupalingenesieren, legt mich immer auf die Knie meines Herzens" [The way you sweep—and not just sifting gold from the sweepings, but of metamorphosing the sweepings into a living plant, always forces me down onto the knees of my heart.]

century, sends his great explication of the tabernacle from the north to the mother house of his order to Prémontré: "We urgently plead, on the bended knees of our heart, as though we were prostrate before your feet, that you may keep me in mind at your evening services." In this way Adam pleads with the brothers for them to intercede on his behalf with Jesus—"Keep the sinner, Adam, who loves you, in mind"—and dares to ask further, "namely, that you may see to it that, after my death, my name, together with the names of those of your community who have also died, shall be entered in the lists of your holy confraternity, for we too are one of yours."[20] The author's plea for intercession by the recipients of, or readers of, or listeners to his work apparently has one of its origins in the convent where commemorative prayer from one fraternity to another was well known. The pleas of Bede, Otfrid, and Adam, in each case sent from afar, attest to a commemorative prayer dedicated to individuals—here, authors in thanks for their work—apart from the confraternities of prayer that existed between whole conventual societies. Otherwise, Bede and Adam could not have submitted their pleas for entry into the lists of Lindisfarne or Prémontré.[21] The expectation—fostered by early

20. In Adam's letter, which accompanies his transmission of the "Tripartitum tabernaculum una cum pictura" from his Scottish monastery to Prémontré (*PL*, 198, cols. 612A–C): "Obnixe itaque vos flectis genibus mentis obsacramus, tanquam pedibus vestris prostrati, ut nostri memores sitis in vespertinis sacrificiis vestris. . . . Mementote itaque diligentis vos, peccatoris Adae. . . . Sed et hoc petitionibus nostris superadderemus, nisi forte temerariae foret praesumtioni imputandum: scilicet ut nomen nostrum in albo sanctae congregationis vestrae, una cum vestrorum, qui jam discessere, nominibus post mortem juberitis adscribi: quia et nos vestri sumus."

21. Hansjörg Wellmer—who agrees with Joachim Wellasch in distinguishing between collective commemoration in an ecclesiastical community and personal commemoration—treats the latter in *Persönliches Memento im deutschen Mittelalter*, Monographien zur Geschichte des Mittelalters, no. 5 (Stuttgart, 1973). As a historian, he investigates necrologies of the ninth to twelfth centuries, which have been compiled by personal commemorators for more or less individual motivations, from the point of view of the religious, historical, or autobiographical conception of the compilers, who personally defined the circle of those who, as a result of "a need for historical self-orientation" (p. 35) because of a later need for commemoration after death in the form of an anniversary commemoration, generally within the horizons of a bishop or an abbot.

As opposed to this side of an interest in commemoration, which is determined by the "commemorator," there is another, of the person seeking commemoration with a more personal request for the inclusion of his name in a commemorative prayer, either personal or communal. This is such a telling source for the understanding of medieval commemorative practice that it calls for individual treatment. Starting on the path trod by Julius Schwietering in his investigation of the poet's plea for intercessory prayer, in Middle High German, it would be desirable to investigate, above all, medieval Latin and other vernacular literatures and also to look, now and again, for such evidence in the extrapoetic genres. Those who seek commemorative prayer may not have such faith in the prayers that they offered during their lifetimes that they can do without the intercession of the saints and their fellow Christians and, last but not least, those who have dedicated their lives to the service of God. But, above all, what is important is to ensure the liturgical, paraliturgical, or private intercession for the salvation of their souls after death. Even texts of commemorative books furnish clues to the fact that pleas or acts by petitioners (up to and including entry into a cloister) could lead to their names' being entered in the monastic *liber vitae* (book of life): thus, in the Salzburg commemorative book, where those are recommended to God's memory who "se nobis sacris orationibus uel confessionibus commendarunt et qui elymosinis suis se commendaverunt" [commend themselves to us by sacred speeches or confessions and who have commended themselves to us by their alms] (Karl Schmid, "Das liturgische Gebetsgedenken in seiner historischen Relevanz am Beispiel der Verbrüderungsbewegung des früheren Mittelalters," *Freiburger Diözesan-Archiv* 99 [1979]: 20 ff., p. 36). The collection of such evidence would be highly desirable and would open up this side of commemoration, and we could also integrate into it, to the fullest possible extent, poetic pleas for intercession. Wellner has noted such evidence only incidentally. When Thietmar von Merseburg in his chronicle (VIII, 12) expresses his plea for intercession in prayer to his readers and successors, this corresponds to Bede's, Otfrid's, and Adam's personal pleas for intercession in prayer (Wellmer, p. 63 n. 111). The other way in which Thietmar would like to persuade the owners of a missal not to forget him after his death is also impressive. Around the initial *Te igitur,* he inscribed these words: "Sacerdos dei, reminiscere thietmari confratris tui, peccatoris et indigni" [Priest of God, remember Thietmar, your confrere, a sinner and unworthy] (p. 63). On the *Te igitur* initials, see Rudolf Suntrup, "*Te igitur* Initialen und Kanonbilder in mittelalterlichen Sakramenthandschriften," in *Text und Bild: Aspekte des Zusammenwirkens zweier Künste im Mittalter und früher Neuzeit,* ed. Christel Meier and Uwe Ruberg (Wiesbaden, 1980), pp. 72–382. As early as the ninth century we find Otfrid having a girdle made for a priest's costume, which seems to have borne his plea for *memoria* as an inscription: "Hanc zona cinctum fac. Christo, pio ordine dignum. sit memor Otfredi quisque hoc decus induat exin" [This girdle make into a robe. Worthy of Christ, worthy of a pious order. Keep Otfried in remembrance, you who put on this dignity thence] (*MG, Poetae* II, 408); Haubrichs, "Nekrologische Notizen," pp. 34f.

Helmut Lippelt's *Thietmar von Merseburg, Reichsbischof und Chronist* (Cologne, 1973) appeared simultaneously with Wellmer's work. The final chapter, "The character of the Chronicler and the Final Structure of His Work" (pp. 194–202) also adduces this evidence and determines that Thietmar's confessions of sin are strikingly connected "with the efforts at commemoration that are a main motif of his historiography—whether he is oppressed by lost memory or whether while he is commemorating others he is diverted to the task of ensuring that his own commemoration is taken care of. Both are immediately related to one another; in his efforts on behalf of the commemoration of the dead, he expects their intercession, and with his confessions of his own sins, he seeks preservation, later on, of his own memory by the living. Is it going too far to see an ancient, far-reaching commemorative system being preserved once more in Thietmar's chronicle, carried over, as it were, into historiography but also coming to an end? Not that the commemorative system as such came to an end; on the contrary, the rise of Cluny cannot be understood except in terms of all the commemorative foundations that came together from the whole of France, and the guild and confraternity systems of the late Middle Ages drew their greatest impulse from the commemoration of the dead; but new structures of commemoration

medieval spiritual poets and authors—that the recipients of their works would reward them by prayer, an expectation that could serve as an inspiration for their work, does not disappear for a long time, even though it is transferred to poets and genres that are nonspiritual.[22] Hartmann von Aue, as a courtly poet, is the first of these, though only in the legend poems (just as legend and Bible poems from then on remain the main place where the poet's plea for commemorative prayer is attested to). In *Der arme Heinrich* he mentions his name for the sake of intercession after his death (vv. 18ff.): "dar umbe hât er sich genant, / daz er sîner arbeit / die er daran hât geleit / iht âne lôn belîbe, / und swer nach sînem lîbe / si hoere sagen oder lese, / daz er im bittende wese / der sêle heiles hin ze gote" [For this reason he has named himself / That the labor / That he has put into this [sc. the poem] / Should not go unrewarded / And whoever hears it or reads it / After his [sc. Hartmann's] life is over / May he pray to God for him / For the salvation of his soul]. (Did any German scholar ever do so? The question emphasizes the distance of the modern reader's attitude from what the poet wished for.) At the end of the *Gregorius* legend, Hartmann's recommendation finally sets the seal on *this good sinner*—above and beyond Hartmann's own prayer for himself as the

were being created" (pp. 201ff.). Lippelt quotes Thietmar: "quia etsi in hoc seculo parum boni operatus sum, tamen defunctorum semper memor sum" [since even if in this world I have effected little that is good, nonetheless I am ever mindful of the dead] (p. 199: *Chronicle* IV, 75), and he also mentions (p. 202 n. 51), as "an instructive example for early personal consideration," Bede's report of the origin of the worship of Oswald (IV, 14); the monks of the monastery at Selsey were called on, in a vision, to ensure that "in suis codicibus, in quibus defunctorum est adnotata depositio" [in their codices, in which the burial of the dead is recorded] it was precisely that day on which Oswald died. The abbot refers to his annal and finds confirmation there and orders a mass and a commemorative feast.

I mention the research of Karl Schmid and Joachim Wollasch as an example of how impulses toward a revitalization of a literary historical investigation into the significance of commemorative prayer could emerge from research by historians into commemoration. Such an investigation would—like the historical one—have to integrate itself into an observation of *memoria* from the standpoint of the history of theology and piety.

22. Schwietering, "Demutsformel," pp. 144ff. Fritz Tschirch, "Das Selbstverständnis des mittelalterlichen deutschen Dichters," in *Beiträge zum Berufsbewußtsein des mittelalterlichen Menschen*, ed. Paul Wilpert, Miscellanea mediaevali, no. 3 (Berlin, 1964), pp. 239–285, p. 274, discerns "a self-assessment and overassessment of the high medieval German poet that rapidly grew excessive." However, except in a very few cases, it does not rest upon an overestimation of the qualities of their own art, but consists above all in the claim to a high and, not least, a moral competence in many areas of the subject matter which was put into poetic form. No poet talks of the expectation of broad fame or of the perpetuation of his name. Tschirch ignores the humility formulas.

poet and for his own salvation—as someone to be used as an advocate before God whose holiness had been demonstrated differently in the work, for example, by miracles, since a saint is the only one who can be summoned as an advocate (*bote*) before God.[23] In asking for the listener's support in commemorative prayer, poets as early as Cassiodorus[24] rely on the promise of the Epistle of James, "pray one for another, that ye may be healed" (5.16), from which they read that intercession for the other person also promises salvation to the one who is interceding: "man giht, er sî sîn selbes bote / und erloese sich dâ mite, / swer vür des andern schulde bite" [It is said he is his own advocate / Who prays for the guilt of another / And effects his own salvation thereby].[25]

23. *Gregorius von Hartmann von Aue,* ed. Hermann Paul, 12th ed., rev. Ludwig Wolff, Altdeutsche Textbibliothek, no. 2 (Tübingen, 1973), lines 3989–4006 (the end of the work):

Hartmann der sîn arbeit
an diz liet hât geleit
gote und iu ze minnen.
der gert daran gewinnen
daz ir im lât gevallen
ze lône von in allen
die ez hoeren oder lesen
daz si im bittende wesen
daz im die schulde geschehe
daz er iuch noch gesehe
in dem himelrîche.
des sendet alle gelîche
disen guoten sündaere
ze boten umb unser swaere,
daz wir in disem ellende
ein also genislich ende
nemen als si dâ nâmen.
des gestiure uns got. âmen

[Hartmann, who took pains over this poem for the love of God and the love of you, he seeks to gain thereby that you will let him have, as his reward, that all who read or hear it will pray that he shall receive the blessing of eternal joy and that he shall see you again in the blessed kingdom of heaven. Therefore, everyone of you send this good sinner as a messenger of our travail so that we in this misery shall have as comforting an end as they [sc. those already in heaven] themselves did. May God grant this. Amen.]

24. Schwietering, "Demutsformel," p. 144 n. 2. On intercession, Otto Michel-Theodor Klauser, "Gebet II (Fürbitte)," in *Reallexikon für Antike und Christentum,* vol. 9 (1976), cols. 2–36.

25. *Armer Heinrich,* vv. 26ff. Gregorius, the penitent, who is chained to a rock in the sea, pleads with the messengers from Rome who, by God's command, have come to fetch him to be pope to intercede for him in his lifetime: ". . . und geruochet iuch erbarmen / über mich vil

Since commemorative prayer ("eines gedenken ze gote" [to remember someone before God] means "to pray for someone") also promotes the salvation of the one who is praying, the hope for the salvation of those who are praying is certainly in the background of monastic *memoria.* Intercession for those who are dead is a part of the search for one's own salvation. For the members of the monastic community, the liturgical commemorative prayer establishes the expectation that they too will be remembered, and such confidence increases as each day passes. As far as the poet is concerned, man's memory is to help him, the poet, remain in God's memory. The poet of the German *Song of Roland* (*Rolandslied*) humbly gives his name at the end of the work for the sake of the hoped-for commemorative prayers by his listeners: "Ob iu daz liet geualle, / so gedencket ir min alle: / ich haize der pfaffe Chunrat" [If the poem pleases you, then remember me all of you; my name is Priest Conrad].[26] The "thou therefore Oh, Lord! have mercy upon us" in the last line of the *Song of Roland* embraces both poet and listener in a community of "us" that is created out of the spirit of the poem.[27] Hugo von Trimberg, who had

---

armen / und gedenket mîn ze gote. / wir haben von sînem gebote swer umbe den sündaere bite, / dâ loese er sich selben mite" [and pray have mercy on me wretched man and remember me before God. We have a command from him, that whoever prays for another sinner, effects his own salvation]. Friedrich Naumann, ed., *Hartmann von Aue, "Gregorius"* (Wiesbaden, 1958), points, in his commentary, to Honorius Augustodunensis's *Sermo pro defunctis* (*PL*, 172, col. 1084): "cum autem pro his, qui in poena sunt, oratis, et vos liberatios, quia, qui pro alio orat, se ipsum liberat" [when, however, you pray for those who are in torment, you free yourselves as well, because whoever prays for another frees himself]. Hugo von Trimberg, *Der Renner,* ed. Gustav Ehrismann, 1 (Berlin, 1970), vv. 21ff., substantiates his plea for commemorative prayer: "wenne geschriben stât: / swer vür eins andern schulde bite, / Sîn selbes sêle loese er dâ mite / Und tilige sîn missetât" [When it is written: whoever prays for the guilt of another, effects the salvation of his own soul and wipes out his own misdeeds]. Freidank's dictum, "Merkt swer für den andern bit, / sich selben loeset er dâ mit" [Behold, he who prays for another effects his own salvation] (39.18), inspired Thomas Mann to write the child Echo's evening prayer in *Dr. Faustus:*

> Merkt swer für den andern bitt',
> Sich selber löset er damit.
> Echo bitt' für die ganze Welt.
> Daß Gott auch ihn in Armen hält. Amen

> [Behold whoever prays for another, Redeems himself thereby. Echo, pray for the whole world, that God will also hold him in his arms. Amen.]

For the rest see Ohly, *Sage und Legende,* p. 128. See also n. 113 below.

26. *Das Rolandslied des Pfaffen Konrad,* ed. Carl Wesle, 2d ed., ed. Peter Wapnewski, Altdeutsche Textbibliothek, no. 69 (Tübingen, 1967), vv. 9077ff.

27. Ohly, *Sage und Legende;* on the *Song of Roland,* pp. 65ff.

intended his early work, *Der Samener,* for "his companions, who were with me at that time, so that they might remember me by it," intends his *Renner,* written two years later, for his "good friends, that they shall remember me, and that whoever shall read it, or hear it read, shall be gracious to my soul."[28]

This sort of evidence drawn from German works of the twelfth and thirteenth centuries that regard the work of art as an aid to the achievement of salvation lacks both embedment in the Latinity of the Middle Ages and the breadth of its historical background. One origin can, however, be found in Augustine's thoughts on the purpose and fruit of his *Confessions.* At the beginning of book 10, the main point of which lies in its chapters on *memoria* (X, 8–26), he reveals his faith in the sense of confraternity, the fraternal hearts of his readers (*fraterna corda*), who, out of love, believe in his self-revelation in the *Confessions.* He expects them to rejoice with him and to sympathize with him to the point of exultation and then lapse back again into lament when they hear of his approach to God and of how far he has fallen back under the weight of his burden. Augustine regards the certainty that his readers have prayed for him as one of the fruits of his confessions. His self-revelation before God and his brothers should result in both their intercession and God's mercy redounding to his benefit. "Hic est fructus confessionum mearum" [This is the fruit of my confessions].[29] The author can also devote

28. *Renner* (see n. 25 above) lines 24589ff., 16–21. Schwietering, "Demutsformel," pp. 145f. Further evidence for *eines gedenken* (to remember someone in prayer) *memorem esse* of the Latin prefaces to Middle High German literary works, ibid., p. 149. The preacher, too, can ask his congregation to remember him in their prayers and pray for his salvation: "remember me and all faithful souls also in your holy prayers today" (*Zeitschrift für deutsches Altertum* 28, p.13). Bruder Hansen at the end of his songs to Mary turns to the Mother of God and asks intercession for him and his wife, whom he has given up for the sake of God: "say a word too for the both of us (5725), so that we shall not have to be ashamed at the Day of Judgment." *Bruder Hansens Marienlieder aus dem vierzehnten Jahrhundert,* ed. Michael S. Batts, Altdeutsche Textbibliothek, no. 58 (Tübingen, 1963). Willame Giffard, the author of an Anglo-Norman apocalypse from the second half of the thirteenth century, commends himself to God's memory by naming himself in the epilogue to his work: "May God have the soul and we the memory! Amen." *La Bible de Macé de la Charité,* vol. 7, *Apocalypse,* ed. Reinerus Lambertus Hermanus Lops (Leyden, 1982), p. lviii. It is very common, in legend literature, to find that the author expects, through his work, to promote his own salvation without mediation. Early evidence of this in Peter Christian Jacobsen, *Flodoard von Reims: Sein Leben und seine Dichtung "De triumphis Christi"* (Leyden, 1978), p. 217.

29. Following suggestions by George Misch, *Geschichte der Autobiographie* (Bern, 1950), p. 650, Julius Schwietering, "Demutsformel," in *Philologische Schriften,* p. 444, related Augustine's words from the *Confessions* to the prayers of Middle High German poets. In *Confessions* X, 4, 5 Augustine says of the readers: "An congratulari mihi cupiunt, cum audierint, quantum ad te accedam munere tuo, et orare pro me, cum audierint, quantum retarder pondere meo? Indicabo

to others the reward of prayer that he receives for his work. Augustine reports the death of his mother, Monica, prays for her and his father, but also passionately implores his readers to remember (*memini*) the two of them in their prayers. The final wish that his mother then makes of him would then be more richly fulfilled by his *Confessions*—that awaken the prayers of many—than through his own prayers.[30]

---

me talibus. Non enim parvus est fructus, domine deus meus, *ut a multis tibi gratiae agantur de nobis*" [Is it that they wish to join with me in thanking you, when they hear how close I have come to you by your grace, and to pray for me, when they hear how far I am set apart from you by the burden of my sins. If this is what they wish, I shall tell them what I am. For no small good is gained, O Lord my God, *if many offer thanks to you* (2 Corinthians 1:11)] "et a multis rogeris pro nobis. Amet in me fraternus animus quod amandum doces, et doleat in me quod dolendum doces. . . . Respirent in illis et suspirent in his, et hymnus et fletus ascendant in conspectum tuum de fraternis cordibus, turibulis tuis" [and many pray to you for me. Let all who are truly my brothers love in me what they know from your teaching to be worthy of their love, and let them sorrow to find in me what they know from your teaching to be occasion for remorse. . . . Let my brothers draw their breath in joy for the one and sigh with grief for the other. Let hymns of gladness and cries of sorrow rise from their fraternal hearts, as though they were vessels burning with incense before you]. Just as in the *Song of Roland* the *Tu autem domine, miserere nobis* follows the plea for commemorative prayer, so in Augustine the *Tu autem* follows, though it is not yet a set part of the liturgy. "Tu autem, domine, delectatus odore *sancti temple* tui, *miserere mei secundum magnam misericordiam tuam* propter nomen tuum et nequaquam deserens coepta tua consumma imperfecta mea: Hic est fructus confessionum mearum, non qualis fuerim, sed qualis sim, ut hoc confitear non tantum coram te secreta exultatione cum tremore et secreto maerore cum spe, sed etiam in auribus credentium filiorum hominum, sociorum gaudii mei et consortium mortalitatis meae, civium meorum et mecum peregrinorum, praecedentium et consequentium et comitum viae meae. . . . Sic itaque audiar" [And I pray you, O Lord, to be pleased with the incense that rises in your *holy temple* (1 Corinthians 3:17) and, for your name's sake, to *have mercy upon me, as you are ever rich in mercy* (Psalms 51:1). Do not relinquish what you have begun, but make perfect what is still imperfect in me [4.6]: So if I go on to confess not what I was but what I am, the good that comes of it is this. There is joy in my heart when I confess to [you?], yet there is fear as well; there is sorrow and yet hope. But I confess not only to you, but also to the believers among men, all who share my joy and all who, like me, are doomed to die; all who are my fellows in your kingdom and all who accompany me on my pilgrimage, those who have gone before and those who will come after and are my companions through life. . . . let my words be understood as they are meant] (this and subsequent passages trans. after R. S. Pine-Coffin, *Saint Augustine Confessions* [Baltimore, 1970], pp. 209f.).

30. *Confessions* IX, 13, 37: "Et inspira, domine meus, deus meus, inspira servis tuis, fratribus meis, filiis tuis, dominis meiss, quibus et corde et voce et litteris servio, ut quotquot haec legerint, meminerint ad altare tuam Monnicae, famulae tuae, cum Patricio, quondam eius conjuge. . . . Meminerint cum affectu pio parentum meorum. . . . ut quod a me illa poposcit extremum uberius ei praestetur in multorum orationibus per confessiones quam per orationes meas" [O my Lord, my God, inspire your servants my brothers—they are your sons and my masters,

Although art history—revising old ideas about the general anonymity of artists in the medieval work of art—did point out quite a number of cases where the artist's name is mentioned,[31] the number of names of poets that is known is far larger than the number of names of artists, which, throughout Europe, are found only in individual cases, whereas the Manesse manuscript gives 140 names of lyric poets. This is true in spite of the not inconsiderable anonymity of literary genres—especially the heroic epic and the prose novel—as well as forms of writing intended for reading or singing in divine service. Where artists do name themselves—as in the case of the sculptor of the tympanum of the west portal of the cathedral at Autun, who carved under the feet of Christ the inscription "Gislebertus hoc fecit" [Giselbert made this]—it is not certain whether we are dealing here with artistic pride or the hope of commemorative prayer. This is certainly the case with Hugo the Goldsmith, who, in the inscription on the silver cover of his book of pericopes, which sports a picture of Christ, names himself, with the words "orate pro eo" [pray for him], as the artist who praises Christ with his artefact in the way that others do with their voice.[32] Sculptors themselves, or others, ask for

---

whom I serve with heart and voice and pen—inspire those of them who read this book to remember Monica, your servant, at your altar and with her Patricius, her husband who died before her. . . . Let them remember with pious heart my parents. . . . So it shall be that the last request that my mother made to me shall be granted in the prayers of the many who read my confessions more fully than in mine alone]. Schwietering, p. 444: "In the same way Frau Ava, at the end of her poem asks intercession for her sons, the dead one and the living one, and only in the last place for herself." Requests of the poet for intercession for others are also found in the *Kaiserchronik* (Ohly, *Sage und Legende*, pp. 21ff.).

31. Harald Keller, "Künstlerstolz und Künstlerdemut," in *Festschrift der Wissenschaftlichen Gesellschaft an der Johann Wolfgang Goethe-Universität* (Frankfurt am Main, 1981), pp. 191–220.

32. Ibid. pp. 192, 199. Emil Ploss, "Der Inschriftentypus 'NN me fecit' und seine geschichtliche Entwicklung bis ins Mittelalter," *Zeitschrift für deutsche Philologie* 77 (1958): 25–46. This terse form of inscription has generally as little to do with a dialogue with the artist's own work (pp. 31, 44) as the name, and the accompanying plea for gracious memory, on a Regensburg bell from the year 1247: "Me resonante pia populi memor esto Maria F[ridericus?] me fecit" [When I am ringing, blessed Mary, remember your people, F(redericus?) made me] (p. 38). One example of artistic pride: the cathedral in Ferrara, which was founded in 1135, bears the inscription in the St. George lunette of the portal: "Artificem gnarem qui sculpserit hec Nicolaum / Huc concurrentes laudent per secula gentes" [May the people who assemble here through the centuries praise Nicolas, the skillful master, who carved this]. A vernacular inscription which was still extant in 1712 and which dates from before 1570 ran: "Li mile cento trenta cenqe nato / Fo questo templo a San Gogio donato / Da Glelmo ciptadin per so amore / E tua fo l'opra Nicolao scolptore" [In 1135 was born / This temple to St. George donated / By Guglielmo, citizen, for love of him / And yours is the work, Nicolò, sculptor]. Giulio Bertoni, "L'iscrizione volgare del duomo

Christ's reward in heaven.[33] Two architects of the minster in Basle are called, in an anticipatory inscription over their pictures, "living stones in the city of heaven."[34] The puzzling inscription made by the master of the Tiefenbronner altar in the fifteenth century leaves open the question as to whether it is the work or its beholder that is being called upon—with the words "pray to God for him (it)"—to intercede for the artist Lukas Moser.[35]

---

di Ferrara (1135)," *Rendiconti della R. Accademia nazionale dei Lincei, Classe di scienze morali, stroiche e filologiche,* 6th ser., 12 (Rome, 1936): 385–400.

33. Keller, "Künstlerstolz," pp. 200, 202, 212.

34. Ibid., p. 200.

35. Ibid., p. 216. The inscription runs: "schri kunst schri und klag dich ser / din begert iecz niemen mer / so o we 1432 / lucas moser maler von Wil maister / des werx. bit got vir in [Cry art, cry and make loud lament / No one desires you any more / Thus alas 1432 / Lucas Moser painter of Wail the master / Of this work. Pray to God for him]. Keller says of this, "all attempts to interpret this have failed up to the present day for, at the end of the *dolce stil nuovo,* West Swabia and Alemannia were enjoying a heyday. Even the explanation that the Council of Constance had created many commissions for the artists—as a result of the meeting of princes of the church from the whole of Europe—which naturally lapsed after the meeting had ended, does not really offer a plausible solution."

It would be necessary to take the drastic course of reading "me" for "you" and "mine" for "yours" if a completely different meaning were to be suggested: that art is not called upon to lament about the time, but the work of art is called upon to intercede for the artist after his death. "To cry" can mean "to call upon in prayer," as it does in the poet's prayer which Wolfram von Eschenbach offers to the titular hero of his Willehalm legend: "4:12 din güete enphahe miniu wort, / herre sanct Willehalm. / mines sündehaften mundes galm / din heilikeit an schrîet: / sit daz du bist gevriet / von allen hellebanden, / so bevoget ouch mich vor schanden, / ich Wolfram von Eschenbach" [May your goodness receive my words, / My lord, St. Willehalm / The sound of my sinful mouth / Prays to your sanctity: / Since you are freed / From all the bonds of hell / Keep me from all shame, / I, Wolfram von Eschenbach].

Further examples of *sin gebet schrîen, an Kristes helfe schrîen, ze gote schrîen, got an schrîen* in George Friedrich Benecke, Wilhelm Müller, and Friedrich Zarncke, *Mittelhochdeutsches Wörterbuch,* 2,2 (Leipzig, 1866), pp. 213ff. The corresponding phrases in English and in French are "to cry to God," "crier au seigneur," or "crier vers Dieu." The prayer "cry" in Wolfram together with the naming of the poet here also prompts the cautious suggestion, that "cry art" could, according to the meaning, be a variation on "pray to God." It is only the confusion of previous attempts at interpretation that inspires the philologist to make such bold suggestions. That a work can intervene on behalf of the salvation of its creator's soul is revealed by the dedicatory picture of the twelfth-century Prüfening Isidor manuscript (Clm 13013, fol. 1). Keller reproduces it (p. 198). On p. 197, he says of this picture that is asking for eternal reward for the scribe of the manuscript: "The dead monk lies, dressed in his cowl, on a straw mat at Christ's feet. Behind him we see St. Michael with the scales for weighing dead souls, which decide whether the dead man belongs in heaven or hell. In order that the scale pan of good works should descend as low as possible, the good angel is making it heavier with the work which the scribe has copied. The devil, who is already hovering over the head of the deathbed, has to depart. At Christ's behest, an angel bears the soul of the scribe who has been saved to heaven." Four lines of a plea for mercy to God—in first person form—stand as an inscription above the picture of the scribe: "Scriptoris miseri dignare deus misereri. Noli culparum podus pensare mearum" [God, deign to have mercy on the poor scribe, do not weigh the burden of my sins]. The living scribe thus prays for himself as a dead man, and this is how he is portrayed in the picture (but still while he was alive?). The upper half of the picture shows St. Isidor and Braulio sitting on thrones. Isidor is handing the scroll to Braulio, "Fac mea scripta legi que te mandante peregi" [Cause the writings that I have done at thy behest to be read]. The writer thus fulfilled a commission of the blessed author himself.

Gerhard Piccard, *Der Magdalenenaltar des "Lukas Moser" in Tiefbronn: Ein Beitrag zur europäischen Kunstgeschichte, mit einer Untersuchung, "Die Tiefbronner Patrozinien und ihre Herkunft" von Wolfgang Irtenkauf* (Wiesbaden, 1969), radically questioned several conclusions arrived at in earlier research, among them the authenticity of the famous inscription "schri. kvnst. schri" (he deciphers its date correctly as 1432 instead of, as was formerly held, 1431), which he tried to show was done only in 1814 (pp. 124, 125). Piccard's work stimulated a whole series of investigations and a special conference about the Tiefbronner altar. Reiner Haussherr gave a very thorough paper, "Der Magdalenenaltar in Tiefbronn: A report on the conference of 9. and 10. March, 1971 in the *Zentralinstitut für Kunstgeschichte* in Munich," *Kunstchronik* 24 (1971): 177–212. Rolf E. Straub, "Einige technologische Untersuchungen am Tiefbronner Magdalenenaltar des Lukas Moser," *Jahrbuch der Staatlichen Kunstsammlungen in Baden-Württemberg* 7 (1970): pp. 31–56, here pp. 31, 42, plate 14f., with proof of the fact that the first construction belonged to the original material of the altarpiece. Charles Sterling, "Observations on Moser's Tiefbronn Altar-Piece," *Pantheon* 30 (1972): 19–32, here p. 31, interprets the "bitter outcry" of the inscription as a result of Moser's conversance with the latest iconography and the latest stylistic developments in Flanders, so that in 1432 he may have felt himself to be the most progressive painter in Germany and the one who reflected most on the artistic media at his disposal. Thus he sees the inscription—as Erwin Panofsky (*Early Netherlandish Painting*) had already done before him—as the expression of a "misunderstood progressive." "He certainly had every reason to be proud of his technical and artistic innovations, which represented in his eyes the only true *kunst*" (p. 31). Similar personal expressions by Jan van Eyck and Konrad Laib make the inscription seem not unusual to Sterling. "Many of them must be lost" (p. 31). Hausherr's paper on Sterling (pp. 203, 207–210) mentions earlier proofs by Sterling, like those on miniatures by Jean Colombe from the late fifteenth century, with expressions like "I lose time in serving you" or "time lost for Colombe" (p. 203). Ernst-Ludwig Richter "Zur Rekonstruktion des Tiefbronner Magdalenenaltars," *Pantheon* 30 (1972): 33–38, follows Straub; according to him, "the painting and inscription of this work have been preserved essentially undamaged and unaltered" (p. 33). Rudolf Kloos delivered a talk in Munich entitled "The Inscriptions of the Tiefbronner Altar from the Point of View of Epigraphy" (Haussherr discusses this, pp. 187–190) with the following result: "The form and content of the horizontal and vertical inscriptions are for the most part—and including the signature of Lucas Moser—original to the year 1432, only the later overpainting has caused a lot of vagueness" (p. 190). Werner Besch, as a German scholar, spoke of "The linguistic and semantic ordering of the German inscription" (discussion by Haussherr, pp. 180, 190f.). According to Besch (contrary to Piccard, pp. 103–124), "there is no cogent reason to deny that the German inscription was not made around 1430 and in that area" (p. 190). Besch looks at the semasiology of the word *kunst:* "In the inscription, *kunst* can therefore scarcely be understood in the sense of

Going in the opposite direction, from the life hereafter to life on earth, people who are damned in hell, but who desire not to be forgotten on earth, can also enter pleas for a *memoria* on earth. Precisely because the question of their salvation has been settled by their being sent to the inferno, they plead for a mitigation of their suffering in hell in the hope that they will not be forgotten on earth. The Florentine Ciacco ends his conversation with Dante in the Inferno with the words "But when you have returned to the sweet world, / I pray you recall me to men's memory: / I say no more to you, answer no more. / Then his straight gaze grew twisted and awry; / He looked at me awhile, then bent his head: / He fell as low as all his blind companions."[36] Dante travels across the Styx in a boat with Virgil, and they meet the Florentine Filippo Argenti in the mire of hell. Argenti clings to their boat, crying, "behold, I weep." Dante recognizes him as someone who had always been arrogant and pushes him away. Virgil embraces him and thanks him, for, "When in the world he was presumptuous: / There is no good to gild his memory, / And so his shade down here is hot with fury."[37] His suffering is sharpened by the thought that he is not remembered. In the seventh circle of hell, the forest of suicides, they meet the confidant of the Emperor Frederick II, Pietro della Vigna, who, after having been ousted and defamed by him, subsequently committed suicide. Virgil wished to heal Pietro's soul, which Dante had mistakenly injured by offering him the prospect of Dante's renewing his reputation on earth, and Pietro, moved by thanks and after confessing his guilt, prays for the restoration of his memory on earth: "If one of you returns into the world, / Then let him help my memory that still / Lies prone beneath the battering of envy."[38] In the desert of the sodomites, where Dante and Virgil meet three Florentine generals, the conversation ends in

high art. For the rest, the lament about art is a topos, belonging to the same topos as the 'praise of time past'" (p. 191). There is further discussion of the word "art" in Moser (pp. 202f.).

36. Quoted from *The Divine Comedy of Dante Alighieri: Inferno,* trans. Allen Mandelbaum (1982), p. 55 (all further quotations from this source).

37. VIII, 46ff. (p. 71).

38. XIII, 76–79 (p. 117). In Aeschylus's *Eumenides,* Clytemnestra's shade rises from the Stygian gate and speaks to the Erinyes in the temple about the disgrace which she suffers by being in the realm of the dead, because she is a murderer and must now be neglected for all time (vv. 94ff.) On gravestones in antiquity, too, the dead express their concern for an honorable memory upon earth: "memoriam facitote mihi, ne derisus in imo / infernas intra sedes de crimine passus / nomine Dalmatio semper amatus ab omnes" [Pay heed to my memory, lest derided down below / Within the infernal realm having suffered for the crime / Under the name Dalmatius I [be] beloved of all]. Richmond Lattimore, *Themes in Greek and Latin Epitaphs,* Illinois Studies in Language and Literature, vol. 28, no. 1 (Urbana, Ill., 1942), p. 63.

their prayer: "So, if you can escape these lands of darkness / And see the lovely stars on your return, / When you repeat with pleasure, 'I was there,' / Be sure that you remember us to men."[39] The concern of those beneath the earth for their memory on earth and their pleas for its nurture, as a means of mitigating their suffering, lends to the meeting with those who are wandering on the other side something that is perhaps more moving than the prayers of the pious on earth for intercession for salvation in the promised life which they believe will come hereafter. It can scarcely be determined whether it is simply a melancholy memory of the daylight of the human world that moves the lost souls in their darkness to pray to men to remember them amicably, or whether there is not also a mute hope for intercession by the living. A secret, even though vain, hope for mercy would be human. It is only in the *Purgatorio* that there is theological space for this, where King Manfred, whose repentance—even though it was put off until he lay on his deathbed—has, in spite of his excommunication, brought him to this higher place, builds on the long arm of God's goodness and asks Dante to tell his daughter about the effect of intercession (*buon preghi*) in reducing the period of suffering, "for those over there can do a lot to help us" (*Purgatorio* III, 145). Jacopo del Cassero, who was treacherously murdered, prays "that thou be gracious to me of thy prayers in Fano, so that holy orison be made for me, that I may purge away my heavy offenses."[40] Such pleas impose upon the poet a responsibility for mitigating the suffering of the lost souls and for reducing the length of suffering of those who still await purgation. The "those over there can help" lessens, it is true, his own burden, since it invites the reader to take his part in commemorative prayer too. This might be one of the points of this sort of narration. When others who are petitioning for the mediation of intercession back on the other side, in their homeland, press forward—"(their) one prayer was that others should pray, so that their way to blessedness be sped"[41]—Dante escapes by making promises (VI, 10ff.): he is forced to ask Virgil what the meaning and value of intercession is, since Virgil has, in the

39. XVI, 82 (p. 147).

40. Quoted from *The Divine Comedy of Dante Alighieri*, trans. Carlyle, Okey, and Wicksteed (New York, 1932). Cf. V, 50. Buonconte and a Sienese woman pray that Dante will take home news of them (V, 87, 103, 130ff.). Sapia the Sienese asks for Dante's own prayer—"For this reason you may include me in your own prayer"—and he asks him to restore his reputation in Tuscany (XIII, 147ff.). In the region of the wrathful, Marco of Venice prays that Dante will pray for him (XVI, 51). The tears and prayers of his wife have raised the glutton, Forese Donati, to a higher circle of purgation (XXIII, 85–93).

41. VI, 25ff. (p. 224).

Aeneid, denied the value of prayer in the face of the verdict of the gods.[42] Virgil points to the change in the period of salvation: "And there where I affirmed that point, default could not be amended by prayer, because the prayer was severed from God" (VI, 40). Otherwise he consoles the questioner who asks such sublime questions with the expectation of the meeting with Beatrice.[43] It is not until the last canto of the *Paradiso* that an answer is given. Here, Beatrice, praying in concert with many other souls, folds her hands in her great intercession for the poet; St. Bernard directs this prayer to the Virgin, who, as the intercessor, gives wings to the call to grace so that it can fly to God. Dante is then accorded the ecstatic sight of eternal light, of which *memoria,* the gift of light, enables him to communicate a little.[44] Looking down into the depths from the heavenly heights of paradise, he sees a book in which the leaves of the love of the whole universe are all bound together.[45] Even if his word is only a reflection of this universal bond, he nevertheless feels that joy is enriched by it ("as I say this, I feel that I rejoice").

Like the heathens, the Christians of late antiquity used the same word for their funeral celebrations, *anamnesis* (*memoria*). The meaning of such cultic *memoria* is not the attestation of private mourning and of not wishing to be forgotten. Remembering the dead is an expression of concern for the well-being, in the next world, of the one who has departed this life.[46] Even the days devoted to the memory of the dead in heathen antiquity—the third, seventh,

42. In the underworld Aeneas meets Palinurus, who begs him to take him over the Styx into the land of the blessed. But the prophetess tells him: "Do not hope that the decrees of the gods will be turned aside by praying" (*Aeneid* VI, 376). As consolation they offer him burial, a tomb, the honoring of his grave, and calling the bank upon which he came to grief by his name for all eternity. His memory among men is thus assured.

43. Appearing to him at the end of the *Purgatorio,* Beatrice takes him through the river Lethe, where he forgets all that is evil, and the river Eunoë to refresh his memory of all that is good (XXXIIf.). The question of intercession is not brought up again until the last canto of the *Paradiso.* On the question of meetings of those wandering in the hereafter with persons of the other world, Peter Dinzelbacher, *Vision und Visionsliteratur im Mittelalter,* Monographien zur Geschichte des Mittelalters, no. 23 (Stuttgart, 1981), takes into account only those which take place in heaven (pp. 146–168). Meetings in hell or in purgatory are mentioned only in passing (however, there is no mention of Dante): pp. 94, 97, 102, 158f.

44. See below pp. 320–321.

45. *Paradiso* XXXIII, 85: "Within its depths I saw ingathered, bound by love in one volume, the scattered leaves of all the universe" (p. 605). On the history of the interpretation of this strophe see John Ahern, "Binding the Book: Hermeneutics and Manuscript Production in *Paradiso* 33," *PMLA* 97 (1982): 800–809.

46. Johannes Quasten, *Musik und Gesang in den Kulten der heidnischen Antike und christlichen Frühzeit,* Liturgische Quellen und Forschungen, no. 25 (Münster, 1930), p. 230.

thirtieth, and fortieth after death—survived in the usage of the church,[47] even if the meaning of the memorial ritual was subject to radical changes because of the change in faith. There was a difference between the pagans bringing the funeral feast to the grave on the third day and the Christians celebrating the Eucharist with the feast of love for the dead and the singing of psalms. The church's struggle against pagan cultic music also had consequences for the Christian celebration of the memory of the dead.[48] Commemoration is sacrifice for the dead person, an act of concern for his or her salvation in the next world. Subjective mourning for the dead is included in the objective service of an act of commemoration for his eternal well-being. *Memoria* as a work of intercession preserves emotion in a cultic act.

The liturgical *memoria* of the Benedictine monasteries in the High Middle Ages is also invested with a character of this sort. The monastic sacrifice of intercession gives the dead person a memorial on earth that is not of stone, but—by dint of the entry of his name into the commemorative list that is designed to be read aloud—it ensures that he will be transferred to the heavenly *liber vitae,* and entered into God's eternal memory. The recording of a name in the book of the dead, which those who compile it call—with full confidence—the *liber vitae,*[49] urges God so strongly to transfer it, out of his grace, into the book of life that he keeps with him in heaven,[50] that a vast be-

47. Emil Freistedt, *Altchristliche Totengedächtnistage und ihre Beziehungen zum Jenseitsglauben und Totenkultus der Antike,* Liturgische Quellen und Forschungen, no. 24 (Münster, 1928). On the feast in memory of the dead, see also Karl Baus, *Der Kranz in Antike und Christentum: Eine religionsgeschichtliche Untersuchung mit besonderer Berücksichtigung Tertullians,* Theophaneia, no. 2 (Cologne, 1940), pp. 138–142. On the *memoria* of martyrs, most recently, W. H. C. Frend, "The North African Cult of Martyrs: From Apocalyptic to Hero-Worship," in *Jenseitsvorstellungen in Antike und Christentum: Gedenkschrift für Alfred Stuiber* (*Jahrbuch für Antike und Christentum,* Ergänzungsband 9) (Münster, 1982), pp. 154–167. Further on our theme, Peter von Moos, *Consolatio: Studien zur mittellateinischen Trostliteratur über den Tod und zum Problem der christlichen Trauer,* 4 vols., Münstersche Mittelalterschriften, no. 3 (Munich, 1972). Index volume refers to *Fortleben, Erinnerung, Gedächtnis, memoria, Nachruhm, Name, recordatio, sermo* (*in sermone vivere*), *Totengedächtnis.*

48. Quasten, *Musik und Gesang,* pp. 81–83, 230–247. On the relationship between *memoria* and feast as far as, and including, the mass, see Oexle, "Armut und Armenfürsorge," pp. 71f., 81.

49. On the designation of the confraternal prayer books as *liber vitae* or *liber viventium,* Leo Koep, *Das himmlische Buch in Antike und Christentum: Eine religionsgeschichtliche Untersuchung zur altchristlichen Bildersprache,* Theophaneia, no. 8 (Bonn, 1952), pp. 107f., 113–116. Blumenberg, *Lesbarkeit,* pp. 22–35: "Heaven as a book, the book in heaven."

50. The Salzburg *Liber confraternitatum* (Book of confraternities) finishes the commemoration of the dead with a prayer for the transference of the names from the liturgical book of life into the heavenly book of the living, as a surety for God's granting of grace: "Dignare Domine in

lief in the combined force of prayer of the whole convent and of fraternally related convents, spread over a wide area, emerges from it. The confidence of being able, by means of such an all-embracing act of prayer, to hold God to such a far-reaching act of grace, so that no member of a monastic community would be excluded from it, bears witness to the effect of the idea of communality in an age when the attainment of earthly or celestial salvation outside a community, organized for its pursuit, hardly ever seemed likely. In the case of recognizably deliberate omissions or deletions of names from diptychs or commemorative book lists,[51] the reverse must have been the case, and we are dealing not just with a *damnatio memoriae* on earth, as was the case in antiquity, but with God's assurance that they will be forgotten, in the sense of real damnation, for eternity. Bearing this in mind, we can get some notion of the scruples that the convent had to exercise in making up lists for inclusion in their commemorative books. For was not the entry of a name a means of urging God to transcribe it into his celestial book?[52] Thus, only then can we reckon what it meant theologically when the authors of visions of the

---

memoriam sempiternam commemorare et refrigerare animabus quas de hoc saeculo pacifica adsumptione migrare iussisti omnium christianorum quique confessi defuncti sunt quorumque nomina scripta sunt in libro vitae et super sancto altario sunt posita, adscribi iubeas in libro viventium et a te Domine venim peccatorum consequi mereantur" [Grant, O Lord, that you will commemorate in eternal memory and refresh the souls of all Christian catholics who have died and confessed their sins, whom you have commanded to depart from this life by peaceful assumption, and of whom the names are written in the book of life, that you will command them to be written in the book of the living, and that they will deserve to receive from you the right of sinners] (after Koep, p. 114). Oexle, p. 90, talks of the "efforts of the petitioners to achieve entry into the *liber vitae*, which is regarded as the equivalent of the heavenly book of life"; citations, p. 79.

51. We know of names' being erased from mass diptychs in connection with excommunication. The consequences for life hereafter are taken into account when St. Columba curses a murderer: "His name will be struck out of the book of life. . . . surprised by sudden death, he will be taken to hell." Augustine is of the opinion that, for example, an unjust deletion from the diptychs is less decisive than a deletion which takes place through one's own conscience: "What does it harm a man, that human ignorance has no wish to read his name from that list, if he has not a bad conscience which will delete him from the book of the living?" (*Letters* 78.4; from Koep, 112f.). On the punitive measure of refusal of *memoria* or exclusion from this by deletion of the name in the period from the third to the eleventh centuries, Oexle, p. 83. Macé de la Charité, the poet of the powerful Old French Bible poem from the early fourteenth century, wishes that God would punish, with deletion from the book of life, him who, contrary to Apocalypse 22:18, either lengthens or shortens the text. "Diex sotraye sa porcio Et son ou dou livre de vie" (42616f.). *La Bible de la Macé de la Charité*, vol. 7, *Apocalypse*, pp. 215f.

52. There is an analogy to this in the inscription of a name into the baptismal roll as a preindication of its being written in God's book of life. Gregory of Nyssa says to those being baptized,

afterlife—and this includes Dante as a poet—thought that they knew whom they could expect to find settled in heaven or in hell in their wanderings beyond the grave. The courage of belief in presupposing God's decision—from the knowledge of his revealed being—was stupendous, both in commemorative prayer as well as in the arts, where the artists peopled places beyond the grave with well-known individuals, something which Luther, in his access of rage over his doctrine of grace, was inclined to do.

If the monastic commemorative books that have been handed down since the eighth century were called *liber vitae* (the book of life) then there is, underlying the title, a pronouncement of an unbelievable faith in the effectiveness of monastic commemorative prayer for the dead brothers. Because their names were entered in the book of life—or excluded from it—by God's own hand, the entering of the name of someone who has died, or even of someone who is still alive, into the monastic book of life is an anticipation of what is to be expected from God, of a boldness that is today incomprehensible but that was by no means so alien to medieval thought. The form of paradigmatic prayer that holds up to God his earlier elevations of the pious[53] is meant to remind God of the duty, which rests within his being, of raising men to grace. The name that we bear serves all who know of us as a means of remembering our identity. The entry of that name into a commemorative book is meant to serve as a guarantee to the bearer that God will remember him as precisely that person whom the brothers commemorate in their intercession. In Early Middle High German, the verb *manen* (to move someone to do something by recalling something to him) is one of the most frequent words

---

"Give me your names, so that I may enter them in the visible books and write them in black ink: but may God enter them on the everlasting tablets, writing with his finger." St. Basil says, "You shall be entered in this book, so that you may be transcribed into that book which is above us." This and other citations in Koep, pp. 97–100. The commemoration of the dead in the sacrificial mass, after the transubstantiation, with the reading aloud of their names from the diptychs in order to recommend them to God's grace (Josef Andreas Jungmann, *Missarum Sollemnia* [Vienna, 1948], 2:295–308), can include the prayer that they be entered into the celestial book (Koep, pp. 100–109, here p. 108). "Thus we can say about the connection between the diptych of the mass and the book of life the same thing that is said about the baptismal roll: the inscription signifies the hope and the prayer that God will make the entry in his book." Oexle, p. 85, speaks of "the responsibility that the danger of forgetting laid on those whose duty was the memoria." A prose writing of the twelfth century sees Mary as keeping the book of life (*Analecta hymnica* 54.227): "Ave, mundi domina, Nostra scribe nomina In libro viventium" [Hail, mistress of the world! Write our names in the book of the living!].

53. Even in antiquity, God is reminded of his earlier acts and therefore of his potential future acts.

meaning "to pray." According to legend, Gregory the Great, by his impassioned commemorative prayer for Trajan as a *rex iustus,* moved God, flying in the face of the whole of theology, to rescue the unbaptized one from hell. God suffers with some irritation the fact that the power of prayer forces him to bring about the salvation of the heathen.[54] Dante observes with a startling visionary clarity—not as a result of prayer—the concrete individual consequences in the afterlife for people who have lived on earth, and pronounces judgment on them, as though he were God, by assigning them to heaven, hell, or purgatory. There is no theologian now living who would dare do this for figures from our most recent memory in the way in which Dante did.

Even earlier wanderers in the next world who were parts of visionary legends meet, in the places where those who have been damned or saved are congregated, historical figures or those who have recently died. Supposedly certain—as a result of knowledge gleaned from the history of revelation—of the difference between good and evil, poets and artists have time and again, either innocently, impartially, presumptuously, or with faith, presumed upon God's idea of salvation for mankind in order to separate, in advance, into their allotted places in the afterlife, the good and the wicked, Christians and heathens, the cursed and the elect, the damned and the saved, as though God's grace could be bound by such preliminary decisions. The reliefs on early Christian sarcophagi have been seen as a "form of pleading, with which the inhabitant of the coffin argues the case for his future fate." The dead, in representations of the Last Judgment, are depicted as men of the age of thirty-three—the age at which Christ was crucified and rose from the dead. This is true of Henry the Lion who, though he died at a ripe age, is depicted, on his sepulchre in Brunswick, as dying at the age of thirty-three. It is by means of superimpositions of pictorial reality of this sort on the reality of life itself that human claims to resemble Christ—even to the point of resurrection—are made upon God and he is expected to honor them.[55] Seen in such a con-

54. Ohly, *The Damned and the Elect,* pp. 132ff. (and bibliography); Leopold Kretzenbacher, "Legendenbilder aus dem Feuerjenseits: Zum Motiv des 'Losbetens' zwischen Kirchenlehre und erzählendem Volksglauben" (Österreichische Akademie der Wissenschaften, philologisch-historische Klasse, *Sitzungsberichte,* 370) (Vienna, 1980); Donat de Chapeaurouge, "Die Rettung der Seele: Biblische Exempla und mittelalterliche Adaptation," in *Vestigiis Bibliae,* ed. Heimo Reinitzer (Hamburg, 1980), 2:35–88, p. 68.

55. On the sarcophagi, Theodor Klauser, "Frühchristliche Sarkophage in Bild und Wort," *Halbjahresschrift: Antike Kunst* 3 (1966): 21f. Percy Ernst Schramm contrasts pictorial reality and actual reality in *Sphaira-Globus-Reichsapfel* (Stuttgart, 1958), p. 4. Cf. also de Chapeaurouge (see n. 54 above), pp. 66, 70, 78.

text, the entry, in "the service of commemorative prayer" of the name of the dead Benedictine brothers into the *liber vitae* of the monastery bears witness to a pious trust in the power of prayer, and also an expectation, expressed in prayer, that God will transfer the names of all the dead who are entered in the monastic book to the book of life that he maintains.[56] The entry of names so that intercession can be made in the memory of the community of prayer stands surety for the change of the cloistered life into celestial life, and that is the way that Hugh of Fouilloy (Hugo de Folieto) looked upon it in his book *De claustro animae*.[57]

The Middle Ages depicted terrestial space in the *mappa mundi*, and time from the creation to, potentially, the end of the world in the world chronicle, and using the pictorial concept of God as the one who embraces the world also showed the cosmos as a whole in his hands and recognized the view that terrestrial time and space were two limited universals. If, today, the historian embeds his subject within a concept by which he encompasses totality as a continuum of history that links every possible change, he forgets much too easily—as perhaps the medieval universalist did—the dependence of all living memory on the group. Yet it would be sheer folly to believe that his con-

56. On the designation of memorial books as *liber vitae* or *memoriale*, see Schmid, "Das liturgische Gebetsgedenken," pp. 35ff., 40, 44. The Salzburg commemorative book asks God to transfer the names of the dead from the *liber vitae*, which lies on the altar, into his *liber viventium* (p. 36 n. 54 above). The letter of Clement is aware of the existence in God's eternal memory of the names that are inscribed there (Greek citation). *Die apostolischen Väter*, new edition of the Funk edition, ed. Karl Bihlmeyer, vol. 1 (Tübingen, 1956), p. 60. Adamus Scotus calls the mother house of his order in Prémontré a *liber vitae* for the sister convents: "Sit eis exemplar, at forma, speculum quoque, et quasi quidam liber vitae: in quo evidenter, quid eligere debeant, quidve respuere, legant. Videant in lectione ejusdem libri, quam prompta esse debeat affabilitas in porta" [Be an example to them, and a form and a mirror as well, and be as if you were a certain book of life, in which, manifestly, they may read what they should choose, or what they should cast out. May they see in the reading of this same book how visible should be the quality of kindness within the gate] (*PL*, 198, col. 613B). What is to be read further in this *liber vitae* is presented in breadth for the life of the convent. The meaning of the *liber vitae* which is attested to here (ca. 1180), "exemplary model of an ideal way of life," suggests that we should pursue the meaning of *liber vitae* systematically. At the same time (ca. 1180) there is a "Book of Memory" in a profane sense—which is to be found elsewhere as well—in the work of the classical Persian epic poet Nizami: "The magic of this single hour would be enough to erase much of what is in the book of memory. What do the fortunate ones care for past sorrows?" Nizami, *Die sieben Geschichten der sieben Prinzessinnen*, trans. and ed. Rudolf Gelpke (Zürich, 1959), p. 34. Koep (see n. 49 above), does not go as far as the Middle Ages.

57. *De claustro animae*, in *PL*, 176, cols. 1017–1218. Bibliography in Ohly, "Problems of Medieval Significs and Hugh of Folieto's Dove Miniature," in this volume, pp. 68–135.

cept—first completely developed in historicism—of the quintessential historicity of the universe of all things, even of nature, his form of scientific memory of the ages of all time, was a common human one, and not one that is bound up with scholars in the academy, and one that spreads all the more widely among various schools, as more and more groups who have their own memories disappear. More limited group memories,[58] like those of the family or of friends, of village or town, of church congregation and religion, of classes and cultural levels, of tribes and peoples, of a community of experience, destiny, or generation, foster a power that has a much stronger effect in their presence than our own, largely fruitless, universal historical memory. For epochs that tend to level things out less than our own does, for example, the Middle Ages, this was more definitely true than it is today, when we are faced with happenings that take place with increasing frequency in a large geographical area. The wide range of literary forms—which permit the past to appear in an idiosyncratic light according to the individual genre—bears witness to a more than social differentiation of its superpersonal memory, a difference of historical outlooks that are otherwise specific. We are only partway to learning how to recognize this difference as unique and as one that is valid among others. The dependence of genres, forms, and choices of historical memory—which is not necessarily congruent with group dependence—cannot be erased from the sources, but rather, we must admit its validity so as to grasp what is special in each case. This is also true of forms of memory in the various genres of literary history that still await a systematic investigation of their genre-specific memory.[59] The convent-bound liturgical *memo-*

58. Maurice Halbwachs, *Les cadres sociaux de la mémoire* (Paris, 1952), *La mémoire collective* (Paris, 1950), and *Das kollektive Gedächtnis* (Stuttgart, 1967), contrasts collective memory with that of history. He determines that "history in general begins at the point where tradition ceases—at a moment in which social memory is extinguished and disintegrates" (p. 66). Rudolf Heinz, "Maurice Halbwachs' Gedächtnisbegriff," *Zeitschrift für philosophische Forschung* 23 (1969): 73–85. On the connection between history and memory, Hanno Helbling, *Der Mensch im Bild der Geschichte,* Erfahrung und Denken, no. 30 (Berlin, 1969), pp. 18–41, "Gedächtnis." Proof note: On the subject of group memory, there appeared, while this was in the press, Otto Gerhard Oexle, "Liturgische Memoria und historische Erinnerung: Zur Frage nach dem Gruppenbewußtsein und dem Wissen der eignen Geschichte in den mittelalterlichen Gilden," in *Tradition als historische Kraft: Festschrift for Karl Hauck,* ed. Norbert Kamp and Joachim Wollasch (Berlin, 1982), pp. 323–340.

59. Herbert Grundmann, "Geschichtsschreibung im Mittelalter" in *Deutsche Philologie im Aufriß,* ed. W. Stammler, vol. 3 (Berlin, 1957), cols. 1272–1336, discusses first the genres, then the epochs. Friedrich Ohly, "Halbbiblische und außerbiblische Typologie" (1975), cited from Ohly, *Schriften* (see n. 10 above), pp. 361–400, here pp. 362 f.: "Historiography as a configuring epochal

ria of monastic intercession for the living and the dead, who are to be recommended to God's memory by this means, builds—as the group memory of those included in such commemorative prayer—a bridge between the human-temporal memory of the brothers or sisters with whom one was associated and the eternal memory of God, to which they are recommended for entry into the book as a service of brotherly love extending beyond time. The faith that this will be done for them can also keep the laymen who are associated with the convent bound to their commemorative community.

The Augustinian doctrine of the Trinity set a high value on *memoria* in the Middle Ages. According to this doctrine, the three powers of the soul—memory, understanding, and will (*memoria, intelligentia,* and *voluntas*), with which *mens, notitia,* and *amor* (mind, conception, and love) are coordinated—are by their nature created by God to serve as analogical knowledge of the three divine persons.[60] The threefold quality of the powers of the

---

memory brings the picture of what has been, and thus the expectation of what is to come, in the field of forms into individual expressions—unchangeable from genre to genre—of what is determined as being memorable. The world chronicle as a history of salvation, *historia* as the history of a people, the annals of the history of what has happened, the legends of the saints, the life of the ruler, regional or local history, the liturgical commemoration of the dead, the *chanson de geste,* the romance of antiquity or Arthurian romance, the *planctus* and the panegyric, legend and occasional poem, gnomic verse and satire, and whatever other forms there may be—each has its own idiosyncratic view of history." Individual representations of the genres of historical sources began to appear in 1975 in the series *Typologie des sources du moyen âge occidental.* See Karl Heinrich Krüger, "Das Institut d'études médiévales in Löwen und seine 'Typologie des sources du moyen âge occidental': Ein Bericht," *Frühmittalterliche Studien* 10 (1976): 437–445.

60. Michael Schmaus, *Die psychologische Trinitätslehre des heiligen Augustinus,* Münstersche Beiträge zur Theologie 11 (Münster, 1927; reprinted 1967, with an afterword, pp. iii*–xxv*, including bibliography since 1927), pp. 264–284, 313–331. The historical relationship between the powers of the soul and Cicero's distinction between the three parts of *prudentia* (*memoria, intelligentia, providentia*) still needs to be investigated: on this subject, Frances A. Yates, *The Art of Memory* (London, 1966), pp. 20f., (Cicero) p. 54, (Alcuin) p. 56, (John of Salisbury) pp. 174f., p. 183 (Raimundus Lullus and mention of the powers of the soul). Michael Schmaus, "Das Fortwirken der Augustinischen Trinitätspsychologie bis zur Karolingischen Zeit," in *Vitae et Veritati: Festchrift, Karl Adam* (Düsseldorf, 1956), pp. 44–56. Alfred Schindler, *Wort und Analogie in Augustins Trinitätslehre,* Hermeneutische Untersuchungen zur Theologie, no. 4 (Tübingen, 1965), p. 41. Peter Kern, *Trinität, Maria, Inkarnation. Studien zur Thematik der deutschen Dichtung des späteren Mittelalters,* Philologische Studien und Quellen, no. 55 (Berlin, 1971), pp. 163, 250f. (citations from the German mystics). Stephan Otto, "Die Funktion des Bildbegriffs in der Theologie des zwölften Jahrhunderts," Beiträge zur Geschichte der Philosophie und Theologie des Mittelalters XV/1 (Münster, 1963). Bibliography and citations from the Middle Ages in Hartmut Freytag, *Kommentar zur frühmittelhochdeutschen Summa Theologiae,* Medium Aevum, Philologische Studien, no. 19 (Munich, 1970), pp. 42–44.

soul in man is so subordinated to the Holy Trinity that its three members—which "mutually embrace each other in their totality"[61] and cooperate in every work—help us to understand the unified effect of the persons of the Trinity by analogy with the triad of the powers of the soul.[62] Thanks to the triad *memoria, intelligentia,* and *voluntas,* as an image of God, man—who holds God in his memory—can recognize and love him at the height of joy. "Hoc est plenum gaudium nostrum, quo amplius non est, frui Trinitate, ad cuius imaginem facti sumus" [This is our full joy, than which there is no greater, to enjoy the Trinity, in whose image we are made].[63] The great doctrine of *memoria* in book 10 of the *Confessions* reaches its high point in the knowledge of the *vita beata,* first from the memory of all men's experience,[64] then from the true *vita beata,* but only from the gift of an experience of God that was not to be found by searching in the depths of memory, as long as God had not entered there—it is a joy that is not granted to the impious. The theological dimension of memory is not gained in what is present in it, but through a "learning" about God that is a sort of revelation.[65]

61. Schmaus (see n. 60 above), p. 275, p. 276: "thus, in this way thought and love inhabit memory."

62. Schmaus, p. 283: "It cannot be denied the spirit has a memory, a reason, and a will. Through the possession of these three powers it is an image of the three-personed God," insofar as "the one spirit makes itself felt in a threefold function" (p. 285): "It is the memory of the spirit of itself, the knowledge of itself and the love of itself that is, in a more intensive form, an image of the Trinity as memory, as knowledge, and love of other objects."

63. *De trinitate* I, 8, 18; Schmaus, p. 308, n. 3.

64. The question "utrum in memoria sit beata vita" [whether happiness is in the memory]. (*Confessions* X, 20, 29):)—"Ubi ergo et quando expertus sum vitam meam beatam, ut recorder eam et amem et desiderem?" [Where and when, therefore, did I experience a state of blessed happiness, so that I am able to remember it and love it and long for it?]—is answered by Augustine (X, 21, 31): "Quae quoniam res est, quam se expertum non esse nemo potest dicere, propterea reperta in memoria recognoscitur, quando beatae vitae nomen auditor" [Since there is no thing that anyone can say he has not experienced because he finds it in his memory and recognizes it when he hears the phrase "a state of happiness"].

65. *Confessions* X, 22, 32: "Est enim gaudium, quod non datur impiis, sed eis, qui te gratis colunt, quorum gaudium tu ipse es. Et ipsa est beata vita, gaudere ad te, de te, propter te ipsa est et non est altera" [For there is a joy that is not given to those who do not love you, but only to those who love you for your own sake. You yourself are their joy. Happiness is to rejoice in you and for you and because of you. This is true happiness and there is no other]; X, 24, 35: "Ecce quantum spatiatus sum in memoria mea quaerens te, domine, et non te inveni extra eam. Neque enim aliquid de te inveni, quod non meminissem, ex quo didici te. Nam ex quo didici te, non sum oblitus tui" [See how I have explored the vast field of my memory in search of you, O Lord. And I have not found you outside it? For I have discovered nothing about you except what I have remembered since the time I first learned about you. Ever since then I have not forgotten you]; X, 25, 36:

While Augustine does not assign one power of the soul to one member of the Trinity, though for him *memoria* does have the greatest affinity with God the Father,[66] later tradition likes to simplify his complicated web of thought, so that *memoria* is linked to God the Father, *intelligentia* to the Son, and *voluntas* to the Holy Spirit. The doctrine—widespread, especially from the twelfth century onward—of the three powers of the soul and their correspondences in the Trinity[67] is reflected, for example, in the German-language interpretation of the St. Trudperter Song of Songs (ca. 1160).[68] In this work we find the terms *gehuht* (memory), *vernunst* (reason), and *wille* (will) grouped together on at least ten occasions. There, too, it is said of *memoria* that if the soul has a body, *memoria* forms its stomach or its feet.[69] Mary received the

---

"dignatus es habitare in memoria mea, ex quo te didici" [And yet you have deigned to be present in my memory ever since I first learned of you]; X, 26, 37: "Ubi ergo te inveni, ut discerem te? Neque enim tam eras in memoria mea, priusquam te discerem. Ubi ergo te inveni, nisi in te supra me?" [Where then did I find you so that I could learn of you. For you were not in my memory before I learned of you. Where else then did I find you, to learn of you, unless it was in yourself, above me?]. Bibliography on the doctrine of *memoria* in Meier, "Vergessen, Erinnern, Gedächtnis" (see n. 8 above), pp. 188f.

66. Schmaus (see n. 60 above), p. 330: against unequivocal assigning of powers of the soul to persons of the Trinity, p. 403 ff. et alibi.

67. Schmaus, p. 418: "The writers of sentences and the summists in the second half of the twelfth century, like, for example, Bandinus, Gandulf, Petrus Pictaviensis, Praepositinus, Petrus Comestor, and above all Petrus Lombardus, take up trinitarian speculation in their work. It plays a leading role in the works of the mystics and the psychologists of the twelfth century. It went from Petrus Lombardus's sentences to the high scholastic commentaries on sentences. In the third distinction of the first book, the commentators start to talk of the image of the Trinity in the soul."

68. *Das St. Trudperter Hohelied: Kritische Ausgabe, Text, Wörterverzeichnis und Anmerkungen*, ed. Hermann Menhardt, Rheinische Beiträge und Hilfsbücher zur germanischen Philologie und Volkskunde, no. 22 (Halle, 1934).

69. I have translated the citations from the *St. Trudperter Hohelied* (except for the terms for the powers of the soul). The material in parentheses is explanation. There are three places where the soul is given an anthropomorphic body, the members of which form the powers of the soul in different variations. The image of God is imprinted on a coin. "The soul resembles this (it is created after his image). The body is complete above, but divided beneath. That means it has a head on top and two feet below. Thus, our *wille* is our legs and feet. The head is our *ratio*, that is, our reason. It coordinates our two wills, one for the body and one for the soul. Your memory is a stomach in which you eat and digest your thoughts" (141, 21–29; Augustine, *Confessions* X, 14, 21: "memoria quasi venter est animi" [the memory is a sort of stomach of the soul]). Or we can adapt it: "Now let us see what the head of our soul is. That is our *will*, which—like the head of all members—coordinates our soul. Our *reason* is the heart. Our memory is feet and legs" (129, 20–23). If the soul is viewed anthropomorphically as the bride, the powers of the soul are, in a

word from the Holy Ghost through the ears of her memory.[70] Among the persons of the Trinity, memory is ascribed to God the Father.[71] The flame of the Holy Spirit's love also sets fire to *ratio* and *voluntas*.[72]

In the last canto of the *Divine Comedy*, Dante prays, as he wakes from the ecstatic view of eternal light that has been given to him and after he has otherwise asked the Muses and Apollo for inspiration from this light, that it give

---

sevenfold series of substantive statements about the will, parts of her body. "Your will is" the feet that carry the memory. It is the eyes with which your *reason* can see. Your *will* is "the mouth and the arms with which you embrace and love your beloved" (13, 26–30).

70. The Holy Ghost accompanies the word into the soul of Mary, which is open to its reception even though her body is closed to it: "This virgin opened the ears of *memory* and of worship with which she had been listening for a long time. There the Holy Ghost was the conductor of the word through the closed body into the open soul. Her *reason*, her *memory*, her *will*—all her *senses* were open to God" (9, 9–14).

71. The triads of the three powers of the soul intertwine artistically and, with a host of theological connections, with those of the theological virtues (faith, hope, and charity), the properties of the Trinity (power, wisdom, and goodness), the acts of the history of salvation (creation, redemption, and bridehood), and the three choirs of angels (cherubim, seraphim, and thrones) in the bridal encounter of the powers which reach up to God and the powers which come to meet them from above. A mystical trait of the bridal assemblage of the powers of the soul with the Trinity asserts itself here: "Now the marriage begins. Now raise your *memory* together with your holy faith to the power of the Creator. It will be joined to him like a bride. Raise up your *reason* with hope to the wisdom of your redeemer. It will be joined to him like the beloved to the beloved. Raise up your *will* with holy love to the highest good of the spirit. Your soul will be joined to him in a wedded and just community of love. There it will melt like wax in the heat of the Holy Ghost. Thus, the seraphim will take your *will* thither. Thus, cherubim will take your *reason* to wisdom. Thus, the thrones will take your *memory* to the seat of the all-highest. That is the very best of weddings" (13, 4–17). The following anagogical promise bears witness to the coordination of the powers of the soul to the persons of the Trinity and the theological virtues: "Our faith leads our *memory* in days to come to his wisdom. There truth makes us be silent, for we are liars. Love constantly leads our *will* to goodness. No one can make us fall silent. There his grace and mercy intercede for us" (132, 6–14). "Let our *memory*, *reason*, and our *will* prepare themselves to receive the Holy Ghost (in his seven gifts). *Memory* remembers sins in fear before the Lord, in shame before the Father. Our *reason* draws us to God with true inwardness and with just works. Our *will* rests with God, with men, and with our neighbors. Thus, man becomes one with God in *wisdom*" (the highest gift of the Holy Ghost; 5, 13–21). If our soul melts away it becomes whole with the God of *goodness*, *wisdom*, and *power*: "that is: divine goodness with our *will*. That is the highest wisdom with our *reason*. That is, awful power with our *memory*. This joy is the highest"(18, 27–30).

72. Man must offer himself to the fire of the Holy Spirit's love. "It sets his *memory* on fire, brings his *reason* to a white heat and his *will* to the melting point" (1.17f.) This fourth concept is added to a group of twelve conceptual and verbal triads: "He (God) wishes us to practice our *memory*, our *reason*, and our good *will*" (53.9–11).

him *memoria* of the indescribable so that he may pass on but a spark of this light; *memoria* is the ability to speak in words what is otherwise ineffable.[73] This is not the technical *memoria* of rhetoric that organizes the text as a work. Here *memoria* is the medium through which the numinous finds entry into language. Torquato Tasso directs his poet's prayer for inspiration to allow him to compose his crusading epic, *Gerusalemme liberata,* not only to Mary as the highest of the muses (I, 2); he also calls upon memory for help, when he has to introduce the Christian heroes in a passage thirty stanzas long: "O Memory, Time's enemy and Oblivion's, steward and guardian of all things, let your powers aid me, that I may recount each leader and every squadron of that host; let their ancient fame shine forth in splendor and resound, that now is made silent and dark by the passing years; let my speech be graced with that which (taken from your stores) every generation may hear, none may extinguish" (I, 36).[74] Just as it would miss the mark in the case of Dante, so would it also not be true of Tasso for us to assume that the *memoria* asked for, or prayed for, by the poet was simply to provide a mass of memories. It would miss the point of Homer's appeal to the Muses in the second book of the Iliad, where his appeal for help with their "remembering" is directed to the divine Muses of Olympus—as the omniscient ones—all of whom appeared before the gates of Troy, and is made because of the inexpressible military might assembled before the city (II, 484–493). It is not a question of the completeness of the catalog of heroes, as such, that the poet would otherwise fear to have missed. Poets—like Homer, Dante, and Tasso—need memory from

73. *Paradiso* XXXIII:

Thenceforward was my vision mightier than our discourse, which faileth at such sight, and faileth memory at so great an outrage . . . 55
O light supreme who so far doth uplift thee o'er mortal thoughts, relend unto my mind a little of what thou then didst seem, 67
And give my tongue such power that I may leave only a single sparkle of thy glory unto the folk to come; 70
For by returning to my memory somewhat, and by a little sounding in these verses, more of thy victory will be conceived. 73

74. The appeal in canto XVII, 3, where the heathen armies are presented as though the poet's natural memory were not equal to such a task, corresponds to this: "Now, Muse, recall for me what were the times, what was then the state of things, what armies, what powers the mighty emperor possessed, what subject peoples and what allied, when out of the South he brought to war his forces, his kings and the farthest Orient. You alone can tell me how the leaders and their bands, and half the world assembled under arms." Quotations from Torquato Tasso, *Jerusalem Delivered,* trans. and ed. Ralph Nash (Detroit, 1987).

heaven in order not to miss the glory of what is worth preserving, something that the divine beings alone have control over. "For you are goddesses," says Homer, "You are present and know everything. But we are without knowledge about the glory of which we hear tell" (485f.). The Muses, the light, have *memoria*, memory from on high, as a surety that what is to be said will be proclaimed in the name of the highest authority. For otherwise, says Homer, "I cannot proclaim and call by name, even if I had ten tongues and ten mouths, a tireless voice, and a heart of iron, if you—Muses of Olympus, daughters of aegis-shaking Zeus—do not remind me how many there were before Troy" (488–492).[75] St. Paul replaces memory from on high with love, as the highest legitimation of speech, "Though I speak with the tongues of men and of angels and have not love, I am as sounding brass or a clanging symbol" (1 Corinthians 13:1). In Hölderlin's poem dedicated to the fire of inspiration, "As Though on a Holiday," it is said of the poet's soul that high memory and love, the divine and the human, are united in the work: "The thoughts of the common spirit they are, quietly ending in the poet's mind. So that swiftly visited, for a long time familiar to infinite powers, it quakes with recollection, and set on fire by the holy ray, the fruit conceived in love, the work of gods and men, the song, that it may bear witness to both, succeeds."[76]

For the Greeks the mother of the Muses is Mnemosyne, "memory," and she survives in her daughters.[77] Thanks to Mnemosyne and the Muses, poets know the power of verse that tears them from the clutches of forgetfulness.[78] "Mortals do not remember what does not enter the magnificent fleece of poetry" (Pindar). It preserves the poet himself from being forgotten. "But the

75. Elke Barmeyer, *Die Musen: Ein Beitrag zur Inspirationstheorie,* Humanistische Bibliothek Reihe 1, Abhandlungen 2 (Munich, 1968), p. 17 on Homer: "The singer confesses that the artistic happening realizes itself as memory, that memory flows toward him from a superhuman source." The chapter "Inspiration as Memory" (pp. 113–124) is divided into three sections, "Kleos: Manifest meaning," "Artistic Memory," and "Mnemosyne."

76. Friedrich Hölderlin, *Sämtliche Werke,* ed. Friedrich Beissner, vol. 2, pt. 1, *Gedichte nach 1800* (Stuttgart, 1951), p. 119. See Barmeyer, pp. 118f. Reference is made to the concept of memory in the poetics of Emil Staiger, as well as to the significance of *mémoire* and *souvenir* in the work of Proust.

77. Theiler, "Erinnerung" (see n. 1 above), col. 44. "Art. Mneme, Mnemosyne," in *Historisches Wörterbuch der Philosophie* (1980), vol. 5, cols. 1441–1444, by G. Plamböck (*Antike*), R. Meyer-Kalkus (nineteenth and twentieth centuries), and P. Stemmer ("Aby Warburg"). With reference to music, Augustine says that what the spirit sees is immortal, like numbers, but the evanescent sound needs to be imprinted on the memory, so that poets had cleverly made the Muses daughters of Jupiter and of memory (*De ordine* II, 15, in *PL*, 32, col. 1014).

78. The following citations are in the section "Mnemosyne" in Barmeyer, pp. 120–124.

golden Muses have made me truly happy and, when I am dead, I shall not pass to Lethe" (Sappho). Helen says of herself and Paris: "Zeus decreed a sad fate for us, so that in the future we shall also live in song for generations yet to come" (*Iliad* VI, 357f.). For us it follows: poetry is for man an artistic vessel by which he can recall the world of his potential experience. Roman antiquity, too, knows that poets make man immortal. Horace places his, "I finished a monument more lasting than bronze" (*Carmina* III, 30) at the beginning of his work, as an inscription that will assure him eternity, in order to proclaim the fact that his work will last longer than any metal. Ovid concluded his *Metamorphoses* with the proud word "Vivam" [I shall live] in the expectation of everlasting glory when his name was raised indelibly above the stars. Horace's ode about poets as those who confer glory refers to Pindar, whose Epinicians saved Aeacus from the Styx, and to Ennius, whose annals rescued Romulus from silence. Horace's words sound like brass: "dignum laude virum vetat Musa mori: coelo Musa beat" [the muse forbids a man worthy of praise to die: the Muse raises him to heaven] (*Odes* IV, 8, 28f.). With faith in the far-reaching power of his word, Virgil promises Euryalus and Nisus, his Trojan friends who have fallen in battle, that their memory will be eternal, a promise that he bases on the following: "Oh happy pair! If ever any power reside within my songs, let no day pass without your being remembered, because the house of Aeneas inhabits the fortress of the Capitoline rock and the father of Rome is in command."[79] Ovid expresses a charming thought in the *Ars amatoria,* where he advises young girls to carry their pretty faces into the crowd and there find favor, for only what is shown can delight. This is true in art as well. If Apelles, the great painter, had not shown his famous picture of Venus arising from the waves in the temple in Cos, "the goddess would, to this day, still be lying hidden in the waves of the sea."[80] Art creates myth, and the artist survives only in what is brought to the light, and this is true of the poet as well: "Do the holy singers strive for aught but fame? / This is the only desire

79.

Fortunati ambo! Si quid mea carmina possunt
nulla dies unquam memori vos eximet aevo,
dum domus Aeneae Capitoli immobile saxum
accolet imperiumque pater Romanus habebit.

80. Publius Ovidius Naso, *Ars Amatoria:*

Si Venerem Cous nusquam posuisset Apelles,
Mersa sub aequoreis illa lateret aquis.
(III, 401)

that inspires us when we write / Gods and kings formerly set great store by poets." And even if this does not still hold true today, there is still: "But it is beautiful to be on the alert for fame, who would know of Homer / If it were not for the *Iliad,* that immortal work?"[81]

In Virgil's fifteenth eclogue, Mopsus, the shepherd, sings the lament for Daphnis to the shepherds. He wishes his grave to have a poem on it ("et tumulum facite et tumulum superaddite carmen" [both make a tomb and place a verse on it] [42]), for this would proclaim that the shepherd's fame reaches to the stars. The highest form of remembrance that the poet accords his hero is his apotheosis. In antiphonal song, Mopsus and Menalcas raise those who are lost above the stars, and forest and mountain proclaim with them: "deus, deus, ille, Menalca" [a god, a god, Menalca is a god] (64). The fact that shepherds here are founding a cult for shepherds—"As to Bacchus and Ceres, year by year shall the husbandmen pay their vows; thou, too, shalt bind them to their vows" (79)—adds a certain facility to the thought that poets create gods.[82]

81.

Quid petitur sacris nisi tantum fama poetis?
Hoc votum nostri summa laboris habet.
Cura deum fuerunt olim regumque poetae . . .

[What is sought by the sacred poets but fame alone? Toil we never so hard this is all we ask. Poets were once the care of gods and kings.] (III, 403)

Sed fame vigilare iuvat. Quis nosset Homerum,
Ilias aeternum si latuisset opus?

[But the watching of fame brings rewards. Who would have known Homer if his eternal work had lain hidden?] (III, 413)

When the poet Propertius meets the god Amor, he makes a strong point of the question of who would sing of love if the god destroys him (1, 9). The poet is the founder and the monitor of his fame; the god's respect and honor is linked to the praises and extolling of his being through the mouth of the poet: "haec mea Musa levis gloria magna tua est" [This my light muse is your great glory]. Erich Burck, "Amor bei Plautus und Properz," in *Commentationes in honorem Edwin Linkomies,* Arctos: Acta philologica fennica, n.s., no. 1 (Helsinki, 1954), pp. 32–60, here p. 56. In the underworld, Scipio tells Achilles that his fame has grown because of Homer: "crevit tua carmine virtus" [your fame has grown in song] (Silius Italicus, *Punica* XIII, 797).

82. Hermann Raabe writes on this eclogue in *Plurima mortis imago: Vergleichende Interpretationen zur Bildersprache Vergils,* Zetemata, no. 59 (Munich, 1974), pp. 14–19. Oblivion consumes fame: "gloria vitae durat apud superos, nec edunt oblivia laudem" (Silius Italicus, *Punica* XIII, 664).

When gods and kings forgot that they rely upon poets and that they survive thanks to sculptors and painters, the builders of temples and, above all, poets, the works, too, lost in significance in the world and the poets also lost a part of their fame. For did not the *Aeneid* create Aeneas for all time, and is the same not true, to a large extent, of the Greek gods?—and where did the Roman myths survive more powerfully than in Ovid's *Metamorphoses*? Juvencus's firm belief—expressed at the beginning of his Gospel harmony—which derives from Ovid's proud "Vivam"[83] and from the belief of the poets of antiquity in the perpetuation of their own names (of a *longa fama*), now changed through Christ, for the Christian poet, into the reward of immortality (*aeterna laudis*),[84] reveals an attitude to the poet's fame that, even though many in the Middle Ages subscribed to this humble attitude, began to lose its effect, especially in the baroque, so that the perpetuation of one's own or another's name would never again be one of the poet's goals.[85] The beginning of Gottfried von Strassburg's *Tristan*, "If we failed in our esteem of those,"[86] demands, in the final instance, that he too should be remembered. Dante, who commemorated more dead and living people than any other poet, thanks Brunetto Latini for his doctrine of man's self-perpetuation ("m'insegnavate come l'uom s'eterna"; *Inferno* XV, 85). And Villani, in his Florentine chronicle, again wishes to serve the perpetual memory (*memoria*) of Dante and of his great work.[87] Aeneas Silvio in 1453 writes to Cardinal Olesnicki in Cracow in memory not of figures of literature but of the authors of antiquity and the church—"the endless stream of those who wrote for

83. Ovid, *Amores* I, 15, 42.

84. On Juvencus, see Ohly, *Schriften*, p. 379f. The Christian renunciation of earthly fame is promulgated by—among many others—Petrarch's "Africa" verses (II, 400–482). Even the highest fame, he says, is limited by transitoriness and final oblivion. Even a new Ennius, who, at a future time, would try to detain the Muses, who were long ago introduced into Rome by his predecessor, would not be able to prevent the death of everything in oblivion, where the monument becomes dust and the writing on it is wiped out. Petrarch therefore points to eternal salvation in heaven, which outlasts all earthly fame, where man will be "sine fine beatus Et sine mensura" [Blessed without limit and without measure] (481f.).

85. Citations in Grimm's *Deutsches Wörterbuch*, 3, col. 1204, under the lemma "ewigen" (Johannes Rothe, von Birken); 12/1, col. 285, under "verewigen" (Stieler, Logau, Lichtwer); 4 1,1 col. 1932, under "Gedächtnis" (Frisius).

86. See p. 338.

87. Von Müller, *Gloria Bona Fama Bonorum* (see n. 13 above), p. 173, 178f. Himself a victim of public *fama*, Dante for the sake of his self-respect ("timore d'infamia"; *Convivium* I, 2) writes proudly against his disdain (p. 184f.).

posterity. Behold what a powerful horde of those who died are yet not dead!"[88] Siegmund von Birken praises Justus Georg Schottelius's services to the German language: "He researched into it and searched and found. / Many a book that he gave to the world has perpetuated his name."[89] Another saying of the aging Goethe postulates: "Say nothing of the transitory! No matter how it occurred. We are here to perpetuate ourselves!"[90] The theme of the perpetuation of the self or of another is timeless. As long ago as the New Empire in Egypt (1550–1080 B.C.) words of wisdom remind us of the survival of Hardedef from the Old Empire in his Book of Wisdom (ca. 2400 B.C.):

Man decays, his corpse is dust,
All his kin have perished:
But a book makes him remembered,
Through the mouth of its reciter.
Better is a book than a well-built house,
Than tomb-chapels in the west;
Better than a solid mansion,
Than a stela in the temple!

Is there one here like Hardedef? . . .
Is there another like Ptahhotep? . . .
Death made their names forgotten
But books made them remembered.[91]

We hear the same thing from the later Orient as well. A king in the Persian epic, Nizami, writes—as the poet of his Alexander epic of the twelfth century—

88. Quoted by Franz Josef Worstbrock, "Die Antikenrezeption in der mittelalterlichen und humanistischen Ars dictandi," in *Die Rezeption der Antike,* ed. August Buck, Wolfenbüttler Abhandlungen zur Renaissanceforschung, no. 1 (Hamburg, 1981), pp. 187–207, here p. 197.

89. *Justus Georg Schottelius 1612–1676: Ein Teutscher Gelehrter am Wolfenbütteler Hof,* catalog for an exhibition in the Herzog August Library in Wolfenbüttel from October 23, 1976 to January 2, 1977, p. 96.

90. *Goethes Werke,* ed. Erich Trunz, vol. 1 (Hamburg, 1958), p. 307. The openness of Oswald von Wolkenstein, expressed in so many ways, corresponds to his unusual confession against his falling into oblivion: "And if I were to remain silent for a long time / Then I would simply be forgotten / In a few years no one would remember me / And so I will start / To sing again, if I can."

91. Keith Bosley, ed., *The Elek Book of Oriental Verse* (London, 1979), p. 231.

To write poetry is of use only
When this writing creates fame and honor.
It is better to put a lock on your mouth
Than to write and then burn your poem.
My inmost soul conceals much that is valuable,
But I will not reveal it until someone asks me to.[92]

In his *Orlando Furioso,* Ariosto links his lines on the river Lethe—into whose eternal oblivion name after name falls—with praise of poets like Homer or Virgil, to whom rulers and heroes owe both their ennoblement and the perpetuation of their memory.

But, as the silver swans with joyful song
Convey these medals safely to the shrine,
Poets on earth renown and fame prolong
Which time would to oblivion consign.
Wise and farsighted princes (few among
So many!) who the steps of the benign
Augustus follow and hold writers dear,
Of Lethe's waters *you* need have no fear.

Our (sc. the German) word *Denkmal,* which refers to the continuous remembrance of someone, corresponds to the word *monumentum,* which is derived by Augustine from μνήμη and *memini* and more precisely to μνήμη and *memoria* as words in antiquity meaning "tomb."[93] If the mute memorial

92. Wilhelm Bacher, *Nizami's Leben und Werke und der zweite Theil des Nizamischen Alexanderbuches,* Beiträge zur Geschichte der persischen Literatur und der Alexandersage (Leipzig, 1871), p. 44.

93. Augustine, *De cura pro mortuis gerenda* 4.6, in *PL,* 40, col. 596: "Sed non ob aliud vel memoriae vel monumenta dicuntur ea quae insignita fiunt sepulcra mortuorum, nisi quia eos qui viventium oculis morte subtracti sunt, ne oblivione etiam cordibus subtrahantur, in memoriam revocant, et admonendo faciunt cogitari: nam et memoriae nomen id apertissime ostendit, et monumentum eo quod moneat mentem, id est admoneat, nuncupatur. Propter quod et Graeci vocant, quod nos memoriam seu monumentum appellamus; quoniam lingua eorum memoria ipsa qua meminimus dicitur." One such is "But then the only reason why the name Memorials or Monuments is given to those sepulchres of the dead which become specially distinguished, is that they recall to memory, and by putting in mind cause us to think of, them who by death are withdrawn from the eyes of the living, that they may not by forgetfulness be also withdrawn from men's hearts. For both the term Memorial most plainly shews this, and Monu-

is given an inscription, it makes the stone talk. "Traveler stand still, stand still in the sight of the mighty stone at the crossroads, and you will see how it starts to talk from the inscription." The stone and the text both cause the traveler to stop and remember.[94] Both can try to be the foundation of posthumous fame: "aeterna fama, accipe posteritas quod per tua saecula narres" is the inscription on one monument,[95] and "hic situs hoc memori saxo mea facta sacravi" is another one for a soldier who, in Hungary, swam across the Danube in his armor and proclaimed proudly, "While it was still in the air, I hit an arrow that had been shot from a bow with another one and broke the first one in two."[96] Those who are buried remind us of what is domestic, harmless, pious: inscriptions on tombs proclaim heroic things about the famous. Others praise civic sense in those who have earned it. The dead, the stones, survivors express their memento by means of the inscription. The consciousness of the transitoriness even of the stone, which is otherwise so seldom expressed—"Even mortal hands can destroy a stone," says Simonides[97]—is behind the frequent threat of the gods' curses on, and punishment of, those who despoil the monument. For the Romans the *damnatio memoriae* was one of the most severe punishments.[98] Portraits of the dead are painted on monuments with

---

ment is so named from monishing, that is, putting in mind. For which reason the Greeks also call that μνημεῖον which we call a Memorial or Monument: because in their tongue the memory itself, by which we remember, is called μνήμη." Cf. "On Care to Be Had for the Dead," trans. Rev. N. Browne, in *Nicene and Post-Nicene Fathers,* vol. 3, *Augustin: On the Holy Trinity, Doctrinal Treatises, Moral Treatises,* ed. Philip Schaff (Peabody, Mass., 1994), pp. 539–551, here 542. As a motto in Helmut Häusle's "Das Denkmal als Garant des Nachruhms," in *Beiträge zur Geschichte und Thematik eines Motivs in lateinischen Inschriften,* Zetemata, no. 75 [Munich, 1980]. On eternal fame and memory in antique grave inscriptions, see Lattimore, *Themes in Greek and Latin Epitaphs* (see n. 38 above), pp. 241–246. A fundamentally opposed citation is "Oblivio omnium rerum mors" [Death is the oblivion of everything], p. 79, with respect to which we may remember the commemorative capability of the dead, something which is not lacking in the afterlife in Dante, in antiquity and in the Middle Ages.

94. Häusle, pp. 42ff., 53.

95. Ibid., p. 65.

96. Ibid., p. 67.

97. Ibid., p. 133; further citations, p. 137 n. 313. On the transitoriness of stone and the permanence of literary monuments, Françoise Jouvosky, *La gloire dans la poésie française et néolatine du XVI*[e] *siècle: Des Rhétoriqueurs à Agrippa d'Aubigne,* Travaux d'Humanisme et Renaissance, no. 102 (Geneva, 1969), pp. 398–404; on the tomb monuments, pp. 404–419. On the tombs, Heinrich Wischermann, *Grabmal, Grabdenkmal und Memoria im Mittelalter,* Berichte und Forschungen zur Kunstgeschichte, no. 5) (Freiburg, 1980).

98. Friedrich Vittinghoff, *Der Staatsfeind in der römischen Kaiserzeit: Untersuchungen zur "damnatio memoriae"* (Berlin, 1936). Max Kaser, "Infamia und ignominia in den römischen

loving care together with words of mourning—that of a beautiful bondswoman, a housekeeper, by her lord[99] and, in the sixth century, that of a bishop of Vienne in Provence:

Pauper laetus abit, nudus discedit opertus,
captivus plaudit liber sese esse redemptum.
cuius agit grates tantoque antistite gaudet.
Inter se adversos illata pace repressit.
Perfugium miseris erat et tutela benignis,
nobis eloquio et stemmate nobilis alto.
nobilior meritis et vitae clarior actu.
Vivat ut aeternum et Christi gratetur amore.[100]

[The pauper goes off rejoicing, the naked person departs well clothed,
The captive, having been ransomed, is gratified to be free.
For what and how much he gives thanks the presiding priest rejoices.
Enemies to one another he suppressed with an enforced peace.
He was a refuge for the miserable and a guardian of the fortunate.
To us he was noble, high of eloquence as well as descent.
Even nobler with respect to his merits and for the way he lived his life.
May he live in eternity and be rewarded by the love of Christ.]

Christians gladly strive for the preservation of memory by words on a gravestone for the length not only of human memory but also of that other memory that aspires to the eternity of life hereafter. While the inscription on the tomb of Pope Pelagius I (ca. 560) believes in his continued existence in heaven as well as on earth—"Vivit in arce poli caelesti luce beatus" [He lives at the summit of the pole in the bliss of heavenly light], "Vivit et hinc cunctis per pia facta locis" [He also lives on in all places through deeds of piety][101]—and Alcuin's inscription for the tomb of Pope Hadrian I links his glory in heaven

Rechtsquellen," *Zeitschrift für Rechtsgeschichte*, Romanistische Abteilung 73 (1956): 220–278. On the portrait in the rites of the sepulchre since the Middle Ages and on the *damnatio memoriae* in the execution of a sentence, from the dishonoring of a portrait of delinquents to the point where they are actually executed in effigy, Wolfgang Brückner, *Bildnis und Brauch: Studien zur Bildfunktion der Effigies* (Berlin, 1966).

99. Häusle, pp. 94ff.

100. Ibid., p. 98.

101. Von Müller (see n. 13 above), p. 90. O. B. Hardison, *The Enduring Moment: A Study of the Idea of Praise in Renaissance Literary Theory and Practice* (Chapel Hill, N.C., 1962).

to his fame on earth,[102] Alfred the Great seeks to leave his *memoria* to posterity in the shape of exemplary good works.[103] Endowments, foundations, and monuments can serve to consolidate the memory of the name of the builder and of his house. Just as Henry the Lion erected the Lion Monument in Brunswick "ad sempiternam et originis et nominis sui memoriam" [to the eternal memory of both his name and origin],[104] so was the Cappenberg head of Barbarossa a memorial to the ruler's personal desire to be remembered and to his majesty.[105] Written monuments as well as stone monuments serve the *aeterna memoria* (everlasting memory) of the dead and the martyrs. In his works, Jerome is at pains to compensate for Blesilla's short life by her *aeterna memoria.*[106] The idea of fame that transcends time was thus not erased when Christianity succeeded antiquity.[107]

However, counterweights also reversed the notion, whether it is the Pauline "Qui gloriatur, in Domino glorietur" [But he that glorieth, let him glory in the Lord] (2 Corinthians 10:17), or whether it is in the sense of the balance of God's and man's demands, according to the already biblical formula *got unde der werlde gevallen* (to please God and the world).[108] In accordance with

102. Von Müller, p. 93f.

103. Ibid., p. 108.

104. Ibid., pp. 113f.

105. Ibid., pp. 115ff. Those who are active in history are also themselves generally anxious about their continuing existence in the memory of their descendants. They arrange for pictorial and textual evidence as testimonials to a continuation of the record of their memory in time. The transmission of the past to the present, to the stock of memory in the future, is part of the office of history. No matter what honorable legitimations they may use for their justification at the present day, they have no need to be ashamed to confess that *memoriae tradere* (consign to memory) springs from a fundamental desire to narrate what has passed. Historical memory preserves for the individual experiences and urges that go beyond his own day and preserves what has been gained from offerings—in the realm of the understanding of the world and of himself—that have been granted him, by enrichments, as time has passed.

106. Jerome, *Epistolae* 39.8.2; Theiler, col. 52.

107. Failing to recognize the origin of wisdom in God, its eulogist in the Wisdom of Solomon promises himself immortality at her hands (Wisdom 8:13): "Because of her I shall have an eternal memory and I shall leave an eternal memory behind to those who shall come after me." The city of Tyre, forgotten of God, originally acquires an evil memory by the singing of its harlot's song (Isaiah 23:15f.): "And it shall come to pass in that day that Tyre shall be forgotten seventy years, according to the days of one king: after the end of seventy years shall Tyre sing as a harlot. 'Take a harp, go about the city, thou harlot that has been forgotten: make sweet melody, sing many songs, that thou mayest be remembered.'" God too will remember it.

108. Gottfried von Strassburg, *Tristan und Isolde,* ed. Friedrich Ranke (Zürich, 1965), line 8013. Cf. Proverbs 3:4: "invenies gratiam et disciplinam bonam coram Deo et hominibus" [you

the demand for the internalization of fame, as it lies within the witness of our conscience (1 Corinthians 1:12) or in the chivalric sense of reputation that is related to the present[109] (whereas *pris* [praise] transcends time), what otherwise serves fame is valid for the time in which it takes place.

Einhard's *Life of Charlemagne* is not intended to serve the fame of his own name—he does not mention that—but the *memoria* of the great man, so that his fame shall not disappear into the darkness of oblivion because no one has spoken of it.[110] The lives of bishops, too, are intended for posthumous fame. The *Life of Bruno of Cologne* (969) does not exhaust the "sempiterna memoria digna" [sempiternally worthy memory] of the man and relies upon additions by Bruno's students.[111] The *Life of Benno of Osnabrück* (pre-1100) wishes to avoid such "gesta certe memoria digna" [deeds certainly worthy of remembrance] being overlooked because of their not being mentioned[112] and aims to establish a congregation that will remember Benno in their prayers and who know that intercession also absolves those who themselves intercede.[113] The *Gesta of Albero of Trier,* written by Balderich after 1150, take their place, with proud formulas of humility, beside the *gesta* of the great

---

shall find grace and a good heart in the sight of God and man]; on the twelve-year-old in the temple (Luke 2:52): "Et Iesus proficiebat sapientia et aetate et gratia apud Dominum et homines [And Jesus increased in wisdom, age, and grace before God and man]; Romans 14:18: "qui enim in hoc servit Christo, placet deo et probatus est hominibus" [for whosoever serves God in this is pleasing to God and approved of by men].

109. On *fama* and *infamia* in canon and civil law, von Müller, pp. 136–154. On *gloria, honor,* and *fama* in Thomas Aquinas's political ethics, pp. 155–163 (here p. 163) from Thomas, *De regimine principum* I, 10: "For who doubts that good kings not only live on, so to speak, in the praise of men in this life but even more after death and are remembered with longing; the name of the bad kings, however, is either wiped out at once or, if they were particularly memorable for their evildoing, is remembered only with curses."

110. On the prologue to Einhard's work, Arno Borst, *Lebensformen im Mittelalter* (Frankfurt, 1973), pp. 121–125.

111. *Lebensbeschreibungen einiger Bischöfe des 10–12 Jahrhunderts,* ed. and trans. Hatto Kallfenz, Ausgewählte Quellen zur deutschen Geschichte des Mittelalters, no. 22 (Darmstadt, 1973), p. 178, lines 14f.

112. Ibid., "Praefatio," p. 372, line 5. See also Karl Schmid, *Die Vita Bennonis als Memorialzeugnis.*

113. *Lebensbeschreibungen einiger Bischöfe,* p. 440, lines 24ff: "Qui pro alio scilicet orat, se ipsum absolvit. Si igitur pro eo orantes nosmet arbitramur absolvi, absurdum est, ei subtrahere, quod nobis ipsis non dubitamus impendi atque manere" [Whoever prays for another surely absolves himself as well. If, therefore, praying for the other, we deem ourselves also to be redeemed, it is absurd from him to withhold what we have no doubt to be vouchsafed and to remain for ourselves]. On the notion that the intercessor absolves himself see above, n. 25.

rulers of antiquity, or the deeds of Charlemagne. Admitting that he is no Homer or Virgil, no Josephus, Statius, or Livy, who should really take his place, Balderich, nevertheless, is out to devote himself to Albero's deeds, "ne penitus eterna oblivione deleantur" [lest they be totally erased by eternal oblivion].[114] He also writes an epitaph for Albero that promises him, in golden letters, eternal fame: "fama perhennis erit" [eternal fame will be [his]].[115]

While the emperor Maximilian I was still writing his historical works as a sort of German-language "book of fame," and thus erecting for himself a literary monument to his own *gedechtnus* (memory), he was pursuing the *memoria* of his own name, still joined to the praise of rulers from families that served as the foundation of his own line. The words of the "White King" that disregard God's memory—"wer ime in seinem leben kain gedächtnus macht, der hat nach seinem tod kain gedächtnus und desselben menschen wird mit dem glockendon vergessen" [anyone who does not create for himself a memory during his lifetime is not remembered after his death, and that same man is forgotten with the passing bell]—are also aiming at written commemoration that will create a tradition in an epoch that is, in general, struggling against its suppression through oblivion.[116] However, no small price was paid for this in Maximilian's entourage. The original, specific, commemorative heart of quite diverse medieval genres was removed from them so that the once multicolored field of formal genres could be absorbed, with an imperial gesture, into the more unified service of an extension of a less colorful court *memoria*.[117] The *gedechtnus* of himself and of his royal house, the intention

114. Ibid., p. 588, line 9.

115. Ibid., p. 614, line 10.

116. Jan-Dirk Müller, *Gedechtnus: Literatur und Hofgesellschaft um Maximilian I* (Munich, 1982), pp. 80ff.

117. Ibid., p. 207: "This signifies a rigid and expedient linking of literary genres within the imperial *gedechtnus* (memory) work. Literary and artistic genres are subordinated to this necessity, original functions of the genre are dismantled, generic structures, insofar as they are dysfunctional for the purpose, are simplified or assimilated to the structure of related genres." Jan-Dirk Müller, *Deutsch-lateinische Panegyrik am Kaiserhof und die Entstehung eines neuen höfischen Publikums in Deutschland: Europäische Hofkultur im 16. und 17. Jahrhundert: Vorträge und Referate gehalten anläßlich des Kongresses der Wolfenbütteler Arbeitskreises für Renaissanceforschung und des Internationalen Arbeitskreises für Barockliteratur in der Herzog August Bibliothek Wolfenbüttel vom 4. bis 8. September 1979* (Hamburg, 1981), pp. 133–140, pp. 137f.: "This linkage of self-portrait and claim to fame by a new type of princely servant gives literature prestige and support at court, but at the cost of a rigid instrumentalization in the service of the *laudes* of the ruler. . . . This instrumentalization embraces all genres: heroic epic and eclogue, odes and epigrams, or mythological festival plays: *memoria* is always the dominant feature in determining the genre."

that links all the literary monuments of his work of praise, proceeds, in these circumstances, hand in hand with models for his own time and for the future.[118] Just as earlier, but probably only in the case of the *Annolied*, which showed the course of the history of the world, of salvation, and of the bishops as all converging on Bishop Anno, the employment of what has been passed down—as suited for a particular occasion—from antiquity, the Bible, and the Middle Ages, as a projection onto Maximilian, is like a confluence of historical memory in an accumulation of traditions to the memory of this ruler that smacks of both the mythic and the sacral.[119]

Tacitus says that the Germans clung to the memory of their origins from the gods in old songs that have been passed down to succeeding generations as a form of historical memory.[120] Geoffrey of Viterbo called his outstanding work of history, written in the year 1185 and covering the period from the creation of the world to the emperor Barbarossa, *Memoria saeculorum* (*Memory of the Ages*).[121] According to John of Garland, *historia* as *sermo verus* (true narrative) (as distinct from *fabula* as *integumentum* [fictive narrative]) passes on the *gesta Scriptaque* (doings and writings) of "great men" *venturis commemoranda viris* (as worthy of recall by generations yet to come).[122]

The most richly developed literary genre of the Middle Ages, the legends of the saints, served to establish and preserve the memory of those who excelled in life and were raised up to God, in death, for a liturgical veneration that would outlast their lifetimes and for the preservation for posterity of their example as the fulfillment of an extraordinary human life. The picture of the saints was preserved for the Christian church in all the arts in a whole host of attestations that is exceeded only by the pictorial memory of what is passed down in the Bible.[123] The saints, like God, are appealed to with a plea

118. Von Müller, pp. 211f.

119. Ibid., pp. 265ff. et passim.

120. Tacitus, *Germania*, annotated by Rudolf Much, 3d ed., with the collaboration of Herbert Jankuhn, ed. Wolfgang Lange (Heidelberg, 1967), cap. 2.8ff.: "celebrant carminibus antiquis quod unum apud illos memoriae at annalium genus est, Tuistonem deum terra editum" [they celebrate in ancient songs, which constitute one of their memorial and historical genres, that the god Tuisto once arose from the earth]; discussed on pp. 50f.

121. Karl Langosch, "Gottfried von Viterbo," in *Die deutsche Literatur des Mittelalter: Verfasserlexikon*, 2d ed., ed. Kurt Ruh et al. (Berlin, 1981), cols. 173–182, here cols. 176f.

122. Hennig Brinkmann, *Mittelalterliche Hermeneutik* (Tübingen, 1980), p. 178. Here we may only point out the function of historiography as *memoria;* it would also deserve separate treatment as to its different genres.

123. On the concept "pictorial memory," Günter Hess, "Allegorie und Historismus: Zum 'Bildgedächtnis' des späten 19. Jahrhunderts," in Fromm, Harms, and Ruberg, *Verbum et Signum*

that we should not be forgotten. In the Crescentia legend in the German *Kaiserchronik* (mid–twelfth century) we are able to observe, on the basis of the history of the subject matter, how the story was changed into a saint legend and we participate in the birth of a new poetic saint, Crescentia. The poet changes the story of the preservation of an anonymous woman's chastity—in the face of great suffering—because he is planning an exemplary story, and it is not until this poem that he invents the name Crescentia for her.[124] Anyone who points out that the word *heilic* (holy) in the twelfth century was not reserved for the saints and is not convinced of Crescentia's sanctity by the statement "sît wart hailic daz wîp" [henceforth the woman was holy] (line 12802) or by her being addressed as "hailige gotes diu" [holy servant of God] (12505, 12671) or "hailige chunigîn" [holy queen] (12461) has nevertheless to admit that, in legend literature, an appeal to a literary figure in the form of a prayer is invariably addressed only to a saint. Her story ends with the appeal to Crescentia and her husband "nû heven wir ûf die hende / unt piten si, daz si unser niht vergezzen, / wande si daz himelrîche hânt besezzen" [now let us raise our hands and pray that they will not forget us, because they have occupied heaven] (12806ff.). The "now let us raise our hands and pray" is the moment when a congregation is first formed around these literary saints whom this poet is the first to regard as sanctified. Saint and legend are here one, in that the saint is created by the poet through his legend. The first people to hear this legend are, at the same time, the first to pray to the new saints. The belief in heavenly intercessors that was created by the poet acquired, in the prayer for intercession, a congregation of believers that embraces both the poet and his audience. "What is left is ordained by the poets" is applicable to the writers of legends and to the poets of the *Gregorius* and the *Song of Roland*. After the Battle of Ronceval not only does the converted

(see n. 7 above), pp. 555–591, "Bildersaal des Mittelalters: Zur Typologie illustrierter Literaturgeschichte im 19. Jahrhundert," in *Deutsche Literatur im Mittelalter: Kontakte und Perspektiven: Hugo Kuhn zum Gedenken,* ed. Christoph Cormeau (Stuttgart, 1980), pp. 501–546, figs. 31–52, and "Panorama und Denkmal: Erinnerung als Denkform zwischen Vormärz und Gründerzeit," in *Literatur in der sozialen Bewegung,* ed. Alberto Martino in Verbindung mit Günter Häntzschel und Georg Jäger (Tübingen, 1977), pp. 130–206.

124. *Die Kaiserchronik eines Regensburger Geistlichen,* ed. Edward Schröder, in *MGH, Deutsche Chroniken,* I/1 (Hanover, 1892), lines 11352–12812. Cf. Ohly, *Sage und Legende in der Kaiserchronik* (see n. 7 above), pp. 189–198. Karen Baasch, *Die Crescentialegende in der deutschen Dichtung des Mittelalters,* Germanistische Abhandlungen, no. 20 (Stuttgart, 1968), pp. 27–122. Max Wehrli, *Roman und Legende im deutschen Hochmittelalter* (1961), pp. 157f., 160ff.; the quotation is from his *Die Heroen der Griechen* (Zürich, 1969), pp. 155–176.

Queen Brechmunda say of the martyrs of the *Song of Roland,* "dise heiligen sculen uns gotes hulde erwerwen" [these saints shall gain God's grace for us] (8656), but when, at the end of the poem, Oliver, Roland, and Turpin have received a *translatio* into the church of the soldier-saint Romanus in Blaye and a pilgrimage to their "holy skeletons" has become a custom, the poet again founds a community of listeners and prayer with the plea that the saints will not forget them at the Day of Judgment:

si furten drie sarche 8666
zu dem guten sent Romane:
da suchet man zeware
ir uil heiligiz gebaine.
an dem iungistin urtaile
sculn si unser niht uergezzen,
want si haben daz himilriche besezzen.

[They took three coffins to the good St. Romanus: there in truth men visit their very holy skeletons. At the Day of Judgment may they not forget us, for they have possessed the Kingdom of Heaven.]

As soon as the heroes have been buried on the battlefield, where many miraculous things happen from then on, the poet invites his listeners to appeal to these poetic saints for help in the face of sin, for God has made them capable of doing this:

zaichen gescahen da genuoge 7596
unt geschent iemir mere.
nu biten wir di hailigen herren,
want iz in got uerlazen hat
daz si uns wegen umbe unser missetat.

[Many signs were seen there / And have been from that time on. / Now let us pray to the holy lords, / For God has given them authority / To judge us according to our misdeeds.][125]

125. On the legendary character of the *Rolandslied,* see Friedrich Ohly, "Die Legende von Karl und Roland," in *Studien zur Frühmittelhochdeutschen Literatur: Cambridge Colloquium, 1971,* ed. L. P. Johnson, H. H. Steinhoff, and R. A. Wisbey (Berlin, 1974), pp. 292–343.

The poet can make us believe that we shall not be forgotten in the sight of God. The moment when the poet lets us speak with him and when he teaches us to speak with him in his prayer of appeal to the figures of his poem is the moment in which a congregation is created. This is the extent to which literary works can exert their influence. From time immemorial, in the history of Christianity, writers of prose and verse have recognized imaginary or historical personages as saints, have represented them as such, and have recommended them to the faithful as worthy of veneration. It is not significant for the literary character of these works, as legends, whether or not the church took up their suggestions and raised these saints to the honors of the altar. There is a not inconsiderable number of legends in Latin and the vernacular that do not belong to the *Acta Sanctorum*. The literary historian has to include them in the history of legend literature.[126]

Like the horn of battle to the warrior, and the spur to the racehorse, the perfection of the great who have lived before us (*virtus majorum*) drives the poet to undertake fresh work in praise of the deeds of the dead. Ennodius (d. 521), the author of legends, also begins the life of St. Anthony of Lerina in this way, since, bound by the chains of language, the picture of his former fame may be handed down to his successors and will not disappear for centuries, if it turns into a subject matter that is read for the sake of his brilliant deeds. The narrowness of mortal nature will be overcome, without danger of challenge, by survival in art, so that contact with the best, even though they have died, will never be lost. Their bodies will become dust again, and the spirit from above will return to its origin, but the preservation, in books, of what they exemplify also changes their death into life. Even if those who have gone home to their Creator and who now shine before him in a double light are not in need of such commemoration, they awaken for us into a new life, and the truth of their lives shines forth for us as an example.[127] If the hero lives only

126. Just as the literary legend of the canonization of Charlemagne prepared the soil, so Mennel's *Fürstliche Chronik* (*Chronicle of the Princes*) attempts to give the house of Hapsburg, for Maximilian I, as great a role as possible in the lives of the saints. Von Müller, p. 266: "Because of the larger number, saints are included who have not been officially canonized by the church: it is not a living cult that is the starting point for inquiries, but these are supposed to substantiate a cult of this sort for the first time."

127. Ennodius, *De vita beati Antoni,* "Praefatio," in *MGH, Auctores antiquissimi* 7 (Berlin, 1885), pp. 185f.: "Vt proeliantes adsurgunt bucinis, ut equorum celeritas ac potiorem ferrate calce provocatur, ita dum maiorum virtus sollicitat ingenia novella, confortat. qui cana exercitia et veterum gesta relegit, ad disciplinarum frugem propositis laudum praemiis inardescit. imago praecedentis gloriae ut as posteros veniat, linguarum catena retinetur. non licet per aetates

in posthumous fame, the saint experiences a double resurrection, one in the life hereafter, but also one here on earth if, through his legend, his death becomes an *obitus vitalis* for those who come after, a survival also of his death in literary memory that also lays claim to continued existence through those who come later.

The clear distinction that was made, in antiquity and the Middle Ages, between the memory of the sufferings of the great, in the Middle Ages in history, and in antiquity in myth, in the Middle Ages in the *historia,* and in antiquity in the *fabula* or *fictio,* never excluded the possibility of a convergence and transmission of patterns between the two, or of a convergence between the mythical heroic legends of antiquity and a hagiography that claims to be historical,[128] or between this and the medieval German romance,[129] between British historiography and the Arthurian romances, and other things of this sort. Thus, the relationship of the *memoria* motivation at the beginning of Ennodius's legend and the deliberation on *memoria* in Gottfried von Strass-

---

perire, si quid lectio serenis actibus amica susceperit, itaque eloquentiae diuturnitatis mortalis naturae sine congressionis periculo vincit angustiam, per quam optimorum conversatio ipsis decedentibus nescit occasum. restituitur quidem corpus origini et destinatus a superis spiritus ad proprium recurrit auctorem: quorum tamen probitas libris mandata fuerit, eorum vitalis est obitus . . . nobis vero ista reviviscant, nobis profutura serventur, quibus si ab studio deest sectari meliora. de illorum, qui facem conversationis suae praeferunt, venire debet exemplo" [As combatants in battle rise up to the trumpets, as the swiftness of their horses is urged to a more intense level by the ironclad spur, so also, when the ancestors' virtue rouses young minds, he strengthens much who revisits armies of old and great deeds of the ancients, who kindles the virtues instilled by training by setting in view the rewards of praise. Let the image of preceding glory come, as it were, to its successors; then the chain of languages remains intact. That it be broken by the generations is not allowed, where a friendly reading welcomes the contact with untroubled energy. And so the duration of eloquence conquers the narrowness of mortal human nature without the danger of a hostile encounter, through which [duration of eloquence] the conversation of the best knows no decline, even though they themselves depart. For the body is indeed restored to its origin and the spirit from above does, as appointed, return to its proper author; those, however, whose rectitude shall have been validated in books, their death shall have the quality of life. . . . for us these things truly seem to come to life again, they are saved to do us good in the future, us, for whom without study the pursuit of a better life is also lacking, study that ought to come from the example of those who bear the torch of their conversation before them—and us].

128. Hermann Usener's work on ancient myth and Christian legend pursued the question of the dependence of their materials. Up till now, the profound relationships between the stories of the heroes of Greek mythology and of the legends of the saints has not been investigated. Without even suggesting the legend, however, the preface to Karl Kerényi, *Die Heroen der Griechen* (Zürich, 1958; Darmstadt, 1959), does suggest a comparison.

129. Wehrli, *Roman und Legende,* pp. 155–176.

burg's prologue, written seven centuries later, is no cause for surprise. The space of time that separates the two closely related texts is of small consequence (and the dependence of the one on the other is improbable), but it does help us to recall how—in whatever narrative genre it may be—what is humanly great, unique, and preserved up to and beyond the Middle Ages is maintained in the treasury of the literary memory as something that is exemplary and beyond the constraints of time. The introduction of what is specific to a given time came about as a result of new adaptations and elaborations that included new interpretations or new material and modified the original in the sense of a "work on the myth"[130] rather than as a result of magnificent new elements or of something that was deliberately forgotten. Even where meditation on the history of salvation—from no matter what date—was able to evaluate and arrange traditional material into specific epochs of salvation, the moral interpretation that was provided in this same traditional material always extracted from it something that was morally valid for its time.

Gottfried von Strassburg's prologue to *Tristan and Isolde,* which—in accordance with the rules of poetics—begins with a series of maxims, starts with momentous lines on remembrance:

Gedæhte man ir ze guote niht,
von den der werlde guot geschiht,
so wærez allez alse niht,
swaz guotes in der werlt geschiht.

[If we failed in our esteem of those by whom good is done in the world, then it would all be as nothing, whatever good is done in the world.]

It cannot be said more succinctly or soberly that the duration—simply the survival—of what has appeared once in the world as a gift to it simply depends upon its being remembered; otherwise, what is given to it disappears, without trace, into nothingness. If mankind is not, like Sisyphus, to constantly lose what it has once received from the great ones of history, not to raise itself through the ages to a stage where things stay put without slipping back again, it has to have memory to preserve what it has gained, at any given time, in the potentials of human existence, or of its understanding of the world and of itself. Gottfried also thinks of the office of the poet in terms of

130. Hans Blumenberg, *Arbeit am Mythos* (Frankfurt, 1979).

administering a memory or of establishing a new one. Liturgical, hagiographical, and profane thoughts on the functional effects of literary memory converge at the end of the great *Tristan* prologue. A reminiscence of breaking bread—a common metaphor for the interpretation of the Scriptures from the time of the church fathers—and the awakening of associations with the Eucharist and of the survival of the saints are combined when, for those who come later, Gottfried produces from the story of Tristan and Isolde, which is exemplary in their life and death for noble hearts (for whom his poem is written), the possibility of existence that he offers as the bread of life. What leads up to the metaphor of the bread are lines on the life force of the great figures of the poem, long since dead, whose names are perpetuated by art—as those of the saints are by their cults—beyond death to be guiding stars that affect the present:

uns ist noch hiute liep vernomem
süeze und iemer niuwe
ir inneclichiu triuwe
ir liep, ir leit, ir wunne, ir not;
al eine und sin si lange tot.
ir süezer name der lebet iedoch
und sol ir tot der werlde noch
ze guote lange und iemer leben,
den triuwe gernden triuwe geben,
den ere gernden ere:
ir tot muoz iemer mere
uns lebenden leben und niuwe wesen;
wan swa man noch hoeret lesen
ir triuwe, ir triuwen reinekeit,
ir herzeliep, ir herzeleit,
Deist aller edelen herzen brot.
hie mite so lebet ir beider tot
und ist uns daz süeze alse brot.
Ir leben, ir tot sint unser brot.
sus lebet ir leben, sus lebet ir tot.
sus lebent si noch und sind doch tot
und ist ir tot der lebenden brot.

[Today we still love to hear of their tender devotion, sweet and ever fresh, their joy, their sorrow, their anguish, and their ecstasy. And although they are long dead, their sweet name lives on and their death will endure for ever to the profit of well-bred people, giving loyalty to those who seek loyalty, honour to those who seek honour. For us who are alive their death must live on and be for ever new. For wherever still today one hears the recital of their devotion, their perfect loyalty, their hearts' joy, their hearts' sorrow—this is bread to all noble hearts. With this their death lives on. We read their life, we read their death, and to us it is sweet as bread. Their life, their death are our bread. Thus lives their life, thus lives their death. They live still and yet are dead, and their death is the bread of living.][131]

131. The translation is taken from Gottfried von Strassburg, *Tristan,* trans. A. T. Hatto (London, 1960), p. 44. Gottfried may have been influenced by Hartmann von Aue's prologue to *Iwein,* where King Arthur is recommended to us as an exemplary figure. The perpetuation of the fame of the historical Arthur had been invented by the legend of his not yet having died, of his withdrawal from the world, and of his reappearance at a future time (references in the *Iwein* edition with a translation and notes by Thomas Cramer [Berlin, 1968], p. 171). Like Chrétien de Troyes before him, Hartmann had reinterpreted this in the sense of the perpetuation of his own name, which still calls on us today:

er hât bi sînen zîten
gelebet alsô schône
daz er der êren krône
dô truoc und noch sîn name treit
des habent die wârheit
sîne lantliute:
si jehent er lebe noch hiute:
er hât den lop erworben
ist ime der lîp erstorben,
sô lebet doch iemer sîn name.
er ist lasterlîcher schame
iemer vil gar erwert,
der noch nâch sînem site vert.

[In his day he lived in such an exemplary fashion, that he wore the crown of good reputation and his name still bears it. His countrymen know the truth of this. They declare that he is still alive today. He has earned praise. Though his body is dead, his name lives on forever. Whoever lives according to his fashion will be spared vicious shame.]

I shall treat the metaphor of bread later.

The memory of Tristan and Isolde in literature is not instigated by the "Ubi sunt qui ante nos" [Where are they who were here before us?]—the theme of the poets of the *memento mori.* We find this in a Latin strophe of the twelfth century and in an English one from the "Love Ruine" of the Franciscan Thomas of Hales (thirteenth century):

Transierunt rerum materies,
Ut a sole liquescit glacies
Ubi Plato, ubi Porphyrius,

What corresponds here to the function of the reading of legend in forming and consolidating a community is the achievement by which a community of

---

Ubi Tullius aut Virgilius:
Ubi Thales, ubi Empedocles,
Aut egregius Aristoteles?
Alexander ubi rex maximus,
Ubi Hector, Trojae fortissimus;
Ubi David rex doctissimus
Ubi Helena Parisque roseus?
Ceciderunt in profundum ut lapides,
Quis scit an detur eis requies?

[Material things have passed away,
As from the sun ice liquifies
Where is Plato, where Porphyrius,
Where Tullius or Virgilius;
Where Thales, where Empedocles,
Or the extraordinary Aristoteles?
Alexander where the king supreme,
Where Hector, of Troy the bravest;
Where David, of kings the learnedest;
Where Helena and Paris the rosy?
Have they fallen like stones into an abyss,
Who knows what rest is given them?]

Hwer is Paris and Heleyne
    That weren so brytht and feyre on bleo
Amadas and Dideyne,
    Tristram, Iseude, and alle theo,
Ector, with his scharpe meyne,
    And Cesar, riche of wordes feo. . . .

Douglas Gray, *Themes and Images in the Medieval English Religious Lyric* (London, 1972), pp. 182–190, pursues the theme from the Old English *Wanderer* to Byron (here esp. pp. 186ff.). The *memento mori* poets also keep awake the memory of those who "sank like stones into the depths." Dante finds Tristan in the inferno (V, 67). Does Byron also point to heaven and hell (p. 190)?

Where is Napoleon the Grand. God knows:
    Where little Castlereagh? the devil can tell . . .

Guy Lefèvre de Boderie organized his verse encyclopedia, *L'encyclie des secrets de l'éternité* (Antwerp, 1571), on the basis of the support of theology by natural history. He remembers those who doubt God's creation with the intention of eradicating their memory: "les noms desquels ie desire estre soubmergez au profond oubly, ainsi que leurs corps sont enseuelis en terre" [the names of those whom I wish to be submerged in a profound oblivion, just as their bodies are buried in the ground] ("Prologue," p. 4).

"aller edelen herzen" [all noble hearts] is united by an increasing intensity of speech in the first person plural until we come to the almost sacral words: "Ir leben, ir tot sint unser brot."[132]

When the poet himself gives the hero of his romance an epitaph set in diamonds, this epicized metaphor seals one of the chief functions of his art, which is to create a *memoria.* Wolfram von Eschenbach did not just write the heroic life of Parzival's father, Gahmuret, a figure who was invented by him. After Gahmuret, fighting for the just cause, falls in a battle between heathens in the east, the heathen ruler on whose side he has fought has him buried in a sarcophagus made of precious stones, and the embalmed body of the young knight shines through the ruby that is set on top of the sarcophagus. At the urging of Gahmuret's Christian companions the heathen king also donates an emerald cross to crown the grave. This, in its turn, bears the hero's diamond helmet, beneath which he died, and inscribed in it is his epitaph. The twenty-six lines of the epitaph proclaim his fame among both Christians and heathens who idolize him, and they end with the plea for commemorative prayer for the dead man: "nu wünscht im heiles, der hie ligt" [now pray for

132. However much it may serve to form a community, the alliance of poet (narrator) and audience in the first person plural nevertheless takes different forms in different genres. How differently the beginning and end of the *Nibelungenlied* sound from the beginning of the prologue to *Tristan:*

> uns ist in alten mæren wunders vil geseit 1
> von heleden lobebæren, von grôzer arebeit.
> von fröuden, hôchgezîten von weinen und von klagen,
> von küener recken strîten muget ir nû wunder hoeren sagen
>
> Ine kan iu niht bescheiden waz sîder dâ geschach: 2379
> wan ritter unde frouwen weinen man dâ sach.
> dar zuo die edelen knehte ir lieben friunde tôt.
> dâ hât daz mære ein ende: daz ist der Nibelunge nôt.

[We have been told in old stories many marvels of famous heroes, of great sorrow. Of joys, festivals of weeping and wailing of the battles of brave warriors, of these you may now hear wonders.

I cannot tell you what happened after this, except that knights and ladies were to be seen weeping there, as well as noble squires, whose dear friends were dead. This is the end of the story: this is the tragedy of the Nibelungen.]

On the use of the first person plural in religious literature, Ohly, "Zum Dichtungsschluß *Tu autem*" (see n. 14 above), p. 43. Oexle (see n. 7 above) emphasizes the nature of *Memoria* as means of creating community, for example: "Commemoration makes a community, memory creates community, it is a constructive element of communities" (p. 86).

the salvation of him who lies here] (*Parzival* 108, 28). The fictive dead man is so present that Wolfram ensures both his posthumous fame and his eternal salvation—precious stones last longer as a monument than metal. The tomb of jewels and its epitaph in diamonds seal Gahmuret's poetic memory for as long as Wolfram's poem exists—*gemma perennius*?

We need poetry as a vessel for remembering the history of human feelings, experiences, and expectations—just as we need all the arts as an aid to our survival as a people, which would otherwise recklessly renounce the wealth of mortal human potential that has been gained during the course of our history. Remembrance is a call to satisfy its claims to form oneself to the greatest extent possible in the image of what has been preserved therein. The poet Guido Guinizelli praised in Dante the fact that he gathered experience for living and dying better from within his own borders:

Beato te, che delle nostre marche . . .
per morir meglio, esperïenza imbarche!
(Purgatorio XXVI, 73)

[Blessed thou, . . . who, for a holier life, art embarking on knowledge of our borders!]

The high value placed upon what is to be handed down by temporal memory is attested to by the devotion of writers who, through the millennia, have battled on stone, papyrus, or parchment against oblivion; not least of these were the medieval monks, to whom alone we owe the fact that much that was great was not lost to us.[133] Memory as heritage must be managed, Greek antiquity must be recalled in Rome, the Bible and antiquity and indigenous tradition must be recalled in the Middle Ages, and finally the scientific memory of our own epoch, which is scarcely to be borne, which affects whole ages and worlds and is no longer encompassable even in encyclopedic terms, must also be managed. Memory as a way of rediscovery is a condition of culture, in which tradition and establishment interlock. We experience a spiritual happiness in recognition as rediscovery if, in the encounter with what has not yet been seen, its picture is enriched by the memory of what is related historically

133. Jacob Burckhardt, "*Über das Studium der Geschichte*," p. 244, laments the irreplaceable losses of works of art, literature, and historiography from antiquity, "because the continuity of spiritual memory (an essential interest of human existence and a metaphysical proof of the significance of its continuance) has grown fragmentary over long periods of time."

or in any other way. When scrutinized it shows us similarities with what has been remembered; it enters as though into a family of *memoria* in which what is peculiar to it acquires the charm of a person rather than standing before the horizon of a child without memory, who will, through its education, first be exposed to the *memoria* of a culture as a spiritual world.

Literature is—like other arts—a memory that is enhanced by being formed, a memory in which what would otherwise lapse into oblivion is raised to a permanence that is founded upon art. Just as other arts leave behind commemorative pictures in their visible monuments, so poets establish memory by the perpetuation, for posterity, of names, deeds, and experiences. Hölderlin's "Was bleibet aber, stiften die Dichter" [What remains is ordained by the poets] in his poem *Andenken* is by no means true only of the memory of historical figures that is secured by art. Historical figures and figures first invented by Tasso both belong among the warriors thirsting for the "booty of memory" in his catalog of heroes. More than persons from the past who live on in memory in the sense of *historia* are those who first entered the world, and entered it only, through literature, in the sense of *fabula,* and are inventions of the imagination that are not attested to in any other art or tradition. Characters like Achilles and Aeneas, Parzival and Tristan, Simplizissimus and Don Quixote, Nathan and Hyperion, the man without qualities, and Kafka's K, are dependent in the extreme on the memory to which they are entrusted. Otherwise, the treasury of all possible human portraits that is made up of heroes, saints, knights, and other expressions of what is humanly possible would be lost to us inexorably and for ever.

The aesthetics of fifteenth-century Italian choreography taught a relationship between the categories of *misura* and *memoria* in such a way that the realization of what was dissimilar to the rest of life, above all the temporal mensurability of steps in the art of dance, depends upon memory as a recollection that is concentrated upon the possibilities present in forms which were to be realized at a given moment.[134] Not as limited, it is true, as the

134. Rudolf zur Lippe, *Naturbeherrschung am Menschen,* vol. 1, *Körpererfahrung als Enfaltung von Sinnen und Beziehungen in der Ära des italienischen Kaufmannskapitals* (Frankfurt, 1979), pp. 181–195 (on *misura*), 195–212 (on *memoria*); vol. 2, *Geometrisierung des Menschen und Repräsentation des Privaten im französischen Absolutismus,* pp. 213 ("Misura stood for a commensurability that was a force in the context of *memoria*"), 198 ("The theoretical disposition according to metre, which *misura* contained, appeared as objectivization in *memoria* when it was actually carried out"), 200 ("The point of memory is to make possible a conception of improvisation, which is reliably removed from coincidence, in that it is indissolubly linked to what is special at a given moment and is communicated, in this way, to the systematic"), and 202

memoria of the dancer, which allows him his spontaneity's freedom of movement within the limits of choreography, the poet's historical memory of the repertoire of forms which are to hand nevertheless directs his inventive imagination into paths from which—in ages marked by tradition—it is not to be recommended that he diverge. *Memoria* teaches us to dance shackled by the chains of history, and these demand that the poet and all artists shed their weight, whether by the worthiness and the perfection with which they bear it or by a trick of art by which they outwit it, a trick that makes tradition or establishment appear as one in the light of day and which lets the consequences be recognized only later on. Art without memory, as something that is functionally incompetent, can easily get beyond the control of history; art with too much memory soon loses the charm of novelty.

Literary forms have devoted themselves separately to certain tasks of memory. In epochs of *contemptus mundi,* the *memento mori* reminds those who are doomed to die that they should consider their own situation. On the threshold of the modern period, around 1490, the Flemish diplomat Philippe de Commynes introduces a new genre, memoirs—side by side with the much older one of autobiography—in which experiences are confided to memory.[135] Literature not only serves the poets' own *memoria* and the *memoria* of their themes and figures from myth, imagination, or history and the values or nonvalues that are represented by them; it also contains a memory that is internal to the work or which refers to the work itself. Research into temporal structure, as the architectural structure of literature, was unsatisfactory so long as there was not a simultaneous regard, in literature, for the actual experience (whether of the poet or his figures) of a time that was encountered as fluid or urgent, sluggish or demanding, drawing near, organizing, or unstable, coupled with the time that had been remembered, as was the case in the literature of the Middle Ages.[136] Large-scale forms of literature—

("*Memoria* is, therefore, the principle by which the canon and the rules can succeed with a certain spontaneity").

135. Borst, pp. 125–132.

136. Uwe Ruberg, *Raum und Zeit im Prosa-Lancelot,* Medium Aevum, Philologische Studien, no. 9 (Munich, 1965), looks into the question of the representation and significance of time. He sums up remembering (p. 183): "What lies before in time forces itself into human consciousness in two ways: by an alleviating, illuminating memory, an intentional act of the conscious spirit, and by the heavy, gloomy *gedencken,* the self-denying devotion to a picture, which has been engraved on the foundations of our soul. Memory accentuates and elevates the present; *gedencken* devalues it and leads, in its final intensification, to lunacy, to a complete loss of the consciousness of time." More on this topic in Meier, n. 231; and see below.

like the epic or the novel—as time that has assumed form, demand both from the author and the listener, or reader, the power of memory, so that what has come earlier can be remembered later, thus enabling a sense of the succession of events to be manifested in the whole. Large-scale works of cosmic content like those of Homer or Virgil, Wolfram von Eschenbach, the anonymous author of the great prose *Lancelot,* Tasso and Ariosto, or more modern authors like Lohenstein and Grimmelshausen, Thomas Mann and Musil demand of the reader a memory—which springs from the work itself—of persons, events, and constellations as a condition of an all-embracing overview of the world of the work,[137] something that is even impossible for a figure within a novel if that figure once loses its insight into the temporal ordering of the work and its own situation within that order. In Wolfram's work, when Parzival turns away from God, he also drops out of time for the period of his renunciation of God (even the romance scarcely remembers him for a space of some three thousand lines). It is Trevrizent who leads him to history—of the ecclesiastical year, of his family, of the Grail, of salvation, and of himself—and through this to God. By the way in which Trevrizent opens up for Parzifal the horizon of the history of salvation and expands his perspective of memory back to the Creation itself, by reminding him of the fallen angels, the Fall of Man, and God's mercy—"nemt altiu mær vür niuwe" [take old tales for new ones]—we see how the interior memory of a literary work can be expanded—both for its author and for the characters within it—so that large parts of the exterior memory of a community involved with things independent of the work—religion, history, and experience—are integrated into it.[138] Dante's *Divine Comedy* is certainly the work whose inner memory is most widely stretched, with its inclusion of biblical and antique allusions, of medieval literature and history, up to the life of the poet, between time and eternity—just as it is located cosmically between heaven and hell—to the point where we have to think of what has not been included from the external memory. As a vicarious *memoria* of its cultural epoch, *The Divine Comedy* contains within itself a sort of cosmic memory that no poetic work after it has ever again contained—not Goethe's *Faust II,* which recalls, by the connections it makes, different ages within itself, or Flaubert's *Tentation de*

137. If it is difficult to separate the approximately 250 different persons in Wolfram's *Parzival,* then it is a hopeless undertaking to try to find your way among the approximately 900 persons in Ariosto's *Orlando Furioso.*

138. On Sancho Panza's form of memory, which characterizes the person, see Harald Weinrich, *Das Ingenium Don Quijotes: Ein Beitrag zur literarischen Charakterkunde,* Forschungen zur romanischen Philologie, no. 1 (Münster, 1956), pp. 104ff.

Saint Antoine, which followed it. The cosmic commemoration brought forth by Dante, by means of his wandering through places in the afterlife and his meeting with those—historical and literary personages from all ages—who live there, has its roots in the century that saw the development of large-scale forms like the chronicle or the *liber mundi* encyclopedia, in which they were still included.[139] These, like the cathedral[140] and the theological summa in the thirteenth century, finally and for a long time, enlarge the boundaries of what is to be retained in the memory.

The claim to readiness to remember raised by a literary work goes far beyond the hermetic whole of the work whenever it enters into a relationship with something that already exists in the past. There are so many kinds of reference of this sort to something older in literature that only a few can be mentioned here. The author must have an educated memory if he wants—by making artful reference to works of the past or to their thoughtful quotation[141]—to bring his own words into an intellectual relation with those of someone who has gone before, and must expect an equally educated mem-

139. Christel Meier, *Grundzüge der mittelalterlichen Enzyklopädistik: Zu Inhalten, Formen und Funktionen einer problematischen Gattung (Literatur und Laienbildung im Spätmittelalter und in der Reformationszeit),* proceedings of a symposium held at Wolfenbüttel, 1981, Germanistische Symposien, Berichtsbände, no. 4, ed. Karl Stackmann (Stuttgart, 1983). Thomas de Chantimpré's encyclopedia sets out to write about the *memorabilia et congrua moribus* of creatures and their characteristics, which are communicated by Vincent de Beauvais's *memoriąe utilia;* ibid., nn. 61, 65.

140. Cf. Ohly, "The Cathedral as Temporal Space," chap. 4 in this volume.

141. Hermann Meyer, *Das Zitat in der Erzählkunst: Zur Geschichte und Poetik des europäischen Romans* (Stuttgart, 1961), investigates the art of quotation in the works of the great humorous writers Rabelais, Cervantes, and Sterne, as well as in the work of German authors from Wieland to Thomas Mann. Meyer's thesis, "that the quotation first developed into a true epical artistic medium of aesthetic significance in the humorous novel" (p. 16), would help to explain why it plays such a different role in medieval poetry. "The poet's participation in the treasures of the Western cultural tradition proclaims itself in the art of quotation. He can refer to them and draw from them with justified confidence that his readers are not completely outside this tradition. The continuity of the cultural tradition affords a certain community, if not of outlook on life and the world, at least on the general level of culture" (p. 24). "The humanistic cultural world which, in spite of a strong illumination of its inner questionability, is still intact in Thomas Mann's novels falls completely apart in Döblin's representation of the social environment" (p. 25). Claudianus (ca. 400 A.D.), like no other author in antiquity, compares persons and happenings of his own time with those of mythology, history, and literature, and in doing so he not only presupposes the widest possible knowledge of them but also raises them to an ideal and exemplary plane. Karl Günther, "De Claudii Claudiani comparationibus," in *Programm zum Jahresberichte über das Königliche Alte Gymnasium zu Regensburg* (1893/94), pp. 9–13.

ory among his public, for otherwise the charm of the perception of such a quietly significant intertextualization would be lost. If the memories of the poet and the reader do not interact, then the reader does not acquire an insight into what the poet intended by an allusion that presupposes an arena of common poetic tradition.[142] More significant, if not more frequent, than for the reinforcement of his own position—for example for the sake of humility or for a Renaissance way of thinking—may be the recourse in the Middle Ages to older material that has been remembered with a feeling of superiority over the past, something that had a far-reaching significance in the relationship of the New Testament to the Old. The acceptance of the memory of the old, which had been superseded, is so much part of the essence of typological thought that arts that are determined by it always formally realize the type that is recalled in its antitype. No other form of art recalls the past with such illustrative power as this does.[143] Literary culture always derives its sustenance from the poetic memory of form, even in other places, with a conditional freedom,[144] and this memory permits it sometimes to preserve, sometimes to change, and sometimes to supersede tradition.

The technical possibilities of the feats of memory that are necessary for the creation and handing on of literature are not to be glossed over here, even if they carry less weight in the understanding of written literature than they

142. Gian Biagio Conte, *Memoria dei poeti e sistema letterario: Catullo, Ovidio, Lucano,* La ricerca letteraria, no. 23 (Turin, 1974), pp. 5–14: "Memoria dei poeti e arte allusiva (A proposito di un verso di Catullo e di uno di Virgilio)." In what follows, Conte treats the linguistic, rhetorical, and poetically formal conditions of the memorability of poetry as a guarantee of its continued existence, in the course of which analogies of function between tropes, metaphors, and allusions are emphasized (pp. 30–45: "Arte allusiva e figure retoriche").

143. On the effects of typological thought on the arts see Ohly, *Schriften* (see n. 10 above), pp. 312–400; in addition, "Skizzen zur Typologie im späteren Mittelalter," in *Medium Aevum deutsch: Beiträge zur deutschen Literatur des hohen und späten Mittelalters: Festschrift für Kurt Ruh zum 65. Geburtstag* (Tübingen, 1979), pp. 251–310; "Typologische Figuren aus Natur und Mythus," in *Formen und Funktionen der Allegorie,* proceedings of a symposium held at Wolfenbüttel, 1978, ed. Walter Haug (Stuttgart, 1979), pp. 126–166.

144. Conte (see n. 142 above), p. 74: "La creazione sarà certa forzatura vittoriosa della convenzione, ma condotta entra il dominio stesso della convenzione. Sarà, come si è detto, libertà condizionata, giacchè anche la libertà esiste solo se accetta di subire le necessarie condizioni dell'esistenza. E saranno certo queste forzature vittoriose a costituire poesia e a far storia facendo nascere il nuovo" [Creation will of course be a victorious forcing of convention, but one conducted within the realm of convention itself. It will be, as has been said, a conditioned freedom, given that even liberty exists only when it accepts being subjected to the necessary conditions of existence. And it is certainly those victorious forcings that will constitute poetry and produce history by bringing innovation into being].

do in what is transmitted orally. In rhetoric, it is only by *memoria*—by the rote learning of literary works as a part of the oratorical act, side by side with *inventio*—that a literary work "actually becomes a poetic work, since learning by heart means that the *opus* becomes fixed."[145] Vitruvius ascribes to blocks of verse that repose, like dice, in strict balance, unequivocal sense and immutable solidity for the memory.[146] Research into oral poetry is familiar with questions of the art of memory in the composition and handing down of the literature as well as with the peculiarities of style that are determined by it.[147] More recent attempts to build a bridge from the rich *ars memoriae* tradition,[148] with its roots in rhetoric, to the literary creations of the Middle

145. Heinrich Lausberg, *Handbuch der literarischen Rhetorik: Eine Grundlegung der Literaturwissenschaft* (Munich, 1973), par. 1244, p. 747; further: "To be sure, the rhetorical *memoria* is keyed to the unique *actio,* which comes to the fore, especially in the division of labor, while the learning of literary works by heart involves a social fixing of the work and its availability for the *pronuntiatio* which can be repeated as often as desired." On the fundamental significance of learning by heart for the educational and cultural history of antiquity and early Christianity, together with the admiration of those endowed with an extraordinary memory, see Theodor Klauser, "Auswendiglernen," in *Reallexikon für Antike und Christentum* (1950), vol. 1, cols. 1030–1039.

146. Vitruvius, *De architectura* 5, "Praefatio," pp. 3f.: "Is (sc. cybus) cum est iactus, quam in partem incubuit, dum est intactus, inmotam habet stabilitatem, uti sunt etiam tesserae quas in alveo ludentes iaciunt. Hanc autem similitudinem ex eo sumpsisse videntur, quod is numerus versuum, uti cybus, in quemcumque sensum insederit, inmotam efficiat ibi memoriae stabilitatem" [When that [sc. cybus] is cast, in whatever part it comes into a resting position, it takes on a motionless stability, as long as it remains untouched, as do also the dice which players cast on a gaming table. Moreover they [architecture and shooting dice] seem to have taken over this similarity from the fact that the number of verses in a poem, in whatever poetic sense it will have been set, effects, analogous to a die, an unwavering stability of memory]. After Bernfried Nugel, *The Just Design: Studien zu architektonischen Vorstellungsweisen in der neoklassischen Literaturtheorie am Beispiel Englands,* Komparatistische Studien, no. 11 (Berlin, 1980), p. 28.

147. James A. Notopoulus, "Mnemosyne in Oral Literature," *Transactions and Proceedings of the American Philological Association* 69 (1938): 465–493. (On Greek literature, he picks up Parry's principle that form should be regarded as the key to function and style as the character of thought.) More recent literature on oral literature handed down from memory in Franz H. Bäuml, "Varieties and Consequences of Medieval Literacy and Illiteracy," *Speculum* 55 (1980): 237–265.

148. Literature on the *ars memoriae* in Meier, n. 231. L. Volkmann, "Ars memorativa," *Jahrbuch der kunsthistorischen Sammlungen in Wien,* N.F., 3 (1929): 111–200. P. Rossi, *Clavis universalis: Arti mnemoniche e logica combinatoria da Lullo a Leibniz* (Milan, 1960). Harry Caplan, "Memory: Treasure-House of Eloquence," in *Of Eloquence: Studies in Ancient and Medieval Rhetoric,* ed. Harry Caplan (Ithaca, 1970), pp. 196–246. H. Blum, "Mnemotechnik," in *Historisches Wörterbuch der Philosophie,* vol. 5 (1980), cols. 1444f. G. Reinert (as the object of psychological

Ages and beyond into the baroque do not seem to me to reach the same level of legitimacy, because they are less stringent.[149]

Besides the component *memini* and its productive intensifications that we have stressed here, as in the first sentence of *Tristan*—"Gedæhte man ir ze guote niht, von den der werlde guot geschiht, so wærez allez alse niht, swaz guotes in der werlde geschiht"—or in the sense of intercessory commemora-

research), cols. 1446–1448. On *naturalis* and *artificiosa memoria* in Cicero, Charles Causeret, *Étude sur la langue de la rhéthorique et de la critique littéraire dans Cicéron* (Paris, 1886), pp. 205f.

The history of the art of memory, which was pursued from ancient rhetoric to the baroque period as a technique for strengthening memory, has received a fundamental treatment, rich in perspectives, by Yates. Insofar as the art of memory recommends the orientation of the memory toward notions of space, it tends toward architectural metaphors and to the sixteenth-century "Theatre" of the memory. In his review of Yates's historical perspectives, Walter J. Ong, S.J., makes some suggestions with reference to memory in oral literary traditions or *memoria* in the religion of the Jews and the Christians, which controvert the unhistorical *ars memoriae,* in "Memory as Art," *Renaissance Quarterly* 20 (1967): 253–260; also in Ong, *Rhetoric, Romance and Technology: Studies in the Interaction of Expression and Culture* (Ithaca, 1971), pp. 102–112. Frances A. Yates, *Theatre of the World* (London, 1969), chap. 8, "The Stage of the English Public Theatre: The Stage in Robert Fludd's Memory System" (pp. 136–161); see also the index (s.v. "memory"). On the spatial metaphors for memory see also Inge Leimberg, "George Herbert, 'The Sinner': Der Tempel als Memoriagebäude," *Archiv für das Studium der neueren Sprachen und Literaturen,* 202, Jahrgang 121 (1969): 241–250. On spatial memory in psychology, Gordon H. Bower, "Analysis of a Mnemonic Device," *American Scientist* 58 (1970): 496–510. On the discussion of the unity of the *Confessions* and the position of the tenth book within them, Wendelin Schmidt-Dengler, "Die *aula memoriae* in den *Konfessionen* des heiligen Augustin," *Revue des études augustiniennes* 14 (1968): 69–89. On the basis of the metaphors of space and architecture for the person and the memory that are used in other books, he argues against a later introduction of the tenth book. Of Augustine's metaphors for memory (*campi et lata praetoria memoriae; memoria quasi venter est animi; thesaurus*) it is the metaphor of the *aula memoriae* which is pursued as to its origin in rhetoric. On the metaphorics of memory, Harald Weinrich, "Münze und Wort: Untersuchungen an einem Bildfeld," in *Sprache in Texten* (Stuttgart, 1971), pp. 276–290, and Metaphora memoriae," ibid., pp. 291–294. We shall not pursue the field of the metaphorics of memory—which is by no means exhausted here—any further. A work on *memoria* and Lethe (together with the metaphorics of memory) is being prepared by Christel Meier. Yates offers a treasure trove of memory metaphors (see above: on Augustine, pp. 46–49).

149. For decades, historical research showed a decided preference for the *ars memoriae* as the method of memory training, culminating in Yates's work (see n. 60 above). It is only relatively recently that an attempt has been made in English studies, from the *ars memoriae,* to bridge the gap to the older history of literature: J. A. van Dorsten, "The Arts of Memory and Poetry," *English Studies* 48 (1967): 419–425. Inge Leimberg (see n. 148 above). R. H. Abrams, "Memory and Making in the Poetics of Renaissance England" (Ph.D. diss., State University of New York at Buffalo, 1971). M. Spiegler, "Spenser's Pictorial Rhetoric: Imagines agentes in 'The Faerie Queene, Book I'" (Ph.D. diss., University of California, Los Angeles, 1971). Joseph G. Weber, "The Poet-

tion (for example, "die suln mîn ze gote gedenken"), there is another meaning that has yet to appear in the dictionaries, to which we should here turn our attention. It lies in the direction of the well-known *sich verdenken* or *verdaht sîn* (to be lost in thought) in the sense of being lost to the point of forgetting the world while recalling an emotion or feeling which leads to a loss of consciousness—as it does in Parzival's trance when he sees the drops

---

ics of Memory," *Symposium: A Quarterly Journal in Modern Foreign Literatures* 33 (1979): 293–298, has nothing to offer. Heinrich F. Plett, "Topik und Memoria: Strukturen mnemonischer Bildlichkeit in der englischen Literatur des 17. Jahrhunderts," in *Topik: Beiträge zur interdisziplinären Diskussion,* ed. Dieter Breuer and Helmut Schanze (Munich, 1981), pp. 307–333. Plett pursues the relationship between *memoria* and literature in the works of Spenser (personifications of imagination and memory rest upon pictorial ideas of rhetoric), spatial pictorial ideas of an architecture of memory specific to a particular epoch, the function of memory pictures as markers in theory, and mnemotechnics as an instrument of the creation of literary texts in George Herbert's "Temple" (1633), in Christopher Harvey's "Synagogue" or "Shadow of the Temple" (1640) as poetic memory structures, and in Bunyan's "Pilgrim's Progress" (1678) as space for movement through loci of memory. He is thus concerned with precipitates of the *ars memoriae* in the arrangement of literary works. However, it is possible that this was scarcely less determined by the medieval traditions of architectural allegoresis. Interferences of notions of the space of memory and allegorical space exegesis, especially where both remind us of the same thing, cannot be excluded; however, they still await detailed study. The temptation, in the face of the lead which research into the *ars memoriae* has taken in philology over research into other aspects of memory in literature, the use of the art of memory as the key to numerous things which up to now may have been understood differently, seems to be in the wind just now. Scholars in English were stimulated by Yates, who sees, for example, Dante's *Divine Comedy* from the point of view of the *ars memoriae:* "*The Divine Comedy* would thus become the supreme example of the conversion of an abstract summa of similitudes and examples, with Memory as the converting power, the bridge between the abstraction and the image. But the other reason for the use of corporeal similitudes given by Thomas Aquinas in the *Summa,* besides their use in memory, would also come into play, namely that the Scriptures use poetic metaphors and speak of spiritual things under the similitudes of corporal things. If one were to think of a Dantesque art of memory as a mystical art, attached to a mystical rhetoric, the images of Tullius would turn into poetic metaphors for spiritual things. Boncompagno, it may be recalled, stated in his mystical rhetoric that metaphor was invented in the Earthly Paradise" (Yates [see n. 60 above], p. 96). Here not only is there consideration of the possibility of mixed forms, but the difference between what is historical and what is functional becomes blurred. The markers of mnemotechnics are scarcely ever mentioned in the theory and practice of allegory. If sixteenth-century mnemotechnics regarded Dante's *Inferno* as a guide to the places of punishment in hell, then the inference remains that Dante himself had assigned hell to *memoria,* purgatory to *intellegentia* and paradise to *providentia,* that is, to the three parts of *prudentia* (p. 95, cf. p. 116, 163ff., 368). A hypothesis which does not yet support the further conclusion that other poets might therefore have allowed themselves to be guided by *ars memoriae.* Practically all the pictures in the arts and in literature of the Middle Ages are supposed to serve memories, generally in traditions specific to

of blood in the snow that recall to him the picture of Condwiramurs (*Parzival* 283, 16f.: "sus begunde er sich verdenken unz daz er unversunnen hielt" [thus he began to lose himself in thought until he had lost his senses]). The occasion for the distraction that causes a man to become lost in thought is a woman; it also appears, harmless, and as a parody, in Ulrich von Lichtenstein's *Frauendienst.* Here the hero, in his epiphany as the goddess Venus on

---

a particular genre. This is also true of the visions which—long before Dante—knew orders of places in the hereafter. Without convincing circumstantial evidence for the fact that the pictorial orders arise from the *ars memoriae* and not, in many cases, from other needs for ordering, we should be careful before explaining them as arising from the needs of mnemotechnics.

In book 6 of the *Aeneid,* Virgil's underworld already knew of special places for dead children, for those who were condemned though innocent, for suicides, for those who died in war, and for criminals, as well as Elysium as the place of purification of the good. Raabe, *Plurima mortis imago,* p. 144. Silius Italicus (d. 101) leads Scipio in his descent into the underworld, where he will talk to his parents and companions, the great ones of the past from the days of Troy to Rome, to eight gates of Hades, which are each assigned to a separate group of human beings. The ninth gate leads the *turba piorum* to the Elysian Fields on the other side of Oceanus. Through the brilliant gold, moonlit tenth gate souls enter heaven, from which after five thousand years they will be born again (*Punica* XIII, 531–549). The order in Hades, the Elysian Fields, and heaven is very close to Dante. The series of places in hell undergoes a particular change in our own times in G. K. Chesterton's *Father Brown* story *The Sign of the Broken Sword,* in *The Father Brown Stories* (London, 1929), p. 267. "Anyhow, there is this about such evil, that it opens door after door in hell, and always into smaller and smaller chambers. This is the real case against crime, that a man does not become wilder and wilder, but only meaner and meaner."

On *memoria,* as the source of poetic creativity, Helen Gardner, ed., *John Donne: The Divine Poems* (Oxford, 1952), pp. lf. Cf. Leimberg, p. 242. Inge Leimberg also very kindly pointed out to me John Donne's *Anniversaries,* ed. Frank Manley (Baltimore, 1963), p. 81, *The First Anniversary,* lines 461ff.:

God did make
A last, and lastingst peece, a song. He spake
To Moses, to deliver vnto all.
That song: because he knew they would let fall,
The Law, the Prophets, and the History.
But keepe the song still in their memory.
Such an opinion (in due measure) made
Me this grat Office boldly to inuade.

The commentary (pp. 167ff.) refers to Deuteronomy 31:19. Donne appeals to St. John Chrysostom's Isaiah commentary (*PL,* 56, 57). Further exegetical evidence for the Old Testament as a *canticum,* p. 168. Donne in *The First Anniversary* rewrote the song of Moses, which was created under the law of reason as a critical *Anatomy of the World* for his time, and made space for the New Testament in *The Second Anniversary: The Progress of the Soul* (pp. 48f.). On memory and creativity, Botho Strauss, *Paare Passanten* (Munich, 1981), pp. 50ff., 110f., 118.

her journey from Venice to Bohemia, is a guest of Kadolt von Felsberg and, in the goddess's costume, promptly falls in love with the mistress of the house. In the delightful scene in which they go to church and the mistress of the house takes Venus, whose baptismal name is Ulrich, to mass, this is what happens to him:

Mîn lîp hie in gedanken stuont 283,9
gar sinne lôs, als die tuont,
die an diu wîp verdenkent sich.
als het ouch ich verdâht dâ mich,
daz ich niht weste wâ ich was;
biz man die êwangelje las:
dô daz ein ander pfaff huob an,
dâ von alrêrst ich mich versan.

[I stood here deep in thought, / Senseless, as they are / Who lose themselves in thought because of a woman, / As though I too had lost myself in thought, / So that I did not know where I was; / Until they started reading the Gospel: / When another priest started doing that, / Then for the first time I came to my senses.]

"Then for the first time I came to my senses." The abrupt change from being lost to the world in one's memory and the demand for one's presence, which is effected, in Parzival's case, by his horse's turning away from the drops of blood and by Gawan's insightful placing of the cloth over the drops to hide them from Parzival's sight, is also characteristic of scenes in one of the most magnificent literary works of the Middle Ages, the monumental prose *Lancelot* romance, written in the decades between *Parzival* and the *Frauendienst*.[150]

In the case of Lancelot, the hero of the romance, who is caught in the thrall of an evil love for Queen Guinevere, and of Arthur, whose star—which had risen so brilliantly half a century before—sinks into ruin in this work, we encounter a motif that promises to treat *gedencken* in a totally new manner. It is a motif that leads through the reverie of the memory of love, the bewilderment of sorrow or of a sense of failure (theological despair does not play

150. *Lancelot* 1–2, ed. Reinhold Kluge, Deutsche Texte des Mittelalters, nos. 42, 47, 63 (Berlin, 1948, 1963, 1974). In what follows I base my remarks upon what Ruberg (n. 136 above) said so excellently in the sections about the waters (pp. 54ff.) and about reactivated time (memory and *gedencken*, pp. 173ff.) in the prose *Lancelot*.

a role here) into a state of mind where we sense madness behind melancholy. Whether riding or resting, Lancelot's activity is often called *gedencken,* without any details of the cause, which is left to our own imagination. First of all, there are seemingly harmless scenes where the hero is rudely awakened from a state of being lost to earthly consciousness by rough intervention from outside. In the forest, in the heat of the day, Lancelot takes off his helmet "und begunde sêre zu gedenken" [and began to lapse into recollection]. He leaves the road and follows a path. At this point a giant comes and hits him in the face, "das er sin gedenken ließ und wart geware das er den groß weg gelaßen hett" [so that he stopped recollecting and became aware of the fact that he had left the highroad] (I, 140). Lancelot rides late to a river to quench his midday thirst. After he has drunk, "er saß nyder und begund sere zu gedencken lange" [he sat down and began to be lost in recollection]. After a good while, a knight comes from the other bank, splashing his way through the ford, so that he sprays Lancelot with water. Lancelot lifts up his head and says: "'Herre riter, ir hant mich naß gemacht und hant mir darzu myn gedencken benomen!' 'Ich acht wenig off uch oder uff uwer gedencken!' sprach der ander" ["Sir, knight, you have made me wet and also stopped my recollecting!" "I care little for you or for your recollecting!" replied the other] (I, 151). Lancelot learns that the ford is named for Arthur's queen. The result is a duel, because Lancelot has been splashed with water while recollecting. Again at a ford, while two armies on the different banks are preparing for battle, Lancelot stays on the platform, under the eyes of the queen, leaning on his spear, lost to the world in front of Guinevere. People shout to him, take his shield away, throw a fish that has been taken from the river at his visor, and he is splashed in the eyes—the dreaming fool, *der arme schnudel,* does not budge. It is only when he is hit on the chest by a spear that he stabs his royal antagonist to death. The horses fall over each other (I, 249). Those around Lancelot have no idea of the depth of his thought, of the love that excludes him from their world. All unsuspecting, they treat him like Job's wife, who pours a bucket of water over Job as he sits grieving like a melancholiac—as Dürer painted it on the Jabach altar.[151] Lancelot later collapses unconscious. Guinevere alone can heal his wild disposition for some hours, the Lady of the Lake for a longer

151. Xanthippe had done the same thing to Socrates. Dürer first depicts Job's wife pouring water over him in the Jabach altar of the years 1503–4. Günter Bandmann, *Melancholie und Musik: Ikonographische Studien,* Wissenschaftliche Abhandlungen der Arbeitsgemeinschaft für Forschung des Landes Nordrhein-Westfalen, no. 12 (Cologne, 1960), pp. 55ff., fig. 13.

time (I, 466ff.). When he thinks that he has lost Guinevere and must do without his friend's solace, nothing saves him from madness:

Alda wart sin ruw groß und großer, das er sere krancken begund an dem libe, und das heubt begund im iteln von wachen and von vasten, so das er begund rasen, und darnach begunde er wuden eins nachtes da er off sym bett lag, und begunde im die nase so sere bluden das alle syn cleider blutig waren und das bett da off er lag. Er stunt uff zu mitternacht also blutig und sprang zu eim fenster uß in sim nydercleid und in sim hemde, sin swert albar in syner hende, und was das groß wunder das er sichselb da mit nit dödet da er zum fenster uß viel.—Alsus ist Lancelot dobesuchtig hinweg gelauffen. [Then his sorrow grew greater and greater, and he began to grow very very bodily ill, and his head began to grow empty because of lack of sleep and food, so that he began to rage and then—one night as he lay on his bed—to rave, and his nose began to bleed so badly that all his clothes and the bed on which he lay were covered in blood. He got up at midnight, covered in blood as he was, and jumped out of a window in his undergarment and his shift, his naked sword in his hands, and the great miracle was that he did not kill himself when he fell out of the window. Thus Lancelot ran away in a frenzy.] (I, 596f.)

Part of the suffering attendant upon melancholic *gedencken,* with its isolating and incapacitating removal from the present and from the world around us, is the possibility of drifting off into melancholy, and then breaking out into madness, which—with the leap from the window—leads into a night alienated from human companionship.[152]

Like Lancelot's *gedencken,* King Arthur's also takes place in the heat of the day on the bank of a flowing stream while he is being disrobed by supporters of his own rank and reputation. If Lancelot's suffering has its roots in his beloved, the king's has its seed in the paralyzing bewilderment of happenings, like the love of the queen—signs that he is not equal to any of the tasks that confront him. In the great adventure of the enchanted city and the castle of Dolorose Garde, where a great number of Arthurian knights are languishing in prison, Arthur is the one who arrives late, neglects his duty, and is later the one who fails. On the bank of the river at the foot of Dolorose Garde he pitches a tent for the night. "Das wetter was heiß, und der könig ging des abends uff das waßer siczen und ließ syn beyn darinn hangen" [The

152. Among the perspectives of the work as a whole, the history of melancholy and other forms of human disturbance and confusion in the prose *Lancelot* still remains to be written.

weather was hot and the king went in the evening to sit by the water and let his legs dangle in it]. Did anyone ever see a king sitting like this? Four knights erect a rapidly prepared baldachin over him. "Der könig saß also und wart sere dencken und lang" [Thus the king sat and was deep in thought for a long time] (I, 170). It would not take much for his opponent, who is calling to him from the other bank, to kill him as he sits like this. Dolorose Garde remains closed to him. "Und der könig war sere zornig und ging siczen off ein brunnenfluß und begunde sere und lang zu gedencken" [and the king was very angry and went and sat at a fountain and began to recollect deep and long]. In this way he loses his next chance, for no one dares disturb him: "unser herr hat so groß gedenck underhanden" [our lord is lost in such deep thought]. The man who is wasting so much of the time that he has in which to set the captives free is met with the cry "Konig Artus, din zytt get hinweg!" [King Arthur, your time is running out!]. The cry, which is taken up by a number of people, fills the valley; his wife hears it. She comes riding up, but Arthur "saß noch in sym gedanck" [but Arthur was still sitting lost in thought]. She is highly incensed, and she is not the only one (I, 176f.). It is not Arthur but Lancelot who frees Dolorose Garde in the service of his beloved queen. Later on we hear once again: "Und das volck von der stat begund sere zu ruffen: Konig Artus, din zyt geet hinweg, din zytt get hinweg! Der konig was aber nieder off jhener bach geseßen und was sere zu ungemach" [And the people of the city began to cry loudly: "King Arthur, your time is running out, your time is running out!" But the king was sitting at the brook and was very morose]—recollecting his knights, whom he has given up for lost (I, 185). Soon, after a long day's ride, Lancelot hears a maiden singing, "und er begunde zu gedencken und ließ das roß geen wo das es wolt" [and he began to recollect and let his horse go wherever it wanted to]. The horse is exhausted; it is Saturday evening, the middle of August. "Er saß und gedacht" [he sat and recollected]. The horse goes over a moor that is dried out by the heat and falls into a ditch and lies for a long time on top of Lancelot (I, 192). All the signs of the romance point to collapse. Recollecting and collapsing are close to one another. The horses and the walls collapse; finally, the whole Arthurian world collapses. "Konig Artus din zytt get hinweg!" the cries foretell it. Lancelot's love for Arthur's queen brings about the collapse of a whole world. The king's melancholic inactivity does nothing to prevent it. Arthur later holds an exemplary court for two weeks while his wife is thinking of a meeting with Lancelot, who in the meantime has become the one to whom she is devoted. Arthur is sitting at the table during the meal. "Er saß über der tafeln und wart gedencken. Da das drit geriecht fur getragen wart, er leit sinen backen in sin hant und leynte off synen ellebogen, er vergaß synes eßsens und alles das umb yn was und darzu sinselbes; er begunde sere zu suffczen und zu weynen. Also saß er fast lang" [He sat at the table and fell to recollecting. When the third dish was brought in, he laid his cheek in his hand and leaned upon his elbow; he forgot his food and everything that was round about him and even himself; he began to sigh deeply and to weep. He sat like this for a long time]. The knights are at their wits' end. Finally Gawan knows what to do. The most beautiful maiden shall go up to Arthur and ask him what he is thinking about. "Die jungfrau ging fur den konig da er noch off sinem ellenbogen lag, und knyet fur yne, sie was sere beengstet wie sie yn angespreche. Sie nam das tischlachen und zoh es so sere nach ir das dem konig die hant von dem backen fure, und slug im der arm off jhene tafeln. Er ließ sin gedencken und sah alumb sich" [The maiden went up to the king while he was still leaning on his elbows, and knelt in front of him; she was very fearful about how she should speak to him. She took the tablecloth and drew it so hard toward her that the king's hand was pulled from his cheek, and his arm was knocked off the table. He ceased recollecting and looked around] (I, 306). The maiden makes her plea, the knights want to know about his recollecting. Outraged, he chases her away. When she is sent back a second time, he reveals that the situation cannot be ameliorated; what he is thinking about is the shame of the Arthurian knights, because they have not engaged in the quest that was demanded of them. In this way he misleads both her and himself.

Remembrance in the prose *Lancelot* inclines to ruin. If it is *memoria*, then it is memory of what is in the process of being ruined, a paralyzingly, hopeless presentiment of the explosive force of the potential that is invested in man, that unhinges a whole world. Creaking, where treason breaks out ubiquitously in every respect, the Arthurian kingdom collapses. Remembrance has an hour in the heat of the day, a place at the flowing waters, a place even at one's own table. The pose of remembrance, the head in the hand supported by the elbows, the pose, too, of prophetic vision is as we find it in Walther von der Vogelweide:

Ich saz ûf eime steine,
und dahte bein mit beine:
dar ûf sazt ich den ellenbogen:
ich hete in mine hant gesmogen
daz kinne und ein mîn wange.

dô dâhte ich mir vil ange,
wie man zer werlte solte leben:
deheinen rât konde ich gegeben

[I was sitting on a rock and had crossed one leg over the other; on this I placed my elbow; I had rested my chin and one of my cheeks in my hand. I then pondered very deeply how man should live on this earth. There was no advice that I could give.]

Injustice, force, treason, discord all had to be considered by Walther. Heedless, however, of the fact that what supported the poet's elbow, the legs crossed on the stone seat, could be pulled away from under him, like the tablecloth on Arthur's own table, "das dem konig die hant von dem backen fure, und slug im der arm off jhene tafeln. er ließ sîn gedencken und sah alumbe sich." Even the pose of remembrance, like its content, starts to slip.[153]

It seems to me that a poetic root of melancholy lies in the "remembering" of the prose *Lancelot.*[154] We find a magnificent example of it later in Dürer's engraving *Melencolia* (fig. 29), with its short midday shadows and,

153. Plautus already mocks the pose of the poet with his chin supported by his arm in *Miles gloriosus* (II, 2, 54ff.). Palaestrio builds up his thoughts in poses. He puts a column under his chin as a support, but he breaks off: "non placet mihi illaec aedificatio" [this structure does not please me]. He recognizes that he is imitating the poetic pose of the barbarians, and that it is not original. A manuscript from St. Gall (?) of about 1100 shows Notker Balbulus, his head in his left hand, leaning on a desk. Peter Gülke, *Mönche, Bürger, Minnesänger: Musik in der Gesellschaft des europäischen Mittelalters,* Wiener musikwissenschaftliche Beiträge, no. 4 (Vienna, 1981), fig. 6.

154. What else we know about it from earlier history comes from quite different sources and corresponds very little to its appearance in *Lancelot.* When Yates points to the melancholic temperament as the best precondition of *memoria* (after Boncompagno, pp. 58f.; Albertus Magnus, pp. 69ff.; Thomas Aquinas, p. 73; Camillo, p. 162), it is the dry-cold or the dry-hot melancholy according to the main testimony of Albertus Magnus from *De bono,* in *Opera omnia,* vol. 28 (Münster, 1951), p. 240: "The goodness of the memory lies in the dry and the cold; for this reason melancholiacs are reckoned to be the best for the memory."

Raymond Klibansky, Erwin Panofsky, and Fritz Saxl, *Saturn and Melancholy: Studies in the History of Natural Philosophy, Religion and Art* (London, 1964; reprint, Nendeln, 1979), p. 337, produce this suggestion: "It was only Raimundus Lullus, in the year 1297, who linked the good memory of the saturnine, by nature watery and earthy human beings, with water and earth, because water was responsive and earth carefully preserved what was imprinted on it": "Et habent bonam memoriam, quia aqua est restrictiva, avara, et impressiva, et species fantasticas diligunt et matematicas. Et terra est subjectum spissum, in quo durat et pressio specierum, que memorate fuerant" [And they have a good memory, since water is receptive, acquisitive, and impressible, and they love phantastic and mathematical kinds of things. And earth is a dense material in which persists also the impression made by the kinds of things that had been committed to memory]. According to Alexander Neckam (d. 1217) *memoria* has its seat in the dry and cold ventricle of the brain at the back of the head, and Aristotle labeled melancholiacs ingenious "propter felicitatem memoriae, quae frigida est et sicca, aut propter eorum astutiam" [on account of the felicity of their memory, which is cold and dry, or because of their astuteness] (ibid., p. 69). On the other hand, on p. 69, we read (n. 6): "The view that melancholy, as corresponding to the heavy and impressionable elements water and earth, favored memory, was everywhere widely held," though there is, to be sure, only one further citation from Raimundus Lullus: "Rursus ait Memoria, 'effective mea natura est melancholia, quoniam per frigiditatem restringo species et conservo metaphorice loquendo, quoniam aqua habet naturam restringendi, et quia terra habet naturam vacuativam, habeo loca, in quibus possum ponere ipsas species'" [Once again Memory affirms, "in the end effect my nature is melancholy, since through the cold I receive the species and preserve them, metaphorically speaking, since water has a receptive nature, and since the earth has an evacuative nature, I have places in which I can put these very same species"].

On melancholy and literature in the modern period, Hans-Jürgen Schings, *Melancholie und Aufklärung: Melancholiker und ihre Kritiker in Erfahrungseelenkunde und Literatur des 18. Jahrhunderts* (Stuttgart, 1977). Ludwig Völker, *Muse Melancholie-Therapeutikum Poesie: Studien zum Melancholieproblem in der deutschen Lyrik von Hölty bis Benn* (Munich, 1978), is concerned with the dialectical interchange of relationship between melancholy and literature, between the melancholic experience of life and the aesthetic mastery of it: "The muse Melancholy—Melancholy as the condition of the creative process as a poetically productive mood—therapy of poetry—the removal and overcoming of melancholy by literature, whether by reading or whether by—and this above all—one's own writing, by the linguistic-literary shaping of melancholy" (p. 7).

Melancholy and heat combine with the melancholic pose in Nietzsche's poem *An die Melancholie,* which begins (Völker, p. 65):

> Verarge mir es nicht Melancholie,
> dass ich die Feder, dich zu preisen, spitze
> und dass ich nicht, den Kopf gebeugt zum Knie,
> einsiedlerisch auf einem Baumstumpf sitze.
> So sahst du oft mich, gestern noch zumal,
> In heisser Sonne morgendlichem Strahle—

> [Melancholy! don't take it amiss if I sharpen my pen to write your praise, and do not sit like some hermit on a tree stump with my head bent over to my knee. You've seen me like that often, even as late as yesterday, sitting in the hot sun's morning rays.]

On a form of melancholy from ["Hinzubrennung" or] "afterscorching" (*per adustionem*) see the chapter on melancholy (pp. 47–61) in Harald Weinrich, *Das Ingenium Don Quijotes. Ingenium* increases with an increase in temperature.

In Caspar David Friedrich's woodcut *Melancholy* (the woman with the spider's web between bare trees), ca. 1801, the woman has her elbows on the withered stump of a bough (Jan Biaistocki, *Stil und Ikonographie: Studien zur Kunstwissenschaft* [Cologne, 1981], fig. 33). The motif of the "thinker" as a melancholiac, introduced by the French *Lancelot* poet around 1230, lives on in literature (for example, Milton's *Il Penseroso*) and in the fine arts up to the time of Rodin's *Thinker.*

in the background, the water, over which a batlike[155] being holds the word *Melencolia.* Three stages in the history of the signification of the pose of the thinker as he sits and recollects were manifested in the work of Michelangelo. Three years before Dürer's *Melencolia* (1514), Michelangelo painted the prophet Jeremiah on the ceiling of the Sistine Chapel (fig. 30) in the old position of the prophetic vision. In the 1520s, he created his sculpture of melancholy in the figure of Lorenzo of Medici on his tomb, where he gazes out over the evening in the picture of a river god (fig. 31). The most fearful heightening of the melancholiac is the desperate creature whom Michelangelo introduced into his powerful Last Judgment, still sitting above the water on the surging edge of hell, toward which forces are already dragging him (fig. 32). Only three centuries after the magnificent prose *Lancelot,* with its diagnosis of an epoch that is pleading now for ruin, now for the redemption that is promised even to the great sinners, arts of equal rank brought melancholic recollection into a pictorial monument of equal quality, though one that is more thoroughly mature because of the epoch in which it was created.

Bending our bow back to the very beginning, we select a text from the early sixteenth century—and our remarks will go no further than this—that once again chooses for itself, in the spirit of the newly burgeoning mysticism of its time, the theologoumenon that, as a constant, embraces the whole theme of this article—recall and oblivion in the relationship of God and man—and that was impressively documented by Hildegard of Bingen[156] some four centuries earlier. The *Spiritual Alphabet* of the Spanish Franciscan Francisco de Osuna (1528), which served St. Theresa as an introduction to her mysticism, devotes, in several of its parts, instructional tracts to the mystical contemplation of each letter of the alphabet. The eleventh tract of the third part, "Tercer Abecedario Spiritual," is dedicated to *memoria* under the letter *M,* the eleventh letter of the alphabet.[157] Under the motto "Remember God

155. On the motif of the bat, see Bandmann (n. 151 above), pp. 87ff., figs. 6, 38ff.

156. See n. 7 above .

157. The third part first appeared in Seville in 1528. I am using the anonymous English translation: *The Third Spiritual Alphabet by Fray Francisco de Osuna* (London, 1931), the *M* chapter on *memoria,* pp. 213–242. Closely related to *memoria* is the Spanish concept of *recogimiento,* which runs through the whole book including the memorial treatise and is translated as "recollection." In this concept we find collection, visualization, and contemplation all combined. The sixth tract, under letter *F,* treats "Frequenta el recogimientio . . ." (pp. 96–113); cf. the eighth letter (pp. 138–167), "Of teaching and learning recollection . . ."; the fifteenth (pp. 293–309) "Speaks of certain impediments of recollection . . ." in 21 chapter 7 (pp. 452–457), "Praise of recollection by other famous doctors of the church."

FIGURE 29

Albrecht Dürer, *Melencolia I* (1514), copperplate etching. (Photograph: Copyright Foto Marburg/Art Resource, New York.)

FIGURE 30
Michelangelo, The prophet Jeremiah, Sistine Chapel (1511).

FIGURE 31

Michelangelo, The tomb of Lorenzo, Medici Chapel (ca. 1520).

FIGURE 32

Michelangelo, Despairing sinner at the Last Judgment, Sistine Chapel (1511). (Photograph: Detail of a damned soul, Sistine Chapel, Vatican Palace, Vatican State. Copyright Alinari/Art Resource, New York.)

constantly and pray to him with sighs," he introduces a theory of the stages of *memoria* as a virtue in contrast to oblivion, which is unworthy of man. For *memoria* is a treasure of wisdom and the ark of truth; for man it is the book of life and the womb of our soul, in which children are conceived who will not be killed by being forgotten. God's eternal memory alone knows no forgetting, for the ideas of all things that repose in him survive the death of things. God's memory is a book of life in which the angels read of God's wishes to instruct them, for in it the eternity of all things is written down. Man, too, made in God's image, must not forget not to spit out God's doctrine but to hold it in the stomach of his memory.[158] The constant recollection of God (through his attributes and through things) is the essence of monastic contemplation, for God's help is ever present, as our bedstead when we sleep and in the breath of our speech. The higher stage of the realization of God, in the recollection of him, takes place in the spiritual memory of the search for God in the constant attention to him with both faith and memory, in the innermost part of the heart.[159] The most complete form of this recollection is the devotedly loving desire for God that sets the flame of love ablaze like a wind, it is a recollection that melts the soul like a ray of sunshine, that causes the bride to sigh for the beloved, right into the deep passion of the desire for God, that surmounts all prior knowledge from memory.[160] From the liturgical recollection of God in the sacrament, through the contemplation of him in the visible, as the expression of the ideas that repose in God's memory, and the spiritual realization of what is known by God, the *memoria* of the soul rises up and intensifies itself to the point of the desire—burning with love and pleasing to God—for his generous grace that leads to the highest form of knowledge, impressed upon the heart by God as the highest gift of heaven,[161] as it was already described in the twelfth century by the emotional mysticism of the Song of Songs. The stages of liturgical and sensitive, spiritual and emotional *memoria* are stages of a mystical approach to God up to the complete and sanctifying proximity of him, who also draws near to the one who is approaching.

The dimensions of memory are stretched between the gracious memory of God and the damnation of his forgetting, between the intercession of the

158. See n. 158, pp. 215f. The metaphor of *venter memoria* is in Augustine, *Confessions* X, 14, 21.

159. Like n. 159, pp. 220f.

160. Pp. 223–229.

161. Pp. 230–232.

liturgical *memento* in the convent and the entreaties not to be forgotten on earth in the inferno. The trinitarian father is reflected, as the power of the creator, in *memoria* as the power of the soul. The mother of the muses is Mnemosyne. From Homer, through Dante to Tasso, we find *memoria* as the divine power to which poets pray for the guarantee of the truth of their works. Poets grant posthumous fame to the great and to heroes, and their work sues for the reward of praise in posterity. Recall without hope becomes visible as melancholy. Every poetic genre has its own form of cosmic memory. We need memory as the atmosphere of our life. Gottfried von Strassburg offers the memory of the potential that appears within his poem as the bread of life. We understand language and literature by virtue of memory. Where painters can create things for us to see as something new and where we can accept them into our memories as enrichment, words are appeals to our memory for what has already been seen and known. If, nevertheless, language and literature also open up a new world in their own way, it is thanks to their ability to juxtapose, in a new way, elements of what has been called to mind by language, so that the new juxtaposition created from elements of what was already present or even what has just been discovered takes its place as a phenomenon in the world. Cultures without writing live from a memory that is orally transmitted. Cultures that need writing live from their written memory and the pictorial memory that is nourished by it (nonrepresentational art is rejected by history; it is superficially without memory). Families in both cultures bequeath their heritage of memory as wealth. Our divisions of the humanities serve it. The spiritual heritage of antiquity, which is tied to writing, would have fallen into the abyss of oblivion and could not have been rescued without the sacrifice made to *memoria* by the Christian monks and the scholars of Islam, who were both, thanks to their belief in the value of what was handed down to them in writing, deeply imbued with the sense of their writing and developed it into a high art.[162] If we bear this is mind we are overcome by dismay at the thought of past or future possibilities of such

162. The far-reaching character of the Christian church service as something that is read distinguishes it from that of old religions which did not depend upon written revelation. Public and private reading right into the monastic cell is the condition for the fact that the church, and especially the convents, of the Middle Ages were also communities of writers who were, in this way, ex officio devoted to the preservation of their written memory, just as church and convents lived a life of devotion to book illumination and, in the other arts, to the pictorial memory of their spiritual world as well. Jacob Burckhardt (see n. 5 above), p. 180, characterizes the old religions as "housing for all the memories of the people and as their soul." The early national religions were—in contrast to world religions—"closely interwoven with the memories, culture, and his-

losses of memory and our thanks are the greater for all the preservation of the gains made by thought and for the pictures of mankind that come to us from the past. Written religions live and die with the *memoria* of their word. Our academic community, which spans places, countries, and continents, lives from a common verbal and written memory, to which it is dedicated. The only interest that it represents is the purely human cause. Hölderlin's poem *Stimme des Volkes* (*The Voice of the People*) calls up the memory of a heroic communal sacrifice and ends:

So hatten es die Kinder gehört
    Sind gut die Sagen, denn ein Gedächtnis sind
        Dem Höchsten sie, doch auch bedarf es
            Eines, die heiligen auszulegen.

[Thus had the children heard it told. Legends are good, for they are a memory for the Highest, but there is also need of one to interpret the holy ones.]

---

tory of the peoples in question, with gods who had to protect or frighten this particular people or state, heroic and proud in their behavior as long as the people flourished" (p. 269).

The Italian painter Alberto Savinio wrote in 1921 in his "Primi saggi di filosofia delle arti":

> "Memory is our culture. It is the ordered collection of our thoughts. Not only of our *own* thoughts: It is also the ordered collection of the thoughts of other people, of all people, who went before us. And since memory is the ordered collection of our, and of other people's, thoughts, it is our religion—*religio*.
>
> "Memory arose at the moment when Adam, driven from paradise, crossed the threshold of paradise. . . . For this reason memory arose, so that by its means the desire for the wealth that had been lost might be propagated from person to person.
>
> "In the beginning memory was in despair. But after a God had approached it with love, hope became the companion of memory.
>
> "Nine daughters were the issue of Jupiter's love for Mnemosyne. Hardly had these descended to earth, than the earth breathed a sigh of joy. Thus, art issued from the fruitful womb of memory . . .
>
> "If memory is not helpful, if art does not come from memory, art is ignoble—plebeian—limited and tedious, empty, like dreams. For art . . . has nothing in common with dreams. Thus, an art which might perhaps marry into the family of dreams and reproduce the special character of dreams that is memorylessness, would be not only empty, but also immoral. . . . Memory beautifies forms: it expands them on all sides beyond their present condition. Through memory we see, if we are looking at pictures, what these pictures were and what they will be: it is the poesy of looking."

According to *Realismus: Zwischen Revolution und Reaktion, 1919–1939,* catalog for an exhibition in the State Art Museum, Berlin (Munich, 1981), p. 79.

The philologist's ethos makes it his duty to preserve, through the ages, an undamaged memory as a legacy for the present and the future. It is part of his business also to interpret what has been entrusted to him by history in terms of his own day. Libraries and archives are, like museums, sometimes sleeping, sometimes reawakened memories of history and sciences, of the sciences of memory that preserve and of the rational sciences that contextualize, which Novalis wanted to combine, as a total science, into an encyclopedism that would join both memory and spirit.[163] If memory is directed to what is a given, and spirit aimed at what is to be achieved, past and future are enfolded in both in the present of existence. The memory of what has been and the anticipation of what is to come unite, for the poet, in the present as the threshold of time. Novalis saw it in this way: "Nichts ist poetischer als Erinnerung und Ahndung oder Vorstellung der Zukunft" [nothing is more poetic than memory and intimation or notion of the future], a mixture of vanishing and animation, sorrow and joy, moderation and elevation, tendency to stagnation and dissolution into combination through "eine geistige Gegenwart . . . und diese Mischung ist das Element, die Atmosphäre des Dichters" [a spiritual present . . . and this mixture is the poet's element, his atmosphere].[164] Or "Alle Erinnerung ist Gegenwart. Im reinern Element wird alle Erinnerung uns wie nothwendige Vordichtung erscheinen" [All memory is the present. In the more pure element all memory would appear to us as necessary prepoetry].[165] The philologist is ill advised to relapse into the tone of his object—

163. *Novalis,* ed. Hans-Joachim Mähl, vol. 2, *Das philosophisch-theoretische Werk* (Munich, 1978), pp. 508ff. Seneca distinguishes between what is given and what is still to be achieved in the eighty-fourth letter to Lucilius, which treats the relationship of reading and writing in the intellectual being. Like bees he must make what has been collected into honey, like the leaf of a reed make honey from the dew of heaven, like a choir, with many voices, create harmony, like the body make blood and vital juices from the food which it has consumed. *Concoquamus illa! alioquin in memoriam ibunt, non in ingenium.* The metaphor of the stomach for memory (see n. 160) is here given meaning in the stomach's task of changing (*mutare*) the food which it is given into strength.

164. See n. 16 above.

165. Novalis (n. 165), p. 349, "Vorarbeiten" (1798), in "Allgemeinen Brouillon" (no. 425, p. 555): "Zukunftslehre gehört zur Geschichte" [instruction about the future belongs to history]. In the *Fragmente und Studien* 1799/1800 (no. 255, p. 794): "Ächt historischer Sinn ist der prophetische" [The true historic sense is the prophetic]. Ibid. (no. 21, pp. 754f.): "Ein Roman muß durch und durch Poesie seyn. . . . Es scheint in einem ächt poetischen Buche, alles so natürlich—und doch so wunderbar—Man glaubt es könne nicht anders seyn, und als habe man nur bisher in der Welt geschlummert—und gehe einem nun erst der rechte Sinn für die Welt auf. Alle Erinnerung und Ahndung scheint aus eben dieser Quelle zu seyn" [A novel must be poetic through and through, everything so natural and yet so wonderful. You believe that it could not

as though he has to imitate the poet—without maintaining a distance from it. However, he cannot be criticized, in the rare case where he succeeds, for his effort to make what is remembered so clear to the present or to what is timeless that even a hint of what is temporally possible is opened up by him. A tone of restraint rather than one of demonstration may help him to a sober, even an alienating, poeticization of the object of his contemplation in the sense that here and there on occasion the "memory could appear as prepoetry." At moments when such a self-revelation of memory and expectation comes to fruition, when the experiences of a teacher and the hopes of his disciples meeting, at last, in their search, finally unite, then perhaps a small piece of the future is not lost.

---

be otherwise and that up till now you have been asleep in the world—and now, for the first time, the real meaning of the world has been revealed to you. All memory and presentiment seem to come from this source].

With the sentence "Everything we do is based on recall and memory" Lee Strassberg, as a teacher, demanded that his actor work less from imagination than from memory (Günter Rühle in an obituary in the *Frankfurter Allgemeine Zeitung,* February 19, 1982). Memory and unbounded curiosity for discovery are mated in the scholar and those who are otherwise productive.

EPILOGUE

PHILOLOGY AS "AESTHETIC SCIENCE" (*KUNSTWISSENSCHAFT*) AND "HUMAN SCIENCE" (*HUMANWISSENSCHAFT*)

In Memoriam Friedrich Ohly (1914–1996)

Friedrich Ohly's scholarly achievement has been remarkable, not only for its extraordinary merits as teaching and research but also for the way it has survived and even flourished in the face of adversity. His was a "humane and free sharing of scholarship," honored rather than dishonored by being at times out of step with the times: with the time of National Socialism and its helpers, by whom he was convicted of insubordination, and dragged, as it were, by the hair into a rapacious war; with the time of their Soviet rivals, by whom he was convicted of insubordination, and sentenced to twenty-five years' hard labor in Siberia; with the times of "barbarism, falsehood, and cultural amnesia" that had suffused those totalitarianisms of the "right" and "left" and could not be altogether absent from a modern world which in some tortured way had helped give birth to such horrors, not even from the groves of academe, to which Ohly "came home in 1953 after spending nine years as a prisoner of war in Russia . . . allowed to begin teaching at the university at age forty," guided by "the resolve . . . to convey no untested truth."[1]

1. Friedrich Ohly, "Introduzione," in *Geometria e memoria: Lettera e allegoria nel Medioevo,* ed. Lea Ritter Santini, trans. Bruno Argenton and Maria Augusta Santini (Bologna, 1985) (henceforth *GM*), pp. 1–16, here 1. This can also be found in a German version of "Introduzione" entitled "Einleitung," a typescript supplied by Friedrich Ohly, p. 21. Cf. Meier, *De thesauro suo,* pp. 419f., on the effects of Nazi and Soviet attempts at mind control on Ohly's position within academic politics after repatriation: "After returning home Ohly resumed his teaching career at the University of Frankfurt in 1954—with a resolve, hardened by experience, to combat barbarism, falsehood, and cultural amnesia with all his might." Cf. Friedrich Ohly, "Zum Vorlesungsstreik im November 1969," in "Stellungnahmen 1966–1973," unpublished typescript ([Münster], December 1982), pp. 15–17, for an attempt to "politicize" one of Ohly's lecture courses.

Testing and criticizing, explaining and interpreting are tasks at the core of Ohly's philology. As both teacher and student, a caring teacher of his students and devoted student of his teachers, as well as of the tradition that teaches both, Ohly consistently identified his scholarly lifework as "philology" and himself as a "philologist." It is not surprising that, with this self-designation, Ohly was, and in some ways still may be, at least superficially out of step with the times: with all their visionary "claims for the future" and their uncritical claimants, with all the unabashed sects and sectarians espousing the latest, best versions of "methodology" and "theory," with all the confident arbiters of taste, fashion, and cultural-political climates, especially of a "professional climate" just waiting in the wings or, even better, already center stage. What is surprising—even fascinating—is not that the belated calling of a Friedrich Ohly should have been superficially out of step with the times, but rather that it should have been so in step at a deeper level as to have had the resonance and exercised the influence which it had and exercised during Ohly's lifetime, which it is likely to maintain and even augment in the present and future, through the legacy of his research and teaching.

What was, and is, this philology of Ohly's, to have had, and be capable of still having, so remarkable an impact? This is the question I should like to address in the following epilogue-like remarks, a risky business, coming as they do after the words of Ohly himself. I shall try to reduce that risk somewhat by stating my views, really little more an invitation to further conversation, with constant reference to, and often with lengthy quotations from, Ohly's own self-reflective comments, including, of course, the passionately candid, dispassionately compelling self-portrait of the scholar printed above as a "Preface" to the first publication in English of his formative essays.[2]

Ohly's very first allusion—in the above-mentioned "Preface"—to his vocation as a "philologist" situates him in opposition to some reigning tendencies of the times: "What the author has done, what is most closely connected with the person who did it, reveals more than all those claims for the future for something—all too willingly put into programmatic form—that are not fulfilled in what is later produced. This book affords the reader the opportunity of meeting me as a self-possessed philologist who, in times of restless changes in the assumption of methodological and theoretical positions,

2. Cf. above, "Foreword," p. xi and n. 8, for the relation between Ohly's "Geleitwort" to *Ausgewählte und neue Schriften zur Literaturgeschichte und Bedeutungsforschung,* ed. Dietmar Peil and Uwe Ruberg (Stuttgart, 1995) (henceforth *AusgNSchr*), and his preface to the present collection (henceforth "Preface").

always remained the same, and whose activity offered no clues for forecasting the professional climate. The serious reader understands, and will certainly not mistake the seeming peace of the tableau which I present for a still life."[3]

Ohly appears as a philologist composed and devoted to his vocation and, at the same time, led to critical reflection: about futuristic proclamations and programmatics, whose validation through actual fulfillment is, however, often indefinitely postponed; about the tendency to waive one's own judgment, to simply accept "methodological and theoretical positions" in vogue in "times of restless changes," and to read, write, teach, and perhaps even think accordingly; about the prospect of having one's "doings" set out as a barometer to predict the "the professional climate" rather than as worthy or unworthy based on standards independent of, albeit not totally beyond, the professional marketplace. Ohly appears as a "philologist" composed out of devotion to his calling, one who always remained constant, always remained himself—a picture which is meant, he cautions, as no "still life" but rather as a tableau whose "peace" is at best "seeming," at its deepest no deeper than merely superficial.[4]

What is criticized by way of the oppositions, implicit as well as explicit, that structure the preceding excerpt is inflation of the scholarly subject and deflation of its object to the status of a mere object of professional ambition.The virtues that Ohly ascribes to the philologist are thus virtues of critical, chiefly self-critical, restraint with respect to—and for—the material that the philologist encounters. Among such virtues of philological restraint are "sobriety," "modesty," and "scrupulousness"; they form a basis for the hermeneutical sensitivity known as "tact."[5]

3. Ohly, "Geleitwort," p. 2; "Preface," pp. xiii–xiv.

4. Cf. on "gelassen" (participial adjective, = "composed") Hermann Paul, *Deutsches Wörterbuch,* 9th rev. ed., ed. Helmut Henne, Georg Objartel, and Heidrun Kämper-Jensen (Tübingen, 1992), p. 329.

5. For "sobriety" and "scrupulousness" cf. Ohly, "Einleitung" typescript, p. 2; "Introduzione," p. 22; and "Geleitwort," p. 4; "Preface," pp. xvii–xviii. Cf. also Friedrich Ohly, *The Damned and the Elect: Guilt in Western Culture,* trans. Linda Archibald (Cambridge, 1992), p. 139: "Memory brings modesty and reassurance." On "tact" cf. Friedrich Ohly, "Kolloquium über Probleme der mittelalterlichen Bedeutungsforschung: Einleitung der Schlußaussprache am 5. Juni 1971," in "Stellungnahmen," pp. 36–42, here p. 38: "we need to be able to estimate the significative possibilities of things in the world of the poetic work with a tact (= "delicacy": *Feingefühl*) born of long preoccupation with, and experience of, a world of significations. Here one can only warn of precipitous attempts to reduce quite different kinds of texts to the same common denominator of the fourfold sense of the Scriptures." See also the striking formulation in Friedrich Ohly, *Schriften*

But other oppositions are implied here that also help define and differentiate philological scholarship. There is, first, Ohly's critical allusion to fixation on "methodological and theoretical positions" and to "restless changes" in their "assumption," trends characteristic of our times. What Ohly suggests here is stated more openly elsewhere in his texts: working with individual details, working close to the empirical data, engaging in philological practice, contextualizing "pragmatically, from the concrete object," as opposed to the abstract "assumption of methodological and theoretical positions," is the very heart and soul of philology. Indeed, privileging the former, doubting the latter, has been the norm within the tradition of philological introspection.[6]

In keeping with the empirical-pragmatic orientation to "the concrete object," the disciplinary alliance that has been traditional has been, as signaled in the epithet "philological-historical," the relationship of philology and history, not the relationship of philology and philosophy. Thus, Ohly on both: "There comes a moment when the fascinating concept of a thought image [*Gedankenbild*] appears [*aufscheint*] to one at a given point in history; when we come across it again we are also conscious that it endures as part of tradition. Patience and more patience are necessary for assembling evidence over a long period of years. The only help in discovering it is reading—reading that covers large fields of history, which often yield an unexpected harvest. 'I have the habit common to all those who cannot think: I can reflect

zur mittelalterlichen Bedeutungsforschung (Darmstadt, 1977) (henceforth *SchrMB*), pp. xxxiii–xxxiv. Cf. further Friedrich Blass, "Hermeneutik und Kritik," in *Handbuch der Klassischen Altertums Wissenschaft,* vol. 1, *Einleitende und Hilfs-Disziplinen,* 2d ed. (Munich, 1892) (henceforth *HbA*), pp. 147–295, here p. 168; Hermann Usener, "Philologie und Geschichtswissenschaft," in *Vorträge und Aufsätze* (Leipzig, 1907), pp. 1–35, here pp. 19, 20, 22; August Boeckh, *Enzyklopädie und Methodenlehre der philologischen Wissenschaften,* pt. 1, *Formale Theorie der philologischen Wissenschaft,* ed. Rudolf Klussmann (1886; reprint, Darmstadt, 1966), p. 87.

6. Cf. Wilhelm Dilthey, "The Rise of Hermeneutics," trans. Fredric R. Jameson and Rudolf A. Makkreel, in *Wilhelm Dilthey: Selected Works,* vol. 4, *Hermeneutics and the Study of History,* ed. Rudolf A. Makkreel and Frithjof Rodi (Princeton, N.J., 1996), pp. 235–258, here p. 249, where the aporia of the "hermeneutic circle" receives not a theoretical but, rather, a practical resolution. "Practice" (*Praxis*) and "empirical observation," or "experience" (*Empirie*), are cited by Blass, "Hermeneutik und Kritik," p. 167, as the basis of philological concepts, including "philology" itself. This resolution is offered to avoid "endless and fruitless intellectual torments as to the definition of concepts that in the end still have their origin nowhere but in the realm of practice and empirical data." See Otto Ribbeck, *Friedrich Wilhelm Ritschl: Ein Beitrag zur Geschichte der Philologie,* vol. 2 (Leipzig, 1881), pp. 17–19; and Ohly, "Geleitwort," p. 3; "Preface," p. xvi: "I cannot propose a method of working on such problems that will always be valid. . . . Patience and more patience are necessary for assembling evidence." On contextualizing "pragmatically, from the concrete object," cf. Ohly, "Einleitung," in *SchrMB,* p. xiii and below.

only when I have a pen in my hand,' says Italo Svevo. The philologist may cull blossoms in the manner of an anthologist, but they must not be combined philosophically, but rather in such a way that colors and forms fall into place as patterns of the historical process as it emerges from intellectual changes of climate that permit the determination of the time and place of a growth that has been discovered."[7]

Allied, doubtless, with Ohly's philological-historical empiricism, his fascination with the material, and his critical distance from theory or methodology imposed upon, rather than shaped by, the material, is his antipathy to having his work become a barometer of sorts for "forecasting the professional climate." For Ohly the saving grace of philology resides in its material, in the radiance that shines out from the "fascinating concept" of some "thought image," some "thought" that emerges at a "point in history" in the form of an "image." Even scholars may falter if—as professionals—they remain too "professional" to be fascinated, if they exploit rather than cherish, use rather than delight in, the material to which they owe so much, or, to paraphrase the late C. Wright Mills, if they live from, rather than for, their work. In philology there are many ways to get even with the material, the extremes being low pedantry and high theory. Ohly would have shuddered—politely—at both; in the present context it seems likely he has more the latter than the former in view, but there are precedents for the criticism of either in philological tradition itself.[8]

Also closely interwoven with Ohly's philological-historical empiricism is his fascination with a sort of material sometimes relegated to the margins of philological inquiry: material produced by the visual arts, products of a history of visual culture that extends from Greco-Roman antiquity, through

7. Ohly, "Geleitwort," p. 3; "Preface," p. xvi. On Italo Svevo, born Ettore Schmitz (1861–1928) into a German-Italian-Jewish family, cf. *The Penguin Companion to European Literature,* ed. Anthony Thorlby (Harmondsworth, 1969), pp. 750–751. On philology and history cf. esp. Usener, "Philologie und Geschichtswissenschaft," passim; and Blass, "Hermeneutik und Kritik," pp. 164–168.

8. Few philologists surpassed Nietzsche's criticism of philological pedantry, the reverse side of his lifelong devotion to philology. Far removed from extremes, the philological liberal August Boeckh propounded conciliation and integration between micrology and macrology; cf., e.g., Boeckh, *Enzyklopädie und Methodenlehre,* pp. 26–27; and Usener, "Philologie und Geschichtswissenschaft," pp. 24–25. N.B. the ambivalence of terms alluding to philological "micrology" (*Mikrologie*) in Ribbeck, *Friedrich Wilhelm Ritschl,* pp. 2, 18; Boeckh, *Enzyklopädie und Methodenlehre,* p. 27; Usener, "Philologie und Geschichtswissenschaft," pp. 24, 27, 29; Blass, "Hermeneutik und Kritik," p. 171 ("It is precisely our high regard for what is minute that makes us great").

the medieval centuries and the epochs of Renaissance, Reformation, and baroque culture to modern times. Ohly's work is not only about philology; it is also about the renewal of philology, and a significant aspect of this renewal was constituted by the examples he gave of a new emphasis on the visual: the fruits of his "true inclination, to pursue philology as an aesthetic science" (*Kunstwissenschaft*).

This aspect of Ohly's work will be taken up again, when Ohly's constitution of philology as an "art" as well as an "aesthetic science" is discussed; for now, I would like to focus on the fascination that visual material held for Ohly. This extends to both the visualizing and revisualizing of textual material and the textualizing and retextualizing of visual material, whose fascination for Ohly lay precisely in its character as an open secret, a mute statement made to our senses by a world of sensuous things. There is no better example than the opening lines of "Problems of Medieval Significs and Hugh of Folieto's 'Dove Miniature'": what is fascinating about the art of the Middle Ages is grounded in its abundance of mystery (*Reichtum an Geheimnis*), in its distant, foreign, alien character, the paradox of its alluring promise and hermetic refusal, the muteness of its signs.[9]

Indeed, the "fascination of the material" is something of a topos in Ohly's writing, as again in the preface to this volume: "The young man, like the old man, was always fascinated [*fasziniert*] by the new, the unknown [*vom Unbekannten*], places where the first furrows could be plowed in virgin territory [*Gelände*]. Medieval significs offered a scholarly field for research that could be cultivated according to plans that could with time grow broader."[10] What fascinated about the material to which Ohly was drawn was its character of "the unknown," a character it may well have retained, even after application of the philologist's subtle—and tactful—arts. Just such an expanse of unknown material, of the philological uncanny, as it were, is set before the reader's eyes early in Ohly's "Introduction" to the Italian texts of his selected essays, as their author characterizes the material that "lured," the pursuit that "fascinated" him: "Instead of literary-historical panoramas, what lured me were expeditions of discovery into the unknown [*in das Unbekannte*] similar to archaeological expeditions that seek through sample excavations to ascertain profiles of the historical terrain [*des historischen Geländes*], to blaze trails of understanding into territory as yet untracked . . . what fascinated

9. Cf. Ohly, "Problems of Medieval Significs and Hugh of Folieto's 'Dove Miniature,'" in this volume, pp. 68–135, here p. 68.

10. Ohly, "Geleitwort," p. 22; "Preface," p. xiv.

[*faszinierten*] me were the historical variations on such thousand-year-old themes with their merger of tradition and foundation, variations on fleeting but constant mythic melodies with their stylistic alteration that derives from the alteration of a whole way of understanding the world."[11] The above passage reads, in its entirety, like a generous amplification of the former, the former like a highly abbreviated version of the latter. Here the "untracked" and "unknown" character of the "historical terrain" is signified in a horizontal "metaphor of the way" and the vertical "archaeological metaphor" of excavation, both belonging to the encompassing metaphorics of "archaeological expeditions" and "expeditions of discovery," both images of philology on the path of art.[12]

The material Ohly's philology investigates is untracked, unearthed, unknown. Researched on alien terrain, it remains—neither metaphysically nor meta-metaphysically but, rather, philologically—other. Observed within many contexts and from multiple perspectives, viewed more closely but never fully, given the approximative character of all philological understanding, it takes on the uncanny fascination and allure of what is "at once alien and familiar": "A comparatistic view of the German literature of the Middle Ages has always been mandatory, since the latter bloomed for by far the most part on the soil of foreign languages and learning until well into the thirteenth century. Surfacing at first like an isle out of an ocean of Latin usage and only gradually laying down its own connected bases of tradition, it then later received, for a century and longer, stimulating influences from France and transformed them with devotion into its own property. So it comes as no surprise that, for example, more than half of my scholarly publications had to be concerned with non-German traditions, which permit us to see German from the outside, at once alien and familiar."[13] It is this view "from the out-

11. Ohly, "Einleitung" typescript, pp. 2–3; "Introduzione," p. 22.

12. Despite obvious parallels the metaphorics of "Einleitung" typescript, pp. 2–3/"Introduzione," p. 22 and "Geleitwort," p. 2/"Preface," pp. xiii–xiv differ significantly. The former is dominated by a "metaphorics of the way" and an "archaeological metaphorics," the latter by an "agricultural metaphorics" of collective effort, joint cultivation, and patient development over time.

13. Friedrich Ohly, "In der Ringvorlesung 'Aufgaben und Möglichkeiten der Germanistik' am 26. Mai 1970," in "Stellungnahmen," pp. 26–27. On the "approximative character of all philological understanding" cf., e.g., Dilthey, "The Rise of Hermeneutics," p. 249: "Theoretically we here [with Schleiermacher's 'practical' and 'elegant' resolution of the 'difficulty' of the hermeneutical circle] reach the limits of all interpretation, which is able to fulfill its task only up to a certain point. For all understanding always remains partial and can never be completed. *Individuum est ineffabile.*" For Ohlyean formulations of philological approximationism cf. Ohly's reference to

side," of a material "at once alien and familiar," that stirs the fascination of distance and difference, lures the philological-historical quest for what is distant, immersion in what is different.[14] The approach *de longue durée* to the mysteries of such alienation, the long philological-historical quest for its millennial vicissitudes of theme and variation, genesis and transmission, for "stylistic alteration that derives from the alteration of a whole way of understanding the world," only heightens the fascination—and wonder. Unmistakable as Ohly sets out on an "expedition of discovery" or settles down—"with a group of younger colleagues devoted to the cause"—to tend a "field for research that could be cultivated according to plans that could with time grow broader," this fascination and wonder at the alien familiarity of the material lies at the very outset of the quest and at every step along the way.[15]

Wehrli, "Deutsche Literaturgeschichte im Mittelalter?" below, pp. 12–13; and Friedrich Ohly, "Remarks of a Philologist about *Memoria*," in this volume, pp. 285–369.

14. Cf. Dilthey, "The Rise of Hermeneutics," pp. 235–236, 248–249. See also Friedrich August Wolf, "Darstellung der Alterthums-Wissenschaft," in *Kleine Schriften in lateinischer und deutscher Sprache*, vol. 2, *Deutsche Aufsätze*, ed. Gottfried Bernhardy (Halle, 1869), pp. 808–895, here pp. 886 inf.–887 sup.; Friedrich Schleiermacher, *Hermeneutik*, ed. Heinz Kimmerle, *Abhandlungen der Heidelberger Akademie der Wissenschaften: Philosophisch-historische Klasse*, Jahrgang 1959, Abh. 2 (Heidelberg, 1959), pp. 79, 119, 128, 129, 130, 131, 140, 146, here esp. p. 128; Friedrich Ast, *Grundlinien der Grammatik, Hermeneutik und Kritik* (1808; reprint, Ann Arbor, Mich., 1982), § 69, 165–166. See also F. D. E. Schleiermacher, *Hermeneutics: The Handwritten Manuscripts*, ed. Heinz Kimmerle, trans. James Duke and Jack Forstman, American Academy of Religion Texts and Translations Series, ed. Robert Ellwood, Jr., no. 1 (Missoula, Mont., 1977), pp. 180, 200; Boeckh, *Enzyklopädie und Methodenlehre*, p. 12; ibid., pp. 19–20; Friedrich Nietzsche, *Encyclopaedie der klassischen Philologie und Einleitung in das Studium derselben*, in *Nietzsche Werke: Kritische Gesamtausgabe*, ed. Giorgio Colli and Mazzino Montinari, 2d sec., vol. 3: *Vorlesungsaufzeichnungen (SS 1870–SS 1871)*, ed. Fritz Bornmann with Mario Carpitella (Berlin, 1993), pp. 339–437, here p. 368: "The most important (and most difficult) thing is to immerse oneself lovingly in classical antiquity and sense the difference"; ibid., p. 373: "The task of *understanding* an author or received information seems easy at first; it is, however, something very difficult, given this immense distance and the difference in ethnicity. We have not developed out of the same element that is to be explained here . . . our *understanding* of classical antiquity is a continuous, perhaps unconscious process of *drawing parallels*. This holds also for reading of any kind, all the more for ancient works, in which everything is alien to us"; ibid., p. 389: "What matters is precisely what we don't have in common, one has to immerse oneself in this."

15. See, e.g., at the opening of "On the Spiritual Sense of the Word in the Middle Ages" (in this volume, p. 1) Ohly's fascination and wonder at Hegel's obliviousness vis-à-vis explaining "the sublime on the basis of Jewish monotheism," an explanation with which he "brought us to the root of Christian art," an art that "he now leaves out of consideration." For "fascination and wonder" in Ohly's openings cf. also "Typology as a Form of Historical Thought" (in this volume, pp. 31–67), "Problems of Medieval Significs" (p. 68), "The Cathedral as Temporal Space:

The way nineteenth- and twentieth-century classical philology perceived its mission to reappropriate "what history has transmitted, in order not to lose possession of it," "to take with us, and revivify, our human past, transforming it into a future" (Ohly), is epitomized in Carl Ludwig Urlichs's (1892) definition of philology's objective: "Philology has as its objective the scholarly cognition of minds foreign to our own, as they have embodied themselves individually and communally under particular circumstances and as they have expressed themselves in enduring monuments: it is therefore essentially recognition and appropriation."[16] To attain this "recognition and appropriation" is, according to Urlichs as well as others, the task of a philology that identifies itself not only as science, as knowledge, but also as art. Indeed, the artistic character of philology is specified by Ohly quite directly in a prior polemical context. In October 1966 Ohly protested a "fashionable, ephemeral" bureaucratization of research and teaching in "Germanistic philology" (*Germanistik*), citing the artistic nature of the humaniora, including the philologies: "Motionless rigidity will descend upon the faculties. . . . The subject matter of the model plan of studies for germanistic philology . . . clearly has fashionable, ephemeral features. . . . Curricular schemes spoil the character of scholarship. By imposing directions they bring the free play between intellectual stimulation and scholarly methods to a halt. Human sciences are no proper soil for didactic four-year plans. They have an unmistakable character of their own that American faculties designate with the title 'Division of the Humanities.' The humaniora are good soil for experience gained through encounter. Their sciences are arts."[17] The ancient con-

---

Siena" (in this volume, p. 136), "Dew and Pearl: A Lecture" (in this volume, p. 234), "Poetry as the Necessary Fruit of a Suffering" (in this volume, p. 251), and "A Philologist's Remarks on *Memoria*" (in this volume, pp. 285–369).

16. Urlichs, *HbA*, vol. 1, pp. 1–145, here p. 5. Cf. Ohly's formulations, below, p. 381.

17. Friedrich Ohly, "Stellungnahme zu Empfehlungen des Wisssenschaftsrates (Oktober 1966)," in "Stellungnahmen," p. 6. Cf. D. Klemenz, "Humaniora," in *Handwörterbuch der Philosophie*, vol. 3, *G-H*, ed. Joachim Ritter (Basel, 1974), henceforth *HWPh*, cols. 1216–1217; and further Rudolf Pfeiffer, *Humanitas Erasmiana*, Studien der Bibliothek Warburg, ed. Fritz Saxl, vol. 22 (London, 1931), p. 7 and n. 3, with references to P. S. Allen, "The Humanities," *Classical Association Proceedings* 14 (London, 1917): 123–133; and Boeckh, *Enzyklopädie und Methodenlehre*, p. 24 ("the so-called humaniora"). See also ibid., p. 25 ("Philology claims to be a science; it is, however, at the same time, an art, namely, insofar as the historical construction of antiquity is itself something artistic"); and Blass, "Hermeneutik und Kritik," p. 167, on hermeneutics and criticism as arts. Urlichs, p. 7, distinguishes "Altertumswissenschaft" (science of antiquity) from "Philologie," assigning "categorically and exclusively to the latter those subjects whose implementation demands just as much art as erudition." On humaniora and the like cf. also Friedrich

ception of "art" (τεχνη) is fundamentally empirical, practical, and pragmatic. The traditional empiricism, practicality, and pragmatism of philology is understandable when we consider it as a kind of art, as rooted in the ancient understanding of "art" outlined by the Romance philologist and systematizer of Greco-Roman rhetoric Heinrich Lausberg, in succinct and lucid formulations.[18]

Such an art, insofar as it is "gained from experience," is empirical; insofar as it is guided by "a system of didactic rules . . . to the end" of doing something as well as possible, it is practical; insofar as "the end" to the attainment of which its "didactic rules" have been "subsequently thought out in a logical fashion" is that of "performing some action," it is pragmatic.[19] And insofar as "theory" is involved at all, it will be a "theory" conceived and formulated as procedure "thought out in a logical fashion, to the end of correctly performing some action that aims at completion and can be repeated at will." Such a methodical procedure may be "represented in theoretical terms" but it will be "validated in practice" and judged pragmatically in terms of the fruit it bears, in terms of its concrete achievements.[20]

Many of Ohly's most revealing statements of self-interpretation occur not in theoretical but rather in practical contexts. In 1977 Ohly characterized

---

August Wolf, *Encyclopädie der Philologie,* ed. S. M. Stockmann (Leipzig, 1845), pp. 4–7; and Wolf, "Darstellung," pp. 814–816 and esp. the long n. 814–815. Cf. also Gottfried Bernhardy, *Grundlinien der Encyklopädie der Philologie* (Halle, 1832), pp. 15, 20.

18. Cf. Heinrich Lausberg, *Handbuch der literarischen Rhetorik: Eine Grundlegung der Literaturwissenschaft,* 3d ed. (Stuttgart, 1990), pp. 1–5, here pp. 1–2, and now also *Handbook of Literary Rhetorik: A Foundation for Literary Study,* ed. David E. Orton and R. Dean Anderson, trans. Matthew T. Bliss, Annemiek Jansen, and David E. Orton (Leiden, 1998), pp. 25–29, here pp. 25–26. See further Rudolf Pfeiffer, *History of Classical Scholarship from the Beginnings to the End of the Hellenistic Age* (Oxford, 1968), p. 3. On "philology" cf. Lausberg, *Handbuch,* pp. 31–32; *Handbook,* pp. 7–8.

19. Cf. Lausberg, *Handbuch,* pp. 25–26; *Handbook,* pp. 1–2; Dilthey, "The Rise of Hermeneutics"; and Blass, "Hermeneutik und Kritik," as above, n. 6. The empiricism, practicality, and pragmatism of philology are based largely on its conception as an "art" developed from "general," "necessary," "natural" activities. Cf. Blass, "Hermeneutik und Kritik," p. 167, for "understanding" and "judging" as "quite general and necessary," i.e., natural, "activities of the human mind, which must be readily available and technically cultivated in a special degree where their objects are separated from the practitioner by as great a distance as in the case of classical literature."

20. Cf. Lausberg, as above, n. 18; also Ohly, "In der Ringvorlesung 'Aufgaben und Möglichkeiten,'" p. 34, and "Einleitung," in *SchrMB,* pp. xiii–xvi and xvi–xviii, for the very practical and pragmatic role of "theory" in the Ohly school's "renewal" of the "medieval type of allegorical lexicon."

the aim and interdisciplinary openness of his collaborative scholarly project: "This project, which is receptive to all historically oriented disciplines of the human sciences (and not of these alone), which is eager for their stimulation and assistance, and which also contributes to reconstructing an aesthetics of the Middle Ages, proposes to work at building a foundation common to, and decisive for, many fields of research into the Middle Ages. . . . Up to now our work has been done pragmatically, from the concrete object. Theory was to be developed from historical findings, not philosophically, that is, to the greatest extent possible from the ways medieval procedure understood itself historically in theoretical terms."[21] Historically relevant contextualization, be it cast in terms of a documented theory or methodology of artistic, literary, and cultural encoding and decoding or in less "theoretical," less "methodological," that is, less general, terms, for instance in terms of documented examples or models, remains the basis of Ohly's philology, as of traditional philology generally. Accessing cultural materials "at once alien and familiar" from the perspectives offered by "their own" historical contexts, be they reflective metacontexts or lower-level comparative contexts, affords—from an Ohlyean standpoint—the most promising point of departure for the philological enterprise: making what is more alien than familiar more familiar and less alien, making "their own" "our own."[22]

Historical contextualization helps, on the one hand, to warrant the otherness of a humanity far removed from our own, by virtue of multiple parameters and factors: "space" and "time," "religion" and "culture," "race," "gender," and "class," aside from all sorts of individual differences that obtain within the foregoing categories. It does so by supplementing, complicating, potentiating the distances and differences already inherent in otherness. On the other hand, through just such supplementation, complication, and potentiation, historical contextualization generates compromise formations, intermediaries, and go-betweens: empathetic links, hybrid understanding.

21. Ohly, "Einleitung," in *SchrMB,* pp. xii–xiii.

22. Cf. Joachim Wach, *Das Verstehen: Grundzüge einer Geschichte der hermeneutischen Theorie im 19. Jahrhundert,* vol. 3 (Tübingen, 1933), p. 339 (Sachregister s.v. "Zusammenhang," "Ganzes"). See also Schleiermacher, *Hermeneutik,* pp. 61–62: "Only through context[ualizing] and comparing the particular [*Zusammenhang und Vergleichung des Besonderen*] does one arrive at the inner unity," i.e., "that which is representable in each particular open to view," "the totality of" which can, however, "never be reached," making "the task" of representation and interpretation "an infinite one." Thus, "carrying out the task is in any case possible only through approximation."

In this way it helps warrant the proximity and congruity, even the familiarity, of such alien otherness to our own being. In sum, historical contextualization serves—paradoxically—the paradoxical ends of philological art: judging as well as understanding, criticism as well as interpretation, separation as well as identification:

> "Κρινειν, . . . 'judging,' *iudicare*," is to a certain degree the opposite of understanding; for in this case one identifies with a mentality alien to oneself; in the former case one separates oneself and regards what is to be judged as something separate from the judge. Both stances are equally natural to the human being.[23]

With this allusion to the role of historical contextualization in the tradition of philology in general and in particular within the philological arts of criticism and interpretation, judging and understanding, the question arises of the forms assumed by those "constant tasks of philology" in Ohly's reflection and of the ways these forms may or may not differ from their traditional counterparts.

Recalling the tradition of the parts or functions of philology, variously formulated as "activities," "practices," "offices," or "tasks" of the philologist vis-à-vis the familiar yet alien, alien yet familiar material that "history has transmitted" to us, Ohly distinguishes and describes them as follows: "The philologies have their constant tasks. The latter are no accidents, but rather make up the core of the philologies and must continue to exist: preserving and sifting, cleansing and making available, explaining and interpreting what history has transmitted, in order not to lose possession of it. What is at stake is how to take with us, and revivify, our human past, transforming it into a future. What is at stake is not so much the present as it is representing the past for the sake of enriching the here and now. In that context the maxim applies that history 'is always history only from the viewpoint of some present time' and therefore can never be fully written. . . . This entails that the horizons of [historical] intuition can also change."[24] Ohly's outline of the constant tasks of the philologies follows the basic division of philology into interpretation

23. Blass, "Hermeneutik und Kritik," p. 168.

24. Cf. Ohly, "In der Ringvorlesung 'Aufgaben und Möglichkeiten,'" p. 26, on Wehrli, "Deutsche Literaturgeschichte im Mittelalter?" p. 9. See Max Wehrli, "Deutsche Literaturgeschichte im Mittelalter?" *German Life and Letters*, vol. 23 (October 1969), reprinted in Wehrli, *Formen mittelalterlicher Erzählung* (Zürich, 1969), pp. 7–23.

and criticism, the latter being itself divided into "recension" (*recensio* = "examination") and "emendation" (*emendatio*).[25] His formulation renders Lachmannian *recensio* and *emendatio* in untechnical and unassuming yet evocative language (*Sichtung*, "sifting"; and *Reinigung*, "cleansing"). It embeds them within a structure that, like the structure of memory, of which Ohly's philology is a refinement, connects past, present, and future for the sake of reappropriating and revitalizing a past that has been preserved and made available. What was lost, or alienated, was in danger of being lost, is repossessed and revivified. Confirmed as our own, it is connected to a future, connected, however, also to the past and thus rendered capable of representing the past and becoming available to enrich the present. Criticism, sifting and cleansing the material, authenticates it as received from the past and makes it accessible to explanation and interpretation, transforming it into a future, enriching the here and now. In order to enrich the present, it must be recalled from the past; in order to be so recalled, it must be seen as foreign to the present. In order to become our own, it must be alien; in order to be alien, it must be seen as other than, but capable of becoming, our own. Criticism takes precedence in this brief delineation, not only sequentially but also in respect to the elaboration of its foundational task ("preserving"), its central tasks ("sifting, cleansing"), and its supplementary task ("making available").

Building upon this tradition of philological arts in the best traditions of German aestheticism and humanism, Ohly conceives of an old-new art of philology viewed from a dual perspective: "philology as an aesthetic science" (*Philologie als Kunstwissenschaft*) and "philology as a human science" (*Philologie als Humanwissenschaft*). Prefigured in several earlier self-presentations, it is also situated strategically, its two components separated from each other, within the "Preface" printed above. The passages in question are driven by an impulse to unification, to the integration of missing parts, which, drawing upon Ohly's aestheticism and his humanism, is potentiated twofold.[26] Other passages, for example, in "Einleitung" and the version

25. The division of philology into hermeneutics (= "art of understanding") and criticism (= "art of judging") is ubiquitous in classical-philological literature. On the subdivision of textual criticism into *recensio* and *emendatio* in the work of Karl Lachmann cf. Rudolf Pfeiffer, *History of Classical Scholarship, 1300–1850* (Oxford, 1976), p. 190. Cf. further John Edwin Sandys, *A History of Classical Scholarship*, vol. 3 (Cambridge, 1908), pp. 126–131; and Sebastiano Timpanaro, "La genesi del metodo del Lachmann," *Biblioteca del Saggiatore*, vol. 18 (1963). Cf. also the articles on "Kritik," etc., in *HWPh*, 4:1249–1282, 1282–1292, 1292–1293, 1293–1294, 1294–1299.

26. Cf. Ohly, "Geleitwort," pp. 3, 3–4; "Preface," pp. xv, xvi: What is presented as missing from Ohly's oeuvre in the former passage is (aside from the edition of the St. Trudpert Song of Songs

of it in Ohly's *Geometria e memoria: Lettera e allegoria nel Medioevo,* "Introduzione," as well as in Ohly's "Geleitwort" in *Ausgewählte und neue Schriften zur Literaturgeschichte und Bedeutungsforschung* and the version of it in this volume, "Preface," sketch in the contours of "philology as an aesthetic science" and "philology as a human science" without the nomenclature: "With the sobriety [*Nüchternheit*], at once moved and thoughtful, that is proper to the philologist, in whom fantasy [*Phantasie*] and scrupulosity [*Akribie*] meet, I am drawn to the spirit become form that characterizes the Middle Ages, those Middle Ages that reach in more ways than a few down to the age of Goethe. What is visible in my work disguises something of its ground—a deeply engrossed visual contemplation of art—in favor of another inclination: understanding what arises from the course of history as a new word in the perennial dialogue of the ages on the question, What abides as human?"[27] What Ohly intimates with the reference to the "ground" of his work as residing in "a deeply engrossed visual contemplation of art" goes beyond working out the implications of the traditional conception of philology as an art, beyond providing texts with appealing illustrations of varying degree of historical relevance, beyond resolute efforts to explore more (and less) obvious connections between verbal and nonverbal arts, to a twofold crux: visualizing verbal material whose visual components may be anything but obvious, verbalizing visual material whose verbal constituents may be equally remote, but in both cases no less, perhaps even all the more, illuminating, with respect to "the scholarly cognition of minds foreign to our own, as they have embodied themselves individually and communally" in such visualizable verbal and verbalizable visual material. What Ohly is drawn to, is, as he emphasizes throughout his self-reflections, not art for art's sake but art as a means of meaning, art as "spirit become form," the arts, both visual and verbal, as embodying "possibilities of being human" that have "become reality in forms filled with meaning": "Together with the sobriety, at once moved and thoughtful, befitting the philologist who unites imagination and scrupulosity—the philologist oriented to what in the course of history has become form—it is his integrative view which provides a basis for justice. History's timeless conversation on the question of what abides as human shows him in the arts possibilities of being human that have become reality in forms filled

with commentary) the intensive interpretation and criticism of an individual work. What is presented as still lacking in the latter is acceptance of metaphor as significant for philology as a human science—on a par with dealing with essentials of the human condition in literary art.

27. Ohly, "Einleitung" typescript, p. 2; "Introduzione," p. 22.

with meaning. In change he finds constants of humanity that have never been outlived—neither in good nor in evil."[28] This exceedingly condensed statement, perhaps Ohly's last word on his philology, reiterates most of his metaphilological themes, touching again upon the character of the philologist, the philological virtues, the relation between philology and history, the transformation of history into form, the way in which "what abides as human" is implicated in history, in which "possibilities of being human" (*Möglichkeiten des Menschseins*), take on form and reality in the arts, "have become reality in forms filled with meaning," "constants of humanity that have never been outlived—neither in good nor in evil." "Philology as an aesthetic science" (*Philologie als Kunstwissenschaft*) and "philology as a human science" (*Philologie als Humanwissenschaft*) are not only inseparable; from Ohly's viewpoint they are also interdependent: the former without the latter would degenerate into some "formalism" for the day and hour of the sort that Ohly acutely protested in polemical contexts; the latter without the former would be scarcely accessible—recognizable, perhaps, only in by-products of "dehumanization," as "deformations," that have the effect of diminishing rather than enhancing the "possibilities of being human."[29]

Each of these "philologies as . . ." has its share in both "fields," medieval significs and literary studies, to which Ohly devoted himself. Each such field is bound to the other by a common "interest in the illumination of existence by means of those possibilities of the spoken word whose aim is meaning—something that is also a task of art."[30] Further, each is integrated with the other by virtue of their common concern with "metaphorics" (*Metaphorik*), "thought images" (*Bildgedanken*), and "imaged thoughts" (*Gedankenbilder*) as major forms among such linguistic possibilities. They are distinguished, however, in that medieval significs is understood as the awesome project of "opening up the world through cognitive insights," revealing "a field for interpreting the world," while the function of literary history is understood as a preoccupation with literary art "as a vessel that contains more secrets to help us understand what is human, in the fullness of all its developments throughout the course of history."[31]

Both philological perspectives, philology as aesthetic science and philology as human science, have a share in culture. Philology itself, as well as its

28. Ohly, "Einleitung" typescript, p. 4; "Introduzione," p. 9. Cf. also Ohly, "Dew and Pearl," p. 250.

29. Cf. Ohly, "In der Ringvorlesung 'Aufgaben und Möglichkeiten,'" pp. 23–24.

30. Cf. Ohly, "Geleitwort," p. 2; "Preface," p. xiv.

31. Cf. Ohly "Geleitwort," p. 2; "Preface," pp. xiv–xvi.

Ohlyean perspectives, as an aesthetic—as well as artistic—refinement of the fundamental human capacity for remembrance, is based upon a *humanum*, and thus is relevant to a vital area of culturological thought and cultural practice.[32] "A Philologist's Remarks about *Memoria*" opens with a reflection on *memoria* as a natural human capacity and closes with an unforgettable meditation on *memoria* cultivated as art, as philology. Characterized by a balance of sobriety and devotion, of "sobriety and love," it portrays the "ethos" and the "tone" of the philologist, the tentative approximation—each to the other—of philology and poetry, alienation and poetic identification, remembrance of a past that cannot be changed and premonitions of a future yet to be remembered:

> The philologist's ethos makes it his duty to preserve, through the ages, an undamaged memory as a legacy for the present and the future. It is part of his business also to interpret what has been entrusted to him by history in terms of his own day. . . . If memory is directed to what is a given, and spirit aimed at what is to be achieved, past and future are enfolded in both in the present of existence. . . . Or . . . "All memory is the present. In the more pure element all memory would appear to us as necessary prepoetry." The philologist is ill advised to relapse into the tone of his object—as though he has to imitate the poet—without maintaining his distance from it. However, he cannot be criticized, in the rare case where he succeeds, for his effort to make what is remembered so clear to the present or to what is timeless that even a hint of what is temporally possible is opened up by him. A tone of restraint rather than one of demonstration may help him to a sober, even an alienating, poeticization of the object of his contemplation in the sense that here and there on occasion the "memory could appear as prepoetry." At moments when such a self-revelation of memory and expectation comes to fruition, when the experiences of a teacher and the hopes of his disciples meeting, at last, in their search, finally unite, then perhaps a small piece of the future is not lost.[33]

32. For "the *humanum*" at a foundational moment in the history of Germanistic philology (*Germanistik*) cf. Jacob Grimm, "Über den Namen der Germanisten," in *Kleinere Schriften*, vol. 7 (Berlin, 1884), p. 569, and ibid., "Bericht über die Zusammenkunft der Germanisten in Frankfurt am 24., 25. und 26. Sept. 1846," p. 578 ("the cultivation of what is human, the *humanum* or even the humaniora"). On Ohly's idea of the *Humanum* cf. especially above, "A Philologist's Remarks about *Memoria*": to 10/3 ("the striving for survival in remembrance . . . is proper to human beings and claims recognition as a *humanum*"); to 10/3 ("in the human world religions and culture are bound to memory"); to 11/6 ("human beings who are less protected and more dependent").

33. Ohly, "A Philologist's Remarks about *Memoria*," pp. 368–369.

Scholars and intellectuals in this country, even broader constituencies, have come to experience and formulate the anxieties and apprehensions of the present as problems of culture. This means the loss of shared signs, the ruin of shared values, the decay of memory and the culture it engenders. It means failure of the very idea and the culture of "humanity," dissolution of the human bonds that, despite their ever-present fragility and vulnerability, form the supportive infrastructure of whatever dignity human life can claim. At the same time textual and cultural studies have been increasingly conceived as largely, if not wholly, "critical," that is, "censorious." But a textual and a cultural studies informed by philological tradition, "medieval significs," for example, or a much-maligned "literary history," and by a philology of culture indebted to them, knows that criticism itself is not only depreciative but also appreciative, that the primary function of criticism as well as of culture is finally no less constructive than deconstructive, no less creative than destructive. Where culture criticizes or destroys, it is critical for the sake of reconstruction, destructive for the sake of creation. A cultural studies that is uncritically critical, globally destructive, is prone to lapse, whether it will or no, into the ultimate unculture, the misculture and inhumanity of "cultural despair."[34] It is prone to slip, long before its moment of triumph, from the pan-critical into a selectively uncritical stance, the former, of course, vis-à-vis what is nearest and undearest, the latter vis-à-vis what is farthest and ipso facto dearest, most susceptible of unrealistic idealization, reactionary enthrallment. Where even these latter possibilities are foreclosed, the criticistic perspective often really does seem paradoxically to assume the guise of its own worst enemy: the "view from nowhere."[35]

The question of the critical imperative, a question which subsumes but transcends academic debates on the relative merits of textual-cultural "deconstruction" versus textual-cultural "reconstruction," has been posed with regard to Ohly's work in a particularly disturbing, immediately relevant form. It is the question of the Holocaust, more precisely and pointedly the question of responding to the Holocaust, with which George Steiner closes his preface to Ohly's study of two diametrically opposed reactions to guilt:

34. Cf. Fritz Stern, *The Politics of Cultural Despair: A Study in the Rise of the German Ideology* (Berkeley, 1961); and Georg Lukács, *Die Zerstörung der Vernunft* (Berlin, 1962). See also Web site notes to "A Philologist's Remarks about *Memoria*," to 10/3 ("in the human world religions and culture are bound to memory").

35. Cf. Chicago Cultural Studies Group, "Critical Multiculturalism," *Critical Inquiry* 18, no. 3 (spring 1992): 530–555, here esp. pp. 550–552.

repentance that trusts in God's capacity to forgive (Gregorius) and despair that eschews such trust and forfeits such grace (Judas):

It is ironic that Dr. Friedrich Ohly's work itself lies under a certain shadow. Nowhere does he bring himself to touch on the obvious central crux that, of the disciples, only Judas is, by his very name, defined as a Jew. It is in the name of Judas' alleged betrayal and of the deicide which it provokes, that Jews were hounded to pitiless death from those very times onward in which Judas looms in Christian literature and iconography. It is countless Jewish men, women and children who suffered ostracism and martyrdom in the black light of Judas' fate as it has been proclaimed and imaged by Christianity. Half a century after Auschwitz, it seems as if German scholarship is still lamed when it draws near the unspeakable; a condition which gives to this essay on "life and guilt" a constraining pathos.[36]

It is true that Ohly does not deal with the medieval promotion of Judas as "Jew par excellence" or with its postmedieval tradition, an identification which served to justify the humiliation and persecution visited upon Jews during the premodern and early modern periods through the eighteenth century and thereafter. At the same time, it is not true that Ohly has failed to recognize and formulate the malicious side of the Middle Ages and their tradition. This includes the hateful character of a Christian anti-Semitism situated within the context of similar phenomena in the Middle Ages, a medieval hatefulness and inhumanity which has persisted well beyond the Middle Ages, to emerge once more in our own times with the destruction of European Jewry in the Holocaust. Elsewhere, in a study of "dismemberment in mediaeval literature," Ohly has written on the subject as follows:

During the Middle Ages the Christian Church persecuted all suspected of heresy mercilessly in wars and legal actions. Tens of thousands fell victim to this persecu-

36. Cf. Friedrich Ohly, *Der Verfluchte und der Erwählte: Vom Leben mit der Schuld,* Rheinisch-Westfälische Akademie der Wissenschaften,Vorträge, G207 (Opladen, 1976), and idem, *The Damned and the Elect: Guilt in Western Culture,* trans. Linda Archibald (Cambridge, 1992), here pp. xiii–xiv. Cf. on Judas and Jews Hyam Maccoby, *Judas Iscariot and the Myth of Jewish Evil* (New York, 1992), esp. pp. 79–81. Maccoby argues the driving force behind the myth of Jewish evil lay in "the need to detach Pauline Christianity from the Jewish revolt against Rome," leading "the evangelists to transfer the" actual or potential "conflict between Jesus and Rome to an alleged struggle between Jesus and the Jewish religion." To Maccoby's formula of "Pauline Christian" disavowal and incrimination—"not we, but 'Judas,' not we, but 'the Jews,' are traitors to Rome"—a second and even more intense denial and inculpation might be added: "not we, but 'Judas,' not we, but 'you Jews,' have betrayed 'our God.'"

tion. New heights were reached after the Reformation on the piles of the Inquisition. When Christians had to suffer this way at the hands of the Church, one cannot really be astonished at the persecution of the Jews, during which Bishops and Christian kings made ample use of dismemberment. English chroniclers report several persecutions of Jews between 1180 and 1280. The Jews have always been the victim of rumours concerning abominable acts allegedly perpetrated by them against Christians or the Christian faith. Such rumours were used particularly in England as an excuse for the persecution of Jews throughout the country. The sources mention dozens of Jews from Lincoln, Norwich, Northampton and other cities who were torn apart by horses or dragged by horses through the streets of London before they finally died on the gallows. . . . One person who can be quoted as an authority was Geoffrey Chaucer who, when he describes in "The Prioress's Tale" how a Jew was punished for allegedly having murdered a Christian child, wrote approvingly: (1822) "*yvel shal have, that yvel wol deserve. Therfor with wilde hors he dide hem drawe, and after that he heng hem by the lawe.*". . . The inherent human tendency towards bestiality did not really burst forth in all its entirety until about the 12th century, becoming even stronger in the late Middle Ages when this punishment was adapted from literature to meet the supposed needs of the judicial system and executions by dismemberment received the blessings and were actively employed by the Emperor and the Church. . . . Modern times have proved worse than the Middle Ages and even more so than classical antiquity. History gives us no occasion to hope that a repetition can be excluded. During both the glorious French and the glorious Bolshevik revolutions not enough horses could be found to kill the thousands of innocent victims, so that it became necessary to make use of such technical inventions as the guillotine. During the last few decades there has been the Holocaust, the Archipelago Gulag was a reality and the Cultural Revolution swept over a great Empire. Even when discussing the execution of a traitor by dismemberment the only attitude which befits modern man is one of modest humility.[37]

It is true that such passages are rarely met with on the surface of Ohly's work; but the sense of man's potentiality for evil which is formulated in the above text, a potentiality to which the Holocaust bears undeniable witness, albeit mute, and which is all the more painful to articulate the closer one has

37. Cf. Friedrich Ohly, "The Death of Traitors by Dismemberment in Mediaeval Literature," trans. Timothy Sodmann from *Atti Accademia Peloritana dei Pericolanti Classe di Lettere Filosofia e Belle Arti* 63 (Messina, 1989): 9–27, here pp. 18, 25–26, 27. In *AusgNSchr*, pp. 423–435 (German version).

been touched by it, lies, I think, just beneath the surface of much that Ohly has written. This is especially true of essays situated on the borderline between philology and moral theology, such as the study to which George Steiner addressed the "Foreword" cited above.[38] A rendering of its subtitle more literal than the catchy "Guilt in Western Culture" is "On Living with Guilt." The contrast between the two translations says something about the tendency of contemporary literary—and cultural—critical discourse on the one hand and the moral-theological tone of Ohly's essay on the other. In the former case "guilt" lies in "it," that very large abstraction, "Western culture"; in the latter case the problem of "living with guilt" is one's own—guilt lives with and in oneself. Ohly's philological-historical interpretation and criticism of the Judas legend presents the figure of Judas not as the representative of an "evil," "malicious," "deicidal" Jewish people, but rather as the realization of a human, all-too-human potentiality (*humanum*). It is a certain despairing, unrepentant, self-destructive way of "living with guilt":

> "How can I live with my guilt?" [. . .] The question first put to Adam, put more starkly at his expulsion from Paradise; the question which belongs among the most enduring problems of this world; a legacy for all times, though not every age has taken it with the same seriousness. "How can I live with my guilt?": the question no one can avoid, though not everyone takes it equally to heart. . . . All myth is bound together, above all, by that most human of all constants, living with guilt. *Nil humani a me alienum puto.* It would be strange indeed if the damned and the elect did *not* march side by side through history. . . . What counts in art, and in life, is not what happens—happens to a person—but what he makes of it. . . . Judas' story is in fact the closest to Oedipus': both have an ill-omened oracle, both are exposed, grow up in a strange land, quarrel with their brothers, kill their fathers and marry their mothers. But when it comes to the question of living with guilt, Judas diverges from Oedipus, for Judas' solution is despair and suicide. It is in their search for self—the evil exposed to the light of day—that Oedipus and Gregorius, finding themselves other than they would wish, cast aside appearances, assume their true identity, and live it. There is no guilty verdict, no acquittal, but they themselves acknowledge and stand for what they are.[39]

38. Cf. Friedrich Ohly, "Desperatio und Praesumptio: Zur theologischen Verzweiflung und Vermessenheit," in *Festgabe für Otto Höfler zum 75. Geburtstag*, ed. H. Birkhan, Philologica Germanica, no. 3 (Wien, 1976), pp. 501–558. In *AusgNSchr*, pp. 177–216.

39. Ohly, *Der Verfluchte und der Erwählte*, pp. 7, 136–137; *The Damned and the Elect*, pp. 1, 139–140. Steiner's reference to the subtitle (p. xiv: "this essay on 'life and guilt'") also obscures the

Ohly's rereading of the Judas legend, as solidly based as it is upon the bedrock of Christian tradition, represents something very like the transformation of the anti-Semitic myth of "Judas' alleged betrayal and of the deicide which it provokes" into an old-new humanistic myth. Ohly's rereading assimilates the Judas legend to an old-new humanistic culture infinitely closer to the letter and spirit of *Nostra Aetate* and its Christianity than to the tradition of Christian anti-Semitism. Judas is no longer demonized, but rather presented as the all-too-human bearer of a *humanum.* Neither he nor the Jewish people, with whom he had been identified and diabolized, is singled out as other or less than the rest of humanity, as singularly guilty of the death of Jesus, of the death of God. Rather, all are guilty. And as long as willful self-conceit, despair of active repentance and God's forgiveness, is disguised as the deepest sense of guilt, one's condition is irremediable. Such a rereading cancels and reverses the original projection of betrayal, the betrayal of God ("not we but 'Judas,' not we but 'the Jews'").[40]

What Ohly achieved in *Der Verfluchte und der Erwählte* fits the paradigm he was to propose over a decade later. It is a paradigm of "intimacy with history," of overcoming history through history, of "memory" bringing "reassurance" as well as "modesty," "confidence" as well as "sobriety," and, above all, a "culture" that imparts the values we hope and fear to profess: sorrow for the suffering, rejoicing in the joy, and respect for the dignity of all our fellow human beings. Such a culture is undone not only by blindness to moral flaws,

---

book's genuine pathos of human, all too human, betrayal of humanity. Cf. also Ohly, "Einleitung," in *GM,* 5: "Living with guilt belongs, like love and death, to the existential experiences which pass no one by who is human. The academy treatise, *The Damned and the Elect: On Living with Guilt,* that one of my books which has remained most hidden and yet surely closest to my heart, deals with . . . the question of human beings living with guilt, which belongs to the most constant of constancies in this world."

40. Cf. above, n. 36, and esp. *Nostra Aetate,* no. 4, in *Vatican Council II,* ed. Austin Flannery, pp. 741–742: "The Church always held and continues to hold that Christ out of infinite love freely underwent suffering and death because of the sins of all men, so that all might attain salvation." On "the good olive tree" see ibid., 740: "the Church cannot forget that she received the revelation of the Old Testament by way of that people with whom God in his inexpressible mercy established the ancient covenant. Nor can she forget that she draws nourishment from that good olive tree on which the wild olive branches of the Gentiles have been grafted (cf. Rom. 11: 17–24). The Church believes that Christ who is our peace has through his cross reconciled Jews and Gentiles and made them one in himself (cf. Eph. 2:14–16)." Cf. also Franz Mussner, *Tractate on the Jews: The Significance of Judaism for Christian Faith,* trans. Leonard Swidler (Philadelphia, 1984), esp. pp. 193 and 251–253.

failings, and failures in relation to our fellow human beings, but also and perhaps even more effectively by the narcissism of despair, by our inability actively to regret, repent, grieve, to face the guilt, feel the shame, and accept the sober hope that insight engenders:

> Horrifying constants in history make one ashamed of what humans have done and the Middle Ages played, in the case at hand, a particularly sad role. And still . . . the more imperative that the vicious elements of an often depressing history are held at bay. For thousands of years this has been humanity's best quality. It remains our duty if we are to avoid being devoured by malice in the future. The times when warmth succeeds in breaking through the clouds that cover mankind, when grace and glory fall upon humanity, counsel a certain intimacy with history. This intimacy should teach us confidence in the *historia calamitatum* as a zone where hope and promise also dwell. We have been given the task of expanding the paths of light cut by Divinity and mankind into the semi-darkness of the human world. Such a task would seem well worth a pledge. We need sobriety so that we may, in spite of all opposition, remain able to follow truth in love, "αληθευειν εν αγαπη."[41]

Critical judgment, to whatever genre of philological criticism it may pertain, assumes standards, norms, values—be it a "judgment of truth or falsehood, that is, historical criticism," in particular a judgment of authorship or authenticity, or "another form of criticism, the aesthetic, 'evaluative' kind, where the question is quality . . . especially whether it [the object] is beautiful"—or "just." And standards, norms, values, be they cognitive, aesthetic, or ethical, are decisive, not only in philological studies but also in questions of culture. Studies of culture some recent incarnations have tended, in the wake of poststructuralist textology, not only to selectively privilege criticism over interpretation, but also to selectively privilege deconstructive over reconstructive critical judgment, in relation to issues of culture as well.[42]

Nowhere is this more evident than with regard to the "possibilities of being human" (*Möglichkeiten des Menschseins*), the *humanum*. Never unconditionally beneficent, the idea has nonetheless represented the origin and goal, the beginning and end, the α and ω of the long cultivation of humanistic studies deriving from studies of Europe's primal others, that is, Hebraic and Greco-Roman antiquity, and extended to literatures and cultures other than

41. Ohly, "The Death of Traitors by Dismemberment," p. 27.
42. Cf. Blass, "Hermeneutik und Kritik," p. 169.

the original others. This cultivation was undertaken despite, not because of, the failures, distortions, and corruptions which also belong—as potentialities and actualities—to all things human. Ohly's humanistic and humane philology of culture foregrounds culturological reconstructionism and the reconstruction of culture as opposed to the implicit or explicit apotheosis of cultural criticism and the criticism of culture as the preeminent tasks of literary and cultural studies in our time. It raises questions about the origins, methods, and above all the ends of a critical separation divorced from interpretive identification. And it offers the *humanum* as fundamental to finding common ground within and among individual cultures that are in their particulars also profoundly different. It does not fail to probe the basic but habitually repressed function of religious belief in constituting the *humanum* and the forms of culture it helps create.[43]

Recuperating the "possibilities of being human" (*Möglichkeiten des Menschseins*) the *humanum* is probably as close to the heart and soul, the goal, of Ohly's philological enterprise as one can come. The following unpublished passage suggests the consequences for Ohly's teaching and research of his orientation to the *humanum*, the ethos of a lifework whose pedagogical and scholarly threads are interwoven inseparably and well:

> Speaking of a rehumanization with some pathos but clearly, what I contemplate is transferring the successes of a formalist approach to contexts of human significance. . . . Almost all medieval literature subscribes to an idea which is, inconceivably, antihumanistically, banned only by a rampantly formalistic brand of scholarship: the principle that literature helps us live. Our discipline would turn into the absurdity of a senseless game, and so would be guilty of a transgression against the *humanum*, if it did not see form as form that is fulfilled, if it saw literature as without a hint of the design and potential of the human being . . . Common to the themes I have called exemplary—the function and experience of space and time, the quest that leads as movement through space and time, the scene of combat with a friend or relative as that of a breakthrough beyond appearance to the reality of being, as well as the situation of man at the crossroads as the critical moment of existence,—is the humanum as that which alone legitimates our preoccupation with literature. According to Schiller: "the idea of poetry is nothing other than to give humanity its fullest possible expression" . . . Wherever and however anyone might succeed in driving this *humanum*—its α and ω—from our scholarly disci-

43. Cf. Françoise Meltzer and David Tracy, eds.,, "Symposium on 'God,'" *Critical Inquiry* 20, no. 1 (1994): 569–622, for an approach to the return of this repressed function.

pline, one would have succeeded in eliminating the discipline, germanistic philology, itself.[44]

Here the *humanum* is revealed not as the ethereal result of a "theory" within which it was, is, and will be always already contained. The *humanum* and its possibilities are, on the contrary, generated and validated approximatively in the course of philological-historical inquiry, in the course of recovering the details of texts, disciplines, and cultures, within contexts and metacontexts wedded to the textual, disciplinary, and cultural details themselves—in the course of remembering.

Taking as its point of departure what is historically, culturally, psychologically one's "own"—and yet somehow different and distant,—and setting it into reciprocally illuminating relationships with the other, Ohly's work yields a rich harvest of humanistic understanding and integration at the level of texts and images, disciplines, and, above all, cultures. It offers one alternative to the globally criticistic approach once endemic to cultural studies in German lands but no longer either quite so global or quite so criticistic, either within Germany or within the United States. If the genus and genius, the governing metaphor, of Ohly's philology, humanistic as well as aesthetic, is *memoria,* its end is the *humanum:* remembering, repeating, and working through the bits and pieces we have inherited, illuminating self through other and other through self, with "sobriety" and "love" contributing what we can to recalling and reconstructing a human world, a world of meaning, in which humanity's best possibilities may flourish, its worst be held at bay.

44. Ohly, "In der Ringvorlesung 'Aufgaben und Möglichkeiten,'" pp. 28–31, is, as always, mindful of the work of his students, Uwe Ruberg, *Raum und Zeit im Prosa-Lancelot;* Ingrid Hahn, *Raum und Landschaft in Gottfrieds Tristan;* and Wolfgang Harms, *Der Kampf mit dem Freund oder Verwandten* and *Homo viator in bivio,* and of his own work—"Die Suche in Dichtungen des Mittelalters"—in relation to theirs. Cf. for "interhumanity" (*Zwischenmenschlichkeit*) Ohly, "In der Ringvorlesung 'Aufgaben und Möglichkeiten,'" p. 30; Martin Buber, "Geleitwort zur Sammlung [*Die Gesellschaft*]," pp. i–xiv, esp. pp. x, xi, xii, xiii ff.; Paul Mendes-Flohr, *From Mysticism to Dialogue* (Detroit, 1989), pp. 13ff. and chap. 2, "The 'Interhuman' as a Sociological Category," pp. 31–47, esp. pp. 38–39, 41–42. Cf. Schiller's "idea of poetry" in *Werke und Briefe,* vol. 8, *Theoretische Schriften,* ed. Rolf-Peter Janz et al., Bibliothek deutscher Klassiker, no. 78 (Frankfurt am Main, 1992), p. 734.

PUBLICATION HISTORY

1. "On the Spiritual Sense of the Word in the Middle Ages"

Originally published as "Vom geistigen Sinn des Wortes im Mittelalter," *Zeitschrift für deutsches Altertum und deutsche Literatur* 89 (1958): 1–23. Franz Steiner Verlag GmbH, Wiesbaden.

Reprinted separately as a Sonderausgabe in der Reihe Libelli, no. 218 (1966). Wissenschaftliche Buchgesellschaft, Darmstadt.

Reprinted in Friedrich Ohly, *Schriften zur mittelalterlichen Bedeutungsforschung* (1977), pp. 1–31. Wissenschaftliche Buchgesellschaft, Darmstadt.

Published in Italian translation as "Sul significato spirituale della parola nel Medioevo," in Friedrich Ohly, *Geometria e memoria: Lettera e allegoria nel Medioevo*, ed. Lea Ritter Santini (1985), pp. 249–275. Società editrice il Mulino, Bologna.

2. "Typology as a Form of Historical Thought"

Originally published as "Typologie als Denkform der Geschichtsbetrachtung: Vortrag gehalten auf den 34. Deutschen Historikertag in Münster am 7. Oktober 1982," in *Natur—Religion—Sprache—Universität: Universitätsforträge 1982/1983*, Schriftenreihe der Westfälischen Wilhelms-Universität Münster, Heft 7 (1983), pp. 68–102. Aschendorff, Münster.

Reprinted in *Typologie: Internationale Beiträge zur Poetik*, ed. Victor Bohn (1988), pp. 22–632. Suhrkamp, Frankfurt am Main.

Published in French translation as "La typologie, forme de pensée de l'histoire," trans. P. Pénsson, in *Traverses*, no. 2 (1992): 42–62.

Published in Italian translation as "La tipologia come forma di pensiero nella riflessione storica," in Friedrich Ohly, *Tipologia: Forma di pensiero della storia* (1994), pp. 177–219. Sicania, Messina.

Reprinted in Friedrich Ohly, *Ausgewählte und neue Schriften zur Literaturgeschichte und Bedeutungsforschung*, ed. Uwe Ruberg and Dietmar Peil (1995), pp. 445–472. S. Hirzel, Stuttgart.

3. "Problems of Medieval Significs and Hugh of Folieto's 'Dove Miniature'"

Originally published as "Probleme der mittelalterlichen Bedeutungsforschung und das Taubenbild des Hugo de Folieto," in *Frühmittelalterliche Studien* 2 (1968): 162–201. Walter de Gruyter, Berlin and New York.

Reprinted in Friedrich Ohly, *Schriften zur mittelalterlichen Bedeutungsforschung* (1977), pp. 32–92. Wissenschaftliche Buchgesellschaft, Darmstadt.

4. "The Cathedral as Temporal Space: On the Duomo of Siena"

Originally published as "Die Kathedrale als Zeitenraum: Zum Dom von Siena," in *Frühmittelalterliche Studien* 6 (1972): 94–158. Walter de Gruyter, Berlin and New York.

Reprinted in Friedrich Ohly, *Schriften zur mittelalterlichen Bedeutungsforschung* (1977), pp. 171–273. Wissenschaftliche Buchgesellschaft, Darmstadt.

Published in Italian translation as "La cattedrale come spazio dei tempi: Il duomo di Siena," in Accademia Senese degli Intronati, Monografie d'arte senese, no. 8 (1979). Accademia senese degli intronati, Siena.

5. "Dew and Pearl: A Lecture"

Originally published as "Tau und Perle: Ein Vortrag," in *Festschrift für Ingeborg Schröbler zum 65. Geburtstag,* ed. D. Schmidtke and Helga Schüppert, Beiträge zur Geschichte der deutschen Sprache und Literatur, Band 95, Sonderheft (1973), pp. 406–423. Max Niemeyer Verlag, Tübingen.

Reprinted in Friedrich Ohly, *Schriften zur mittelalterlichen Bedeutungsforschung* (1977), pp. 274–292. Wissenschaftliche Buchgesellschaft, Darmstadt.

6. "Poetry as the Necessary Fruit of a Suffering"

German typescript as yet unpublished.

Published only in Italian translation as "La poesia come necessario frutto di una sofferenza," in Friedrich Ohly, *Geometria e memoria: Lettera e allegoria nel Medioevo,* ed. Lea Ritter Santini (1985), pp. 53–89. Società editrice il Mulino, Bologna.

7. "A Philologist's Remarks on *Memoria*"

Originally published as "Bemerkungen eines Philologen zur Memoria," in *Memoria: Der geschichtliche Zeugniswert des liturgischen Gedenkens im Mittelalter,* ed. Karl Schmid and Joachim Wollasch, Münstersche Mittelalter-Schriften, Band 48, München B (1984). Wilhelm Fink Verlag, Munich.

Published in Italian translation in Friedrich Ohly, *Geometria e memoria: Lettera e allegoria nel Medioevo,* ed. Lea Ritter Santini (1985), pp. 109–188. Società editrice il Mulino, Bologna.

INDEX

Page numbers in italics refer to figures